Mexico's Beach Resorts For Dummies, 2nd Edition

Essential Spanish Words and Phrases

English	Spanish	Pronunciation
Good day (Good morning)	**Buenos días**	*bway*-nohss *dee*-ahss
Good evening/afternoon	**Buenas tardes**	*bway*-nahss *tar*-days
Good night	**Buenas noches**	*bway*-nahss *noh*-chase
Good-bye	**Adiós**	ah-dee-*ohss*
Excuse me	**Disculpe**	dees-*kool*-peh
Do you speak English?	**¿Habla usted inglés?**	*ah*-blah oo-*sted* een-*glays*?
I speak a little Spanish.	**Hablo un poco de español.**	*ah*-blow oon *poh*-koh day ess-pah-*nyol*
I don't understand Spanish very well.	**No entiendo español muy bien.**	noh ehn-tee-*ehn*-do ess-pah-*nyol* mwee byen
What did you say?	**¿Mande?** (formal)	*mahn*-day?
What time is it?	**¿Qué hora es?**	kay *oar*-ah ess?
Where is...?	**¿Dónde está...?**	*dohn*-day ess-*tah*?
...the airport	**...el aeropuerto**	el ah-ay-row-*por*-tow
...the station	**...la estación**	lah ess-tah-*seown*
...a hotel	**...un hotel**	oon oh-*tel*
...a gas station	**...una gasolinera**	*oon*-uh gah-so-lee-*nay*-rah
...a restaurant	**...un restaurante**	oon res-tow-*rahn*-tay
...the toilet	**...el baño**	el *bahn*-yoh
...a good doctor	**...un buen médico**	oon bwayn *may*-dee-co
...the road to...	**...el camino a...**	el cah-*mee*-noh ah
...a postcard	**...una tarjeta postal**	*oon*-uh tar-*heh*-ta pohs-*tahl*
I would like...	**Quisiera...**	key-see-*ehr*-ah
...to eat	**...comer**	ko-*mayr*
...a room	**...una habitación**	*oon*-nuh ah-bee-tah-*seeown*
How much is it?	**¿Cuánto cuesta?**	*kwahn*-to *kwess*-tah?
Do you accept...?	**¿Acepta usted...?**	ah-*sayp*-tah oo-*sted*?
...traveler's checks	**... los cheques de viajero**	los *chay*-kays day bee-ah-*hehr*-oh
...credit cards	**...tarjetas de crédito**	tar-*hay*-tahs day *kray*-dee-toh
May I see your menu?	**¿Puedo ver el menú?**	*puay*-tho veyr el may-*noo*?
The check, please.	**La cuenta, por favor.**	lah *quayn*-tah pohr fa-*vorh*

Mexican Cuisine Terms

- **Agua fresca:** Fruit-flavored water, usually watermelon or cantaloupe where ingredients such as lemon and hibiscus flower are added.

- **Antojitos:** Typical Mexican supper foods, usually made with *masa* or tortillas and containing a filling or topping such as sausage, cheese, beans, and onions; includes such items as *tacos, tostadas, sopes,* and *garnachas* (thick tortillas).

- **Botana:** An appetizer.

- **Buñuelos:** Round, thin, deep-fried, crispy fritters dipped in sugar.

- **Carnitas:** Pork that's been deep-cooked (not fried) in lard, then simmered, and then served with corn tortillas for tacos.

- **Ceviche:** Fresh, raw seafood marinated in fresh lime juice, garnished with chopped tomatoes, onions, chiles, and sometimes cilantro, and served with crispy, fried, whole-corn tortillas or crackers.

- **Churro:** Tube-shaped, bread-like fritter, dipped in sugar and sometimes filled with *cajeta* (caramel) or chocolate.

- **Frijoles charros:** Beans flavored with beer; a northern Mexican specialty.

- **Gusanos de maguey:** Maguey worms, considered a delicacy; delicious when deep-fried to a crisp and served with corn tortillas for tacos.

- **Huevos Mexicanos:** Scrambled eggs with chopped onions, hot peppers, and tomatoes.

- **Menudo:** Stew made with the lining of the cow's stomach. It can be served in a red or white broth. A traditional hangover cure.

- **Pan dulce:** Lightly sweetened bread in many configurations, usually served at breakfast or bought in any bakery.

- **Pibil:** Pit-baked pork or chicken in a sauce of tomato, onion, mild red pepper, cilantro, and vinegar.

- **Pozole:** Pork or chicken broth with hominy and shredded pork or chicken. The traditional recipe calls for the pork's head, but now it's commonly prepared with chicken or pork loin. Pozole is served red in Jalisco and white in Guerrero. Thursdays are the traditional day to eat pozole in Acapulco and Ixtapa.

- **Tacos al pastor:** Thin slices of flavored pork roasted on a revolving cylinder dripping with onion slices and the juice of fresh pineapple slices. Served in small corn tortillas, topped with chopped onion and cilantro.

- **Tamal:** Incorrectly called a "tamale" (*tamal* singular; *tamales* plural). A meat or sweet filling rolled with fresh *masa,* wrapped in a cornhusk or banana leaf, and then steamed; many varieties and sizes throughout the country.

- **Torta:** A sandwich, usually on *bolillo* bread, typically comprising sliced avocado, onions, and tomatoes with a choice of meat and often cheese.

For Dummies: Bestselling Book Series for Beginners

FOR DUMMIES

The fun and easy way™ to travel!

U.S.A.

Also available:

America's National Parks For Dummies

Arizona For Dummies

Boston For Dummies

California For Dummies

Chicago For Dummies

Florida For Dummies

Los Angeles & Disneyland For Dummies

New Mexico For Dummies

New Orleans For Dummies

New York City For Dummies

San Francisco For Dummies

Seattle For Dummies

Washington, D.C. For Dummies

RV Vacations For Dummies

Walt Disney World & Orlando For Dummies

EUROPE

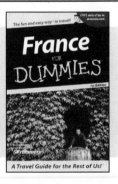

Also available:

England For Dummies

Europe For Dummies

Ireland For Dummies

London For Dummies

Paris For Dummies

Scotland For Dummies

Spain For Dummies

OTHER DESTINATIONS

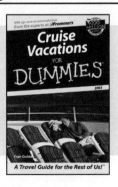

Also available:

Bahamas For Dummies

Honeymoon Vacations For Dummies

Mexico's Beach Resorts For Dummies

Vancouver & Victoria For Dummies

Mexico's
Beach Resorts
FOR
DUMMIES®
2ND EDITION

by David Baird and Lynne Bairstow

WILEY

Wiley Publishing, Inc.

Mexico's Beach Resorts For Dummies, 2nd Edition

Published by
Wiley Publishing, Inc.
111 River St.
Hoboken, NJ 07030-5774
www.wiley.com

WILEY

About the Authors

For **Lynne Bairstow,** Mexico has become more her home than her native United States. After living in Puerto Vallarta and exploring Mexico for most of the past 14 years, she's developed not only an appreciation but also a true love for the country and its complex, colorful culture. Her travel articles on Mexico have been published in *The New York Times, San Francisco Chronicle, Los Angeles Times, Luxury Living, Frommer's Budget Travel* magazine, and *Alaska Airlines Magazine.* In 2000, the Mexican government awarded Lynne the Pluma de Plata, a top honor granted to foreign writers, for her work in the Frommer's guidebooks to Mexico.

David Baird is a writer, editor, and translator who feels uncomfortable writing about himself in the third person (too much like writing your own obituary). Now based in Austin, Texas, he has spent years living in various parts of Mexico, Brazil, Peru, and Puerto Rico. But whenever possible, he manages to get back to the Yucatán's turquoise-blue waters because he thinks he looks good in that color and because he's excessively fond of the local cooking.

Dedication

This book is dedicated to my many friends in Mexico who, through sharing their insights, anecdotes, knowledge, and explorations of Mexico, have shared their love of this country. In particular, Carlos, Claudia, Ricardo, and Paulina have shared with me and have shown me what a magical place Mexico is and how much more I have to discover and enjoy.

— Lynne Bairstow

To my brother John, whose sheer willpower overcame my objections and forced me to take that vacation many, many years ago that first brought me to the Caribbean shores of Mexico.

— David Baird

Authors' Acknowledgments

Many thanks to all the many people who helped me gather the information, tips, and treasures that have made their way into this book. I am especially grateful for the assistance of Alejandra Macedo and her tireless work in ensuring that the information in this book is correct and for her valuable ideas and contributions.

— Lynne Bairstow

I would like to acknowledge my indebtedness to the irrepressible Desiré Sanromán, a Cozumeleña who knows her island and befriended me for reasons that aren't quite clear. (Sympathy? Pity? Concern for all the readers I may mislead?) I also thank that most capable of guides, Claudia Hurtado Valenzuela, who opened the doors of the Riviera Maya to me, and whose views on all matters touristic were well worth hearing.

— David Baird

Publisher's Acknowledgments

We're proud of this book; please send us your comments through our Dummies online registration form located at www.dummies.com/register/.

Some of the people who helped bring this book to market include the following:

Editorial

Editors: Christina Guthrie, Project Editor; Michael Kelly, Development Editor

Copy Editor: Chad Sievers

Cartographer: Elizabeth Puhl

Editorial Manager: Christine Meloy Beck

Editorial Assistants: Melissa Bennett, Elizabeth Rea

Senior Photo Editor: Richard Fox

Assistant Photo Editor: Michael Ross

Cover Photos
Front: Glen F. McLaughlin/Corbis
Back: Mark Lewis/Getty Images

Cartoons: Rich Tennant, www.the5thwave.com

Production

Project Coordinator: April Farling

Layout and Graphics: Amanda Carter, Andrea Dahl, Lauren Goddard, Denny Hager, Stephanie D. Jumper, Michael Kruzil, Kristin McMullan, Lynsey Osborn, Julie Trippetti

Proofreaders: Laura Albert, Andy Hollandbeck, Carl William Pierce, Dwight Ramsey, TECHBOOKS Production Services

Indexer: TECHBOOKS Production Services

Publishing and Editorial for Consumer Dummies

Diane Graves Steele, Vice President and Publisher, Consumer Dummies

Joyce Pepple, Acquisitions Director, Consumer Dummies

Kristin A. Cocks, Product Development Director, Consumer Dummies

Michael Spring, Vice President and Publisher, Travel

Brice Gosnell, Associate Publisher, Travel

Kelly Regan, Editorial Director, Travel

Publishing for Technology Dummies

Andy Cummings, Vice President and Publisher, Dummies Technology/General User

Composition Services

Gerry Fahey, Vice President of Production Services

Debbie Stailey, Director of Composition Services

Contents at a Glance

Maps at a Glance

Table of Contents

Part X: The Part of Tens *449*

Chapter 32: Ten Top Mexican Moments 451

Chapter 33: Ten (Or So) Myths and Misconceptions about Mexico 455

Chapter 34: Ten Most Deliciously Mexican Dishes 459

Introduction

● ●

Mexico not only offers travelers some of the world's best beaches, but it also presents a rich, thousand-year-old culture and amazing natural wonders to explore. Whether it's the desert caves of Los Cabos or the Caribbean reefs off Cancún and Cozumel, Mexico's largely untouched coastline is a virtual playground for travelers. In addition to the many natural attractions, Mexico's beach resorts have added golf, tennis, diving, and abundant watersports to their lures. But can the rest of your knowledge about this vast country fit inside a mango seed? For many people, Mexico is both familiar and a mystery, and some opinions of this land are influenced by inaccurate or outdated stereotypes. If you're a traveler who's more attuned to the culture, you may have visited one or two Mexican beach resorts, but you're probably curious about some of the others.

How do you sift through the destination choices — and then all the hotel options — without throwing in the beach towel in a daze of confusion? How do you plan a vacation that's perfect for you — not one that simply follows the recommendations of a friend or travel agent? You've come to the right place. This guide rescues you from both information overload and detail deficit — those annoying syndromes that afflict far too many would-be travelers. We give you enough specifics to help you plan the type of trip you want and steer clear of the type of trip you don't want.

Sure, plenty of other guidebooks are available that cover Mexico and its beach destinations, but many of them may as well be encyclopedias: They include practically everything you can possibly see and do. When the time comes to decide upon accommodations, attractions, activities, and meals, you probably have a tough time finding the best options because they're buried in with the rest of the mediocre to not-so-hot suggestions.

Mexico's Beach Resorts For Dummies, 2nd Edition, is a whole new enchilada. In this book, we streamline the options, focusing on each vacation spot's high points (and warning you about the low points). We leave out the less-visited, harder-to-reach beach resorts so that we can concentrate on the most popular (and most exciting) destinations. With the straightforward tips that we offer — how to get there, what to expect when you arrive, where to stay, where to eat, and where to have big fun — arranging your dream vacation can't be easier.

About This Book

You can use this book in three ways:

- ✔ **As a trip planner:** Whether you think you know where you want to go in Mexico, or you don't have a clue, this book helps you zero in on the ideal beach resort for you. It guides you through all the necessary steps of making your travel arrangements, from finding the cheapest airfare and considering travel insurance to figuring out a budget and packing like a pro. Chapters are self-contained, so you don't have to read them in order. Find the chapters you want in the table of contents, and just flip to them as you need them.

- ✔ **As a beach-resort guide:** Pack this book along with your sunscreen — it comes in just as handy while you're away, though not to prevent sunburn. Turn to the appropriate destination chapters whenever you need to find the best beaches, a good place to eat, a worthwhile boat cruise, a challenging golf course, the lowdown on a hot nightspot, or tips on any other diversions.

- ✔ **For an enjoyable overview:** If you want a feel for Mexico's most popular beach resorts, read this book from start to finish to get a taste of all the highlights.

Travel information is subject to change at any time — call ahead for confirmation when making your travel plans. Your safety is important to us (and to the publisher), so we encourage you to stay alert and be aware of your surroundings. Keep a close eye on cameras, purses, and wallets — all favorite targets of thieves and pickpockets.

Conventions Used in This Book

In this book, we include reviews of our favorite hotels and restaurants, as well as information about the best attractions at each of Mexico's top beach resorts. In these reviews, we use abbreviations for commonly accepted credit cards. Here's what those abbreviations stand for:

AE: American Express

DC: Diners Club

MC: MasterCard

V: Visa

We also include some general pricing information to help you as you decide where to unpack your bags or where to dine on the local cuisine. We use a system of dollar signs to show a range of costs (in U.S. dollars) so that you can make quick comparisons.

Unless stated otherwise, the lodging rates that we give are for two people spending one night in a standard double room. Prices are provided for both high season — the most popular travel time that runs roughly from Christmas to Easter — and the generally lower-priced summer season (or low season). Note that the following dollar sign pricing system indicates only the high-season rates for lodging, and applies to main courses only for restaurants.

Some hotel rates are much higher than others no matter what time of year it is. Don't be too quick to skip an accommodation that seems out of your price range, though. Some rates include breakfast, both breakfast and dinner, or even three meals per day. Other resorts are *all-inclusive,* which means that after you pay for your room, you never have to dip into your pocket again for meals, beverages, tips, taxes, most activities, or transportation to and from the airport. So, although a price tag may seem sky-high at first, you may actually find it affordable upon second glance.

Check out the following table to decipher the dollar signs:

Cost	Hotel	Restaurant
$	Less than $75	Less than $15
$$	$76–$125	$16–$30
$$$	$126–$175	$31–$50
$$$$	$176–$250	$51 and up
$$$$$	More than $251 per night	

Foolish Assumptions

As we wrote this book, we made some assumptions about you and what your needs may be as a traveler. Here's what we assumed about you:

- ✔ You may be an inexperienced traveler looking for guidance when determining whether to take a trip to a Mexican beach resort and how to plan for it.

- ✔ You may be an experienced traveler who hasn't had much time to explore Mexico or its beaches and wants expert advice when you finally do get a chance to enjoy some fun in the sun.

- ✔ You're not looking for a book that provides all the information available about Mexico or that lists every hotel, restaurant, or attraction available to you. Instead, you're looking for a book that focuses on the places that offer the best or most unique experiences in these beach resorts.

How This Book Is Organized

We divide this book into 11 parts. The chapters within each part cover specific subjects in detail. Skip around as much as you like; you don't have to read this book in any particular order. In fact, think of these pages as a buffet. You can consume whatever you want — and no one cares if you eat the flan for dessert before you have the enchiladas.

For each beach resort, we include a section called "Fast Facts." These sections give you handy information that you may need when traveling in Mexico, including phone numbers and addresses to use in an emergency, area hospitals and pharmacies, names of local newspapers and magazines, locations for maps, and more.

Part 1: Getting Started

In this part, we compare and contrast Mexico's most popular beach resorts so that you can decide which place best suits your tastes and needs. Sure, they all have gorgeous beaches, but that's where the similarities end. To help you plan a vacation that's tailored to your preferences, this part guides you through the process of figuring out which resort or resorts are best for you.

We also give you a brief overview of local customs, cuisines, and fiestas and celebrations. We take you through the best — and worst — times of year to travel, and we explain the differences between high season and low season. We also tell you about special holidays that may help you decide when to visit Mexico. We offer up some budget-planning tips, and finally, we offer special trip-planning advice for families, singles, gay and lesbian travelers, seniors, and travelers who are physically challenged.

Part 11: Ironing Out the Details

This section is where we lay out everything you need to know about making all the arrangements for your trip. We help you decide whether to use a travel agent, a packager, or the Internet. We offer advice on finding the best airfare — and airline — for your destination. Likewise, we explain how to estimate the total cost of your vacation and how to stay within your budget. Finally, we take you through all the ins and outs of other vacation essentials, from getting a passport and considering travel insurance to staying safe and packing like a pro.

Part 111: Cancún

Welcome to Mexico's most popular beach resort. This area is a great destination for first-time travelers to Mexico. Why? Because it has all the comforts of home: familiar restaurant and hotel chains along with great shopping, easy access to diverse cultural and geographical activities and excursions to the ancient ruins of Tulum, world-class scuba diving, and plenty of Mexican fiestas. We provide all the details for getting to, eating at, staying in, and playing at all of Cancún's hot spots.

Part IV: Cozumel and the Riviera Maya

Staying on a tropical island is a dream for many, and Cozumel offers a distinctive island destination for a laid-back vacation with a myriad of water activities, many centered around the famous reef that outlines the southwest coast. Back on the mainland, the Riviera Maya provides a stunning stretch of pristine beaches, unique towns, and mega-resorts from Cancún to Tulum. Check out the ultra-trendy town of Playa del Carmen or visit one of the eco-parks. There's plenty here for everyone. In this part, we cover all the information you need to travel to and around these two beach resorts.

Part V: Puerto Vallarta and the Central Pacific Coast

Turn to this part for the inside scoop (Lynne, one of the authors of this book, is a long-time resident!) on visiting the beautiful city of Puerto Vallarta. From viewing historic landmarks to dining in world-class restaurants to finding the perfect beach along the 50 miles of coastline surrounding Banderas Bay, a trip to this part of Mexico is sure to please even the most discriminating vacationer.

Part VI: Ixtapa and Zihuatanejo

Who says you can't get it all in one destination? Traveling to the towns of Ixtapa and Zihuatanejo provides the best of two worlds: Ixtapa gives you high-class hotels along a beautiful strip of sand, and nearby Zihuatanejo wraps you in the warmth of its small-town charms. This part offers advice on staying and dining in both of these great vacation spots.

Part VII: Acapulco

The grande dame of Mexico's west coast, Acapulco draws many visitors to its glittering bay and glamorous nightlife. Enjoy the excitement of a bustling city combined with the amenities of a beachfront resort. This part gives you the lowdown on vacationing in Mexico's first beach resort.

Part VIII: Huatulco and the Southern Pacific Coast

For details on a vacation that centers on the natural beauty of the land and the sea, turn to Part VIII. This part offers a close-up look at two towns along the southern Pacific coast: Huatulco and Puerto Escondido.

Part IX: Los Cabos and Southern Baja

Want to take time out for a great golf vacation? Ready to reel in a big one? Want to relax in one of Mexico's most deluxe resorts? Or, just need to let your hair down and enjoy some super-charged nightlife? Then turn to Part IX for all the details on vacationing in Los Cabos and on the Baja Peninsula.

Part X: The Part of Tens

Every *For Dummies* book has a Part of Tens. In this section, you can find out about ten marvelous Mexico moments, ten common myths about Mexico, and ten delicious Mexican dishes to try.

Part XI: Appendixes

Do you want to locate a quick phone number or Web site, touch up on a few common Spanish words and phrases, get your hunger pangs going for some authentic Mexican cuisine? Check out this part for all that information and more.

Worksheets to help make your travel planning easier are located at the very back of the book. You can find them easily because they're printed on yellow paper.

Icons Used in This Book

Throughout this book, helpful icons highlight particularly useful information. Here's a look at what each symbol means:

Keep an eye out for the Bargain Alert icon as you look for money-saving tips and great deals.

Watch for the Heads Up icon to identify annoying or potentially dangerous situations such as tourist traps, unsafe neighborhoods, budgetary rip-offs, and other things to avoid.

Look to the Kid Friendly icon for attractions, hotels, restaurants, and activities that are particularly hospitable to children or people traveling with kids.

The Romance icon signals the most romantic restaurants, hotels, and attractions that Mexico's beach resorts have to offer.

The Tip icon alerts you to practical advice and hints to make your trip run more smoothly.

Note the ¡Viva Mexico! icon for food, places, or experiences that offer a true taste of Mexico.

Where to Go from Here

There's nothing like a beach vacation — whether you spend it lazing in the sun or pursuing active, water-bound activities — and it's even better when planned with the right advice and insider tips. Whether you're a veteran traveler or new to the game, *Mexico's Beach Resorts For Dummies,* 2nd Edition, helps you put together just the kind of trip you have in mind. So, start turning these pages, and before you know it, you'll feel those balmy beach breezes on your face!

Part I
Getting Started

The 5th Wave   By Rich Tennant

THE MEXICAN EXPERIENCE

Your glass of water...

In this part . . .

*P*lanning a trip can be daunting — so we're here to
help give you a sense of the place you're considering
visiting. Mexico is a vast and varied country with a bevy of
unique beach resorts. We introduce you to the highlights
of the most popular ones, so you can pick the destination
that best matches your idea of the perfect seaside getaway.

In Part I, we cover the basics: Each of Mexico's beach
resorts has a charm all its own, so deciding which one
best suits your preferences is the first step in planning
your ideal vacation. Next come the details — such as
when to go and which type of hotel is best for you. We
also give tips and tricks for accurately planning your vacation budget. Nothing can take away the pleasure of lazy
days faster than worries about spending too much money,
so spend some time here to ward away those stressful
thoughts. Finally, we offer some tips for travelers with special needs in order to help ensure that you choose exactly
the right place that fulfills both your personal requirements and your expectations.

Chapter 1

Discovering Mexico's Beach Resorts

In This Chapter

▶ Introducing Mexico's beach resorts

▶ Deciding which area to visit

▶ Examining the pros and cons of each destination

*M*exico has a lot going for it in terms of attracting travelers: warm weather, miles and miles of coastline, and a location so close to the United States that sometimes it almost seems like a part of it. Although the official language is Spanish, the use of English is almost as common as Spanish in resort areas. A visit to Mexico can offer the experience of visiting a foreign country accompanied by many of the familiarities of home.

Mexico's beaches are generally spectacular. But they're also as varied as the country itself. Deciding which one is right for you depends a lot on what you're looking for in a vacation. As you read this chapter, think about what you really want in a destination. Romance? Family fun? Lively singles scene? And consider how you want to travel. Budget? Luxury? Somewhere in between? These considerations can help narrow down your planning. One thing's for certain — no matter what you're seeking, you can find at least one Mexican beach resort that fits the bill.

Because of Mexico's sheer size, covering more than one of its beach resorts in a single trip isn't practical, with the exception of the Riviera Maya, found south of Cancún. In this chapter, we help you decide which resort best matches your wish list. Although Mexico has many more beaches than you could possibly dream of exploring in one trip, in this book, we only include those with the easiest air access and the best services and facilities for tourism.

If you don't know where to begin in choosing between Acapulco and Cancún, or Los Cabos and Puerto Vallarta, don't worry. In this book, we tell you what you need to know to help you decide which destination is right for you. In this chapter, we give you a rundown of the highlights and drawbacks of each of Mexico's most popular beach resorts. Because the type of accommodations you want may determine where you go — or don't go — we also explain the different lodging options available at each destination.

Understanding the Lay of the Land

Mexico is a country known for both its geographical and cultural diversity. And, as a country with more than 8,000 miles of shoreline, you can choose between a quiet stretch of sand, a pounding surf break, or a dynamic beach resort with nonstop nightlife.

Mexico's beach resorts are located in one of three main regions of the country: the Caribbean coast, along the eastern seaboard; the Pacific coastline; or on Mexico's Baja Peninsula, an extension of California that is almost completely separated from mainland Mexico.

The eastern destinations are known for their crystalline waters, which border the coral reefs of the Caribbean, and flat, scrubby landscapes. This area was the land of the ancient Maya, and their impressive remains are close enough to the popular beach destinations to explore. The Pacific beach resorts tend to have mountainous backdrops and dramatic tropical jungles bordering cobalt blue waters. Baja's beach resorts combine a stunning desert landscape with oceans teeming with sea life.

Picking the Right Beach Resort

Although Acapulco was Mexico's first beach to attract international travelers, the white-sand beaches and nearby ruins make Cancún the most popular choice today. Puerto Vallarta and Huatulco offer a strong dose of natural charm and eco-tourism, and Los Cabos has become Mexico's mecca for golfers and fishermen. Ixtapa and Zihuatanejo, Cozumel, and Puerto Escondido offer a laid-back retreat beneath palm fronds and sunny skies, and the rapidly growing Riviera Maya region draws adventurers and relaxation-seekers alike. In a nutshell, each resort has its own look, character, and special something. The following sections are snapshots to help you focus on the resort that's right for you.

Also see "Mexico's Beach Resorts: The Scorecard," at the end of this chapter, for a concise rating of each aspect of the resort areas that we cover in this book. After you decide which amenities are the highest priorities, you can use the table to find the resort that most meets your particular wishes.

Choosing Cancún

Cancún is Mexico's most popular beach resort, and the reason most people travel to Mexico. It perfectly showcases both the country's breathtaking natural beauty and the depth of its thousand-year-old history. Cancún is also especially comforting for first-time visitors to Mexico because it offers a taste of life back home that makes foreigners feel instantly at ease in this beach resort.

Cancún offers an unrivaled combination of high-quality accommodations, dreamy beaches, and diverse shopping, dining, and nightlife. The added lure of ancient culture is also evident in all directions. And the best part? Cancún is also a modern mega-resort. Even if you're a bit apprehensive about visiting foreign soil, you'll feel completely at home and at ease in Cancún. Many people speak English, vendors and stores accept dollars, the roads are well paved, and most lawns are manicured. Malls are the places for shopping and dining, and you quickly spot recognizable names for dining, shopping, nightclubbing, and sleeping.

Two principal parts comprise Cancún: **Isla Cancún** (Cancún Island), with a 14-mile-long strip of beachfront hotels reminiscent of Miami Beach, and **Ciudad Cancún** (Cancún City), on the mainland, with hotels to accompany the functional elements of any community.

Cancún, located on the Yucatán Peninsula, is also the departure point for wonderful day-trips to the nearby islands of Cozumel and Isla Mujeres (Island of Women), where you can enjoy first-class diving, as well as the remains of ancient cultures.

If you're looking for an incredible introduction to Mexico's beaches and a Mexican-lite vacation while enjoying world-class shopping in a pampered environment, Cancún is your beach. (Check out the chapters in Part III for more detailed information on this resort.)

Top aspects of a vacation in Cancún include

- ✔ Great beaches of powdery, white sand and turquoise-blue water
- ✔ First-class facilities, modern accommodations, and tons of shopping and dining options
- ✔ Numerous outdoor activities including jungle tours, visits to Mayan ruins, and eco-oriented theme parks
- ✔ No need to worry about communication at this English language-friendly destination

Mexico

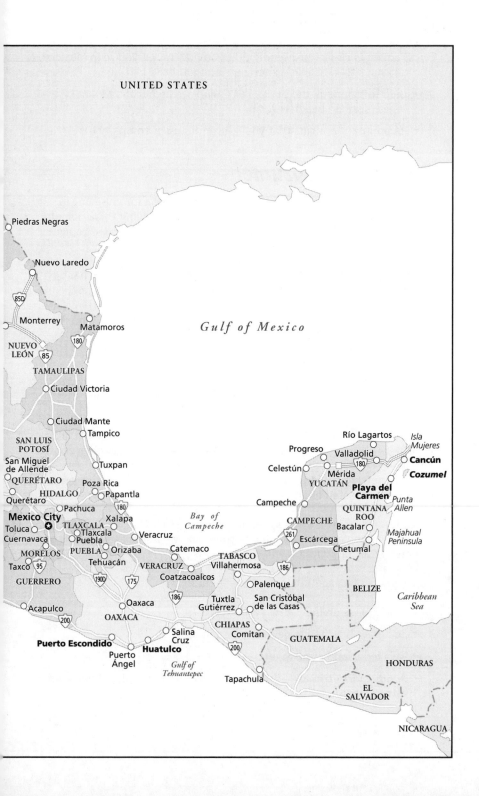

UNITED STATES

Gulf of Mexico

Piedras Negras

Nuevo Laredo

85D

Monterrey
Matamoros

NUEVO
LEÓN 85
180

TAMAULIPAS

Ciudad Victoria

Ciudad Mante

SAN LUIS
POTOSÍ
Tampico

San Miguel
de Allende
Tuxpan

QUERÉTARO
Poza Rica

HIDALGO
Papantla

Querétaro

Pachuca
180

Mexico City
Xalapa
Bay of
Campeche

Toluca
TLAXCALA

Cuernavaca
Tlaxcala
Puebla
Veracruz

MORELOS
PUEBLA
Orizaba

Taxco 95
Tehuacán
Catemaco

GUERRERO
VERACRUZ
Villahermosa

1900 175
Coatzacoalcos

Acapulco
Oaxaca
Tuxtla
Gutiérrez

200
OAXACA
186

Salina
Cruz
CHIAPAS
Comitan

Puerto Escondido

Puerto
Ángel
Huatulco

Gulf of
Tehuantepec
200

Tapachula

Río Lagartos
Isla
Mujeres

Progreso
Valladolid

Celestún
180
Cancún

Mérida
Cozumel

YUCATÁN
Playa del
Carmen

Campeche
Punta
Allen

QUINTANA
ROO

CAMPECHE
Bacalar

261
Escárcega
Majahual
Peninsula

TABASCO
Chetumal

186

Palenque
BELIZE

San Cristóbal
de las Casas
Caribbean
Sea

GUATEMALA

HONDURAS

EL
SALVADOR

NICARAGUA

But also consider the following:

- ✔ Cancún is so visitor-friendly that you may forget you're in Mexico and miss the Mexican experience altogether.
- ✔ Built for tourism, the prices in Cancún are higher than in most other Mexican beach resorts.
- ✔ Its popularity means that you'll have plenty of company here!

Diving into Cozumel

If underwater beauty is your most important criteria for choosing a beach, then let Cozumel dazzle you. Considered by many to be one of the world's top-ten diving spots, few places can top the aquatic splendor of the waters surrounding this island.

And when you come up for air, or if you're a nondiver, Cozumel has several inland attractions, a variety of watersports, a new golf course, and ample choices for dining and libations. As Mexico's most important port of call for cruise ships, Cozumel also has the best duty-free shopping and one of the largest selections of fine jewelry shops in the country. The island's one town, San Miguel, has a charming old-Mexico feel to it.

Cozumel has more budget-friendly accommodations and places to dine than newer, nearby Cancún. However, even though the island is really active during the day, it's generally a quiet place at night.

Just a 45-minute ferry ride away from mainland Mexico, Cozumel makes for a great jumping-off point for explorations along the Yucatán's coastline. Just across the channel from Cozumel is captivating Playa del Carmen, quickly growing in popularity due to its central location and funky-sophisticated charms.

In addition to being a diver's dream destination, staying in Cozumel can be like enjoying multiple beach resorts in one vacation! (Take a look at Chapter 12 for more on Cozumel.)

Top aspects of a vacation in Cozumel include

- ✔ World-class diving
- ✔ Secluded beaches to get away from it all
- ✔ Relaxed island atmosphere
- ✔ A short ferry trip away from the mainland's cultural and historical attractions

But also consider the following:

- ✔ The nightlife is almost nonexistent.
- ✔ Cozumel is super-casual; you won't find a dress-up place on the island.
- ✔ Stores tend to be more expensive than elsewhere because they cater to cruise-ship visitors.
- ✔ When the cruise ships arrive, Cozumel is very crowded.

Exploring the Riviera Maya

Cancún's popularity has given rise to a growing curiosity and desire to explore other parts of the pristine coastline to the south. New venues started popping up along the shoreline heading south to Tulum. Now officially dubbed the Riviera Maya, this stretch of peaceful places to stay is ideal for either more adventurous travelers or those who simply want to stay put in an all-inclusive enclave.

The hottest spot along the Riviera Maya is Playa del Carmen, which lies more than 64km (40 miles) south of Cancún. Playa — as locals refer to it — is a small town that's both funky and sophisticated. In the early '80s, Playa del Carmen was nothing more than the ferry landing for Cozumel, but it has since developed into an engaging resort town of its own merit, with powdery-sand beaches and an eclectic collection of lodging, dining, and shopping.

Playa seems to attract younger visitors who are looking for a combination of simplicity and variety. Recently, though, Playa has also attracted developers. As they rapidly change the beachscape to the north and south with the addition of mega-resorts, they're also changing Playa's previously playful vibe. But Playa still has enough of its original flavor to make it different from any other resort in the area.

South of Playa del Carmen lie a succession of commercial nature parks, planned resort communities, and a few rustic beach hideaways including Xcaret, Puerto Aventuras, Xpu-Ha, Akumal, Xel-Ha, and Tulum. This stretch of coast is also sprinkled with newly developed, all-inclusive resorts, and is seeing the most dynamic growth in tourism development in all Mexico.

If you love getting away from it all, the Riviera Maya is a natural choice for exploration and relaxation. (See Chapter 13 for more details.)

Top aspects of a vacation in the Riviera Maya include

- ✔ Beautiful beaches and an array of eco-parks ideal for nature lovers
- ✔ Favored by more adventurous travelers, some of whom have settled here to offer eclectic accommodations, shopping, and dining options
- ✔ Smaller crowds and lower prices
- ✔ All-inclusive haven with great savings if traveling with children

But also consider the following:

- ✔ Limited shopping and dining exist outside of Playa del Carmen.
- ✔ Nightlife? What nightlife? Unless you consider stargazing an aspect of nightlife.
- ✔ Without a rental car, you're stuck where you stay.

Playing in Puerto Vallarta

Puerto Vallarta is the place to go if you're looking to experience a beach resort with authentic Mexican flavor. Unlike other resorts, such as Cancún, Ixtapa, and Huatulco, Puerto Vallarta grew up around an original beach community. To this day, it has a seductively simple pace of life that's reflected in the warmth of its people and the spirit of the place itself.

Puerto Vallarta, with its traditional Mexican architecture and gold-sand beaches bordered by jungle-covered mountains, is currently the second most visited resort in Mexico (trailing only Cancún). Vallarta, as locals prefer to call it, maintains its small-town charm despite being home to sophisticated hotels, great restaurants, a thriving arts community, an active nightlife, and a growing variety of eco-tourism attractions that range from mountain biking in the Sierra foothills to whale-watching.

Natural beauty and modern infrastructure aside, Puerto Vallarta is remarkable for the number of options it offers for different types of tourists. Whether you're a couple looking for a romantic getaway, a family trying to find a great value, or senior travelers in search of new shores to explore, Vallarta has something to fit everyone. This resort is also known for being very gay-friendly, and it has a selection of hotels, excursions, and nightlife options that cater specifically to same-sex couples.

If you're an avid golfer with family members who don't share your passion for the links, you can take advantage of the six championship-quality courses that are now available for play, making Vallarta an up-and-coming golf resort. And the resort provides ample activities for the non-golfers in your group.

With an ideal mix of modern services and traditional charms, Puerto Vallarta is both a great first-time introduction to Mexico and a wonderful place for those looking to explore more of this country's natural and cultural riches. (Look at the chapters in Part V for more on this area.)

Top aspects of a vacation in Puerto Vallarta include

- ✔ Considered Mexico's friendliest beach resort
- ✔ An authentic sense of community
- ✔ Ideal combination of natural beauty and modern infrastructure
- ✔ An epicurean's delight with more than 250 restaurants, as well as varied nightlife and great shopping
- ✔ Wide variety of lodging options to fit all tastes and pocketbooks
- ✔ Countless activities, including mountain biking, hiking, birdwatching, jungle trekking in ATVs, diving, snorkeling, ocean kayaking, and surfing
- ✔ Excellent and uncrowded golf courses

But also consider the following:

- ✔ The beaches, at least those in central Puerto Vallarta, aren't the best in Mexico. They feature a golden sand that's darker than most. However, the northern and southern shores offer exquisite options, and they're only a short distance away.
- ✔ The presence of numerous beach vendors and timeshare salespeople means that you'll have plenty of practice saying, "No, gracias!"
- ✔ The town is jam-packed during the major Mexican holidays — Easter, September 16, November 20, and Christmas — which means higher prices, fewer lodging opportunities, and tangled traffic.

Introducing Ixtapa and Zihuatanejo

If you can't decide between a modern beach resort and a typical Mexican seaside village, then consider Ixtapa and Zihuatanejo, located north of Acapulco on Mexico's Pacific coast. These side-by-side destinations offer the best of both worlds less than 7km (4 miles) from one another. Although they share common geography, they couldn't be more different in character. Ixtapa is a model of modern infrastructure, services, and luxury hotels, while Zihuatanejo — or Zihua, to the locals — is the quintessential Mexican beach village.

If you favor luxury over charm, opt for Ixtapa and take advantage of the well-appointed rooms in this pristine setting of great natural beauty. You can easily and quickly make the 7km (4-mile) trip into Zihuatanejo for a sampling of the simple life in this seaside *pueblo* (small town). However, if you prefer a more rustic retreat with real personality, settle in Zihuatanejo.

Although this dual destination is a good choice for the traveler looking for a little of everything, from resort-style indulgence to unpretentious simplicity, keep in mind that these two resorts are more welcoming to couples and adults than families with small children. A number of places are off-limits to children under the age of 16 — something of a rarity in Mexico.

Ixtapa and Zihuatanejo offer active days and relaxed evenings. During the day, you can choose between scuba diving, deep-sea fishing, bay cruises to remote beaches, and golfing. The nightlife in both towns borders on the subdued, but Ixtapa is the livelier of the two. The favored evening activity here tends to be a late dinner on the beach.

Enjoy a sense of two-for-one in this dual destination that's truly an optimal combo of the best of Mexican beach resorts. (See the chapters in Part VI for more on these two destinations.)

Top aspects of a vacation in Zihuatanejo include

- ✔ Beautiful beaches within a bay that ensures calm waters with ample stretches of sand for sun worshipers
- ✔ Traditional Mexican beach-town atmosphere
- ✔ Smaller, more unique accommodations in a variety of price ranges
- ✔ A casual, relaxed atmosphere
- ✔ One of the best-priced destinations in Mexico

But also consider the following:

- ✔ The nightlife is very quiet.
- ✔ Going to the beach sums up the daytime activity; however, you can take short trips to find horseback riding, bird-watching, and other, more active endeavors.
- ✔ It's among the least kid-friendly destinations in Mexico.
- ✔ The summers are extremely hot, and air conditioning isn't prevalent.

Top aspects of a vacation in Ixtapa include

- ✔ Modern infrastructure and expansive beaches
- ✔ Larger chain hotels and nicely appointed accommodations

> ✔ Two good golf courses with some of the lowest greens fees in Mexico
>
> ✔ Enough variety in the nightlife, especially fun for the 20- and 30-year-old crowd

But also consider the following:

> ✔ It lacks the true "feeling" of being in Mexico.
>
> ✔ Mexican tourists can make the Easter and Christmas holidays crowded.
>
> ✔ Summers are very hot.

Getting acquainted with Acapulco

Acapulco is known for its sultry beaches for tanning during the day and its glitzy discos for partying at night. To this day, Acapulco has a nonstop, 24-hour-a-day energy, which clearly demonstrates why it was the largest and most renowned Mexican resort from the 1940s to the 1970s, when movie stars made it their playground. Although golf and tennis are played here with intensity, the real participant sport is the nightlife, which has made this city famous for decades.

Despite the seemingly decadent, nocturnal attractions, Acapulco is also a charmingly ideal place for a fun-filled family vacation. Many activities and destinations cater to children, including water parks, zoos, and exciting tours down a nearby river. Accommodations fit every budget, and, in the true spirit of Mexican family hospitality, children are welcome almost everywhere in town.

In addition to the broadest range of late-night entertainment in Mexico, this beach resort also has excellent airline connections, outstanding dining, and a wide array of daytime activities. You can stay at luxurious hillside villas, resort hotels, or modest inns on the beach and in the old center of Acapulco. It's got something for everyone.

Although the view of the bay is stunning, the bay's cleanliness is still somewhat in question, despite valiant efforts by city officials. The water's cleanliness is an important consideration if your ideal beach getaway includes tons of time in the ocean. If you plan on spending your afternoons in the sea, you may want to choose a different resort or, at least, a place located south of town in one of the areas fronting the Pacific Ocean rather than Acapulco Bay.

Acapulco is for you if you want to dine at midnight, dance until dawn, and sleep all day on a sun-soaked beach. (For more information, check out the chapters in Part VII.)

Top aspects of a vacation in Acapulco include

- ✔ Nightlife so hot it rivals the sunshine
- ✔ Unforgettable views of the breathtakingly beautiful bay
- ✔ An average of 360 days of sunshine per year
- ✔ Wide variety of lodging options
- ✔ Excellent air-travel connections

But also consider the following:

- ✔ The cleanliness of the bay remains questionable.
- ✔ The most popular resort with residents of Mexico City, it tends to fill up with city dwellers on weekends and major holidays.
- ✔ Acapulco has a somewhat outdated feel to it, and as a big city, it can seem less clean than other Mexican beach resorts.

Hanging out in Huatulco

The resort found farthest south along Mexico's Pacific coastline, Huatulco is the perfect place for those travelers who want to enjoy pristine beaches and jungle landscapes but would rather view them from a luxury-hotel balcony. If you want to enjoy nature's beauty during the day and then retreat to well-appointed comfort by night, Huatulco is for you.

The area offers undeveloped stretches of pure, white sands. Isolated coves lie in wait for the promised growth of Huatulco, which luckily, isn't occurring as rapidly as Cancún's expansion. Huatulco is a FONATUR development project that aims to cover 52,000 acres of land. Of that area, more than 40,000 acres are to remain as ecological preserves. (FONATUR is a government agency that develops strategic plans and assists in arranging financing for tourism development projects. It's the agency responsible for the site selection and planning of Cancún; Ixtapa and Los Cabos are other FONATUR destinations.)

Huatulco has developed a name because of its eco-tourism attractions: river rafting, rappelling, and jungle hiking, to name a few. However, the shopping, the nightlife, and even the dining options outside the hotels are scarce, and what is available is high priced for the quality.

If you're especially drawn to snorkeling, diving, boat cruises to virgin bays, and simple relaxation, Huatulco fits the bill. (See Chapter 26 for more information.)

Top aspects of a vacation in Huatulco include

- ✔ Magnificent, unspoiled beaches where you can get away from it all
- ✔ Beautifully appointed accommodations
- ✔ Slow-paced, small-town atmosphere with modern infrastructure
- ✔ Plenty of eco-oriented activities such as river rafting, rappelling, and jungle hiking
- ✔ Water-lovers paradise with plenty of snorkeling, diving, and boating
- ✔ Superb service and friendliness from the locals

But also consider the following:

- ✔ The nightlife is almost nonexistent.
- ✔ The dining and shopping options are limited.
- ✔ Reaching Huatulco is more difficult than many resorts, and a limited number of direct flights service the area.
- ✔ It's slightly more expensive than other beach resorts in Mexico.

Kicking back in Puerto Escondido

Puerto Escondido — usually referred to as Puerto — is known for its great surf, breathtaking beaches, friendly locals, and inexpensive prices. Located just north along the Pacific coastline from Huatulco, Puerto Escondido is another "real" place — not a planned development — which gives it a unique and authentic character. And it almost seems as though the locals would rather keep the place small.

In addition to its legendary surf break, Puerto is increasingly gaining a reputation with travelers seeking both spiritual and physical renewal. Abundant massage and bodywork services, yoga classes, and exceptional and varied vegetarian dining options — not to mention seaside tranquility — are hallmarks of this resort. We consider it the single best beach value in all Mexico.

European travelers make up a significant number of the visitors, and hearing a variety of languages on the beach and in the bars is common. Puerto is also a place that younger travelers favor — and one of the few resorts that offers welcoming options for the backpack- and hammock-type of traveler.

Puerto is definitely the place for surf lovers, but it's also great for those who are looking for a funky, relaxed beach attitude infused with a cosmopolitan appreciation for espresso drinks and world music. (See Chapter 27 for details on Puerto Escondido.)

Top aspects of a vacation in Puerto Escondido include

- ✔ The best surfing beaches in Mexico
- ✔ The best overall value
- ✔ Vibrant nightlife with plenty of live music
- ✔ Simple atmosphere with no pretensions of being a grand place
- ✔ Plenty of healthful and healing-oriented services

But also consider the following:

- ✔ Accommodations are generally in independent inns that feature fewer services.
- ✔ Puerto Escondido isn't a resort that caters to children. That aspect, combined with a concern about the powerful ocean surf, makes this a destination that we don't recommend for family travelers.
- ✔ Challenging air access is the rule. It usually involves complicated connections through Mexico City and/or Oaxaca, which makes travel time lengthy.

Lazing in Los Cabos

What was once considered an offbeat outpost for only the most rugged of sportsmen and vagrants has somehow evolved into Mexico's most posh beach resort. Los Cabos, located on the Baja Peninsula just south of California, actually refers to three areas: the quaint town of **San José del Cabo,** the high-energy tourist enclave of **Cabo San Lucas,** and the 18-mile-long stretch of highway connecting the two, known as **the Corridor,** which is lined with luxury resorts.

Each town has its own distinct personality: San José is a gentrified version of a small Mexican town, and Cabo San Lucas is a party place that attracts the most visitors. Alternately known as "the end of the line" and "the last resort," Cabo San Lucas boasts a let-loose nightlife that frequently goes until breakfast the next morning. Cabo San Lucas, in particular, is so American-friendly that you may find you rarely get the chance to practice your Spanish, and dollars are accepted as readily as pesos. In fact, many visitors find that it feels more like an extension of Southern California than Mexico.

Although sport-fishing originally took credit for putting Los Cabos on the map, golf is now the stronger attraction. The Corridor that connects the two "Cabos" has an impressive collection of championship golf courses interspersed at respectable distances among the gorgeous resorts dotting the coastline. Accommodations in the two bookend towns range from smaller inns to larger chain hotels.

The beaches are breathtaking — cobalt-blue ocean meeting terra-cotta desertscapes speckled with cacti. Surfing is challenging here, and the numerous inlets seem custom-made for sea kayaking. Favored land-bound activities beyond golf include ATV tours and horseback riding.

In terms of everything from taxis to dining out, Los Cabos is much more expensive than other Mexican beach resorts. One contributing factor is its remote location; other than the abundant seafood caught offshore, almost everything else needs to be trucked down the long peninsula. (The chapters in Part IX go into detail about Los Cabos.)

Top aspects of a vacation in Los Cabos include

- ✔ The sheer beauty of the combination desert and seascapes

- ✔ Outstanding sporting opportunities, from the legendary sport-fishing to premier golf, plus exceptional spas to take out the kinks

- ✔ No need to worry about speaking Spanish at this English language and U.S. dollar-friendly destination

But also consider the following:

- ✔ It's indisputably Mexico's most expensive beach resort.

- ✔ If you plan on doing any exploring, you may need to consider renting a car because the distance from one "Cabo" to another is significant.

- ✔ You may feel more like you're in Southern California than Mexico; Los Cabos has become very Americanized.

- ✔ Despite the level of sophistication of the hotels (especially along the Corridor), the region's dining and nightlife options are lacking, and they're likely to appeal to a college-age crowd at best.

Mexico's Beach Resorts: The Scorecard (3 points indicate the highest rating)

Points for:	Cancún	Cozumel	Riviera Maya	Puerto Vallarta	Ixtapa	Zihuatanejo	Acapulco	Huatulco	Puerto Escondido	Los Cabos
Luxury	3	1	1	2	3	2	2	2	1	3
Nightlife	3	1	1	3	1	1	3	1	2	3
Great food	2	1	1	3	2	1	3	1	2	2
Beaches	3	1	3	1	1	2	2	3	1	2
Bargain rates	1	2	2	3	1	3	2	1	3	1
Local color	1	2	1	3	1	3	3	1	3	1
Mexican culture	2	1	2	3	1	2	3	1	1	0
Golf	1	1	1	3	1	0	1	1	0	3
Senior appeal	2	1	1	3	1	1	2	1	0	3
Hiking	1	1	1	3	1	1	2	3	3	3
Natural beauty	2	3	3	3	1	2	3	3	3	3
Sightseeing	3	1	3	2	1	1	3	3	2	3
Diving/snorkeling	3	3	3	1	1	1	1	3	1	3
Watersports	3	3	2	3	3	3	2	3	3	3
Peace and quiet	1	2	3	1	2	3	1	3	3	2
Family friendly	3	1	3	3	3	2	3	2	1	3
Easy access	3	1	1	3	2	2	2	1	1	3

Chapter 2

Deciding When to Go

· ·

In This Chapter

▶ Understanding Mexico's weather

▶ Knowing the high and low travel seasons

▶ Planning your trip around festivals and special events

· ·

*M*exico's beach resorts enjoy sun-drenched and moderate winters, and they logically attract the most visitors when the weather at home is cold and dreary. However, almost any time of the year has its pros and cons for travel. In this chapter, we review what you can expect from the weather during different months of the year. We also highlight some of Mexico's most festive celebrations that you may want to plan your trip around.

Forecasting the Weather

Mexico has two main climatic seasons: a **rainy season** (May to mid-October) and a **dry season** (mid-October through April). The rainy season can be of little consequence in the country's dry, northern region, but the southern regions typically receive tropical showers, which begin around 4 or 5 p.m. and last a few hours. Though these rains can come on suddenly and be quite strong, they usually end just as quickly as they begin, and they cool the air for the evening. We favor the rainy season because that's when the landscape is at its most lush and tropical flowers are everywhere. The lightning flashes offshore also make for a spectacular show.

Hurricane season — June through October — particularly affects the Yucatán Peninsula and the southern Pacific coast.

June, July, and August are very hot and humid on the Yucatán Peninsula, with temperatures rising into the mid-80s and 90s Fahrenheit (low 30s Celsius). Most of coastal Mexico experiences temperatures in the 80s in the hottest months. Very high summer temperatures are reserved for Mexico's northern states that border the United States. During winter months, temperatures average 70° F to 75° F (21° C–24° C) during the days, and about 55° F to 65° F (13° C–18° C) in the evenings, in most of the resorts in this book. Los Cabos is often cooler (50° F/10° C) during winter months.

Considering Mexico's Travel Seasons

Mexico has two principal travel seasons: high and low. The **high season** begins around December 20 and continues to Easter, although in some places the high season can begin as early as mid-November. The **low season** begins the day after Easter and continues to mid-December; during the low season, prices may drop between 20% and 50%. At beach destinations popular with Mexican travelers, such as Acapulco, the prices revert back to high-season levels during July and August, the traditional, national summer vacation period. Prices at inland cities seldom fluctuate from high to low season, but they may rise dramatically during the weeks of **Easter** and **Christmas.** In Isla Mujeres and Playa del Carmen, both on the Yucatán coast, the high season starts in mid-November as well, but they also have a "second" high season, in August, when many European visitors arrive. We mention all these exceptions in the relevant chapters that follow.

We find **November** to be the best month to travel to Mexico. The scenery is still green from the recently ended rainy season, and temperatures are just beginning to turn a bit cooler, which can produce crystal-clear skies. This is especially true in Los Cabos, when even the desert is in bloom. Crowds are also at a minimum, and you're likely to find some good deals.

One time you may want to avoid is **spring break.** You find the highest concentration of high-octane party crowds in Cancún, but Puerto Vallarta also gets its fair share of craziness. Frankly, why travel to see American youth behaving badly? Other times you may want to avoid are the weeks of Christmas and Easter. During these traditional Mexican holiday periods, both crowds and prices are at their highest, but the crowds consist more of families and couples than young and rowdy revelers.

Mexico's Calendar of Events

Mexicans are known for throwing a great party — *fiesta!* — and their love of fireworks is legendary. You may choose to plan your visit around a colorful national or religious celebration. Watersports enthusiasts may consider visiting during one of the numerous regattas and sport-fishing festivals held at many of the resorts. Remember that during national holidays, Mexican banks and government offices — including immigration — are closed.

Mexicans celebrate Christmas and Easter similarly to the way they're celebrated in the United States, but Christmas is much more religiously oriented, and they place less emphasis on Santa and gift exchanges.

January/February/March

Día de Reyes (Three Kings Day) commemorates the three kings bringing gifts to the Christ child. On this day, children receive gifts, much like the traditional exchange of gifts that accompanies Christmas in the United States. Friends and families gather to share the *Rosca de Reyes,* a special cake. A small doll representing the Christ child is placed within the cake; whoever receives the doll in his or her piece must host a *tamales*-and-*atole* (meat or sweet filling wrapped in a cornhusk and a hot drink) party the next month. January 6.

Music, dances, processions, food, and other festivities are features of **Día de la Candelaria (Candlemass)** and lead up to a blessing of seed and candles in a celebration that mixes pre-Hispanic and European traditions marking the end of winter. All those who attended the Día de Reyes celebration reunite to share *atole* and *tamales* at a party hosted by the recipient of the doll found in the *rosca.* February 2.

Día de la Constitución (Constitution Day) is a celebration in honor of the current Mexican constitution that was signed in 1917 following the Mexican Revolution of 1910. If you're in Mexico on this day, you find a parade wherever you are. February 5.

Carnaval (Carnival) is the last celebration before Lent, and it's celebrated with special gusto in Cozumel and in Mazatlán, north of Puerto Vallarta. Here, the celebration resembles New Orleans's Mardi Gras with a festive atmosphere and parades. Transportation and hotels are packed, so try to make reservations six months in advance and arrive a couple of days before the beginning of celebrations. Three days preceding Ash Wednesday and the beginning of Lent.

Benito Juárez was a reformist leader and a Mexican president who became a national hero. The national holiday honoring **Benito Juárez's birthday** is the same date as the **spring equinox,** an important celebration of the ancient Mexicans. In Chichén-Itzá (chee-*chin* eat-*zah*), the ancient Mayan city located 179km (112 miles) from Cancún, the celebration of the first day of spring is particularly impressive. The Temple of Kukulcán — Chichén-Itzá's main pyramid — aligns with the sun, and the shadow of the body of its plumed serpent moves slowly from the top of the building downward. When the shadow reaches the bottom, the body joins the carved-stone snake's head at the base of the pyramid. According to ancient legend, at the moment that the serpent is whole, the earth is fertilized to assure a bountiful growing season. Visitors come from around the world to marvel at this sight, so advance arrangements are advisable. Elsewhere, festivals and celebrations to welcome spring mark the equinox. In the custom of the ancient Mexicans, people perform dances and say prayers to the elements and the four cardinal points (north, south, east, west) in order to renew their energy for the upcoming year. Wearing white with a red ribbon is customary. March 21. (You can see the serpent's shadow at Chichén-Itzá from March 19 to March 23.)

April/May/June

Semana Santa (Holy Week) celebrates the last week in the life of Christ from Palm Sunday through Easter Sunday with somber religious processions, spoofs of Judas, and reenactments of specific biblical events, plus food and craft fairs. Businesses close during this traditional week of Mexican national vacations. If you plan on traveling to or around Mexico during Holy Week, make your reservations early. Airline seats on flights into and out of the country are reserved months in advance. Buses to almost anywhere in Mexico are always full, so try arriving on the Wednesday or Thursday prior to the start of Holy Week. Easter Sunday is quiet. The week following is a traditional vacation period. Week before Easter.

Labor Day is a national holiday celebrating workers. It features countrywide parades and fiestas. May 1.

Cinco de Mayo is a national holiday that celebrates the defeat of the French at the Battle of Puebla in 1862. May 5.

July/August/September

Mexico begins **Día de Independencia (Independence Day)** — the holiday that marks Mexico's independence from Spain — at 11 p.m. on September 15, with the president of Mexico's famous independence *grito* (shout) from the National Palace in Mexico City. The rest of the country watches the event on TV or participates in local celebrations, which mirror the festivities at the national level. September 16 is the actual Independence Day and is celebrated with parades, picnics, and family reunions throughout the country. September 15 and 16.

During the **fall equinox,** Chichén-Itzá once again takes center stage as the same serpent shadow play that occurs during the spring equinox repeats itself for the fall equinox, representing the fall harvest. September 21 and 22.

October/November/December

What's commonly called the **Día de los Muertos** (Day of the Dead) is actually two days: All Saints Day, honoring saints and deceased children, and All Souls Day, honoring deceased adults. Relatives gather at cemeteries countrywide, carrying candles and food, and often spend the night beside the graves of loved ones. Weeks before, bakers begin producing bread formed in the shape of mummies and round loaves decorated with bread "bones." Decorated sugar skulls emblazoned with glittery names are sold everywhere. Many days ahead, homes and churches erect special altars laden with bread, fruit, flowers, candles, photographs of saints and of the deceased, and favorite foods and photographs of the deceased. On these two nights, children walk through the streets dressed in costumes and masks, often carrying mock coffins and pumpkin lanterns, into which they expect money to be dropped. November 1 and 2.

Puerto Vallarta goes all out during **Fiestas del Mar (SeaFest),** a month-long calendar of activities that includes art festivals, sports competitions, the Governor's Cup golf tournament, and an outstanding gourmet-dining festival, which features guest chefs from around the world working with local chefs in select restaurants. Among the sporting events are sailing regattas, windsurfing exhibitions, and beach volleyball competitions. November 10 to 30.

Día de Revolución (Revolution Day) is a national holiday commemorating the start of the Mexican Revolution in 1910 with parades, speeches, rodeos, and patriotic events. November 20.

During the **Día de Nuestra Señora de Guadalupe (Feast of the Virgin of Guadalupe),** people throughout the country honor Mexico's patroness with religious processions, street fairs, dancing, fireworks, and masses. It's one of Mexico's most moving and beautiful displays of traditional culture. In December 1531, the Virgin of Guadalupe appeared to a young man, Juan Diego, on a hill near Mexico City. He convinced the bishop that he had seen the apparition by revealing his cloak, upon which the Virgin was emblazoned. In Puerto Vallarta, the celebration begins on December 1 and extends through December 12, with traditional processions to the church for a brief mass and blessing. In the final days, the processions and festivities take place around the clock. A major fireworks exhibition takes place on December 12 at 11 p.m. December 1 to 12.

Christmas Posadas celebrates the Holy Family's trek to Bethlehem. On each of the nine nights before Christmas, people customarily reenact the Holy Family's search for an inn with door-to-door candlelit processions in cities and villages nationwide. December 15 to 24.

Chapter 3

Planning Your Budget

. . . .

In This Chapter

▶ Checking out hotel, transportation, and dining costs

▶ Finding out when and what to tip

▶ Figuring out those extra expenses: activities, attractions, and shopping

▶ Considering taxes

▶ Discovering budget-saving tips

. . . .

The brochures are in front of you, and visions of lazy, sunny days fill your thoughts — so who wants to think about money? Take a few minutes to figure out your expected expenses now, so you can enjoy a worry-free vacation later.

Your choice of beach resort greatly affects your budget. A room in Los Cabos is considerably more expensive than one in Puerto Vallarta, and ditto for all the other expenses down the line. After you figure out your hotel and airfare, calculate the other estimated costs associated with your trip to plan a proper budget.

Using the worksheets at the back of this book to jot down anticipated costs can help you know whether you need to trim any of your expenses. Or even better, you may discover that you can afford to slip into that oceanfront room or plan that sunset sail you've been dreaming of.

To make certain that you don't forget any expenses, try taking a mental stroll through your entire trip. Start with the costs of transportation from your home to the airport, your airline tickets, and transfers to your hotel. Add your daily hotel rate (don't forget taxes!), meals, activities, entertainment, taxis, tips, your return to the airport, and finally, your return trip home from the airport and any parking fees you may have incurred. Just to be safe, add an extra 15% to 20% for extra, unexpected costs that may pop up.

Calculating Your Hotel Cost

The biggest part of your vacation budget will go toward your hotel and airfare, so we suggest getting those expenses down as low as possible. In the various destination chapters, we use dollar signs ($–$$$$$) to indicate the price category (in U.S. dollars) of each hotel. (Check out the Introduction of this book for a rundown on the price categories and their corresponding dollar signs.)

You can get a room for $30 a night, or you can get a room for $700 a night! Keep in mind that some room rates include breakfast — or all meals, beverages, and entertainment — so be sure to compare mangos with mangos. Also, when finalizing your reservations, be sure to check whether the total cost includes taxes and tips.

Even within a resort, the price of rooms can vary widely. Room location — oceanfront versus a view of a dumpster — is one differential. Ask yourself how much your room location matters. Do you view your room as simply a place to sleep, shower, and dress? Or will you not feel officially "on vacation" unless you can fall asleep to the sound of the surf? If so, a pricier room may well be worth it. However, remember that many garden-view rooms in our recommendations are only steps away from the beach and possibly even more tranquil than their oceanfront counterparts.

When it comes to rates, the most common term is **rack rate.** The rack rate is the maximum rate that a resort or hotel charges for a room. It's the rate you get if you walk in off the street and ask for a room on a night that the place is close to being full.

Often, the rack rate is the first rate a hotel offers, but you usually don't have to pay it. Always ask whether a lower rate or special package is available — it can't hurt, and you may at least end up with a free breakfast or spa service.

In this book, we use rack rates as a guidepost, not expecting that you'll have to pay them. Minimum night stays, special promotions, and seasonal discounts can all go a long way toward bringing the rack rate down. Also, be sure to mention your frequent-flier or corporate-rewards programs if you book with one of the larger hotel chains. Please note that rates change often, so the prices quoted in this book may be different from the prices you're quoted when you make your reservation.

Room rates also rise and fall with occupancy rates. If your hotel choice is close to empty, it pays to negotiate. Resorts tend to be much more crowded during weekends.

Feeling romantic? Special packages for **honeymooners** are really popular in Mexican beach resorts. Even if you've been hitched for a while, your trip can be a second honeymoon, right? If you ask, you may end up with a complimentary bottle of champagne and flower petals on your bed.

Mexico couldn't be more accommodating to travelers with children. Many of the larger chains don't charge extra for children staying in the same room as their parents, and some offer special meal programs and other amenities for younger travelers. Although rollaway beds are common, you may have a challenge finding a crib. Ask about this contingency when making your reservation.

Totaling Transportation Costs

After taking care of your airfare (for tips on finding low airfare, see Chapter 5), your transportation costs vary depending upon your choice of Mexican beach resorts. Even though some resort areas — such as Cancún — offer economical shuttles and great public transportation options, others — such as Los Cabos — have such expensive local transportation that getting around may cost even more than getting there.

One advantage of a **package tour** (when you make one payment that covers airfare, hotel, round-trip transportation to your accommodations, and occasionally meals or tours) is that the round-trip ground transportation between the airport and your hotel is usually included. If you're not certain whether your package covers ground transportation, ask. Note that the Mexican taxi union is strong, so you're unlikely to find much shuttle transportation provided by your hotel.

Generally, renting a car doesn't make sense, with the noted exceptions being in Los Cabos and possibly Cozumel if you're looking to explore the far side of the island there. Renting a small car runs about $70 a day on average, including insurance, so you may want to squeeze your car-dependent explorations into a day or two at the most. Planning your rental-car excursions to coincide with your arrival or departure is also wise so that you can use your wheels for either leg of your airport-hotel transportation needs.

As a rule, taxis tend to be the most economical and efficient transportation for getting around the other beach destinations, such as Puerto Vallarta, Cancún, Acapulco, and Huatulco. In each of the chapters detailing these resorts, we provide taxi rates for getting around town.

Estimating Dining Dollars

In each resort's dining section, Parts III through IX, we describe our favorite restaurants, all of which include dollar signs ($–$$$$$) to give you an idea of the prices you can expect to pay (in U.S. dollars). Refer to the Introduction of this book for a detailed explanation of these price categories.

The prices quoted refer to main courses at dinner, unless otherwise specified. We eliminate the most expensive shrimp and lobster dishes from our estimates to avoid pre-trip sticker shock. In most cases, you can find additional entrees above and below our quoted price range. To estimate your total dining expenses, add in estimated costs for beverages, appetizers, desserts, and tips as well.

Hotels increasingly are offering dining plans. To help you wade through the terminology, review the following basics:

- ✔ **Continental plan (CP):** Includes a light breakfast — usually juices, fruits, pastries or breads, and coffee.

- ✔ **Breakfast plan (BP):** Includes a full, traditional American-style breakfast of eggs, bacon, French toast, hash browns, and so forth.

- ✔ **Modified American plan (MAP):** Includes breakfast (usually a full one) and dinner.

- ✔ **Full American plan (FAP):** Includes three meals a day.

- ✔ **All-inclusive:** Includes three all-you-can-eat meals a day, plus snacks, soft drinks, and alcoholic beverages. Sometimes, additional charges apply for premium liquors or wines.

- ✔ **European plan (EP):** No meals are included.

Mexican beach-resort hotels are known for their expansive breakfast buffets. But the buffets can also be expensive, averaging about $20, even for small children. If breakfast is your main meal or only meal of the day, these all-you-can-eat extravaganzas may be worthwhile; otherwise, you're probably better off sleeping in or finding breakfast elsewhere.

The highest dining-out prices are in Los Cabos. Because almost all ingredients need to be transported from the mainland, the costs are much higher.

Be sure to explore restaurants away from your hotel. You're likely to get a much better dining value, and you can truly savor the diverse flavors of Mexico. For eateries that best represent the flavorful (and we don't mean spicy) cuisine of Mexico, look for the ¡Viva Mexico! icon that accompanies some of the restaurant reviews throughout this book.

While you're in Mexico, be sure to try the local beers. Corona is the best-known brew, but other excellent choices are Bohemia, Modelo Especial, Pacifico, Indio, and Dos Equis Negro. Beer in Mexico is often cheaper than soft drinks! Your vacation is looking better and better, isn't it?

Tipping Tips

Many travelers skimp on tips in Mexico, but please don't. Most of the employees in this country's hospitality industry receive the majority of their income from tips. For bellmen or porters, the equivalent of $1 per bag is appropriate. For hotel housekeeping, tip between $1 and $2 per night, depending upon the type of hotel you're staying in. For restaurant service, 15% is standard, but consider 20% if the service is particularly noteworthy. Oddly enough, the one area you don't need to consider is tips for taxis — tipping taxi drivers here isn't customary unless they help with baggage or you've hired them on an hourly basis and they double as a tour guide.

You'll no doubt run into all sorts of enterprising young boys looking for a tip to point you in the direction of your restaurant, help you into a parking spot, or do some other sort of unnecessary favor. In cases like these, tip as you see fit, or as the spirit moves you.

Spending Wisely on Activities, Attractions, and Shopping

You're going to a beach resort, so regardless of your budget, you always have the option of simply soaking up the tropical sun during the day and then taking in the moonlit nights. It's the most economical plan and a relaxing and enjoyable option for many. Still, with so much to do and see, you probably want to spend some time and money getting out and enjoying Mexico's many treasures.

Pricing for **sightseeing tours** varies by the destination, the length of time of the excursion, whether or not a meal and beverages are included, and other extras. However, you can use some pretty typical ranges as guidelines. A city tour generally runs from $12 to $20; half-day boat cruises that include lunch can cost between $40 and $60; and full-day excursions to neighboring areas run between $60 and $150.

If you plan to take part in any **sports-related activities** such as golf, diving, or sport-fishing, you may find the prices to be higher than back home, but you're also apt to find a bargain when comparing other beach-resort venues. For example, greens fees at the Acapulco

Princess Golf Club are $63, but the fees at Cabo del Sol in Los Cabos are more than $200 for 18 holes. Dives range from around $50 to $70 for a two-tank dive, but you tend to really get what you pay for in terms of quality of equipment and dive guides, so it's best to pay up. Cozumel has the greatest selection of expert dive shops, and the competition makes Cozumel's prices the most reasonable for the quality of experience. Going fishing? Cost variables beyond your point of departure include boat size, charter options, and type of gear and refreshments, but count on spending between $50 and $75 per person for a half-day charter.

As for **nightlife,** the cost depends more on your personal tastes. The "hot" nightlife areas, such as Acapulco and Cancún, are pricier than others, and $20 cover charges are common during busier times. Puerto Vallarta and Los Cabos have more casual and less expensive, but just as lively, nightlife options. You're not bound to spend too much cash in Ixtapa, Cozumel, or Huatulco, either, simply because there's not much to do after dark in these locations. When you're out on the town, beer is the best bargain, costing about $1 to $3 per beer. Premium brand drinks can run you around $3 to $5 each (though when outside your hotel, you may want to avoid drinks requiring ice). Women can easily find bargains such as "two-for-one" or "all-you-can-drink" specials.

Shopping is your call — you can plan to spend or save here. Besides silver jewelry and other souvenirs, the best excuse for shopping in Mexico is the great prices on duty-free perfumes, watches, and other goods in Cancún and along the Riviera Maya. Other destinations have less to offer in the duty-free area, but we discuss each resort's shopping specialties in greater detail within their respective chapters, in Parts III through IX.

Taxing Issues

A 15% **value-added tax** (*impuesto al valor agregado,* **or IVA**) is added to goods and services in most of Mexico (10% in Cancún, Cozumel, and Los Cabos), and it's supposed to be included in the posted price. Unlike other countries (Canada and Spain, for example), Mexico doesn't refund this tax when visitors leave the country, so you don't need to hang on to those receipts for refund purposes.

Published prices you encounter in your travels around Mexico's beaches are likely to include all applicable taxes, except for hotel rates, which are usually published without the 15% IVA and the 2% lodging tax.

An **exit tax** of approximately $18 is imposed on every foreigner leaving Mexico via the air. This tax is usually — but not always — included in the price of airline tickets. Be sure to reserve at least this amount in cash for your departure day if you're not certain that it's included in your ticket price.

Cutting Costs

While planning your trip, keep in mind certain things that may help you save some money. Before you leave for vacation, don't forget to consider the incidentals that can really add up — hotel taxes, tips, and telephone surcharges.

Here are a few other suggestions to help keep a lid on expenses so that they don't blow your vacation budget:

✔ **Travel in the off-season.** If you can travel at non-peak times (September through November, for example), you can usually find better hotel bargains.

✔ **Travel on off days of the week.** If you can travel on a Tuesday, Wednesday, or Thursday, you may find cheaper flights to your destination. When you inquire about airfares, ask whether flying on a different day is cheaper.

✔ **Try a package tour.** With one call to a travel agent or packager, you can book airfare, hotel, ground transportation, and even some sightseeing for many of these destinations for a lot less than if you tried to put the trip together yourself. (See Chapter 5 for specific suggestions of package tour companies to contact.)

✔ **Always ask for discount rates.** Membership in AAA, frequent-flier plans, AARP, or other groups may qualify you for a discount on plane tickets and hotel rooms if you book them in the United States. In Mexico, you can generally get a discount based on how full the hotel is at the time you show up; however, you're also taking a chance on a vacancy not being available.

✔ **Get a room off the beach.** Accommodations within walking distance of the shore can be much cheaper than those right on the beach. Beaches in Mexico are public, so you don't need to stay in a hotel that's on the sand to spend most of your vacation at the beach.

✔ **Share your room with your kids.** In Mexico, this setup is usually the norm rather than the exception, so book a room with two double beds. Most hotels don't charge extra for up to two children staying in their parents' room.

✔ **Use public transportation whenever practical.** Not only will you save taxi fare, but simply getting to where you're going can be like a mini-excursion as you enjoy the local scene! In Cancún, you're apt to run into mostly tourists on the clean, public buses of the hotel zone. In Puerto Vallarta, you may be serenaded along the bus route — it's part of the charm!

✔ **Cut down on the souvenirs.** We realize expecting you to return home without any local treasures may be too much to ask, but think hard about whether that oversized sombrero will be as charming back home. Your photographs and memories are likely to be your best mementos.

✔ **Use public phones and pre-paid phone cards to call home.** Avoid using the phone in your hotel room to call outside the hotel. Charges can be astronomical, even for local calls. Rather than placing the call yourself, say, for a dinner or tour reservation, ask the concierge to make a reservation for you — he or she will do it as a service. If you do have to make a call, keep in mind that you'll even be charged a surcharge for using your own calling card and its 800 number. Most 800 numbers aren't toll free when dialed from Mexico. And avoid using the public phones that urge you, in English, to call home using *their* 800 number. This is the absolute most expensive way to call home, and the service charges the call to your home phone. The best option? Buy a Ladatel (brand name for Mexico's public phones) prepaid phone card, available at most pharmacies, and dial direct using the instructions in Appendix A of this book.

✔ **Steer clear of the minibar and room service.** Those little bottles can really add up! Consider buying your own supplies and bringing them to your room, and you'll save a bundle. Likewise, room service is the most expensive way to dine — a service charge and tip are added on top of generally inflated prices. Also, some hotels provide complimentary bottled water, but others charge as much as $5 per bottle, so be sure you know what you're drinking.

✔ **Drink local.** Imported labels can be twice the price as the national brands, which often are also imported but just imported from areas other than the United States. At least ask what's being served as the house brand — you may be pleasantly surprised.

✔ **Follow Mexican custom and have lunch as your main meal.** If the restaurant of your dreams is open only for dinner, save that one for your one "splurge" evening and try out other restaurants for your midday meal. Lunch tabs are usually a fraction of their dinner counterparts, and they frequently feature many of the same specialties.

✔ **Skimp on shrimp and lobster.** Sure, we know — you're sitting seaside and dreaming of that tasty lobster. Just understand that they're the priciest items on the menu, and the less expensive and local fresh fish is often just as good or better.

✔ **Buy Mexican bottled water.** Forget the water labels that you know — Mexico's bottled waters are just as good as the imports and about half the price.

Chapter 4

Tips for Travelers with Special Interests

· ·

· ·

*M*ost people consider themselves unique with special needs, but some types of travelers really do warrant a little extra advice. In this chapter, we cover information that's helpful to know if you're traveling with children, if you're a senior traveler, if you have special needs because of a disability, if you're gay or lesbian, if you're traveling solo, or if you're planning on tying the knot in Mexico. Throughout the chapter, we clue you in on what to expect, offer some useful tips, and whenever possible, steer you to experts concerning your particular circumstances.

Vacationing with Children

Children are considered the national treasure of Mexico, and Mexicans warmly welcome and cater to your kids. Although many parents were reluctant to bring young children to Mexico in the past, primarily due to health concerns, we can't think of a better place to introduce children to the exciting adventure of exploring a different culture. Some of the best destinations for children include Puerto Vallarta, Cancún, and Acapulco. Hotels can often arrange for a babysitter. Some hotels in the moderate-to-luxury range have small playgrounds and pools for children and hire caretakers who offer special-activity programs during the day, but few budget hotels offer these amenities. All-inclusive resorts make great options for family travel because, as a rule, they offer exhaustive activities programs. They also make mealtime easy by offering buffet-style meal services almost around the clock.

Before leaving for your trip, check with your pediatrician or family doctor to get advice on medications to take along. Disposable diapers cost about the same in Mexico as they do in the United States, but the quality is poorer. You can get brand-name diapers identical to the ones sold in the United States, but you'll pay a higher price. Many stores sell familiar, brand-name baby foods. Dry cereals, powdered formulas, baby bottles, and purified water are all easily available in midsize and large cities or resorts.

Cribs, however, may present a problem; only the largest and most luxurious hotels provide them. However, rollaway beds to accommodate children staying in a room with their parents are often available. Child seats or highchairs at restaurants are common, and most restaurants go out of their way to accommodate the comfort of your children. You may want to consider bringing your own car seat along because they're not readily available to rent in Mexico.

We recommend that you take coloring books, puzzles, and small games with you to keep your children entertained during the flight or whenever you're traveling from one destination to the next. Another good idea is to take a blank notebook, in which your children can paste little souvenirs from the trip, such as the label from the beer Daddy drank on the beach or small shells and flowers that they collect. And don't forget to carry small scissors (pack the scissors during the flight due to security reasons) and a glue stick with you, or the blank notebook may remain blank.

The following is a list of Web sites where you can find helpful advice on traveling with children:

- ✔ **Family Travel Network** (www.familytravelnetwork.com) offers travel tips and reviews of family-friendly destinations, vacation deals, and thoughtful features such as "What to Do When Your Kids Are Afraid to Travel" and "Kid-Style Camping."

- ✔ **Kids Travel Buddies** (www.kidstravelbuddies.com) and **Activities for Kids** (www.activitiesforkids.com) provide other general resources for tips on traveling with children.

- ✔ **Travel with Your Kids** (www.travelwithyourkids.com) is a comprehensive site offering sound advice for traveling with children.

Seeking Specials for Seniors

Mexico is a popular country for retirees and for senior travelers. For decades, North Americans have been living indefinitely in Mexico by returning to the border and re-crossing with a new tourist permit every 6 months. Mexican immigration officials have caught on, and they now limit the maximum time you can spend in the country to 6 months in any given year. This measure is meant to encourage even partial residents to comply with the proper documentation procedures. The following can provide some information for seniors thinking of retiring in Mexico:

- ✔ **AIM** (*Adventures in Mexico*) is a well-written, candid, and very informative newsletter for prospective retirees. Recent issues evaluated retirement in Puerto Vallarta, Puerto Angel, Puerto Escondido, and Huatulco. For subscriptions, which are $18 to the United States and $21 to Canada, write to Apdo. Postal 31–70, 45050 Guadalajara, Jalisco, Mexico. Back issues are three for $5.

- ✔ **Sanborn Tours** (2015 South 10th St., McAllen, TX, 78503; ☎ 800-395-8482) offers a "Retire in Mexico" orientation tour.

- ✔ Puerto Vallarta resident and author Polly Vicars's ***Tales of Retirement in Paradise*** offers an entertaining account of the pleasures of "retired" life in this seaside town — a very popular beach resort with senior travelers. All proceeds from the book go to the America-Mexico Foundation (www.puerto-vallarta.com/amf), which provides scholarships to needy and deserving Mexican students. You can buy the $20 book online through Amazon.com (www.amazon.com) or purchase it directly from the author via e-mail at phvicars@pvnet.com.mx. The book is also available for sale in Puerto Vallarta at bookstores and various shops.

For seniors more interested in traveling rather than moving, you're not alone. People older than 60 are traveling more than ever before. And why not? Being a senior citizen entitles you to some terrific travel bargains.

- ✔ If you're not a member of **AARP** (601 E St. NW, Washington, DC 20049; ☎ **800-424-3410** or 202-434-AARP; www.aarp.org), formerly the American Association of Retired Persons, do yourself a favor and join. AARP offers members a wide range of benefits, including *Modern Maturity* magazine and a monthly newsletter. Anyone older than 50 can join.

- ✔ **Grand Circle Travel** (347 Congress St., Suite 3A, Boston, MA 02210; ☎ **800-221-2610;** www.gct.com) is one of the hundreds of travel agencies that specialize in vacations for seniors. But beware: Many agencies are of the tour-bus variety, with free trips thrown in for those who organize groups of 20 or more. If you're seeking more independent travel, consult a regular travel agent.

- ✔ **SAGA International Holidays** (222 Berkeley St., Boston, MA 02116; ☎ **800-343-0273**) offers inclusive tours and cruises for those 50 and older.

Ensuring Access for Travelers with Disabilities

A disability needn't stop anybody from traveling. More options and resources are available than ever before. *A World of Options,* a 658-page book of resources for travelers with disabilities, covers everything from biking trips to scuba outfitters. It costs $35 and is available from **Mobility International USA** (P.O. Box 10767, Eugene, OR 97440; ☎ 541-343-1284 voice and TTY; www.miusa.org). Another source to check out is **Access-Able Travel Source** (www.access-able.com), a comprehensive database of travel agents who specialize in disabled travel; it's also a clearinghouse for information about accessible destinations around the world.

We need to honestly say that Mexico does fall far behind other countries when it comes to accessible travel. In fact, you may feel like you're maneuvering one giant obstacle course. At airports, you may encounter steep stairs before finding a well-hidden elevator or escalator — if one exists. Airlines often arrange wheelchair assistance for passengers to the baggage area. Porters are generally available to help with luggage at airports and large bus stations after you clear baggage claim.

Escalators (and there aren't many in the beach resorts) are often non-operational. Stairs without handrails abound. Few restrooms are equipped for travelers with disabilities, and when one is available, access to it may be via a narrow passage that doesn't accommodate a wheelchair or a person on crutches. Many deluxe hotels (the most expensive) now have rooms with baths for people with disabilities. Budget travelers may be best off looking for single-story motels, although accessing showers and bathrooms may still pose a problem outside of specially equipped deluxe hotels. Generally speaking, no matter where you are, someone will lend a hand, although you may have to ask for it.

Few airports offer the luxury of boarding an airplane from the waiting area. You either descend stairs to a bus that ferries you to a waiting plane that you board by climbing stairs, or you walk across the airport tarmac to your plane and climb up the stairs. Deplaning presents the same problems in reverse.

In our opinion, the wide, modern streets and sidewalks of Cancún make it among the most "accessible" resorts. In addition to the superior public facilities, you can find numerous accommodation options for travelers with disabilities.

In addition to Cancún, over the past two years, the downtown area of Puerto Vallarta has become almost fully "accessible" for those with disabilities, adding ramps to all sidewalks, the central plaza, and along the seaside *malecón* (boardwalk), thanks to the efforts of a local activist. These enhancements also make Cancún especially appealing for those with strollers, or others in search of friendlier curbs and walking areas.

Travelers with disabilities may also want to consider joining a tour that caters specifically to them. One of the best operators is **Flying Wheels Travel** (P.O. Box 382, Owatonna, MN 55060; ☎ **507-451-5005;** Fax: 507-451-1685; www.flyingwheelstravel.com). The agency offers various escorted tours and cruises, as well as private tours in minivans with lifts. Another good company is **FEDCAP Rehabilitation Services** (211 W. 14th St., New York, NY 10011). Call ☎ **212-727-4200** (Fax: 212-727-4373) for information about membership and summer tours.

Accessible Journeys (☎ **800-846-4537** or 610-521-0339; www.disabilitytravel.com) caters specifically to slow walkers and wheelchair travelers and their families and friends. **Access Adventures** (206 Chestnut Ridge Rd., Rochester, NY, 14624; ☎ **585-889-9096**) offers customized itineraries for a variety of travelers with disabilities. **The Moss Rehab Hospital** (☎ **215-456-9603;** www.mossresourcenet.org) provides friendly, helpful phone assistance through its **Travel Information Service. The Society for Accessible Travel and Hospitality** (☎ **212-447-7284;** Fax: 212-725-8253; www.sath.org) offers a wealth of travel resources for people with all types of disabilities, and informed recommendations on destinations, access guides, travel agents, tour operators, vehicle rentals, and companion services. Annual membership costs $45 for adults, $30 for seniors and students.

Vision-impaired travelers can contact the **American Foundation for the Blind** (11 Penn Plaza, Suite 300, New York, NY 10001; ☎ **800-232-5463;** www.afb.org) for information on traveling with seeing-eye dogs.

Gathering Advice for Gays and Lesbians

Mexico is a conservative country with deeply rooted Catholic religious traditions. Public displays of same-sex affection are rare, especially outside the major resort areas. Women in Mexico frequently walk hand in hand, but anything more crosses the boundary of acceptability. However, gay and lesbian travelers are generally treated with respect and shouldn't experience any harassment, assuming the appropriate regard is given to local culture and customs. Puerto Vallarta, with its selection of accommodations and entertainment oriented especially toward gay and lesbian travelers, is perhaps the most welcoming and accepting destination in Mexico. Susan Weisman's travel service, **Bayside Properties** (☎ **322-223-4424;** www.baysidepuertovallarta.com), rents gay-friendly condos, villas, and hotels for individuals and large groups. Her services are customized to individual needs, and she can offer airport pickups and in-villa cooks.

The International Gay & Lesbian Travel Association (IGLTA) (☎ 800-448-8550 or 954-776-2626; Fax: 954-776-3303; www.iglta.org) can provide helpful information and additional tips. The **Travel Alternatives Group (TAG)** maintains a database and a gay-friendly accommodations guide. For details, call ☎ 415-437-3800 or e-mail the group at info@ mark8ing.com. **Arco Iris** is a gay-owned, full-service travel agency and tour operator specializing in Mexico packages and special group travel. Contact the agency by phone (☎ 800-765-4370 or 619-297-0897; Fax: 619-297-6419) or through the Web site at www.arcoiristours.com. **Now, Voyager** (☎ 800-255-6951; www.nowvoyager.com) is a San Francisco-based, gay-owned-and-operated travel service. **Olivia Cruises & Resorts** (☎ 800-631-6277 or 510-655-0364; www.olivia.com) charters entire resorts and ships for exclusive lesbian vacations all over the world.

Traveling Solo

Mexico is a great place to travel on your own without really being or feeling alone. Although identical room rates for single and double occupancy are slowly becoming a trend in Mexico, many of the hotels in this book still offer single rooms at lower rates.

Mexicans are very friendly, and meeting other foreigners is easy. But if you don't like the idea of traveling alone, try **Travel Companion Exchange (TCE)** (P.O. Box 833, Amityville, NY, 11701; ☎ 631-454-0880; Fax: 631-454-0170; www.travelcompanions.com), which brings prospective travelers together. Members complete a profile and then place an anonymous listing of their travel interests in the newsletter. Prospective traveling companions then make contact through the exchange. Membership costs $99 for 6 months or $159 for a year. TCE also offers an excellent booklet, for $4.95, on avoiding theft and scams while traveling abroad.

As a female traveling alone, Lynne (one of this book's authors) can tell you firsthand that she generally feels safer traveling in Mexico than in the United States. But use the same common-sense precautions you use when traveling anywhere else in the world, and stay alert to what's going on around you.

Mexicans, in general, and men, in particular, are nosy about single travelers, especially women. If taxi drivers or anyone else with whom you don't want to become friendly asks about your marital status, family, and so on, our advice is to make up a set of answers (regardless of the truth): "I'm married, traveling with friends, and I have three children."

Saying you're single and traveling alone may send out the wrong message about availability. Face it — whether you like it or not, Mexico is still a macho country with the double standards that a macho attitude implies. Movies and television shows exported from the United States have created an image of sexually aggressive North American women. If someone bothers you, don't try to be polite — just leave or head into a public place.

You may even consider wearing a ring that resembles a wedding band. Most Mexican men stay away at the sight of a ring, and it also deters many uncomfortable questions.

Planning a Wedding in Mexico

Mexico's beaches may be old favorites for romantic honeymoons, but have you ever considered taking the plunge in Mexico? A destination wedding saves money and can be less hassle compared with marrying back home. Many hotels and attractions offer wedding packages, which can include everything from booking the officiant to hiring the videographer. Pick the plan you want and, presto, your wedding decisions are done! Several properties also provide the services of a wedding coordinator (either for free or at a reasonable cost) who not only scouts out sweetheart pink roses but also can handle marriage licenses and other formalities. A destination wedding can be as informal or as traditional as you like. After returning from their honeymoon, many couples hold a reception for people back home who couldn't join them. At these parties, couples sometimes continue the theme of their wedding locale (decorate with piñatas or hire a mariachi band, for example) and show a video of their ceremony so that everyone can share in their happiness.

If you invite guests to your destination wedding, find out about group rates for hotels and airfare, which can save 20% or more off regular prices. Plan as far ahead as possible so that people can arrange their schedules and join you.

Under a treaty between the United States and Mexico, Mexican civil marriages are automatically valid in the United States. You need certified copies of birth certificates, driver's licenses, or passports; certified proof of divorce or the death certificate of any former spouses (if applicable); tourist cards (provided when you enter Mexico); and results of blood tests performed in Mexico within 15 days before the ceremony.

Check with a local, on-site wedding planner through your hotel to verify all the necessary requirements and obtain an application well in advance of your desired wedding date. Contact the **Mexican Tourism Board** (☎ **800-446-3942;** www.visitmexico.com) for information.

Part II
Ironing Out the Details

The 5th Wave   By Rich Tennant

"Do you mind NOT practicing your 'Olé's!' while I'm vacuuming?"

In this part . . .

Ready to travel to Mexico? Well then, it's probably time to do a little planning. In the next three chapters, we help you with the basics you need to consider when booking your ideal trip to one of Mexico's beach destinations. We help you decide whether to use a travel agent or to take care of the arrangements on your own, cover the pros and cons of package deals, and point you in the direction of the best places to find the information you need to accurately plan and budget your trip. Finally, we cover the nitty-gritty details — from getting your passport to packing your bags — you need to know so that you can enjoy a hassle-free vacation.

Chapter 5

Making Your Travel Arrangements

. . . .

In This Chapter

▶ Choosing to use a travel agent or planning your own trip

▶ Knowing what to expect from a travel agent

▶ Understanding package tours

▶ Taking a look at airlines and airfares

▶ Finding the best room for your needs

▶ Booking on a Web site

. . . .

*M*exico is known for its simplicity of life and easy-going ways, so why should getting there be any more complicated? Whether you're a do-it-yourselfer or a person who prefers to let someone else take care of the details, reading this chapter can save you time, money, and confusion. We point you in the direction of travel agents — and Internet tools — and explain the benefits and limitations of traveling on a package tour. We offer tips on getting the best airfares and choosing the best airline to whisk you away to your dreamy Mexican beach.

Using a Travel Agent versus Planning on Your Own

Deciding whether to use the services of a travel agent or do your own planning comes down to one key component: time. If you don't have a lot of time, seeking a travel agent may be the way to go. If you've got some time to spare, you may enjoy planning your own trip. Either way, both options have their benefits.

Keep in mind that many wholesalers that sell travel packages to Mexico make these available only through travel agents, meaning that your best value could also come with the added benefit of saving time.

Going with a travel agent

The best way to find a good travel agent is the same way you find a good plumber, mechanic, or doctor — through word of mouth — and the similarities don't end there. Travel agents can be as valuable as these other pros in your life, especially if you're a frequent traveler.

One of the main benefits of using a travel agent is that he or she can save you time. And if a travel agent specializes in Mexico, all the better. You're likely to gain personal insights or discover things about a destination or hotel that simply can't come through in a brochure.

Any travel agent can help you find a bargain airfare, hotel, or rental car. A good travel agent stops you from ruining your vacation by trying too hard to save a few dollars at the expense of a good experience. The best travel agents can tell you how much time to budget for a destination, find a cheap flight that doesn't require you to change planes multiple times, get you a better hotel room for about the same price, arrange for a competitively priced rental car, and even give restaurant recommendations.

Most of the top wholesalers offering travel packages to Mexico that combine air, hotel, and airport transfers (including Apple Vacations and GoGo Worldwide Vacations) make these available only through qualified travel agents. Although there's talk that these companies may soon sell their packages direct to consumers via the Internet, for now you need a travel agent in order to get these packages — which, because of the volume of hotel rooms they buy, generally offer the best overall value to Mexico's most popular beach resorts.

Using a travel agent is the right choice if:

- ✔ You want to purchase an air/hotel package to one of the most popular destinations.
- ✔ You're not too Internet savvy.
- ✔ You prefer discussing things with a live person.
- ✔ You may need to make changes in your itinerary.
- ✔ You're traveling with a group, coming together from several parts of the country.
- ✔ You're departing from one city, but returning to a different city.

Opting to plan on your own

The Internet has given people many of the same tools that used to be the exclusive domain of travel agents. Now finding as good a travel deal as an agent can usually find — or perhaps an even better deal — is possible. What's the key to this self-guided, money-saving process? You must be willing to invest the time and patience it takes to uncover the best deals.

 Don't underestimate the value of a first-hand recommendation from a friend or coworker. Talk to someone you know who has been to the place you're thinking of visiting for a fresh assessment and a firsthand opinion. Then, after taking all your "research" into consideration, make your own decisions and plans based on your own experiences and preferences.

 Another great source of information is an Internet message board, where travelers share experiences and offer tips or answer questions based on their recent experience at a hotel or destination. These message boards can be helpful resources for up-to-the-minute recommendations and observations. You can find an excellent and active travel message board on the Frommer's Web site (www.frommers.com/community).

Getting the Most from a Travel Agent

To get the most out of your travel agent, do a little homework. Read up on your destination (you've already made a sound decision by buying this book) and pick out some accommodations and attractions you think you may like. If necessary, get a more comprehensive — yet compact — travel guide, such as *Frommer's Portable Cancún; Los Cabos & Baja; Puerto Vallarta, Manzanillo, & Guadalajara;* or *Acapulco, Ixtapa & Zihuatanejo* (Wiley), after you narrow down the choice of your destination.

If you have access to the Internet, check prices on the Web before meeting with an agent to get a sense of ballpark prices (see the "Finding the Best Airline and Airfare" section, later in this chapter). Then take your guidebook and Web information to the travel agent and ask him or her to make the arrangements for you. Because travel agents have access to more resources than even the most complete Web travel site, they may be able to get you a better price than you could get by yourself. And they can issue your tickets and vouchers right there at the office. If they can't get you into the hotel of your choice, they can recommend an alternative, and you can look for an objective review in the guidebook that you conveniently brought with you.

Try to find a travel agent who recently has been to the beach resort that interests you. Even if the agent has traveled there, be aware that he or she likely stayed at only one or two hotels, probably one of the larger hotels that may have provided the agent with a complimentary room.

Before you call or meet with your travel agent, have one or two places in mind to compare. This book is a useful tool in narrowing down your choices. We've done the preliminary research to help you choose a place that has the features you're most interested in, and we've weeded out the mediocre hotels and restaurants to give you a head start. Jot down your preferences and maybe check the Web for some ideas of seasonal promotions and prices so that you have a ballpark idea of what to expect.

Keep in mind that travel agents work on commission. The good news is that *you* don't pay the commission; the airlines, accommodations, and tour companies do. The bad news is that unprincipled travel agents often try to persuade you to book the vacations that provide them with the most money in commissions. Over the past few years, some airlines and resorts have begun to limit or eliminate travel-agent commissions altogether. The immediate result has been that travel agents don't even bother booking certain services unless the customer specifically requests them. And some travel agents have started charging customers for their services. Don't be too put off by this; if you're working with a pro with real, hands-on knowledge of your resort, it could be well worth the extra fee to truly enjoy your vacation.

Considering an Escorted Tour or a Package Tour

There's a big difference between an escorted tour and a package tour. With an *escorted tour,* the tour company takes care of all the details and tells you what to expect at each attraction. You know your costs upfront, and an escorted tour can take you to the maximum number of sights in the minimum amount of time with the least amount of hassle. *Package tours* generally consist of round-trip airfare, ground transportation to and from your hotel, and your hotel room price, including taxes. Some packages also include all food and beverages and most entertainment and sports, when booked at an all-inclusive resort. You may find that a package tour can save you big bucks and is an ideal vacation option.

Evaluating escorted tours

When choosing an escorted tour, ask a few simple questions before you buy:

- ✔ **What is the cancellation policy?** Do you have to put a deposit down? Can they cancel the trip if they don't get enough people? How late can you cancel if you're unable to go? When do you pay? Do you get a refund if you cancel? If *they* cancel?

- ✔ **How jam-packed is the schedule?** Do they try to fit 25 hours into a 24-hour day, or will you have ample time to relax by the pool or shop? If getting up at 7 a.m. every day and not returning to your hotel until 6 or 7 p.m. sounds like a grind, certain escorted tours may not be for you.

- ✔ **How big is the group?** The smaller the group, the less time you spend waiting for people to get on and off the bus. Tour operators may be evasive about this information because they may not know the exact group size until everybody has made their reservations. But they should be able to give you a rough estimate. Some tours have a minimum group size and may cancel the tour if they don't book enough people.

- ✔ **What exactly is included?** Don't assume anything. You may have to pay to get yourself to and from the airport. A box lunch may be included in an excursion but drinks may cost extra. Beer may be included but not wine. How much flexibility do you have? Can you opt out of certain activities, or does the bus leave once a day, with no exceptions? Are all your meals planned in advance? Can you choose your entree at dinner, or does everybody get the same chicken cutlet?

Picking a package tour

For popular destinations such as Mexico's beaches, package tours are the smart way to go. In many cases, a package that includes airfare, hotel, and transportation to and from the airport costs less than just the hotel alone if you booked it yourself. That's because packages are sold in bulk to tour operators who resell them to the public. Purchasing a package tour is similar to buying your vacation at one of those large, members-only discount stores — except the tour operator is the one who buys the 1,000-count box of garbage bags and resells them ten at a time at a cost that undercuts what you'd pay at your average, neighborhood supermarket.

Package tours can vary as much as those garbage bags, too. Some offer a better class of hotels than others. Some offer the same hotels for lower prices. Some offer flights on scheduled airlines; others book charter planes (which are known for having the absolute minimal amount of conceivable legroom). In some packages, your choice of travel days and accommodations may be limited. Some let you choose between escorted vacations and independent vacations; others allow you to add on just a few excursions or escorted day-trips (also at discounted prices) without booking an entirely escorted tour. Note that most packagers don't sell directly to the public, but require you to purchase their packages through an affiliated travel agent.

Each destination usually has one or two packagers that are better than the rest because they buy in even bigger bulk. The time you spend shopping around will be well rewarded.

The best place to start looking is the travel section of your local Sunday newspaper. Also check the ads in the back of national travel magazines like *Travel + Leisure, National Geographic Traveler,* and *Condé Nast Traveler.* **Liberty Travel** (☎ 888-271-1584; www.libertytravel.com) is one of the biggest packagers in the Northeast and usually boasts a full-page ad in Sunday papers. Liberty Travel is one wholesaler that sells its packages direct to travelers without a travel-agent intermediary. **American Express Vacations** (☎ 800-346-3607; http://travel.americanexpress.com) is another option.

When comparing packages, here are a few tips:

- ✓ **Read the fine print.** Make sure you know *exactly* what's included in the price you're being quoted, and what's not.

- ✓ **Don't compare Mayas and Aztecs.** When you look at different packagers, compare the deals that they offer on similar properties. Most packagers can offer bigger savings on some hotels than others.

- ✓ **Know what you're getting yourself into — and if you can get yourself out of it.** Before you commit to a package, make sure that you know how much flexibility you have. Often, packagers offer trip-cancellation insurance for around $25 to $30, which guarantees return of your payment if you need to change your plans.

- ✓ **Use your best judgment.** Stay away from fly-by-night and shady packagers. Go with a reputable firm with a proven track record. This is where your travel agent can come in handy.

You can even browse for these packages online; try these sites — some of which allow you to book on your own online — for a start:

- ✓ Check out www.2travel.com and find a page with links to a number of the big-name Mexico packagers, including several of the ones listed in this chapter.

✔ For last-minute, air-only packages or package bargains, check out **Vacation Hotline** at www.vacationhotline.net. After you find your "deal," you need to call the agency to make final booking arrangements; the agency also offers packages from both the popular Apple and Funjet vacation wholesalers.

✔ To shop for Mexico beach vacation packages, another excellent site is BeachDestinations (www.beachdestinations.com), which offers great deals on complete packages to Mexico's most popular beach resorts, as well as last-minute deals. You can also shop for special packages for golf, weddings, or family travel.

Another good resource is the airlines themselves, which often package their flights with accommodations. When you pick the airline, you can choose the one that has frequent service to your hometown and the one on which you accumulate frequent-flier miles. Among the airline packages, your options include

✔ **Aeroméxico Vacations** (☎ 800-245-8585; www.aeromexico. com) offers year-round packages to almost every destination the airline flies to, including Acapulco, Cancún, Cozumel, Ixtapa and Zihuatanejo, Los Cabos, and Puerto Vallarta. Aeroméxico has a large selection of more than 100 resorts in these destinations and others in a variety of price ranges. The best deals are from Houston, Dallas, San Diego, Los Angeles, Miami, and New York, in that order.

✔ **Alaska Airlines Vacations** (☎ 800-468-2248; www.alaskaair.com) sells packages to Ixtapa and Zihuatanejo, Los Cabos, and Puerto Vallarta. Alaska flies direct to Mexico from Los Angeles, San Diego, San Jose, San Francisco, Seattle, Vancouver, Anchorage, and Fairbanks. The Web site offers unpublished discounts that aren't available through the phone operators.

✔ **America West Vacations** (☎ 800-356-6611; www.americawest vacations.com) has deals to Acapulco, Ixtapa and Zihuatanejo, Los Cabos, and Puerto Vallarta, mostly from its Phoenix gateway. Many of their packages to Los Cabos also include car rentals. The America West Web site offers featured specials at added discounts that aren't available through the phone operators. You can also book hotels without air by calling their toll-free number.

✔ **American Airlines Vacations** (☎ 800-321-2121; www.aavacations. com) has year-round deals to Acapulco, Cancún, Los Cabos, Puerto Vallarta, and the Riviera Maya. You don't have to fly with American if you can get a better deal on another airline; land-only packages include hotel, airport transfers, and hotel room tax. American's hubs to Mexico are Dallas/Fort Worth, Chicago, and Miami, so you're likely to get the best prices — and the most direct flights — if you live near those cities. The Web site offers unpublished discounts that aren't available through the phone operators.

✔ **Continental Vacations** (☎ **800-634-5555** and 888-989-9255; www.continental.com) has year-round packages available to Cancún, Cozumel, Puerto Vallarta, Cabo San Lucas, Acapulco, and Ixtapa and Zihuatanejo; and the best deals are from Houston; Newark, New Jersey; and Cleveland. You have to fly Continental. The Internet deals offer savings not available elsewhere.

✔ **Delta Vacations** (☎ **800-872-7786**; www.deltavacations.com) has year-round packages to Acapulco, Puerto Vallarta, Los Cabos, Cozumel, and Cancún. Atlanta is the hub that will likely offer the best deals.

✔ **Mexicana Vacations** (☎ **800-531-7921**; www.mexicana.com) offers getaways to all the resorts buttressed by Mexicana's daily direct flights from Los Angeles to Los Cabos, Cancún, Puerto Vallarta, and Ixtapa and Zihuatanejo.

✔ **US Airways Vacations** (☎ **800-455-0123**; www.usairways vacations.com) offers packages to Cancún, Cozumel, and the Riviera Maya. Charlotte is the hub that will likely offer the best deals.

Several companies specialize in packages to Mexico's beaches; they usually fly in their own, chartered airplanes, which allows them to offer greatly discounted rates. Here are some of the packagers we prefer:

✔ **Apple Vacations** (☎ **800-365-2775**; www.applevacations.com) offers inclusive packages to all the beach resorts and has the largest choice of hotels in Acapulco, Cancún, Cozumel, Huatulco, Ixtapa and Zihuatanejo, Los Cabos, Puerto Vallarta, and the Riviera Maya. Their packages are available only through travel agents. Apple perks include baggage handling and the services of an Apple representative at the major hotels.

✔ **Funjet Vacations** (bookable through any travel agent, or at the Web site at www.funjet.com) is one of the largest vacation packagers in the United States. Funjet has packages to Acapulco, Cancún, Cozumel, the Riviera Maya, Huatulco, Los Cabos, Ixtapa and Zihuatanejo, and Puerto Vallarta.

✔ **GOGO Worldwide Vacations** (☎ **888-636-3942**; www.gogowwv.com) has trips to all the major beach destinations, including Acapulco, Cancún, Puerto Vallarta, and Los Cabos, offering several exclusive deals from higher-end hotels. Bookable through any travel agent.

✔ **Pleasant Mexico Holidays** (☎ **800-448-3333**; www.pleasant holidays.com) is another of the largest vacation packagers in the United States with hotels in Acapulco, Cancún, Cozumel, Ixtapa and Zihuatanejo, Los Cabos, and Puerto Vallarta.

The biggest hotel chains and resorts also offer packages. If you already know where you want to stay, call the hotel or resort and ask whether it offers land/air packages.

Finding the Best Airline and Airfare

The first step for the independent travel planner is finding the airlines that fly to your desired beach resort. Mexico is becoming more easily accessible by plane. Many new regional carriers offer scheduled service to areas previously not served. In addition to regularly scheduled service, direct charter services from U.S. cities to resorts are making it possible to fly direct to most beach resorts from the largest airports in the United States. However, if you find that no direct flights are available, you can always reach your destination through an almost painless connection in Mexico City.

If you're booked on a flight through Mexico City, always try to check your luggage to your final destination. Checking your luggage through is possible if you're flying with affiliated or code-share airlines — separate airlines that work closely together to help travelers reach final destinations via connecting flights. This way, you don't have to lug your bags through the Mexico City airport, and it saves some time during the connecting process.

For information about saving money on airfares using the Internet, see "Researching and Booking Your Trip Online," later in this chapter.

The main airlines operating direct or nonstop flights to points in Mexico include

- **Aeroméxico** (☎ 800-237-6639; www.aeromexico.com). Flights to Cancún, Puerto Vallarta, Ixtapa and Zihuatanejo, Acapulco, Los Cabos, Huatulco.

- **Air Canada** (☎ 888-247-2262; www.aircanada.ca). Flights to Puerto Vallarta.

- **Alaska Airlines** (☎ 800-426-0333; www.alaskaair.com). Flights to Cancún, Puerto Vallarta, Los Cabos.

- **America West** (☎ 800-235-9292; www.americawest.com). Flights to Puerto Vallarta, Acapulco, Los Cabos.

- **American Airlines** (☎ 800-433-7300; www.aa.com). Flights to Cancún/Cozumel, PuertoVallarta, Acapulco, Los Cabos.

- **ATA Airlines** (☎ 800-225-2995; www.ata.com). Flights to Cancún, Puerto Vallarta.

- **British Airways** (☎ 800-247-9297, or 0345-222-111 or 0845-77-333-77 in Britain; www.britishairways.com). Flights to Cancún (from London).

- **Continental Airlines** (☎ 800-525-0280; www.continental.com). Flights to Cancún/Cozumel, Puerto Vallarta, Acapulco, Los Cabos.

- ✔ **Delta** (☎ 800-221-1212; www.delta.com). Flights to Cancún/ Cozumel (serviced by Aeroméxico), Puerto Vallarta, Acapulco, Los Cabos, Ixtapa and Zihuatanejo, Huatulco.

- ✔ **Frontier Airlines** (☎ 800-432-1359; www.frontierairlines.com). Flights to Los Cabos, Cancún, Puerto Vallarta, Ixtapa and Zihuatanejo.

- ✔ **Mexicana** (☎ 800-531-7921; www.mexicana.com). Flights to Cancún, Cozumel, Puerto Vallarta, Ixtapa and Zihuatanejo, Acapulco, Huatulco, Los Cabos.

- ✔ **Northwest Airlines** (☎ 800-225-2525; www.nwa.com). Seasonal flights to Cancún/Cozumel, Puerto Vallarta, Acapulco, Los Cabos.

- ✔ **US Airways** (☎ 800-428-4322; www.usairways.com). Flights to Cancún/Cozumel.

Competition among the major U.S. airlines is unlike that of any other industry. A coach seat is virtually the same from one carrier to another, yet the difference in price may run as high as $1,000 for a product with the same intrinsic value.

Business travelers, who need flexibility to purchase their tickets at the last minute or change their itinerary at a moment's notice, or who want to get home before the weekend, pay the premium rate, known as the full fare. Passengers who can book their ticket long in advance, who don't mind staying over Saturday night, or who are willing to travel on a Tuesday, Wednesday, or Thursday pay the least — usually a fraction of the full fare. On most flights, even the shortest hops, the full fare is close to $1,000 or more, but a 7- or 14-day advance purchase ticket is closer to $200–$300. Obviously, it pays to plan ahead.

The airlines also periodically hold sales, in which they lower the prices on their most popular routes. These fares have advance purchase requirements and date-of-travel restrictions, but you can't beat the price: usually no more than $400 for a cross-country flight. Keep your eyes open for these sales as you're planning your vacation. The sales tend to take place in seasons of low travel volume.

Consolidators, also known as *bucket shops,* are a good place to check for the lowest fares. Their prices are much better than the fares you can get yourself and are often even lower than what your travel agent can get you. You can see their ads in the small boxes at the bottom of the page in your newspaper's Sunday travel section. Some of the most reliable consolidators include **Cheap Tickets** (☎ 800-377-1000; www.cheaptickets.com) and **1-800-FLY-CHEAP** (www.flycheap.com). Another good choice, **STA Travel** (☎ 800-781-4040; www.statravel.com), especially caters to young travelers, but their bargain-basement prices are available to people of all ages.

Here are some travel tips — tested and true — for getting the lowest possible fare:

- ✔ **Timing is everything.** If you can, avoid peak travel times. In Mexico, the weeks surrounding the Christmas/New Year holidays and Easter are so jam-packed that we find it not very enjoyable to be at a beach resort anyway. Airfares are relatively expensive anytime between January and May, with September through mid-November offering up the best deals. Specials pop up throughout the year, however, based on current demand, and last-minute specials on package tours are an increasingly popular way to travel.

- ✔ **Advantage — advance.** Forgetting what we said in the previous sentence, you can also save big by booking early — with excellent fares available for 30-, 60-, or even 90-day advance bookings. Note that if you need to change your schedule, a penalty charge of $75 to $150 is common.

- ✔ **Choose an off-peak travel day.** Traveling on a Tuesday, Wednesday, or even Thursday can also save you money. Even if you can't travel both ways on these lower-fare days, you can still save if you fly off-peak at least one way.

- ✔ **Look for the midnight hour:** In the middle of the week, just after midnight, many airlines download cancelled low-priced airfares into their computers, so this is a great time to buy newly discounted seats. Midnight is the cutoff time for holding reservations. You may benefit by snagging cheap tickets that were just released by those who reserved — but never purchased — their tickets.

Choosing the Room That's Right for You

Whether you've chosen a package deal or you're planning your trip on your own, getting a room is a crucial part of your vacation planning. In this section, we help you decipher the various rates and provide some tips on how to get the best one. We also compare the pros and cons of different types of places to stay.

From small inns to large all-inclusives, most Mexican beach resorts offer every type of vacation accommodation. And the prices can vary even more! Recommendations for specific places to stay are in the chapters devoted to the individual beach towns. We try to provide the widest range of options — both in types of hotels as well as budgets — but we always keep comfort in mind. What you find in this book is what we believe to be the best value for the money. Here are the major types of accommodations:

✔ **Resorts:** These accommodations tend to be the most popular option — especially with package tours — because they offer the most modern amenities, including cable television, hair dryers, in-room safes, and generally, a selection of places to dine or have a drink. Large by definition, they may also boast various types of sporting facilities, spa services, shopping arcades, and tour-desk services. These places also tend to be the most expensive type of accommodation, but they can be heavily discounted if your timing is right.

✔ **Hotels:** These quarters tend to be smaller than resorts, with fewer facilities. In terms of style, look for anything from hacienda-style villas to all-suite hotels or sleek, modern structures. All hotels at Mexican beach resorts have at least a small swimming pool, and if they're not located directly on a beach, hotels may offer shuttle service to a beach club or an affiliated beachfront hotel.

✔ **All-inclusives:** In Mexico, all-inclusives are gaining rapidly in popularity, and they seem to be getting larger and larger in size. As the name implies, all-inclusives tie everything together in one price — your room, meals, libations and other beverages, entertainment, sports activities, and sometimes, off-site excursions. The advantage that many travelers find with this option is an expected fixed price for their vacation — helpful if you need to stay within a strict budget. Many all-inclusives have their own nightclubs or, at least, offer evening shows and entertainment, such as theme nights, talent contests, or costume parties. As for the food, you may never go hungry, but you're unlikely to go gourmet either. Our advice: Ask someone you know who's recently been to a particular all-inclusive.

✔ **Condos, apartments, and villas:** One of these accomodations can be a good option, especially if you're considering a stay longer than a week, and the reach of the Internet has made these lodging options extremely viable. Many condos, apartments, and villas come with housekeepers or even cooks. Knowing exactly what you're getting is hard — and often complaining after you arrive is futile — so again, word of mouth can be helpful here. At the very least, ask for references or search on the Internet for anyone who can offer up an experience. In addition to the Internet, select options are always advertised in the major metropolitan newspapers, such as the *Los Angeles Times, Chicago Tribune,* and the *New York Times.* Our recommendation? Save this option for your second visit when you have a better idea about the various parts of town and the area in general.

Finding the ideal family accommodations

All-inclusive hotels and resorts are becoming more and more popular with families. All-inclusives are large hotels that work with economies of scale to offer lodging, food, and drink (alcoholic or otherwise), all for a single relatively low rate. All-inclusives offer convenience and economy, especially for families with many mouths to feed. And, because they're enclosed areas, they make it easy for parents to keep an eye on their children.

These hotels have a certain sameness about them, so much can be said that applies to them all. They're usually built around a large pool with activities and an activities organizer; often, a so-called quiet pool is on-site, too. One large buffet restaurant and a snack bar serve the needs of most guests, but you can usually find a couple of specialty restaurants (with no extra charge) to which you have to make reservations. Colored bracelets serve to identify guests. In the evenings, the hotel's theater presents a show.

These hotels work best for travelers who are looking for a beach vacation to get away from the cold weather. It's not a getaway from *people* — these hotels are large and work with a high occupancy rate. Yes, staying at these all-inclusives is convenient and hassle-free. They make everything easy, including taking tours and day-trips. They do all the organizing for you. On the downside, you don't get the spontaneity or the sense of adventure that comes with other styles of traveling. These self-contained hotels lack personality and local color (though many will make clumsy attempts at tying in with the cultural icons of the region, especially Maya names and motifs). The question you have to answer is whether the advantages outweigh the disadvantages.

Researching and Booking Your Trip Online

More and more savvy travelers turn to the Internet when planning the perfect vacation to find out where the good deals are. Sites such as **Travelocity** (www.travelocity.com), **Expedia** (www.expedia.com), and **Orbitz** (www.orbitz.com) allow consumers to comparison-shop for airfares, book flights, discover last-minute bargains, and reserve hotel rooms and rental cars (most sites require you to complete some sort of one-time registration form). Internet research can be a rather time-consuming task, but the benefits of researching your trip online can be well worth the effort.

Finding the best airfare online

In addition to the standard task of searching for a decent airfare at one of the major travel Web sites noted, airlines and more specific travel sites offer additional ways to save money on your air transportation to your resort destination.

✔ Airlines offer **last-minute specials,** such as weekend deals or Internet-only fares, to fill empty seats. Most of these E-savers are announced on Tuesday or Wednesday and must be purchased online.

✔ Some sites send you **e-mail notification** when a cheap fare to your favorite destination becomes available, and some let you know when fares to a particular destination are at their lowest.

Sign up for weekly e-mail alerts at airline Web sites or check megasites that compile comprehensive lists of E-savers, such as Smarter Living (www.smarterliving.com) or WebFlyer (www.webflyer.com).

✔ All major airlines offer **incentives** — bonus frequent-flier miles, Internet-only discounts, or sometimes, perks such as free wireless phone rentals — when you purchase online or buy an E-ticket.

✔ Qixo (www.qixo.com) allows you to search for flights and hotel rooms on 20 other travel-planning sites (such as Travelocity) at once. Qixo sorts results by price, after which you can book your travel directly through the site.

✔ Advances in mobile technology provide travelers with the ability to check flight statuses, change plans, or get specific directions from handheld computing devices, mobile phones, and pagers. Some sites e-mail or page a passenger if a flight is delayed.

Several sites are devoted to helping you find last-minute travel bargains — such as when you're knee-deep in snow during a dreary January day, and decide spending the weekend on a sun-soaked beach in Mexico is just what you need. In addition to the airline sites and the most popular online travel agencies, check these out:

✔ **Site59.com** (www.site59.com), named for the 59th minute, specializes in last-minute, long-weekend travel. It bundles air, hotel, and other extras, with bookings available anywhere from 14 days to 3 hours prior to your desired travel.

✔ **11th Hour Vacations** (www.11thhourvacations.com) offers last-minute deals on longer trips, and also includes the option of condo rentals, in addition to hotels. You can book just a place to stay or a complete package.

✔ **LastMinuteTravel.com** (www.lastminutetravel.com) posts its top 25 deals every week, plus package specials. You can also narrow your search for preferred activities, such as golf packages.

The good news is that you don't even have to book your trip online to reap the research benefits of the Web. The Internet can be a valuable tool for comparison-shopping, for approaching a travel agent with a base of knowledge, and even for chatting with other travelers to truly rate the quality of the buffets at that all-inclusive you're considering.

Browsing for your lodging

When it comes to looking for great deals on **hotel rooms,** use a Web site devoted primarily to lodging because you may find properties that aren't listed on more general online travel sites. Some lodging sites specialize in a particular type of accommodation, such as bed-and-breakfasts, which you won't find on the more mainstream booking services. Others, such as TravelWeb, offer weekend deals on major chain properties, as we discuss later in this section.

And don't forget to check directly with Mexico's (and international) top hotel chains for special online deals. Start with www.caminoreal.com and www.fiestaamericana.com, or turn to Appendix A in this book for a more complete listing of hotel chains.

✔ Specific to Mexico, **Mexico Boutique Hotels** (http://mexico boutiquehotels.com) has listings of small, unique properties that are unlikely to show up on the radar screens of most travel agents or large Web travel sites. In addition to very complete descriptions, the site also offers an online booking service. Another site specializing in Mexico accommodations is www.mexicohotels.com.

✔ Although the name **All Hotels on the Web** (www.all-hotels.com) is something of a misnomer, the site *does* have tens of thousands of listings throughout the world. Bear in mind each hotel has paid a small fee ($25 and up) to be listed, so it's less of an objective list and more like a book of online brochures.

✔ **hoteldiscount!com** (www.180096hotel.com) lists bargain room rates at hotels in more than 50 U.S. and international cities. The cool thing is that hoteldiscount!com pre-books blocks of rooms in advance, so sometimes it has rooms — at discount rates — at hotels that are "sold out." Select a city and input your dates, and you get a list of the best prices for a selection of hotels. This site is notable for delivering deep discounts in cities where hotel rooms are expensive. The toll-free number is printed all over this site (☎ 800-96-HOTEL); call it if you want more options than are listed online.

- ✔ **InnSite** (www.innsite.com) has B&B listings in all 50 U.S. states and more than 50 countries around the globe. Find an inn at your destination, see pictures of the rooms, and check prices and availability. This extensive directory of B&Bs only includes listings if the proprietor submitted one (it's free to get an inn listed). The innkeepers wrote the descriptions, and many listings link to the inns' own Web sites. Also check out the **Bed and Breakfast Channel** (www.bedandbreakfast.com).

- ✔ **Places to Stay** (www.placestostay.com) lists one-of-a-kind places, with a focus on resort accommodations, in the United States and abroad that you may not find in other directories. Again, listing is selective: This isn't a comprehensive directory, but it can give you a sense of what's available at different destinations.

- ✔ **TravelWeb** (www.travelweb.com) lists more than 26,000 hotels in 170 countries, focusing on chains such as Hyatt and Hilton, and you can book almost 90% of these listings online. The site's Click-It Weekends, updated each Monday, offers weekend deals at many leading hotel chains.

Avoid online auctions. Sites that auction airline tickets and frequent-flier miles are the top perpetrators of Internet fraud, according to the National Consumers League.

Chapter 6

Money Matters

Most people save all year to be able to enjoy a wonderful vacation, so in this chapter we share with you the finer points of stretching your dollars into pesos. We tell you about the nuances of changing currency to get more for your money and present the pros and cons of traveler's checks, credit cards, and cash. Finally, we help you regroup after your wallet is lost or stolen.

Making Sense of the Peso

The currency in Mexico is the **Mexican peso,** and in recent years, economists have been talking about its amazing recovery and resiliency against the U.S. dollar. At this book's time of print, each peso is worth close to 9 U.S. cents, which means that an item costing 11 pesos would be equivalent to US$1. Like most things in Mexico, the paper currency is colorful, and it comes in denominations of 20 (blue), 50 (pink), 100 (red), 200 (green), and 500 (burgundy) pesos. Coins come in denominations of 1, 2, 5, 10, and 20 pesos and 50 **centavos** (100 centavos equal 1 peso).

New 50- and 500-peso bills look very similar, but 50-peso bills have a slightly pinkish hue and are smaller in size. However, always double-check how much you're paying and your change to avoid unpleasant surprises. The same applies to 10- and 20-peso coins. Twenty-peso coins are slightly larger than the 10-peso coins, but they look very similar.

Getting change continues to be a problem in Mexico. Small-denomination bills and coins are hard to come by, so start collecting them early in your trip and continue as you travel. Shopkeepers — and especially taxi drivers — always seem to be out of change and small bills; that's doubly true in a market. In other words, don't try to pay with a 500-peso bill when buying a 20-peso trinket.

Before you leave your hotel, getting 100 pesos — a little more than US$9 — in change is a good idea in order to have change for cab and bus fares.

In this book, we use the universal currency sign ($) to indicate both U.S. dollars and pesos in Mexico (though the reviews and listings provide U.S. dollar costs). When you're in Mexico, you notice the common use of the currency symbol ($), generally indicating the price in pesos. Asking for clarification is okay if you're not sure because some higher-end places do tend to price their goods in U.S. dollars. Often, if a price is quoted in U.S. dollars, the letters "USD" follow the price.

The exchange rate fluctuates a tiny bit daily, so you're probably better off not exchanging too much of your currency at once. Don't forget, however, to have enough pesos to carry you over a weekend or Mexican holiday, when banks are closed. In general, avoid carrying the U.S. $100 bill, the bill most commonly counterfeited in Mexico, and therefore, the most difficult to exchange, especially in smaller towns. Because small bills and coins in pesos are hard to come by in Mexico, the U.S. $1 bill is very useful for tipping. A tip of U.S. coins is of no value to the service provider because he or she can't exchange them into Mexican currency.

To make your dollars go further, remember that ATMs offer the best exchange rate; however, you need to consider any service fees. Mexican banks offer the next-best fare, and they don't charge commission, unless you're cashing traveler's checks, in which case they usually charge a small commission. After banks, *casas de cambio* (houses of exchange) are your next-best option, and they usually charge a commission. You can almost always get a lower exchange rate when you exchange your money at a hotel front desk.

Traveler's Checks, Credit Cards, or Cash?

You need to think about *what kind* of money you're going to spend on your vacation before you leave home.

Relying on ATMs and cash

These days, all the Mexico beach resorts detailed in this book have 24-hour ATMs linked to an international network that almost always includes your bank at home. **Cirrus** (☎ 800-424-7787; www.mastercard.com/atmlocator) and **Plus** (☎ 800-843-7587; www.visa.com/atms) are the two most popular networks; check the back of your ATM card to see which network your bank belongs to. The 800-numbers and Web sites can give you specific locations of ATMs where you can withdraw money while on vacation. Using ATMs permits you to withdraw only as much cash as you need for a few days, which eliminates the insecurity (and the pickpocketing threat) of carrying around a wad of cash. Note, however, that a daily maximum of about US$1,000 is common.

One important reminder: Many banks now charge a fee ranging from 50 cents to *three dollars* for nonaccount-holders to use their ATMs. Your own bank may also assess a fee for using an ATM that's not one of its branch locations. This means, in some cases, you get charged *twice* just for using your bankcard when you're on vacation. Although an ATM card can be an amazing convenience when traveling in another country (put your card in the machine and out comes foreign currency at an extremely advantageous exchange rate), banks are also likely to slap you with a "foreign currency transaction fee" just for making them do the pounds-to-dollars-to-pesos conversion math.

Using a credit card

Credit cards are invaluable when traveling. They're a safe way to carry "money," and they provide a convenient record of all your travel expenses when you arrive home.

Visa, MasterCard, and American Express are the most accepted cards in Mexico. You can charge most hotel, restaurant, and store purchases on your credit card. (The hotel and restaurant listings in this book note those locations that don't accept credit cards.) You generally can't charge gasoline purchases in Mexico — but for most resorts covered in this book, you really don't need a car.

Travel with at least two different credit cards if you can. Depending on where you go, you may find MasterCard accepted more frequently than Visa (or vice versa), American Express honored or refused, and so on.

You can get **cash advances** from your credit card at any bank, and you don't even need to go to a teller — you can get a cash advance at the ATM if you know your **PIN number.** If you've forgotten your PIN number or didn't even know you had one, call the phone number on the back of your credit card and ask the bank to send it to you. It usually takes 5 to 7 business days, though some banks will do it over the phone if you tell them your mother's maiden name or some other security clearance.

You have to contend with a hidden expense when borrowing cash from a credit card: Interest rates for cash advances are often significantly higher than rates for credit-card purchases. More importantly, you start paying interest on the advance *the moment you receive the cash.* On an airline-affiliated credit card, a cash advance doesn't earn frequent-flier miles.

Relying on debit cards

Another option for you is using a debit card (an ATM card with a credit card logo), which works just like a credit card except the purchase comes directly out of your checking account rather than being applied against your credit limit. In many cases, your debit and ATM card are the same piece of plastic. Instead of getting cash, however, the debit card pays for purchases anywhere a credit card is accepted.

Traveling with traveler's checks

Traveler's checks are something of an anachronism from the days when people wrote personal checks instead of going to an ATM. Because people could replace traveler's checks if lost or stolen, they used them as a sound alternative to filling their wallet with cash at the beginning of a trip.

Still, if you prefer the security of traveler's checks, you can get them at almost any bank. **American Express** offers checks in denominations of $20, $50, $100, $500, and $1,000. You pay a service charge ranging from 1% to 4%, though AAA members can obtain checks without a fee at most AAA offices. You can also get American Express traveler's checks over the phone by calling ☎ **800-221-7282.**

Visa (☎ **800-227-6811**) also offers traveler's checks, available at Citibank locations across the country and at several other banks. The service charge ranges between 1.5% and 2%; checks come in denominations of $50, $100, $500, and $1,000. **MasterCard** also offers traveler's checks; call ☎ **800-223-9920** for a location near you.

Although traveler's checks are very safe, consider that:

- ✔ You usually get charged a commission to cash your traveler's checks, and when you add that to the exchange-rate loss, you end up getting fewer pesos for your money.

- ✔ Many smaller shops don't take traveler's checks, so if you plan to shop, cash the traveler's checks before you embark on your shopping expedition.

Knowing What to Do If Your Wallet Gets Stolen

Odds are that if your wallet is gone you've seen the last of it, and the police aren't likely to recover it for you. However, after you realize it's gone and you cancel your credit cards, call to inform the police. You may need the police-report number for credit-card or insurance purposes later. After you've covered all the formalities and before you head to the nearest bar to drown your sorrows, retrace your steps — you may be surprised at how many honest people are in Mexico, and it's likely that you may find someone trying to find you to return your wallet.

Almost every credit-card company has an emergency toll-free number you can call if your wallet or purse is stolen. Your credit-card company may be able to wire you a cash advance immediately; in many places, the company can get you an emergency credit card within a day or two. The issuing bank's toll-free number is usually on the back of the credit card, but that won't help you much if the card was stolen. Write down the number on a separate piece of paper before you leave home, and keep it in a safe place just in case.

If your credit card is stolen or lost, major credit-card companies have emergency toll-free numbers. Here's a list of numbers to call in the United States as well as internationally:

- ✔ **American Express** cardholders and traveler's check holders should call ☎ **800-327-2177** (U.S. toll free); ☎ **336-393-1111** (international direct-dial) for gold and green cards.

- ✔ The toll-free, U.S. emergency number for **Visa** is ☎ **800-336-8472;** from other countries, call ☎ **410-902-8012.** Your card issuer can also provide you with the toll-free, lost/stolen-card number for the country or countries you plan to visit.

- ✔ **MasterCard** holders need to dial ☎ **800-826-2181** in the United States or 800-307-7309 from anywhere in the world, or ☎ 314-542-7111. Also check with your card issuer for the toll-free, lost/stolen-card number for the country or countries you want to visit.

To dial an 800 U.S. toll-free number from inside Mexico, you must dial 001-880 and then the last seven digits of the toll-free number. For toll-free numbers beginning with 888, dial 001-881, and then the remaining digits; for toll-free numbers beginning with 877, dial 001-882, then the remaining digits; and for toll-free numbers beginning with 866, dial 001-883, then the remaining digits.

If you opt to carry **traveler's checks,** keep a record of their serial numbers so that you can handle this type of emergency.

Chapter 7

Tying Up the Loose Ends

A re you ready? Really ready? Before you can string that hammock between the palms, you need to take care of a few more details to get to your personal paradise.

In this chapter, we cover the essentials and the requirements of getting into Mexico — and then back home again. We also review the ins and outs of dealing with travel insurance, discuss what you need to know to ensure a safe trip, help you decide whether you need to rent a car, and offer tips to make sure you pack everything you need for your Mexican beach vacation.

Arriving In and Departing From Mexico

All travelers to Mexico are required to present **proof of citizenship,** such as a valid passport (the preferred documentation — see the next section), an original birth certificate with a raised seal, or naturalization papers. If you're using a birth certificate, bring a current form of photo identification, such as a driver's license or an official ID card. If your last name on the birth certificate is different from your current name (women using a married name, for example), you also need to bring a photo ID card *and* legal proof of the name change, such as the *original* marriage license or certificate.

When reentering the United States, you must prove both your citizenship *and* your identification, so always carry a picture ID such as a driver's license or valid passport.

Birth certificates enable you to enter Mexico, but alone, don't enable you to reenter the United States. And although you can enter Mexico using a driver's license as identification, this document alone isn't acceptable identification for reentering the United States. While in Mexico, you must also obtain a **Mexican tourist permit (FMT),** which is issued free of charge by Mexican border officials after proof of citizenship is accepted. Airlines generally provide these forms aboard your flight into Mexico.

The tourist permit (FMT) is more important than a passport in Mexico, so guard it carefully. If you lose your FMT, you may not be permitted to leave the country until you can replace it — a bureaucratic hassle that can take anywhere from a few hours to a week. (If you do lose your tourist permit, get a police report from local authorities indicating that your documents were stolen; having one *may* lessen the hassle of exiting the country without all your identification.) You should also contact the nearest consular office to report the stolen papers so that the consulate can issue a reentry document.

Note that children under the age of 18 traveling without parents or with only one parent must have a notarized letter from the absent parent or parents authorizing the travel. The letter must include the duration of the visit, destination, names of accompanying adults, parents' home addresses, telephone numbers, and so forth. A picture of the child must also be attached to this letter. When applicable, provide divorce, death certificate, or guardianship papers.

Obtaining a Passport

Although you can enter Mexico without a passport, the only legal form of identification recognized around the world is a valid passport. For that reason alone, having your passport whenever you travel abroad is a good idea. In the United States, you're used to your driver's license being the all-purpose ID card. Abroad, it only proves that some American state lets you drive. Getting a passport is easy, but it takes some time to complete the process.

The U.S. State Department's Bureau of Consular Affairs maintains an excellent Web site (www.travel.state.gov) with good information about passports, including downloadable applications and locations of passport offices; just follow the link to "Passport Information." In addition, the Web site provides extensive information about foreign countries, including travel warnings about health and terrorism. You can also call the National Passport Information Center at ☎ **900-225-5674** (35¢ per minute) or ☎ **877-487-2778** ($4.95 per call).

If you're a resident of Canada, the United Kingdom, Ireland, Australia, or New Zealand, you can find passport information for your home country in the upcoming section, "Applying for passports from other countries."

Applying for a U.S. passport

Apply for a passport at least a month, preferably two, before you leave. Although processing generally takes three weeks, during busy periods it can run longer (especially in spring). For people older than 15, a passport is valid for ten years, unless you change your name.

If you're a U.S. citizen applying for a first-time passport and you're 13 years of age or older, you need to apply in person at one of the following locations:

- ✔ **A passport office.** An appointment is required for a visit to one of the following facilities, and your departure date must be within two weeks: Boston, Chicago, Houston, Los Angeles, Miami, New York City, Philadelphia, San Francisco, Seattle, Stamford (Connecticut), and Washington, D.C. No appointments are required at the offices in Honolulu and New Orleans.

- ✔ **A federal, state, or probate court.**

- ✔ **A major post office, some libraries, and a number of county and municipal offices.** Not all accept applications; call your local post office or log on the Web site at www.usps.com for more information.

When you go to apply, bring the following items with you:

- ✔ **Completed passport application:** To apply for your first passport, fill out form DSP-11 (available online at www.travel.state.gov and www.usps.com). You can complete this form in advance to save time. However, *don't sign* the application until you present it to the person at the passport agency, court, or post office.

- ✔ **Application fee:** For people age 16 or older, a new passport costs $85 ($55 plus a $30 execution fee, to the facility handling the application). A renewal passport fee is $55.

- ✔ **Proof of U.S. citizenship:** Bring your old passport if you're renewing (see the following section); otherwise, bring a certified copy of your birth certificate with registrar's seal, a report of your birth abroad, or your naturalized citizenship documents.

- ✔ **Proof of identity:** Among the accepted documents are a valid driver's license, a state or military ID, an old passport, or a naturalization certificate.

✔ **Two identical 2-inch-by-2-inch photographs with a white or off-white background:** You can get these pictures taken in just about any corner photo shop, as well as in some drugstores such as Walgreens; these places have a special camera to make the photos identical. Expect to pay up to $15 for them. You *can't* use the strip photos from one of those photo vending machines.

Renewing a U.S. passport by mail

You can renew an existing, non-damaged passport by mail if it was issued within the past 15 years, *and* you were older than age 16 when it was issued, *and* you still have the same name as shown on the passport (or you can legally document your name change, such as with a valid marriage license).

Include your expired passport, renewal form DSP-82, two identical photos (see the preceding section), and a check or money order for $55 (no extra handling fee). Mail everything (certified, return receipt requested, just to be safe) in a padded envelope to National Passport Center, P.O. Box 371971, Pittsburgh, PA 15250-7971.

Allow at least a month to six weeks for your application to be processed and your new passport to arrive.

Getting your passport in a hurry

Although processing usually takes about three weeks, it can actually take far longer, especially during busy times of year, such as the spring. If you're crunched for time, consider paying an extra $60 (plus the express mail service fee) to have your passport sent to you within seven to ten working days. In even more of a hurry? Try **Passport Express** (☎ **800-362-8196** or 401-272-4612; Fax: 401-272-4839; www. passportexpress.com), a nationwide service that can get you a new or renewed passport within 24 hours. Getting a new passport with this service costs $149 plus the $145 government fee if you need it in one to six days, or $109 plus the $145 government fee if you need it in seven to ten days. If you're renewing your passport, the Passport Express fees are the same, but the government fee is reduced to $115. For a rushed passport, you must have proof of travel (your tickets or a travel itinerary).

For more details about getting a passport, call the **National Passport Agency** (☎ **202-647-0518**). To locate a passport office in your area, call the **National Passport Information Center** (☎ **900-225-5674,** 35¢ per minute). The **U.S. State Department**'s Web page also offers information on passport services, and you can download an application. In addition, many post offices and travel agencies keep passport applications on hand.

Applying for passports from other countries

This section offers more information for citizens of Canada, the United Kingdom, Ireland, Australia, and New Zealand.

Canadian citizens

Passport information and applications are available from the central **Passport Office** in Ottawa (☎ **800-567-6868;** www.ppt.gc.ca). Regional passport offices and travel agencies also offer applications. Valid for five years, a passport costs $60 Canadian. Applications must include two identical passport-sized photographs and proof of Canadian citizenship. Allow five to ten days for processing if you apply in person or about three weeks if you submit your application by mail.

United Kingdom citizens

To pick up an application for a ten-year passport, visit your nearest passport office, major post office, or travel agency. You can also contact the **London Passport Office** at ☎ **0171-271-3000** or **0870-521-0410,** or search its Web site at www.ukpa.gov.uk. Passports are £42 for adults and £25 for children under 16.

Irish citizens

You can apply for a ten-year passport, costing IR£45, at the **Passport Office** (Setanta Centre, Molesworth St., Dublin 2; ☎ **01-671-1633;** www.irlgov.ie/iveagh; e-mail: passportsdublin.@iveagh.gov.ie). You can also apply at 1A South Mall, Cork (☎ **021-272-525**) or at the counter of most main post offices. Those younger than age 18 and older than age 65 must apply for a IR£12 three-year passport.

Australian citizens

Apply at your local post office, search the government Web site at www.passports.gov.au, or call toll free ☎ **131-232.** Passports for adults are A$148 and are valid for ten years; for those under age 18, a five-year passport is A$74.

New Zealand citizens

You can pick up a passport application at any travel agency or Link Centre. For more info, contact the **Passport Office** (P.O. Box 805, Wellington; ☎ **0800-225-050;** www.passports.govt.nz; e-mail: passports@dia.govt.nz). Passports for adults are NZ$80 and are valid for ten years; for those under age 16, a five-year passport is NZ$40.

Dealing with lost passports

Keep your passport with you at all times, preferably secured in a money belt. The only times to give it up are at the bank or money exchange, for tellers to verify information when you change traveler's checks or foreign currency, or to airline reservations agents and immigration officials when entering or leaving a country.

If you lose your passport in a foreign country, go directly to your country's embassy or consulate. Bring all forms of identification you have, and the embassy's staff can start arranging for a new passport. This is a huge hassle that you want to avoid at all costs.

Always carry a photocopy of the first page of your passport with you when you travel. Doing so greatly speeds up the paperwork in case your passport goes missing.

Clearing U.S. Customs

You *can* take it with you — up to a point. Technically, no limits exist on how much loot U.S. citizens can bring back into the United States from a trip abroad, but the customs authority *does* put limits on how much you can bring in for free. (This limit is mainly for taxation purposes, to separate tourists with souvenirs from importers.)

As a U.S. citizen, you may bring home $800 worth of goods duty-free, as long as you've been out of the country at least 48 hours and haven't used the exemption in the past 30 days. This amount includes one liter of an alcoholic beverage (you must, of course, be older than 21), 200 cigarettes, and 100 cigars. Anything you mail home from abroad is exempt from the $800 limit. You may mail up to $200 worth of goods to yourself (marked "for personal use") and up to $100 to others (marked "unsolicited gift") once each day, so long as the package doesn't include alcohol or tobacco products. You have to pay an import duty on anything over these limits.

Note that buying items at a **duty-free shop** before flying home doesn't exempt them from counting toward U.S. customs limits (monetary or otherwise). The "duty" that you're avoiding in those shops is the local tax on the item (such as state sales tax in the United States), not any import duty that may be assessed by the U.S. customs office.

If you have further questions, or for a list of specific items you can't bring into the United States, look in your phone book (under U.S. Government, Department of Homeland Security, U.S. Customs & Border Protection) to find the nearest customs office. Or check out the Customs & Border Protection Web site at www.customs.gov.

Considering Travel Insurance

There are three primary kinds of travel insurance: trip-cancellation insurance, medical insurance, and lost-luggage insurance.

Trip-cancellation insurance is a good idea if you've paid a large portion of your vacation expenses upfront, such as for an air/hotel package deal, an all-inclusive resort, or a cruise. Strongly consider this coverage, particularly if you have young children, because you never know when accidents or illnesses can crop up.

But the other two types of insurance — **medical** and **lost luggage** — don't make sense for most travelers. Your existing health insurance probably covers you if you get sick while on vacation. (Although, if you belong to an HMO, find out whether you're fully covered when away from home.) Homeowner's insurance usually covers stolen luggage if you have off-premises theft. Check your existing policies before you buy any additional coverage. The airlines are responsible for $2,500 on domestic flights (and $9.07 per pound, up to $640, on international flights) if they lose your luggage; if you plan to carry anything more valuable than that, keep it in your carry-on bag.

Some credit cards (American Express and certain gold and platinum Visa and MasterCards, for example) offer automatic flight insurance against death or dismemberment in case of an airplane crash. If you still feel you need more insurance, try one of the companies listed later in this section. But don't pay for more insurance than you need. For example, if you only need trip-cancellation insurance, don't purchase coverage for lost or stolen property. Trip-cancellation insurance costs approximately 6% to 8% of the total value of your vacation.

Among the reputable issuers of travel insurance are

- ✔ **Access America** (6600 W. Broad St., Richmond, VA 23230; ☎ 800-284-8300; Fax: 800-346-9265; www.accessamerica.com)

- ✔ **Travel Guard International** (1145 Clark St., Stevens Point, WI 54481; ☎ 800-826-1300; www.travel-guard.com)

- ✔ **Travel Insured International, Inc.** (P.O. Box 280568, 52-S Oakland Ave., East Hartford, CT 06128-0568; ☎ 800-243-3174; www.travelinsured.com)

- ✔ **Travelex Insurance Services** (11717 Burt St., Ste. 202, Omaha, NE 68154; ☎ 800-228-9792; www.travelex-insurance.com)

Getting Sick Away from Home

Apart from how getting sick can ruin your vacation, it also can present the problem of finding a doctor you trust when you're away from home. Bring all your medications with you, as well as a prescription for more because you may run out. Bring an extra pair of contact lenses in case you lose one. And don't forget the Pepto-Bismol for common travelers' ailments such as upset stomach or diarrhea.

If you have health insurance, check with your provider to find out the extent of your coverage outside of your home area. Be sure to carry your identification card in your wallet. (See the "Considering Travel Insurance" section, earlier in this chapter, for more information.)

If you suffer from a chronic illness, talk to your doctor before taking the trip. For such conditions as epilepsy, diabetes, or a heart condition, wearing a **Medic Alert identification tag** immediately alerts any doctor to your condition and gives him or her access to your medical records through Medic Alert's 24-hour hotline. Membership is $35, with a $15 renewal fee. Contact the Medic Alert Foundation (2323 Colorado Ave., Turlock, CA 95382; ☎ **800-432-5378;** www.medicalert.org).

If you do get sick, ask the concierge at your hotel to recommend a local doctor — even his or her own doctor if necessary. Another good option is to call the closest consular office and ask for a referral. Most consulates have a listing of reputable English-speaking doctors. Most beach destinations in Mexico have at least one modern facility staffed by doctors used to treating the most common ailments of tourists. In the case of a real emergency, a service from the United States can fly people to U.S. hospitals: **Air-Evac (☎ 888-554-9729)** is a 24-hour air ambulance. You can also contact the service in Guadalajara (☎ **01-800-305-9400,** 3-616-9616, or 3-615-2471; www.globallifeflight.com). Several companies offer air-evac service; for a list, refer to the U.S. State Department Web site at www.travel.state.gov/medical.html.

From our years of experience of living in and/or traveling throughout Mexico, we can honestly say that most health problems that foreign tourists to Mexico encounter are self-induced. If you take in too much sun, too many margaritas, and too many street tacos within hours of your arrival, don't blame the water if you get sick. You'd be surprised how many people try to make up for all the fun they've missed out on in the past year on their first day of vacation in Mexico.

Avoiding turista!

It's called "travelers' diarrhea," or *turista,* the Spanish word for "tourist." We're talking about the persistent diarrhea, often accompanied by fever, nausea, and vomiting, that used to attack many travelers to Mexico. Some folks in the United States call this affliction "Montezuma's revenge," but you won't hear it referred to this way in Mexico. Widespread improvements in infrastructure, sanitation, and education have practically eliminated this ailment, especially in well-developed resort areas. Most travelers make a habit of drinking bottled water, which also helps to protect against unfamiliar bacteria. In resort areas, and generally throughout

Mexico, only purified ice is used. Doctors say this ailment isn't caused by just one "bug," but by a combination of consuming different foods and water, upsetting your schedule, being overtired, and experiencing the stresses of travel. A good high-potency (or "therapeutic") vitamin supplement and extra vitamin C can help. And yogurt is good for healthy digestion. If you do happen to come down with this ailment, nothing beats Pepto-Bismol, readily available in Mexico.

The U.S. Public Health Service recommends the following measures for preventing travelers' diarrhea:

- ✔ Choose food carefully. In general, avoid salads, uncooked vegetables, and unpasteurized milk or milk products (including cheese). However, salads in a first-class restaurant, or in a restaurant that serves a lot of tourists, are generally safe to eat. Choose food that's freshly cooked and still hot. Peelable fruit is ideal. Don't eat undercooked meat, fish, or shellfish.

- ✔ Don't overdo the sun.

- ✔ Drink only purified water. This means tea, coffee, and other beverages made with boiled water; canned or bottled carbonated beverages and water; or beer and wine. Most restaurants with a large tourist clientele use only purified water and ice.

- ✔ Get enough sleep.

- ✔ In addition, something as simple as clean hands can go a long way toward preventing *turista*.

Because **dehydration** can quickly become life threatening, be especially careful to replace fluids and *electrolytes* (potassium, sodium, and the like) during a bout of diarrhea. Do this by drinking Pedialyte, a rehydration solution available at most Mexican pharmacies, sports drinks, or glasses of natural fruit juice (high in potassium) with a pinch of salt added. Or try a glass of boiled, pure water with a quarter teaspoon of sodium bicarbonate (baking soda) and a bit of limejuice added.

Keeping the kids healthy

If you're traveling with **infants and/or children** in Mexico, be extra careful to avoid anything that's not bottled. You can readily purchase infant formulas, baby foods, canned milk, and other baby supplies from grocery stores. Your best bet is to carry extra baby eats when you go out. Most Mexican restaurants cheerfully warm bottles and packaged goods for your child.

Be especially careful of sun exposure because **sunburn** can be extremely dangerous. Protect the little ones with special SPF bathing suits and cover-ups and regularly apply a strong sunscreen. (While you're at it, don't forget a fairly strong sunscreen for yourself.)

Dehydration can also make your child seriously ill. Make sure your child drinks plenty of water and juices throughout the day. Especially when they're in the pool or at the beach having fun, they may not remember that they're thirsty, so reminding them is your job. Sunburn also contributes to and complicates dehydration.

Staying Safe and Healthy: Cautionary Words for the Wise

If you find yourself getting friendly with the locals — and we mean friendly to the point of a fling — don't be embarrassed to carry or insist on stopping for condoms — then use them! Too many vacationing men and women are filled with morning-after regrets because they didn't protect themselves. Don't allow your fear of being judged make you unprepared. Also know that Mexico's teen-to-twenty-something population has a rapidly escalating **HIV/AIDS** rate — especially in resort areas — due to the transient nature of the population and poor overall education about this disease.

And when it comes to **drugs,** many outsiders have the impression that the easy-going nature of these tropical towns means an equally laid-back attitude exists toward drug use. Not so. Marijuana, cocaine, Ecstasy, crystal methamphetamine, and other mood-altering drugs are illegal in Mexico. In some resorts, such as Puerto Vallarta, police randomly search people — including obvious tourists — who are walking the streets at night. However, unless you seek drugs out, whatever behind-the-scenes action there is won't likely affect you.

If you do choose to indulge, don't expect any special treatment if you're caught. In fact, everything bad you've ever heard about a Mexican jail is considered to be close to the truth — if not a rose-colored version of it. Mexico employs the Napoleonic Code of law, meaning that you're guilty until proven innocent. Simply stated, using drugs isn't worth the potential high. That's what tequila's for!

Renting a Car

First, know that car-rental costs are high in Mexico because cars are more expensive here. However, the condition of rental cars has improved greatly over the years, and clean, comfortable, new cars are the norm. At press time, the basic cost for a one-day rental of a Volkswagen (VW) Beetle, with unlimited mileage (but before the 15% tax and $15 to $25 daily charge for insurance), was $45 in Cancún, $40 in Puerto Vallarta, and $40 in Acapulco. Renting by the week gives you a lower daily rate. Avis was offering a basic seven-day weekly rate for a VW Beetle (before tax or insurance) of $220 in Cancún and Puerto

Vallarta and $200 in Acapulco. Prices may be considerably higher if you rent in these same cities around a major holiday.

Car-rental companies usually write up a credit-card charge in U.S. dollars.

Be careful of deductibles, which vary greatly in Mexico. Some deductibles are as high as $2,500, which immediately comes out of your pocket in case of car damage. Hertz has a $1,000 deductible on a VW Beetle; the deductible at Avis is $500 for the same car.

Always get the insurance; any coverage provided by your credit card or your own insurance policy isn't valid in Mexico. Insurance is offered in two parts. Collision and damage insurance covers your car and others if the accident is your fault, and personal accident insurance covers you and anyone in your car. Read the fine print on the back of your rental agreement and note that insurance may be invalid if you have an accident while driving on an unpaved road.

Personally, we think that Los Cabos is the only destination that is really enjoyed best if you have a car to get around. For all other beach destinations, we prefer to use taxis, which are reasonably priced except in Los Cabos.

Finding the best car-rental deal

Car-rental rates vary even more than airline fares. The price depends on the size of the car, the length of time you keep it, where and when you pick it up and drop it off, where you take it, and a host of other factors.

Asking a few key questions can save you hundreds of dollars. For example, weekend rates may be lower than weekday rates. Ask whether the rate is the same for pickup Friday morning as it is for Thursday night. If you're keeping the car five or more days, a weekly rate may be cheaper than the daily rate. Some companies may assess a drop-off charge if you don't return the car to the same renting location; others, notably National, don't. Ask whether the rate is cheaper if you pick up the car at the airport or a location in town. Don't forget to mention membership in AAA, AARP, frequent-flier programs, and trade unions. These memberships usually entitle you to discounts ranging from 5% to 30%. Ask your travel agent to check any and all these rates. And most car rentals are worth at least 500 miles on your frequent-flier account!

As with other aspects of planning your trip, using the Internet can make comparison-shopping for a car rental much easier. All the major booking Web sites — **Travelocity** (www.travelocity.com), **Expedia** (www.expedia.com), **Yahoo Travel** (www.travel.yahoo.com), and **Cheap Tickets** (www.cheaptickets.com), for example — have search engines that can dig up discounted car-rental rates. Just enter the size of the car you want, the pickup and return dates, and the city where you want to rent, and the server returns a price. You can even make the reservation through these sites.

Some companies offer refueling packages, in which you pay for an entire tank of gas upfront. The price is usually fairly competitive with local gas prices, but you don't get credit for any gas remaining in the tank. If you reject this option, you pay only for the gas you use, but you have to return the car with a full tank or face charges of $3 to $4 a gallon for any shortfall. If a stop at a gas station on the way to the airport will make you miss your plane, by all means take advantage of the fuel purchase option. Otherwise, skip it.

Driving safely

If you decide to rent a car and drive in Mexico, keep these few things in mind:

✔ Most Mexican roads aren't up to U.S. standards of smoothness, hardness, width of curve, grade of hill, or safety markings.

✔ Driving at night is dangerous — the roads aren't good, and they're rarely lit; trucks, carts, pedestrians, and bicycles usually have no lights; and you can hit potholes, animals, rocks, dead ends, or uncrossable bridges without warning.

✔ Never turn left by stopping in the middle of a highway with your left signal on. Instead, pull off the highway onto the right shoulder (generally, this is a turn lane), wait for traffic to clear, and then proceed across the road.

✔ No credit cards are accepted for gas purchases, which is sold by the liter but is generally only slightly more expensive than in the United States (and about on par with a liter of gas in Canada).

✔ Places called *vulcanizadora* or *llantera* repair flat tires. Finding such places open 24 hours a day on the most traveled highways is common. Even if the place looks empty, chances are you can find someone who can help you fix a flat.

✔ When possible, many Mexicans drive away from minor accidents, or try to make an immediate settlement, to avoid involving the police.

✔ If the police arrive while the involved persons are still at the scene, everyone may be locked up until responsibility is determined and damages are settled. If you were in a rental car, notify the rental company immediately and ask how to contact the nearest adjuster. (You did buy insurance with the rental, right?)

Packing for Mexico's Beaches

Start packing by taking out everything you think you need and laying it out on the bed. Then get rid of half of it.

It's not that the airlines won't let you take it all — they will, with some limits — but why would you want to get a hernia from lugging half your house around with you? Suitcase straps can be particularly painful with sunburned shoulders.

So what are the bare essentials? They include

- ✔ A belt
- ✔ A camera
- ✔ Comfortable walking shoes
- ✔ Something to sleep in
- ✔ A swimsuit
- ✔ Toiletries and medications (pack these in your carry-on bag so that you have them if the airline loses your luggage)
- ✔ A versatile sweater and/or jacket

Unless you're attending a board meeting, a funeral, or one of the city's finest restaurants, you probably don't need a suit or a fancy dress. Even the nicest restaurants tend to be casual, especially for men. Women, on the other hand, tend to enjoy those sexy resort dresses, and they're definitely appropriate in any of the resorts in this book. But when it comes to essentials, you get more use out of a pair of jeans or khakis and a comfortable sweater.

Electricity runs on the same current in Mexico as in the United States and Canada, so feel free to bring a hairdryer, personal stereo, or whatever else you'd like to plug in. Don't bother to bring a travel iron — most hotels offer irons and ironing boards, or they offer the service at a very reasonable rate.

When choosing your suitcase, think about the kind of traveling you're doing. If you'll be walking with your luggage on hard floors, a bag with wheels makes sense. If you'll be carrying your luggage over uneven roads or up and down stairs, wheels won't help much. A fold-over garment bag can help keep dressy clothes wrinkle-free, but it can be a nuisance if you're packing and unpacking a lot. Hard-sided luggage protects breakable items better, but it weighs more than soft-sided bags.

When packing, start with the biggest, hardest items (usually shoes) and then fit smaller items in and around them. Pack breakable items in between several layers of clothes or keep them in your carry-on bag. Put things that could leak, such as shampoos or suntan lotions, in resealable plastic bags. Lock your suitcase with a small padlock or small cable ties (which are cheaper if your luggage gets singled out for inspection) and put a distinctive identification tag on the outside so that your bag will be easy to spot on the carousel (and even an ID tag on the inside in case the outside one gets ripped off).

You're allowed one to two pieces of carry-on luggage, both of which must fit in the overhead compartment or under the seat in front of you. Make sure your bag contains a book, any breakable items you don't want to put in your suitcase, a personal headphone stereo, a snack in case you don't like the airline food, bottled water, any vital documents you don't want to lose in your luggage (such as your return ticket, passport, wallet, and so on), and some empty space for the sweater or jacket that you don't want to be wearing while you're waiting for your luggage in an overheated terminal. Also carry aboard any prescription medications, your glasses or spare contact lenses, and your camera and extra film. You may want to carry a change of clothes (shorts, T-shirt, and swimsuit) — just in case. If the airline loses your luggage, you're likely to have it within 24 hours, but having these essentials can get you right into vacation fun anyway.

Because lost-luggage rates have reached an all-time high, consumers are trying to divert disaster by bringing all their possessions on board. But planes are more crowded than ever, security measures have been increased, and overhead compartment space is at a premium. Most airlines now limit you to a single carry-on for crowded flights and impose size restrictions on the bags you do bring on board. The dimensions vary, but the strictest airlines say carry-ons must measure no more than 22 x 14 x 9 inches, including wheels and handles, and weigh no more than 40 pounds. Many airports are already furnished with X-ray machines that literally block any carry-on bigger than the posted size restrictions. It sounds drastic, but keep in mind that many of these regulations are enforced only at the discretion of the gate attendants. However, if you plan to bring more than one bag aboard a crowded flight, be sure your medications, documents, and valuables are consolidated in one bag in case you're forced to check the second one.

Here's a quick checklist of items you don't want to forget:

- ✔ Casual slacks other than jeans (for men, especially if you plan on hitting the trendiest discos, which may not allow shorts or jeans)
- ✔ Comfortable walking shoes
- ✔ Driver's license (if you plan to rent a car)
- ✔ Hat or cap

- A pareo that can double as a long or short skirt, or a wrap (for women)
- Sandals
- Scuba certification (if you plan to dive)
- Sunglasses
- Sunscreen
- Two swimsuits (at least)

Part III
Cancún

The 5th Wave   By Rich Tennant

"I know it's a popular American expression, but you just don't say 'Hasta la vista, baby'—to a nun."

In this part . . .

The most popular of Mexico's beach resorts, Cancún perfectly showcases the country's breathtaking natural beauty and the depth of its thousand-year-old history. Cancún is both the peak of Caribbean splendor and a modern mega-resort. It boasts translucent turquoise waters, powdery white-sand beaches, and a wide array of nearby shopping, dining, and nightlife choices, in addition to a ton of other activities. Most accommodations are offered at exceptional value, and Cancún is easily accessible by air.

Many travelers who feel apprehensive about visiting foreign soil feel completely at home and at ease here: Most people speak English, most stores and vendors accept U.S. dollars, roads are well paved, and lawns are manicured. A lot of the shopping and dining takes place in malls, and you'll swear that some hotels seem larger than a small town. Simply stated, Cancún is the reason why most people travel to Mexico. The following chapters introduce you to this Caribbean-coast jewel and include plenty of tips for making the most of your stay on this nonstop island.

Chapter 8

The Lowdown on Cancún's Hotel Scene

By Lynne Bairstow

· ·

In This Chapter

▶ Sizing up the hotel locations

▶ Evaluating Cancún's top hotel choices

· ·

*I*n 1974, a team of Mexican-government computer analysts selected Cancún as an area for tourism development because of its ideal combination of features to attract travelers — and they were right on the money. Cancún is actually an island: a 23-km-long (14-mile) sliver of land shaped roughly like the number 7. Two bridges, spanning the expansive Nichupté Lagoon, connect Cancún to the mainland. (Cancún means "golden snake" in the Mayan language.)

With more than 24,000 hotel rooms in the area to choose from, Cancún has something for every taste and every budget. In this chapter, I review the two main areas — **Cancún Island (Isla Cancún)** and **Cancún City (Ciudad Cancún),** located inland, to the west of the island.

Cancún is definitely the destination to try out an air-hotel package. Although the rack rates at Cancún's hotels are among the highest in Mexico, the package deals are among the best because of the large number of charter companies operating here. (See Chapter 5 for more information on package deals, as well as some recommendations.) I should also point out that if you do arrive without a hotel reservation — I don't recommend it during peak weeks surrounding the Christmas and Easter holidays — you're likely to be able to bargain your way into a great rate.

Choosing a Location

Island hotels are stacked along the beach like dominoes; almost all offer clean, modern facilities. Extravagance reigns in the more recently built hotels, many of which are awash in a sea of marble and glass. However, some hotels, although they're exclusive, display a more relaxed attitude.

The water is placid on the island's upper end facing Bahía de Mujeres, while beaches lining the long side of the island facing the Caribbean are subject to choppier water and crashing waves on windy days. Be aware that the farther south you go on the island, the longer it takes (20 to 30 minutes in traffic) to get back to the "action spots," which are primarily located between the Plaza Flamingo and Punta Cancún on the island — close to the point that connects the two parts of the 7 — and along Avenida Tulum on the mainland.

Almost all major hotel chains are represented along **Isla Cancún,** also known as the **Hotel Zone,** so my selections can be viewed as a representative summary, with a select number of notable places to stay. The reality is that Cancún is so popular as a package destination from the United States that prices and special deals are often the deciding factor for vacationers traveling here.

 Ciudad Cancún is the more authentic Mexican town of the two locations, where the hotels' employees live and where people not on vacation conduct their day-to-day business. The area offers independently owned, smaller, and much less expensive stays — the difference in prices between these accommodations and their island counterparts is truly remarkable. And many hotels in Ciudad Cancún offer a shuttle service to sister properties in Isla Cancún, meaning you can still access the beach, for a fraction of the price, in return for a little extra travel time. Many of the best restaurants are located here, especially if you're looking for a meal in a type of restaurant that differs from those you can find back home. You can also get the best value for your meal budget in Ciudad Cancún.

Living la vida local

For condo, home, and villa rentals as an alternative to hotel stays, check with **Cancún Hideaways** (☎ 817-468-0564; Fax: 817-557-3483), a company specializing in luxury properties, downtown apartments, and condos — many offered at prices much lower than comparable hotel accommodations. Owner Maggie Rodriguez, a former resident of Cancún, has made this niche market her specialty. You can preview her offerings at **www.cancun-hideaways.com**.

Cancún's Best Accommodations

Each hotel listing includes specific rack rates for two people spending one night in a standard room, double occupancy during high season (Christmas to Easter), unless otherwise indicated. *Rack rates* simply mean published rates and tend to be the highest rate paid — you can do better, especially if you're purchasing a package that includes air-fare (see Chapter 5 for tips on avoiding paying rack rates). The rack rate prices quoted here include the 12% room tax — note that this is 5% lower than in most other resorts in Mexico, where the standard tax is 17%. Please refer to the Introduction of this book for an explanation of the price categories.

Hotels often double the normal rates during Christmas and Easter weeks, but low-season rates can be anywhere from 20% to 60% below high-season rates. Some rates may seem much higher than others, but many of these higher rates are *all-inclusive* — meaning that your meals and beverages are included in the price of your stay. All tips, taxes, and most activities and entertainment are also included in all-inclusive rates.

All hotels listed here have air conditioning, unless otherwise indicated.

Antillano
$ Ciudad Cancún

A quiet and very clean choice, the Antillano is close to the Ciudad Cancún bus terminal. Rooms overlook the main downtown street (Avenida Tulum), the side streets, or the interior lawn and pool. The latter choice is the most desirable because these rooms are the quietest. Each room has coordinated furnishings, one or two double beds, a sink area separate from the bathroom, and red-tile floors. A bonus: This inexpensive hotel provides guests the use of its beach club on the island. To find Antillano from Avenida Tulum, walk west on Claveles a half block; it's opposite the restaurant Rosa Mexicana. Parking is on the street.

Av. Claveles 1 (corner of Av. Tulum). ☎ *998-884-1132. Fax: 998-884-1878.* www. hotelantillano.com. *48 units. Rack rates: High season $70 double; low season $52 double. AE, MC, V.*

Blue Bay Getaway & Spa Cancún
$$$$$ Isla Cancún

Blue Bay is a spirited yet relaxing all-inclusive resort for adults only — no kids under 16 are allowed — that's favored by young adults in particular. One of its best features is its prime location — right at the northern end of the Hotel Zone, close to the major shopping plazas, restaurants, and nightlife, with a terrific beach with calm waters for swimming. Surrounded by acres of tropical gardens, the comfortable, clean, and modern guest rooms are located in two sections: the central building, where rooms are decorated in rustic wood, and the remaining nine buildings, which feature rooms in a colorful Mexican decor. The main lobby, administrative offices, restaurants, and the Las Margaritas bar are all located in the central building, meaning you're close to all the action — and more noise — if your room is in this section. Included are all your meals, served at any of the four restaurants, and libations, which you can find in the five bars. During the evenings, guests may enjoy a variety of theme-night dinners, nightly shows, and live entertainment in an outdoor theater with capacity for 150 guests. Activities and facilities include three swimming pools (with seven outdoor whirlpools), a tennis court, an exercise room, windsurfing, kayaks, catamarans, boogie boards, complimentary snorkeling and scuba lessons, and a marina. Safes are available for an extra charge, as is a dry-cleaning and laundry service. Blue Bay allows guests to use the amenities and facilities at its sister resort, the Blue Bay Club and Marina (a resort for families), located just outside Ciudad Cancún, near the ferry to Isla Mujeres. A free bus and boat shuttle service is provided between both Blue Bay resorts.

Paseo Kukulkán, Km 3.5. ☎ ***800-BLUE-BAY*** *in the U.S., or 998-848-7900. Fax: 998-848-7994.* www.bluebayresorts.com. *216 units. Free parking. Rack rates: High season $280 double; low season $180 double; rates are all-inclusive (room, food, beverages, and activities). AE, MC, V.*

Calinda Viva Cancún
$$$–$$$$ Isla Cancún

From the street, the Calinda Viva may not be much to look at, but the location is ideal because it's set on Cancún's best beach for safe swimming. And it's close to all the shops and restaurants clustered near Punta Cancún and the convention center. The ocean side has a small but pretty patio garden and pool. You can choose between rooms with either a lagoon or ocean view. The rooms are large and undistinguished in decor, but they're comfortable. They feature marble floors and either two double beds or a king-size bed. Several studios with kitchenettes are also available upon request. In addition to a restaurant and three bars, you also can use two lighted tennis courts, watersports equipment rental, and a small marina with its own fishing fleet.

Paseo Kukulkán, Km 8.5, next to the Playa Linda dock. ☎ ***998-883-0800***. *Fax: 998-883-2087. 216 units. Free parking. Rack rates: High season $145–$250 double; low season $138–$158 double. AE, MC, V.*

Accommodations in Isla Cancún (Hotel Zone)

Blue Bay Getaway & Spa Cancún (Km 3.5) **1**
Calinda Viva Cancún (Km 8.5) **3**
Camino Real Cancún (Km 9.5) **5**
CasaMagna Marriott (Km 14.5) **10**
El Pueblito (Km 17.5) **12**
Fiesta Americana Grand Coral Beach (Km 9.5) **4**
Flamingo Cancún (Km 11.5) **7**

Hilton Cancún Beach & Golf Resort (Km 17) **11**
Le Méridien Cancún Resort & Spa (Km 14) **9**
Miramar Misión Cancún Park Plaza (Km 9.5) **6**
Presidente InterContinental Cancún (Km 7.5) **2**
Ritz-Carlton Cancún (Km 13.5) **8**
Sun Palace (Km 20) **14**
Westin Regina Cancún (Km 20) **13**

Camino Real Cancún
$$$$$ Isla Cancún

The Camino Real is among the island's most appealing places to stay, located on 4 acres right at the tip of Punta Cancún. The setting is sophisticated, but the hotel is very welcoming to children. Camino Real is a favored name within Mexico, where vacations are synonymous with family. The hotel's architecture is trademark Camino Real — contemporary and sleek, with bright colors and strategic angles. Rooms in the newer 18-story Camino Real Club have extra services and amenities, including a complimentary full breakfast each day in the Beach Club lobby. The lower-priced rooms have lagoon views. In addition to the oceanfront pool, the Camino Real has a private saltwater lagoon with sea turtles and tropical fish. Three lighted tennis courts, a fitness center, beach volleyball, a sailing pier, and a watersports center keep things active. The hotel's three restaurants — including the popular María Bonita (see Chapter 10) — and the lively Azúcar Caribbean Bar are all on-site.

Av. Kukulkán, Km 9.5, Punta Cancún. ☎ 800-722-6466 in the U.S., or 998-848-7000. Fax: 998-848-7001. www.caminoreal.com/cancun. *389 units. Daily fee for guarded parking adjacent to hotel. Rack rates: High season $325 double, $395 Camino Real Club double; low season $195 double, $264 Camino Real Club double. AE, DC, MC, V.*

Cancún INN Suites El Patio
$ Ciudad Cancún

A European-style guesthouse, Cancún INN Suites El Patio caters to travelers looking for more of the area's culture. Many of the guests at this small hotel stay for up to a month and enjoy its combination of excellent value and warm hospitality. You won't find any bars, pools, or loud parties in this place; what you will find is excellent service and impeccable accommodations. Rooms face the plant-filled interior courtyard, dotted with groupings of wrought-iron chairs and tables. Each room has a slightly different decor and set of amenities, but all have white-tile floors and rustic wood furnishings in their various configurations. Some rooms have light kitchenette facilities, and you can also use a common kitchen area with purified water and a cooler for stocking your own supplies. A small restaurant — actually closer to a dining room — serves breakfast and dinner. Although a public phone is located in the entranceway, the staff can also arrange for a cellular phone in your room. The game and TV room has a large-screen TV with cable, a library stocked with books on Mexican culture, backgammon boards, playing cards, and board games. The hotel offers special packages for lodging and Spanish lessons. The staff serves complimentary coffee and toast in the mornings, though you can order (and pay for) a full breakfast as well. Note that even though smoking isn't allowed in the rooms, it's allowed on the premises.

Av. Bonampak 51 at Cereza. ☎ 998-884-3500. Fax: 998-884-3540. www.cancun-suites.com. *18 units. Rack rates: $50 double; ask about discounts for longer stays. AE, MC, V.*

Accommodations in Ciudad Cancún

Antillano **3**
Cancún INN Suites
El Patio **6**
Hacienda Cancún **1**
Hotel Margaritas **2**
Parador **4**
Radisson
Hacienda **5**

Area of Detail

Isla Cancún
(Zona Hotelera)

Avenida Bonampak
Barracuda
Cazon
Cazon
Pargo
Pargo
Cherna
Cherna
Robalo
Juriel
Robalo
Sierra

To Hotel Zone
(Cancún Island)

Barracuda
Rubia
Sierra
Nube
Brisa
Avenida Cobá
Avenida Cobá

Rubia
Mero
Mero
Huachinango
Huachinango
Mojarra

Avenida J.C. Nader

Tourist
Office

Avenida Tulum

Bus Station

Azucenas
Azucenas
Tulipanes
Tulipanes
Claveles
Claveles
Crisantemas

Avenida Xcaret
Jaleb
Jaleb
Reno
Reno
Venado

Margaritas
Margaritas

PARQUE
PALAPAS

Alcatraces
Alcatraces
Avenida Coba

Hospital

Rosas
Jazmines
Jazmines
Gladiolas
Gladiolas
Orquideas

Avenida Yaxchilán

Red Cross

Tanchacte
Marañon
Chiabal
Coco
Chiabal
Piña

Caimito

Nicchehabi
Saramullo
Conoco
Tauch
Tauch
Yoquen

Avenida Sunyaxchen

Guanabana
Guanabana
Anona
Avenida Coba

Grosella
Grosella
Nancen

Post Office

Valpich
Soliman
Avenida Xel-xa

Guaya
Ciruela
Anona
Ixtab
Chaac
Avenida Tankah

0   1/8 mile
0   125 meters

CasaMagna Marriott
$$$$$ Isla Cancún

This property is quintessential Marriott. Travelers who are familiar with the chain's standards feel at home here and appreciate the hotel's attention to detailed service. In fact, if you're on your first trip to Mexico, and you're looking for a little familiarity of home, this is a great choice because it feels like a slice of the United States transported to a stunning stretch of Caribbean beach. Guest rooms have contemporary furnishings, tiled floors, and ceiling fans; most have balconies. All suites occupy corners and have enormous terraces, ocean views, and TVs in both the living room and the bedroom. The CasaMagna Marriott offers five on-site restaurants, plus a lobby bar with live music. Alongside the meandering oceanfront pool are two lighted tennis courts. The hotel caters to family travelers with specially priced packages (up to two children can stay free with parents) and the Club Amigos supervised children's program. A more deluxe offering from Marriott, the 450-room luxury **JW Marriott Cancún,** is located on the beach next to the CasaMagna. Its hallmark is a 20,000-square-foot spa and fitness center.

Paseo Kukulkán, Km 14.5. ☎ *800-228-9290 in the U.S., or 998-881-2000. Fax: 998-881-2085.* www.marriott.com. *452 units. Rack rates: High season $270–$319 double, $350 suite; low season $139–$160 double, $300 suite; ask about available packages. AE, MC, V.*

El Pueblito
$$$$$ Isla Cancún

The El Pueblito looks like a traditional Mexican hacienda and has the gracious, hospitable service to match. Several three- or four-story buildings (no elevators) are terraced in a V-shape down a gentle hillside toward the sea, with a meandering swimming pool with waterfalls running between them, to a beachside, thatched-roof restaurant. Consistent renovations and upgrades and a changeover to an all-inclusive concept have made this hotel more appealing than ever and another exceptional all-inclusive value. Rooms are very large and have rattan furnishings, travertine marble floors, large bathrooms, and either a balcony or terrace facing the pool or sea. In addition to a constant flow of buffet-style meals and snacks, you also can enjoy a nightly theme party, complete with entertainment. Miniature golf and a water slide, plus a full program of kid's activities, make this place an ideal choice for families with children. Babysitting services are available for $10 per hour. The hotel is located toward the southern end of the island past the Hilton Resort.

Paseo Kukulkán, Km 17.5, past the Hilton Resort. ☎ *998-881-8800. Fax: 998-885-0731.* www.pueblitohotels.com. *350 units. Free parking. Rack rates: High season $300 double, low season $184 double; rates are all-inclusive. AE, MC, V.*

Fiesta Americana Grand Coral Beach
$$$$$ Isla Cancún

A spectacularly grand hotel, the Fiesta Americana has one of the best locations in Cancún with its 1,000 feet of prime beachfront and proximity to the main shopping and entertainment centers — perfect for the traveler looking to be at the heart of all that Cancún has to offer. The great Punta Cancún location (opposite the convention center) has the advantage of facing the beach to the north, meaning that the surf is calm and perfect for swimming. When it comes to the hotel itself, the operative word is *big* — everything at the Fiesta Americana seems oversized, from the lobby to the rooms. Service is gracious, if cool, as the hotel aims for a more sophisticated ambience. The finishings of elegant dark-green granite and an abundance of marble extend from the lobby to the large guest rooms, all of which have balconies facing the ocean. Two swimming pools border the beach, including a 660-foot-long free-form swimming pool with swim-up bars and a casual poolside snack bar, plus a full watersports equipment rental service on the beach. Two additional restaurants, plus five bars, are inside the hotel, along with a mini-shopping center. If tennis is your game, this hotel has the best facilities in Cancún; three indoor tennis courts with stadium seating are part of an extensive fitness center and spa.

Paseo Kukulkán, Km 9.5. ☎ *800-343-7821 in the U.S., or 998-881-3200. Fax: 998-881-3273.* www.fiestaamericana.com.mx. *602 units. Rack rates: High season $431–$555 double, $511–$650 Club Floors double; low season $261–$424 double, $347–$504 Club Floors double. AE, MC, V.*

Flamingo Cancún
$$$–$$$$ Isla Cancún

The Flamingo seems to have been inspired by the dramatic, slope-sided architecture of the Camino Real, but the Flamingo is considerably smaller and less expensive. And with two pools, it's a friendly, accommodating choice for families. The clean, comfortable, and modern guest rooms — all with balconies — border a courtyard facing the interior swimming pool and palapa pool bar. A second pool with a sundeck overlooks the ocean. You can choose an all-inclusive plan, which includes meals. The Flamingo is in the heart of the island hotel district, opposite the Flamingo Shopping Center and close to other hotels, shopping centers, and restaurants.

Blvd. Kukulkán, Km 11.5. ☎ *998-883-1544. Fax: 998-883-1029.* www.flamingo cancun.com. *221 units. Free, unguarded parking across the street in the Plaza Flamingo. Rack rates: High season $150 double, low season $120 double; all-inclusive plan is $220 double high season, $200 double low season. AE, MC, V.*

Hacienda Cancún
$ Ciudad Cancún

An extremely pleasing little hotel — and a great value — Hacienda Cancún is perfect for travelers on a budget. The facade has been remodeled to look like a hacienda, and rooms continue the theme, with their rustic-style Mexican furnishings. Guest rooms are clean and very comfortable; all have two double beds and windows (but no views). There's a nice, small pool and cafe under a shaded palapa in the back. To find it from Avenida Yaxchilán, turn west on Sunyaxchen; it's on your right next to the Hotel Caribe International, opposite 100% Natural. Parking is on the street.

Sunyaxchen 39–40. ☎ *998-884-3672. Fax: 998-884-1208. E-mail:* hhda@Cancun. com.mx. *35 units. Rack rates: High season $45 double; low season $38 double. MC, V.*

Hilton Cancún Beach & Golf Resort
$$$$$ Isla Cancún

The Hilton in Cancún is especially perfect for anyone whose motto is "the bigger the better." Grand, expansive, and fully equipped, this is a true resort in every sense of the word. The Hilton Cancún (formerly the 1994-vintage Caesar Park Resort) is situated on 250 acres of prime Cancún beachfront property with its own 18-hole, par-72 golf course across the street and a location that gives every room an ocean view (some have both ocean and lagoon views). Like the sprawling resort, rooms are grandly spacious and immaculately decorated in a minimalist style. Marble floors and bathrooms throughout are softened with area rugs and pale furnishings. The more elegant Villa rooms are set off from the main hotel in two- and three-story buildings (no elevators) and have their own check-in and concierge service, plus nightly complimentary cocktails. The hotel is especially appealing to golfers because it's one of only two hotels in Cancún with an on-site course. (The other is the Mélia, which has an 18-hole executive course.) The seven interconnected pools with a swim-up bar, two lighted tennis courts, a large, fully equipped gym, and a beachfront watersports center make the Hilton Cancún a good choice for those looking for an action-packed stay. Their Kids Club program is one of the best on the island, making it great for families.

Paseo Kukulkán, Km 17, Retorno Lacandones. ☎ *800-774-1500 in the U.S., or 998-881-8000. Fax: 998-881-8080.* www.hiltoncancun.com. *426 units. Rack rates: High season $375–$380 double, $440 Villa Front, $430 Villa Garden; low season $259–$300 double, $419 Villa Front, $399 Villa Garden. AE, DC, MC, V.*

Hotel Margaritas
$$ Ciudad Cancún

Located in downtown Cancún, this four-story hotel (with elevator) is comfortable and unpretentious, offering one of the best values in Cancún. Rooms have white-tile floors and a small balcony, and they're exceptionally clean and bright and pleasantly decorated. The attractive pool is surrounded by lounge chairs and has a wading section for children. The hotel offers complimentary safes at the front desk and more services than most budget hotels, including babysitting.

Av. Yaxchilán 41. ☎ 998-884-9333. Fax: 998-884-1324. www.margaritascancun. com. *100 units. Rack rates: High season $80 double; low season $65 double. AE, MC, V.*

Le Méridien Cancún Resort & Spa
$$$$$ Isla Cancún

Of all the luxury properties in Cancún, the Le Méridien is the most inviting, with a polished yet welcoming sense of personal service. Although other hotels tend to overdo a sense of formality in striving to justify their prices, Le Méridien has an elegantly casual style that makes you comfortable enough to relax thoroughly. From the intimate lobby and reception area to the most outstanding concierge service in Cancún, guests feel immediately pampered upon arrival. The hotel itself is smaller than others and feels more like an upscale boutique hotel than an immense resort — a welcome relief to those overstressed by activity at home. The decor throughout the rooms and common areas is one of understated good taste — both classy and comforting, not overdone. Rooms are generous in size, and most have small balconies overlooking the pool with an ocean view. There's a very large marble bathroom with a separate tub and a glassed-in shower. The hotel attracts many Europeans and younger, sophisticated travelers, and is ideal for a second honeymoon or romantic break. Certainly, a highlight of — or even a reason for — staying here is time spent at the **Spa del Mar,** one of Mexico's finest and most complete European spa facilities, featuring two levels and more than 15,000 square feet of services dedicated to your body and soul. A complete fitness center with extensive cardio and weight machines is on the upper level. The spa is located below and is comprised of a healthy snack bar, a full-service salon, and 14 treatment rooms, as well as separate men's and women's steam rooms, saunas, whirlpools, cold plunge pools, inhalation rooms, tranquility rooms, lockers, and changing areas.

The health club may become a necessity if you fully enjoy the gourmet restaurant, **Aioli,** with its specialties based on Mediterranean and Provençal cuisines (check out Chapter 10 for a detailed review of this restaurant). The menu is simply delicious — not pretentious. Adjoining the spa is a large swimming pool that cascades down three levels. Above the spa is a tennis center with two championship tennis courts with lights. Watersports equipment is available for rent on the beach. There's also a supervised children's program with its own Penguin Clubhouse, play equipment, and a wading pool.

Retorno del Rey, Km 14. ☎ 800-543-4300 in the U.S., or 998-881-2200. Fax: 998-881-2201. www.meridiencancun.com.mx. *213 units. Free parking. Rack rates: High season $420 double, $660 suite; low season $230 double, $370 suite; ask about special spa packages. AE, DC, MC, V. Small pets accepted, with advance reservation.*

Miramar Misión Cancún Park Plaza
$$$$ **Isla Cancún**

Another good choice for travelers looking for well-priced rooms right on the beach, the ingeniously designed Miramar offers partial views of both the lagoon and ocean from all its rooms. A notable feature is the large, rectangular swimming pool that extends through the hotel and down to the beach and contains built-in, submerged sun chairs. There's also an oversized whirlpool (the largest in Cancún), a sundeck, an exercise room, and a snack bar on the seventh-floor roof. Rooms are on the small side but are bright and comfortable with a small balcony and bamboo furniture; bathrooms have polished limestone vanities. In addition to three restaurants, you can also hang out in the popular nightclub **Batacha,** featuring live tropical music for dancing from 11 p.m. to 4 a.m. Tuesday to Sunday.

Av. Kukulkán, Km 9.5. ☎ *998-883-1755. Fax: 998-883-1136.* www.hotelesmision. com. *300 units. Rack rates: High season $211; low season $160 double. AE, MC, V.*

Parador
$ **Ciudad Cancún**

The convenient location and rock-bottom prices make this otherwise nondescript hotel among the most popular downtown hotels. Guest rooms, located on one of three floors, are arranged around two long, narrow garden courtyards leading back to a small pool (with an even smaller, separate children's pool) and grassy sunning area. The rooms are contemporary and basic, each with two double beds and a shower. The hotel is next to Pop's restaurant, almost at the corner of Uxmal. Street parking is limited.

Av. Tulum 26. ☎ *998-884-1043 or 998-884-1310. Fax: 998-884-9712. 66 units. Rack rates: High season $45 double; low season $35 double; ask about promotional rates. MC, V.*

Presidente InterContinental Cancún
$$$$$ **Isla Cancún**

On the island's best beach facing the placid Bahía de Mujeres, the Presidente's location is reason enough to stay here, and it's just a 2-minute walk to Cancún's public Pok-Ta-Pok Golf Club. Cool and spacious, the Presidente sports a postmodern design with lavish marble and wicker accents and a strong use of color. Guests have a choice of two double beds or one king-size bed. All rooms have tastefully simple white cedar accents, minibars, and complimentary Internet access. The expansive pool area has a pyramid-shaped waterfall and is surrounded by cushioned lounge chairs and five Jacuzzis. In addition to lighted tennis courts and a small fitness center, the marina has watersports equipment rentals. Coming from Ciudad Cancún, the Presidente is on the left side of the street before you get to Punta Cancún. With its ambience, the Presidente is an ideal choice for a romantic getaway or for couples who enjoy indulging in golf, tennis, or even shopping.

Av. Kukulkán, Km 7.5. ☎ *800-327-0200 or 800-904-4400 in the U.S., or 998-848-8700. Fax: 998-883-2515. www.interconti.com. 299 units. Rack rates: High season $280–$300 double; low season $250–$280 double; ask about special promotional packages. AE, MC, V.*

Radisson Hacienda
$$$ Ciudad Cancún

The nicest hotel in downtown Cancún, the Radisson Hacienda is also one of the area's best values. It offers all the expected comforts of a known hotel chain, yet in an atmosphere of Mexican hospitality. Resembling a Mexican hacienda, rooms are set off from a large rotunda-style lobby, lush gardens, and a pleasant pool area, which has a separate wading section for children. All rooms have brightly colored fabric accents; views of the garden, the pool, or the street; and a small sitting area and balcony. Bathrooms have a combination tub and shower. For the price, the extra in-room amenities of a coffeemaker, hairdryer, and iron are nice pluses. In addition to two restaurants, there's also a generally lively lobby bar, as well as tennis courts and a small gym. Guests of the Radisson Hacienda enjoy a complimentary shuttle service to the beach on Isla Cancún or to the Pok Ta Pok Golf Course. The hotel is located right behind the state government building and within walking distance of downtown Cancún dining and shopping.

Av. Nader 1. ☎ *800-333-3333 in the U.S., or 998-887-4455. Fax: 998-884-7954. www.radissoncancun.com. 248 units. Rack rates: 140 double, $168 jr. suite. AE, MC, V.*

Ritz-Carlton Cancún
$$$$$ Isla Cancún

The grand-scale Ritz-Carlton is a fountain of formality in this casual beach resort, perfect for someone who wants a Palm Beach–style experience in Mexico. The decor — in both public areas as well as guest rooms — is sumptuous and formal with thick carpets, elaborate chandeliers, and fresh flowers throughout. The hotel fronts a 1,200-foot white-sand beach, and all rooms overlook the ocean, pool (heated during winter months), and tropical gardens. In all rooms, marble bathrooms have telephones, separate tubs and showers, and lighted makeup mirrors. Ritz-Carlton Club floors offer guests five mini-meals a day, private butler service, and Hermés bath products. **The Club Grill,** a fashionable English pub, is one of the best restaurants in the city, and the **Lobby Lounge** is the original home of proper tequila tastings, featuring one of the world's most extensive menus of fine tequilas, as well as Cuban cigars. I love their white-draped cabañas for two on the beach! There's a very good fitness center and the new luxury Kayantá Spa, plus three lighted tennis courts. The Ritz Kids program has supervised activities for children, and babysitting services are also available. The hotel has won countless recognitions and accolades for service. Special packages for golfing, spa, and weekend getaways are worth exploring.

Retorno del Rey 36, off Paseo Kukulkán, Km 13.5. ☎ *800-241-3333 in the U.S. and Canada, or 998-881-0808. Fax: 998-881-0815.* www.ritzcarlton.com. *365 units. Free guarded parking. Rack rates: High season $299–$629 double, $389–$850 Club floors; low season $249–$319 double, Club floors $369–$429. AE, MC, V.*

Sun Palace

$$$$$ **Isla Cancún**

If you're looking for an all-inclusive resort on a great stretch of Caribbean beach, this member of the popular Palace Resorts group is a prime pick — and the most elegant of the resort chain's options in Cancún. What you get here is a fantastic beach, one of the widest on the island. Located toward the southern end of the island, next to the Westin Regina, the Sun Palace is farther away from the action of the hotel zone — which may be just what you need in order to revel in all the included goodies that go with staying here. Suites feature a modern Mexican decor, and all have marble floors and a combination bath with whirlpool tub. All suites also have either ocean-view balconies or terraces, and come with premium extras such as bathrobes and hairdryers. In addition to the beachside pool, there's also an indoor pool and a large Jacuzzi with a waterfall. A nicely equipped health club and tennis court complement the resort's ample activities program. In addition to its three restaurants and 24-hour room service, the Sun Palace also has nightly theme parties. One of the best perks to staying here, however, is that the excursions to Tulum, Chichén-Itzá, and Isla Mujeres are also included in their activities program. When you stay at any of the Palace resorts, you have the option of playing at any of the other members of their chain — in Cancún, other resorts are the Beach Palace, the Cancún Palace, and the Moon Palace Golf Resort.

Paseo Kukulkán, Km 20. ☎ *800-346-8225 or 998-891-4100. Fax: 998-891-4109.* www.palaceresorts.com. *227 suites. Rack rates: $310–$398 double all-inclusive. AE, DC, MC, V.*

Westin Regina Cancún

$$$$$ **Isla Cancún**

A stunning hotel, the Westin Regina is great for anyone wanting the beauty of Cancún's beaches and a little distance between them and the more boisterous, flashy parts of Cancún's hotel strip. The strikingly austere but grand architecture of the Westin Regina is the stamp of leading Latin American architect Ricardo Legorreta. A series of five swimming pools front the beach, and the Westin offers two lighted tennis courts and a small fitness center with limited spa services. The hotel is divided into two sections: the main building and the more exclusive six-story, hot-pink tower section. Standard rooms are unusually large and beautifully furnished with cool, contemporary furniture. The rooms on the sixth floor have balconies, and first-floor rooms have terraces. Rooms in the tower all have ocean or lagoon views and extensive use of marble, furniture with Olinalá lacquer accents, Berber-carpet area rugs, oak tables and chairs, and terraces with lounge chairs. It's important to note that this hotel is a 15- to 20-minute ride from the lively strip that lies between the Plaza Flamingo and Punta Cancún, so it's a better choice for those who want to relish a little more seclusion than Cancún typically offers. However, you can easily join the action when you're so inclined — buses stop in front and taxis are readily available.

Paseo Kukulkán, Km 20. ☎ *800-228-3000 in the U.S., or 998-848-7400. Fax: 998-885-0666.* www.westin.com. *293 units. Rack rates: High season $388–$450 double; low season $209–$299 double. AE, DC, MC, V.*

Chapter 9

Settling into Cancún

By Lynne Bairstow

● ●

In This Chapter

▶ Knowing what to expect when you arrive

▶ Finding your way around

▶ Discovering helpful information and resources

● ●

Yes, you need a passport or other appropriate credentials (see Chapter 7) to enter Cancún, but after that, you couldn't be in a more American-friendly foreign destination if you tried. If this is your first trip to Mexico — or to a foreign country — you'll probably find that the ensuing culture shock is practically nonexistent. But there are still a few details that you'll be more comfortable knowing before you arrive. In this chapter, I take you from the plane, through the airport, and to your hotel, helping you quickly get your bearings in this easy-to-navigate resort.

Arriving in Cancún

Cancún has one of Mexico's most modern and busiest airports, which seems to be in a constant state of construction to improve and expand its services. Still, navigating Cancún's airport is easy — both international and national flights are under the same roof. After checking in with immigration, collecting your bags, and passing through the customs checkpoint, you're ready to enjoy your holiday!

Navigating passport control and customs

Immigration check-in can be a lengthy wait, depending on the number of planes arriving at the same time, but is a generally easy and unremarkable process in which officials ask you to show your passport and complete a tourist card, known as the **FMT** (check out Chapter 7 for more information).

Your FMT is an important document, so take good care of it. You're supposed to keep the FMT with you at all times, because you may be required to show it if you run into any sort of trouble. You also need to turn the FMT back in upon departure, or you may be unable to leave without replacing it.

Next up is the baggage claim area. Here, porters stand by to help with your bags, and they're well worth the price of the tip — about a dollar a bag. After you collect your luggage, you pass through another checkpoint. Something that looks like a traffic light awaits you here. You press a button, and if the light turns green, you're free to go. If it turns red, you need to open each of your bags for a quick search. It's Mexico's random search procedure for customs. If you have an unusually large bag, or an excessive amount of luggage, you may be searched regardless of the traffic-light outcome.

Just past the traffic light, you exit to the street, where you can find transportation to your hotel. Choose between a *colectivo* (shared minivan) and a private taxi. If three or more of you are traveling together, you're better off with the private cab service. With so many hotels for the collective van to stop at, it can easily take an hour to get to your room, and believe me, the drivers wait until the vans are packed before departing! Check out the "Accommodations in Isla Cancún" map in Chapter 8 to find out where your hotel is relative to the airport.

If you do choose the *colectivo* service, which consists of air-conditioned vans, buy your ticket at the booth that's located to the far right as you exit baggage claim. You can purchase tickets for private cab service at a booth inside the airport terminal. Tickets for both the *colectivo* vans and the private taxis are based on a fixed rate depending on the distance to your destination. A taxi ticket is good for up to four passengers.

Getting to your hotel

The airport is on the mainland, close to the southern end of the Cancún area. It's about 14 km (9 miles) to downtown **Ciudad Cancún** (Cancún City), which is located on the mainland. The start of the **Zona Hotelera (Hotel Zone),** located on **Isla Cancún** (Cancún Island), is 10 km (6½ miles) from the airport — about a 20-minute drive east from the airport along wide, well-paved roads.

Hiring a taxi

Rates for a **private taxi** from the airport are around $25 to downtown Cancún or $35 to $45 to the Hotel Zone, depending on your destination. The *colectivos* run from Cancún's international airport into town and the Hotel Zone and cost about $9 per person. There's minibus transportation (for $9.50) from the airport to the Puerto Juárez passenger ferry that takes you to Isla Mujeres. You can also hire a private taxi for this trip for about $40.

No *colectivo* service returns to the airport from Ciudad Cancún or the Hotel Zone, so you must hire a taxi, but the rate should be much less than the trip from the airport. The reason? Only federally chartered taxis may take fares *from* the airport, but any local taxi may bring passengers *to* the airport. Ask for a fare estimate at your hotel, but expect to pay about half what you were charged to get from the airport to your hotel (if you originally took a taxi).

Renting a car

Most major car-rental firms have outlets at the airport, so if you're renting a car, consider picking it up and dropping it off at the airport to save on airport-transportation costs. Another way to save money is to arrange for the rental before you leave home. If you wait until you arrive, the daily cost of a rental car may be around $65 to $75 for a Volkswagen Beetle. Major car-rental services include

- ✔ **Avis** (☎ **800-331-1212** in the U.S., or 998-886-0221; www.avis.com)

- ✔ **Budget** (☎ **800-527-0700** in the U.S., or 998-884-6955; www.budget.com)

- ✔ **Dollar** (☎ **800-800-4000** in the U.S., or 998-886-0179; www.dollar.com)

- ✔ **Hertz** (☎ **800-654-3131** in the U.S. and Canada, or 998-884-1326; www.hertz.com)

- ✔ **National** (☎ **800-328-4567** in the U.S., or 998-886-0655; www.nationalcar.com)

Although you certainly don't have to rent a car in Cancún — taxis and buses are plentiful — this is one destination where having a car may make sense for a day or two. It can be a convenience, although it's not likely to save you bundles on transportation costs, based on the relatively high prices of car rentals in Cancún. The roads in and around Cancún are excellent, and parking is readily available in most of the shopping/entertainment malls. The main reason for renting a car, however, is the flexibility that it provides in exploring the surrounding areas — a day-trip down the coast or to nearby sights is definitely recommended. But if you're not comfortable driving, you can easily cover this ground in one of the many sightseeing tours available.

If you do rent a car, keep any valuables out of plain sight. Although Cancún's crime rate is very low, the only real problem tends to be rental-car break-ins.

Looking for more information?

Here's a list of the best Web sites for additional information about Cancún:

✔ **All About Cancún** (www.cancunmx.com)

Before taking off on a vacation, every traveler has a few questions. If Cancún is your destination, this site is a good place to start. It contains a database of answers to the most commonly asked questions. Just look for "The Online Experts" section. The site can be slow, but it has input from lots of recent travelers to the region.

✔ **Cancún Convention and Visitors Bureau** (www.cancun.info)

The official site of the Cancún Convention and Visitors Bureau provides excellent information on events and area attractions. The site's hotel guide is one of the most complete and detailed listings I've seen, and it has an active message board of recent visitors to Cancún.

✔ **Cancún.com** (www.cancun.com)

Cancún.com is a comprehensive guide that has tons of information about what to do and see in Cancún. Just remember that advertisers pay to be included and provide most of the details. Highlights include forums, live chats, property-swaps, and bulletin boards, plus information on local Internet access, news, and events. You can even reserve a golf tee time or plan your wedding online.

✔ **Cancún Travel Guide** (www.go2cancun.com)

This group specializing in online information about Mexico has put together an excellent resource for Cancún rentals, hotels, and area attractions. Although only paying advertisers are listed, you can find most of the major players here.

Getting Around Cancún

As I discuss a bit in the "Getting to your hotel" section earlier in this chapter, there are really two Cancúns: **Isla Cancún** (Cancún Island) and **Ciudad Cancún** (Cancún City). The latter, on the mainland, has restaurants, shops, and less-expensive hotels, as well as all the other establishments that make local life function — pharmacies, dentists, automotive shops, banks, travel and airline agencies, car-rental firms, and so on — which are all located within an approximately nine-square-block area. The city's main thoroughfare is **Avenida Tulum.** Heading south, Avenida Tulum becomes the highway to the airport, Playa del Carmen, and Tulum. (It actually runs all the way down to Belize.) Heading north, Avenida Tulum intersects the highway to Mérida and the road to Puerto Juárez and the Isla Mujeres ferries.

The famed **Zona Hotelera** (Hotel Zone, also called the **Zona Turística,** or Tourist Zone) stretches out along Isla Cancún, which is a sandy strip of land 23 km (14 miles) long and shaped like a 7. The Playa Linda

Bridge, at the north end of the island, and the Punta Nizuc Bridge, at the southern end, connect Isla Cancún to the mainland. Between these two bridges lies **Laguna Nichupté.** Avenida Cobá from Cancún City becomes Paseo Kukulkán, the island's main traffic artery — actually, the only main road on the island, so getting lost here really takes some effort! To get the hang of pronouncing it quickly enough, say koo-cool-*can*, as in, *can*-cun is sooo cool! Cancún's international airport is located just inland from the south end of the island.

Ciudad Cancún's street-numbering system is a holdover from its early days. Addresses in the city are still expressed by the number of the building lot and the *manzana* (block) or *supermanzana* (group of city blocks). The city is still relatively compact, and you can easily cover the downtown commercial section on foot. Streets are named after famous Mayan cities. Chichén-Itzá, Tulum, and Uxmal are the names of the boulevards in downtown Cancún, as well as nearby archeological sites.

On the island, addresses are given by their kilometer (Km) number on Paseo Kukulkán or by reference to some well-known location. The point on the island closest to Ciudad Cancún is Km 1; Km 20 is found at the very bottom of the 7 at Punta Nizuc, where the Club Med is located.

Taking a taxi

Taxi prices in Cancún are clearly set by zone, although keeping track of what's in which zone can take some work. Taxi rates within the Hotel Zone are a minimum fare of $5 per ride, making it one of the most expensive taxi areas in Mexico.

Taxis operating in the Hotel Zone feel perfectly justified in having a discriminatory pricing structure: Local residents pay about half of what tourists pay, and guests at higher-priced hotels pay about twice the fare that guests in budget hotels are charged. You can thank the taxi union for this bit of fun — they establish the rate schedule. Rates should be posted outside your hotel; however, if you have a question, all taxi drivers are required to have an official rate card in their taxi, although it's generally in Spanish.

Within downtown, the cost is about $1.50 per cab ride (not per person); within any other zone, it's $5. Traveling between two zones also costs $5. If you cross two zones, the cost is $7.50; crossing three zones runs about $11. Settle on a price in advance, or check at your hotel, where destinations and prices are generally posted. Trips to the airport from most zones cost $15. Taxis also have a rate of $18 per hour for travel around the city and Hotel Zone, but you can generally negotiate this rate down to $10 to $12. If you want to hire a taxi to take you to Chichén-Itzá or along the Riviera Maya, expect to pay about $30 per hour — many taxi drivers feel that they're also providing guide services.

Catching a bus

Bus travel within Cancún continues to improve and is increasingly the most popular way of getting around for both residents and tourists. Air-conditioned and rarely crowded, the Hotel Zone buses run 24 hours a day. You can easily spot the bus stops; look for roadside signs that have a bus on them. Bus stops are in front of most of the main hotels and shopping centers. Most buses cost 60¢. In town, almost everything is within walking distance. Ruta 1 and Ruta 2 *(Hoteles)* city buses travel frequently from the mainland to the beaches along Avenida Tulum (the main street) and all the way to Punta Nizuc at the far end of the Hotel Zone on Isla Cancún.

Ruta 8 buses go to Puerto Juárez/Punta Sam, where you can catch ferries to Isla Mujeres. The buses stop on the east side of Avenida Tulum. These buses operate between 6 a.m. and 10 p.m. daily. Beware of private buses along the same route; they charge far more than the public ones. The public buses have the fare amount painted on the front; at the time of publication, the fare was six pesos (60¢).

Zipping around on a moped

Mopeds are a convenient and popular way to cruise around the congested traffic, but they can be dangerous. Rentals start at $25 for a day, and the shops require a credit-card voucher as security for the moped.

When you rent a moped, make sure you receive a crash helmet (it's the law) and instructions on how to lock the wheels when you park. Read the fine print on the back of the rental agreement regarding liability for repairs or replacement in case of accident, theft, or vandalism.

Fast Facts: Cancún

American Express

The local office is located in Ciudad Cancún at Avenida Tulum 208 and Agua (☎ 998-881-4025, 998-881-4040), one block past the Plaza México. The office is open Monday to Friday 9 a.m. to 6 p.m. and Saturday 9 a.m. to 2 p.m.

Area Code

The telephone area code is **988.**

Babysitters

Most of the larger hotels can easily arrange for babysitters, but many sitters speak limited English. Rates range from $4 to $10 per hour.

Banks, ATMs, and Currency Exchange

Most banks are downtown along Avenida Tulum and are usually open Monday to Friday 9:30 a.m. to 5 p.m., and many now have ATMs for after-hours cash withdrawals. In the Hotel

Zone, you can find banks in the Plaza Kukulkán and next to the convention center. There are also many *casas de cambio* (exchange houses) in the Hotel Zone, in the plazas, and near the convention center. Avoid changing money at the airport as you arrive, especially at the first exchange booth you see — its rates are less favorable than any in town or others farther inside the airport concourse. In general, you can find the best exchange rates at ATMs, casas de cambio, and hotels.

Business Hours

Most downtown offices maintain traditional Mexican hours of operation (9 a.m. to 2 p.m. and 4 p.m. to 8 p.m., daily), but shops remain open throughout the day from 10 a.m. to 9 p.m. Offices tend to close on Saturday and Sunday, but shops are open on Saturday, at least, and increasingly offer limited hours of operation on Sunday. Malls are generally open from 10 a.m. to 10 p.m. or later.

Climate

It's hot but not overwhelmingly humid. The rainy season is May through October. August through October is the hurricane season, which brings erratic weather. November through February is generally sunny but can also be cloudy, windy, somewhat rainy, and even cool, so a sweater and rain protection is handy.

Consular Agents

The **U.S. consular agent** is located in the Plaza Caracol 2, 3rd level, rooms 320–323, Paseo Kukulkán, Km 8.5 (☎ 998-883-0272). The office is open Monday to Friday 9 a.m. to 1 p.m. The **Canadian** consulate is located in the Plaza Caracol 11, 3rd level, room 330, Paseo Kukulkán, Km 8.5 (☎ 998-883-3360). The office is open from Monday to Friday 9 a.m. to 5 p.m.

Emergencies/Hospitals

To report an emergency, dial ☎ **065,** which is supposed to be similar to 911 emergency service in the United States. For first aid, the **Cruz Roja** (Red Cross; ☎ 998-884-1616; Fax:

998-884-7466) is open 24 hours a day on Avenida Yaxchilán between avenidas Xcaret and Labná, next to the Telmex building. **Total Assist,** a small, nine-room emergency hospital with English-speaking doctors (Claveles 5, SM 22, at Avenida Tulum; ☎ 998-884-1058, 998-884-1092; E-mail: htotal@prodigy. net.mx), is also open 24 hours. American Express, MasterCard, and Visa are accepted. Desk staff may have limited command of English. An **air ambulance service** is also available by calling ☎ 800-305-9400 (toll free within Mexico). *Urgencias* means "Emergencies."

Information

The **State Tourism Office,** Calle Picaria 23 (☎ 998-881-9000), is centrally located downtown. The office is open daily 9 a.m. to 9 p.m., and it has maps, brochures, and information on the area's popular sights, including Tulum, Xcaret, Isla Mujeres, and Playa del Carmen. A second tourist information office, the **Convention and Visitors Bureau** (☎ 998-884-6531, 998-884-3438), is located on Avenida Naves on the corner of Avenida Cobá, next to Pizza Rolandi, and is open Monday to Friday 9 a.m. to 8 p.m. Hotels and their rates are listed at each office, as are ferry schedules. For information prior to your arrival in Cancún, visit the Convention Bureau's Web site at www.cancun.info.

Pick up copies of the free monthly *Cancún Tips* or the *Cancún Tips* booklet, which is published four times a year. Both contain lots of useful information and great maps. The publications are owned by the same people who own the Captain's Cove restaurants, a couple of sightseeing boats, and timeshare hotels, so the information, though good, isn't completely unbiased.

Internet Access

C@ncunet (☎ 998-885-0055), located in a kiosk on the second floor of Plaza Kukulkán (Paseo Kukulkán, Km 13), offers Internet access for $4 per 15 minutes or $7 per hour from 10 a.m. to 10 p.m.

Maps

One of the best around is the free American Express map, usually found at the tourist information offices and the local American Express office. The publication *Cancún Tips* (see "Information") also has excellent maps and is generally available through your hotel concierge.

Newspapers/Magazines

Most hotel gift shops and newsstands carry English-language magazines and English-language Mexican newspapers.

Pharmacy

Next to the Hotel Caribe Internacional, **Farmacia Canto** (Avenida Yaxchilán 36, at Sunyaxchen; ☎ 998-884-9330) is open 24 hours. American Express, MasterCard, and Visa are accepted. Plenty of drugstores are in the major shopping malls, open until 10 p.m., in the Hotel Zone. You can stock up on Retin-A, Viagra, and many other prescription drugs without a prescription.

Police

To reach the **police** *(seguridad pública),* dial ☎ 998-884-1913 or 998-884-2342.

Post Office

The **main post office** (☎ 998-884-1418) is downtown at the intersection of avenidas Sunyaxchen and Xel-Ha. It's open Monday to Friday 9 a.m. to 4 p.m. Saturdays, from 9 a.m. to 12 p.m., it's open just for the purchase of stamps.

Safety

There is very little crime in Cancún. People are generally safe late at night in tourist areas; just use ordinary, common sense. As at any other beach resort, don't take money or valuables to the beach.

Swimming on the Caribbean side presents a danger from undertow. Pay attention to the posted flag warnings on the beaches.

Car break-ins are about the only crimes here, although they do happen frequently, especially around the shopping centers in the Hotel Zone. VW Beetles and Golfs are frequent targets.

Taxes

There's a 10% value-added tax (IVA) on goods and services, and it's generally included in the posted price. Cancún's IVA is 5% lower than most of Mexico due to a special exemption that dates back to its origins as a duty-free port.

Taxis

Taxi prices in Cancún are set by zone, and keeping track of what's in which zone can take some work. Taxi rates within the Hotel Zone are a minimum fare of $5 per ride, making it one of the most expensive taxi areas in Mexico. Rates within the downtown area are between $1.50 and $2. You can also hire taxis by the hour or day for longer trips, when you'd prefer to leave the driving to someone else. Rates run between $15 and $20 per hour with discounts available for full-day rates, but an extra charge applies when the driver doubles as a tour guide. Always settle on a price in advance, or check at your hotel, where destinations and prices are generally posted.

Telephone

Avoid the phone booths that have signs in English advising you to call home using a special 800 number — these are absolute rip-offs and can cost as much as $20 per minute. The least expensive way to call is by using a Mexican prepaid phone card called Telmex (LADATEL), available at most pharmacies and mini-supermarkets, using the official public phones, Telmex (Lada). Remember, in Mexico, you need to dial 001 prior to a number to reach the United States, and you need to preface long-distance calls within Mexico by dialing 01.

Time Zone

Cancún operates on central standard time, but Mexico's observance of daylight savings time varies somewhat from that in the United States.

Chapter 10

Dining in Cancún

By Lynne Bairstow

. . . .

In This Chapter

▶ Discovering Cancún's best restaurants

▶ Finding a restaurant with true Mexican ambiance

. . . .

U.S.-based franchise chains, which really need no introduction, populate a large part of Cancún's restaurant scene. These chains include Hard Rock Cafe, Planet Hollywood, Rainforest Cafe, Tony Roma's, T.G.I. Friday's, Ruth's Chris Steak House, and the gamut of fast-food burger places. Contrary to common travelers' wisdom, many of Cancún's best restaurants are located either in hotels or shopping malls.

The majority of restaurants are located in the Hotel Zone in Isla Cancún, which is logical because that's where most of the tourists who come to dine out are located. However, don't dismiss the charms of dining in Ciudad Cancún. You're likely to find a great meal — at a fraction of the price of an Isla Cancún eatery — accompanied by a dose of local color.

As in many of Mexico's beach resorts, even the finest restaurants in town can be comfortably casual when it comes to dress. Men rarely wear jackets, although you may frequently see women in dressy resort wear — basically, anything goes.

For those traveling with kids, Cancún has no shortage of options. From Johnny Rockets to McDonald's, this destination has plenty of kid-friendly — and kid-familiar — places.

Prices in Cancún can cover an extended range, boosted by shrimp and lobster dishes, which can top $20 for an entree. If you're watching your budget, even the higher-priced places generally have less-expensive options — just avoid the premium seafood dishes. Remember that tips generally run about 15%, and most restaurant and bar staff really depend on tips for their income, so be generous if the service warrants.

Cancún's Best Restaurants

The restaurants in this chapter are either locally owned, one-of-a-kind restaurants, or exceptional selections at area hotels. Many feature live music as an accompaniment to the dining experience. I arrange the restaurants alphabetically and note their location, as well as their general price category and cuisine. Please refer to the Introduction of this book for an explanation of the price categories.

Please see Appendix C for more information on Mexican cuisine.

100% Natural
$ Isla Cancún   VEGETARIAN/MEXICAN

If you want a healthy reprieve from an overindulgent night — or just like your meals as fresh and natural as possible — this is your oasis. No matter what your dining preference, you owe it to yourself to try a Mexican tradition: the fresh-fruit *liquado*. The blended drink combines fresh fruit, ice, and either water or milk. More creative combinations may mix in yogurt, granola, or other goodies. And 100% Natural serves more than just meal-quality drinks — there's a bountiful selection of basic Mexican fare and terrific sandwiches served on whole-grain bread, both with options for vegetarians. Breakfast is a delight as well as a good value. The space abounds with plants and cheery colors. There are a few locations in town; the branch in Plaza Terramar (☎ 998-883-3636) is open 24 hours.

Plaza Kukulkán, Paseo Kukulkán, Km 13. ☎ 998-885-2904. Reservations not needed. Main courses $2.80–$13. MC, V. Daily 8 a.m.–11 p.m.

Aioli
$–$$$ Isla Cancún   FRENCH

In the Le Méridien Hotel, the Provençal — but definitely not provincial — Aioli offers simply exquisite French and Mediterranean gourmet specialties served in a warm and cozy country French setting. Though it has perhaps the best breakfast buffet in Cancún (for $15), most visitors outside the hotel enjoy Aioli only for dinner, when low lighting and superb service make the restaurant a top choice for a romantic dinner. Starters include the traditional pâtés and a delightful escargot served in the shell with a white wine and herb butter sauce. A specialty is duck breast served in a honey and lavender sauce. Equally scrumptious is the rack of lamb, prepared in a Moroccan style and served with couscous. Pan-seared grouper is topped with a paste of black olives, crushed potato, and tomato; the bouillabaisse is laden with an exceptional array of seafood. Desserts are decadent in true French style, including the signature "Fifth Element," a sinfully delicious temptation rich with chocolate. For the quality and the originality of the cuisine, coupled with the excellence in service, Aioli gets my top pick for Cancún's best value in fine dining.

Isla Cancún Dining

To Puerto Juárez ↑
and Punta Sam
180
Av. López Portillo
Ave. Bonampak
CIUDAD CANCÚN
see Ciudad Cancún Dining map

Playa las Perlas
Playa Juventud
Ferry to Isla Mujeres
Bahía de Mujeres
Km 3
Playa Langosta
Playa Linda
Km 3.5
Km 4
Km 5
Playa Tortuga
Paseo Kukulkán
Carlos 'n' Charlies
Km 7
Km 7.5
Km 8

307
Avenida Tulum
Paseo Mujeres

Canal Nichupté

To Tulum
& Chetumal

Pok-Ta-Pok Golf Course

Laguna Bojórquez

Plaza Caracol
1
Punta Cancún
2
Convention Center
Km 9
Km 9.5
Playa Gaviota
Km 10
3
4
Playa Chac-Mool
Plaza Flamingo

Km 11.5

Laguna del Amor

Laguna de Nichupté

Km12
La Isla Shopping Village
5 **6**
Plaza Kukulkán

7
8
9 Km 14
10
11

Caribbean Sea

Ruinas del Rey
Paseo Kukulkán
Km 16

Laguna Inglé
Canal Nizuc
Playa del Rey

Km 20
Punta Nizuc

← To Airport
Paseo Kukulkán

Beach ✲
Golf ⛳
Ruins ≋

0 ——— 2 mi
0 ——— 2 km
N

UNITED STATES
Gulf of Mexico
MEXICO
THE YUCATÁN PENINSULA
Cancún
Mexico City ★
PACIFIC OCEAN
0 —— 500 mi
0 —— 500 km

100% Natural *(Km 13)* **6**
Aioli *(Km 14)* **8**
Captain's Cove *(Km 16.5)* **11**
Club Grill *(Km 13.5)* **7**
La Destilería *(Km 12.65)* **5**
La Dolce Vita *(Km 14.6)* **10**

La Fisheria *(Km 8.5)* **1**
Lorenzillo's *(Km 10.5)* **4**
Mango Tango *(Km 14.2)* **9**
María Bonita *(Km 9.5)* **2**
Plantation House *(Km 10.5)* **3**
Savio's *(Km 8.5)* **1**

Le Méridien Hotel, Retorno del Rey, Km 14. ☎ *998-881-2225.* www.meridien cancun.com.mx. *Free parking. Reservations required. Main courses: $14–$30. AE, DC, MC, V. Open: Mon–Sun 6:30 a.m.–11 p.m.*

Captain's Cove

$$ Isla Cancún   INTERNATIONAL/SEAFOOD

Recognized for its consistent value — think heaping servings, friendly service, and great sunset views from the upper deck — Captain's Cove regularly packs customers into its several dining levels. Diners face big, open windows overlooking the lagoon and Royal Yacht Club Marina. For breakfast, try the extremely popular all-you-can-eat buffet that beats the price and quality of most hotel buffets. Main courses of USDA Angus steak and seafood are the norm at lunch and dinner, and a menu catering especially to children is available. Dessert standouts include flaming coffees, crêpes, and Key lime pie. Captain's Cove sits almost at the end of Paseo Kukulkán, on the lagoon side opposite the Omni Hotel.

Paseo Kukulkán, Km 16.5. ☎ *998-885-0016. Reservations recommended. Main courses: $16–$20; breakfast buffet $8.95. AE, MC, V. Open: Daily 7 a.m.–11 p.m.*

Club Grill

$–$$$ Isla Cancún   INTERNATIONAL

Cancún's most elegant and stylish restaurant, located in the Ritz-Carlton hotel, is also among its most delicious. The gracious service and old-world charm begin the moment you enter the anteroom with its comfortable couches and chairs and selection of fine tequilas and Cuban cigars. The scene continues into a candlelit dining room with padded side chairs and tables shimmering with silver and crystal. Elegant plates of peppered scallops, truffles, and potatoes in tequila sauce; grilled lamb; or mixed grill arrive at a leisurely pace after the appetizer. The restaurant has both smoking and nonsmoking sections. After dinner, take a turn on the dance floor, as a band plays romantic music beginning at 8 p.m. Club Grill is the place for that truly special night out. A dress code is enforced: No sandals or tennis shoes, and gentlemen must wear long pants.

Ritz-Carlton Cancún, Paseo Kukulkán, Km 13.5. ☎ *998-881-0808. Reservations required. Main courses: $11–$40. AE, DC, MC, V. Open: Tues–Sun 7–11 p.m.*

El Pescador

$–$$ Ciudad Cancún   SEAFOOD

Locals all seem to agree: El Pescador is the best spot for fresh seafood in Cancún. A line often forms here for the well-prepared fresh seafood served in a street-side patio and upstairs venue. Feast on shrimp cocktail, conch, octopus, *camarones à la criolla* (Creole-style shrimp), charcoal-broiled lobster, and stone crabs. Can't decide? Try a little of everything

Ciudad Cancún Dining

El Pescador **3**
La Habichuela **2**
Los Almendros **7**
Périco's **1**
Rolandi's Pizza **5**
Rosa Mexicana **4**
Stefano's **6**

Avenida Bonampak

Barracuda
Rubia
Barracuda
Cazon
Cazon
Pargo
Pargo
Cherna
Cherna
Robalo
Juriel
Robalo
Sierra
Rubia
Mero
Mero
Huachinango
Huachinango
Mojarra
Sierra
Avenida Cobá
Avenida Cobá
Nube
Brisa
To Hotel Zone (Cancún Island)

Avenida J.C. Nader

Tourist Office

Avenida Tulum

Bus Station

Margaritas
Margaritas
Azucenas
Azucenas
Tulipanes
Tulipanes
Claveles
Claveles
Crisantemas
Alcatraces
Alcatraces
Avenida Coba
Avenida Xcaret
Jaleb
Jaleb
Reno
Reno
Venado

PARQUE PALAPAS

Hospital

Rosas
Jazmines
Jazmines
Gladiolas
Gladiolas
Orquideas
Avenida Yaxchilán

Tanchacte
Marañon
Chiabal
Coco
Chiabal
Piña
Red Cross
Caimito
Guanabana
Guanabana
Anona
Avenida Coba

Nicchehabi
Conoco
Yoquen
Saramullo
Tauch
Tauch
Grosella
Avenida Sunyaxchen

Valpich
Soliman
Post Office
Grosella
Nancen
Avenida Xel-ha
Guaya
Ciruela
Ixtab
Chaac
Anona
Avenida Tankah

0   1/8 mile
0   125 meters

Area of Detail

Isla Cancún (Zona Hotelera)

in the *Zarzuela* combination seafood plate, cooked in white wine and garlic. El Pescador features a Mexican specialty menu as well. Another branch, **La Mesa del Pescador,** is located in the Plaza Kukulkán on Isla Cancún and is open the same hours, but it's more expensive.

Tulipanes 28, off Av. Tulum. ☎ 998-884-2673. Reservations not needed. Main courses: $5–$30. AE, MC, V. Open: Daily 11 a.m.–11 p.m.

La Destilería
$–$$ Isla Cancún MEXICAN

If you want to experience tequila in its native habitat, don't miss this place — even though it's across the country from the region that produces the beverage. La Destilería is more than a tequila-inspired restaurant; it's a mini-museum honoring the "spirit" of Mexico. It serves more than 150 brands of tequila, including some treasures that never find their way across the country's northern border, so be adventurous! The margaritas are among the best on the island. When you decide to have some food with your tequila, the menu is refined Mexican, with everything from quesadillas with squash blossom flowers to shrimp in a delicate tequila-lime sauce.

Paseo Kukulkán, Km 12.65, across from Plaza Kukulkán. ☎ 998-885-1086 or 998-885-1087. Reservations recommended during high season. Main courses $8–$30. AE, MC, V. Daily 1 p.m. to midnight.

La Dolce Vita
$–$$ Isla Cancún ITALIAN/SEAFOOD

The casually elegant La Dolce Vita is known as Cancún's favorite Italian restaurant. Appetizers include pâté of quail liver and carpaccio in vinaigrette or mushrooms Provençal. The chef specializes in homemade pastas combined with fresh seafood. You can order green tagliolini with lobster medallions, linguine with clams or seafood, or rigatoni Mexican-style (with *chorizo,* mushrooms, and chives) as a main course, or as an appetizer for half price. You can dine in air-conditioned comfort or on an open-air terrace with a lagoon view. Dinner is accompanied by live jazz from 7 to 11:30 p.m., Monday through Saturday.

Paseo Kukulkán, Km 14.6, on the lagoon, opposite the Marriott Casamagna. ☎ 998-885-0150 or 998-885-0161. www.cancun.com/dining/dolce. Reservations required for dinner. Main courses: $9–$29. AE, MC, V. Open: Daily noon to midnight.

La Fisheria
$–$$ Isla Cancún SEAFOOD

La Fisheria is one of the exceptions to the rule about never finding good food in a shopping mall eatery. The expansive menu at La Fisheria includes shark fingers with a jalapeño dip, grouper fillet stuffed with seafood in a lobster sauce, Acapulco-style *ceviche* (in a tomato sauce), New England clam chowder, steamed mussels, grilled red snapper with pasta — you get the idea. The menu changes daily, but there's always *tikin xik,* that great Yucatecan grilled fish marinated in *achiote* sauce (made from achiote chile paste). And for those diners not inclined toward seafood, a wood-burning, oven-made pizza may do, or perhaps one of the grilled chicken or beef dishes. If you're at the mall shopping, La Fisheria is your best bet — and a reason to stop by if you're not.

Plaza Caracol, Shopping Center 2nd floor. ☎ 998-883-1395. Reservations not needed. Main courses: $6.50–$21. AE, MC, V. Open: Daily 11 a.m. to 11 p.m.

La Habichuela

$$–$$$ Ciudad Cancún   GOURMET SEAFOOD/CARIBBEAN/MEXICAN

Dine al fresco in a garden setting and enjoy some of downtown Cancún's finest food. Romantic in its setting on a vine-draped patio, La Habichuela boasts tables that are covered in pink-and-white linens, and soft music playing in the background. For an all-out culinary adventure, try *habichuela* (string bean) soup; shrimp in any number of sauces, including Jamaican tamarind, tequila, and a ginger-and-mushroom combination; and the Maya coffee with *xtabentun* (a strong, sweet, anise-based liquor). The grilled seafood and steaks are excellent as well, but La Habichuela is a good place to try a Mexican specialty such as *enchiladas suizas (Swiss crepes)* or *tampiqueña*-style beef (thinly sliced, marinated, and grilled). For something totally divine, try the *Cocobichuela,* which is lobster and shrimp in a curry sauce served in a coconut shell and topped with fruit.

Margaritas 25. ☎ 998-884-3158. www.lahabichuela.com. *Free parking. Reservations recommended in high season. Main courses: $15–$39. AE, MC, V. Open: Daily noon to midnight.*

Lorenzillo's

$–$$$$ Isla Cancún   SEAFOOD

Live lobster is the overwhelming favorite here, and part of the appeal is selecting your dinner out of the giant lobster tank. A dock leads down to the main dining area, overlooking the lagoon and topped by a giant palapa. When the place is packed (which is often), a wharf-side bar handles the overflow. In addition to the lobster — it comes grilled, steamed, or stuffed — good bets are the shrimp stuffed with cheese and wrapped in bacon, the admiral's fillet coated in toasted almonds and a light mustard sauce, or the seafood-stuffed squid. Desserts include the tempting "Martinique": Belgian chocolate with hazelnuts, almonds, and pecans, served with vanilla ice cream. A sunset pier offers a lighter menu of cold seafood, sandwiches, and salads. There's a festive, friendly atmosphere, and children are very welcome — after all, most of the patrons are wearing bibs! A personal favorite, I never miss a lobster stop here when I'm in Cancún.

Paseo Kukulkán, Km 10.5. ☎ *998-883-1254.* www.lorenzillos.com.mx. *Free parking in lot across the street, plus valet parking. Reservations recommended. Main courses: $8–$50. AE, MC, V. Open: Daily noon to midnight.*

Los Almendros

$ Ciudad Cancún   YUCATECAN

To steep yourself in Yucatecan cuisine and music, head directly to this large, colorful, air-conditioned restaurant. Regional specialties served here include lime soup, *poc chuc* (a marinated, barbecue-style pork), chicken or pork *pibil* (a sweet and spicy barbeque sauce served over shredded meat), and appetizers such as *panuchos* (soft, fried tortillas with refried beans and either shredded turkey or pork *pibil*). The *combinado Yucateco* is a sampler of four typically Mexican main courses. Los Almendros is located opposite the bullring.

Av. Bonampak and Sayil. ☎ *998-887-1332. Reservations recommended during high season. Main courses: $5–$10. AE, MC, V. Open: Daily 11 a.m.–10 p.m.*

Mango Tango

$–$$$ Isla Cancún   INTERNATIONAL

Mango Tango has sizzling floor shows and live reggae music, but its kitchen is the real star. Try the peel-your-own shrimp, Argentine-style grilled meat with *chimichurri* sauce (sauce with roasted vegetables and a variety of spices), and other tropical specialties. Creole gumbo comes with lobster, shrimp, and squid, and the coconut-and-mango cake is a fitting finish to the meal. The beauty of dining here is that you can stay and enjoy one of the currently hot nightspots in Cancún.

Paseo Kukulkán Km 14.2, opposite the Ritz-Carlton Cancún. ☎ *998-885-0303. Reservations recommended. Main courses: $12–$45; dinner show $40. AE, MC, V. Open: Daily 2 p.m.–2 a.m.*

Dining at sea

One unique way to combine dinner with sightseeing is to board the **Lobster Dinner Cruise** (☎ 998-849-4621). Cruising around the tranquil, turquoise waters of the lagoon, passengers feast on lobster dinners accompanied by wine. The cost is $64.50 per person, and the cruise departs two times daily from the Royal Mayan Marina. A sunset dinner cruise leaves at 4 p.m. during winter months and 5 p.m. during the summer. A moonlight cruise leaves at 7:30 p.m. during the winter and 8:30 p.m. during the summer.

María Bonita

$$–$$$ Isla Cancún   REGIONAL/MEXICAN/ NOUVELLE MEXICAN

Possibly the most "Mexican" of Isla Cancún's dining options, María Bonita combines the music, food, and atmosphere of Mexico's various regions — it's almost like taking a condensed food tour of this vast country! Being that María Bonita is located in a hotel (the Camino Real Cancún), prices are higher and the flavors are more institutionalized than the traditional Mexican restaurants found in Ciudad Cancún, but the restaurant is still a good choice for diners wanting more of Mexico's flavors — without leaving the Hotel Zone. The restaurant overlooks the water, and the interior is divided by cuisine type. For example, one favorite is *La Cantina Jalisco,* which features an open, colorful Mexican kitchen (with pots and pans on the wall) and tequila bar (with more than 50 different tequilas). For the less adventurous in your party, a few international dishes are thrown in for variety. Trios, marimba, and jarocho music, as well as the ever-enchanting mariachis, serenade the diners. Check out the front of the menu for explanations on the different peppers used. The kitchen marks each dish for its heat quotient (from zero to two chiles). The restaurant is to the left of the hotel entrance, and you can enter from the street.

In the Camino Real Cancún hotel, Punta Cancún. ☎ *998-848-7000, ext. 7960 Reservations recommended. Main courses: $25–$31. AE, DC, MC, V. Open: Daily 6 p.m.–1 a.m.*

Périco's

$–$$$ Ciudad Cancún   MEXICAN/SEAFOOD/STEAKS

With colorful murals that almost dance off the walls, a bar area overhung with baskets (and with saddles for bar stools), inviting leather tables and chairs, and waiters dressed like Pancho Villa, it's no wonder that Périco's is always booming and festive. It's arguably the most tourist-friendly spot in Ciudad Cancún. The extensive menu offers well-prepared steak, seafood, and traditional Mexican dishes for moderate rates (except for the lobster), but the food here is less the point than the fun. Périco's is a place not only to eat and drink, but also to let loose and join in the fun. Don't be surprised if other diners drop their forks, don huge Mexican sombreros, and snake around the dining room in a conga dance. You can still have fun whether or not you join in, but Périco's is definitely not the place for that romantic evening alone. There's marimba music from 7:30 to 9:30 p.m. and mariachis from 9:30 p.m. to midnight. Expect a crowd.

Yaxchilán 61. ☎ *998-884-3152. Reservations recommended. Main courses: $14–$39. AE, MC, V. Open: Daily 1 p.m.–1 a.m.*

Plantation House

$$–$$$ Isla Cancún   CARIBBEAN/FRENCH

Elegant Caribbean fare — styled after the time when it was infused with European influences — is served up in this pale yellow-and-blue clapboard restaurant overlooking Nichupté Lagoon. The decor combines island-style colonial charm with elegant touches of wood and crystal. For starters, try the signature poached shrimp with lemon juice and olive oil or a creamy crabmeat soup. Move on to the main event, which may consist of classic veal Wellington in puff pastry with duck pâté, fish fillet crusted in spices and herbs and topped with a vanilla sauce, or lobster medallions in mango sauce. The service is excellent, but the food is only mediocre, especially considering the price. Flambéed desserts are a specialty, and the Plantation House has one of the most extensive wine lists in town. Plantation House is generally quite crowded, which makes it a bit loud for a truly romantic evening.

Paseo Kukulkán, Km 10.5. ☎ *998-883-1433. Reservations recommended. Main courses: $15–$35. AE, MC, V. Open: Daily noon to 12:30 a.m.*

Rolandi's Pizza

$ Ciudad Cancún   ITALIAN

Surprised to find great pizza in Cancún? Don't be. Rolandi's Pizza is an institution in Cancún, and the Rolandi name is synonymous with dining in both Cancún and neighboring Isla Mujeres. At this shaded outdoor sidewalk cafe, you can choose from almost two dozen different wood-oven pizzas and a full selection of spaghetti, calzones, Italian-style chicken and beef, and desserts. There's a full bar list as well. Another Rolandi's Pizza is located in Isla Mujeres at 110 Avenida Hidalgo (☎ **998-877-0430;** Open: Monday to Sunday, 11 a.m. to 11 p.m.) and has the same food and prices. Both locations have become standards for dependably good casual fare in Cancún. For a more formal, Italian-dining affair, try the elegant **Casa Rolandi** in Plaza Carocal, Isla Cancún (☎ **988-883-1817**).

Cobá 12. ☎ *998-884-4047.* www.rolandi.com. *Reservations not needed. Main courses and pizza: $6–$15; pasta $7–$12. AE, MC, V. Open: Daily 1 p.m. to midnight.*

Rosa Mexicana

$–$$$ Ciudad Cancún   MEXICAN HAUTE

Rosa Mexicana is a simply stylish bistro and a top choice for downtown dining. Candlelit tables are set indoors and surrounded by colorful *piñatas* and paper streamers and located on a plant-filled patio in back. The menu features "refined" Mexican specialties. Try the *pollo almendro,* which is chicken covered in a cream sauce sprinkled with ground almonds, or the pork baked in a banana leaf with a sauce of oranges, lime, *chile ancho* (smoky flavored chile pepper), and garlic. The more traditional steak *tampiqueño* is a huge platter that comes with guacamole salad, quesadillas, beans, salad, and rice. Dine to live, romantic Mexican music most nights.

Claveles 4. ☎ ***998-884-6313.*** *Reservations recommended for parties of 6 or more. Main courses: $8–$17; seafood platter $38. AE, MC, V. Open: Daily 5–11 p.m.*

Savio's

$–$$$ Isla Cancún   ITALIAN

Savio's is a great place to stop for a quick meal or coffee, and it's centrally located in the heart of the Hotel Zone. The bar is always crowded with patrons sipping everything from cappuccino to imported beer. Repeat diners look forward to large fresh salads and richly flavored, subtly herbed Italian dishes. The ravioli stuffed with ricotta and spinach is served in a delicious tomato sauce. A stylish place with a black-and-white decor and tile floors, Savio's has two levels and faces Paseo Kukulkán through two stories of awning-shaded windows.

Plaza Caracol. ☎ ***998-883-2085.*** *Reservations not accepted. Main courses: $8.25–$30. AE, MC, V. Open: Daily 10 a.m. to midnight.*

Stefano's

$–$$ Ciudad Cancún   ITALIAN/PIZZA

Call the food Mexitalian if you will, but it seems to be a winning combination. Stefano's began primarily as a local restaurant, serving Italian food with a few Mexican accents, and is now equally popular with tourists. Among the menu items are ravioli stuffed with *huitlacoche* (a type of mushroom that grows on a cornstalk); rigatoni in tequila sauce; and seafood with chile peppers, nestled proudly alongside the Stefano special pizza, made with fresh tomato, cheese, and pesto. For dessert, ricotta strudel is something out of the ordinary. Stefano's offers lots of different coffees and mixed drinks, plus an expanded wine list.

Bonampak 177. ☎ ***998-887-9964.*** *Reservations recommended during high season. Main courses: $7–$17; pizza $5.75–$9.75. AE, MC, V. Open: Daily 1 p.m. to midnight.*

Chapter 11

Having Fun on and off the Beach in Cancún

By Lynne Bairstow

● ●

In This Chapter

▶ Enjoying Cancún's best activities — on land and at sea

▶ Spending a day on nearby Isla Mujeres

▶ Exploring Mayan ruins and environmental "theme parks"

▶ Seeing Cancún's best sights

▶ Experiencing great shopping

▶ Living it up at night in Cancún

● ●

*Y*ou're likely to run out of vacation days before you run out of things to do in Cancún. Snorkeling, Jet Skiing, jungle tours, and visits to ancient Mayan ruins or modern ecological theme parks are among the most popular diversions in this resort that has a little of everything. Beyond Cancún's renowned beaches are more than a dozen malls with name-brand retailers and duty-free shops (featuring European goods with better prices than you can find in the United States), plus a seemingly endless supply of nightclubs to revel in.

In addition to Cancún's own attractions, the resort is a convenient distance from the more Mexican-feeling beach towns in **Isla Mujeres, Playa del Carmen,** and **Cozumel.** The **Mayan ruins** at Tulum and Chichén-Itzá, are also close by. All these diversions are within driving distance for a spectacular day-trip.

So what's worth your time? To help you decide, I devote this chapter to giving you an overview of the best beaches in this mecca of white sand and crystalline waters. I also give you the rundown on the area's popular day-trips and diversions.

Finding Water Fun for Everyone

If you're in Cancún, you probably decided to come here based on the vision of powdery, white-sand beaches and translucent, turquoise waters. If you're in search of a beautiful beach, Cancún may be your nirvana. And with the added bonus of the Nichupté Lagoon on the other side of the island, Cancún is packed with ways to make the most of your time in the water.

Basking on a Cancún beach

The big hotels dominate the best stretches of beaches, so you likely have a fine patch of sand at your hotel. Mexico's beaches are public property, so technically you can use the beach of any hotel by accessing it directly from the sand. *Technically* is the key word here. Although this is the law, the reality is that hotel security guards regularly ask non-guests to relocate. You choose if you want to suffer the potential embarrassment of being asked to leave or, if asked, standing your ground — or beach, as it were.

If you're intent on swimming, be careful on beaches fronting the open Caribbean, where the undertow can be quite strong. By contrast, the waters of **Bahía de Mujeres** at the north end of the island are usually calm and ideal for swimming. Get to know Cancún's water-safety pennant system and make sure you check the flag at any beach or hotel before entering the water.

Here's what each flag means:

- **White:** Excellent
- **Green:** Normal conditions (safe)
- **Yellow:** Changeable, uncertain (use caution)
- **Black or red:** Unsafe (use the swimming pool instead)

In the Caribbean, storms can arrive quickly, and conditions can change from safe to unsafe in a matter of minutes, so be alert. If you see dark clouds heading your way, head to shore and wait until the storm passes.

The public beaches located along the stretch of Isla Cancún on the calm, Bahía de Mujeres side include

- **Playa Linda.** Playa Linda (located at Km 4 on Paseo Kukulkán) has a shuttle service to Isla Mujeres, as well as a few dive shops and snack bars.
- **Playa Langosta.** Playa Langosta (Km 5) is a protected cove near the Hotel Casa Maya that features a tour-boat pier and a water-sports concession, plus some shops and restaurants.

Cancún & Environs

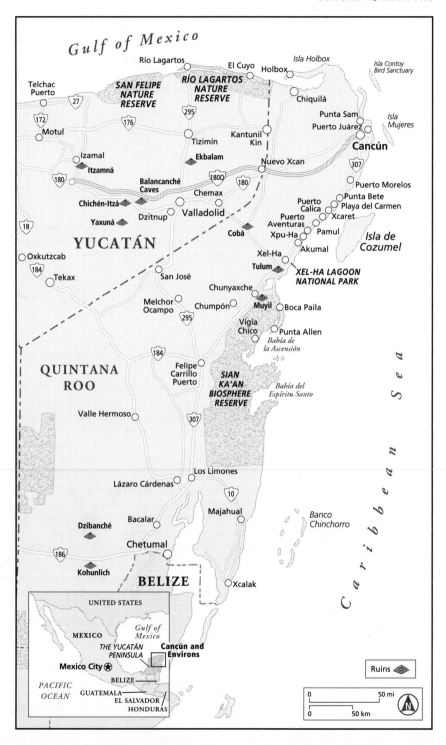

✔ **Playa Tortuga.** At Km 7.5, Playa Tortuga is a popular public beach with changing rooms, public restrooms, and restaurants. On weekends, families frequently overrun this bit of sand.

✔ **Playa Caracol.** The last beach before the island curves toward the Caribbean is Playa Caracol (Km 8), which stretches for about a mile and passes the Fiesta Americana and Camino Real hotels — a lovely stretch with a few restaurants but no public facilities.

Cancún's Caribbean side faces the open sea, and it's subject to frequent riptides and strong currents. The regally named beaches here include

✔ **Playa Chac-Mool** (named after the Mayan deity of rain). Playa Chac-Mool (Km 13) has showers, restrooms, and other facilities that make it as popular as Playa Tortuga on weekends.

✔ **Playa del Rey.** The last public beach (Km 20) on the island before Punta Nizac, this beach is an unspoiled treasure. This remarkable stretch of sand ends at the entrance to Club Med.

At most beaches, in addition to swimming, you can rent a sailboard and take lessons, ride a parasail, or partake in a variety of other watersports.

Skiing and surfing

Many beachside hotels offer watersports concessions that include the rental of rubber rafts, kayaks, and snorkeling equipment. Outlets for renting **sailboats, Jet Skis, windsurfers,** and **water skis** are located on the calm Nichupté Lagoon. Prices vary and are often negotiable, so check around.

For windsurfing, go to the Playa Tortuga public beach, which has a **windsurfing school** (no phone) with equipment for rent.

A very popular option for getting wet and wild is a **jungle cruise,** offered by several companies. The cruise takes you by Jet Ski or WaveRunner through Cancún's lagoon and mangrove estuaries out into the Caribbean Sea and by a shallow reef. The excursion runs about 2½ hours (you drive your own watercraft) and is priced from $35 to $45, with snorkeling and beverages included. Some of the motorized mini-boats seat you side by side; other crafts seat one person behind the other. The difference? The second person can see the scenery or the back of their companion's head, depending on your choice.

The operators and names of boats offering excursions change often. The popular **Aquaworld** (Paseo Kukulkán, Km 15.2; ☎ **998-848-8327;** www.aquaworld.com.mx) calls its trip the Jungle Tour and charges $45 for the 2½-hour excursion, which includes 45 minutes of snorkeling time. Aquaworld even gives you a free snorkel, but its watercrafts have the less-desirable seating configuration of one behind the other. Departures are 8:30 a.m., 9 a.m., 11 a.m., 12 p.m., and 2:30 p.m. daily. To find out what's available when you're here, check with a local travel agent or hotel tour desk; you can find a wide range of options. You can also go to the Playa Linda pier either a day ahead or the day of your intended outing and buy your own tickets for this excursion or for Aquaworld's trips to Isla Mujeres. If you go on the day of your trip for the tour to Isla Mujeres, arrive at the pier around 8:45 a.m.; most boats leave by 9 or 9:30 a.m.

Exploring the deep blue

Known for its shallow reefs, dazzling colors, and diversity of life, Cancún is one of the best places in the world for beginning **scuba diving.** Punta Nizuc is the northern tip of the **Gran Arrecife Maya (Great Mesoamerican Reef),** the largest reef in the Western Hemisphere and one of the world's largest. In addition to the sea life present along this reef system, several sunken boats add a variety of dive options. Inland, a series of caverns and wellsprings, known as *cenotes,* are fascinating venues for the more experienced diver. Drift diving is the norm here, with popular dives going to the reefs at **El Garrafón** and the **Cave of the Sleeping Sharks** — although be aware that the famed "sleeping sharks" have departed, driven off by too many people watching them snooze. For those unfamiliar with the term, drift diving occurs when divers drift with the strong currents in the waters and end up at a point different from where they started. The dive boat follows them. In traditional dives, the divers resurface where they began.

Resort courses that teach the basics of diving — enough to make shallow dives and slowly ease your way into this underwater world of unimaginable beauty — are offered in a variety of hotels. Scuba trips run around $60 for two-tank dives at nearby reefs and $100 and up for locations farther out. **Scuba Cancún** (Paseo Kukulkán, Km 5; ☎ 998-849-7508; www.scubacancun.com.mx), located on the lagoon side, offers a 4-hour resort course for $60. In addition to calling or visiting, you can make reservations from 7:30 to 10:30 p.m. using the fax line: 998-849-4736. Full certification takes 4 to 5 days and costs $368. Scuba Cancún is open from 8:30 a.m. to 8 p.m. and accepts major credit cards.

Scuba Cancún also offers diving trips to 20 nearby reefs, including Cuevones at 30 feet, and the open ocean at 30 to 60 feet (offered in good weather only). The average dive is around 35 feet. One-tank dives cost $52, and two-tank dives cost $64. Discounts apply if you bring your own equipment. Dives usually start around 9 a.m. and return by 2:15 p.m. Snorkeling trips cost $27 and leave every afternoon after 3:30 p.m. for shallow reefs located about a 20-minute boat ride away.

The largest dive operator is **Aquaworld,** (see contact information in the "Skiing and surfing" section, earlier in this chapter). Aquaworld offers resort courses and diving from a man-made, anchored dive platform, Paradise Island. The price is $92, and includes a basic scuba introductory course in the pool, as well as a general theory class on diving. Aquaworld also has the **Subsee Explorer,** a submarine-style boat with picture windows that hang beneath the surface. The boat doesn't actually submerge — it's more like an updated version of the glass-bottom boat concept — but it does provide nondivers with a look at life beneath the sea. This outfit is open 24 hours a day and accepts all major credit cards.

Most of the beaches in Isla Mujeres are either too rocky or offer no snorkeling opportunities, so Garrafón or a trip to Isla Contoy are the only real options here. There are few beachfront hotels on Isla Mujeres, but those that exist aren't located in good snorkeling areas except Casa de los Suenos, which is adjacent to Garrafón. In addition to **snorkeling** at **Garrafón National Park** (see the "Traveling to the Island of Women" section, later in this chapter), travel agencies offer an all-day excursion to the natural wildlife habitat of **Isla Contoy** that usually includes time for snorkeling. The island, located an hour and a half past Isla Mujeres, is a major nesting area for birds and a treat for true nature lovers. Only two boats hold permits for excursions to the island. They depart at 9 a.m. and return by 5 p.m. The price of $60 includes drinks and snorkeling equipment.

The Great Mesoamerican Reef also offers exceptional snorkeling opportunities. In Puerto Morelos, 37km (23 miles) south of Cancún, this reef hugs the coastline for 14km (9 miles). The reef is so close to the shore (about 455 m/500 yd.) that it forms a natural barrier for the village and keeps the waters calm on the inside of the reef. The water here is shallow, from 1.5 to 9 meters (5–30 ft.), resulting in ideal conditions for snorkeling. Stringent environmental regulations implemented by the local community have kept the reef here unspoiled.

Only a select few companies offer snorkel trips, and they must adhere to guidelines that ensure the reef's preservation. **Cancún Mermaid** (☎ **998-843-6517** or 998-886-4117; www.cancunmermaid.com) is considered the best — it's a family-run eco-tour company that has operated in the area since the 1970s and is known for highly personalized service. The tour typically takes snorkelers to two sections of the reef, spending about an hour in each area. When conditions allow, the boat drops off snorkelers and then follows them along with the current — an activity known as *drift snorkeling,* which enables snorkelers to see as much of the reef as possible. The trip costs $50 for adults, $40 for children, which includes boat, snorkeling gear, life jackets, a light lunch, bottled water, sodas, and beer, plus round-trip transportation to and from Puerto Morelos from Cancún hotels. Departures are Monday through Saturday at 9 a.m. or noon; a minimum of four snorkelers is required for a trip, and reservations are required.

Reeling in the big one

You can arrange a day of **deep-sea fishing** at one of the numerous piers or travel agencies for around $220 to $360 for 4 hours, $420 for 6 hours, and $520 for 8 hours for up to 4 people. Marinas sometimes assist in putting together a group. Charters include a captain, a first mate, bait, gear, and beverages. Rates are lower if you depart from Isla Mujeres or from Cozumel Island, and frankly, the fishing is better closer to these departure points.

Swimming with dolphins

In Cancún, the **Parque Nizuc** (☎ 998-881-3030) marine park offers guests a chance to swim with dolphins (for $135) and view these wonderful creatures in their dolphin aquarium, Atlántido. It's a fun place for a family to spend the day, with its numerous pools, waterslides, and rides. Visitors can also snorkel with manta rays, tropical fish, and tame sharks. Admission is $33 for adults, $25 for children 3 to 11, and it's open 10 a.m. to 5:30 p.m. American Express, MasterCard, and Visa are accepted. The park is located on the southern end of Cancún (Paseo Kukulkán, Km 25), between the airport and the Hotel Zone.

La Isla Shopping Village, Paseo Kukulkán, Km 12.5, also has an **Interactive Aquarium** (☎ 998-883-0413, 998-883-0436 or 998-883-0411) with dolphin swims and the chance to feed a shark for $110. Interactive encounters and swims start at $50.

You can find the best option for doing the dolphin thing on Isla Mujeres, where you can swim with dolphins at **Dolphin Discovery** (☎ 998-849-4757; Fax: 998-849-4758/4751; www.dolphindiscovery.com). Each session lasts an hour, with an educational introduction followed by 30 minutes of swim time. The price is $119, and transportation to Isla Mujeres is an additional $15. Advance reservations are required because capacity is limited each day. Assigned swimming times are 9 a.m., 11 a.m., 1 p.m., and 3 p.m., and you must arrive an hour before your scheduled swim time.

Enjoying Land Sports

Even by land, Cancún has its share of winning ways to spend the day. Although golf is a latent developer here, more courses are popping up along the coast south of Cancún. Tennis, however, is tops as a hotel amenity, and you can find courts throughout Cancún. Horseback riding and all-terrain vehicle (ATV) tours are also great choices for land adventures.

Teeing off

Although the golf options are limited, the most well-known — and well-used — facility is the 18-hole **Club de Golf Cancún** (☎ 998-883-1230 or 998-883-1277; www.cancungolfclub.com), also known as the Pok-Ta-Pok Club. Designed by Robert Trent Jones Sr., it's located on the northern leg of the island. Greens fees are $125 per 18 holes. Clubs rent for $26, shoes run $16, and caddies charge $20 per bag. The club is open daily; American Express, MasterCard, and Visa are accepted. The club also has tennis courts.

The **Melía Cancún** (☎ 998-881-1100, ext 193) offers a 9-hole executive course; greens fee is $35, and the club is open daily from 8 a.m. to 4 p.m. American Express, MasterCard, and Visa are accepted.

A more interesting option is at the **Hilton Cancún Beach & Golf Resort** (☎ 998-881-8016; Fax: 998-881-8093). Its championship 18-hole, par-72 course was designed around the Ruinas del Rey (Ruins of the King) archeological site. Greens fees for the public are $139 for 18 holes and $101 for 9 holes, and Hilton Cancún guests pay $88 for 18 holes and $66 for 9 holes; all greens fees include a golf cart. Golf clubs and shoes are available for rent, and the club is open daily 6 a.m. to 6 p.m.

The first Jack Nicklaus Signature golf course in the Cancún area has opened at the **Moon Palace Golf Resort**, along the Riviera Maya (www.palaceresorts.com). Two additional PGA courses are planned for the area just north of Cancún, Puerto Cancún, scheduled to be completed around 2006.

Making time for tennis

Many hotels in Cancún offer excellent **tennis** facilities, and many of the courts are lit for night play. Among the best are the facilities at Le Méridien and the Fiesta Americana Coral Beach hotels. The hotel reviews in Chapter 8 include a number of hotels that have tennis courts on-site.

Galloping along

Rancho Loma Bonita (☎ 998-887-5465 or 998-887-5423; www.lomabonitamex.com) is Cancún's most popular option for **horseback riding.** Five-hour packages are available for $72 for adults, $65 for children 6 to 12. The packages include 2 hours of riding to caves, *cenotes* (spring-fed, underground caves), lagoons, and Mayan ruins, and also along the Caribbean coast. A donkey polo game (yes, you get to play!) and some time for relaxing on the beach are also included. The ranch also offers a four-wheeler ride on the same route as the horseback tour for

$55 double, or $72 if you want to drive solo. Rancho Loma Bonita is located about 30 minutes south of Cancún. The prices include transportation to the ranch, riding, soft drinks, and lunch, plus a guide and insurance. Visa is accepted, but cash is preferred.

Trailing away

Cancún Mermaid (☎ **998-843-6517** or 998-886-4117; www.cancun mermaid.com), in Cancún, offers ATV jungle tours for $49 per person. The ATV tours travel through the jungles of Cancún and emerge on the beaches of the Riviera Maya. The 2½-hour tour includes equipment, instruction, a tour guide, and bottled water; it departs daily at 8 a.m. and 1:30 p.m. The company picks you up at your hotel. Another ATV option is Rancho Loma Bonita; see "Galloping along," earlier in this chapter.

Traveling to the Island of Women

One of the most popular — and in my mind, best — ways to spend the day is to check out a real Mexican beach town across the narrow channel from Cancún. **Isla Mujeres, or "Island of Women,"** located just 10 miles offshore, is one of the most pleasant day-trips from Cancún. At one end of the island is **El Garrafón National Underwater Park,** which is excellent for snorkeling and diving. At the other end is a captivating village with small shops, restaurants, and hotels, along with **Playa Norte,** the island's best beach.

To get to Isla Mujeres, you have four options:

- ✓ The **public ferries** from Puerto Juárez take between 15 and 45 minutes and make frequent trips.

- ✓ Traveling by **shuttle boat** from Playa Linda or Playa Tortuga is an hour-long ride. The boats offer irregular service.

- ✓ The **water taxi** is a more expensive but faster option than the public ferry or a shuttle boat. It's located next to the Xcaret terminal.

- ✓ Daylong **pleasure-boat trips** to the island leave from the Playa Linda pier.

Pleasure-boat cruises to Isla Mujeres include practically every conceivable type of vessel: Modern motor yachts, catamarans, trimarans, and even old-time sloops — more than 25 boats a day — take swimmers, sun lovers, snorkelers, and shoppers out into the translucent waters. Some tours include a snorkeling stop at Garrafón, lunch on the beach, and a short time for shopping in downtown Isla Mujeres. Most cruises leave at 9:30 or 10 a.m., last about 5 or 6 hours, and include continental breakfast, lunch, and snorkel gear rental. Others, particularly the sunset and night cruises, go to beaches away from town for pseudo-pirate shows and include a lobster dinner or Mexican buffet. If you want to actually see Isla Mujeres, go on a morning cruise or go on your own using the public ferry at Puerto Juárez. Prices for the day cruises run around $45 per person.

The inexpensive Puerto Juárez **public ferries** are just a few miles from downtown Cancún, and they give you greater flexibility in planning your day. From Isla Cancún or Ciudad Cancún, take a taxi or the Ruta 8 bus (from Av. Tulum) to Puerto Juárez. Choose the fast ferry (a 15-minute ride) that costs $4.50 per person compared to the slower one (a 45-minute ride) that costs $2. Departures are every half-hour from 6 a.m. to 8:30 a.m. and then every 15 minutes until 8:30 p.m. Upon arrival, the ferry docks in downtown Isla Mujeres near all the shops, restaurants, hotels, and Playa Norte. Take a taxi or rent a golf cart to get to Garrafón Park at the other end of the island. You can stay on the island as long as you like (even overnight) and return by ferry, but be sure to check the time of the last returning ferry — the hours are clearly posted.

The group that runs Xcaret (see the "Xcaret" section later in this chapter) now manages **Garrafón,** so it has taken on more of a full-service theme-park atmosphere. A basic entrance fee of $29 for adults and $15 for children entitles you to access the reef, nature trails, and a museum, and to use kayaks, inner tubes, life vests, the pool, hammocks, and public facilities and showers. You can rent snorkel gear and lockers for an extra charge. Several restaurants are on-site; an additional $20 (or $17 for kids) to the entrance fee gives you access to the buffet and open bar. An all-inclusive option is available for $59 for adults and $32 for children, which adds dining at any of the restaurants, plus unlimited domestic drinks and use of snorkel gear, lockers, and towels. Garrafón also has full dive facilities and gear rentals, plus an expansive gift shop.

Other excursions from Isla Mujeres go to **Garrafón Reefs** underwater, so you can have a near-scuba-diving experience and see many colorful fish. However, the reefs are some distance from the shore, and they're impossible to reach on windy days with choppy seas. Also keep in mind that the reefs have suffered from over-visitation, and their condition is far from pristine.

The **Atlantis Submarine** (☎ **987-872-5671;** www.atlantisadventures. com) provides a front-row seat to the underwater action. Departures vary, depending on weather conditions. Atlantis Submarine departs Monday to Saturday every hour from 9 a.m. until 1 p.m.; tours last an hour and 45 minutes and cost $76 per person. You need to take a ferry to Cozumel to catch the submarine. Still other boat excursions visit **Isla Contoy, a national bird sanctuary** that's well worth the time. You can call any travel agent or see any hotel tour desk to get a wide

Isla Mujeres (The Island of Women)

Isla Mujeres Town Plan

selection of tours to Isla Contoy. Prices range from $44 to $65, depending on the length of the trip. If you plan to spend time in Isla Mujeres, the Contoy trip is easier and more pleasurable to take from there.

Touring Ruins or an Eco-Theme Park

One of the best ways to spend a vacation day is by exploring the nearby archeological ruins or one of the new ecological theme parks near Cancún. Historical and natural treasures unlike any you may have encountered before are within easy driving distance. Cancún is a perfect base for day-trips to these places that provide a great introduction to Mexico's rich historical past and diverse natural attractions.

Make the Mayan ruins to the south of Cancún at **Tulum** your first goal. Then, perhaps, you can check out the *caleta* (cove) of **Xel-Ha** or take the day-trip to **Xcaret.**

Organized day-trips are popular and easy to book through any travel agent in town, or you can plan a journey on your own via bus or rental car.

Seeing the archeological sites

You can choose from three great archeological sites within close proximity to Cancún: Tulum, Ruinas del Rey, and Chichén-Itzá.

- ✔ **Tulum:** Summer hours: daily from 8 a.m. to 7 p.m.; winter hours: daily from 7 a.m. until 6 p.m. Admission $2.
- ✔ **Ruinas del Rey:** Daily 8 a.m. until 5 p.m. Admission $4.50.
- ✔ **Chichén-Itzá:** Daily 8 a.m. to 5 p.m. Admission $8.50.

For all sites, admission for children under 12 is free, and admission is free for everyone on Sundays and Mexican national holidays. Video camera permits cost $4, and parking is additional, varying with the site.

Tulum

Poised on a rocky hill overlooking the transparent, turquoise Caribbean Sea, ancient **Tulum** is a stunning site — and my personal favorite of all the ruins. It's not the largest or most important of the Mayan ruins in this area, but it's the only one by the sea, which makes it the most visually impressive in my opinion. Intriguing carvings and reliefs decorate the well-preserved structures, which date back to between the 12th and 16th centuries in the post-classic period.

The site is surrounded by a wall on three sides, which explains its name — *tulum* means fence, trench, or wall. Its ancient name is believed to have been *Záma,* a derivative of the Mayan word for "morning" or "dawn," and the sunrise at Tulum is certainly dramatic. The wall is believed to have been constructed after the original buildings to protect the interior religious altars from a growing number of invaders. Although Tulum is considered to have been principally a place of

Tulum Ruins

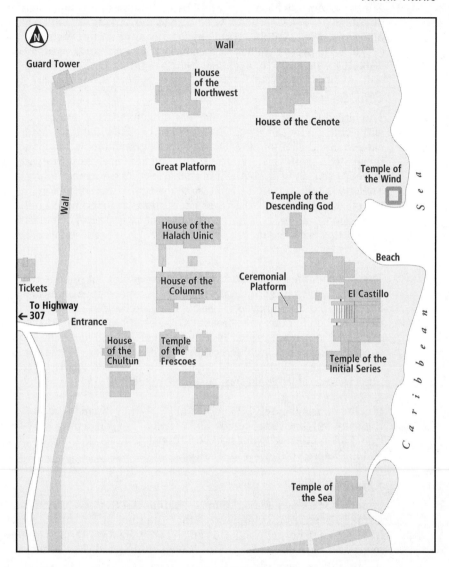

worship, members of the upper classes later took up residence here to take advantage of the protective wall. Between the two most dramatic structures — the castle and the Temple of the Wind — lies Tulum Cove, where you can swim and spend time relaxing on this absolutely magical beach. The cove is a small inlet with a beach of fine, white sand, and it was a point of departure for Mayan trading vessels in ancient times. Entrance to the site without a tour is $2; use of a video camera requires a $4 permit. A popular day excursion combines a visit to the ruins at Tulum with the ecological water park Xel-Ha (see the "Xel-Ha" section later in this chapter).

Tulum is located 130km (81 miles) south of Cancún, along Highway 307. The ruins' entrance is to your left, before you pass through the town of Tulum. After you turn left, you come to the parking lot, which also offers restroom facilities, a snack bar, and some shops. A shuttle train ($1) is available to take to you the site of the ruins, but it's also an easy walk of a little more than a kilometer (½ mile).

Chichén-Itzá

The fabled pyramids and temples of Chichén-Itzá (no, it doesn't rhyme with "chicken pizza"; the accents are on the last syllables — chee-*chin* eat-*zah*) are the region's best-known ancient monuments. Walking among these stone platforms, pyramids, and ball courts gives you an appreciation for this ancient civilization that you can't get from reading books. The city is built on such a scale as to evoke a sense of wonder: To fill the plaza during one of the mass rituals that occurred here a millennium ago would have required an enormous number of celebrants. Even today, with the mass flow of tourists through these plazas, the ruins feel empty.

The site occupies 4 square miles and it takes most of the day to see all the ruins, which are open daily 8 a.m. to 5 p.m. Service areas are open 8 a.m. to 10 p.m. Admission is $8.50, free for children under age 12, and free for all on Sundays and holidays. A permit to use your own video camera costs an additional $4. Chichén-Itzá's sound and light show is worth seeing and is included in the cost of admission. The show is held at 8 p.m. every night and is in Spanish, but headsets providing translations in several languages are available for rent ($3).

Chichén-Itzá is located 179km (112 miles) west of Cancún, along Highway 180, between Cancún and Merida. You can arrange day-trips from Cancún through your hotel or through a travel agent in the United States (before you go) or in Mexico.

Ruinas del Rey

Cancún has its own Mayan ruins — **Ruinas del Rey** (no phone) — a small site that's less impressive than the ruins at Tulum or Chichén-Itzá. Mayan fishermen built this small ceremonial center and settlement very early in the history of Mayan culture and then abandoned it. The site was resettled again near the end of the post-classic period, not long before the conquistadors arrived. You can see the platforms of numerous small temples amid the banana plants, papayas, and wildflowers. The Hilton Cancún golf course has been built around the ruins, but the ruins have a separate entrance for sightseers. The ruins are located at Paseo Kukulkán, Km 17, about 21km (13 miles) from town, at the southern reaches of the Hotel Zone, close to Punta Nizuc. Look for the Hilton hotel on the left (east) and then the ruins on the right (west). Admission to the site without a tour is $4.50, free on Sundays. It's open daily from 8 a.m. to 5 p.m.

Chichén-Itzá Ruins

Exploring an eco-theme park

The popularity of the Xcaret and Xel-Ha eco-parks has inspired a growing number of entrepreneurs to ride the wave of interest in ecological
and adventure theme parks. Be aware that "theme park" more than
"ecological" is the operative part of the phrase. The newer parks of
Aktun Chen and Tres Ríos are — so far — less commercial and more
focused on nature than their counterparts.

Aktun Chen

This park, consisting of a spectacular 5,000-year-old grotto and an abundance of wildlife, marks the first time that above-the-ground cave sys-
tems in the Yucatán have been open to the public. The name Aktun

Chen means "cave with an underground river inside." The main cave containing three rivers is more than 500 meters (600 yards) long with a magnificent vault. Discreet illumination and easy walking paths make visiting the caves more comfortable, without appearing to alter the caves too much from their natural state. The caves contain thousands of stalactites, stalagmites, and sculpted rock formations, along with a 12-meter (40-foot) deep _cenote_ (an underground, spring-fed cave) with clear blue water.

Aktun Chen was once underwater itself, and you notice fossilized shells and fish embedded in the limestone as you walk along the paths. Caves are an integral part of this region's geography and geology, and knowledgeable guides lead you through the site while providing explanations and offering mini-history lessons on the Maya's association with these caves. Tours have no set times — guides are available to take you when you arrive — and groups are kept to a maximum of 20 people.

Nature trails surround the caves throughout the 988-acre park, where spotting deer, spider monkeys, iguanas, and wild turkeys is common. A small, informal restaurant and gift shop are also on-site.

Traveling to Aktun Chen on your own is easy. From Cancún, go south on Highway 307 (the road to Tulum). Just past the turnoff for Akumal, a sign on the right side of the highway indicates the turnoff for Aktun Chen; from there, it's a 3-kilometer (2-mile) drive west along a smooth but unpaved road. Travel time from Cancún is about an hour, and the park is open from 9 a.m. until dark. The entry fee of $18 includes the services of a guide. Call ☎ **998-892-0662** or 984-877-8550 for more information, or you can visit the park via the Internet at www. aktunchen.com.

Tres Ríos

Tres Ríos — meaning three rivers — is the most "natural" of the area's nature parks. Located on more than 150 acres of land, this park is a true nature reserve that offers guests a beautiful area for kayaking, canoeing, snorkeling, horseback riding, or biking along jungle trails. Essentially, the park is just one big natural spot for participating in these activities. It's definitely less commercial than the other eco-theme parks.

The park is located just 25 minutes south of Cancún. The entrance fee is $22 for adults and $19 for children, which includes canoe trips; the use of bikes, kayaks, and snorkeling equipment; and the use of hammocks and beach chairs after you tire yourself out. Extra charges apply for scuba diving, horseback riding, and extended guided tours through the preserve and its estuary. Tres Ríos also has bathroom facilities, showers, and a convenience store; however, the facilities are much less sophisticated than the area's other, more developed eco-theme parks.

Most Cancún travel agencies sell a half-day "kayak express" tour to Tres Ríos. Priced at $48, the trip includes admission to the park and its activities, round-trip transportation, lunch, and two nonalcoholic drinks. Call ☎ **998-887-8077** in Cancún or visit the park's Web site at www.tres-rios.com for details and reservations. Tres Ríos is open daily 9 a.m. to 5 p.m.

Xcaret

Xcaret (*ish*-car-et), located 80km (50 miles) south of Cancún (☎ **998-898-1900;** www.xcaretcancun.com), is a specially built ecological and archaeological theme park and one of the area's most popular tourist attractions. Xcaret has become almost a reason in itself to visit Cancún. With a ton of attractions — most of them participatory — in one location, it's the closest thing to Disneyland in Mexico. In Cancún, signs advertising Xcaret and folks handing out Xcaret leaflets are everywhere. The park has its own bus terminal in Cancún where buses pick up tourists at regular intervals. Plan to spend a full day here. Children love it, and the jungle setting and palm-lined beaches are beautiful. Past the entrance booths (built to resemble small Mayan temples) are pathways that meander around bathing coves, the snorkeling lagoon, and the remains of a group of real Mayan temples.

Xcaret may celebrate Mother Nature, but its builders rearranged quite a bit of her handiwork in completing it. If you're looking for a place to escape the commercialism of Cancún, this may not be it. The park is relatively expensive and may be very crowded, thus diminishing the advertised "natural" experience.

Entrance gains you access to swimming beaches, limestone tunnels to snorkel through, marked palm-lined pathways, a wild-bird breeding aviary, horseback riding, scuba diving, a botanical garden and nursery, a sea turtle nursery, a butterfly pavilion, and a tropical aquarium, where visitors can touch underwater creatures such as manta rays, starfish, and octopi. Extra charges apply for some of these activities. One of the park's most popular attractions is the excellent "Dolphinarium," where visitors (on a first-come, first-served basis) can swim with the dolphins for an extra charge of $80.

Oh, but there's more. Xcaret features a replica of the ancient Mayan game, pok-ta-pok. In this game, six "warriors" bounce around a 9-pound ball with their hips. The Seawalker, a type of watersport designed for non-swimmers, is another attraction. By donning a special suit and helmet with a connected air pump, you can walk on the ocean floor or examine a coral reef in a small bay.

The visitor center has lockers, first-aid assistance, and a gift shop. Visitors aren't allowed to bring in food or drinks, so you're limited to the rather high-priced restaurants on-site. No personal radios are allowed, and you must remove all suntan lotion if you swim in the lagoon to avoid poisoning the lagoon habitat.

The admission price of $49 per person entitles you to use the facilities, boats, life jackets, snorkeling equipment for the underwater tunnel and lagoon, and lounge chairs. Other attractions, such as snorkeling at $32, horseback riding at $49, scuba diving at $55 for certified divers ($75 for a resort course), and the dolphin swim at $80, cost extra. There may be more visitors than equipment (in the case of beach chairs, for example), so bring a beach towel and your own snorkeling gear to be on the safe side.

Travel agencies in Cancún offer day-trips to Xcaret that depart at 8 a.m. and return at 6 p.m. The cost is $89 for adults ($45 for children), which includes transportation, admission, and a guide. You can also buy a ticket to the park at the **Xcaret bus terminal** (☎ **998-881-2401,** 998-883-3143), located next to the Fiesta Americana Coral Beach hotel on Isla Cancún. The "Xcaret Day and Night" trip includes round-trip transportation from Cancún, a *charreada* festival (where horse-riding and roping skills are showcased), lighted pathways to Mayan ruins, dinner, and a folkloric show. The cost is $89 for adults and $45 for children age 6 to 11 (free for kids age 5 and under). Buses leave the terminal at 9 and 10 a.m. daily, with the "Day and Night" tour returning at 9:30 p.m. The park itself is open Monday to Saturday 8:30 a.m. to 8:30 p.m., Sunday 8:30 a.m. to 5:30 p.m.

Xel-Ha

The sea has carved the Caribbean coast of the Yucatán into hundreds of small *caletas,* or coves, that form the perfect habitat for tropical marine life, both flora and fauna. Many caletas along the coast remain undiscovered and pristine, but Xel-Ha (shell-*hah*), located near Tulum, plays host daily to throngs of snorkelers and scuba divers who come to luxuriate in its warm waters and swim among its brilliant fish. Xel-Ha is a swimmers' paradise with no threat of undertow or pollution. It's a beautiful, completely calm cove that's a perfect place to bring kids for their first snorkeling experience. Experienced snorkelers may be disappointed because the crowds seem to have driven out the living coral and many of the fish here.

Xel-Ha (☎ **998-884-9422;** www.xelha.com.mx) is 117km (73 miles) south of Cancún along Highway 307. The entrance is a half-mile from the highway. Admission is $29 per adult and $15 for children age 5 to 11 (free for children under age 5) and includes use of inner tubes, life vests, and shuttle trains to the river. On weekends, admission is only $22 for adults and $11 for kids. You can also choose an all-inclusive option for admission, equipment, food, and beverages that runs $56 for adults and $28 for children. The park is open daily 8:30 a.m. to 5 p.m., offers free parking with admission, and accepts American Express, MasterCard, and Visa. After you arrive at the 10-acre park, you can rent snorkeling equipment and an underwater camera, but you may also bring your own. Food and beverage service, changing rooms, showers, and other facilities are available. Platforms have been constructed that allow decent sea-life viewing for non-snorkelers.

In addition, the resort offers "snuba," a clever invention that combines snorkeling and scuba. Snuba is a shallow-water diving system that places conventional scuba tanks on secure rafts that float at surface level; the "snuba-diver" breathes normally through a mouthpiece, which is connected to a long air hose attached to the tank above. This setup enables a swimmer to go as deep as 20 feet below the surface and stay down for as long as an hour or more. It's a great transition to scuba, and many divers may even enjoy it more because snuba leaves you remarkably unencumbered by equipment.

When you swim, be careful to observe the "swim here" and "no swimming" signs. You can see the greatest variety of fish right near the ropes that divide the swimming areas from the non-swimming areas and near any groups of rocks. An interactive dolphin attraction has been added — a 1-hour swim costs $90, and an educational 15-minute program runs $15. Make your reservations at least 24 hours in advance for one of the four daily sessions: 9:30 a.m., 12:30 p.m., 2 p.m., and 3:15 p.m.

If you're driving, just south of Xel-Ha turn off on the west side of the highway so you don't miss the ruins of **ancient Xel-Ha.** You're likely to be the only one there as you walk over limestone rocks and through the tangle of trees, vines, and palms. There's a huge, deep, dark cenote to one side, a temple palace with tumbled-down columns, a jaguar group, and a conserved temple group. A covered palapa on one pyramid guards a partially preserved mural. Admission is $3.50.

Xel-Ha is close to the ruins at **Tulum** (check out the "Seeing the archeological sites" section earlier in this chapter) and makes a good place for a dip after you finish climbing the Mayan ruins. You can even make the short 13km (8-mile) hop north from Tulum to Xel-Ha by public bus. When you get off at the junction for Tulum, ask the restaurant owner when the next buses come by; otherwise, you may have to wait as long as 2 hours on the highway.

Sightseeing in Cancún

To the right side of the entrance to the Cancún Convention Center is the small **Museo Arqueológico de Cancún** (☎ 998-883-0305), a small but interesting museum with relics from archaeological sites around the state. Admission is $3.50. The museum is open Tuesday to Sunday from 10 a.m. to 7 p.m.

During the winter tourist season, **bullfights** are held every Wednesday at 3:30 p.m. in Cancún's small bullring (☎ 998-884-8372), which is located near the northern end of Paseo Kukulkán opposite the Restaurant Los Almendros (av. Bonampak and Sayil). A sport introduced to Mexico by the Spanish viceroys, bullfighting is now as much a part of Mexican culture as tequila. The bullfights usually include four bulls, and the spectacle begins with a folkloric dance exhibition, followed by a performance

Cancún Area

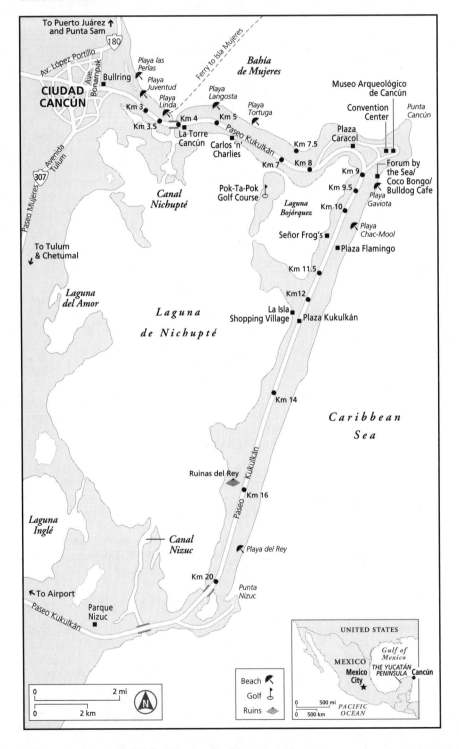

To Puerto Juárez ↑
and Punta Sam

180

Av. López Portillo

Ave. Bonampak

Bullring

CIUDAD
CANCÚN

Avenida Tulum

307

Paseo Mujeres

Playa las
Perlas

Playa
Juventud

Playa
Linda

Km 3

Km 3.5

La Torre
Cancún

Km 4

Km 5

Carlos 'n'
Charlies

Playa
Langosta

Ferry to Isla Mujeres

*Bahía
de Mujeres*

Playa
Tortuga

Paseo Kukulkán

Km 7.5

Km 7

Km 8

Museo Arqueológico
de Cancún

Convention
Center

*Punta
Cancún*

Plaza
Caracol

Km 9

Km 9.5

Km 10

Forum by
the Sea/
Coco Bongo/
Bulldog Cafe

Playa
Gaviota

Playa
Chac-Mool

*Canal
Nichupté*

Pok-Ta-Pok
Golf Course

*Laguna
Bojórquez*

Señor Frog's

Plaza Flamingo

To Tulum
& Chetumal

*Laguna
del Amor*

*Laguna
de Nichupté*

Km 11.5

Km12

La Isla
Shopping Village

Plaza Kukulkán

Km 14

*Caribbean
Sea*

*Laguna
Inglé*

*Canal
Nizuc*

Ruinas del Rey

Paseo Kukulkán

Km 16

Playa del Rey

To Airport

Km 20

Punta
Nizuc

Paseo Kukulkán

Parque
Nizuc

0   2 mi
0   2 km

Beach
Golf
Ruins

UNITED STATES

*Gulf of
Mexico*

MEXICO

Mexico
City

THE YUCATÁN
PENINSULA

Cancún

0   500 mi
0   500 km

*PACIFIC
OCEAN*

by the *charros* (Mexico's sombrero-wearing cowboys). You're not likely to see Mexico's best bullfights in Cancún — the real stars are in Mexico City.

Keep in mind that if you go to a bullfight, *you're going to see a bullfight,* so stay away if you're an animal lover or you can't bear the sight of blood. Travel agencies in Cancún sell tickets: $35 for adults, with children admitted free of charge. Seating is by general admission. American Express, MasterCard, and Visa are accepted.

Get the best possible view of Cancún atop the **La Torre Cancún,** Paseo Kukulkán, Km 4 (☎ **998-849-4848**), a rotating tower at the El Embarcadero park and entertainment complex. One ride costs $9; a day and night pass goes for $14. Open daily from 9 a.m. to 11 p.m.

Shopping in Cancún

Despite the surrounding natural splendor, shopping has become a favored activity in Cancún, and the place is known throughout Mexico for its diverse array of shops and festive malls catering to large numbers of international tourists. Tourists arriving from the United States may find apparel more expensive in Cancún, but the selection here is much broader than in other Mexican resorts.

Numerous duty-free shops offer excellent value on European goods. The largest shop is **UltraFemme** (☎ **998-884-1402** or 998-885-0804), specializing in imported cosmetics, perfumes, and fine jewelry and watches. Its Ciudad Cancún location on Avenida Tulum, Supermanzana (intersection) 25, offers lower prices than the locations at Plaza Caracol, Kukulkán Plaza, Maya Fair Plaza, and Plaza Flamingo or at the store at the international airport.

Handcrafts and other *artesanía* works are more limited and more expensive in Cancún than in other regions of Mexico because they're not produced here, but they're available. Several **open-air crafts markets** are easily visible on Avenida Tulum in Ciudad Cancún and near the convention center in the Hotel Zone. One of the biggest markets is **Coral Negro,** located at Paseo Kukulkán, Km 9.5 (☎ **998-883-0758;** Fax: 998-883-0758). It's open daily from 7 a.m. to 11 p.m.

The main venue for shopping in Cancún is the **mall** — not quite as grand as its U.S. counterpart, but close. Cancún's malls are air-conditioned, sleek, and sophisticated, with most located on Paseo Kukulkán between Km 7 and Km 12. You can find everything from fine crystal and silver to designer clothing and decorative objects, along with numerous restaurants and clubs. Stores are generally open daily from 10 a.m. to 10 p.m., with clubs and restaurants remaining open much later. Here's a brief rundown on the malls, running from the northern to the southern end of the island — and some of the shops they contain:

✔ **Maya Fair Plaza/Centro Comercial Maya Fair,** frequently called "Mayfair" (Paseo Kukulkán, Km 8.5; ☎ 998-883-2801), is Cancún's oldest mall and features a lively, bricked center with open-air restaurants and bars, such as Tequila Sunrise, and several stores selling silver, leather, and crafts.

✔ The long-standing **Plaza Caracol** (Paseo Kukulkán, Km 8.5; ☎ 998-883-1038) holds Cartier jewelry, Guess, Waterford Crystal, Señor Frog clothing, Samsonite luggage, Gucci, and La Fisheria restaurant. It's just before you reach the convention center as you come from Ciudad Cancún.

✔ The entertainment-oriented **Forum by the Sea** (Paseo Kukulkán, Km 9; ☎ 998-883-4425) has shops including Tommy Hilfiger, Levi's, Diesel, Swatch, and Harley Davidson, but most people come here for the food and fun. You can choose from Hard Rock Cafe, Coco Bongo, Rainforest Cafe, Sushi-ito, and Santa Fe Beer Factory, plus an extensive food court. It's open 10 a.m. to midnight (bars remain open later).

✔ Planet Hollywood anchors the **Plaza Flamingo** (Paseo Kukulkán, Km 10.5; ☎ 998-883-2945), but branches of Bancrecer, Subway, and La Casa del Habano (for Cuban cigars) are located inside.

✔ The newest and most intriguing mall is the **La Isla Shopping Village** (Paseo Kukulkán, Km 12.5; ☎ 998-883-5025; www.laislacancun.com.mx), an open-air festival mall that looks like a small village, where walkways lined with shops and restaurants crisscross over little canals. The mall also has a "riverwalk" alongside the Nichupté Lagoon and an interactive aquarium and dolphin-swim facility. Shops include Zara clothing, Benetton, Guess, Swatch, Ultra Femme, and much more. Dining choices include Johnny Rockets, The Food Court (not actually a "food court," but an Anderson's restaurant), and the beautiful Mexican restaurant, La Casa de las Margaritas. There's also a first-run movie theater, a video arcade, and several nightclubs, including Max-O's and Alebrejes. It's located across from the Sheraton, on the lagoon side of the street.

✔ Inside **Kukulkán Plaza** (Paseo Kukulkán, Km 13; ☎ 998-885-2200; www.kukulcanplaza.com) is a large selection of more than 300 shops, restaurants, and entertainment venues. There's a branch of Banco Serfin; OK Maguey Cantina Grill; a movie theater with U.S. movies; an Internet-access kiosk; Tikal, a shop with Guatemalan textile clothing; several crafts stores; a liquor store; several bathing-suit specialty stores; record and tape outlets; a leather-goods store (including shoes and sandals); and a store specializing in silver from Taxco. In the food court are a number of U.S. franchise restaurants, including Ruth's Chris Steakhouse, plus a specialty-coffee shop. For entertainment, the plaza has a bowling alley, the Q-Zar laser game pavilion, and a videogame arcade. There's also a large indoor parking garage. The mall is open 10 a.m. to 10 p.m.

Discovering Cancún after Dark

Ready to party? The nightlife in Cancún is as hot as the sun at noon on a cloudless July day, and clubbing is one of the main attractions of this let-loose town. The current hotspots are centralized in **Forum by the Sea** and **La Isla Shopping Village,** but finding a party anywhere in town isn't hard. Hotels also compete for your pesos with happy-hour entertainment and special drink prices as they try to entice visitors and guests from other resorts to pay a visit. (Lobby-bar hopping at sunset is one great way to plan next year's vacation.)

Partying at a club

Clubbing in Cancún can go on each night until the sun rises over that incredibly blue sea. Several of the big hotels have nightclubs — sometimes still called discos here — and others entertain in their lobby bars with live music. On weekends, expect to stand in long lines for the top clubs, pay a cover charge of $10 to $20 per person, and pay $5 to $8 for a drink. Some of the higher-priced clubs include an open bar or live entertainment.

Check out the "Cancún Area" map in Chapter 10 for various club locations.

The **Bar Crawl Tour,** offered by the American Express Travel Agency (☎ **998-881-4050;** Fax: 998-884-6942), is a great introduction to the Cancún club scene. It's not as cheesy as it may sound, and it's a great way to check out the top spots without making a major investment in cover charges. For $49, a bus takes you from bar to club to bar to club — generally a range of four to five top choices — where you bypass any lines and spend about an hour at each establishment. Entry to the clubs, one welcome drink at each location, and transportation by air-conditioned bus is included in the fee, allowing you to sample the best of Cancún's nightlife.

What's hot now? As any good clubber knows, popularity can shift like the sands on the beach, but Cancún clubs do seem to have staying power. So take this list as a starting point — extensive research showed me that these were the current hot spots at press time, listed alphabetically:

- ✔ **Bulldog Cafe,** in the Hotel Krystal on the island (☎ **998-848-9850**), is a former hot spot's attempt to lure back the crowds (it used to be the opulent disco Christine). To the impressive space, signature laser-light shows, infused oxygen, and large video screens, the club added updated music and a funkier ambiance. The music ranges from hip-hop to Latino rock, with a heavy emphasis on dance tunes. Bulldog is open nightly from 10 p.m.

until the party winds down. The cover charge is $12 per person, or $25 for an open bar all night long. American Express, MasterCard, and Visa are accepted.

✔ **Coco Bongo** in Forum by the Sea (Paseo Kukulkán, Km 9.5; ☎ 998-883-5061; www.cocobongo.com.mx) continues its reputation as the hottest spot in town. This spot's main appeal is that there's no formal dance floor, so you can dance anywhere you can find the space — that includes on the tables, on the bar, or even on stage with the live band! Coco Bongo can pack in up to 3,000 people — and regularly does. You have to see it to believe it. Despite its capacity, lines are long on weekends and in the high season. The music alternates between Caribbean, salsa, techno, and classics from the 1970s and 1980s. Coco Bongo draws a mixed crowd, but the young and hip dominate. Choose between a $15 cover or $25 for open bar (national drinks).

✔ **Dady'O** (Paseo Kukulkán, Km 9.5; ☎ 998-883-3333) is a highly favored rave with frequent, long lines. It opens nightly at 9:30 p.m. and generally charges a cover of $15. **Dady Rock Bar and Grill** (Paseo Kukulkán, Km 9.5; ☎ 998-883-1626), the offspring of Dady'O, opens early (7 p.m.) and goes as long as any other nightspot, offering a new twist on entertainment with a combination of live bands and DJ-orchestrated music. It also features an open bar, full meals, a buffet, and dancing.

✔ **La Boom** (Paseo Kukulkán, Km 3.5; ☎ 998-849-7588/87; www.laboom.com.mx) has two sections: One side is a video bar, and the other is a bilevel disco with cranking music. Both sides are air-conditioned. Each night finds a special deal going on: no cover, free bar, ladies' night, bikini night, and others. Popular with early 20-somethings, it's open nightly 10 p.m. to 6 a.m. A sound-and-light show begins at 11:30 p.m. in the disco. The cover varies for the disco and the bar depending on the night — women get in free most nights, and men pay covers that vary between $10 and $20 with an open bar.

Not into the party scene? The most refined and upscale of all Cancún's nightly gathering spots is the **Lobby Lounge** at the **Ritz-Carlton Hotel** (☎ 998-881-0808, ext. 5310). Live dance music and a list of more than 120 premium tequilas for tasting or sipping are the highlights here.

Hanging out after dinner

Numerous restaurants, such as **Carlos 'n Charlie's, Planet Hollywood, Hard Rock Cafe, Señor Frog's, T.G.I. Friday's,** and **Iguana Wana,** double as nighttime party spots offering wild-ish fun at much lower prices than the clubs. Check these out:

✔ **Carlos 'n Charlie's** (Paseo Kukulkán, Km 5.5; ☎ **998-849-4124**) is a reliable place to find both good food and fraternity-house–type entertainment in the evenings. A dance floor goes along with the live music that starts nightly around 8:30 p.m. A cover charge kicks in if you're not planning to eat. It's open daily 11 a.m. to 2 a.m.

✔ **Hard Rock Cafe,** in Forum by the Sea (☎ **998-881-8120;** www. hardrock.com), entertains with a live band at 10:30 p.m. every night except Wednesday. At other times, you get lively recorded music to munch by. The menu combines the most popular foods from American and Mexican cultures. It's open daily 11 a.m. to 2 a.m.

✔ **Planet Hollywood** (Plaza Flamingo, Paseo Kukulkán, Km 11.5; ☎ **998-885-3003;** www.planethollywood.com) is the still-popular brainchild (and one of the last-remaining) of Sylvester Stallone, Bruce Willis, and that terminating politician Arnold Schwarzenegger. It's both a restaurant and a nighttime music/dance spot with mega-decibel live music. It's open daily 11 a.m. to 2 a.m. American Express, MasterCard, and Visa are accepted.

Enjoying a cultural event

Several hotels host **Mexican fiesta nights,** which include a buffet dinner and a folkloric dance show; the price, including dinner, ranges from $35 to $50.

In the Costa Blanca shopping center, **El Mexicano** restaurant (☎ **998-883-2220**) hosts a tropical dinner show every night and also features live music for dancing. The entertainment alternates each night — *mariachis* entertain off and on from 7 to 11 p.m., and a folkloric show takes place from 8 to 9:30 p.m.

You can also get in the party mood at **Mango Tango** (Paseo Kukulkán, Km 14.2; ☎ **998-885-0303**), a lagoon-side restaurant/dinner-show establishment opposite the Ritz-Carlton Cancún. Diners can choose from two seating levels, one nearer the music and the other overlooking the whole production. The music is loud and varied but mainly features reggae or salsa. The 1-hour-and-20-minute dinner show begins at 8:30 p.m. nightly and costs $40. If you're not dining and come just for the music and drinks, a $10 cover charge applies.

For entertainment that lets tourists and locals mingle, head for the downtown **Parque de las Palapas** (the main park) for *Noches Caribeños* (Caribbean Nights), where live tropical music is provided at no charge for anyone who wants to listen and dance. Performances begin at 7:30 p.m. on Sundays. Sometimes, performances are scheduled for Fridays and Saturdays, but the calendar varies.

Part IV
Cozumel and the Riviera Maya

The 5th Wave   By Rich Tennant

"Well, if you're not drinking Tequila with your breakfast burrito, then why is your cereal bowl rimmed in salt."

In this part . . .

The island of Cozumel and the mainland south of Cancún — called the Riviera Maya — offer a different way of experiencing the transparent blue waters and white-sand beaches of the Mexican Caribbean. Small towns, such as Playa del Carmen and Tulum, and isolated resorts, both small and large, present quite a contrast to Cancún's studded line-up of hotels. Dotting the landscape are nature parks, ruins, and lovely natural features. Life in these parts is slower and holds more local color.

Access by air is easy. Cozumel has its own international airport and the Riviera Maya enjoys easy access to Cancún's airport. As with Cancún, many people speak English, making communication with the locals easy. The two chapters in this part provide the information you need to make your stay in the region relaxing and enjoyable.

Chapter 12

Cozumel

By David Baird

C ozumel is a Caribbean island 12 miles off the Yucatán coast. More relaxed than the booming mainland, Cozumel has the feel of a small island — roads that don't go very far, lots of mopeds, few buses and trucks, and a certain sense of isolation. It's not that small — 45km (28 miles) long and 18km (11 miles) wide — but the vast majority of the land is uninhabited low tropical forest. The island's one small town is San Miguel.

Cozumel is a popular destination for divers and sun-seekers and is a busy port of call for cruise ships. Divers come to Cozumel — the No. 1 dive destination in the Western Hemisphere — to enjoy the towering reefs lying just off the island's western shore.

For sun-seekers, the island offers the beautiful Caribbean. The water on the protected side of the island is perfectly calm, unless a north wind is blowing. It's like having the Caribbean for a swimming pool. And at several beaches you can find all the usual watersports and beach activities. If you're a golfer, you may want to check out a beautiful golf course designed by Jack Nicklaus. If you're not, try out an assortment of tours and other activities. Because the island is also a popular cruise-ship port, you find tons of duty-free shops and jewelry stores.

Choosing a Location

The town of San Miguel and all Cozumel's hotels except for one are on the island's protected western shore. Some are north of town, some are south of town, and some are in town. The hotels in town aren't beach hotels, but they're less expensive and offer convenient access to the town's restaurants, nightspots, dive shops, and stores. To go to the beach, you need to get a taxi or rent a bike, moped, or car.

If the most you want to do is hang out around the pool with the occasional dip into the Caribbean, select one of the beach hotels either north or south of town. All hotels outside of town have swimming pools and all can provide services for divers and snorkelers. For the most part, the southern coast has better beaches, but many of the southern hotels are far from town, making it a little more expensive to do some shopping and other activities. Some southern hotels are on the inland side of the road, and some are on the beach side, which makes for a large difference in price. The properties farthest away from town are all-inclusives, which means that the price of your stay includes meals, beverages, tips, taxes, airport transportation, and even some activities, as well as your lodging.

Because Cozumel is a big destination for divers, all the large hotels and many of the smaller ones offer dive packages; I don't mention this in the reviews later in this chapter, but you can ask about them when shopping around for a hotel. All the large waterfront hotels have a dive shop and a pier. If you would rather dive with an operator other than the one at your hotel, that's fine — any dive boat can pull up to any hotel pier to pick up divers.

Evaluating the Top Accommodations

The prices I quote for the hotels are rack rates for two people spending one night in a double room, and they include the 12% room tax. Please refer to the Introduction of this book for an explanation of the price categories. See Chapter 5 for tips on avoiding paying rack rates.

The beach hotels in Cozumel, even the smaller ones, work with several vacation packagers for the U.S. and Canadian markets. You can get sizable discounts by booking airfare, ground transfer, and lodging in one package. Working with some tour operators requires flexibility, but the big ones for Cozumel — FunJet and Apple Vacations — offer enough flights to accommodate many people's vacation plans. If you want an all-inclusive hotel, you can get a better deal through a travel agent or packager than by contacting the hotel directly. For more information about working with vacation packagers and travel agents, check out Chapter 5.

Cozumel Island

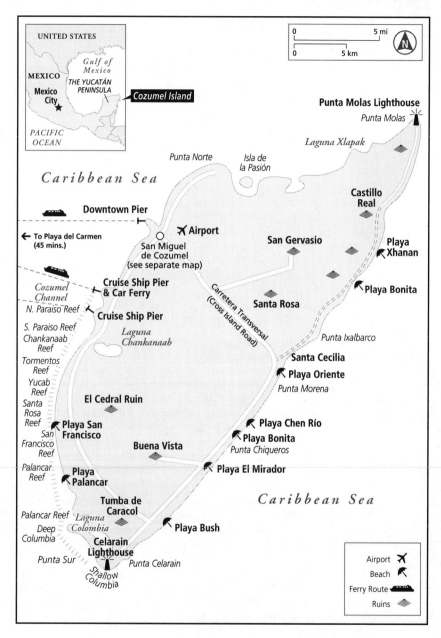

For small groups of friends, a fun alternative to a hotel is to share a villa or condo. Try **Cozumel Vacation Villas and Condos** (Av. 10 Sur no. 124, 77600 Cozumel, Q. Roo; ☎ **800-224-5551** in the U.S., 987-872-0729 or 987-872-1375; www.cvvmexico.com), which offers accommodations by the week.

All hotels have air conditioning unless otherwise indicated.

Allegro Cozumel by Occidental
$$$$$ **South of town**

This all-inclusive has some sister hotels across the way on the mainland, but this one enjoys something the others don't: the placid water of Cozumel's protected coast. There is also a sister hotel next door, the **Grand Cozumel by Occidental,** which is newer and has larger, nicer rooms, but for the money, I like this hotel because it has a better beach. Guests at the **Grand** can enjoy the **Allegro,** but not vice versa. Rooms are midsize with standard bathrooms and are situated in large two-story Polynesian-style thatched buildings surrounding a large pool. You have a choice of two double beds or one king. The hotel gets a mix of families and couples and offers a wide range of activities and water equipment. It's a good choice for families who want only to be on the beach. Taking a taxi to town from here can be expensive; the hotel is at the island's far southern end. Three restaurants and a snack bar are available.

Carretera Costera Sur, Km 16.5. ☎ *800-858-2258 in the U.S. or 987-872-9770. Fax: 987-872-9792.* www.occidentalhotels.com. *300 units. Rack rates: High season $262–$300 double; low season $248–$262 double. Rates include food, beverages, and non-motorized watersports equipment. AE, MC, V.*

B&B Caribo
$ **In town**

Cindy Cooper, the owner of this B&B, is a good host who enjoys running and yoga. Her rates are a deal and include breakfast and several little extras. She rents her rooms by the day, the week, or the month. Rooms come with cool tile floors, painted furniture, and big bottles of purified drinking water. The six apartments come with small kitchens (minimum stay of one week required for the apartments). A shared guest kitchen serves the other six rooms. Most rooms have a double bed and a twin bed, but no TVs or phones. A number of common rooms, including a television/computer room and a rooftop terrace, are available. Breakfasts are delicious. To find the Caribo from the central plaza, walk 7 blocks inland on Juárez to the smartly painted blue-and-white house on the left at Av. 40.

Av. Juárez No. 799. ☎ *987-872-3195.* www.visit-caribo.com. *12 units. Rack rates: High season $50 double, $60 apartment; low season $35 double, $40 apartment. Rates include breakfast. AE, MC, V.*

El Cid La Ceiba Beach Hotel
$$$–$$$$ **South of town**

Located on the beach side of the southbound road, this hotel is great for snorkeling and shore diving — a submerged airplane is just offshore. It's

San Miguel de Cozumel

ACCOMMODATIONS ■

Allegro Cozumel
  by Occidental **14**
B&B Caribo **7**
El Cid La Ceiba
  Beach Hotel **15**
El Cozumeleño
  Beach Resort **1**
Flamingo Hotel **4**
Iberostar Cozumel **16**
InterContinental
  Presidente Cozumel
  Resort **17**
Playa Azul Golf &
  Beach Hotel **2**
Plaza Las Glorias **13**

DINING ◆

El Moro **6**
French Quarter **10**
Jeanie's Waffle
  House **12**
La Choza **11**
Lobster House
  (Cabaña del
  Pescador) **3**
Pepe's Grill **9**
Prima **8**

Information ⓘ
Pedestrian Only ////
Post Office ✉

a popular hotel with divers and nondivers alike. The rooms are nicely furnished, large, and comfortable. All rooms have ocean views and balconies. The emphasis here is on watersports, particularly scuba diving. The resort has received plenty of praise from scuba magazines, and the dive shop is a Mares Hub center. Diving is available right from the hotel beach. Choose between two restaurants. (There's also a bar.) Other diversions include two large pools, a lighted tennis court, a small exercise room with sauna, a whirlpool, and watersports-equipment rentals.

Costera Sur Km 4.5. ☎ *800-435-3240 in the U.S., or 987-872-0844. Fax: 987-872-0065.* www.elcid.com. *98 units. Free limited parking. Rack rates: High season $165–$188 double; low season $100–$150 double. AE, MC, V.*

El Cozumeleño Beach Resort

$$$$$ North of town

An all-inclusive resort, El Cozumeleño is for people who want an active vacation with plenty to do, including an extravagant pool and sunning area, and a full array of watersports and equipment rentals. As if that isn't enough to keep you busy, just across the road is the new golf course. Recently, the owners have more than doubled the number of rooms in the hotel and added to the amenities. The rooms in the old part are large, much longer than they are wide; rooms in the new part are also large, and their shape allows for a less awkward arrangement of furniture. All rooms have balconies with a great ocean view, attractive decor, large bathrooms, and either a king bed or two double beds. The hotel has two restaurants and three bars (including a swim-up bar). There are three pools (including a wading pool and a very large pool with a roofed section that provides shade), a large whirlpool, and a tennis court. One drawback is that the beach is small for this size of resort. Moped rentals, an ample children's program, a game room, and miniature golf are some of the additional highlights.

Carretera Santa Pilar Km 4. ☎ *800-437-3923 in the U.S. and Canada, or 987-872-9530. Fax: 987-872-9544.* www.elcozumeleno.com. *252 units. Rack rates: High season $275 double; low season $200–$250 double; rates are all-inclusive. AE, MC, V.*

Flamingo Hotel

$ In town

A small hotel just off Avenida Rafael Melgar, the Flamingo offers three stories of attractive, comfortable rooms around a small, plant-filled inner courtyard. Highlights include an inviting rooftop terrace and a popular bar/coffee bar. The more expensive upstairs rooms have air conditioning and TVs. All rooms are medium to large in size and have two double beds, white-tile floors, medium-size bathrooms, and ceiling fans. A penthouse suite comes with a full kitchen and sleeps up to six. The English-speaking staff is helpful and friendly. To find it, walk 3 blocks north on

Melgar from the town's central plaza and turn right on Calle 6; the hotel is on the left.

Calle 6 Norte No. 81. ☎ ***800-806-1601*** *in the U.S., or* ☎ *and fax: 987-872-1264.* www.hotelflamingo.com. *22 units. Rack rates: High season $49–$69 double; low season $39–$49 double. AE, MC, V.*

Iberostar Cozumel
$$$$ South of town

Just beyond the Allegro Cozumel by Occidental (see review earlier in this section), practically at the end of the island, is this all-inclusive hotel laid out much like its neighbors: one- and two-story buildings, each holding between four and eight units, surround a large common area of pools, a snack bar, and the beach. Also, like the Occidental properties, this hotel is operated by a Spanish company that mastered the business of running all-inclusives on the Spanish coast. It has sister properties on the Yucatán mainland, but this is the smallest of the company's Mexican properties; hence, it doesn't feel quite as much like production-line tourism. Iberostar does a particularly good job with the food and the service, which is why I think it's a step up from most of the other all-inclusives. The grounds are beautifully kept. The rooms are medium size and are attractive, and the bathrooms are ample, well lit, and come with showers.

Carretera Costera Sur Km 17.75 ☎ ***987-872-9900***. *Fax: 987-872-9906.* www.iberostar.com. *300 units. Rack rates: High season $280–$300 double; low season $250–$275 double. Rates include food, beverages, and non-motorized watersports equipment. AE, MC, V.*

InterContinental Presidente Cozumel Resort
$$$$$ South of town

This is Cozumel's finest hotel in terms of location, on-site amenities, and service. Palatial in scale and modern in style, the Presidente spreads across a long stretch of coast with only distant hotels for neighbors. Rooms come in four categories — superior, deluxe, deluxe oceanfront, and deluxe beachfront — distributed among four buildings (two to five stories tall). Superior rooms come with a garden view; deluxe rooms come with an ocean view. Most deluxe and superior rooms are large with roomy, well-lit bathrooms. Deluxe oceanfront rooms and beachfront rooms are even larger and have spacious balconies or patios. (The main difference is that the beachfronts are at ground level with direct access to the beach and the oceanfronts are on the second floor.) Most rooms come with a choice of one king bed or two double beds and are furnished in an understated, modern style. A long stretch of sandy beach area dotted with palapas and palm trees fronts the entire hotel. This destination features a large pool, plus a wading pool and a watersports-equipment rental booth. You can choose from two restaurants and a bar, plus 24-hour room service. A special in-room dining option with a serenading trio is available for beachfront rooms. Two lighted tennis courts, a fully equipped gym, and a moped-rental service for getting around the island are also on-site. A children's activities center makes this a good choice for families.

Carretera a Chankanaab, Km 6.5. ☎ *800-327-0200 in the U.S., or 987-872-9500. Fax: 987-872-9501.* www.cozumel.intercontinental.com. *253 units. Free parking. Rack rates: High season $334 gardenview double, $455–$736 oceanfront double, suites from $851; low season $276 gardenview double, $391–$673 oceanfront double, suites from $788. Discounts and packages available. AE, DC, MC, V.*

Playa Azul Golf & Beach Hotel

$$$$–$$$$$ **North of town**

For golfers, this hotel is the place to stay in Cozumel. It's perhaps the most relaxing of the island's hotels, and includes unlimited free golfing (guests pay only for the mandatory cart rental). The hotel's small beach with shade palapas is one of the best on this side of the island. Service is attentive and personal. Almost all the rooms come with balconies and ocean views. The rooms in the original section are all suites — large suites with very large bathrooms. The new wing mostly has standard rooms that are comfortable and large and decorated with light tropical colors and furniture. All rooms come with either a king bed or two double beds, and suites offer two convertible single sofas in the separate living-room area. A restaurant, two bars, and a small pool are also available.

Carretera San Juan Km 4. ☎ *987-872-0199 or 987-872-0043. Fax: 987-872-0110.* www.playa-azul.com. *50 units. Free parking. Rack rates: High season $185 double, $220–$290 suite; low season $130 double, $160–$260 suite. AE, MC, V.*

Plaza Las Glorias

$$$$$ **South of town**

If you're not visiting Cozumel during the high season, the low-season rates make this hotel a good bargain. This all-suite, five-story hotel combines the top-notch amenities of the expensive hotels farther out with the convenience of being 5 blocks from town. For people who must have a beach, this isn't the right hotel. (Don't dismiss it, though; the hotel has a smart, terraced, sunning area above the water with easy access to the sea.) The split-level rooms are large and have separate sitting areas. The decor is decent, though it won't overwhelm you, and the furniture and beds are comfortable. Bed choices include two doubles, two twins, or one king. All rooms face out over the water and have a balcony or a terrace. The dive shop here comes highly recommended. You can enjoy a casual dining restaurant and bar, plus a swim-up bar in the large pool.

Av. Rafael Melgar Km 1.5. ☎ *800-342-AMIGO in the U.S. and Canada, or 987-872-2000. Fax: 987-872-1937.* www.sidek.com.mx. *174 units. Free parking. Rack rates: High season $280 double; low season $130 double. AE, MC, V.*

Settling into Cozumel

You get to the island either by airplane or by ferry from the mainland, which means that you'll arrive at the airport or the municipal pier. In either case, nothing could be more straightforward. Cozumel's airport is small and presents no complications, and the municipal pier is right across from the town's main plaza.

Cozumel's **airport** is immediately inland from downtown. There is only one transportation provider: **Transportes Terrestres,** which operates a fleet of air-conditioned Suburbans. Buy your ticket as you exit the terminal. Fares are $4 per person to downtown hotels, $7 for hotels along the north shore, and $9 and up for hotels along the south shore.

More charter flights come to the island than standard commercial flights. You can buy just a plane ticket from one of the travel packagers recommended in Chapter 5. Of course, they would prefer to sell you an entire package, but they'll be happy to fill empty seats on a plane if they have to. Commercial carriers from the United States include **Continental** (☎ **800-525-0280;** www.continental.com); **US Airways** (☎ **800-428-4322;** www.usairways.com); and **American** (☎ **800-433-7300;** www.aa.com). Some of these flights are seasonal, and the American Airlines flight from Dallas is running on a test basis. In addition, **Mexicana** flies from Mexico City with several international connecting flights, and its affiliate, AeroCaribe, flies frequently to/from Cancún.

If Cozumel is your port of entry, you'll receive a **Mexican tourist permit (FMT)** upon arrival. This document is important, so take good care of it. You're supposed to keep it with you at all times — you may be required to show it if you run into any sort of trouble. You also need to turn it in upon departure.

Passenger ferries travel to and from Playa del Carmen. Of the two companies that service the area — **Barcos México** (☎ **987-872-1508**) and **Ultramar** (☎ **987-869-2775**) — there is little difference. They operate from the same pier in Cozumel, they charge the same amount for a one-way ticket ($9), and they take the same amount of time (30 to 40 minutes) to make the crossing. And for reasons known only to the two ferry companies, they have virtually identical schedules, leaving from either Cozumel or Playa about every hour on the hour. Ultramar is planning to use another pier in Playa del Carmen, if it can get permission to complete it, which would be the only difference. In Cozumel, both companies dock at the downtown pier, called the **Muelle Fiscal.** Both companies' boats are enclosed and air-conditioned and have comfortable upholstered seats. Short-term luggage storage is available at the Cozumel dock for $2 per day.

The car/passenger ferry to Cozumel from Punta Venado (11km/7 miles south of Playa del Carmen) takes a little longer, runs less frequently, and costs $80 for a standard car. It's operated by **Marítima Chankanaab** (☎ 987-872-0916), with four departures per day: 7 a.m. and 1, 5, and 9 p.m. Arrive an hour before departure. The schedule is subject to change, so double-check it. The ferry docks in Cozumel at the **Muelle Internacional** (the **International Pier,** which is just south of town near El Cid La Ceiba Hotel).

Knowing your way around town

San Miguel is logically planned and easy to find your way around. It's laid out on a grid, with *avenidas* (avenues) running north-south, and *calles* (streets) running east-west. The exception is **Avenida Juárez,** which runs east from the passenger-ferry dock directly inland and eventually turns into a road that crosses to the island's eastern shore.

Avenida Juárez divides the town into northern and southern halves. Everything north of Avenida Juárez is labeled *norte,* and everything south is *sur.* What's more, the parallel *calles* to the north of Avenida Juárez have even numbers: 2 Norte, 4 Norte, 6 Norte, and so on, while the ones to the south have odd numbers: 1 Sur, 3 Sur, 5 Sur, and so on. An exception is Calle Adolfo Rosado Salas, running between 1 Sur and 3 Sur.

The *avenida* that runs along the shore is Avenida Rafael Melgar. The *avenidas* running parallel to Melgar are numbered in multiples of five that increase as you move inland: Avenida 5, Avenida 10, Avenida 15, and so on.

The northern extension of Avenida Melgar, called **Carretera Santa Pilar** or **San Juan,** leads to the northern hotels and the golf course. It's only a couple of miles long, but the southward extension of Melgar goes for several miles all the way to the island's tip. It's called **Costera Sur.** The majority of the island's big hotels are along the south road. Also along this road is the **Chankanaab National Park,** encircling the beautiful lagoon of the same name. Beyond Chankanaab are several beach clubs, where you can enjoy the water and find food and beverages. These vary from simple to quite elaborate.

After the Costera Sur reaches the southern tip of the island, it curves to the left and heads up the less-protected eastern shore of the island. Here, the coast is rockier and the surf is harder. Eventually, this road meets up with the road that crosses the island and is the extension of Avenida Juárez, known as the **Carretera Transversal.** This road passes by San Gervasio, the island's most prominent ruins, as well as the airport.

Getting around town

You can walk to most destinations in town. However, getting to outlying hotels and beaches, including the Chankanaab National Park, requires a taxi or rental car.

Car rentals run from $35 to $60 per day for an economy-sized car, depending on the season. All the major rental agencies are present in Cozumel, including **Avis** (☎ 987-872-0219) and **Budget** (☎ 987-872-5177). Usually, you save a little money by renting a car in advance, but if you want to have a car for only a day or two, renting a car through your hotel and having the car-rental company deliver it is easy enough.

Moped rentals are a popular alternative on Cozumel. You can find rental mopeds all over the village for a cost of anywhere from $15 to $30 for 24 hours. If you rent a moped, be careful. Riding a moped made a lot more sense when Cozumel had less traffic; now it's a risky activity — motorists have become pushier.

Moped accidents easily rank as the most common cause of injury in Cozumel. Before renting a moped, give it a careful inspection to see that all the gizmos — horn, light, starter, seat, and mirror — are in good shape and be sure to note all damage to the moped on the rental agreement. If the moped vibrates at cruising speed, it's probably due to an unbalanced wheel, and you should return it. Most importantly, read the fine print on the back of the rental agreement, which states that you aren't insured, that you're responsible for paying for any damage to the bike (or for the entire bike if it's stolen or demolished), and that you must stay on paved roads. It's illegal to ride a moped outside of town without a helmet (subject to a $25 fine).

Taxis remain a good and reasonably priced option unless you plan on doing some major exploring. Scan over these few sample fares for two people (for more than two passengers, you pay an extra charge that varies according to your destination): town to southern hotels, $7 to $15; town to northern hotels, $4 to $5; town to Chankanaab, $8. Call ☎ 987-872-0236 for taxi pickup. Fares on the island are standardized; you won't be able to negotiate.

Fast Facts: Cozumel

American Express

The local representative is Fiesta Cozumel (Calle 11 No. 598; ☎ 987-872-0725).

Area Code

The telephone area code is **987**.

Banks, ATMs, and Currency Exchange

There are several banks and *casas de cambio* (exchange houses) on the island, as well as ATM machines. Most places accept dollars, but you usually get a better deal paying in pesos.

Business Hours

Most offices maintain traditional Mexican hours of operation (9 a.m. to 2 p.m. and 4 to 8 p.m. daily), but shops remain open throughout the day. Offices tend to close on Saturday and Sunday, but shops are open on Saturday, at least, and increasingly offer limited hours of operation on Sunday.

Climate

From October to December, strong winds and some rain can prevail all over the Yucatán. In Cozumel, wind conditions in November and December can make diving dangerous. May to September is the rainy season. Temperatures during the day in the summer are 80° F to 90° F (27° C–32° C); in winter 70° F to 75° F (21° C–24° C).

Diving

If you intend to dive, remember to bring proof of your diver's certification. Underwater currents can be very strong here, and many of the reef drops are quite steep, making them excellent sites for experienced divers but too challenging for novice divers.

Hospital/Recompression Chamber

There are four recompression chambers (*cámaras de recompresión*). **Buceo Médico,** staffed 24 hours, is on Calle 5 Sur, 1 block off Avenida Rafael Melgar between Melgar and Avenida 5 Sur (☎ 987-872-2387 or 987-872-1430). Another one is the **Hyperbaric Center of Cozumel** (Calle 4 Norte, between avenidas 5 and 10; ☎ 987-872-3070).

Information

The State Tourism Office (☎ and fax: 987-869-0212) is located on the second floor of the Plaza del Sol commercial building, facing the central plaza, and is open Monday to Friday 9 a.m. to 3 p.m. and 6 to 8 p.m.

Internet Access

There are a number of cybercafes near the central plaza. One of the most reliable is

Modutel (Av. Juárez No. 15, at the intersection with Av. 10). Hours are 10 a.m. to 8 p.m. The farther you go from the main plaza, the cheaper the rates.

Police

Dial ☎ 060. Remember that finding an English-speaking operator at the police station is highly unlikely.

Post Office

The post office *(correo),* Avenida Rafael Melgar at Calle 7 Sur, at the southern edge of town (☎ 987-872-0106), is open Monday to Friday 9 a.m. to 6 p.m. and Saturday 9 a.m. to noon.

Taxes

A 15% IVA (value-added tax) on goods and services is charged, and it's generally included in the posted price.

Taxis

The government and taxi driver union fix the fares on the island. Taxis charge extra for more than two passengers. Call ☎ 987-872-0236 for taxi pickup.

Telephone

Avoid the phone booths that have signs in English advising you to call home using a special 800 number — these are absolute rip-offs and can cost as much as $20 per minute. The least expensive way to call is by using a Telmex (LADATEL) prepaid phone card, available at most pharmacies and minisupers, using the official Telmex (Lada) public phones. Remember, in Mexico you need to dial 001 prior to a number to reach the United States, and you need to preface long distance calls within Mexico by dialing 01.

Time Zone

Cozumel operates on central standard time.

Dining in Cozumel

Like many of Mexico's beach resorts, even Cozumel's finest restaurants are casual when it comes to dress. Men seldom wear jackets, although ladies occasionally wear dressier resort wear. Basically, if you err on the side of casual, you won't go wrong.

For inexpensive alternatives to the restaurants, try one of these suggestions. If you're in the mood for just a little bread or pastry to go with your coffee, try **Zermatt** (☎ **987-872-1384**), a terrific little bakery on Avenida 5 at Calle 4 Norte. If you want something really inexpensive and filling, try **Comida Casera Toñita,** on Calle Adolfo Rosado Salas between avenidas 10 and 15 (☎ **987-872-0401**). *Comida casera* means home cooking, and this place definitely has the feel of someone's home, in fact, it's Toñita's home, open Monday to Saturday 8 a.m. to 6 p.m.

Please refer to the Introduction of this book for an explanation of the price categories. Remember that tips generally run about 15%, and most wait-staff really depend on these gratuities for their income, so be generous if the service warrants.

Please see Appendix C for more information on Mexican cuisine.

El Moro
$ In town   REGIONAL

El Moro consistently offers good food, attentive service, and large portions for moderate prices. What it doesn't offer is stylish surroundings or a convenient location, but a cab ride costs only a couple of bucks. Here you can try some of the best Yucatecan food on the island — anything from *pollo ticuleño,* a specialty from the town of Ticul, which is a layered plate of smooth tomato sauce, mashed potatoes, crispy baked corn tortilla, and batter-fried chicken breast, all topped with shredded cheese and green peas; to *poc chuc,* pork marinated in a tangy sauce and grilled. There are also a number of seafood dishes and Mexican classics on the menu, such as butterfly shrimp, fried fish, or enchiladas. El Moro is 12 blocks inland from Melgar between calles 2 and 4 Norte.

75 BIS Norte No. 124. ☎ *987-872-3029. Reservations not accepted. Main courses: $5–$15. MC, V. Open: Fri–Wed 1–11 p.m.; closed Thurs.*

French Quarter
$–$$ In town   LOUISIANA/SOUTHERN

In a pleasant upstairs open-air setting, the French Quarter serves Southern and Creole classics. The jambalaya and étouffée are delicious. The menu also lists such specialties as blackened fish, and the owner goes to great lengths to get the freshest lump crabmeat, which usually appears in one form or another as a daily special. The filet mignon with red-onion marmalade is a real charmer. In addition to the outdoor setting, an air-conditioned dining room and a bar area are downstairs. The French Quarter is on Avenida 5, a block and a half south of the town square.

Av. 5 Sur 18. ☎ 987-872-6321. Reservations recommended during high season. Main courses: $10–$25. AE, MC, V. Open: Daily 4–11 p.m.

Jeanie's Waffle House
$ **In town   BREAKFAST/DESSERTS**

The specialty here is crisp, light waffles served in a variety of ways, including waffles *ranchero* with eggs and salsa, waffles Benedict with eggs and hollandaise sauce, and waffles with whipped cream and chocolate. Hash browns, homemade breads, and great coffee are other reasons to drop in for breakfast, which is served until 3 p.m.

Av. Rafael Melgar between calles 5 and 7 Sur. ☎ 987-872-4145. Reservations not accepted. Breakfast: $4–$7. No credit cards. Open: Mon–Sat 6 a.m.–9 p.m.; Sun 6 a.m. to noon.

La Choza
$ **In town   MEXICAN**

Local residents consider this one of the best Mexican restaurants in town. Platters of poblano chiles stuffed with shrimp, *mole poblano,* and *pollo en relleno negro* (chicken stuffed with a preparation of scorched chiles) are among the specialties. The table sauces and guacamole are great, and the daily specials can be delicious, too. This is an open-air restaurant with well-spaced tables under a tall thatched roof. From the ferry pier, walk 2 blocks inland on Avenida Juárez, turn right on Avenida 10, and walk 2 more blocks. La Choza is on the corner.

Calle Adolfo Rosado Salas 198 (at Av. 10 Sur). ☎ 987-872-0958. Reservations accepted only for groups of 6 or more. Main courses: $8–$14; breakfast $4. AE, MC, V. Open: Daily 7:30 a.m.–11 p.m.

Lobster House (Cabaña del Pescador)
$$–$$$ **North of town   LOBSTER**

The thought that most often occurs to me when I eat a prepared lobster dish is that the cook could have simply boiled the lobster to better effect. This restaurant's owner seems to agree. The only item on the menu is lobster boiled with a hint of spices and served with melted butter accompanied by sides of rice, vegetables, and bread. The price of dinner is determined by the weight of the lobster tail you select, with side dishes provided at no charge. Candles and soft lights illuminate the dining rooms. A rustic, tropical-island feel, gardens, fountains, and a small duck pond make the scene inviting and intimate. The owner, Fernando, welcomes you warmly and sends you next door to his brother's excellent Mexican-food restaurant, El Guacamayo, if you must have something other than lobster.

Carretera Santa Pilar, Km 4 (across from Playa Azul Hotel). No phone. Reservations not accepted. Main courses: lobsters sold by weight $20–$30. No credit cards. Open: Daily 6–10:30 p.m.

Pepe's Grill

$$–$$$ In town   STEAKS/SEAFOOD

The chefs at Pepe's seem fascinated with fire; what they don't grill in the kitchen, they flambé at your table. The most popular grilled items are the prime rib, filet mignon (good, quality meat), and lobster. For something out of the ordinary, try the shrimp Bahamas, which are flambéed with a little banana and pineapple in a curry sauce with a hint of white wine. Pepe's is a second-story restaurant with a large air-conditioned dining room under a massive beamed ceiling. The lighting is soft, and a guitar trio plays background music. Large windows look out over the town's harbor. The children's menu offers breaded shrimp and broiled chicken. For dessert, Pepe's offers a few more flaming specialties: bananas Foster, crêpes suzette, and café Maya (coffee, vanilla ice cream, and three liquors).

Av. Rafael Melgar at Calle Rosado Salas. ☎ 987-872-0213. Reservations recommended. Main courses: $15–$35; children's menu $6.50. AE, MC, V. Open: Daily 5–11:30 p.m.

Prima

$–$$ In town   NORTHERN ITALIAN

Everything is super fresh here — the pastas, vegetables, and the seafood. Owner Albert Domínguez grows most of the vegetables in his local hydroponic garden. The menu changes daily and specializes in northern Italian seafood dishes. It may include shrimp scampi, fettuccine with pesto, or lobster and crab ravioli with cream sauce. The fettuccine Alfredo is wonderful, the salads are crisp, and the steaks are USDA choice. Pizzas are cooked in a wood-burning oven. Desserts include Key lime pie and tiramisu. Dining is upstairs on the breezy terrace.

Calle Rosado Salas No. 109A (corner with Av. 5) ☎ 987-872-4242. Reservations recommended during high season. Pizzas: $6–$14; pastas $8–$10; steaks $13–$18. AE, MC, V. Open: Daily 4–11 p.m.

Having Fun on and off the Island

One of the advantages of vacationing in Cozumel is that you can indulge in a true island experience and still be just a short hop from mainland Mexico and its attractions. **Playa del Carmen** is a convenient half-hour ferry ride away and makes for a relaxing excursion. From there, you can take a bus to one of the large nature parks such as **Xel-Ha** or **Xcaret,** or one of the major ruins, such as **Chichén-Itzá** or **Tulum** (see Chapter 11 for more on these attractions).

A trip to Xcaret is the easiest excursion. A visit to Xel-Ha is often combined with a visit to Tulum. The trip to Chichén-Itzá, if not done by plane, is by far the longest and most exhausting. Easier still, you can arrange a tour with one of the travel agencies on the island. I recommend **InterMar Cozumel Viajes** (Calle 2 Norte, No. 101-B, between avenidas 5 and 10; ☎ **987-872-1098;** Fax: 987-872-0895; E-mail: intermar@cozumel.com.mx).

Cozumel does have its own ruins, which are easy to visit. (But, honestly, they can't compare with the major sites on the mainland.) In pre-Hispanic times, Mayan women made a pilgrimage to the island to leave offerings to Ixchel, the goddess of fertility. You can see the remains of about 40 sites on the island today, and archaeologists still uncover the small dolls that were part of the offerings. The most important ruins on the island are at San Gervasio (see the "Seeing the sights" section, later in this chapter).

Travel agencies can schedule activities such as **glass-bottom boat tours, submarine tours, dinner cruises,** or **a romantic supper on the beach.** For **diving and snorkeling,** you can do better by arranging your own trip (see the "Exploring the depths" section, later in this chapter).

If you schedule a snorkeling or diving trip through a travel agency, you'll most likely end up on a boat full of cruise-ship passengers. Your best bet is to find an operator who uses a small boat.

Combing the beaches

Although most of Cozumel's shoreline is rocky, the island has some nice beaches. And most beaches have what is called a "beach club" on them. A beach club in its simplest form is just a *palapa* (thatched roof) shack on the beach where you can enjoy soft drinks, beer, and fried fish. In a more elaborate form, the beach club may have a full-service restaurant, rent snorkeling gear, and even have a pool. A still larger version offers all kinds of watersports rentals, including banana boats, Jet Skis, and parasailing equipment. Cozumel has two beach clubs made in this latter mold: **Mr. Sancho's** and **Playa Sol.** Mr. Sancho's has free admission; Playa Sol has entrance fees from $8 to $37 for the all-inclusive rate. Both are on the southern highway Costera Sur, about 13 to 16 km (8 to 10 miles) south of town. A quieter beach club with a pool and full restaurant is **Nachi Cocom** (located almost a mile beyond Mr. Sancho's). It charges $5 for admission.

For beach access without admission, south of Nachi Cocom are **Playa San Francisco** and **Playa Palancar;** both are good places to enjoy the beach. Beach clubs of the simpler variety include **Paradise Cafe** on the southern tip of the island across from Punta Sur Nature Park and **Playa Bonita, Chen Rio,** and **Punta Morena** on the eastern coast. Except on Sundays when the locals hit the beaches, these places are quiet and uncrowded. Most of the east coast is unsafe for swimming because of the surf.

Also on the island, **Chankanaab National Park** has a nice beach, too, and a variety of other activities. Admission is $10. See the "Seeing the sights" section, later in this chapter, for more information.

Exploring the depths

Cozumel is the most popular dive destination in the Western Hemisphere. Don't forget to bring your dive card and dive log. The dive shops on the island rent scuba gear, but they don't take you out on the boat until they see some documentation. If you have a medical condition, bring a letter signed by a doctor stating that you're cleared to dive. A two-tank, morning dive costs around $60; some shops are now offering an additional one-tank, afternoon dive for $9 for folks who took the morning dives. (It's about $25 if you just opt for the one-tank, afternoon dive.) A lot of divers save some money by buying a hotel and dive package with or without air transportation and food. These packages usually include two dives a day.

Diving in San Miguel is different from diving in a lot of places — it's drift diving, which can be a little disconcerting for novice divers. The current that sweeps along Cozumel's reefs pulling nutrients into the reefs and making them as large as they are also dictates how you dive here. The problem: The current pulls at different speeds at different depths and in different places. When it's pulling strong, the current can quickly scatter a dive group. This is why having a dive master experienced with the local conditions who can pick the best place for diving is important, given the current conditions.

Fortunately, the island has a lot of reefs to choose from. Here are just a few:

- ✔ **Palancar Reef:** Famous for its caves and canyons, plentiful fish, and a wide variety of sea coral

- ✔ **San Francisco Reef:** Features a shallower drop-off wall than many reefs and fascinating sea life

- ✔ **Santa Rosa Wall:** Monstrous reef famous for its depth, sea life, coral, and sponges

- ✔ **Yucab Reef:** Highlights include beautiful coral

Cozumel has more than 60 dive operators. I can recommend a couple. Bill Horn's **Aqua Safari,** on Avenida Rafael Melgar at Calle 5 Sur (☎ 987-872-0101; Fax: 987-872-0661; www.aquasafari.com) and in the Hotel Plaza Las Glorias (☎ 987-872-3362 or 987-872-2422), is a PADI (Professional Association of Diving Instructors) five-star instructor center with full equipment and parts rental and sales. **Liquid Blue Divers** (☎ 987-869-0593; www.liquidbluedivers.com) offers a real personal service. Owner Roberto Castillo has a small, fast boat and takes a maximum of 12 per dive trip. He's PADI certified, and his wife Michelle handles the reservations through e-mail, responding to any inquiry within 24 hours.

Underwater Yucatán offers a different twist on diving — **cenote diving.** On the mainland, the peninsula's underground *cenotes* (say-*noh*-tehs), or sinkholes, which were sacred to the Maya, lead to a vast system of underground caverns. Here, the gently flowing water is so clear that divers appear to be floating on air through the *cenotes* and caves that look just like those on dry land, complete with stalactites and stalagmites.

The experienced cave divers of **Yucatech Expeditions** (☎ and fax: **987-872-5659;** E-mail: yucatech@cozumel.czm.com.mx) offer a trip five times a week. *Cenotes* are 30 to 45 minutes from Playa del Carmen, and a dive in each *cenote* lasts around 45 minutes (divers usually do two or three). Dives are within the daylight zone, about 130 feet into the caverns and no more than 60 feet deep. Company owner Germán Yañez Mendoza inspects diving credentials carefully, and divers must meet his list of requirements before cave diving is permitted. For information and prices, call or drop by the office at Avenida 15 No. 144, between calles 1 Sur and Adolfo Rosado Salas. There are several other *cenote* dive operators on the mainland who are closer to the *cenotes,* especially in Akumal and near Tulum.

Snorkeling is also an option on Cozumel. Anyone who can swim can snorkel. Rental of the snorkel (breathing tube), goggles, and flippers should cost only about $5 to $10 for half a day. A number of small boats offer good snorkeling trips because they necessarily take few people for each trip. One person who does a good tour is **Victor Casanova.** He speaks English and takes his time and doesn't rush his customers. You can contact him through e-mail at wildcatcozumel@hotmail.com, or by phone at ☎ **987-872-1028.** Or you can try the **Kuzamil Snorkeling Center** (☎ **987-872-4637**), which offers a trip that goes to several spots and includes lunch for $65 for adults and $50 for children under 12.

Sailing away

Boat trips are a popular pastime on Cozumel. You can choose from evening cruises, cocktail cruises, glass-bottom boats, and other options. You can contract these tours through a local travel agency. One rather novel boat trip is a ride in a submarine, offered by **Atlantis Submarines**

(☎ **987-872-5671;** www.atlantisadventures.com). The sub holds 48 people, operates almost 3km (2 miles) south of town in front of the Casa del Mar hotel, and costs $72 per adult and $36 for kids. Call ahead or inquire at one of the travel agents in town. This is a far superior experience to the **Subsee Explorer** offered by **Aquaworld,** which is really a glorified glass-bottom boat.

Catching a big one

The best months for offshore fishing are March through June, when the catch includes blue and white marlin, sailfish, tarpon, swordfish, dorado, wahoo, tuna, and red snapper. You can contact Victor Casanova (☎ **987-872-1028;** E-mail: wildcatcozumel@hotmail.com), or **Aquarius Travel Fishing** (Calle 3 Sur no. 2, between Avenida Rafael Melgar and Avenida 5; ☎ **987-872-1092;** www.aquariusflatsfishing.com).

Hitting the links

Cozumel has a lovely 18-hole golf course designed by Jack Nicklaus. It's just north of town at the Cozumel Country Club. Greens fees are $149 including taxes and cart rental. A couple of hotels on the island have golf packages. The Playa Azul has the best arrangement, offering free golf to its guests, who have to pay only for the cart rental.

Seeing the sights

Companies offer several kinds of tours of the island, but to be frank, the best part of Cozumel isn't on land; it's what's in the water. But, if you're starting to look like a prune from all the time in the water or you want to try something different, travel agencies can book you on a group tour of the island for around $40. Prices may vary a bit depending on whether the tour includes lunch and a stop for snorkeling and swimming at Chankanaab Park. If you're only interested in Chankanaab, you can go by yourself and save money (keep reading; more info is coming up in this section). Taxi drivers charge $60 for 4-hour tours of the island, which most people would consider only mildly amusing depending on the personality of the taxi driver.

A **horseback tour** of the island's interior is fun and inexpensive. A few outfits offer horseback riding, but the best is **Rancho Palmitas** (no phone). This outfit has the best horses and conducts the most interesting tours. It has two locations, both south of town. One is near the InterContinental Presidente Cozumel Resort and the other is across the road from the Allegro Hotel by Occidental. Both locations are open 7 days a week. Tours depart at 8 and 10 a.m., noon, and at 2 and 4 p.m.

Chankanaab National Park is the pride of many of the islanders. *Chankanaab* means "little sea," which refers to a beautiful, land-locked pool connected to the sea through an underground tunnel — a sort of miniature ocean. Snorkeling in this natural aquarium isn't permitted, but you can do so at other locations in the park, which also includes a lovely beach for sunbathing. Arrive early to stake out a chair and palapa before the cruise-ship crowd arrives. Likewise, the snorkeling is best before noon. The park has bathrooms, lockers, a gift shop, several snack huts, a restaurant, and snorkeling gear available to rent.

Bordering the lagoon is a botanical garden with shady paths. The garden is home to 351 species of tropical and subtropical plants from 22 countries in addition to 451 species of plants from Cozumel. Several Mayan structures have been re-created within the gardens to give visitors an idea of Mayan life in a jungle setting. A small natural history museum is also on the property. Admission to the park costs $10, and it's open daily 8 a.m. to 5 p.m.

Also at Chankanaab are dolphins. **Dolphin Discovery** (☎ **998-849-4757** in Cancún; www.dolphindiscovery.com) has several programs for sharing a swim with these highly intelligent animals. You need to make reservations in advance, and the surest way is through the Web site. But, if you're already in Cozumel, you can find out whether there's an open slot by calling ☎ **987-872-9702.** The dolphin swim costs $119. You can also select a swim and snorkel program for $89 that gets you in the water with the dolphins but offers less interaction. Dolphin Discovery offers a program only in Cozumel where you can swim with sea lions ($59); reservations also are a must. Finally, a sea lion show costs $5 per adult, $3.50 per kid. Tickets are available through any travel agency in town. The show also includes some scarlet macaws, which, like the sea lions, were rescued from illegal captivity.

One of the most popular island excursions is to the ruins of San Gervasio. When it comes to Cozumel's Mayan ruins, getting there is most of the fun — do it for the mystique and for the trip, not for the size or scale of the ruins. The buildings, though preserved, were crudely made and wouldn't be much of a tourist attraction if they weren't the island's only cleared and accessible ruins. To get to the ruins of **San Gervasio** (100 B.C. to A.D. 1600), follow the Carretera Transversal toward the eastern side of the island. The well-marked turnoff is about halfway between town and the eastern coast. Stop at the entrance gate and pay the $1 road-use fee. Head straight over the pothole-infested road for about 3km (2 miles) until you reach the ruins. Pay the $5 fee to enter; camera permits cost $5 for each still or video camera you want to bring in. A small tourist center at the entrance has cold drinks and snacks for sale.

More significant than beautiful, this site was once an important ceremonial center where the Maya gathered. The important deity here was Ixchel, known as the goddess of weaving, fertility, childbirth, the moon, and medicine. You don't see any representations of Ixchel at San Gervasio today, but here's a little history: Bruce Hunter, in his *Guide to*

Ancient Maya Ruins (University of Oklahoma Press), writes that priests hid behind a large pottery statue of the goddess and became her voice, speaking to pilgrims and answering their petitions. Ixchel was the wife of Itzamná, the sun god and preeminent deity among all Mayan gods.

Tour guides charge $10 for groups of one to six people, but, with a copy of the green booklet *San Gervasio,* sold at local checkout counters and bookstores, you can see the site on your own. Seeing the whole place takes 30 minutes. Taxi drivers offer a tour to the ruins for about $25; the driver waits for you outside the ruins.

In town, check out the small historical museum, **Museo de la Isla de Cozumel,** on Avenida Rafael Melgar between calles 4 and 6 Norte (☎ 987-872-1475). It's more than just a nice place to spend a rainy hour. The museum's first floor has an excellent exhibit displaying endangered species in the area, the island's origin, and its present-day topography and plant and animal life, including an explanation of coral formation. The second-floor galleries feature the town's history, artifacts from the island's pre-Hispanic sites, and colonial-era relics like cannons, swords, and ship paraphernalia. The museum is open daily from 9 a.m. to 6 p.m. Admission is $3; guided tours in English are free. A rooftop restaurant serves breakfast and lunch.

Taking in the shops

If you like shopping for silver jewelry, you can spend a great deal of time examining the wares of all the jewelers along Melgar who cater to cruise-ship shoppers. Numerous duty-free stores sell items such as perfumes and designer wares. You can find a good variety of duty-free shops at the Punta Langosta shopping center on the southern part of Avenida Rafael Melgar in front of the Punta Langosta pier. If you're interested in Mexican folk art, a number of stores now display a wide variety of interesting pieces. Check out the following shops, all of which are on Melgar within a few blocks of the plaza:

- ✔ **Los Cinco Soles** (☎ 987-872-2040)
- ✔ **Indigo** (☎ 987-872-1076)
- ✔ **Viva Mexico** (☎ 987-872-5466)

Prices for serapes (cotton ponchos), T-shirts, and other tourist-type goods are less expensive on the side streets off Melgar.

While you're shopping in San Miguel, someone will probably approach you to offer a deal in a timeshare apartment. Although investing in timeshares is generally a bad idea, weighing financial decisions when you're in vacation mode is a really bad idea. Something about vacationing makes people suspend their critical judgment. Don't mix business with pleasure. Wait until you're back home, where you can do your research, before entering the timeshare market.

Enjoying the nightlife

Cozumel is a town frequented by divers and other active visitors who play hard all day and wind down at night. The nightlife scene is generally low-key and peaks in the early evening. The cruise-ship crowd offers an exception to this rule. On Sunday evenings, the place to be is the main plaza, which usually hosts a free concert and has plenty of people strolling about and visiting with friends. Most of the clubs are either in the Punta Langosta shopping center, such as **Carlos 'n Charlie's** (☎ 987-869-1646) and **Señor Frog's** (☎ 987-869-1651), or along the Avenida Rafael Melgar waterfront, such as **Hard Rock Cafe** (☎ 987-872-5271) and **Viva Mexico** (☎ 987-872-0799). Also, try out a great little salsa bar called **La Pura Vida** (☎ 987-878-7831) at the corner of Avenida 5 Sur and Calle Adolfo Rosado Salas.

Chapter 13

Playa del Carmen and the Riviera Maya

By David Baird

* *

* *

*T*he Riviera Maya is the area of the Yucatán Peninsula's upper Caribbean coast from just south of Cancún to the town of Tulum, a distance of 132km (82 miles). It's a beautiful place with a mix of small resort communities, nature parks, small beach hotels, and large all-inclusive resorts. A long reef system protects this coast and offers many snorkeling and diving opportunities. Where there are gaps in the reef — Playa del Carmen, Xpu-Ha, and Tulum — you find the best beaches. The action of the surf washes away silt and seagrass and erodes rocks, leaving a sandy bottom. Where the reef is prominent, you can expect good snorkeling just offshore with plenty of fish and other sea life.

Playa del Carmen is the largest town in the Riviera Maya. In the last few years, it has developed a kind of dual personality. Originally it was a hideaway for hippies looking for an undeveloped piece of paradise — a counterculture getaway clothed in native architecture with thatched roofs, rustic clapboard, and adobe walls. Then the developers showed up and built a resort community on the south side of town called Playacar, complete with golf course, condos, and large all-inclusive hotels. The town continues to attract a lot of young people interested in living the simple life and working only as much as necessary. Playa, as the locals refer to it, is a fun place to stay, with plenty to do or not to do, and a lovely beach for those who choose the latter option. In the evenings, people stroll down the town's Quinta Avenida (Fifth Ave.) shopping, choosing between the many restaurants and bars, or simply enjoying the evening air.

Tulum is another booming town on this coast. It sprung up along the highway near the ruins of the same name. Nearby is a beautiful beach with small hotels and their thatched-roofed (*cabañas* or *palapas*) cabins and small structures. Tulum marks the end of the Riviera Maya. South of here is a large natural preserve called Sian Ka'an and then the lower Caribbean coast, which hasn't the same quality of beaches as the upper coast.

The Riviera Maya has grown increasingly popular as its lodging and dining options have multiplied. It also holds a wealth of attractions. In fact, many of the day-trips offered in Cancún are to places on this coast, such as snorkeling tours; horseback riding; the nature parks of **Tres Rios, Xcaret,** and **Xel-Ha;** and even the ruins of Tulum. Many Europeans have settled here and set up small hotels and restaurants, lending the area a certain cosmopolitan flavor. But this cosmopolitanism is spread throughout the towns of this coast and not concentrated in an urban center such as Cancún. In the Riviera Maya, you don't find any tall skyscrapers or broad boulevards. Staying here is a different experience from staying in Cancún, adding to the choices that visitors to the Yucatán have.

Deciding Where to Stay

Choosing your lodging depends largely on personal taste and the kind of vacation you have in mind. The Riviera Maya has just about any kind of lodging option:

- Small, charming hotels in a town where you can interact with the local residents and get a feel for what life is like in this part of the world

- Villas and condos that rent by the week — a great option for a family vacation or a group of friends

- Intimate *cabaña* hotels (cabins) on a beach far enough away from the modern world that they have to generate their own electricity or do without

- Large all-inclusives with all the modern conveniences, including expansive pools, game rooms, and watersports equipment

- Small, private spa-resorts that pamper their guests

In this chapter, I list some of my favorite hotels in the Riviera Maya, including beach cabañas, inexpensive one-of-a-kind places, and even my favorite secluded spa-resort. For more information about the different towns and locations along this coast, see the "Settling into the Riviera Maya" section, later in this chapter.

If you decide to stay in a hotel in Playa del Carmen, don't hesitate to choose a place that's not on the beach. Town life here is a big part of the fun, and staying on the beach in Playa has its disadvantages — such as higher rates and the noise produced by a couple of the beach-side bars. And if you choose accommodations off the beach, you don't have to worry about not being able to find that perfect strip of sand. Beaches are public property in Mexico, and you can lay out your towel anywhere you like without anyone bothering you.

Near the town of Tulum, you can choose from about 30 *cabaña* hotels in a "hotel zone" on the beach. All are small hotels that generate their own electricity. They don't offer air conditioning, and they charge more than the small hotels in the other towns, but what you're paying for is the seclusion and the quiet. The beaches near Tulum are marvelous and uncrowded.

For families and groups of friends wishing to rent a condo or villa for a week, the following Web sites are good places to start: **Akumal Vacations** (www.akumalvacations.com), **Caribbean Fantasy** (www.caribbfan.com), or **Loco Gringo** (www.locogringo.com). You can find rentals on many parts of the coast, including an abundance in the town of Akumal, which many families favor because it's quieter and more convenient than some of the booming towns such as Playa or Tulum.

Also popular with families (and couples) are the all-inclusive hotels, of which there are more than 40 on this coast. All-inclusives are large hotels that work with economies of scale to offer lodging, food, and drink all for a single relatively low rate. See Chapter 5 for more details about all-inclusive hotels and resorts.

The best way to get a room at an all-inclusive is by contacting a travel agent who works with vacation packagers. You get a much better deal that way than by contacting the hotel directly. Even if you have lots of frequent-flier miles to burn, you'll still find matching the rates of a full package difficult.

All-inclusives tend to look and feel alike, which is why I don't include any in the hotel reviews later in this chapter. Of the many all-inclusives in the Riviera Maya, however, the following are a few that may bear looking into:

✔ **Aventura Spa Palace** (☎ **984-875-1100;** Fax: 984-875-1101; www.palaceresorts.com) is a hotel in the Palace chain — this one is just for grown-ups. It has a large spa and gym and attractive common areas and guest rooms. There is a large pool but no beach; guests can take a shuttle to the Xpu-Ha property for beach access.

✔ The **Copacabana Beach Resort** in Xpu-Ha (☎ **984-875-1800;** Fax: 984-875-1818; www.hotelcopacabana.com) has raised walkways preserving much of the flora and making it visually interesting. And Xpu-Ha is blessed with a stunning beach.

✔ **Freedom Paradise** (☎ **866-548-3995** or 998-887-1101; Fax: 998-887-1102; www.freedomparadise.com) is billed as the first size-friendly vacation resort. The management has worked hard to create an environment that large people will find comfortable. I like it because it doesn't have all the frou-frou of so many other resorts — it's friendly and unpretentious.

✔ **Iberostar Quetzal or Tucan** (☎ **984-877-2000;** Fax: 984-873-0424; www.iberostar.com): Of the several all-inclusives that are in Playa del Carmen/Playacar, I like this one, which has two names for different halves of the same hotel. The food is better than at most all-inclusives, and the central part of the hotel is made of raised walkways and terraces over the natural mangrove habitat. Its neighbor, the Gala (☎ **984-877-4040;** Fax: 984-873-1169; www.galaresorts.com.mx), is also a good choice.

✔ Also in Xpu-Ha is the **Xpu-Ha Palace** (☎ **984-875-1010;** Fax: 984-875-1012; www.palaceresorts.com), which is built on the grounds of a failed nature park. It has some keen features including lagoons and a jungle, and features several facilities for kids, including a small crocodile hatchery. The hotel is spread out over a large area and necessarily involves a good bit of walking, but this also makes it feel less crowded.

Evaluating the Top Accommodations

In the following reviews, I note *rack rates* (the maximum that a hotel or resort charges for a room) for two people spending one night in a double room. For Christmas and New Year's, rates can be higher than the standard high-season rates. Prices quoted here include the 12% room tax. Please refer to the Introduction of this book for an explanation of the price categories.

Hotels listed here have both air conditioning and TVs, unless otherwise indicated, and if the review doesn't say anything to the contrary, you can safely assume that you can walk directly out of your hotel and onto the beach.

Cabañas Ana y José
$$–$$$ Tulum

These cabañas offer a tranquil escape that feels worlds away from the rest of civilization, and they provide sufficient creature comforts to make for a relaxing stay. The beach in front of the hotel is pure white sand. The

Playa del Carmen

ACCOMMODATIONS ■
Hotel Jungla Caribe **6**
Hotel Lunata **8**
Shangri-La Caribe **1**
Treetops **5**
Villa Catarina Rooms
and Cabañas **2**
DINING ◆
Casa Mediterránea **7**
Estas Son Las Mañanitas **9**
La Casa del Agua **10**
La Tarraya Restaurant/Bar **11**
Media Luna **3**
Yaxché **4**

Calle 14
■ New
  Bus Station
Calle 12
Calle 10
Calle 8
Calle 6
Calle 4
Calle 2
Riviera
Bus Station ■
Avenida Juárez
← To Highway 307
Post Office ✉
Calle 1
Calle 1
Av. 35
Av. 30
Av. 25
Av. 20
Av. 15
Av. 10
5A Av.
Pedestrians Only
Caribbean Sea
Ferry Pier
to Cozumel
(Muelle)

rock-walled cabañas closest to the water (called "oceanfront") are a little larger than the others and come with two double beds. I also like the attractive second-floor "vista al mar" rooms, which have tall palapa roofs. The standard rooms are much like the others but don't face the sea and don't get as much sea breeze. There is 24-hour electricity for lights and ceiling fans but no TV or A/C. It does have a small pool, one of the few on this part of the coast that do. A restaurant takes care of meals. All rooms have tile or wood floors, one or two double beds, and patios or balconies. The hotel, located 6km (4 miles) from the Tulum ruins, can have a rental car waiting for you at the Cancún airport. Reservations are a must in high season.

Carretera Punta Allen, Km 7, Punta Allen Peninsula. ☎ **988-887-5470.** *Fax: 988-887-5469.* www.anayjose.com. *15 units. Free parking. Rack rates: High season $110–$150 double; low season $90–$130 double. MC, V.*

Club Akumal Caribe/Hotel Villas Maya Club
$$–$$$ Akumal

This hotel's rooms and garden bungalows, set along the pristine and tranquil Akumal Bay, are large and comfortable. The 40 Villas Maya bungalows are simply and comfortably furnished and come with kitchenettes. The 21 rooms in the three-story beachfront hotel are more elaborately furnished. They come with refrigerators and a king bed or two queen beds. Both the bungalows and the rooms have tile floors and good-size bathrooms, but neither have phones or TVs. A large pool on the grounds, a children's activities program (during high season), two restaurants, and a bar round out the facilities. You can also ask about two- and three-bedroom villas for rent.

Carretera Cancún-Tulum (Hwy. 307), Km 104. ☎ *800-351-1622 in the U.S., 800-343-1440 in Canada; 984-875-9012 direct.* www.hotelakumalcaribe.com. *70 units. Free parking. Rack rates: High season $110 bungalow, $140 hotel room; low season $66 bungalow, $84 hotel room. AE, MC, V. Only cash at the restaurants.*

Hotel Jungla Caribe
$$ Playa del Carmen

Located right in the heart of the Avenida 5 action, "La Jungla" is an imaginative place, with a highly stylized look that mixes neoclassical with Robinson Crusoe. Its character perfectly keeps with the town's quirkiness. Owner Rolf Albrecht envisioned space and comfort for guests, so all but eight of the standard rooms are large, with gray-and-black marble floors, the occasional Roman column, and large bathrooms. Fifteen of the rooms are suites. Catwalks connect the "tower" section of suites to the hotel. Take a dip in an attractive pool in the courtyard beneath a giant *Ramón* tree. Eight small rooms lack air conditioning and are priced lower than the rates listed here.

Av. 5 Norte at Calle 8. ☎ *and fax: 984-873-0650.* www.jungla-caribe.com. *25 units. Rack rates: High season $80 double, $100–$110 suite; low season $45 double, $55–$60 suite. AE, MC, V.*

Hotel Lunata
$$ Playa del Carmen

The Lunata offers a combination of location, comfort, attractiveness, and price that no other hotel in this category can beat. It's built in hacienda style, with cut stone and wrought iron, and is decorated in contemporary Mexican colors. The rooms show a lot of polish, with good air conditioning and nicely finished bathrooms. They also come with a TV, a small fridge, and a safe. The majority of rooms are deluxe, which are medium to large and come with a king or two doubles. A complimentary continental breakfast is served in the garden, and the third-story terrace makes a nice place to hang out. This hotel is right on Avenida 5; if you like to go to bed early, stay in a room in back.

Avenida 5 (between calles 6 and 8). ☎ *984-873-0884. Fax: 984-873-1240.* www. lunata.com. *10 units. Free guarded parking. Rack rates: $80–$100 double, $75–$125 deluxe and jr. suite. Rates include continental breakfast. AE, MC, V.*

Hotel Ojo de Agua
$ Puerto Morelos

This is a seaside hotel with modern rooms. Two three-story buildings stand on the beach at a right angle to each other. Most rooms have balconies and glass sliding doors. They're simply furnished and clean. Most rooms have two double beds or a double and a twin; those with one double bed go for $10 less. Twenty-four rooms have air conditioning, and 24 have phones (not the same 24). "Studio" units have kitchenettes. A medium-size pool and a restaurant are available. Service is friendly. You can set up snorkeling and scuba trips with the hotel. Turn left when you get to the town plaza and keep going; look for the sign.

Supermanzana 2, lote 16. ☎ *998-871-0027 or 998-871-0507. Fax: 998-871-0202.* www.ojo-de-agua.com. *36 units. Rack rates: High season $55–$60 double, $62–$70 studio or deluxe; low season $46–$50 double, $54–$60 studio or deluxe. Weekly and monthly rates available. AE, MC, V.*

La Posada del Capitán Lafitte
$$$$ Between Playa del Carmen and Puerto Morelos

A large sign on the left side of Highway 307, 13km (8 miles) south of Puerto Morelos, points you in the direction of La Posada del Capitán Lafitte. This lovely seaside retreat sits on a solitary stretch of sandy beach. Here you can enjoy being isolated while still having all the amenities of a relaxing vacation. The one- and two-story white-stucco bungalows, which hold one to four rooms, stretch across a powdery white beach (but the sea floor is a little rocky). They're small but comfortable, with tile floors; small, tiled bathrooms; either two double beds or one king-size bed; and an oceanfront porch. Twenty-nine bungalows have air conditioning; the rest have fans. The hotel offers transportation to and from the Cancún airport for $50 per person (minimum of two passengers). Your room price includes both breakfast and dinner, plus there's a poolside grill and bar. Amenities include a medium-size pool, watersports equipment, and a TV/game room.

Carretera Cancún-Tulum (Hwy. 307), Km 62. ☎ *800-538-6802 in the U.S. and Canada, or 984-873-0214.* www.mexicoholiday.com. *62 units. Free guarded parking. Rack rates: High season $200–$225 double; low season $130–$140 double. Rates include breakfast and dinner. MC, V.*

Maroma

$$$$–$$$$$ near Puerto Morelos

In the area around Puerto Morelos, four spa resorts offer different versions of the hedonistic resort experience. All four pride themselves on their personal service, amenities, and spa and salon treatments. Being in the Yucatán, they like to add the healing practices of the Maya, especially the use of the steam bath known in Mexico as a *temascal.* Of the four, this resort has been around the longest. It has a gorgeous beach and beautifully manicured grounds. Two- and three-story buildings contain the large guest rooms; most have king beds. The small size makes for personal service and a wonderful sense of escape.

Carretera 307, Km 51. ☎ *866-454-9351 in the U.S. or 998-872-8200. Fax: 998-872-8220.* www.orient-express.com. *58 units. Free valet parking. Rack rates: $225 garden-view double; $364–$476 premium or deluxe double; from $728 suite. Rates include ground transfer, full breakfast, 1 snorkeling tour. AE, MC, V.*

Shangri-La Caribe

$$$$ Playa del Carmen

This hotel — a loose grouping of cabañas on one of the best beaches in Playa — is hard to beat for sheer fun and leisure. And it's far enough from the center of town to be quiet yet convenient. The older, south side of the hotel (the "Caribe" section) consists of one- and two-story cabañas. The north ("Playa") side has a few larger buildings, holding four to six rooms. A preference for one or the other section is a matter of taste; the units in both are similar in amenities, privacy, and price. The real difference in price depends on the proximity to the water — beachfront, ocean view, or garden view. Garden view is the best bargain, being only a few steps farther from the water. Many garden-view rooms (mostly in a third section called "Pueblo") have air conditioning, which adds $6 to the price. All rooms have a patio or porch complete with hammock. Most come with two double beds, but a few have a king bed. Windows are screened, and ceiling fans circulate the breeze. Book well in advance during high season.

Calle 38 and the beach. ☎ *800-538-6802 in the U.S. or Canada, or 987-873-0611. Fax: 987-873-0500.* www.shangrilacaribe.net. *107 units. Free guarded parking. Rack rates: High season $180 garden view, $200–$250 ocean view or beachfront; low season $140 garden view, $160–$200 ocean view or beachfront. Rates include breakfast and dinner for two. AE, MC, V.*

Treetops

$–$$ Playa del Carmen

Treetops not only offers a good price but also a good location — half a block from the beach, and half a block from Avenida 5, which is just enough distance to filter out the noise. The rooms at Treetops encircle a pool, a small *cenote,* and a patch of preserved jungle that shades the hotel and lends the proper tropical feel. Rooms are large and comfortable and have air conditioning, fans, refrigerators, and either balconies or patios. Some of the upper rooms, especially the central suite, have the feel of a treehouse. Two other suites are large, with fully loaded kitchenettes, and work well for groups of four.

Calle 8 s/n. ☎ *984-873-1495. Fax: 984-873-0351.* www.treetopshotel.com. *17 units. Rack rates: High season $50–$80 double, $100–$120 suite; low season $40–$70 double, $90–$110 suite. MC, V.*

Villa Catarina Rooms and Cabañas
$–$$ Playa del Carmen

Hammocks stretch out in front of each of the stylishly rustic rooms and *cabañas* at this property nestled in a grove of palms and fruit trees, just a block from the beach. Each of the clean, well-furnished rooms has one or two double beds on wooden bases with carpet or wood floors. Some rooms have a small loft for reading and relaxing; others have palapa roofs or terraces. Furnishings and Mexican folk-art decorations add a great touch that's uncommon for hotels in this price range. Bathrooms are detailed with colorful tiles, and some of the larger rooms have sitting areas. Good cross-ventilation through well-screened windows keeps the rooms relatively cool. Complimentary coffee is available every morning.

Calle Privada Norte between avenidas 12 and 14. ☎ *984-873-2098. Fax: 984-873-2097. 14 units. High season $70–$90 double; low season $50–$70 double. MC, V.*

Zamas
$$–$$$ Tulum

Zamas is a grouping of stylish beach *cabañas* located out on a rocky point on the coast just south of Tulum. Each *cabaña* comes with a small porch area and hammocks, a thatched roof, a large bathroom, and electricity. Mosquito netting hangs over each bed. What the *cabañas* don't have are ceiling fans, which they generally don't need. In this respect, the hotel's location is enviable in that there's almost always a breeze. Rooms come with a variety of bed combinations and are ranked in three categories: garden view, ocean view, and beachfront. Note that the rooms don't have air conditioning, TV, or phones (even the hotel doesn't have a direct phone!). The hotel's restaurant has great food.

Carr. Punta Allen, Km 5. ☎ *415-387-9806 in the U.S. or Canada.* www.zamas.com. *20 units. Rack rates: High season $110–$150 ocean-view double, $80–$115 double; low season $80–$110 ocean-view double, $60–$90 double. No credit cards.*

Settling into the Riviera Maya

For getting through customs and immigration at the Cancún airport, see Chapter 9. The airport is located well south of Cancún, so you don't have to go through the city to get to Playa or the Riviera Maya. If you're **driving,** follow the signs for Puerto Morelos/Playa del Carmen as you exit the airport. Turn right (south) on Highway 307. For more specific directions on entering Playa or going farther south, see "Getting around the area," later in this chapter.

Another option is to take a bus that travels straight from the airport to Playa. After you arrive in Playa, you can catch a bus to any of the major towns along the coast. Turn right after you exit the airport (you walk by a long line of counters with people offering you all kinds of services and info — keep right on walking). Walk to the other side of the airport's main entrance. Look for buses labeled **Autobuses Riviera** in large letters. They offer direct service more than 12 times a day. Cost is $7.50 one-way.

Knowing where to go

If you know where to go, knowing how to get there is easy. The Riviera Maya is a coast with one highway, and anyplace you're heading to is going to be either north or south of the place you're coming from. Here's a list of all the major towns and attractions north to south from the Cancún airport to Tulum:

- **Puerto Morelos:** This sleepy little village has a few small hotels and rental houses. Locals refer to it as "Muerto Morelos" (Dead Morelos) during the off-season for the lack of activity. It's a short distance from the bustle of Cancún and Playa del Carmen, and can be considered a convenient escape from the crowds, perfect for a relaxed vacation of lying about the beach and reading a book (with perhaps the occasional foray into a watersport or two). The coast is sandy and well protected by an offshore reef, which means good snorkeling and diving nearby, but plenty of seagrass is on the beach and in the water.

- **Tres Rios:** A few miles before you get to Playa, you see signs for this eco-park. This natural reserve contains 150 acres where you can ride horseback, paddle a canoe or kayak, bike along jungle trails, or just hang out at the beach. This reserve is the least developed of the three eco-parks on this coast. Don't go during the summer months. See Chapter 11 for more about visiting this park.

- **Playa del Carmen:** The largest town on this coast, Playa's got the best restaurants and the most nightlife. It also has a beautiful beach. It's a popular destination, not a place to find solitude.

The Riviera Maya

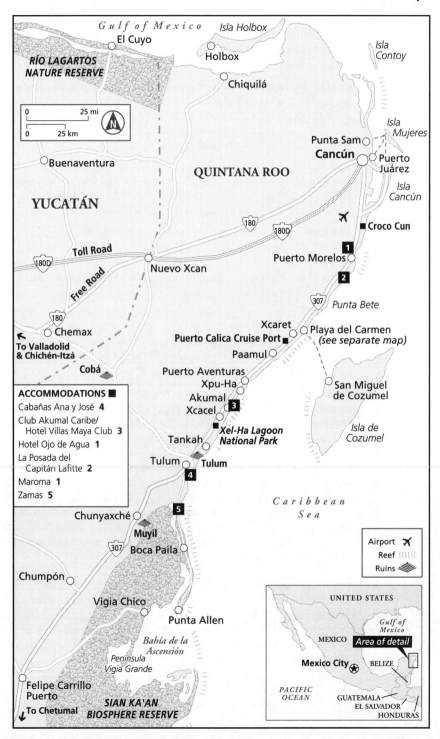

Gulf of Mexico

El Cuyo

Isla Holbox

Holbox

Isla Contoy

RÍO LAGARTOS NATURE RESERVE

Chiquilá

0   25 mi
0   25 km

Isla Mujeres

Punta Sam

Cancún

Puerto Juárez

Buenaventura

QUINTANA ROO

Isla Cancún

YUCATÁN

180

180D

Croco Cun

1

Toll Road

180D

Puerto Morelos

Nuevo Xcan

Free Road

2

307 *Punta Bete*

180

Chemax

Xcaret

Playa del Carmen
(see separate map)

To Valladolid & Chichén-Itzá

Puerto Calica Cruise Port ■

Paamul

Cobá

Puerto Aventuras

Xpu-Ha

San Miguel de Cozumel

ACCOMMODATIONS ■

Cabañas Ana y José **4**

Club Akumal Caribe/
  Hotel Villas Maya Club **3**

Hotel Ojo de Agua **1**

La Posada del
  Capitán Lafitte **2**

Maroma **1**

Zamas **5**

Akumal

Xcacel

3

Isla de Cozumel

■ **Xel-Ha Lagoon National Park**

Tankah

Tulum

Tulum

4

5

Caribbean Sea

Chunyaxché

Muyil

307 Boca Paila

Airport ✕
Reef �𝄐
Ruins ≈

Chumpón

Vigia Chíco

Punta Allen

Bahía de la Ascensión

UNITED STATES

Gulf of Mexico

MEXICO

Area of detail

Peninsula
Vigia Grande

Mexico City ★

BELIZE

Felipe Carrillo Puerto

To Chetumal

SIAN KA'AN BIOSPHERE RESERVE

PACIFIC OCEAN

GUATEMALA
EL SALVADOR
HONDURAS

✔ **Xcaret:** Just 7km (4 miles) south of Playa del Carmen is the largest nature park on the coast. It draws people from Cancún, Cozumel, and all points along this coast. Highlights include floating through an underground river (not for everybody), nightly shows, and loads of seaside activities. Chapter 11 has more details about this park.

✔ **Puerto Aventuras:** A modern marina community with tons of condos and a few hotels, I don't care much for staying here, but it's a good place to hook up with sport-fishing outfits or to try a swim with dolphins. See the section, "Having Fun on and off the Beach," later in this chapter, for more info.

✔ **Xpu-Ha:** This broad beautiful beach with private houses and a few large all-inclusives is a great place to stay for sun worshipers and a good place to go for the day. There's a smattering of beach restaurants and some villas and cabins for rent.

✔ **Akumal:** This small, modern, and ecologically oriented community is built on the shores of Akumal Bay and Half-Moon Bay. It's mostly made up of two-story villas, and a few hotels — all on the water. It's a lot quieter than Playa and is a diving center for the coast.

✔ **Xel-Ha:** A large, well-protected lagoon is the centerpiece for this lovely eco-park. It attracts crowds of snorkelers who come to view the fish in the calm, clear waters. The park also offers dolphin swims and a small grouping of ruins. Check out Chapter 11 for more details about this location.

✔ **Tulum:** The town of Tulum is on the highway 132km (82 miles) from Cancún, just south of the ruins of the same name. It has a hotel district about 3km (2 miles) away on the coast where about 30 small hotels are lined up along a beautiful beach. All these hotels generate their own electricity and can't provide basics such as air conditioning or phones. Most have small restaurants, and the town itself has at least a half dozen more. Construction is booming, both in the town and along the coast. But you can enjoy the beach here in relative solitude and quiet (unless your hotel is busy building additional rooms). Of course, the flip side of peace and quiet is that Tulum doesn't have the variety of restaurants that Playa and Cancún do.

Keeping some cash on hand when traveling this coast is always a good idea. Outside of Playa del Carmen, you don't find many cash machines. In the smaller towns and resorts and at some gas stations, you often can't pay with a credit card. Puerto Morelos has just one ATM in the town and another on the highway at the turnoff junction. After Playa del Carmen, the next cash machines are in Tulum (two). Also, if you're driving, keep some gas in the tank; the coast south of Puerto Aventuras can sometimes experience power failures that last a day, and after the power returns, there can be long lines for gas and cash.

Getting around the area

A single road, Highway 307, runs the length of the Riviera Maya. From the Cancún airport to Playa del Carmen (51km/32 miles), it's a four-lane divided highway with speed limits up to 110 kmph (68 mph). There are a couple of traffic lights and several reduced-speed zones around the major turnoffs.

As you approach Playa, two extra lanes are added each way and then divide up. Stay in the left lanes; you want to make a left turn at either of two traffic lights. If you don't stay left, you have to pass through and keep going until you find a turnaround. The first traffic light is Avenida Constituyentes, which works for destinations in northern Playa. The second is Avenida Juárez, the artery connecting the highway to the town's main square and ferry pier.

From Playa to Tulum (80km/50 miles), the road becomes a smooth two-lane highway with wide shoulders. Speed limits are the same, but with more spots that require you to reduce your speed.

Don't be surprised if you see faster traffic on this stretch of road moving into the middle of the road when passing (as if there were a center lane). Oncoming traffic moves to the right to make room for the passing vehicle. You do the same, but keep a lookout for cyclists on the shoulder. When making a left turn where there is no left-turn lane, move to the shoulder and stop and wait for a gap in the traffic to cross the road. Don't stop in the main lane of the highway! In some places, use the right-hand turnoff that curves around and then cross the highway at a right angle. Also, all these potential hazards make driving at night especially challenging. (And it gets dark early on this coast.)

You may notice tons of buses running this stretch of highway, but I prefer renting a car because many buses stop only in the larger towns or they leave you a half-mile from the beach you're trying to get to. Playa has any number of rental agencies. Reserving a car before getting to Mexico is usually cheaper than waiting until after you arrive (see Chapter 7).

Fast Facts: Riviera Maya and Playa del Carmen

Area Code

The telephone area code for most of the Riviera Maya is **984**. The exception is Puerto Morelos and its surroundings, which has the 998 area code.

Banks, ATMs, and Currency Exchange

There are several banks in Playa with ATMs, along with several money-exchange houses. Many of these offices are located close to the pier and along Avenida 5 at Calle 8.

There's an ATM in Puerto Morelos and one at the highway turnoff for the town (beside the pharmacy). You can also use the two ATMs and one bank in Tulum.

Business Hours

Most offices maintain traditional Mexican hours of operation (10 a.m. to 2 p.m. and from 4 p.m. to 8 p.m. daily), but shops remain open throughout the day. Offices tend to close on Saturday and Sunday. Shops are usually open on Saturday but still generally respect the tradition of closing on Sunday. During peak season, many shops remain open until 9 or even 10 p.m.

Internet Access

There are cybercafes and Internet providers in all the major towns, including quite a few in Playa. Prices are generally cheap, but seem to increase inversely in proportion to the size of the town.

Medical

For serious medical attention, go to **Hospiten** in Cancún. In Playa, Dr. Jorge Mercado is a capable general practitioner who speaks English. His office is at the corner of avenidas 10 and Constituyentes (☎ 984-873-3908).

Pharmacy

The **Farmacia del Carmen** (☎ 984-873-2330), on Avenida Juárez between avenidas 5 and 10, is open 24 hours.

Post Office

The post office is on Avenida Principal, 3 blocks north of the plaza on the right after the Hotel Playa del Carmen and the launderette.

Taxes

There's a 15% IVA (value-added tax) on goods and services, which is generally included in the posted price.

Telephone

Avoid the phone booths that have signs in English advising you to call home using a special 800 number — these are absolute rip-offs and can cost as much as $20 per minute. The least expensive way to call is by using a Telmex (LADATEL) prepaid phone card, available at most pharmacies and mini-supers, using the official Telmex (Lada) public phones. Remember, in Mexico, you need to dial 001 prior to a number to reach the United States, and you need to preface long-distance calls within Mexico by dialing 01.

Time Zone

The Riviera Maya operates on central standard time.

Dining along the Riviera Maya

Every town in the Riviera Maya has at least a few restaurants where you can get good, if not outstanding, food. But Playa del Carmen is the exception; it has an impressive number and variety of restaurants for a town its size. The European influence is quite noticeable, especially with the Italian restaurants. With so many options available, this section lists only my favorites in Playa. In most other places, your choices will be so limited, you won't be struggling with any tough decisions.

✔ In Puerto Morelos, the best and most expensive restaurant in town is **John Grey's** (open only for dinner, closed Sunday; ☎ 998-871-0449), which is a couple of blocks north of the plaza and a couple inland. The owner is a former chef for the Ritz-Carlton. The rest of my suggestions are on or around the main square and include **Cafe del Puerto** for salads, sandwiches, and the like (☎ 998-874-2086); **Los Pelicanos** for overpriced seafood (☎ 998-871-0014); **Hola Asia** for Asian food (☎ 998-871-0679); and **Le Café d'Amancia** for coffee and pastries (☎ 998-850-4110).

✔ Puerto Aventuras has a large open area beside the dolphin pool (see "Swimming with dolphins," later in this chapter) with chairs and tables and a half dozen restaurants where you can get anything from steaks to pizza to pub grub. None is outstanding, but all are passable.

✔ In Akumal, many people rent villas and cook for themselves (there's a convenient grocery store called **Super Chomak** at the entrance to town). There are also a few restaurants: the **Turtle Bay Café and Bakery** (no phone) is my favorite spot for breakfast or a light lunch, **La Buena Vida** for dinner or a drink (☎ 984-875-9061).

✔ Tulum has a few good restaurants with reasonable prices. In the town proper is **Charlie's** (☎ 984-871-2136), my favorite for Mexican food, and **Don Cafeto's** (☎ 984-871-2207), also Mexican. Both places are on the main street. There's a great, authentic-Italian restaurant called **Il Giardino di Toni e Simone** (☎ 044-984-804-1316,** a wireless phone; closed Wed), 1 block off the highway. Look for a large building-supply store called ROCA — the restaurant is on the opposite side of the road 1 block away. A couple of roadside places grill chicken and serve it with rice and beans for an economical lunch. In the hotel zone, try the food at Zamas.

Please refer to the Introduction of this book for an explanation of the price categories that I use in the following listings. Remember that tips generally run about 15% and most wait-staff really depend on gratuities for their income, so be generous if the service warrants.

Please see Appendix C for more information on Mexican cuisine.

Casa Mediterránea
$ **Playa del Carmen   NORTHERN ITALIAN**

Tucked away on a quiet little patio off Avenida 5, this small, homey restaurant serves excellent food. The owners, Maurizio Gabrielli and Giovanna Furian, usually attend to the customers and make recommendations. They came to Mexico to enjoy the simple life, and this inclination shows in the restaurant's welcoming, unhurried atmosphere. The menu is mostly northern Italian, with several dishes from the rest of the country as well as daily specials. They make their pastas (except penne and spaghetti) in-house, and none are precooked. Try fish and shrimp ravioli or penne alla Veneta. You can choose from several wines, mostly Italian. The salads are good and are carefully prepared — dig in without hesitation

Avenida 5 (between calles 6 and 8; look for a sign for Hotel Marieta). ☎ *984-876-3926. Reservations recommended in high season. Main courses: $8–15. No credit cards. Open: Daily 1–11 p.m.*

Estas Son Las Mañanitas
$ **Playa del Carmen   MEXICAN/ITALIAN**

For dependable food in an advantageous spot for people-watching, try this restaurant. It's simple outdoor dining on Avenida 5 — comfortable chairs and tables under *palapa* umbrellas. It's not noisy, and the Italian owner is vigilant about maintaining quality and consistency. He offers an excellent *sopa de lima,* a large seafood pasta, grilled shrimp with herbs, and Tex-Mex specialties such as chili and fajitas. The hot sauces are good.

Av. 5 (between calles 4 and 6). ☎ *984-873-0114. Reservations not needed. Main courses: $7–12. AE, MC, V. Open: Daily 8–11:30 p.m.*

La Casa del Agua
$ **Playa del Carmen   EUROPEAN/MEXICAN**

This new arrival to Playa offers some of the best of both Old and New Worlds. What I tried was delicious — chicken in a wonderfully scented sauce of fine herbs accompanied by fettuccine, and a well-made tortilla soup listed as *sopa mexicana.* There are a number of cool and light dishes that would be appetizing for lunch or an afternoon meal; for example, an avocado stuffed with shrimp and flavored with a subtle horseradish sauce on a bed of alfalfa sprouts and julienned carrots — a good mix of tastes and textures. The dining area is upstairs under a large and airy palapa roof.

Avenida 5 at Calle 2. ☎ *984-803-0232. Reservations recommended in high season. Main courses: $9–$15. AE, MC, V. Open: Daily 2 p.m. to midnight.*

La Tarraya Restaurant/Bar
$ **Playa del Carmen   SEAFOOD/BREAKFAST**

"The restaurant that was born with the town," proclaims the sign outside this establishment. Locals also recommend this restaurant as the best for seafood. It's right on the beach, and the water practically laps at the foundations. Because the owners are fishermen, the fish is so fresh that it's practically still wiggling. The wood hut doesn't look like much, but you can have your fish prepared in several ways here. If you haven't tried the Yucatecan specialty *tik-n-xic* fish (named for locally caught fish — like grouper or mahimahi — prepared in a spicy barbecue style sauce), this would be a good place to do so. Tarraya is on the beach opposite the basketball court.

Calle 2 Norte at the beach. ☎ *987-873-2040. Reservations not needed. Main courses: $4–$9; whole fish $8 per kilo; breakfast $2.50–$5. No credit cards. Open: Daily 7 a.m.–9 p.m.*

Media Luna

$ Playa del Carmen   VEGETARIAN/SEAFOOD

The owner-chef here has come up with an outstanding and eclectic menu that favors grilled seafood, sautés, and pasta dishes with inventive combinations of ingredients. Everything I had was quite fresh and prepared beautifully, taking inspiration from various culinary traditions — Italian, Mexican, and Japanese. Keep an eye on the daily specials. The restaurant also makes sandwiches and salads, black-bean quesadillas, and crêpes. The restaurant is open-air, and the decor is primitive-tropical chic.

Avenida 5 (between calles 12 and 14). ☎ *984-873-0526. Reservations not needed. Main courses: $7–$15; sandwich with a salad $4–$8; breakfast $4–$7. No credit cards. Open: Daily 8 a.m.–11:30 p.m.*

Yaxché

$–$$ Playa del Carmen   MAYA/YUCATECAN

The menu here makes use of many native foods and spices to produce a style of cooking different from what you usually get when ordering Yucatecan food. You find such things as a cream of *chaya* (a native leafy vegetable), or *xcatic* chile (a regional variety of chile pepper) stuffed with savory pit-baked pork called *cochinita pibil*. I also like the classic fruit salad, done Mexican style with limejuice and dried powdered chile. The menu is varied and includes a lot of seafood dishes, and the ones I had were fresh and well prepared.

Calle 8 (between av. 5 and 10). ☎ *984-873-2502. Reservations recommended in high season. Main courses: $8–$20. AE, MC, V. Open: Daily noon to midnight.*

Having Fun on and off the Beach

The Riviera Maya is an ideal destination for people who like being active and exploring new lands. The region has Mayan ruins, caves, clear-water underground rivers *(cenotes),* and fascinating flora and fauna to see, plus plenty of options for scuba diving and snorkeling.

Scuba and snorkeling

For scuba diving in Puerto Morelos, contact Victor Reyes, the English speaking owner of **Mystic Divers** (☎ 998-871-0634; www. mysticdiving.com). He knows the local dive spots well and is quite accommodating. His shop is on the main square. You can also arrange a snorkeling tour here, or ask at the Hotel Ojo de Agua. The reef in front of Puerto Morelos has been declared a national park and is protected. It is quite shallow and perfect for snorkeling.

In Playa del Carmen, contact **Tank-Ha Dive Center** (☎ **984-873-0302;** www.tankha.com). It's on Playa's Avenida 5 between calles 8 and 10. You can arrange both reef and cavern diving here, plus snorkeling trips.

Akumal has been the main diving center on this coast for quite some time. It was the base of operations of a group known as CEDAM, who became widely known for discovering an old Spanish shipwreck complete with treasure. At least 30 dive sites are offshore near Akumal. The oldest dive operator in town is the **Akumal Dive Shop** (☎ **984-875-9032;** www.akumal.com). In addition to the usual certification courses, it offers cavern diving and technical diving instruction.

Cavern diving is big here because the Yucatán has so many underground rivers, especially around the lower Riviera Maya. If you want to try diving or snorkeling in caverns, the easiest and most fun way is to go to **Hidden Worlds Cenotes** (☎ **984-877-8535;** www.hiddenworlds.com.mx). It's 2km (1 mile) south of Xel-Ha on the right side of the road. You can easily spot the sign. Here, you can rent all the gear including a wet suit (the water is a bit chilly) and tour two caverns. These caverns were filmed for the IMAX production, *Journey into Amazing Caves.* The snorkel tour with gear costs $40 and takes you to two different caverns. The main form of transportation is by truck with a guide who throws in tidbits of information and lore about the jungle plant life that you see. Prepare to do some walking, so take shoes or sandals.

For easy-going snorkeling in warmer water, try the nature parks, especially Xel-Ha, which has scads of fish and rays. For more information on the nature parks, see Chapter 11.

Swimming with dolphins

You can swim with dolphins at two of the nature parks on this coast — Xel-Ha and Xcaret (see Chapter 11) — or you can do so in Puerto Aventuras. An excellent outfit called **Dolphin Discovery** (☎ **998-849-4757;** www.dolphindiscovery.com) does a first-rate job of getting people in contact with these marvelous creatures. An hour-long session costs $119. Make your reservations well ahead of time using the Web site.

Gone fishing

Puerto Aventuras is also the main hangout for fishing. Your best bet for deep-sea fishing is **Capt. Rick's Sportfishing Center** (☎ **984-873-5195** or 984-873-5387; www.fishyucatan.com). The best fishing on this coast is from March to August. The captain can combine a fishing trip with some snorkeling, which makes for a leisurely day.

Getting in touch with nature

The Riviera Maya also provides plenty to do for landlubbers. To start, the ruins of Tulum are easy to get to and interesting to view; for more information, check out Chapter 11.

If you want to see some of the jungle, try out rappelling, or get to know a contemporary Mayan community, contact **Alltournative** (☎ **984-873-2036;** www.alltournative.com), or book one of its tours through your hotel or a local travel agency. They do small groups and use vans to pick you up at almost any hotel in the Riviera Maya. Most of their tours combine a little adventure with some of the local culture and natural history. The guides are quite professional.

If you want to see more of the region's natural habitat, you can arrange a trip to the **Sian Ka'an Biosphere** to see a great variety of birds and sea life, and with a little luck, some of the rarer forest critters. In Tulum, contact **Sian Ka'an Tours** (☎ **984-871-2363;** E-mail: siankaan_tours@hotmail.com), which is on the east side of the highway, a block south of the road that heads to the beach. This company offers a general-interest day tour and a sunset tour.

On the highway between Akumal and Xel-Ha is the turnoff for an interesting large cavern called **Aktun Chen.** You explore the cavern by guided tour ($18 adults, $10 for children ages 6 to 12). It takes 45 minutes and involves a good bit of walking. The cavern is well lit and has good footing. On the park's grounds are a number of local species of fauna, including spider monkeys. Chapter 11 has a bit more detail about Aktun Chen.

Several outfits along the road offer horseback riding. The best is just south of Xcaret. It's called **Rancho Punta Venado** (☎ **984-877-9701**). You can see signs from the highway. It's less touristy than other places, and the owner takes good care of his horses.

Teeing off and playing tennis

Your best option for chasing a little white ball and whacking a larger, yellow one is the Playacar Golf Club immediately south of Playa del Carmen. It features an 18-hole championship **golf course** (☎ **984-873-0624**) designed by Robert Von Hagge. Greens fees are $160 in the morning (includes golf cart) and $100 after 2 p.m. Two **tennis** courts are also available at the club at a rate of $10 per hour.

Going shopping

Playa del Carmen offers the most opportunity for **shopping** in the area — along its popular Avenida 5. This pedestrian-only street is lined with dozens of small, trendy shops selling imported batik (Balinese-style) clothing, Guatemalan-fabric clothing, premium tequilas, Cuban cigars, masks, pottery, hammocks, and a few T-shirts. Throw in a couple of tattoo parlors, and you complete the mix. There is a smattering of interesting shops in some of the smaller towns, and on the highway are some large jewelry and rug stores.

Enjoying the nightlife

It seems like everyone in Playa is out on Avenida 5 or on the square until 10 or 11 p.m. Pleasant strolls, meals, and drinks at street-side cafes, shops, and bars with live music make up Playa's nightlife. Down by the ferry dock is a **Señor Frog's** (☎ 984-873-0930), with its patented mix of thumping dance music, gelatin shots, and fraternity-house antics; it's on the beach at Calle 4. **Captain Tutiz** (no phone) is also on the beach, designed like a pirate ship and with a large dance floor and live entertainment that can be good at times, but usually makes you want to throw a few more drinks back just to make it tolerable. The real beach bar in Playa is at the **Blue Parrot** (☎ 984-873-0083), and it has quite a following.

I've been hearing a lot of complaints about timeshare salespersons on this stretch of coast lately — more than the usual amount. Some complaints describe tactics that could almost be considered hostage-taking. I've also heard of people being stranded on the highway after they've declined to buy. Don't mix business with pleasure.

Part V
Puerto Vallarta and the Central Pacific Coast

The 5th Wave   By Rich Tennant

©RICHTENNANT

TINY LAGOON DIVE TOURS

Dive among our many man made reefs

"Did you want to take the Schwinn bicycle dive, the Weber gas grill dive, or the Craftsman riding lawn mower dive?"

In this part . . .

*I*f you're looking to bask in warm hospitality as well as the sun, Puerto Vallarta is an excellent choice that offers exquisite surroundings, friendly people, and tons of things to do and see. As a longtime resident of this picturesque town, Lynne shares an insider's perspective on getting around and exploring the sights.

Puerto Vallarta boasts a wide variety of places to stay and the most delectable array of dining options of any of Mexico's beach resorts. In the upcoming chapters, you find recommendations for the best places to stay in the area, as well as tips on finding the best restaurants — not an easy task considering all the wonderful dining choices Puerto Vallarta offers. Finally, with this part, you can locate the ideal beach along the more than 50 miles of coastline within Banderas Bay.

Chapter 14

The Lowdown on Puerto Vallarta's Hotel Scene

By Lynne Bairstow

- -

In This Chapter

▶ Getting the scoop on hotel locations

▶ Sizing up Puerto Vallarta's top hotel choices

- -

***P*uerto Vallarta** maintains a small-town charm despite offering its visitors a range of sophisticated hotels, great restaurants, a thriving arts community, an active nightlife, and a growing variety of eco-tourism attractions. With its traditional Mexican architecture and gold-sand beaches bordered by jungle-covered mountains, Vallarta is currently the second-most visited resort in Mexico (trailing only Cancún).

Most of the luxury hotels and shopping centers have sprung up to the north and south of the original town, allowing Vallarta to grow and become a sizable city of 250,000 without sacrificing its considerable charms. This growth pattern has made it possible for Vallarta to provide visitors with the services and infrastructure of a modern city while retaining the feel of a peaceful Mexican village.

In this chapter, I review the main parts of town, the types of hotel rooms you're likely to find in each place, and the pros and cons of staying in each area. Then I review some of my favorite places to stay in Puerto Vallarta. The selection is so varied that, regardless of your taste or budget, you're sure to find a perfect fit for a satisfying vacation.

Choosing a Location

The part of town you choose to stay in usually impacts your overall vacation experience, although everything is relatively close by and getting around is easy and inexpensive. The term *Vallarta* actually encompasses the entire area that borders **Bahía de Banderas** (Banderas Bay) — a 52-mile stretch of coastline that extends through two Mexican states. My hotel recommendations extend through this entire area as well.

Nuevo Vallarta and the northern coast

Traveling north from the airport (Gustavo Diaz Ordaz International Airport), you first come to **Nuevo Vallarta.** Many people assume Nuevo Vallarta is a section of Puerto Vallarta, but it's really a stand-alone destination located in the state of **Nayarit.** It's a mega-resort development — complete with marina, golf course, and luxury hotels. Most of the hotels here are all-inclusive, located on one of the widest, most attractive beaches on the bay. Two lengthy entrance roads from the highway pass by fields that are great for bird-watching and nearby lagoons that are great for kayaking. The **Paradise Plaza shopping center** (next to the Paradise Village resort) has added a lot to the area in terms of shopping, dining, and services. In addition, two golf courses opened in 2002: the **Mayan Palace Golf Club** and the **El Tigre** course of Paradise Village.

Visitors to Nuevo Vallarta usually plan to travel the distance into Puerto Vallarta (about 30 minutes and $15 by cab) for anything other than poolside and beach action — options for dining and other diversions outside the Nuevo Vallarta hotels remain limited, but are getting better. Taxis are available 24 hours a day. A regularly scheduled public-bus service runs between 7 a.m. and 11 p.m. daily and costs about $1.50 for a one-way trip.

Bucerías, a small beachfront village of cobblestone streets, villas, and small hotels, is farther north along Bahía de Banderas, 19km (12 miles) beyond the airport. Past Bucerías, following the curved coastline of Bahía de Banderas, is **Punta Mita.** Once a truly rustic village of fishermen and bamboo houses, Punta Mita is developing its own identity as a luxury destination. Five super-exclusive, luxury-boutique resorts, numerous private villas, and three golf courses are in the works. As of 2004, only the Four Seasons Resort (see review later in this chapter) and its adjacent Jack Nicklaus Signature golf course are open. This spot of white-sand beaches and clear waters was once home to an ancient celestial observatory, and you can't imagine a more exquisite setting. Punta Mita is a departure from the other beaches in the area.

Marina Vallarta

If you head south from the airport, the first area you come to is **Marina Vallarta,** a resort city within Puerto Vallarta, located on the immediate right as you come into town from the airport. Guests here feel a world apart from the quaintness of downtown Puerto Vallarta. Marina Vallarta has the most modern luxury hotels of any area in town, plus a huge marina with 450 yacht slips, a golf course, restaurants and bars, and several shopping plazas.

Because the area began life as a swamp and was later filled in for development, the beaches are the least desirable in the area, with darker sand and seasonal inflows of cobblestones washing down from the mountains and rivers and then up on the beaches. However, the exquisite pools at the oceanfront hotels more than make up for this shortcoming.

The **Marina Vallarta Club de Golf** (☎ 322-221-0073), an 18-hole golf course designed by Joe Finger, is within walking distance of most of the hotels. (See Chapter 17 for more information on golf and other activities in Puerto Vallarta.)

Although this isn't the area of choice if you're a true beach aficionado, Marina Vallarta is nice for families and for vacationers looking for lots of centralized activity. The complex is attractive and clean, and the public transportation is good. If you choose to travel by taxi, going from Marina to downtown Puerto Vallarta takes about 20 minutes, which is due to traffic more than distance, and costs about $7.

Hotel Zone

The next area you encounter heading south from the airport toward town is known as the **Hotel Zone** because of all the high-rise hotels located side-by-side along the main roadway. Here, the main street running between the airport and town is called Avenida Francisco Medina Ascencio, but it's sometimes referred to as Avenida de las Palmas for the stately palm trees that line the strip of land that divides the road. The tourism boom that Vallarta enjoyed in the mid-1970s gave birth to the hotels that line this road, and most of them have been exceptionally well maintained. All the hotels offer excellent, wide beachfronts with generally tranquil waters for swimming. This area is home to more casual, less expensive hotels that offer a great beach as a bonus.

The long and wide stretch of golden beach fronting the Hotel Zone has smoother sand and more watersports concessions than either Marina Vallarta or downtown. Although many shopping plazas line the main road in front of the hotels, they mostly service the large residential community to the east. You find the most interesting restaurants and intriguing shops downtown or back in Marina, but from the Hotel Zone, you're only a quick taxi or bus ride away from either of these areas.

El Centro Vallarta

Few beach resorts in Mexico offer what Puerto Vallarta exudes — the feeling that you're actually in Mexico. Staying in the **central downtown** area provides the charm of a traditional village and proximity to a tropical beach. Sophisticated services, all classes and types of restaurants, sizzling nightspots, and enough shops and galleries to tempt even the most jaded consumers are contained within the cobblestone streets and welcoming atmosphere of the central town.

Cool breezes flow down from the mountains along the Río Cuale (Cuale River), which runs through the center of town. The boardwalk, or *malecón,* that borders the main waterfront street boasts fanciful public sculptures, lively restaurants, shops, bars — and timeshare sales booths. The *malecón* is a magnet for both residents and visitors who walk its length while taking in the ocean breeze, a gorgeous sunset, or a perfect, moonlit night.

Accommodations here may be older, but they're inexpensive and generally well kept — plus they have plenty of character. In addition to being able to reach any downtown destination on foot, the neighborhood is as safe as it is charming.

Just south of downtown, the **Playa Los Muertos** area has recently undergone a renaissance. It's now not only a place offering great values in accommodations, dining, and nightlife, but also an added plus for the Los Muertos neighborhood is that it also has funky charm, which you can experience in the sidewalk cafes, great restaurants, and casual nightspots. Economically priced hotels and good-value guesthouses dominate accommodations here. Another bonus for the Los Muertos neighborhood is that most of Vallarta's nightlife activity is now centered in the areas south of the Río Cuale and along Olas Altas.

The southern shore

Hillsides dotted with private villas and a few large hotels surround the coastal highway. Immediately south of town lies the exclusive residential and rental district of **Conchas Chinas.** La Jolla de Mismaloya resort lies 10km (6 miles) south of town on **Playa Mismaloya** (where *The Night of the Iguana* was filmed). No roads service the southern shoreline of Bahía de Banderas, but three small coastal villages are popular attractions for visitors to Puerto Vallarta: **Las Animas, Quimixto,** and **Yelapa,** which are all accessible only by boat. Many visitors mistakenly believe that these villages are islands, but they're actually located along the same coast. Yelapa offers some rustic accommodations in addition to making a great destination for an enjoyable day-trip (see Chapter 17 for more on things to see and do in Yelapa). Las Animas and Quimixto don't offer any accommodations.

Beyond a varied selection of hotels, Puerto Vallarta has many other types of accommodations. Oceanfront or marina-view condominiums and elegant private villas are also available; both options can offer a better value and more ample space for families or small groups. For more information on short-term rentals, check out the Web site at www.virtualvallarta.com, which lists a selection of rental options. Prices start at $99 a night for non-beachfront condos and go up to $1,000 for penthouse condos or private villas. Susan Wiseman's **Bayside Properties,** Francisca Rodríguez 160, at the corner of Olas Altas

(☎ **322-222-0568;** www.puertovallartabayside.com), rents gay-friendly condos, villas, and hotels for individuals and large groups. She can arrange airport pickup and in-villa cooks.

Puerto Vallarta's Best Accommodations

For each hotel, I include specific rack rates for two people spending one night in a double room during high season (Christmas to Easter) unless otherwise indicated. *Rack rates* simply mean published rates and tend to be the highest rates paid — you can do better, especially if you're purchasing a package that includes airfare (see Chapter 5 for tips on avoiding paying rack rates). Prices quoted here include the 17% room tax. Please refer to the Introduction of this book for an explanation of the price categories.

It's not unusual for many hotels to double their normal rates during Christmas and Easter weeks, but low-season rates can be anywhere from 20% to 60% below high-season rates. *Note:* Some rates may seem much higher than others, but many of these rates are "all-inclusive" — meaning that your meals and beverages are included in the price of your stay. All-inclusive rates also take into account all tips and taxes and most activities and entertainment.

All hotels listed here have both air conditioning and TVs, unless otherwise indicated.

Camino Real
$$$$–$$$$$ South Shore/Conchas Chinas

The original luxury hotel in Puerto Vallarta, the Camino Real has retained its place as a premier property despite newer arrivals. It unquestionably has the nicest beach of any Vallarta hotel — soft, white sand and a private cove. On the beach, numerous shade palapas are available, along with a chair, towels, and food and beverage service. Both the nature of the geography and the physical boundaries set it apart from other properties — with a lush mountain backdrop, the Camino Real retains the exclusivity that made it popular from the beginning — yet it's only a 5- to 10-minute ride to town. The hotel consists of two buildings: the 250-room main hotel, which curves gently as it traces the shape of the Playa Las Estacas, and a newer, 11-story Camino Real Club tower, also facing the beach and ocean. An ample pool with an in-pool bar fronts the main building and faces the beach. Standard rooms in the main building are large. Some of the rooms have sliding doors that open onto the beach, and others have balconies. The standard rooms in the tower at the Royal Beach Club feature balconies with whirlpool tubs. All rooms are decorated in the signature vibrant colors of Camino Real hotels. New owners have scheduled this hotel for some renovations and upgrades, though it's still remarkably well maintained. For libations and sustenance, the property has four restaurants and a lobby bar that specializes in a wide selection of premium tequilas. Two lighted, grass tennis courts and a small fitness room with weights are also on-site.

Carretera Barra de Navidad, Km 3.5, Playa Las Estacas. ☎ *800-722-6466 in the U.S. and Canada, or 322-221-5000. Fax: 322-221-6000.* www.pvr-caminoreal.com. *337 units. Free secured parking. Rack rates: High season $180–$265 double, $700–$1,100 suite; low season $135–$150 double, $400–$880 suite. AE, DC, MC, V.*

Casa Tres Vidas
$$$$$ **South Shore/Conchas Chinas**

Terraced down a hillside to Playa Conchas Chinas, Casa Tres Vidas is actu-ally three individual villas that make a great — and affordable — place to stay for families or groups of friends. Set on a stunning private cove, Tres Vidas provides the experience of having your own private villa — complete with service staff. Under new ownership since 2000, Tres Vidas has been upgraded in furnishings and amenities, and it's an outstanding value for the location (close to town), sweeping panoramic views from every room, and excellent personal service. Each of the three villas has at least two levels, more than 5,000 square feet of mostly open-design living area, a pri-vate swimming pool, a heated whirlpool, and air-conditioned bedrooms. (Because the layout is so open, the rest of the rooms don't have air con-ditioning.) The Villa Alta penthouse villa has three bedrooms, plus a rooftop deck with pool and bar. Vida Sol, the center villa, has an 18-foot-high domed living room with fireplace, and features graceful arches and columns. Although it has three bedrooms, it can sleep ten — two of the bedrooms have two king-size beds in them. Directly on the ocean, Vida Mar is a four-bedroom villa that can accommodate eight guests. An added bonus: Gourmet meals are prepared in your villa twice a day — you only pay for the cost of the food, and you choose the menu. Casa Tres Vidas is owned and managed by the owners of the adjacent Quinta María Cortez (see review later in this chapter).

Calle Sagitario 132, below the Conchas Chinas Mercado (market). ☎ *888-640-8100 or 801-531-8100 in the U.S., or 322-221-5815. Fax: 322-221-5327.* www.casatres vidas.com. *3 villas. Very limited street parking available. Rack rates: High season: Villa Alta $510, Villa Sol $485, Villa Mar $510. Low season: Villa Alta $375, Villa Sol $350, Villa Mar $375. Prices are per night for complete villa, full services, and two meals prepared. AE, MC, V.*

Fiesta Americana Puerto Vallarta
$$$$ **Hotel Zone**

The Fiesta Americana's towering, three-story, thatched-palapa lobby is a landmark in the Hotel Zone, but this hotel is even more well known for its excellent beach and friendly service. The nine-story, terracotta-colored

Puerto Vallarta Hotel Zone Accommodations

Camino Real **8**
Casa Tres Vidas **6**
Fiesta Americana
  Puerto Vallarta **4**
Four Seasons Resort
  Punta Mita **1**
Grand & Club Marival **3**
Paradise Village **2**
Premier Hotel & Spa **5**
Quinta María Cortez **7**
Velas Vallarta
  Suite Resort **10**
Verana **9**
Westin Regina Resort **11**

building embraces a large plaza with a big pool and bar area facing the beach. Marble-trimmed rooms in neutral tones with pastel accents come with carved headboards and comfortable rattan and wicker furniture. All rooms have private balconies with ocean and pool views. In addition to the three restaurants, the Fiesta Americana has a lobby bar with live music nightly. A children's program and the excellent pool and beach facilities make this hotel a great choice for families.

Av. Francisco Medina Ascencio, Km 2.5. ☎ *800-FIESTA-1 in the U.S., or 322-224-2010. Fax: 322-224-2108.* www.fiestaamericana.com. *291 units. Limited free parking. Rack rates: High season $180 double; low season $120–$160 double. AE, DC, MC, V.*

Four Seasons Resort Punta Mita
$$$$$ Punta Mita

Located on the undisputed best beach in the area, this boutique hotel artfully combines seclusion and pampered service with a welcoming sense of comfort. The 113 rooms and 27 suites are in three-story *casitas* (little houses), which surround the main building where the lobby, cultural center, restaurants, and pool are located. The stretch of beachfront is the only white-sand beach in the bay, due to a coral reef located just offshore, which also makes the water a dreamy and translucent shade of aquamarine. Every guest room offers an ocean view from a large terrace or balcony. Most suites also offer a private plunge pool, as well as a separate sitting room. Room interiors are plush and spacious with a king or two double beds, a seating area, and an oversized bathroom with a deep soaking tub, a separate glass-enclosed shower, and a dual-vanity sink. This is the place to go to completely get away from it all, but remember that you're at least 45 minutes from Puerto Vallarta's activities. For most guests, this isn't a problem — the Four Seasons is so relaxing and comfortable that thinking of anyplace else is hard. The centerpiece of the resort is the 18-hole (with an optional 19th hole of play on a natural island) Jack Nicklaus Signature golf course. The course has ocean views from every hole, and eight holes border the ocean. A full-service spa, complete tennis center, and watersports center round out the activities. In addition to the two restaurants, you can enjoy a golf clubhouse, a lobby bar, and 24-hour room service. The heated infinity pool (a type of pool that has the edge that seems to disappear into the horizon) is surrounded by private cabañas, and waiters come by every so often to offer chilled towels or a spritz of water. A notable attraction is the cultural center — a library-style environment with free Internet access and a menu of entertaining lectures on Mexican culture, including a popular tequila tasting! The Kids for All Seasons activities program is hands-down the best place for children to enjoy their vacation as much as you will. The Four Seasons was the first resort to be located in Punta Mita, an exclusive development north of Vallarta that's all the buzz in luxury travel. In late 2005, La Solana, a Rosewood Resort, will join it.

Downtown Puerto Vallarta Accommodations

Punta Mita, Bahía de Banderas, Nayarit 63734. ☎ *800-332-3442*, 329-291-6000. Fax:
329-291-6060. www.fourseasons.com/puntamita. *140 units. Valet parking.
Rack rates: High season $360–$527 double, $680–$900 suite; low season $280–$360
double, $480–$650 suite. AE, DC, MC, V.*

Grand & Club Marival
$$$$ **Nuevo Vallarta**

This all-inclusive hotel, located almost by itself at the northernmost end
of Nuevo Vallarta, is a refreshing choice compared to the mega-resorts
that tend to dominate all-inclusive options. The broad, sandy beach is
one of the real assets here — it stretches more than 500 yards. There's
also an extensive activities program, including fun for children. This
Mediterranean-style property is relatively small, but it offers a large variety of rooms ranging from standard rooms with no balconies to large
master suites with whirlpools. Choose from among six restaurants, plus

eight bars, for your dining and drinking desires. The hotel has three pools and a whirlpool for adults, plus two pools for children and four lighted tennis courts. If you're coming from the Puerto Vallarta airport, Club Marival is the first resort to your right on Cocoteros when you enter Nuevo Vallarta from the second entrance.

Paseo de los Cocoteros y Blvd s/n. ☎ *322-297-0100. Fax: 322-297-0262.* www. cameleonmarival.com/marival.htm. *646 units. Rack rates: High season $246 double, low season $230 double. Rates are all-inclusive. Ask about seasonal specials. AE, MC, V.*

Hacienda San Angel

$$$$$ Centro

This enchanting bed and breakfast may not be on the beach, but you'll hardly miss it, because you'll be so pampered in the stunning suites, or satisfied enjoying the view from the rooftop heated pool or Jacuzzi and sundeck. Once Richard Burton's home in Puerto Vallarta, this B&B is located just behind Puerto Vallarta's famed church — Our Lady of Guadalupe — making it easy walking distance to the downtown restaurants, shopping, and galleries. The Hacienda is comprised of three villas; the first two are joined to the third villa by a path that winds through a lovely terraced garden filled with tropical plants, flowers, statuary, and a charming fountain. A large, heated pool and deck offer panoramic views of the city and Bahía de Banderas, while a second sundeck with Jacuzzi literally overlooks the church's crown, across to the water beyond. Each of the Hacienda's nine elegant suites is individually decorated, accented with exquisite antiques and original art, and has a private bath, air conditioning, remote control cable TV, telephone, and bathrobes. Bed linens and coverings are of the finest quality, with touches such as Venetian lace and goose-down pillows. Each morning, you wake up to a continental breakfast served outside your suite at your requested hour, or you can choose a full breakfast (for an additional charge). The Hacienda's private chef also prepares a menu of snacks and light meals during the day, or can prepare a sumptuous private dinner upon request. From Monday through Saturday, guests can attend a complimentary cocktail hour and down one of Hacienda's signature drinks (such as the Celestial Sin — a wicked blend of vodka and blue Curacao), accompanied by snacks. With its commitment to highly personalized services, the Hacienda's concierge can arrange excursions, golf games, or on-site spa treatments. Sophisticated style, coupled with casual Vallarta charm, make Hacienda San Angel the newest "find" in Mexico for the discriminating traveler.

Miramar 336. ☎ *322-222-2692.* www.haciendasanangel.com. *9 suites. Very limited street parking. Rack rates: High season $275–$330 double; low season $150–$210 double. All rates include daily continental breakfast and evening cocktail hour. Rates for the entire Hacienda or separate villas consisting of three suites each are also available. No credit cards.*

Hotel Molino de Agua

$$–$$$ Centro

With an unrivaled location adjacent to both the Río Cuale and the ocean, this hotel is a mix of stone and stucco-walled bungalows and small beach-front buildings spread out among winding walkways and lush tropical gardens. If you want a place that's more intimate than a standard hotel, in a location that's more immersed in town activities, this is the best choice. It's located immediately past the Río Cuale — after crossing the southbound bridge, the hotel is on your right. Although the hotel is centrally located on a main street, open spaces, big trees, birds, and lyrical fountains lend tranquility to the space. The individual bungalows are located in the gardens between the entrance and the ocean; make sure to request one away from the front of the property where street noise can keep you up at night. The bungalows are well maintained, and the simple furnishings include a bed, wooden desk and chair, Mexican tile floors, beamed ceilings, and beautifully tiled bathrooms. Wicker rocking chairs grace their private patios. Rooms and suites in the small, two- and three-story buildings on the beach have double beds and private terraces. There are no TVs or telephones in any of the rooms. In addition to an oceanside pool, a second pool with a whirlpool is adjacent to the Lion's Court restaurant and bar.

Ignacio L. Vallarta 130, just over the southbound bridge on the right side. ☎ *322-222-1957. Fax: 322-222-6056.* www.molinodeagua.com. *58 units. Free secured parking. Rack rates: High season garden bungalows $97 double, oceanfront rooms and suites $135–$155 double; low season bungalows $75 double, rooms and suites $89–$110 double. AE, MC, V.*

Paradise Village

$$$–$$$$$ Nuevo Vallarta

This resort truly lives up to its name. It feels more like a self-contained village than a resort and is indeed a paradise bordering one of the most stunning stretches of broad, sandy beach in the bay. Paradise Village offers a full array of guest services, ranging from an on-site disco to a full-service European spa and health club. In 2002, the resort added the 18-hole El Tigre golf course to its roster of guest amenities (see Chapter 17). Styled in a Mayan-influenced design, the collection of pyramid-shaped buildings houses all-suite accommodations in studio, one-bedroom, and two-bedroom configurations. All the suites are well designed and feature muted color schemes, sitting areas, and kitchenettes — making them ideal for families or groups of friends. The Mayan theme extends to both oceanfront pools with mythical creatures forming water slides and water-falls. The exceptional spa is reason enough to book a vacation here. Services include treatments, hydrotherapy, massage (including massage on the beach), and fitness and yoga classes. Special spa packages are always available, and they can include a full fitness evaluation if you're up for it. Four tennis courts, a lap pool, a basketball court, beach volleyball courts, and a watersports center complement the spa and fitness center. In addition to the two full-service restaurants, beachfront snack bars and special theme nights add to the dining options. The kid's club and petting zoo are especially popular with families.

Paseo de los Cocoteros 001. ☎ *800-995-5714, 322-226-6770. Fax: 322-226-6752.* www.paradisevillage.com. *Free covered parking. 490 units. Rack rates: High season $165–$565 double; low season $140–$483 double. AE, DC, MC, V.*

Playa Los Arcos Hotel & Suites
$$–$$$ **Centro**

An excellent value and always popular, this hotel is a personal favorite of mine. Its stellar location in the heart of Playa Los Muertos is central to the Olas Altas sidewalk-cafe action and close to downtown. The four-story structure is U-shaped, facing the ocean, with a small swimming pool in the courtyard. Rooms with private balconies overlook the pool, and the ten suites have ocean views. Five of the suites have kitchenettes. The standard rooms are small but pleasantly decorated with carved wooden furniture painted pale pink, and they're immaculate. A palapa beachside bar with occasional live entertainment, a gourmet coffee shop, and the popular Kaiser Maximilian's gourmet restaurant (see Chapter 16) are on the premises. The hotel is located 7 blocks south of the river.

Olas Altas 380. ☎ *800-648-2403 in the U.S., or 322-222-0583. Fax: 322-226-7104.* www.playalosarcos.com. *175 units. Limited street parking available. Rack rates: High season $100–$120 double, $168 suite; low season $79 double, $120 suite. AE, MC, V.*

Premier Hotel & Spa
$$–$$$$$ **Centro**

You couldn't ask for a better location if you want to explore the vibrancy that Vallarta's *centro* has to offer. Located on a wide swathe of golden sand beach — and just a few blocks north of the start of the *malecón* — the Premier is easy walking distance or a quick taxi ride to the downtown restaurants, shops, galleries, and clubs. One of the newer hotels in Vallarta (opened in 1999), the architecture is contemporary, but its size gives the hotel an intimate feel. With a first-rate spa and a policy that restricts guests to ages 16 and older, it's a place that caters to relaxation. Four types of rooms are available, and all are decorated in warm colors with tile floors and light wood furnishings. Deluxe rooms have ocean views, with a choice of a king bed or two doubles, a respectable seating area with comfortable chairs, plus a sizable private balcony — request one of several rooms that has an outdoor whirlpool. Premiere suites are larger, and have a separate seating area; seven additional suites have a separate living room plus a dining area with private bar and a spacious terrace. These rooms also have a double whirlpool tub and a separate glass-enclosed shower. The top-of-the-line master suites have all these amenities, plus an outdoor whirlpool on an extra-spacious balcony. Thick terrycloth robes, slippers, hairdryers, coffeemakers, and a daily restocking of complimentary bottled water are among the notable in-room amenities. The beachfront pool is on the small side, but it's heated in the winter, overlooks the beach, and has attendants to keep you supplied with drinks, snacks, and towels. You have three restaurants to choose from, all which offer spa cuisine dining options, plus 24-hour room service. If you're not tempted by the nearby and accessible dining choices in downtown Vallarta, the Premier offers an all-inclusive option, with all meals and drinks included.

The stunning bi-level spa is the hotel's real attraction. Scented with aromatherapy and glowing with candlelight, it uses top-notch, 100% natural products, most based on Mexico's natural treasures such as coconut, aloe, and papaya. The spa has separate men's and women's steam rooms, sauna, locker/dressing rooms, and six private treatment rooms, including hydrotheraphy rooms, for massage and skin care treatments. There's also a salon and well-equipped fitness room.

San Salvador 117. ☎ **877-886-9176** *in the U.S., or 322-226-7001. Fax: 322-226-7043.* www.premiereonline.com.mx. *83 units. Rack rates: High season suite only $135–$374 double, all-inclusive $448–$598 double; low season suite only $121–$325 double, all-inclusive $334–$448 double. AE, MC, V.*

Quinta María Cortez
$$$–$$$$ South Shore/Conchas Chinas

An eclectic, sophisticated, and imaginative B&B on the beach, this is Puerto Vallarta's most original place to stay — and one of Mexico's most memorable inns. Seven large suites, uniquely decorated in antiques, whimsical curios, and original art, all feature a private bathroom, and most include a kitchenette and balcony. Sunny terraces, a small pool, and a central gathering area with fireplace and palapa-topped dining area (where an excellent full breakfast is served) occupy different levels of this seven-story house. A rooftop terrace offers yet another alternative for taking in the sun and is among the very best sunset-watching spots in town. Quinta María is located on a beautiful cove on Playa Conchas Chinas where the rocks sitting just offshore form tranquil tide pools. This B&B wins my highest recommendation, but admittedly, it's not for everyone. Air-conditioned areas are limited due to the open nature of the suites and common areas, but then, the openness is a large part of the allure. Vacationers who love Quinta María find themselves charmed by this remarkable place and consistently gracious service and return year after year. Not appropriate for children.

Calle Sagitario 126, Playa Conchas Chinas. ☎ **888-640-8100** *in the U.S., or 322-221-5317. Fax: 322-221-5327.* www.quinta-maria.com. *7 units. Very limited street parking available. Rack rates: High season $150–$250 double; low season $100–$185 double. Rates include breakfast. AE, MC, V.*

Velas Vallarta Suite Resort

$$$$–$$$$$ **Marina Vallarta**

The beachfront Velas Vallarta is an excellent choice for families because each suite offers a full-size and fully equipped kitchen, ample living and dining areas, separate bedroom(s), and a large balcony with seating. Following a complete makeover in 2003, the suites are decorated in a sophisticated, modern design featuring jewel-tone colors, Huichol art and Mexican textiles, feather beds with goose-down comforters, texturized wall coverings, new 27-inch flat-screen TVs, modern kitchen appliances, and teak wood furniture on balconies and terraces. Special extras include luxury bath amenities and even a pillow menu, from which you can choose the type of pillow you want (based on firmness and stuffing) from a menu of options. This property is actually part hotel and part full-ownership condominium, which means each suite is the size of a true residential unit offering the feeling of a home away from home. The suites all have partial ocean views, and they face onto a central area where three free-form swimming pools, complete with bridges and waterfalls, meander through tropical gardens. A full range of services — including restaurants, mini-market, deli, tennis courts, spa, and boutiques — means you'd never need to leave the place if you didn't want to. The Marina Vallarta Golf Club is across the street, and special packages are available to Velas guests. With a special on-site wedding planner who can arrange every detail in one of a variety of ceremonies, Velas has become a popular place for tying the knot. The resort also offers the Gold Crown All-Inclusive option, with one of the most premium all-inclusive programs in Mexico, offering lobster, finer cuts of beef, and premium liquors, as opposed to the lower-cost food and liquor options provided with most all-inclusives.

Paseo de la Marina 485. ☎ *800-835-2778 in the U.S. and Canada, or 322-221-0091. Fax: 322-221-0751.* www.velasvallarta.com. *361 units. Free indoor parking. Rack rates: Studio $250 double, $325–$650 suite; all-inclusive studio $340 double, suite $430–$1,200. AE, DC, MC, V.*

Verana

$$$$–$$$$$ **Yelapa**

The magical Verana is my current favorite place to stay in Mexico. It has an unparalleled ability to inspire immediate relaxation and a deep connection with the natural beauty of the spectacular coast. Although Yelapa is 30 minutes by water taxi from town, even if you're not familiar with the village, I recommend that you consider it. Verana has six rustic yet sophisticated suites, set into a hillside with sweeping views of the mountains and ocean. Each is a work of art, hand-crafted with care and creativity by owners Heinz Leger, a former film production designer, and prop stylist Veronique Lieve. Each suite has a private terrace and two beds, but you won't find TVs, telephones, stereos, or other distractions. My favorite suite is the Studio; it's the most contemporary, with a wall of floor-to-ceiling windows that perfectly frame the spectacular view. The European-trained chef prepares a nightly dinner of scrumptious creations — global cuisine with a touch of Mexico — at the on-site restaurant, which also serves breakfast and lunch. To while away your days, soak up some sun at the hilltop pool with sun chairs, use a small but ecletic library of diverse reading materials, and relax in a sumptuous indoor-outdoor spa. Tours and excursions to nearby — but secluded — beaches are also available, or it's a comfortable walk into Yelapa's town and lively beach. Compare this to the prices of the other rustic-chic resorts along Mexico's Pacific coast, and you find it's a true value. Adventurous travelers shouldn't miss a stay at this unique place. To arrive, management helps arrange transportation to Boca de Tomatlán, where you catch a private boat that takes you to Yelapa; from there, it's a gentle 9-minute hike up to Verana (a mule helps with your bags).

Yelapa, 48300. ☎ 800-677-5156 or 661-946-7477 in the U.S., or 322-222-2360. www.verana.com. *6 villas. Rack rates: Villa $250 double; 3-bedroom Casa Grande $400 double; 5-night minimum stay (7 nights during holiday seasons; shorter stays based on availability). Extra person $95 per night. Mandatory meal plan (breakfast, lunch, and dinner) is $65 per person per day. AE, MC, V.*

Westin Regina Resort
$$$$–$$$$$ Marina Vallarta

The service standard of Westin hotels, combined with the stunning architecture and vibrant colors of this resort, make it a Puerto Vallarta favorite — ideal for almost any traveler or type of vacation. Although the grounds are large — more than 21 acres with 850 feet of beachfront — the warm service and gracious hospitality always reminds me of an intimate resort. The central free-form pool with hundreds of tall palms surrounding it is spectacular. You may find hammocks strung between the palms closest to the beach where there's also a wooden playground for kids. Rooms are contemporary in style and brightly colored in textured fabrics. They feature oversized wood furnishings, tile floors, original art, tub/shower-combination bathrooms, and in-room safes. Balconies have panoramic views. Two floors of rooms are designated as the Royal Beach Club and come with special VIP services and amenities. The fitness center here is one of the most modern, well-equipped facilities of its kind in Vallarta, and three grass tennis courts are available for day or night play. Guests enjoy play privileges at the Marina Vallarta Golf Club and a kid's club takes care of the activities for younger travelers. Of the two restaurants, the beachside Garibaldi's is known as the best seafood restaurant in the Marina Vallarta area.

Paseo de la Marina Sur 205. ☎ 800-228-3000 in the U.S., or 322-226-1100. Fax: 322-226-1131 or 322-226-1145. www.westinpv.com. *280 units. Free parking. Rack rates: High season $205–$395 double, $530–$770 suite; low season $160–205 double, $335–$530 suite. AE, DC, MC, V.*

Chapter 15

Settling into Puerto Vallarta

By Lynne Bairstow

- -

In This Chapter

▶ Knowing what to expect when you arrive

▶ Finding your way around town

▶ Discovering helpful information and resources

- -

From the moment you arrive, you're likely to settle into Puerto Vallarta's welcoming ways. In this chapter, I take you from the plane, through the airport, and to your hotel, helping you quickly get your bearings in this easy-to-navigate town. I also provide tips on everything from taxis to Internet access. You have insider information here — Puerto Vallarta has been my home for the past 14 years!

Arriving in Puerto Vallarta

Puerto Vallarta's airport is easy to get through, so you can reach the sun-soaked days in no time. Recently recognized as the friendliest international city by the travel magazine *Condé Nast Traveler,* Puerto Vallarta is a pleasure. The people here are genuinely welcoming and proud to share their town with visitors. They strive to make your stay as pleasant as possible. Visitors usually get a taste of Puerto Vallarta's hospitality right from the start — you should find both immigration and customs to be brief, generally easy procedures.

Navigating passport control and customs

After you deplane, you go through a jetway and wind your way down some stairs into the immigration-clearance area, or a bus may take you directly to immigration from your plane. When you reach immigration, an officer asks you to show your passport and your completed tourist card, the **FMT** (see Chapter 7 for all the FMT details).

Your FMT is an important document, so take good care of it. You're supposed to keep the FMT with you at all times because you may be required to show it if you run into any sort of trouble. You also need to turn it back in upon departure, or you may be unable to leave without replacing it.

Next up is the baggage claim area. Here, porters stand by to help with your bags, and they're well worth the price of the tip — about a dollar a bag. After you collect your luggage, you pass through another checkpoint. Something that looks like a traffic light awaits you here. You press a button, and if the light turns green, you're free to go. If it turns red, you need to open each of your bags for a quick search. It's Mexico's random search procedure for customs. If you have an unusually large bag, or an excessive amount of luggage, you may be searched regardless of the traffic-light outcome.

Just past the traffic light, you pass into an enclosed space with people behind counters — it may look like a tourist information center, but the people behind the counters are actually timeshare sales reps. Unless you want to start your vacation shopping for timeshares with these high-pressure sales pros, keep moving.

Just beyond this entryway you see a bustling crowd of people waiting for fellow passengers, transportation representatives, and taxi drivers promoting their services. If you're part of a package tour that includes ground transportation to your hotel, start looking for your rep here. Generally he or she is carrying a sign with your name or the name of your tour company on it. If you haven't arranged transportation, head for the blue and orange booths marked "Taxi" to purchase your set-price tickets to your hotel.

Getting to your hotel

The airport is close to the north end of town near the Marina Vallarta, about 10km (6 miles) from downtown. **Transportes Terrestres** minivans and **Aeromovil** taxis make the trip from the airport to all the hotel areas. Costs for both options are determined by zones — clearly posted at the respective ticket booths. Fares start at $8 for a ride to Marina Vallarta and go up to $25 for a trip to the south-shore hotels. **Airport taxis** (Aeromovil) are federally licensed taxis that operate exclusively to provide transportation from the airport. Their fares are almost three times as high as city (yellow) taxis. A trip from the airport to downtown Puerto Vallarta costs $14, whereas a return trip using a city taxi costs only $4.50. Yellow cabs are restricted from picking up passengers leaving the airport.

If you don't have too much baggage, you can walk across the highway via the overpass at the side exit of the airport. Yellow cabs are lined up on the other side of the highway ready to take you anywhere your heart desires for a third of the price of the airport cabs.

Getting Around Puerto Vallarta

Puerto Vallarta is very easy to get around. Essentially, one main road stretches from the airport in both directions around the bay. Puerto Vallarta has followed this central roadway — which changes names a few times along the way — as it has grown along the beach to the north and south. Linking the airport to downtown, the road is called **Avenida Francisco Medina Ascencio** (sometimes still referred to by its previous name, Avenida de Las Palmas). Along this main thoroughfare are many luxury hotels (in the area called the **Zona Hotelera,** or **Hotel Zone**), plus several shopping centers with casual restaurants.

As you come into the central downtown area, known as *El Centro,* the main road becomes **Paseo Díaz Ordaz,** which runs north to south through the town. The seaside promenade, called the *malecón,* which borders Paseo Díaz Ordaz, is frequently used as a reference point for giving directions. This section of downtown marked off by the *malecón* is the original town and is sometimes referred to as *Viejo Vallarta* — the cultural and civic heart of Puerto Vallarta. City hall, the waterfront, the open-air Los Arcos Theater, the landmark Our Lady of Guadalupe church, and scores of restaurants, galleries, and shops all call this area home.

From the waterfront, the town stretches back into the hills a half-dozen blocks. The areas bordering the **Río Cuale** (Cuale River) are the oldest parts of town — and home to Gringo Gulch, named for the dozens of U.S. expatriates that made their homes here in the late 1950s.

The area immediately south of the river, called **Olas Altas** after its main street (and sometimes **Los Muertos** after the beach of the same name), is now home to a growing selection of sidewalk cafes, fine restaurants, espresso bars, and hip nightclubs (many with live music).

From the center of town, nearly everything both north and south of the river is within walking distance. **Bridges** on Insurgentes (northbound traffic) and Ignacio L. Vallarta (southbound traffic) link the two sections of town.

Taking a taxi

Taxi travel is the preferred way for getting around Puerto Vallarta. Away from the airport, taxis are plentiful and relatively inexpensive. Most trips from downtown to the northern Zona Hotelera and Marina Vallarta cost between $3.50 and $5; a trip between Marina Vallarta and Playa Mismaloya to the south costs $8. Rates are charged by zone and are generally posted in hotel lobbies. You can also hire taxis by the hour or day for longer trips when you prefer to leave the driving to someone else, a good alternative to renting a car. Rates run between $10 and $12 per hour with discounts available for full-day rates.

Beware of restaurant recommendations offered by taxi drivers — many drivers receive a commission from restaurants where they discharge passengers. Be especially wary if a driver tries to talk you out of a restaurant you've already selected and to one of his own personal "favorites."

Catching a bus

Another option for travel around town — combining cheap, easy transportation with some local color — is Puerto Vallarta's city buses. They run from the airport through the Zona Hotelera along Calle Morelos (1 block inland from the *malecón*), across the Río Cuale, and inland on Vallarta, looping back through the downtown hotel and restaurant districts on Insurgentes and several other downtown streets. To get to the northern Zona Hotelera strip from old Puerto Vallarta, take the Zona Hoteles, Ixtapa, or Las Juntas bus. These buses in the Zona Hotelera follow the same route and may also post the names of hotels they pass such as Krystal, Fiesta Americana, Sheraton, and others. Buses marked "Marina Vallarta" travel inside the Marina Vallarta area and stop at the major hotels there. City buses, which cost about 50¢, can service just about all your transportation needs frequently and inexpensively.

Buses generally run from 6 a.m. to 11 p.m., and waiting more than a few minutes for one is rare. An additional bus route travels south every 10 to 15 minutes to either Playa Mismaloya or Boca de Tomatlán (the last point on the southern shore of the bay that can be reached by land — the destination is indicated in the front window) from Plaza Lázaro Cárdenas, a few blocks south of the river at Cárdenas and Suárez, and along Basilio Badillo, between Piño Suárez and Insurgentes.

Buses in Vallarta tend to be rather aggressive, and some even sport appropriately intimidating names — "Terminator," "Rambo," and "Tornado" are three of my favorites. Don't tempt fate by assuming that these buses stop for pedestrians. Although Vallarta is an extremely low-crime city, bus accidents are frequent — and often fatal.

Renting a car

Rental cars are available at the airport and through travel agencies, but unless you're planning a distant side trip, don't bother. Car rentals are expensive, averaging $60 per day, and parking around town is difficult.

If you see a sign for a $10 Jeep rental or $20 car rental, be aware that it's a lure to get people to attend timeshare presentations. Unless you're interested in a timeshare, stopping to inquire is a waste of your time.

Cruising around

The cruise-ship pier, or *muelle,* also called Terminal Marítima, is where **excursion boats** to Yelapa, Las Animas, Quimixto, and the Marietas Islands depart. The pier is north of town near the airport and just an inexpensive taxi or bus ride away from the Vallarta region. Just take any bus marked "Ixtapa," "Las Juntas," "Pitillal," or "Aurora" and tell the driver to let you off at the Terminal Marítima. *Note:* Odd though it may seem, you have to pay a $1 fee to access the pier where the tour boats are docked.

Water taxis offering direct transportation to Yelapa, Las Animas, and Quimixto leave at 10:30 and 11 a.m. from the pier at Playa Los Muertos (south of downtown) on Rodolfo Rodríguez next to the Hotel Marsol. Another water taxi departs at 11 a.m. from the beachfront pier at the northern edge of the *malecón.* A round-trip ticket to Yelapa (the farthest point) costs $12. Return trips usually depart between 3 and 4 p.m., but confirm the pickup time with your water-taxi captain. Other water taxis depart from Boca de Tomatlán, located about 30 minutes south of town by public bus. These Boca de Tomatlán water taxis are a better option than those at Playa Los Muertos if you want more flexible departure and return times from the southern beaches. Generally, they leave on the hour for the southern shore destinations, or more frequently if there's heavy traffic. The price is about $10 round trip with rates clearly posted on a sign on the beach. You can hire a private boat taxi for between $35 and $50 (depending on your destination), which allows you to choose your own return time. The boats take up to eight people for that price, so people often band together at the beach to hire one.

Fast Facts: Puerto Vallarta

American Express
The local office (Morelos 660, at the corner of Abasolo; ☎ 01-800-333-3211 in Mexico, or 322-223-2955) is open Monday to Friday 9 a.m. to 6 p.m. and Saturday 9 a.m. to 1 p.m. This location offers excellent, efficient, travel-agency services in addition to offering currency-exchange and traveler's checks services.

Area Code
The telephone area code is **322**. The area code for Nuevo Vallarta and the northern areas is **329**.

Babysitters
Most of the larger hotels can easily arrange babysitters, but many sitters speak limited English. Rates range from $5 to $8 per hour.

Banks, ATMs, and Currency Exchange
Banks are located throughout downtown and in the other prime shopping areas of Vallarta. Most banks are open Monday to Friday 9 a.m. to 5 p.m. with partial hours on Saturday. You can find ATMs throughout Vallarta, including the central plaza downtown. They're increasingly becoming the most favorable way to exchange currency because they offer bank rates plus 24-hour, self-service convenience. Money exchange houses *(casas de cambio)* are also located

throughout town and offer longer hours than the banks with only slightly lower exchange rates.

Business Hours

Most offices maintain traditional Mexican hours of operation (9 a.m. to 2 p.m. and 4 p.m. to 8 p.m., daily), but shops remain open throughout the day. Offices tend to be closed on Saturday and Sunday, but shops are open on Saturday, at least, and increasingly offer limited hours of operation on Sunday. During peak season, many shops and galleries remain open as late as 10 p.m.

Climate

Vallarta is warm all year with tropical temperatures; however, evenings and early mornings in the winter months can turn quite cool. Summers are sunny, but an increase in humidity during the rainy season, between May and October, is the norm. Rains come almost every afternoon in June and July. These usually brief but strong showers are just enough to cool off the air for evening activities. September is the month in which heat and humidity are the least comfortable and rains are the heaviest.

Consular Agents

Both the U.S. and Canadian consulates maintain offices here in the building on the southern border of the central plaza (note the U.S. and Canadian flags). The **U.S. Consular Agency** office (☎ 322-222-0069; Fax: 322-223-0074; both available 24 hours a day for emergencies) is open Monday to Friday 10 a.m. to 2 p.m. The **Canadian Consulate** (☎ 322-293-0099 or 322-293-0098; 24-hour emergency line: 01-800-706-2900) is open Monday to Friday 9 a.m. to 3 p.m.

Emergencies

Police emergency (☎ 060); **local police** (☎ 322-290-0513 or 322-290-0512); **intensive care ambulance** (☎ 322-225-0386; *Note:* English-speaking assistance isn't always available at this number); **Red Cross** (☎ 322-222-1533).

Hospitals

Ameri-Med Urgent Care (☎ 322-221-0023; Fax: 322-221-0026; www.amerimed-hospitals.com) offers healthcare service 24 hours a day that meets U.S. standards and is located at the entrance to Marina Vallarta in the Neptune Plaza. In addition to excellent diagnostic capabilities, it also has emergency facilities and helicopters to evacuate patients to the United States. The excellent **San Javier Marina Hospital** (☎ 322-226-1010) also offers U.S.-standard healthcare service that's available 24 hours. It's located on the main highway across from the cruise-ship terminal (Terminal Marítima).

Information

The **Municipal Tourism Office** (Juárez and Independencia; ☎ 322-223-2500, ext. 230, ask for the Tourism Office) is in a corner of the white Presidencia Municipal building (city hall) on the northwest end of the main square. In addition to offering a listing of current events and a collection of promotional brochures for local activities and services, these folks can also assist you with specific questions — an English-speaking person is usually on staff. This is also the office of the tourist police. It's open Monday to Friday 8 a.m. to 4 p.m.

The exceptionally helpful and friendly **State Tourism Office** (Plaza Marina L 144, 2nd floor; ☎ 322-221-2676, 322-221-2677, or 322-221-2678) also offers promotional brochures and can assist you with specific questions about Puerto Vallarta and other points within the state of Jalisco including Guadalajara, the Costa Alegre, and the town of Tequila. It's open Monday to Friday 9 a.m. to 5 p.m. and Saturday 9 a.m. to 1 p.m.

Internet Access

Puerto Vallarta is probably the best-connected destination in Mexico as far as the Internet goes. Of the numerous cyber-cafes around town, one of the most popular is **The Net House** (Ignacio L. Vallarta 232, 2 blocks past the southbound bridge;

☎ 322-222-6953; E-mail: info@vallarta cafes.com). It's open daily 8 a.m. to 2 a.m. Rates are $4 per hour, and there are 21 computers with fast connections and English keyboards. **Café Net** (Olas Altas 250, at the corner of Basilio Badillo; ☎ 322-222-0092) has become a social hub. Rates run $2 for 30 minutes. Complete computer services, a full bar, and food service are also available. It's open daily 8 a.m. to 2 a.m. Some hotels also offer e-mail kiosks in their lobbies, but this is a more expensive option than the Net cafes.

Maps

One of the best around is the free American Express map, usually found at the tourist information offices and the local American Express office. Other free maps of the area are available at the Municipal Tourism Office, on the southeast corner of city hall (the corner nearest to the Our Lady of Guadalupe church).

Newspapers/Magazines

Vallarta Today, a daily English-language newspaper (☎ 322-225-3323 or 322-224-2829; www.vallartatoday.com), is a good source for local information and upcoming events. The quarterly city magazine, *Vallarta Lifestyles* (☎ 322-221-0106), is also very popular. It has plenty of helpful information and good colored maps of all the major tourist areas. Both publications are available for sale at area newsstands and hotel gift shops although you can also find them distributed for free at local businesses. The weekly *P.V. Tribune* (☎ 322-223-0585) is distributed free throughout town and offers an objective local viewpoint.

Pharmacy

CMQ Farmacia (Basilio Badillo 365; ☎ 322-222-1330) is open 24 hours and can also deliver to your hotel free of charge with a minimum purchase of $10. **Farmacia Guadalajara** (Emiliano Zapata 232; ☎ 322-224-1811) is also open 24 hours a day.

Police

The policemen in white, safari-style uniforms with white pith helmets belong to a special corps of English-speaking police established to assist tourists. For the main police department, call ☎ 322-290-0513 or 322-290-0512.

Post Office

The post office *(correo)* (Mina 188; ☎ 322-222-1888) is open Monday to Friday 9 a.m. to 6:30 p.m. and Saturday 9 a.m. to 1 p.m.

Safety

Puerto Vallarta enjoys a very low crime rate. Public transportation is perfectly safe to use, and tourist police (dressed in white safari uniforms with white hats) are available to answer questions, give directions, and offer assistance. Most crimes or encounters with the police are linked to using or purchasing drugs, so simply don't do it. *Note:* The tourist police are making a more frequent habit of conducting random personal searches for drugs. Although some questions have arisen about their right to do this, the best course of action is to comply if they want to frisk you — objecting may result in a free tour of the local jail. Report any unusual incidents to the local consular office.

Taxes

There's a 15% value-added tax (IVA) on goods and services, and it's generally included in the posted price.

Taxis

Taxis are plentiful and relatively inexpensive. Most trips from downtown to the northern Zona Hotelera and Marina Vallarta cost between $3.50 and $5; trips between Marina Vallarta and Mismaloya Beach to the south cost $8. Rates are charged by zone and are generally posted in the lobbies of hotels. You can also hire taxis by the hour or day for longer trips when you prefer to leave the driving to someone else. Rates run between $10 and $12 per hour with discounts available for full-day rates.

Telephone

Avoid the phone booths that have signs in English advising you to call home using a special 800 number — these are absolute rip-offs and can cost as much as $20 per minute. The least expensive way to call is by using a Telmex (LADATEL) prepaid phone card, available at most pharmacies and mini-supers, using the official Telmex (Lada) public phones. In Mexico you need to dial 001 prior to a number to reach the United States, and you need to preface long distance calls within Mexico by dialing 01.

Time Zone

Puerto Vallarta operates on central standard time, but Mexico's observance of daylight savings time varies somewhat from that in the United States.

Chapter 16

Dining in Puerto Vallarta

By Lynne Bairstow

In This Chapter

▶ Discovering Puerto Vallarta's best restaurants

▶ Finding a restaurant with true Mexican ambiance

▶ Dining on the *malecón* and in the jungle

*P*uerto Vallarta has the most exceptional dining scene of any resort town in Mexico. More than 250 restaurants serve cuisines from around the world in addition to fresh seafood and regional dishes. Chefs from France, Switzerland, Germany, Italy, and Argentina have come for visits and then stayed to open their own restaurants. In celebration of the diversity of dining experiences available, Vallarta's culinary community hosts a 2-week-long Gourmet Dining Festival each November, as part of the annual Fiestas del Mar (SeaFest).

As in many of Mexico's beach resorts, even the finest restaurants in town can be comfortably casual when it comes to dress. Men seldom wear jackets, although ladies frequently don dressy resort wear — basically, everything goes. Remember that dinner tends to take on the dual nature of Puerto Vallarta — many tourists dine at earlier hours, but locals are apt to just be thinking about dinner at 9 p.m., so many restaurants stay open late.

Nonetheless, dining isn't limited to high-end options — you can also find plenty of small, family-owned restaurants, local Mexican kitchens, and vegetarian cafes. Vallarta also has its share of imported, food-and-fun chains: Hard Rock Cafe, Outback Steakhouse, and even Hooters. I don't bother reviewing these restaurants because the consistency and decor are so familiar. Resist the temptation to go with what you know, though. Trust me — the locally owned restaurants offer both the best food and the best value.

Vallarta on the whole is a very child-friendly place, and families are welcome to bring their children almost anywhere. If your young ones are particular to more American tastes, standards such as McDonald's, Burger King, and Hard Rock Cafe — good choices — are here, but you may also want to try one of their Mexican counterparts — Carlos O'Brian's or Papaya 3, both located downtown.

Puerto Vallarta's Best Restaurants

Unless you're visiting during the height of high season, you generally don't need reservations — especially with the number and range of excellent restaurants in Vallarta. I note reservation information for the few exceptions that tend to be very busy.

Contrary to conventional travel wisdom, most of the best restaurants in the Marina Vallarta area are actually located in hotels. Especially notable are **Andrea,** at Velas Vallarta, for fine Italian cuisine, and **Garibaldi's,** on the beachfront of the Westin Regina Resort, for exceptional seafood. (See Chapter 14 for more information on these resorts.) You can find other choices along the boardwalk bordering the marina yacht harbor. A notable stop is the **Café Max,** next to the Vallarta Adventures offices in Condominiums Marina Golf, Local 11 (☎ 322-221-0362). It serves excellent coffee and espresso drinks, plus pastries and light snacks and sandwiches, and is open Monday through Saturday from 8 a.m. to 1 p.m., and 4 p.m. to 10:30 p.m. (no credit cards are accepted).

The most condensed restaurant area, Zona Romántica, is south of the Río Cuale. The area's street, Basilio Badillo, is even nicknamed "Restaurant Row." A second main dining drag has emerged along Olas Altas, where you can find all varieties of foods and price categories. The wide sidewalks are lined with cafes and espresso bars, which are generally open 7 a.m. to midnight.

Finding inexpensive, vegetarian options

The best inexpensive local spots are downtown. The long-standing favorite spot for light meals and fresh fruit drinks is the tiny **Tutifruti** (Morelos 552; ☎ 322-222-1068), which is open Monday through Saturday 8 a.m. to 8 p.m. An inexpensive, bountiful, and delicious vegetarian buffet is a daily hit at **Planeta Vegetariano,** Iturbide 270, just down the street from the Our Lady of Guadalupe church (☎ 322-222-3073). The buffet is offered from 11:30 a.m. to 10 p.m. and costs $5.50 (no credit cards). A vegetarian breakfast buffet is also available from 8 to 11 a.m. for $3.50. Planeta Vegetariano is closed on Sundays. A second location with the same prices and hours of service is now in Marina Vallarta (☎ 322-209-0555), located in Marina del Rey, local L-4.

All the restaurants I include in the following listings are arranged alphabetically with their location and general price category noted. Please refer to the Introduction of this book for an explanation of the price categories. Remember that tips generally run about 15%, and most wait-staff really depend on these for their income, so be generous if the service warrants.

Please see the menu glossary in Appendix C for more information on Mexican cuisine.

Archie's Wok
$–$$ Centro/Zona Romántica   ASIAN/SEAFOOD

Since 1986, Archie's has been legendary in Puerto Vallarta for serving original cuisine influenced by the intriguing flavors of Thailand, China, and the Philippines. Archie was Hollywood director John Huston's private chef during the years Huston spent in the area. Today, Archie's wife Cindy continues his legacy. The drinks — including a Thai mai tai and other tropical drinks that are made from only fresh fruit and juices — are a good way to kick off a meal here, as are the Filipino spring rolls, which are consistently crispy and delicious. The popular Singapore fish fillet features lightly battered fillet strips in a sweet-and-sour sauce, and the Thai garlic shrimp is prepared with fresh garlic, ginger, cilantro, and black pepper. Vegetarians have plenty of options, including the broccoli, tofu, mushroom, and cashew stir-fry in a black bean and sherry sauce. Finish things off with the signature Spice Islands coffee or a slice of lime cheese pie. Live classical music sets the atmosphere in Archie's Oriental garden Thursday to Saturday from 8 to 11 p.m.

Francisca Rodríguez 130, ½ block from the Los Muertos pier. ☎ *322-222-0411. E-mail:* awok@pvnet.com.mx. *Main courses: $6–$19. AE, MC, V. Open: Mon–Sat 2–11 p.m. Closed Sept–Oct.*

Arrayán
$ Centro   MEXICAN

Opening its doors in late 2003, the traditional but original Arrayán has quickly become the darling of casual, local eateries — and the pot of gold at the end of the rainbow for anyone in search of authentic Mexican cuisine. Owner Carmen Porras enlisted Mexico City chef Carmen Titita (praised by James Beard for her culinary work) to assist in the design of the kitchen and creation of the restaurant's concise menu, which features genuine Mexican food of the region. The open-air (but covered) dining area surrounds a cozy courtyard, while its exposed brick walls and funky-chic decor showcase a modern view of Mexican classics — tin tubs serve as sinks in the bathrooms, and colorful plastic tablecloths and primitive art enliven the dining room. Start with an order of sumptuous plantain fritters filled with black beans or an unusual salad of diced nopal cactus paddles with fresh cheese. Favorite main courses include tacos filled with prime beef filet, or a Mexican duck confit, served in an *arrayán*-orange sauce. (Arrayán, the namesake of the place, is a small bittersweet fruit, native to the region.) Homemade, fresh-fruit ice creams are an especially tasty finish to your meal. The full bar offers an extensive selection of tequilas and regional liquors, while non-alcoholic beverages center around "aqua frescas," blended drinks of fresh fruit and water. You can't miss the pink facade with the large bell at the entry. The excellent service is a plus to this can't-miss dining experience.

Allende 344, just past the intersection with Matamoros. ☎ *322-223-2963. E-mail:* carmyp@prodigy.net.mx. *Main courses: $8–$12. No credit cards. Open: daily 1–11 p.m.*

Benitto's
$ Marina Vallarta   CAFE

Wow! What a sandwich! Benitto's food is reason enough to come, but this tiny yet terrific cafe (located inside the Plaza Neptuno shopping center) also offers an original array of sauces and very personable — albeit slow — service. Popular with locals for light breakfasts, filling lunches, or even fondue and wine in the evenings, Benitto's is the best place in town to find pastrami, corned beef, or other traditional (gringo!) sandwich fare, all served on your choice of gourmet bread. Draft beer and wine are available as are Benitto's specialty infused waters.

Inside Plaza Neptuno, Francisco Medina Ascencio by Marina Vallarta. ☎ *322-209-0287. Main courses: $2.50–$7; breakfast $2–$5. No credit cards. Open: Daily 8:30 a.m.–9 p.m.*

Café des Artistes/Thierry Blouet Cocina de Autor
$$–$$$$ Centro   FRENCH/INTERNATIONAL

If you want one over-the-top dining experience in Puerto Vallarta, Café des Artistes is the hands-down choice. Creative in its menu and innovative in design, this dinner-only location rivals those in any major metropolitan city for its culinary sophistication, and may soon become a reason in itself to visit Vallarta. The award-winning chef and owner, Thierry Blouet, is both a member of the Académie Culinaire de France and a Maître Cuisinier de France. In late 2003, the singular dining experience of the Café des Artistes evolved to complete a trio of special places, adding the upscale Constantini Bar Lounge and the separate but connected Thierry Blouet Cocina de Autor dining area. All are located in a restored house that resembles a castle. The interior of the original Café des Artistes combines murals, lush fabrics, and an array of original artworks, with both an interior dining area as well as a lushly landscaped terraced garden area, open only during the winter and spring. The menu of this section is a changing delight of French gourmet bistro fare, which draws heavily on Chef Blouet's French training, yet uses regional specialty ingredients. A few of

Marina Vallarta Dining

the noteworthy entrees include sea bass fillet served with polenta, and the renowned roasted duck glazed with honey, soy, ginger, and lime sauce, and served with a pumpkin risotto.

At the Cocina de Autor, the atmosphere is sleek and stylish, and the fixed-price tasting menu (prices depend on the number of plates you select, between three and six, from a long list of starters, entrees, and desserts) offers you a choice of the chef's most innovative and sumptuous creations, with each dish creatively combining ingredients to present one memorable flavor. The Cocina also provides perfect wine pairings, if desired. After your meal, you're invited to the cognac and cigar room, an exquisite blend of old adobe walls, flickering candles, and elegant leather chairs. Or move on to the adjacent Constantini Bar Lounge, with its live jazz music and plush sofas, for a fitting close to a memorable meal. Without a doubt, it's all worth the splurge.

Guadalupe Sanchez 740, at Leona Vicario. ☎ *322-222-3228/29.* www.cafedes artistes.com. *Reservations required. Main courses: $19–$29; Cocina de Autor tasting menu ranges from $25 to $68. AE, MC, V. Open: Daily 6–11:30 p.m.; the lounge stays open until 2 a.m.*

Café San Angel

$ Centro/Zona Romántica   CAFE

A comfortable, classic, sidewalk cafe, Café San Angel is a local gathering place from sunrise to sunset. For breakfast, choose between a burrito stuffed with eggs and chorizo sausage, a three-egg Western omelet, crêpes filled with mushrooms, or a tropical fruit plate. Deli sandwiches, crêpes, and pastries round out the small but ample menu. The cafe also has exceptional fruit smoothies (such as the Yelapa — a blend of mango, banana, and orange juice) and perfectly made espresso drinks. As much as I love it here, I have to warn you that the service is reliably slow and frequently frustrating, so choose this place if time is on your side, though it does offer the best people-watching in the area to help you endure the slow service. Bar service and Internet access are also available.

Olas Altas 449, corner of Francisca Rodríguez. ☎ *322-223-1273. Main courses: $3.50–$6; breakfast $3.50–$5. No credit cards. Open: Daily 8–1 a.m.*

Daiquiri Dick's

$–$$ Centro/Zona Romántica   MODERN AMERICAN

A Vallarta dining institution, Daiquiri Dick's has been around for more than 20 years, evolving its winning combination of decor, service, and scrumptious cuisine. The menu is among Vallarta's most sophisticated, and the genuinely warm staff and open-air location fronting Playa Los Muertos add to the feeling of casual comfort. As lovely as the restaurant is, though, and as notorious as the fresh-fruit daiquiris are, the food is the main attraction, incorporating touches of Tuscan, Thai, and Mexican. Start with grilled asparagus wrapped in prosciutto and topped with shaved asiago cheese, then try an entree such as sesame-crusted tuna, grilled rare and served with wild greens; pistachio chicken served with polenta; or my favorite, simple yet indulgent lobster tacos. Chocolate banana bread pudding makes a perfect finish. Daiquiri Dick's is a great place for groups, as well as for a romantic dinner. It's one of the few places that is equally enjoyable for breakfast, lunch, or dinner.

Olas Altas 314. ☎ *322-222-0566.* www.ddpv.com. *Reservations recommended. Main courses: $6.50–$21. AE, MC, V. Daily 9 a.m.–10:30 p.m. Closed Sept.*

de Santos

$–$$ Centro   MEDITERRANEAN

From the moment it opened, de Santos quickly became the hot spot in town for late-night dining and bar action. Although the dining aspect

Downtown Puerto Vallarta Dining

Archie's Wok **12**	Espresso **9**
Arrayán **2**	Fajita Republic **15**
Café des Artistes/	Kaiser Maximilian **11**
Thierry Blouet Cocina	La Palapa **13**
de Autor **3**	Las Palomas **6**
Café San Angel **14**	Los Xitomates **5**
Daiquiri Dick's **10**	Pipis **2**
de Santos **1**	Planeta Vegetariano **7**
El Repollo Rojo (Red	Rito's Baci **4**
Cabbage Café) **16**	Trio **8**

initially didn't live up to the atmosphere and music, it does now. The fare is Mediterranean-inspired; the best bets include lightly breaded calamari, seafood casserole, lobster ravioli, and excellent thin-crust pizzas. Other good choices are the nightly specials — always the most creative offerings on the menu. The cool, refined interior, with exposed brick walls, crisp white-clothed tables, and lots of votive candles, feels more urban than resort, and the joint boasts the most sophisticated sound system in town — including its own DJ who spins to match the crowd's mood. It probably helps that one of the partners is also a member of Maná, the chart-topping, wildly popular Latin group. Prices are extremely reasonable for the quality and overall experience of an evening here. Start with dinner and then stay on and enjoy the most favored club in town, of the same name, located next door (see Chapter 17).

Morelos 771, between Pipila and Leona Vicario. ☎ *322-223-3052.* www.desantos. com.mx. *Reservations recommended. Main courses: $5–$15; wine and mixed drinks $3–$5. AE, MC, V. Open: Dinner 6 p.m.–2 a.m.; bar open until 4 a.m. on weekends.*

El Repollo Rojo (Red Cabbage Cafe)

$–$$ Centro   MEXICAN

This tiny, hard-to-find cafe is worth the effort — a visit here rewards you with exceptional, traditional Mexican cuisine and a whimsical crash course in the contemporary culture of Mexico. The small room is covered wall to wall and table to table with photographs, paintings, movie posters, and news clippings about Mexico's cultural icons. The Mexican painter Frida Kahlo (the same Frida that Salma Hayek portrayed in the film, *Frida*) figures prominently in the decor, and a special menu duplicates dishes that she and husband Diego Rivera prepared for guests. Specialties from all over Mexico are featured, including the divine *chiles en nogada* (poblano chiles stuffed with ground beef, pine nuts, and raisins, topped with a sweet cream sauce and served cold), an intricate chicken *mole* from Puebla, and the hearty *carne en su jugo* (steak in its juice). El Repollo Rojo isn't the place for an intimate conversation, however — the poor acoustics cause everyone's conversations to blend together, although generally what you're hearing from adjacent tables are raves about the food. Also, this is about the only nonsmoking restaurant in town that I'm aware of.

Calle Rivera del Río 204 A, across from the Río Cuale. ☎ *322-223-0411. Main courses: $3–$18. No credit cards. Open: Daily 5–11 p.m.*

Espresso

$ Centro/Zona Romántica   ITALIAN

This eatery is Vallarta's best late-night dining option, and especially popular with *vallartenses* (locals). The two-level restaurant is on one of the town's busiest streets — across from El Torito's sports bar, and cater-cornered from the lively Señor Frog's — meaning that traffic noise is a factor, though not a deterrent. The food is superb, the service attentive, and the prices more than reasonable. Owned by a partnership of lively Italians, it serves food that is authentic in preparation and flavor, from thin-crust, brick-oven pizzas to savory homemade pastas. My favorite pizza is the Quattro Stagioni, topped with artichokes, black olives, ham, and mushrooms. Excellent calzones and panini (sandwiches) are also options. I prefer the rooftop garden area for dining, but many patrons gravitate to the pool tables in the air-conditioned downstairs, which features major sports and entertainment events on satellite TV. Espresso also has full bar service and draft beer — oh yes, and also espresso.

Ignacio L. Vallarta 279. ☎ *322-222-3272. Main courses: $6.50–$13. AE, MC, V. Open: Daily noon to 4 a.m.*

Fajita Republic

$–$$ Centro/Restaurant Row   MEXICAN/SEAFOOD/STEAKS

Fajita Republic has hit on a winning recipe: delicious food, ample portions, welcoming atmosphere, and low prices. The restaurant is casual, fun, and festive in atmosphere, and situated in a garden of mango and palm trees with a view of the passing action on the bordering street. The specialty is, of course, fajitas, grilled to perfection in every variety: steak, chicken, shrimp, combo, and vegetarian. All come with a generous tray of salsas and toppings. This tropical grill also serves sumptuous BBQ ribs, grilled shrimp, and Mexican *molcajetes* (dishes served in these stone bowls traditionally used in Mexico for grinding and pureeing) with incredibly tender strips of marinated beef fillet. Starters include fresh guacamole served in a giant spoon and the ever-popular Mayan cheese sticks (cheese, breaded and deep-fried). Try a "Fajita Rita Mango Margarita" — or one of the other spirited temptations — served in oversized mugs or by the pitcher. A new, second location in Nuevo Vallarta, across from the Velas Resort is drawing equal raves, with the same menu and prices.

Pino Suárez 321, corner of Basilio Badillo, 1 block north of Olas Altas. ☎ *322-222-3131. Main courses: $9–$17. MC, V. Open: Daily 5 p.m. to midnight.*

Vallarta's jungle dining

Want to get wild while you dine? One of the unique attractions of Puerto Vallarta is its "jungle restaurants," located to the south of town toward Playa Mismaloya. Each restaurant offers open-air dining in a tropical setting by the sea or beside a mountain river. A stop for swimming and lunch at one of these places is included in many of the "jungle" or "tropical" tours (see Chapter 17 for more about these tours).

If you travel on your own, a taxi is the best transportation because all the jungle restaurants are located quite a distance from the main highway. Taxis are usually waiting for return patrons.

The most recommendable of the jungle restaurants is **El Nogalito** (☎ and fax: **322-221-5225**). Located beside a clear jungle stream, this exceptionally clean, beautifully landscaped ranch serves lunch, beverages, and snacks on a shady terrace in a relaxing atmosphere. Several hiking routes also depart from the grounds. El Nogalito's guides point out the area's native plants, birds, and wildlife. To get to El Nogalito, take a taxi or travel to Punta Negra, just about 8km (5 miles) south of downtown Puerto Vallarta. A well-marked sign points to Calzada del Cedro, a dirt road leading to the ranch. El Nogalito is much closer to town than the other jungle restaurants and is open daily from noon to 5:30 p.m. (no credit cards).

Just past Boca de Tomatlán, at Highway 200, Km 20, is **Chico's Paradise** (☎ **322-223-6005** or 322-223-6006; www.chicosparadise.com.mx), which offers spectacular views of massive rocks and the surrounding jungle and mountains. Natural pools and waterfalls for swimming are located here, plus a small *mercado* (market) selling pricey trinkets. The menu features excellent seafood (the seafood platter for two is excellent — lobster, clam, giant shrimp, crab, and fish fillet) as well as Mexican dishes. The quality is quite good, and the portions are generous, although prices are higher than in town — remember, you're paying for the setting. Chico's is open daily from 10 a.m. to 6 p.m. (no credit cards).

Kaiser Maximilian

$–$$ Centro/Zona Romántica   INTERNATIONAL

Kaiser Maximilian is the prime place to go if you want to combine exceptional food with great people-watching. This bistro-style cafe has a casually elegant atmosphere with a genuinely European feel to it. Austrian-born owner Andreas Rupprechter is always on hand to ensure that the service is as impeccable as the food is delicious. Indoor, air-conditioned dining is at cozy tables dressed in crisp white linens; sidewalk tables are larger and great for groups of friends. The cuisine merges old-world European preparations with regional, fresh ingredients. My personal favorite is the filet of trout with watercress and beet sauce, served on a bed of spinach. I like it so much that I've never tried any other dish, although friends tell me the mustard chicken with mashed potatoes is excellent, and the rack of lamb with polenta, endives, and lima beans is simply divine. Maximilian also offers northern-European classics such as *rahmschnitzel* (sauteed pork loin and homemade noodles in a creamy mushroom sauce). Desserts are especially tempting, as are the gourmet coffees — Maximilian has its own Austrian cafe and pastry shop next door. It's located at the intersection of Basilio Badillo and Olas Altas, in front of the Playa Los Arcos Hotel.

Olas Altas 380, on the sidewalk level of the Playa Los Arcos Hotel. ☎ **322-223-0760.** www.kaisermaximilian.com. *Reservations recommended in high season. Main courses: $7–$22. AE, MC, V. Open: Mon–Sat 6–11 p.m.*

La Palapa

$–$$ Centro/Zona Romántica   SEAFOOD/MEXICAN

This lovely, open-air, *palapa*-roofed (thatched umbrella) restaurant on the beach is a decades-old local favorite, and with each visit, I find the quality of both the food and service continually improving. Enjoy a tropical breakfast by the sea, lunch on the beach, cocktails at sunset, or a romantic dinner — at night the staff sets cloth-covered tables in the sand. For lunch and dinner, seafood is the specialty. Featured dishes include macadamia and coconut shrimp in a litchi-fruit sauce and pan-seared scallops over a mussel risotto, served with mango chutney — but note that the menu changes regularly, and that La Palapa also offers daily specials. The fresh catch is listed on a chalkboard and is served in much thicker portions than at most local restaurants — simply sumptuous, and prepared to your preference. La Palapa's location in the heart of Playa Los Muertos makes it an exceptional place to either start or end the day; I favor it for breakfast or, even better, for a late-night, sweet temptation and specialty coffee enjoyed while watching the moon over the bay with the sand at my feet. A particular favorite is the all-you-can-enjoy Sunday brunch, which entitles you to a spot on popular Playa Los Muertos for the day! A plus at lunch is you can enjoy the extra-comfortable beach chairs for post-lunch sunbathing. A new, classy bar area features acoustic guitars and vocals nightly from 8 to 11 p.m., frequently performed by the very talented owner Alberto himself. La Palapa had a complete makeover in 2002 and retained its charm and gracious service.

Pulpito 103. ☎ *322-222-5225. Reservations recommended for dinner in high season. Main courses: $7–$25; salads or sandwiches $5–$12; breakfast $2.50–$12. AE, MC, V. Open: Daily 8 a.m.–11 p.m.*

Las Palomas
$–$$ Centro   MEXICAN

One of Puerto Vallarta's first restaurants, this is the power-breakfast place of choice for local movers and shakers — and a generally popular hangout for everyone else throughout the day. Authentic in atmosphere and menu, Las Palomas is one of Puerto Vallarta's few genuine Mexican restaurants and has an atmosphere of a gracious home. Breakfast is the best value. The staff pours mugs of steaming coffee spiced with cinnamon as soon as you're seated. Try the classic *huevos rancheros* (fried eggs served on a soft fried corn tortilla and topped with red sauce — spicy or mild) or *chilaquiles* (tortilla strips, fried and topped with a red or green spicy sauce, cream cheese, and fried eggs). Lunch and dinner offer other traditional Mexican specialties plus a selection of stuffed crêpes. The best place for checking out the *malecón* and watching the sun set while sipping an icy margarita is in the spacious bar or upstairs terrace.

Paseo Díaz Ordaz 594. ☎ *322-222-3675. Main courses: $6–$18; breakfast $3.50–$7; lunch $5–$12. AE, MC, V. Open: Daily 8 a.m.–11 p.m.*

Los Xitomates
$–$$ Centro   MEXICAN

Located in the heart of downtown, this creative Mexican restaurant has earned raves for its intimate atmosphere and chef/owner Luis Fitch Gómez's exceptionally creative versions of the country's culinary treasures. It's named for one of Mexico's contributions to gastronomy — the tomato (Xitomatl, in the ancient Aztec language of Náhuatl). The menu mixes Mexican with Caribbean, Asian, and Mediterranean influences, and the presentation is as creative as the preparation. Starters include the signature coconut shrimp in a tangy tamarind sauce, thinly sliced scallops with cucumber and jícama julienne, or mushrooms stuffed with shrimp or *huitlacoche* (itself, a mushroom that grows on corn stalks). Main courses range from grilled salmon filet in a poblano chile sauce, to a tender rib eye steak with mushrooms, delicately flavored with the Mexican herb, epazote. The house specialty dessert is a Toluca ice cream cake. The warmly decorated dining room is accented with tin star lamps and flickering candles. An excellent wine list and full bar complement the exquisite dining.

Morelos 570, across from Galeria Uno. ☎ *322-222-1695.* www.losxitomates. com. *Reservations recommended. Main courses: $8–$22. AE, MC, V. Open: Daily 7–11:30 p.m.*

Pipis

$–$$ Centro   MEXICAN

Most of the people who come to Pipis tend to think of it as their own "find" — it's just enough off the beaten track to give a taste of a Vallarta neighborhood, and the ambiance is an authentic glimpse at the Mexican belief that life is meant to be enjoyed. If you're looking for a casually good time, this is your place. Within moments of sitting down, your waiter prepares homemade guacamole at your table and serves it with chips. The specialty here is sizzling fajitas — chicken, beef, or seafood, generous in portion, and absolutely delicious. Equally famous are the oversize margaritas, but be warned: These are serious drinks! That may account for the fact that the place is always a riot of laughter and conversation, mixed with the music of strolling mariachis. The gracious owners are always on hand, and the wait-staff seems dedicated to making certain you're happy and well fed. Pipis also has a full menu of other traditional Mexican dishes, but I've never moved beyond the fajitas — they're just too good.

Guadalupe Sánchez 807, corner with Pipila ☎ *322-223-2767.* www.pipis. com.mx. *Main courses: $8–$21. AE, MC, V. Open: Daily 1–11 p.m.*

Porto Bello

$–$$ Marina Vallarta   ITALIAN

One of the first restaurants in the marina, Porto Bello remains a favorite. It features authentically flavorful Italian dishes in a casual atmosphere overlooking the marina and exceptional service. For starters, the fried calamari is delicately seasoned, and the grilled vegetable antipasto can easily serve as a full meal. Signature dishes include Fusilli Porto Bello prepared with black olives, artichokes, lemon juice, olive oil, and basil, and veal scaloppine with a creamy white-wine sauce, mushrooms, and shrimp. Most people prefer seating on the gazebo-like patio overlooking the boats in the marina. Indoor dining is air-conditioned, and occasionally, live music fills the air in the evenings.

Marina Sol, Local 7 (Marina Vallarta malecón)*.* ☎ *322-221-0003. Main courses: $8–$24. AE, MC, V. Open: Daily noon to 11 p.m.*

Rito's Baci

$–$$ Centro   ITALIAN

If the food wasn't a reason to come here (and it definitely is), then Rito himself and his gentle, devoted way of caring for every detail of this cozy *trattoria* would be the draw. His grandfather emigrated from Italy, so the recipes and traditions of Italian food come naturally to him. His passion for food is obvious as he describes the specialties, which include lasagna (vegetarian, *verde,* or meat-filled); ravioli stuffed with spinach and ricotta cheese; spaghetti with garlic, anchovy, and lemon zest; and a side of homemade Italian sausage. Everything, in fact, is made by hand from fresh ingredients. Pizza lovers favor the Piedmonte, with that famous sausage and mushrooms, and the Horacio, a cheeseless pizza with tomatoes, oregano, and basil. Sandwiches come hot or cold and are a two-handed operation. Rito's is located 1½ blocks off the *malecón* on Josefa O. de Domínguez next to Galeria A.L.

Domínguez 181, between Morelos and Juárez. ☎ *322-222-6448. Pasta $6.50–$19; salads and sandwiches $2–$5.60; pizzas $13–$14.50. MC, V. Open: Daily 1–11 p.m.*

Trio
$–$$ Centro   INTERNATIONAL

Trio remains the darling of Vallarta restaurants, and is especially popular with Vallarta's local residents. Diners are beating a path to this modest but stylish cafe because the chef/owners Bernhard Güth and Ulf Henriksson both share an undeniable passion for food, which is exhibited in each dish. Güth and Henriksson have combined local ingredients with their impressive culinary experience; the result is memorable entrees such as San Blas shrimp in a fennel-tomato vinaigrette served over broiled nopal cactus, herb risotto with toasted sunflower seeds and quail, and pan-roasted sea bass with glazed grapes, mashed potatoes, and sauerkraut in a white pepper sauce — but these dishes may not be on the menu when you arrive because Trio is a constantly changing work of art! Trio is noted for its perfect melding of Mexican and Mediterranean flavors. What's great about this place, besides everything I've already mentioned, is that despite a sophisticated menu, the atmosphere is always comfortable and welcoming — Bernhard and Ulf are regularly seen chatting with guests at the end of an evening. A rooftop bar area makes for a comfortable wait for a table or a great spot to enjoy an after-dinner coffee. A real treat!

Guerrero 264. ☎ *322-222-2196.* www.triopv.com. *Reservations recommended. Main courses: $6.50–$19.00. Lunch available in high season only. AE, MC, V. Open: Mon–Sat noon to 4 p.m.; dinner daily 6 p.m. to midnight.*

Chapter 17

Having Fun on and off the Beach in Puerto Vallarta

By Lynne Bairstow

. . . .

In This Chapter

▶ Hitting the beaches Puerto Vallarta style

▶ Enjoying Puerto Vallarta's best sports on land and by sea

▶ Sightseeing and shopping like a tour professional

▶ Heading out beyond Puerto Vallarta

▶ Dancing until dawn, and maybe even later

. . . .

Decisions, decisions . . . With so many fun-filled options competing for your time, choosing among them may be the biggest problem you encounter on a Vallarta vacation. Besides a bevy of beautiful beaches — some secluded coves, others outrageous in their people-watching potential — dry land also offers intriguing and entertaining possibilities.

In this chapter, I give you an overview of the best beaches tucked into the 26 miles of coastline surrounding **Bahía de Banderas** (Banderas Bay) and the best ways to get to each. I also reveal the most interesting sights in town and a few cool activities to try.

Vallarta is gaining recognition as a veritable treasure chest for eco-tourism. A number of tours permit you to explore the culture or nature of the area — while having a sunny-good time in the process. I cover these excursions as well.

Hitting the Beaches

For years, beaches were Puerto Vallarta's main attraction. Although visitors today explore more of the surrounding geography, the golden sands and cobalt waters are still a powerful draw. The coast of Bahía

de Banderas covers more than 50 miles, with 26 miles of beaches ranging from action-packed party spots to secluded coves accessible only
by boat.

Northern beaches

The entire northern coastline from Punta Mita to Bucerías is a succession of sandy coves alternating with rocky inlets. For years, the beaches
to the north, with their long, clean breaks, have been the favored locale
for surfers.

 Public transportation to any of the north-shore beaches is easy and
inexpensive. Buses and minivans marked "Bucerías" or "Punta Mita"
stop at the bus stop in front of the airport gas station. You can ask your
driver to let you off at any of the beaches listed in this section. Buses
generally run every 20 minutes from 6 a.m. to 11 p.m., but check with
your hotel concierge for current schedules. For the return trip, simply
flag a bus down. The fare is less than $2 each way; that price gets you
all the way to Punta Mita.

As you travel south on Highway 200A from Punta Mita, the first public
beach you come to is **Playa Anclote** — a broad, sandy beach with protected swimming areas and a few great *palapa* (thatched roof) restaurants. The water is gentle and shallow for quite a distance out, and boats
regularly anchor offshore and take dinghies in for a fresh fish lunch. Of
the restaurants, El Anclote and El Dorado are long-standing favorites;
each offers beach chairs for your post-margarita nap in the sun. The
new Chef Roger on the beach, however, is bound to raise the culinary
bar of this casual dining area.

You can also hire a *panga* (small motorized boat) at Playa Anclote
from the fisherman's cooperative on the beach and have the captain
take you to the **Marietas Islands** just offshore. These uninhabited
islands are a great place for bird-watching, diving, snorkeling, or just
exploring. You can spot blue-footed booby birds (no joke) all along the
islands' rocky coast, and giant mantas, sea turtles, and colorful tropical fish swim among the coral cliffs. The islands are honeycombed
with caves and hidden beaches — including the stunning Playa del
Amor that only appears at low tide. You enter a shallow passageway
to access this semicircular stretch of sand. And a cave 40 feet below
the surface has an air pocket where divers can dispose of their regula-
tors and have an underwater conversation! Humpback whales congre-
gate around these islands during the winter months, and you can rent
a *panga* for a do-it-yourself whale-watching excursion (trips cost about
$20 per hour). You can also visit these islands aboard one of the
numerous day cruises that depart from the cruise-ship terminal in
Puerto Vallarta.

Puerto Vallarta Area

To Bucerías, Nuevo Vallarta, and Punta Mita

MARINA VALLARTA

Playa de Oro

Terminal Marítima (Cruise Pier)

See Marina Vallarta inset

Bullring

Vista Vallarta Golf Course

0   200 mi
0   200 km

Puerto Vallarta

JALISCO

PACIFIC OCEAN

MICHOACAN

Mexico City

Ave. Francisco M. Ascencio

Marina Vallarta Area

Airport

Albatros

Gaviotas

Garsos

Bocanegra

Flamingos

Pelicanos

Garsas

Paseo de la Marina Norte

Paseo de la Marina

Mastil

Proa

Popa

Vallarta Adventures

Plaza Neptuno

Ancla

Vela

Timon

Paseo de la Marina Sur

0   1/2 mi
0   0.5 km

N

Playa de Oro

Playa Las Glorias

Bahía de Banderas

Avenida de México

Playa Camarones

See Downtown Puerto Vallarta inset

Downtown Puerto Vallarta Area

Invierno

Octubre

Napanjo

Lázaro Cárdenas

Aquiles Serdán

Francisca Rodríguez

Matamoros

31 de

Pipila

Aldama

Ramón Corona

Abasolo

Morelos

Miramar

Aguacate

Insurgentes

Paseo Díaz Ordaz (El Malecón)

Iturbide

Guerrero

Zaragoza

Libertad

Constitución

Vallarta

Pino Suárez

Olas Altas

Amapas

Bahía de Banderas

0   1/4 mi
0   0.25 km

N

Playa Los Muertos Pier (water taxi)

EL CENTRO

Río Cuale

Playa Olas Altas

Playa Los Muertos

Playa Punta Negra

Playa Garza Blanca

Playa Gemelas

Airport ✈
Beach ❊
Church ✝
Golf ⛳

Los Arcos

Playa Mismaloya

To Yelapa and Tomatlán

To Manzanillo and El Eden Chino's

0   1 mi
0   1 km

N

The **Villa Vera Beach Club** (formerly the Los Veneros Beach Club; ☎ 322-221-1401), located 11km (7 miles) south of El Anclote and 29km (18 miles) north of Puerto Vallarta, is a great place to spend a day — all the facilities and amenities of a pampering, private club are available at a daily cost of $16 for adults and $12 for children. Two crystalline pools — one with a wet bar for adults only — showers, towel service, an exceptional stretch of beach, and a full-service restaurant and bar make this patch of sand a favorite of mine for an indulgent beach day. My friends with kids think it's one of the best places around to spend a day in the sun with the little ones. In addition to the kid-friendly main swimming pool, a full playground with water slides and a tropical bird show are always a hit with the youngsters.

Just 2km (1 mile) south of Villa Vera is the rustic, natural setting of **Playa Destiladeras.** It has talc-smooth sand and a couple of thatched-roof restaurants, making for a quick but meaningful getaway from town. **Playa Piedra Blanca** and **Playa Manzanillo** are beaches similar in style and spirit located just before the curve in the bay, past the small town of La Cruz de Huanacaxtle.

The small coastal town of **Bucerías,** with its broad, smooth-sand beaches, has caught on as a great day-trip. Come here from Puerto Vallarta to enjoy the long, wide, and uncrowded beach, along with the fresh seafood served at the beachfront restaurants or at one of the great cafes. One of the top choices is **Karen's Place** on the beach at the Costa Dorada, calles Lázaro Cárdenas and Juárez (☎ 329-298-1499). Open Tuesdays through Sundays from 9 a.m. to 9 p.m., it caters to American tastes and has a super Sunday brunch served from 9 a.m. to 3 p.m. Sunday is also street-market day in town, but in keeping with the casual pace of Bucerías, the market doesn't get going until noon or so. The **Coral Reef Surf Shop** (Heroe de Nacozari 114 F; ☎ 329-298-0261) offers a great selection of surfboards and gear for sale. It also features surfboard and boogie-board rentals, surf lessons, ATV tours, and other adventure tours to surrounding areas.

The gold-sand **beaches of Nuevo Vallarta** are the main reason people choose to stay in Nuevo Vallarta hotels. Nuevo Vallarta is south of Bucerías, and technically you could say that it also falls on the northern coastline. If you want to check the beaches out for yourself, spend a day at the **Etc. Beach Club** (Paseo de los Cocoteros 38; ☎ 322-297-0174). This casual beach club has a volleyball net, showers, restroom facilities, and food and drink service on the beach (both day and night). Public transportation is okay to get to Nuevo Vallarta, because it's the most economic way to get there in relative comfort — the buses are fairly new and some even are air-conditioned. Taxis are a bit expensive — $15 one way, but they're a faster, more convenient way to get to Nuevo Vallarta. To get here from Puerto Vallarta, take the second entrance to Nuevo Vallarta and turn right on Paseo de los Cocoteros; it's past the Vista Bahía hotel. The club is open daily during the winter from 11 a.m.

to 10:30 p.m. and from 11 a.m. to 7 p.m. in the summer. Bring cash for food and drink purchases — credit cards aren't accepted.

Central and town beaches

In Chapter 14, I caution you that the beaches at **Marina Vallarta,** with darker sand and seasonal inflows of stones, are the least desirable in the area. If you're a traveler whose priority is the beauty of the beach, venture to areas other than Marina Vallarta. Though it has its charms, the beaches aren't among them.

The **Hotel Zone** beach runs for 5km (3 miles) from just beyond the cruise-ship terminal to the north to just south of the *malecón* (board-walk). The names of the beaches change along the way, from Playa de Oro to Playa Camarones, but most people just refer to the hotel property that the beaches front.

It's a wide, clean, and generally uncrowded stretch of sand, but the shore does drop steeply just offshore. This is the best place to rent watersports equipment, especially Jet Skis and sailboards.

As you reach the central town, you may notice that relatively few people choose to swim along the central stretch of sand running from the start of the *malecón* to the Río Cuale, because it's more of a commercial area, and there are no services for chairs or beverages on the sand, although it's a popular place for parasailing.

Playa Los Muertos (also known as Playa Olas Altas or Playa del Sol) begins just south of the Río Cuale and is hands-down the most popular town beach. The water can be rough here, but the wide beach is home to a large array of *palapa* restaurants with food, beverage, and beach-chair service. The two most popular spots to grab some grub are the adjacent El Dorado and La Palapa (see Chapter 16 for a detailed review of the latter), both of which are located at the end of Calle Pulpito. On the southern end of this beach is a section known as "Blue Chairs" — the most popular gay beach. Vendors stroll the length of Los Muertos, and beach volleyball, parasailing, and Jet Skis are all popular pastimes.

Playa Mismaloya is in a sheltered cove about 10km (6 miles) south of town along Highway 200. The water here is clear and beautiful and ideal for snorkeling off the beach. Entrance to the public beach is just to the left of the **La Jolla de Mismaloya All Suites Resort** (☎ 322-226-0660; www.lajollademismaloya.com). Colorful *palapa* restaurants dot the small beach, and you can rent beach chairs for sunbathing. You can also stake out a table under a *palapa* for the day. Using a restaurant's table and *palapa* is a reciprocal arrangement — the restaurant provides a comfortable place to hang out, and you buy your drinks, snacks, and lunch there. The 1960s Richard Burton movie, *The Night of the Iguana,* was filmed at Mismaloya. La Jolla de Mismaloya has a restaurant, **The Sets of The Night of the Iguana Restaurant,** on the restored film set that's open daily noon to 11 p.m. The movie runs continuously in **John Huston's Restaurant** (serving drinks and light snacks 11 a.m. to 6 p.m.) located below the The Sets of The Night of the Iguana.

About 5km (3 miles) past Mismaloya is **Boca de Tomatlán,** which is similar in setup to Mismaloya but without a large resort looming in the backdrop. Both Mismaloya and Boca de Tomatlán are accessible by public buses that depart from Lázaro Cárdenas Park, at the corner of Basilio Badillo and Insurgentes, every 15 minutes from 5:30 a.m. to 10 p.m. and cost just 50¢. La Boca is the end of the bus line and the point at which the highway turns inland.

South-shore beaches

Boca de Tomatlán is the jumping-off point for the south-shore beaches of **Las Animas, Quimixto,** and **Yelapa,** all of which are accessible only by boat. In addition to having the ambiance of a south-seas cove, each location offers intriguing hikes to jungle waterfalls and plays host to restaurants that front a wide beach. Las Animas is my favorite of the three spots. The beach has the most tranquil waters for swimming and two rocky headlands for protection. Quimixto's palm-fringed crescent of sand takes a back seat to hiking and horseback rides to the waterfall. Although the waterfall rages impressively from August to January, as the dry winter season progresses, you're likely to be less than blown away.

Yelapa, located on a beautiful sheltered cove, is the most remote location of these three beaches. Once a haven for those looking to escape the confines of society — or equally as likely, the law — it became a popular haven for long-term, expatriate visitors and artists due to its seclusion, natural beauty, and simplicity of life. Yelapa has no cars, has one lone paved (pedestrian-only) road, and got electricity only in the past two years. It offers a few primitive accommodations, plus one stunning six-villa inn, **Verana** (Chapter 14 has a detailed review), as well as beachside restaurants and hikes to one of two jungle waterfalls. Although the mellow attitude still prevails, yoga is rapidly becoming the preferred way to reach an altered state of mind here.

Finding Water Fun for Everyone

You haven't experienced Puerto Vallarta unless you've been to the bay — on a boat, under the water, or playing along the shoreline. Bahía de Banderas is as deep as the surrounding mountains are high, and with the wealth of sea life found here, you're as likely to spot whales or dolphins as you are to see other tour boats. The view of town from the bay is simply stunning. And, when it comes to having fun in the water, your biggest challenge is what to do first.

Cruising Puerto Vallarta

Puerto Vallarta offers a number of different boat trips, including sunset cruises and trips for snorkeling, swimming, and diving. Most of the excursions generally travel one of two routes: to the **Marietas Islands,** which are about a 30- to 45-minute boat ride off the northern shore of Bahía de Banderas, or to **Yelapa, Las Animas,** or **Quimixto** along the southern shore.

All the trips to the southern beaches make a stop at **Los Arcos,** an island rock formation south of Puerto Vallarta, for snorkeling. Don't base your opinion of underwater Puerto Vallarta on this location though. Dozens of tour boats dump large numbers of snorkelers overboard at the same time each day, and the fish have figured out *not* to be there at that time. Los Arcos is, however, an excellent site for night diving.

When comparing all the boat cruises, note that some include lunch and most provide music and an open bar on board. Most boats leave around 9:30 a.m., stop for 45 minutes of snorkeling, arrive at the beach destination around noon for a 2½ hour stay, and return around 3 p.m. At Quimixto and Yelapa, visitors can take a half-hour hike to a jungle waterfall or rent a horse for the trip. Prices range from $20 for a sunset cruise or a trip (with open bar) to one of the beaches to $70 for an all-day outing with open bar and meals.

Here are some great choices for a boat cruise:

✔ One boat, the *Marigalante* (☎ 322-223-0309; www.marigalante.com.mx), an exact replica of Columbus's ship the *Santa Maria,* was built in honor of the 500-year anniversary of his voyage to the Americas. It offers a daytime "pirate's cruise" complete with picnic barbecue and treasure hunt and a sunset dinner cruise with folkloric dance and fireworks. The day tour is $55 per person, and the sunset dinner cruise is $70 per person.

✔ My choice for the best day-trip is an excursion to **Caletas,** the cove where John Huston (the director of such movie classics as *The Maltese Falcon, The Treasure of Sierra Madre,* and the Vallarta-filmed *The Night of the Iguana*) made his home for years. **Vallarta Adventures** (☎ 866-256-2739 from the U.S., or 322-297-1212; www.vallarta-adventures.com) holds the exclusive lease on this private cove and has done an excellent job of restoring Huston's former home, adding exceptional day-spa facilities, and landscaping the beach, which is wonderful for snorkeling or diving. The quality facilities, combined with the relative privacy that this day-trip offers at $70 per person, has made it one of the most popular excursions. Vallarta Adventures also offers an evening cruise that comes complete with dinner and a spectacular contemporary dance show, "Rhythms of the Night."

✔ **Whale-watching tours** are becoming more popular each year because spotting humpback whales is almost a certainty from mid-November (sometimes a few weeks later) through March. For centuries, these majestic whales have migrated to Bahía de Banderas (called Humpback Bay in the 1600s) to reproduce and bear calves. **Open Air Expeditions** (Guerrero 339; ☎ **322-222-3310;** www. vallartawhales.com) is the noted, local, whale-watching authority. These folks offer ecologically oriented tours (for up to 12 people) in small, specially designed, soft boats that allow for better observation from a level that is closer to water, and the sound of their engine is less disturbing to the whales than the engines of the larger boats. The twice-daily, $70 tours (8:30 a.m. and 2:30 p.m.) last 4 hours and include a healthful snack.

Vallarta Adventures (☎ **866-256-2739** from the U.S., or 322-297-1212) offers whale-watching photo excursions in small boats for $70. The trip includes a pre-departure briefing on whale behaviors. This company also features whale-watching on its tours to the Marietas Islands. For $80 you get lunch, time at a private beach, and an ambiance that is more festive than educational while traveling aboard the large catamaran boats.

Skiing and surfing

Watersports — including water-skiing, parasailing, and windsurfing — are available at many beaches along the Bahía de Banderas. The best-known spot for watersports-equipment rental is **Club Bananas Water Sports Center,** which is located on the beachfront of the Las Palmas Hotel (Avenida Francisco Medina Ascencio Km 2.5, Hotel Zone; ☎ **322-221-0821;** ask for the Water Sports Center). WaveRunners, banana boats, and water-skiing equipment are available for hourly, half-day, or full-day rentals. You can also find rental equipment at Playa Los Muertos in between La Palapa and El Dorado restaurants.

Exploring the deep blue

Although Puerto Vallarta lacks the crystal-clear waters of Cancún and other Caribbean coastal venues, it's still a great dive site. The reefs are much smaller than those in Caribbean destinations; however, the abundance of marine life is spectacular. You can see a great variety of sea life, including giant mantas, sea turtles, dolphins, and tropical fish. During the winter months, you're also apt to hear the beautiful underwater songs of humpback whales as you dive. Underwater enthusiasts from beginners to experts can arrange scuba diving with the following folks:

✔ **Vallarta Adventures** (☎ **866-256-2739** from the U.S., or 322-297-1212; www.vallarta-adventures.com) is a five-star PADI dive center that offers instructional programs ranging from the resort-course level to instructor certification. Dives take place at Los

Arcos, a company-owned site at Caletas Cove, Quimixto Coves, the Marietas Islands, and the offshore El Morro and Chimo reefs.

✔ **Chico's Dive Shop** (Díaz Ordaz 772–5, near Carlos O'Brian's; ☎ 322-222-1895; www.chicos-diveshop.com) offers similar dive trips and is also a PADI five-star dive center. Chico's is open daily 8 a.m. to 10 p.m. and has branches at the Marriott, Vidafel, Villa del Palmar, Camino Real, Paradise Village, and Playa Los Arcos hotels.

Sailing away

Put some wind in your sails and experience the bay in the most natural of ways:

✔ **Sail Vallarta** (Club de Tenis Puesta del Sol, Local 7-B, Marina Vallarta; ☎ 322-221-0096; E-mail: sail@pnet.puerto.net.mx) offers several different sailboats for hire. A group day-sail, including crew, use of snorkeling equipment, drinks, food, and music, plus a stop at a beach for swimming and lunch, costs $82. Most trips include a crew, but you can make arrangements to sail yourself or on a smaller boat. Prices vary for full boat charters depending on the vessel and amount of time you want to spend on the water.

✔ **Vallarta Adventures** (☎ 866-256-2739 from the U.S., or 322-297-1212; www.vallarta-adventures.com) also offers two beautiful sailboats for charter and small group sails (up to 12 people for day or evening sails). The service is superb, as is the quality of the food and beverages served on board. And the Vallarta Adventures boats are known for being the sailboats most frequently under sail — many of the other sailing charters prefer to simply motor around the bay.

Reeling in the big one

You can arrange a fishing trip through travel agencies or through the **Cooperativa de Pescadores** (Fishing Cooperative; ☎ 322-222-1202, 322-224-7886) on the *malecón* north of the Río Cuale, next door to the Rosita Hotel. Fishing charters cost $180 to $350 a day for four to eight people; price varies with the boat size. Although the posted price at the fishing cooperative is the same as what you'd find through travel agencies, you may be able to negotiate a lower price at the cooperative. Bring cash — the cooperative doesn't accept credit cards. It's open Monday to Saturday from 7 a.m. to 10 p.m., but make arrangements a day in advance. You can also arrange fishing trips at the Marina Vallarta docks or by calling **Fishing with Carolina** (☎ 322-224-7250 or wireless (044) 322-292-2953; E-mail: fishingwithcarolina@hotmail.com), which features a 30-foot Uniflite Sportsfisher fully equipped with an English-speaking crew. Fishing trips generally include equipment and bait, but drinks, snacks, and lunch are optional, so check to find out what the price includes.

Swimming with dolphins

Ever been kissed by a dolphin? Take advantage of a unique and absolutely memorable opportunity to swim with Pacific bottlenose dolphins in a clear lagoon or oceanarium. **Dolphin Adventure** (☎ **866-256-2739** from the U.S., or 322-297-1212; www.vallarta-adventures.com) operates an interactive dolphin-research facility — considered the finest in Latin America — that allows a limited number of people to swim with the dolphins Monday through Saturday at scheduled times. Cost for the swim is $170, and advance reservations are required — they're generally sold out at least a week in advance.

You may prefer the **Dolphin Encounter** ($75) at the same facility, which allows you to touch and discover more about these dolphins in smaller pools, so you're ensured up-close and personal time with these fascinating creatures — it's also a better choice for children. Dolphin Adventures has two facilities — one in the lagoon of Nuevo Vallarta, and a newer, more expansive oceanarium-style facility on Av. Las Palmas No. 39-A., which also serves as the headquarters of Vallarta Adventures. The oceanarium gets my highest recommendation. The experience leaves you with an indescribable sensation, and it's a joy to see these dolphins — they're well cared for, happy, and spirited. After a few swims with these dolphins, I now consider them to be my friends, and they even remember me — that's how it seems to me anyway. The program is about education and interaction, not entertainment or amusement, and I especially recommend it for children 10 and older.

Enjoying Land Sports

What's great about Puerto Vallarta is that many of the best things to do on land here are free. Vallarta is a town of simple pleasures — walking along the *malécon* at sunset, catching a concert at the open-air theater across from the central plaza, strolling through the impressive Our Lady of Guadalupe church, or wandering into any of the dozens of local art galleries.

In addition to these laid-back diversions, Puerto Vallarta is a virtual playground for activities ranging from mountain biking to golf. Eco-friendly tours can take you into the tropical jungle or to remote mountain villages. I bet that you can find more things to do here than you have days in which to do them.

Teeing off

Puerto Vallarta is rapidly positioning itself to rival Los Cabos as Mexico's golf capital. Five new courses have opened in recent years, and the Vista Vallarta Golf Club was the site of the 2002 World Golf Championships-World Cup.

A set of fairways and greens that has been around for awhile is the Joe Finger–designed course at the **Marina Vallarta Golf Club** (☎ 322-221-0073), an 18-hole, par-74, private course that winds through the Marina Vallarta peninsula and provides great ocean views. It's for members only, but most of the luxury hotels in Puerto Vallarta have memberships that their guests can use. A bar, restaurant, and pro shop are on the premises, and a golf pro is around to offer his services. The greens fees are $136 in high season and $115 during low season. (These rates may vary depending on the type of membership your hotel has.) Fees include golf cart, range balls, and tax. Caddies charge $8 to $10. Club rentals, lessons, and special packages are also available.

North of town in the state of Nayarit, about 16km (10 miles) beyond Puerto Vallarta, is the public, 18-hole, par-72 **Los Flamingos Club de Golf** (☎ 329-296-5006; www.flamingosgolf.com.mx), the oldest course in town. It features beautiful jungle vegetation and has just undergone a course renovation and upgrade. The club is open 7 a.m. to 5 p.m. daily and has a snack bar (but no restaurant) and full pro shop. The greens fee is $90 and includes the use of a golf cart; a caddy charges $12, and club rentals are $30. A free shuttle service is available from downtown Puerto Vallarta; call for pickup times and locations.

The new Jack Nicklaus Signature golf course at the **Four Seasons Punta Mita** (☎ 322-291-6000) is breathtaking as well as challenging. It has eight oceanfront holes, but you can see the ocean from every hole on the course. Its hallmark is Hole 3B, the "Tail of the Whale," with a long drive to a green located on a natural island — the only natural-island green in the Americas. It requires an amphibious golf cart to take you to the green when the tide is high, and the management has thoughtfully added an alternative-play hole for times when the ocean or tides aren't accommodating. The course is open only to guests of the Four Seasons resort or to members of other golf clubs with a letter of introduction from their pro. Selected other Vallarta-area hotels also have guest privileges — ask your concierge. Greens fees for guests of the Four Seasons are $170, $260 for non-guests, including cart, with club rentals (Calloway) an extra $60. Golf lessons are also available.

A second Jack Nicklaus course is at the **Vista Vallarta Golf Club** (☎ 322-290-0030; www.vistavallartagolf.com), along with one designed by Tom Weiskopf. These courses were the site of the 2002 World Golf Championships-World Cup. Vista Vallarta is in the foothills of the Sierra Madre, behind the bullring in Puerto Vallarta. A round costs $167 per person, including cart.

The Robert von Hagge–designed **El Tigre** course at Paradise Village in Nuevo Vallarta (☎ 322-297-0773; www.eltigregolf.com) opened in March 2002. The 7,239-yard course is on a relatively flat piece of land, but the design incorporates challenging bunkers, undulating fairways, and water features on several holes. El Tigre offers lessons and has an expansive clubhouse. Greens fees are $185 a round, or $85 if you play after 2 p.m.

Taking time for tennis

Many hotels in Puerto Vallarta offer excellent **tennis** facilities, several with clay courts, and there's also a full-service public tennis club. The **Canto del Sol Tennis Club** (☎ 322-224-0123), located at the Continental Plaza hotel in the Hotel Zone, offers indoor and outdoor courts (including a clay court), a full pro shop, lessons, clinics, and partner match-ups.

Trailing away

One of the best ways to get some exercise, and see some great local sites in the process, is to take a mountain-bike tour with **Bike Mex** (Calle Guerrero 361; ☎ 322-223-1834). Bike Mex offers expert **guided biking and hiking tours** up the Río Cuale canyon and to outlying areas. The popular Río Cuale bike trip costs $42 for 4 hours and includes bike, helmet, gloves, insurance, water, lunch, and an English-speaking guide. Trips take off at either 9 a.m. or 2 p.m., but starting times are flexible; make arrangements a day ahead.

And . . . did I say Yelapa is accessible only by boat? For anyone serious about their biking, I've traveled with Bike Mex on its all-day, advanced-level bike trip to this magical cove, and it's great. You and your fellow riders depart at 7:30 a.m. in a van and travel to your starting point in the town of El Tuito. The 53km (33-mile) ride includes 30km (18½ miles) of climbs to a peak elevation of a little more than 1,000m (3,600 feet). The journey covers switchbacks, fire roads, single tracks, awesome climbs, and steep downhills before ending up at a beachfront *palapa* restaurant in Yelapa. You have the option of staying the night in Yelapa or returning that afternoon by small boat. This tour costs $150, takes 4 to 6 hours, and includes all the bike gear, drinks, lunch, boat and land transportation, guide, and *ample* encouragement.

Other bicycle trips, such as those along the beachfront of Punta Mita, are also available. Guided **hiking tours** are available along the same routes. The prices start at $30 and vary depending on the route.

Saddling up

You can arrange guided **horseback rides** through travel agents or directly with one of the local ranches. **Rancho Palma Real** (Carretera Vallarta-Tepic 4766; ☎ 322-221-2120) offers by far the nicest horseback riding tour in the area. The horses are in excellent health and condition, plus you get an added tour of local farms on your way to the ranch. The office is 5 minutes north of the airport, and the ranch is in Las Palmas, approximately 40 minutes northeast of Vallarta. Breakfast and lunch are included with the $55 fee.

Rancho El Charro (Avenida Francisco Villa 895; ☎ **322-224-0114;** www.ranchoelcharro.com) and **Rancho Ojo de Agua** (Cerrada de Cardenal 227; ☎ and fax: **322-224-0607**) also offer high-quality tours. Both of these ranches are about a 10-minute taxi ride north of downtown toward the Sierra Madre foothills. The morning and sunset rides last 3 hours and take you up into the mountains overlooking the ocean and town. The cost is $30. They also have their own comfortable base camp for serious riders who want to stay out overnight.

Enjoying an eco-tour

The **Sierra Madre Expedition** is an excellent tour offered by **Vallarta Adventures** (☎ **866-256-2739** from the U.S., or 322-297-1212; www.vallarta-adventures.com). This daily excursion travels in special Mercedes all-terrain vehicles through jungle trails north of Puerto Vallarta, stopping at a small town and in a forest for a brief nature walk. The tour winds up on a pristine secluded beach for lunch and swimming. The $65 outing is worthwhile because it takes tourists on exclusive trails through scenery that would otherwise be off-limits.

In addition to their seasonal whale-watching excursions, **Open Air Expeditions** (☎ **322-222-3310;** www.vallartawhales.com) offers other nature-oriented trips, including **bird-watching** outings and **ocean kayaking** sessions in Punta Mita. The tours at **Ecotours de México** (Ignacio L. Vallarta 243; ☎ **322-222-6606;** www.ecotours-mex.com) include seasonal trips (August to November) to a **turtle preservation camp** where you can witness baby Olive Ridley turtles hatch.

Tukari Tours travel agency (☎ **322-224-7177;** Fax: 322-224-2350; www.tukari.com) specializes in ecological and culturally oriented tours. These folks can arrange bird-watching trips to the fertile birding grounds near **San Blas** (3 to 4 hours north of Puerto Vallarta in the state of Nayarit), shopping trips to **Tlaquepaque and Tonalá** (6 hours inland near Guadalajara), or a day-trip to **Rancho Altamira** (a 50-acre, hilltop working ranch) for a barbecue lunch and horseback riding followed by a stroll through **El Tuito,** a small colonial-era village nearby. They can also arrange an unforgettable morning at **Terra Noble Spa Art and Healing Center** (☎ **322-223-3530** or 322-222-5400; www.terranoble.com), a mountaintop day spa and center for the arts where participants can get a massage or treatment, work in clay and paint, and have lunch in a heavenly setting overlooking the bay.

Vallarta's newest adventure activity is a **canopy tour,** operated by Vallarta Adventures (☎ **866-256-2739** from the U.S., or 322-297-1212; www.vallarta-adventures.com). You glide from treetop to treetop, getting an up-close-and-personal look at a tropical rainforest canopy and the trails far below. Expert guides assist you to the special platforms, and you move from one platform to another using pulleys on horizontal traverse cables, while the guides explain the tropical flora surrounding you. The guides also offer assistance — and moral support! — as you rappel back down to the forest floor. Tours depart from the Vallarta Adventures offices in both Marina Vallarta and Nuevo Vallarta at 8 a.m., returning at 2 p.m. The price ($65 for adults, $33 for children 8 to 12) includes the tour, unlimited non-alcoholic beverages, and light snacks.

A second option for a canopy tour is available in the southern jungles of Vallarta, over the Orquidias River, with **Canopy Tours de Los Veranos** (☎ 322-223-6060; www.canopytours-vallarta.com). This tour picks you up at the Canopy office, near the southside Pemex station, to transport you to their facilities upriver from Mismaloya. Departures are at 9, 10, and 11 a.m., noon, and 1 and 2 p.m. In addition to the 13 cables — the longest being a full 350 meters (1,150 feet) — it also offers climbing walls, waterslides, and horseback riding. Price is $66 for adults, or $46 for children ages 6 to 12. Use of the natural-granite climbing wall (helmets and climbing shoe use included) is $18; a 90-minute jungle horseback riding tour costs $35.

Sightseeing in Puerto Vallarta

Puerto Vallarta, itself, is a sight to see — cobblestone streets lined with tiny shops, rows of windows edged with curling wrought iron, and vistas of red-tile roofs set against the sea. Start with a walk up and down the *malecón*, the boardwalk that borders the main seaside street.

One of the great pleasures of strolling Puerto Vallarta's *malecón* is taking in the fanciful sculptures that line this seaside promenade. Among the notable works on display is *Nostalgia*, located across from Carlos O'Brian's restaurant. Created by Ramiz Barquet, this sculpture depicts a couple sharing a romantic moment while gazing out on the bay. Farther south is the sculpture group at the *Rotonda del Mar*, locally known as *Fantasy by the Sea*. It's an array of sculpture "chairs" by renowned Mexican artist Alejandro Colunga. This wildly creative series — one chair is topped by a large octopus head, another bench has two giant ears for backrests — seems to always draw a crowd. Closer to the main square is the *Boy on the Seahorse* sculpture, an image that has come to represent this resort town. Photo ops abound — don't miss the fountain across from the main square; its three bronze dolphins seem ready to leap right into the bay.

Across the street from the fountain is the **palacio municipal** (city hall), located on the main square (next to the tourism office). Besides housing the local government, the building has a large Manuel Lepe mural painted inside its stairwell. Nearby, up Calle Independencia, sits the **Parish of Nuestra Señora de Guadalupe church** (Hidalgo 370; ☎ 322-222-1326), topped with its curious crown held in place by angels — a replica of the one worn by Empress Carlota during her brief time in Mexico as Emperor Maximilian's wife. On the church steps, women sell religious mementos, and across the narrow street, vendors sell native herbs for curing common ailments. Services in English are held Sundays at 10 a.m. (in January, there's also a 5 p.m. mass in English). Regular parish hours are from 7 a.m. until 9:30 or 10 p.m. daily.

Three blocks south of the church, head east on Calle Libertad, lined with small shops and pretty second-story windows, to the **municipal market** by the river. After exploring the market, cross the bridge to the island on the river; sometimes a painter is at work on the island's banks. Walk down the center of the island toward the sea, and you come to the tiny **Museo Río Cuale** (no phone), which has a small but impressive permanent exhibit of pre-Columbian figurines. It's open Monday to Saturday 10 a.m. to 4 p.m. Admission is free.

Retrace your steps back to the market and Calle Libertad and follow Calle Miramar to the brightly colored steps up to Calle Zaragoza. Midway up the steps is a magnificent view over rooftops to the sea, plus a cute cafe, **Graffiti** (no phone), where you can break for a cappuccino and a snack. There are close to 100 steps, but you walk leisurely to climb them and coming down is a breeze; the idea is to experience the streets of Vallarta and the feel of this place that was built on the side of the mountain. Up Zaragoza to the right a block is the famous **pink arched bridge** that once connected Richard Burton's and Elizabeth Taylor's houses. This area, known as **"Gringo Gulch,"** is where many Americans have houses.

You can also tour the **Taylor-Burton villas** (Casa Kimberley; Calle Zaragoza 445; ☎ **322-222-1336;** www.casakimberley.com). Tours of the two houses once owned by Elizabeth Taylor and Richard Burton cost $8. Just ring the bell between 9 a.m. and 6 p.m., and if the manager is available, he'll take you through the house.

You can get a peek at some of the other villas in Vallarta every Wednesday and Thursday (from late November through Easter) on the **International Friendship Club** private-home tours (☎ **322-222-5466**). You get to view four private villas in town for a donation of $25 per person with proceeds benefiting local charities. Tour arrangements begin at 10 a.m. at the Hotel Molino de Agua (Avenida Ignacio L. Vallarta 130, adjacent to the southbound bridge over the Río Cuale), where you can buy breakfast while you wait for the group to gather. Arrive early because this tour sells out quickly! The tour departs at 11 a.m. and lasts approximately 2½ hours.

Hotel travel desks and travel agencies can book you on the ever-popular **Tropical Tour** or **Jungle Tour** ($21 each), a basic orientation to the area. These tours are really expanded city tours that include a drive through the workers' village of Pitillal, the affluent neighborhood of Conchas Chinas, the cathedral, the market, the Taylor-Burton houses, and lunch at a jungle restaurant. Any stop for shopping usually means the driver picks up commission for what you buy.

Shopping Puerto Vallarta

What makes shopping in Puerto Vallarta so great is that it's generally concentrated in small, eclectic, and independent shops rather than impersonal malls. You can find excellent-quality **folk art,** original **clothing** designs, and fine **home accessories** at great prices. Vallarta is known for having the most diverse and impressive selection of **contemporary Mexican fine art** available outside Mexico City. If you want the more typical Mexico resort shopping experience, don't worry — you can still find plenty of tacky T-shirts and the ever-present **silver jewelry.**

The best shopping is concentrated in a few key areas: central downtown, the Marina Vallarta *malecón,* the popular *mercados,* and on the beach — where the merchandise comes to you. Some of the more attractive shops are found 1 to 2 blocks in **back of the *malecón.*** Although still home to a few interesting shops, the marina boardwalk *(marina malecón)* is dominated by real estate companies, timeshare vendors, restaurants, and boating services. Start at the intersection of calles Corona and Morelos — you can find interesting shops in all directions from here. **Marina Vallarta** does offer two shopping plazas (Plaza Marina and Plaza Neptuno, both on the main highway coming from the airport into town), but both have a limited selection of shops.

Puerto Vallarta's **municipal market** is just north of the Río Cuale where Libertad and A. Rodríguez meet. The *mercado* sells clothes, jewelry, serapes, shawls, leather accessories and suitcases, papier-mâché parrots, stuffed frogs and armadillos, and of course, T-shirts. Be sure to do some comparison-shopping and definitely bargain before buying. The market is open daily 9 a.m. to 7 p.m. Up the *mercado* stairs, a **food market** serves inexpensive Mexican meals — for more adventurous diners, it's probably the best value and most authentic dining experience in Vallarta. You can find an **outdoor market** along Río Cuale Island, between the two bridges. Vendors sell crafts, gifts, folk art, and clothing.

Along any public beach, walking **vendors** approach tourists and try to sell merchandise ranging from silver jewelry to rugs, T-shirts to masks. "Almost free!" they call out in seemingly relentless efforts to attract your attention. If you're too relaxed to think of shopping in town, this can be an entertaining alternative for picking up a few souvenirs. (Remember that bargaining is expected.) The most reputable beach vendors are concentrated at Playa Los Muertos in front of the El Dorado and La Palapa restaurants (on the beach near Calle Pulpito).

You need to be aware that much of the silver sold on the beach is actually alpaca, a lesser-quality silver metal (even though many pieces are still stamped with the designation "9.25," supposedly indicating that it's true silver). The prices for and quality of silver on the beach are much lower than they are elsewhere. If you're looking for a more lasting piece of jewelry, you're better off shopping in a true silver shop.

In most of the better-quality shops and galleries, shipping, packing, and delivery services to Puerto Vallarta hotels are available, and some also ship to your home address.

Clothing

Here are some recommended clothing shops and boutiques:

- ✔ Vallarta's only true department store is **LANS,** Juárez 867 (☎ 322-223-2829), which also has a new location in the Hotel Zone in front of the Gigante shopping center (☎ **322-225-4242**). LANS offers a wide selection of name-brand clothing, accessories, footwear, cosmetics, and home furnishings.

- ✔ **Laura López Labra Designs,** Basilio Badillo 324 (☎ **322-222-3074**), just may have the most comfortable clothing you've ever worn. LLL is renowned for her trademark, all-white (or natural) designs in 100% cotton or lace. Laura's fine gauze fabrics float through her designs of seductive skirts, romantic dresses, blouses, beachwear, and baby dolls. Men's offerings include cotton drawstring pants and lightweight shirts. It's open Monday to Saturday 10 a.m. to 2 p.m. and 5 to 9 p.m.

- ✔ **Mar de Sueños,** Leona Vicario 220 (☎ **322-222-2662**), is a small but delectible shop that carries stunning swimsuits and exquisite lingerie. Without a doubt, this shop offers the finest women's beachwear, intimate apparel, and evening wear in Vallarta for those special occasions — or just to make you feel extra special. The shop also stocks a selection of fine linen clothing, and it's one of the few places in Mexico that carries the renowned Italian line, La Perla. Other name brands include Gottex, Calvin Klein, and DKNY. Open Monday to Saturday from 10 a.m. to 2 p.m. and 5 to 9 p.m.

- ✔ Hip and sultry fashions, direct from South America, are the specialties of the **de Santos Boutique,** Morelos 771 (☎ **322-223-5326**, or 322-223-3052; www.desantos.com.mx), found adjacent to the de Santos restaurant and club. It's open Monday to Saturday 10 a.m. to 2 p.m. and 6 to 10 p.m.

Huichol Indian art: What it is and where to buy it

Puerto Vallarta offers the best selection of Huichol art in Mexico. Descendants of the Aztecs, the Huichol Indians are one of the last remaining indigenous cultures in the world that have remained true to its ancient traditions, customs, language, and habitat. The Huichol live in adobe structures in the mountains north and east

(continued)

(continued)

of Puerto Vallarta. Due to the decreasing fertility of the land surrounding their villages, they now depend more on the sale of their artwork for sustenance.

Huichol art has always been cloaked in a veil of mysticism — probably one of the reasons this form of *artesanía* (handcrafts) is so sought after by serious collectors. Huichol art is characterized by colorful, symbolic yarn "paintings," inspired by visions experienced during spiritual ceremonies. In these ceremonies, artists ingest peyote, a hallucinogenic cactus, which induces brightly colored visions; these are considered to be messages from their ancestors. The symbolic and mythological imagery seen in these visions is reflected in the art, which encompasses not only yarn paintings but also fascinating masks and bowls decorated with tiny colored beads.

The Huichol may be geographically isolated, but they have business savvy and have adapted their art to meet consumer demand — original Huichol art, therefore, isn't necessarily traditional. Designs depicting iguanas, jaguars, sea turtles, frogs, eclipses, and eggs are a result of popular demand. For more traditional works, look for pieces that depict deer, scorpions, wolves, or snakes.

You may also see Huichol Indians on the streets of Vallarta, dressed in white clothing embroidered with colorful designs. A number of fine galleries that sell Huichol pieces are located in downtown Puerto Vallarta (see "Decorative and folk art" and "Crafts and gifts," later in this chapter). A notable place for finding out more about the Huicholes is **Huichol Collection,** Morelos 490, across from the sea-horse statue on the *malecón* (☎ 322-223-2141). This shop offers an extensive selection of Huichol art in all price ranges, and it has a replica of a Huichol adobe hut, informational displays explaining more about their fascinating way of life and beliefs, and usually a Huichol Indian at work creating art.

Huichol art falls into two main categories: yarn paintings and beaded pieces. All other items you may find in Huichol art galleries are either ceremonial objects or items used in their everyday lives.

- ✔ **Yarn paintings** are made on a wood base covered with wax that is meticulously overlaid with colored yarn. Designs represent the magical vision of the underworld, and each symbol gives meaning to the piece. Paintings made with wool yarn are more authentic than those made with acrylic; however, acrylic yarn paintings are usually brighter and have more detail because the threads are thinner. Finding empty spaces where the wax base shows is normal. Usually the artist starts with a central motif and works around it, but having several independent motifs that, when combined, take on a different meaning is common. A painting with many small designs tells a more complicated story than one with only one design and fill-work on the background. Look for the story of the piece on the back of the painting. Most Huichol artists write in pencil in Huichol and Spanish.

- ✔ **Beaded pieces** are made on carved wooden shapes depicting different animals, wooden eggs, or small bowls made from gourds. The artist covers the pieces with wax and applies tiny *chaquira* beads one by one to form different designs. Usually the beaded designs represent animals; plants; the elements of fire, water, or air; and certain symbols that give a special meaning to the whole. Beadwork with many small designs that don't exactly fit into one another is more time consuming and has a more complex symbolic meaning. This kind of work has empty spaces where the wax shows.

Contemporary art

With one of the stronger art communities in Latin America, Puerto Vallarta has an impressive selection of fine galleries featuring quality, original works of art. Here are some that are worth a visit:

- **Galería AL (Arte Latinoamericano),** Josefa Ortiz Dominguez 155 (☎ and fax: **322-222-4406**), showcases contemporary works created by young, primarily Latin-American artists, as well as Vallarta favorite Marta Gilbert. It's open Monday to Saturday 10 a.m. to 9 p.m.

- **Gallería Dante,** Basilio Badillo 269 (☎ **322-222-2477;** www.galleriadante.com), showcases contemporary sculptures and classical reproductions of Italian, Greek, and Art Deco bronzes — all set against a backdrop of gardens and fountains in a former private villa. Located on the "calle de los cafés," the gallery is open daily during the winter 10 a.m. to 5 p.m.

- **Galería des Artistes,** Leona Vicario 248 (☎ **322-223-0006**), features contemporary painters and sculptors from throughout Mexico, including the renowned original "magiscopes" of Feliciano Bejar. Paintings by Vallarta favorite Evelyn Boren, as well as a small selection of works by Mexican masters, including Diego Rivera and Orozco, are also here, among the exposed brick walls and stylish interior spaces. It's open Monday to Saturday noon to 11 p.m.

- Since opening in 1987, **Galería Pacífico,** Aldama 174, 2nd floor, 1½ blocks inland from the fantasy sculptures on the *malecón* (☎ **322-222-1982;** www.artmexico.com), has been considered one of Mexico's finest galleries. The gallery has a wide selection of sculptures and paintings by midrange masters and up-and-comers on display. During high season, it's open Monday to Saturday 10 a.m. to 9 p.m. and Sundays by appointment.

- One of Vallarta's first galleries, **Galería Uno,** Morelos 561 at Corona (☎ **322-222-0908**), features an excellent selection of contemporary paintings by Latin-American artists, plus a variety of posters and prints. Set in a classic adobe building with an open courtyard, it's also a casual, *salón*-style gathering place for friends of owner Jan Lavender. The gallery is open Monday to Saturday 10 a.m. to 9 p.m.

- **T. Fuller Gallery,** Hidalgo 242 (☎ **322-222-9196**), just steps away from Our Lady of Guadalupe church, exhibits a small but stunning collection of contemporary art, paintings, ceramics, and sculptures. Hours are Monday to Saturday 10 a.m. to 2 p.m., and 6 to 9 p.m.

Crafts and gifts

Check out these choices for finding crafts and gifts:

✔ Opened in 1953, **Alfarería Tlaquepaque,** Avenida México 1100
(☎ **322-223-2121**), is Vallarta's original source for Mexican ceramics and decorative crafts — all at excellent prices. Talavera pottery
and dishware, colored glassware, bird cages, baskets, and wood
furniture are just a few of the many items you can find in this
warehouse-style store. The hours are Monday to Saturday 9 a.m.
to 9 p.m., Sunday 10 a.m. to 3 p.m.

✔ Flickering candles glowing from colored-glass holders welcome you
into **Safari Accents,** Olas Altas 224, Local 4 (☎ **322-223-2660**), a
highly original shop overflowing with creative gifts, one-of-a-kind
furnishings, and reproductions of paintings by Frida Kahlo and
Botero. It's open 10 a.m. to 11 p.m. daily.

Decorative and folk art

Find some one-of-a-kind pieces at these unique shops:

✔ The **Banderas Bay Trading Company,** Lázaro Cárdenas 263, near
Ignacio L. Vallarta (☎ **322-223-4352**), has fine antiques and decorative objects for the home, including unique and contemporary
furniture, antique wooden doors, religious-themed items, *retablos*
(painted scenes on tin backgrounds depicting the granting of a
miracle), original art, beeswax candles in grand sizes, hand-loomed
textiles, plus glassware and pewter. Items are hand-picked by
one of the most noteworthy interior designers in the area, Peter
Bowman. Open Monday to Saturday 9 a.m. to 8 p.m.

✔ **Lucy's CuCu Cabaña and Zoo,** Basilio Badillo 295 (no phone), has
one of the most entertaining, eclectic, and memorable collections
of Mexican folk art — about 70% of which is animal-themed. Items
include metal sculptures, Oaxacan wooden animals, *retablos*, and
fine Talavera ceramics. Five percent of all sales benefit the Puerto
Vallarta Animal Protection Association, organized by the shop's
owners. The shop is open Monday to Saturday 10 a.m. to 10 p.m.,
but it's closed May 15 to October 15.

✔ **Puerco Azul,** Constitucion 325, just off Basilio Badillo (☎ **322-222-
8647**), offers a whimsical and eclectic selection of art and home
accessories, much of it created by owner and artist Lee Chapman
(a.k.a. Lencho). You can find many animal-themed works in bright
colors, including his signature "blue pigs" (puercos azules). It's
open Monday to Saturday 10 a.m. to 8 p.m.

✔ **Querubines,** Juárez 501 A, at Galeana (☎ **322-223-1727**), is my
personal favorite for the finest-quality artisan works from throughout Mexico, including exceptional artistic silver jewelry, embroidered and hand-woven clothing, bolts of loomed fabrics, tin mirrors
and lamps, glassware, pewter frames and trays, high-quality wool
rugs, straw bags, and Panama hats. It's open Monday to Sunday
10 a.m. to 9 p.m.

Jewelry and accessories

You can find jewelry and other accessories at the following:

- **Mosaïqe,** Basilio Badillo 277 (☎ 322-223-3146), is a potpourri of global treasures. The shop features an extensive selection of silk, cotton, and cashmere pareos and shawls, plus resort bags, jewelry, and home decor items. It's open daily 10 a.m. to 7 p.m.

- At **Viva,** Basilio Badillo 274 (☎ 322-222-4078; www.viva collection.com), both the shop and jewelry are stunning. You enter through a long corridor lined with displays showcasing exquisite jewelry from 450 international designers. The main room has a large, glass, pyramid-shaped skylight as its roof, and more memorable jewelry displays surround comfy couches. Viva also features the largest selection of authentic French espadrilles and ballet slippers in Latin America, plus a great selection of sunglasses and hats. It's open daily 10 a.m. to 11 p.m.

Tequila and cigars

Looking for quality tequila and cigars? Check out these shops:

- **La Casa del Habano,** Aldama 174 (☎ 322-223-2758), is a fine tobacco shop with certified-quality cigars from Cuba, Mexico, and the Dominican Republic, along with humidors, cutters, elegant lighters, and other smoking accessories. It's open Monday to Saturday noon to 9 p.m.

- At **La Casa del Tequila,** Morelos 589 (☎ 322-222-2000), you can find an extensive selection of premium tequilas, plus information and tastings to help guide you to an informed selection. In the back, a garden patio has a bar for enjoying some of Mexico's best tacos, plus tequila drinks. Business hours are Monday to Saturday 10 a.m. to 10 p.m.

Embarking on a Side Trip

Anyone for a shot of tequila? I'm talking about taking a picture of the town — although you can also sample the beverage of the same name on this side trip. **Vallarta Adventures** (☎ 866-256-2739 from the U.S., or 322-297-1212; www.vallarta-adventures.com) offers a half-day trip (300km/187.5 miles) that takes you to the classic town of **Tequila,** where you visit one of the original haciendas and tequila fields. It's just a comfortable 35-minute flight aboard a private, 16-passenger plane to the town of Tequila. This is the only region in the world where this legendary spirit is distilled, much like the exclusive Champagne region in

France. The visit centers around Herradura Tequila's impressive 18th-century **Hacienda San Jose** where you find out about the myth and the tradition of producing tequila from the stately plants that line this town's hillsides — an experience comparable to California's winery tours. The tour departs every Thursday at 1 p.m. from the Aerotron private airport (adjacent to the PV International Airport) and returns to Puerto Vallarta by 8 p.m. The cost is $255, which includes all air and ground transportation, tours, lunch, and beverages.

For other day-trip options around Vallarta, two worthy choices are San Sebastián and Yelapa.

Mining historic San Sebastián

If you haven't heard about **San Sebastián,** it probably won't be long until you do — its remote location (about 160km/100 miles from Vallarta) and historic appeal have made it the media's new darling destination in Mexico. Originally discovered in the late 1500s and settled in 1603, the town peaked as a center of mining operations, swelling to a population of more than 30,000, by the mid-1800s. Today, with roughly 600 year-round residents, San Sebastián retains all the charm of a village locked in time. Highlights include an old church, a coffee plantation, an underground tunnel system — and not a T-shirt shop to be found.

Vallarta Adventure's **Colonial Treasures Air Expedition** (☎ 866-256-2739 from the U.S., or 322-297-1212; www.vallarta-adventures.com) is a great introduction to this town. A 15-minute flight aboard a 13-seat, turbo-prop Cessna Caravan takes you into the heart of the Sierra Madre before settling in San Sebastián. The plane is equipped with raised wings, which allows you to admire — and photograph — the mountain scenery below. The plane arrives on a gravel landing strip in San Sebastián for a half-day tour — it's more like an informal stroll through town and a chance to talk with the more colorful personalities of the area — and each day is different. The package costs $130 and includes the flight, a walking tour of the town (including a stop at the old Hacienda Jalisco, an inn located in a historic building, once used as the headquarters of a silver mining company — a favored getaway of John Huston, Elizabeth Taylor, Richard Burton, and their friends), and brunch in town.

This innovative tour company also offers a similar — yet different — air tour to the mountain villages of **Mascota** and **Talpa de Allende,** where you find out about the religious significance of these traditional towns. In Mascota, stroll the cobblestone streets lined with adobe houses and colonial haciendas, stopping at the majestic town church, dedicated to the Virgin de los Dolores (Virgin of Sorrows), which was completed in 1880 and took more than 100 years to construct. You stop for lunch and tour a local raicilla distillery to sample this locally popular beverage before traveling on to Talpa. Talpa is known for being home to one of Mexico's most revered icons, the Virgin Rosario de Talpa, believed to grant miracles with her healing powers. Ask for one yourself as you visit the Gothic church that bears her name, or simply wander around this pastoral village, set in a valley that is surrounded by pine-covered mountains. The 6-hour adventure includes airfare and lunch, for $140 per person. Departures are daily, except Wednesdays and Sundays, at 10:30 a.m., from Aerotron (next to Puerto Vallarta's airport).

Pacific Travel (☎ 322-225-2270) offers a **Jeep tour** to San Sebastián for $75 (up to four people per Jeep including a guide). You can choose to drive along steep, narrow, rocky mountain roads or leave that part of the adventure to your guide. This tour departs at 9 a.m. and returns at 5 p.m.

If you want to stay overnight, you have two options. The first is the very basic **El Pabellon de San Sebastián** (☎ and fax **322-297-0200** or 322-297-2856), which has nine rooms facing the town square. Don't expect extras here, but the rates run $12 per double or $7.50 for singles. Reservations are handled through the town's central phone lines — you call and leave a message or send a fax, and hopefully, the hotel receives it. Except on holidays, there's generally room at this inn, but bring cash — credit cards aren't accepted.

A more enjoyable option is the stately **Hacienda Jalisco** (make your reservations through the town telephones listed in the preceding paragraph or via e-mail at ssb@pvnet.com.mx), built in 1850 and once the center of mining operations in this old mining town. Located near the airstrip (a 15-minute walk from town), the beautifully landscaped, rambling hacienda has walls that seem to whisper tales of its past. But if proprietor Bud Acord is feeling social, his stories usually outshine any the hacienda has to tell. He's welcomed John Huston, Liz Taylor, Richard Burton, Peter O'Toole, and a cast of local characters as his guests. The extra-clean rooms have wood floors, rustic furnishings and antiques, and working fireplaces; some are decorated with pre-Columbian reproductions. The ample bathrooms are beautifully tiled and have skylights. Hammocks grace the upstairs terrace. A sort-of museum on the lower level attests to the celebrity guests and prior importance the hacienda has enjoyed over the years. Because of its remote location, all meals are included. Rates are $120 per couple per night including meals; alcoholic beverages are extra. Group rates are available and discounts may be possible for longer stays. No credit cards are accepted.

Relaxing in Yelapa

Yelapa, the same south-shore beach I discuss earlier in this chapter, is also a great overnight escape. It's a cove straight out of a tropical fantasy and only a 45-minute trip by boat from Puerto Vallarta. Yelapa has no cars, has one lone paved (pedestrian-only) road, and got electricity only in the past 2 years. (The cove remains accessible only by boat.) Yelapa's tranquility, natural beauty, and seclusion make it a popular home for hippies, hipsters, artists, writers, and a few expatriates (looking to escape the stress of the rest of the world or, perhaps, the law). Yes, it's a seemingly strange cast of characters, but you're unlikely to ever meet a stranger here — Yelapa remains casual and friendly.

To get to Yelapa, take an excursion boat or an inexpensive water taxi. You can spend an enjoyable day in this wonderful spot, but I recommend a longer stay — it provides a completely different perspective of the place.

When you're in Yelapa, you can lie in the sun, swim, and snorkel; eat fresh, grilled seafood at a beachfront restaurant; or sample the local moonshine, *raicilla.* The beach vendors specialize in the most amazing pies I've ever tasted (coconut, lemon, or chocolate), and the way pie ladies walk the beach while balancing the pie plates on their heads is equally amazing. Vendors sell crocheted swimsuits too. You can also tour this tiny town or hike up a river to see one of two waterfalls. The waterfall closest to town is about a 30-minute walk from the beach.

If you use a local guide for a tour or a hike, agree on a price before you start out. Horseback riding, guided bird-watching excursions, fishing trips, and paragliding are also available.

For overnight accommodations, local residents frequently rent out rooms, or you can check out the rustic **Hotel Lagunita** (☎ 322-209-5055 or 322-209-5056; www.hotel-lagunita.com). With 27 *cabañas* (all with private bathroom), a saltwater pool, massage services, and an amiable restaurant/bar, this is the most accommodating place for most visitors — although you may need to bring your own towel because they're known to be in short supply. Also, note that the hotel only has a few hours of power daily. Rates generally run $55 to $70 per night, but they vary depending on the *cabaña* and the time of year. Hotel Lagunita accepts American Express, MasterCard, and Visa with a 10% surcharge. This location has become quite popular for yoga students and other groups.

My preferred place to stay is **Verana** (☎ 800-677-5156 or 661-946-7477 in the U.S., or 322-222-2360; www.verana.com). It's a magical six-villa inn located on the mountaintop of the western edge of Yelapa Cove. For details about Verana, check out my review in Chapter 14.

If you stay over on a Wednesday or Saturday night during winter months, don't miss the regular dance at the **Yelapa Yacht Club** (no phone). Typically tongue-in-cheek for Yelapa, the "yacht club" consists of a cement dance floor and a disco ball, but the DJ spins a great range of tunes ranging from Glenn Miller to Jay-Z, attracting all ages and types of musical aficionados to the dance. Dinner is a bonus — the food may be the best anywhere in the bay. The menu changes depending on what's fresh. Ask for directions; it's located in the main village on the beach.

Discovering Puerto Vallarta after Dark

Puerto Vallarta's spirited nightlife reflects the town's dual nature: part resort, part colonial Mexican town. In the past few years, Vallarta's nightlife has seen an expansion of live music, especially in clubs along Calle Ignacio L. Vallarta (the extension of the main southbound road) after it crosses the Río Cuale. A live blues club, a sports bar, live mariachi music, a gay dance club, a steamy-hot live salsa dance club, and the obligatory **Señor Frog's** are along one 3-block stretch of the road. Walk from place to place and take in a bit of it all!

The *malecón,* which used to be lined with restaurants, is now known more for its selection of dance clubs and a few more-relaxed club options, all of which look out over the ocean. You can walk along the broad walkway by the water's edge and check out the action at the various clubs, which extend from the Cuban-themed **La Bodeguita del Medio** on the north end to **Hooters** just off the central plaza.

Marina Vallarta has its own array of clubs with a more upscale, indoor, and air-conditioned atmosphere. South of the Río Cuale, the **Olas Altas zone** literally buzzes with action pouring out of its wide selection of small cafes and martini bars. In this zone, there's also an active gay and lesbian club scene.

Taking in a cultural event

As in most Mexican beach resorts, Vallarta has a limited selection of cultural nightlife beyond the **Mexican fiesta,** but as a growing center for the visual arts in Mexico, Vallarta is more diverse than most. Popular events include the winter season of art-exhibition openings. Puerto Vallarta's gallery community comes together to present almost weekly **art walks** where new exhibits are presented, featured artists are in attendance, and complimentary cocktails are served. These social events alternate between the galleries along the Marina Vallarta *malecón* and the galleries in the central downtown area. Check listings in the daily English-language newspaper, *Vallarta Today,* upon arrival to see what may be on the schedule during your stay.

Celebrating a fiesta

Major hotels in Puerto Vallarta feature frequent fiestas for tourists — an open-bar, a Mexican buffet dinner, and live-entertainment extravaganzas. Some fiestas are fairly authentic and are good introductions for first-time travelers to Mexico; others can be a bit cheesy. Shows are usually held outdoors but move indoors when necessary.

✔ The **NH Krystal Puerto Vallarta** (☎ 322-224-0202) hosts one of the best fiestas on Tuesdays and Saturdays at 7 p.m. These things are difficult to quantify, but Krystal's program is probably less tacky than most of its hotel counterparts. The charge is $47, and major credit cards are accepted.

✔ My personal favorite of the nocturnal fiestas is **Rhythms of the Night,** which combines a sunset boat cruise to the cove of Caletas with an evening of dining and entertainment under the stars at John Huston's former home. The smooth, fast Vallarta Adventure catamaran takes you to the site, providing entertainment along the way until you're greeted at the dock by tiki torches and native drummers. There's no electricity here — you dine by the light of the multitude of candles, the stars, and the moon. The buffet dinner is delicious — steak, seafood, and generous vegetarian options, accompanied by wine. Everything is first class. The show, set to the music of native bamboo flutes and guitars, showcases indigenous dances in a contemporary style. The boat departs from the Terminal Marítima at 6 p.m. and returns by 11 p.m. To reserve a spot, contact **Vallarta Adventures** (☎ 866-256-2739 from the U.S., or 322-297-1212; www.vallarta-adventures.com). The cost is $75 and includes the boat cruise, dinner, open bar, and entertainment. Major credit cards are accepted.

Enjoying the club and music scene

You can actually find some of Vallarta's best bets for nightlife in popular restaurants — combining food and fun. Other options are one of the many clubs featuring live music. Whatever your final selection is, one thing is for sure — Vallarta offers something for everyone, and there's rarely a quiet night in town.

Restaurants/bars

The sleek **Bianco,** Insurgentes 109, Col. Emiliano Zapata (☎ 322-222-2748), is a popular choice for more sophisticated nightlife, with its long, glass-top bar and cozy seating areas where conversation is possible. This is the spot — finally — for anyone older than 30 who wants to enjoy an evening out, listening to contemporary music. The air-conditioned lounge also features occasional live music, notably salsa on Thursday nights. You can't miss the dramatic entrance, and the lounge even has valet parking — a first in Vallarta. Open daily from 5 p.m. to 4 a.m.

Vallarta's original nightspot is **Carlos O'Brian's,** Paseo Díaz Ordaz 786, along the *malecón* at Pípila (☎ 322-222-1444 or 322-222-4065), once considered the only place you'd think of going for an evening of revelry. Although the competition is stiffer nowadays, COB's still packs them in — especially the 20-something set. Late at night, the scene resembles a college party. It's open daily noon to 2 a.m.

The newest and most sophisticated lounge in Vallarta is the **Constantini Bar Lounge,** set in the elegant eatery, Cafe des Artistes, Guadalupe Sanchez 740 (☎ **322-222-3228/29;** www.cafedesartistes.com). Opened in late 2003, it's become a popular option for those looking for a lively yet sophisticated option for after-dinner drinks. The plush sofas are welcoming, and the list of champagnes by the glass, signature martinis, and specialty drinks are suitably tempting. Live jazz and blues in an intimate atmosphere are drawing crowds. An ample appetizer and dessert menu make it appropriate for a late-night dining-and-drinks option. Open from 6 p.m. to 2 a.m.

Kit Kat Club, Pulpito 120, Playas Los Muertos (☎ **322-223-0093**), is swank, sleek, and reminiscent of a New York, high-style club, but don't be fooled — the club also has a terrific sense of humor. In the golden glow of candlelight, you can lounge around in cushy, leopard-patterned chairs or cream-colored, overstuffed chaise lounges listening to swinging tunes while sipping on a martini. The place isn't only hip, but it also serves good food, with especially tasty appetizers that can double as light meals and scrumptious desserts. Michael, the owner, describes his lounge and cafe as cool, crazy, wild, jazzy, and sexy. I agree. Often, in high season, a cross-dressing songstress performs a cabaret-style floor show. The club is open daily 11 a.m. to 2 a.m.

La Bodeguita del Medio, Paseo Diaz Ordaz/*malecón*, at Allende (☎ **322-223-1585**), is an authentic Cuban restaurant known for its casual energy, terrific live music, and mojitos — stiff rum-based drinks with fresh mint and limejuice. It's a branch of the original Bodeguita in Havana (reputedly Hemingway's favorite restaurant there), which opened in 1942. If you can't get to that one, the Vallarta version has successfully imported the essence — and it has a small souvenir shop that sells Cuban cigars, rum, and other items. The downstairs has large wooden windows that open to the *malecón* street action, while the upstairs offers terrific views of the bay. Walls throughout are decorated with old photographs and patrons' signatures — if you can, find a spot and add yours! The food is less memorable here then the music and atmosphere, so I suggest drinks and dancing, nothing more. It's open daily from 11:30 a.m. to 2 a.m.

A Mexican classic gone contemporary is **La Cantina de los Remedios,** Morelos 709 (☎ **322-222-1734**). *Cantinas* are a centuries-old tradition in Mexico, and this one retains the fundamentals while updating the concept to a hip club. Cantinas serve little complimentary plates of food as your table continues to order drinks. The grub is served here from 1 to 5 p.m. and may include *carne con chile* (meat in a chile sauce), soup of the day, or quesadillas. In the evenings, enjoy a romantic, clubby atmosphere with recorded music alternating between sultry boleros and the hottest in Mexican rock at levels that still permit conversation. If you require more stimulation, board games are available to play in one of the brightly colored, smaller rooms or on the larger open-air patio. La Cantina is open Sunday to Wednesday noon to 2 a.m. and Thursday to Saturday noon to 4 a.m. No credit cards.

Live music

Currently the most popular live-music club in Vallarta, **Club Roxy,**
Ignacio L. Vallarta 217 (☎ **322-223-2404**), features a hot house band,
led by club owner Pico, that plays a mix of reggae, blues, rock, and anything by Santana. Live music jams Monday to Saturday from 10 p.m. to
2 a.m. Roxy is located south of the river between Madero and Cárdenas,
and it's open nightly 6 p.m. to 2 a.m. There's no cover.

El Faro Lighthouse Bar (☎ **322-221-0541** or 322-221-0542) is a circular
cocktail lounge at the top of the Marina Vallarta lighthouse and is one
of Vallarta's most romantic nightspots. Live or recorded jazz plays, and
conversation is manageable. Drop by at twilight for the magnificent
panoramic views. Open daily 5 p.m. to 2 a.m. with no cover.

Mariachi Loco, Lázaro Cárdenas 254, at Ignacio Vallarta (☎ **322-223-
2205**), is a live and lively mariachi club that also features singers belt-
ing out boleros and ranchero classics. The mariachi show begins at
10 p.m. — the mariachis stroll and play as guests join in impromptu
singing — and by 10 p.m., things really get going. After midnight, the
mariachis play for pay, which is around $10 for each song. The kitchen
serves Mexican food until 1 a.m. The club itself is open daily 7 p.m. to
4 a.m.

Dance clubs and discos

A few of Vallarta's clubs or discos charge admission, but generally you
just pay for drinks — $4 for a margarita, $2.50 for a beer, and more for
whiskey and mixed drinks. Keep an eye out for the discount passes frequently available in hotels, restaurants, and other tourist spots. Most
clubs are open daily 10 p.m. to 4 a.m.

- ✔ **Christine** (☎ 322-224-0202) is a dazzling club that still draws a
  crowd with an opening laser-light show, pumped-in dry ice and
  oxygen, flashing lights, and a dozen large-screen video panels.
  Once a disco — in the true sense of the word — Christine received
  a facelift in 2003, and is now a more modern dance club, with
  techno, house, and hip-hop the primary tunes played. The sound
  system is truly amazing, and the mix of music can get almost anyone dancing. This spot is open nightly 10 p.m. to 4 a.m.; the light
  show begins at 11 p.m. No shorts (for men), tennis shoes, or flip-
  flops are permitted. It's part of the NH Krystal Puerto Vallarta,
  north of downtown, and is very visible off Avenida Francisco
  Medina Ascencio. Cover varies from free to $15, depending on the
  night, and major credit cards are accepted.

- ✔ **de Santos,** Morelos 771 (☎ **322-223-3052** or 322-223-3053; www.
  desantos.com.mx), may be among Vallarta's chicest dining spots,
  but it is really known more for the urban, hip crowd its bar and
  adjacent club draws. Opened in 2003, this stunning state-of-the-art
  club quickly became the place for the super-chic to party. The

lower level holds an air-conditioned bar and dance floor, where a DJ spins the hottest house and techno. Upstairs, an open-air roof-top bar has chill-out music and acid jazz. Enjoy the tunes and the fresh air while lounging around on one of the several oversize beds. One partner, a member of the super-hot Latin rock group Maná, uses Vallarta as a home base for writing new songs. The restaurant bar is open daily from 5 p.m. to 1 a.m.; the club is open Wednesday through Saturday from 10 p.m. to 6 a.m., and often waives the cover charge, which ranges from $5 to $20, for women.

✔ **Emporium by Collage,** Calle Proa s/n, Marina Vallarta (☎ 322-221-0505 or 322-221-0861), is a multilevel monster of nighttime enter-tainment that features a pool hall, video arcade, bowling alley, and an always-packed disco bar (with frequent live entertainment). Open daily 10 a.m. to 6 a.m., the club is easily visible from the main highway, just past the entrance to Marina Vallarta, and it's very popular with a young and mainly local crowd. No cover.

✔ The **J&B Salsa Club,** Avenida Francisco Medina Ascencio, Km 2.5, in the Hotel Zone (☎ 322-224-4616), is the locally-popular place to go for dancing to Latin music — from salsa to samba, the danc-ing here is hot! The club features live bands on Fridays, Saturdays, and holidays. It's open from 9 p.m. to 6 a.m. with a $8 cover.

✔ At **The Palm Video & Show Bar,** Olas Altas 508 (☎ 322-223-4813), the big screen above the dance floor plays the most danceable videos in town. At this colorful, lively, and air-conditioned club, the pool table is regularly in play, and you frequently find you're in for a night of great entertainment, as the club regularly books live shows featuring female impersonators. This is a gay-friendly but not exclusively gay club, with a spirited, festive atmosphere. Open daily from 7 p.m. to 2 a.m., a cover charge of about $5 applies on show nights only.

✔ The sheer size of **Señor Frog's,** Ignacio L. Vallarta and Venustiano Carranza (☎ 322-222-5171 or 322-222-5177), an outpost of the famed Carlos 'n Charlie's chain, may be daunting, but it still fills up with partiers and rocks until the early morning hours. Those cute waiters remain a signature of the chain, and one never knows when they'll assemble on stage and call on a bevy of beauties to join them in a tequila-drinking contest. Occasionally, live bands appear. Although mainly popular with the 20s set, all ages find it fun. There's food service, but it's better known for its dance-club atmosphere. It's open from noon to 4 a.m., with no cover.

✔ A visit to the **Zoo,** Paseo Díaz Ordaz 630, the *malecón* (☎ 322-222-4945), gives you a chance to be an animal and get wild in the night — this joint even has cages to dance in if you're feeling really unleashed. The Zoo has a terrific sound system and a great variety of dance music including techno, reggae, and rap. Every hour is a happy hour here with two-for-one drinks. The club is open 11:30 a.m. until the wee hours of the morn, and cover usually ranges from free to $10.

Sports bar

With enough TVs and sports memorabilia to start a mini-museum, **Mickey's No Name Café,** Morelos 460 at Mina, the *malecón* (☎ 322-223-2508), is a great venue for catching your favorite game, including NBA, NHL, NFL, and MLB games, as well as pay-per-view sporting events. Mickey's also serves great BBQ ribs and imported steaks from the United States. It's open daily 9 a.m. to midnight.

Gay and lesbian clubs

Vallarta has a vibrant gay community and a wide variety of clubs and nightlife options including special bay cruises and evening excursions to nearby ranches. The free *Gay Guide Vallarta* (☎ 322-299-0936; www.gayguidevallarta.com) specializes in gay-friendly listings.

- ✔ **Club Paco Paco,** Ignacio L. Vallarta 278 (☎ 322-222-1899; www.pacopaco.com), is a combination disco, cantina, and rooftop bar that also hosts a spectacular "Trasvesty" drag show every Friday, Saturday, and Sunday night at 1:30 a.m. The club is open noon to 6 a.m. daily and is air-conditioned. **Paco's Ranch,** around the corner at Venustiano Carranza 239, has nightly specials including Western Night on Tuesdays and Leather Night on Thursdays. A nightly "Ranch Hand's Show" is performed at 1 a.m. and 3 a.m. This club, which can be accessed from Club Paco Paco, is open 8 p.m. to 6 a.m. The cover of $6 applies to both clubs and includes a drink.

- ✔ **Los Balcones,** Juárez 182 (☎ 322-222-4671), one of the original gay clubs in town, is a bi-level space with several dance floors and an excellent sound system. It earned a few chuckles when it was listed as one of the most romantic spots in Vallarta by *Brides* magazine. This air-conditioned club is open 9 p.m. to 4 a.m. and posts nightly specials including exotic male dancers.

Part VI
Ixtapa and Zihuatanejo

In this part . . .

Think of a vacation here as getting two destinations (and the best of both worlds) for the price of one: The side-by-side beach resorts of Ixtapa and Zihuatanejo may share a common geography, but they couldn't be more different in character. Ixtapa has a modern infrastructure, tons of services, and luxury hotels. Zihuatanejo — or Zihua to the locals — is the quintessential Mexican beach village with the appropriately quintessential one-of-a-kind accommodations.

The only thing that some visitors may find lacking is the nightlife, which is rather subdued in both towns — especially compared to other more developed resorts such as Acapulco, Los Cabos, and Puerto Vallarta. But, if you're looking for laid-back evenings of good conversation and cocktails in the moonlight, the absent party crowd may be a plus.

Chapter 18

The Lowdown on the Ixtapa and Zihuatanejo Hotel Scenes

By Lynne Bairstow

. . . .

In This Chapter

▶ Sizing up the hotel locations

▶ Checking out top hotel choices in Ixtapa and Zihuatanejo

. . . .

*T*hink of a vacation to this slice of Mexico as cashing in a two-for-one coupon and getting the best of both worlds: The side-by-side beach resorts of **Ixtapa** and **Zihuatanejo** may share a common geography, but they couldn't be more different in character. Ixtapa boasts a modern infrastructure, a wide array of services, and luxury hotels. Zihuatanejo — or Zihua to the locals — is the quintessential Mexican beach village and offers lower-priced rooms and one-of-a-kind inns. If you're the type of traveler who prefers comforts reminiscent of home, opt for Ixtapa and take advantage of well-appointed rooms in a setting of tropical beauty. You can easily and quickly make the 6km (4-mile) trip into Zihuatanejo for a sampling of life in this *pueblo* by the sea. But, if you prefer a more rustic retreat with real personality, consider settling in Zihuatanejo. Its funky charm has attracted a community of Swiss and Italian immigrants, adding an air of sophistication to the laid-back village life.

With a backdrop of palm-covered hills and the Pacific Ocean waters serving as a foreground, you can enjoy a full range of activities and diversions here — scuba diving, deep-sea fishing, bay cruises to remote beaches, and golf are among the favorites. The one exception is the nightlife, which is rather subdued in both towns, especially compared to other more-developed resorts such as Acapulco, Los Cabos, and Puerto Vallarta.

As a dual destination, Ixtapa and Zihuatanejo are the ideal choice for the traveler looking for a little bit of everything, from resort-styled indulgence to unpretentious good times. Zihua is a relaxed, down-to-earth paradise, and it's also known for its collection of unique hillside boutique hotels, which cater to an international crowd looking for pampered luxury and individualized style. Terrific bargains also exist and still offer character, cleanliness, and safety — if not the full range of amenities. Of all the resorts in Mexico, the Ixtapa-Zihuatanejo region has the best selection of one-of-a-kind places to stay.

These two resort towns are more welcoming to couples and adults than they are to families. A number of places are off-limits to children under 16 — something of a rarity in Mexico.

Choosing Your Location

Because the ambiance is so different between these two sister towns, choosing the right place to stay makes a big difference in your overall vacation experience — though the ride between the two is an easy one.

Ixtapa, as I note earlier in the chapter, is the more modern, made-for-tourism town. Developed by the Mexican government in the 1970s as a complement to Zihua's fetching charms, Ixtapa places a bevy of conveniences at your disposal: shopping centers, sleek eateries, golf courses, and high-rise hotels. Almost everything is accessible by foot or is an inexpensive cab ride away.

Each of the Ixtapa hotels listed in this chapter (with the exception of Las Brisas) lies along the wide, attractive Playa el Palmar and is largely self-contained — with shops, bars, restaurants, and water fun on-site — meaning you never need to leave the resort's property if you don't want to. The main difference between Ixtapa and Zihuatanejo is that while Ixtapa hotels offer every conceivable comfort and convenience, they lack the charm and originality of Zihua accommodations. Also you need to remember that Ixtapa hotels, on the whole, are priced much higher.

If you choose the traditional appeal of **Zihuatanejo,** you still need to narrow down your preference in terms of staying in the central town or on one of Zihua's neighboring beaches. In either case, Zihua is small, friendly, colorful, and full of Mexico's authentic charms.

The places to stay in town — known as *el centro* — are generally small and inexpensive with the exception of Villa Vera Puerto Mio (which isn't technically located downtown anyway, so forget about the whole "exception" thing). Many establishments offer bare-bones accommodations without air conditioning and are subject to local street noise, but they're clean, priced right, and within easy walking distance of plenty of places to eat and shop. Note that none of the *centro* Zihua hotels are situated directly on the beach, and only Puerto Mio has an ocean view.

Also worth knowing is that the term "bungalow" is loosely defined in Zihuatanejo, just as it is elsewhere in Mexico. Thus, a bungalow may be an individual unit with a kitchen and bedroom, or it may be a mere bedroom. It may also be like a hotel, located in a two-story building with multiple units with or without kitchens. The bungalow may be cozy or rustic, with or without a patio or balcony.

Two lovely beaches and a couple of Mexico's most notable small hotels are just east of *centro* Zihuatanejo. **Playa Madera** and **Playa La Ropa,** separated from each other by only a craggy shoreline, are both accessible by road. Prices here tend to be higher than those in town, but the value is much better, and people tend to find that the beautiful and tranquil setting is worth the extra cost. The area is rich with charm and a stellar selection of sand for anyone who truly treasures a great beach. The only drawback to this area is that dining is limited to *palapa* (thatched roof) beach restaurants or the on-site restaurants at the hotels, and there's essentially no shopping or nightlife to speak of, which means you have to hop in a taxi and go to town for any diversions other than beach-related fun and limited dining. The town is just 5 to 20 minutes away depending on whether you walk or take a taxi, which costs about $2.

Ixtapa's and Zihuatanejo's Best Accommodations

As far as prices go, I note *rack rates* (the maximum that a hotel or resort charges for a room) for two people spending one night in a double room. You can usually do better, especially if you're purchasing a package that includes airfare. Expect to pay more — up to double the rack-rate prices — if you're planning a visit during Christmas or Easter weeks. Prices quoted here include the 17% room tax. Please refer to the Introduction of this book for an explanation of the price categories.

As I mention earlier in this chapter, Ixtapa and Zihuatanejo tend to not be very kid friendly, so if you plan on bringing the whole family, including the little ones, please pay special attention to the Kid Friendly icons highlighting the best choices. Unless otherwise indicated, all hotels have air conditioning.

Apartamentos Amueblados Valle
$–$$ Zihuatanejo Centro

These accommodations are actually apartments, but you can rent them by the day or week, meaning you can enjoy a well-furnished apartment for the price of an inexpensive hotel room. This property is a great choice for friends traveling together on a budget. Five one-bedroom apartments accommodate up to three people; the three two-bedroom apartments can fit four comfortably. Request an apartment that doesn't face the street; they're less noisy. Each apartment is different, but all are clean and airy with ceiling fans, private balconies, and kitchenettes, but no air conditioning. Maid service is provided daily, and the office offers a paperback-book exchange. Reserve well in advance during high season.

Vincente Guerrero 14, about 2 blocks in from the waterfront between Ejido and N. Bravo. ☎ 755-554-2084. Fax: 755-554-3220. 8 units. Rack rates: High season $60 1-bedroom apartment, $90 2-bedroom apartment; low season $40 1-bedroom apartment, $60 2-bedroom apartment. Ask for special rates during low season and for prolonged stays. No credit cards.

Barceló Ixtapa
$$$$ Ixtapa

A grand, 12-story resort hotel (formerly the Sheraton), Barceló Ixtapa is one of the best choices in the area for families. A modern, well-equipped resort, Barceló boasts handsomely furnished public areas and tropical gardens surrounding a large pool, which has a swim-up bar and a separate section for children. Most rooms have balconies with ocean or mountain views, and nonsmoking and handicapped-accessible rooms are available. You never need to leave this hotel if you choose not to; the Barceló Ixtapa lacks for nothing — four restaurants plus room service, a nightclub, a lobby bar, and the area's most popular Mexican fiesta (held weekly) with a sumptuous buffet and live entertainment outdoors. If you choose to spend all your time here, be sure to take advantage of the optional, all-inclusive pricing rates. Four tennis courts and a fitness room are available for the actively inclined. For all the Barceló offers on-site, it may be the best value in Ixtapa.

Bulevar Ixtapa s/n, at the southeastern end of Playa el Palmar. ☎ 800-325-3535 in the U.S. and Canada, or 755-553-1858. Fax: 755-553-2438. www.barcelo.com. *333 units. Free parking. Rack rates: High season $245 double all-inclusive, $180 double with breakfast only; low season $225 double all-inclusive. AE, DC, MC, V.*

Bungalows Ley
$$–$$$$ Zihuatanejo Beaches/Playa Madera

Located on a small complex on Playa Madera, Bungalows Ley is a great option for friends traveling together. If you're traveling with a group, you may want to book the most expensive suite (called Club Madera), which comes with a rooftop terrace, tiled hot tub, outdoor bar and grill, and a spectacular view. No two suites are the same here, but all are immaculate; the simplest layouts are studios with one bed and a kitchen in the same room. All rooms have terraces or balconies just above the beach, and all are decorated in the ice-cream colors reminiscent of Miami South Beach. Bathrooms, however, tend to be small and dark. Clients praise the management and the service. To find the property, follow Calle Eva S. de López Matéos to the right up a slight hill; the hotel is on the left.

Zihuatanejo and Ixtapa Area Accommodations

Apartamentos
Amueblados Valle **1**
Barceló Ixtapa **14**
Bungalows Ley **6**
Casa Cuitlateca **10**
Hotel Raul 3 Marías **4**
Hotel Susy **3**
La Casa Que Canta **8**
Las Brisas Resort **13**
NH Krystal Ixtapa **15**
Posada Citlali **2**
Sotavento Beach Resort **9**
Villa del Sol **12**
Villa Vera Puerto Mio **5**
Villas Miramar **7**
Villas San Sebastián **11**

Calle Eva S. de López Matéos s/n. ☎ **755-554-4087.** *Fax: 755-554-4563. 8 units. Rack rates: $103 double with A/C; $162 for 2-bedroom suite with kitchen for up to 4 persons or $212 for up to 6 persons. AE, MC, V.*

Casa Cuitlateca
$$$$–$$$$$ Zihuatanejo Beaches/Playa La Ropa

The perfect place for a romantic holiday, Casa Cuitlateca is an exclusive bed and breakfast and one of the unique inns that has made Playa La Ropa a standout. Done in the architectural style that has made Zihua famous, Casa Cuitlateca has *palapa* roofs and earthy colors and is built into the hillside across from Playa La Ropa, just a short walk away. Three of the four units offer a stunning view. Two smaller rooms have their own private terrace and a small sitting area. There's also a suite with a large terrace, and a second suite with no view but a very nice sitting area and small private garden. Each room is carefully decorated with handcrafts and textiles from all over Mexico. The bar is on the first level behind the pool and serves cocktails to the public from 4:30 to 8 p.m. Guests can help themselves to soft drinks and beers on the honor system when the bar is closed. The small pool, like everything else here, is beautifully designed. On the top level of the two suites, all guests can enjoy a sundeck and a hot tub. From the entrance to the property, you climb a steep staircase of 120 steps. The driveway is also very steep, with parking for six cars. The parking lot connects to the house through a hanging bridge.

Calle Playa La Ropa, a short walk in from La Ropa beach. ☎ **877-541-1234** *from the U.S., or 755-554-2448. Fax: 755-554-7394.* www.casacuitlateca.com. *4 units. Rack rates: $340 double, $50 each extra person. Low season: $220 double. Rates include round-trip transfers to the airport and full breakfast daily. AE, MC, V. No children under 16.*

Hotel Raul 3 Marias
$ Zihuatanejo Centro

Although it's a small, basic hotel with strictly functional rooms, the Raul is very clean and known for its friendly guest services. Nine rooms have a balcony overlooking the street, and the small office offers telephone and fax service to guests. Downstairs is the landmark Zihuatanejo seafood restaurant, Garrobos, which is open for lunch and dinner. The hotel also offers deep-sea fishing and diving charters.

Juan Alvarez 52, between 5 de Mayo and Cuautemoc streets. ☎ **755-554-6706.** *E-mail:* garroboscrew@prodigy.net.mx. *17 units. Rack rates: High season $50 double; variable prices in low season. AE, MC, V.*

Hotel Susy

$ Zihuatanejo Centro

Consistently clean with tons of plants along a shaded walkway set back from the street, this two-story hotel offers small rooms with fans (no air conditioning) and louvered-glass windows with screens. Hotel Susy is a good choice if you're looking for a central location, a cheap price, and a comfortable, simple place to stay. Request an upper-floor room and enjoy a balcony that overlooks the street. To get here, face away from the water at the basketball court on the *malecón* (boardwalk), turn right, and walk 2 blocks; the hotel is on your left at the corner of Guerrero.

Juan Alvarez 3 at Guerrero. ☎ **755-554-2339.** *18 units. Rack rates: High season $30 per person, per room; low season $25 double. MC, V.*

La Casa Que Canta

$$$$$ Zihuatanejo Beaches/Playa La Ropa

Another striking inn and another ideal choice for a romantic getaway is "The House that Sings," located on a mountainside overlooking Zihuatanejo Bay. Designed with striking molded-adobe architecture, La Casa Que Canta was the first of a rustic-chic style of architecture now known as Mexican Pacific. All the rooms are individually decorated in unusual, painted, Michoacán furniture; antiques; and stretched-leather *equipales* (a traditional Mexican chair characterized by its round-design and sturdy construction), with hand-loomed fabrics and handsome, natural-tile floors used throughout. All units have large, beautifully furnished terraces with bay views. Hammocks under the thatched-roof terraces, supported by rough-hewn *vigas* (wooden beams), are perfectly placed for watching yachts sail in and out of the harbor. The four categories of rooms (terrace suites, deluxe suites, grand suites, and private-pool suites) are all spacious. Rooms meander up and down the hillside, and although no one staircase is terribly long, you should know that Casa Que Canta doesn't have elevators. Technically, the hotel isn't on Playa La Ropa (or any beach), but on the road leading there. The closest stretch of beach (the very beginning of Playa La Ropa) is down a steep hill. La Casa Que Canta has a small restaurant-bar on a shaded terrace, a small pool on the main terrace, and a second, saltwater pool on the bottom level. A new Well Being Center has been added, offering massage, spa services, and yoga. Little extras such as laundry, room service, and complimentary soft drinks and beer in your minifridge are present to pamper you.

Camino Escénico a Playa La Ropa. ☎ **888-523-5050** *in the U.S., 755-555-7000. Fax: 755-554-7900.* www.lacasaquecanta.com. *21 suites. Rack rates: $360–$690 double. AE, MC, V. No children under 16.*

Las Brisas Resort
$$$$–$$$$$ **Ixtapa**

Set above the high-rise hotels of Ixtapa on its own rocky promontory, Las Brisas (formerly the Westin Brisas) is clearly the most stunning of Ixtapa's hotels, and the hotel most noted for gracious service. The austere but luxurious public areas, all in stone and stucco, are bathed in sweeping breezes and an air of exclusivity. A minimalist luxury also characterizes the rooms, which have Mexican-tile floors and private, plant-decked patios with hammocks and lounges. All rooms face the hotel's cove and private beach, Vista Hermosa. Although this beach is true to its name (the breezes), it's dangerous for swimming. The six master suites come with private pools, the 16th floor is reserved for nonsmokers, and three rooms on the 18th floor are equipped for travelers with disabilities. Like many of Ixtapa's hotels, Las Brisas is so complete that you may never feel the urge to leave — choose from among five restaurants, room service, and three bars including a lobby bar with live trio music at sunset. Three swimming pools (including one for children) connected to one another by waterfalls, lighted tennis courts (with a pro available on request), and a fitness center with massage services round out the offerings.

Bulevar Ixtapa s/n. ☎ **888-559-4329** *in the U.S., or 755-553-2121. Fax: 755-553-1038.* www.brisas.com.mx. *423 units. Free parking. Rack rates: High season $285 deluxe, $490 Royal Beach Club; low season $196 deluxe, $230 Royal Beach Club. AE, DC, MC, V.*

NH Krystal Ixtapa
$$$–$$$$$ **Ixtapa**

Welcoming, exceptional service is what the Krystal chain of hotels is known for in Mexico, and the Ixtapa version is no exception. In fact, many of the staff members have been with the hotel for all its 20-some years of operation and greet returning guests. The Krystal is probably the area's best hotel for families because it has a playground and a special kid's club activities program. Each spacious and nicely furnished room has a balcony with an ocean view, game table, and tile bathroom. Master suites have large, furnished, triangular-shaped balconies that overlook the spacious grounds and the large pool, which has a special kid's section as well as a waterfall and waterslide. A tennis court, racquetball court, and a small gym are also on-site. Note that some rates include a daily breakfast buffet — a great deal if you make the buffet your main meal of the day. Krystal Ixtapa has five restaurants to choose from, including the evenings-only Bogart's, plus room service. Also important to note is that the center of Ixtapa nightlife is found here, at Krystal's famed Christine Disco.

Bulevar Ixtapa s/n, at the northwestern end of Playa el Palmar. ☎ **800-231-9860** *in the U.S., or 755-553-0333. Fax: 755-553-0216. 255 units.* www.nh-hotels.com. *Free parking. Rack rates: High season $190 double, $280 suite; low season $170 double, $255 suite. 2 children under 12 stay free in parents' room. Ask for special packages. AE, DC, MC, V.*

Posada Citlali

$ Zihuatanejo Centro

A pleasant, three-story hotel, Posada Citlali is a major bargain. Although the rooms are small, they're spotless, and they border a very pleasant plant-filled courtyard decked out with comfortable rockers and chairs. Bottled water is in help-yourself containers on the patio, and fans are found in all rooms (there's no air conditioning). Although you may hear the children heading for the nearby school in the morning, the location avoids most of the evening noise and traffic sounds, making Posada Citlali a peaceful retreat in *el centro*. The stairway to the top two floors is narrow and steep.

Vicente Guerrero 3, near the corner of Alvarez. ☎ **755-554-2043.** *E-mail:* citlali@ zihuatanejo.com.mx. *19 units. Rack rates: $35 double. No credit cards.*

Sotavento Beach Resort

$–$$$ Zihuatanejo Beaches/Playa La Ropa

Perched on a hill above the beach, this resort is for people who want to relax near the ocean in a simple, lovely setting without being bothered by televisions or closed up in air-conditioned rooms. A throwback to the style of the 1970s, when Zihua was first being discovered by an international jet set, the Sotavento comprises two multi-story buildings. Quite a variety of rooms are available to choose from — ask to see a few different rooms to find something that suits you, such as the popular doubles on the resort's upper floors, which are about three times the size of a normal double room. The furnishings in all the rooms are simple but comfortable, and all have ocean-view terraces that are half-sheltered and half-open, with chaises for basking in the sun and hammocks for enjoying the shade. Screened windows filter the ocean breezes, and ceiling fans keep the rooms airy even when the breeze is absent (remember — there's no air conditioning). One curious feature of the Sotavento is that the floors are always slightly slanted in one direction or another — by design of the owner. Two restaurants, a small lobby bar, a pool with whirlpool, and a rooftop yoga studio serve guests. The resort is built into the side of a hill, and isn't for people who dislike climbing stairs. Take the highway south of Zihuatanejo about 2km (1 mile), turn right at the hotel's sign, and follow the road.

Playa La Ropa. ☎ **877-699-6685** *from the U.S., 877-667-3702 from Canada, or 755-554-2032. Fax: 755-554-2975.* www.beachresortsotavento.com. *100 units. Rack rates: High season $60–$105 double, $75–$130 suite; low season $75 double, $85 suite. AE, MC, V.*

Villa del Sol

$$$$$ Zihuatanejo Beaches/Playa La Ropa

Villa del Sol is an exquisite inn known as much for its unequivocal attention to luxurious detail as for its exacting German owner, Helmut Leins, who is almost always present to ensure the quality of his guests' stay. Villa del Sol is a haven of tranquility that caters to guests looking for complete privacy and serenity. Each room is a harmony of magnificent design. The spacious, split-level suites have one or two bedrooms, plus a living area and a large terrace, some of which have a private mini-pool. King-size beds are draped in white netting, and comfy lounges and hammocks beckon to you at siesta time. Standard rooms are smaller, and they don't have TVs or telephones, but they're still artfully and individually appointed with artistic Mexican details. Nine beachfront suites have recently been added, but I still prefer the original rooms. No two are alike. Suites have CD players and private fax machines, with satellite TVs or DVD players brought to you upon request. No children under 12 are allowed during high season, and a "no children" and "no excess noise" sentiment prevails in general. Travelers who relish a more typically welcoming Mexican ambiance may find a stay here less enjoyable. The hotel sits on a private, 600-foot-long, palm-shaded beach and also has three pools (including one 60-foot lap pool), two tennis courts, and a massage service. After you work up an appetite, enjoy an outstanding gourmet meal at the open-air, beachfront restaurant-bar or room service in your sumptuous surroundings. The rooms are stocked with deluxe amenities, and the hotel offers every service expected at a five-star resort.

Playa La Ropa. ☎ **888-389-2645** *or 755-555-5500. Fax: 755-554-2758.* www.hotel villadelsol.com. *70 units. Rack rates: High season $300–$900 double; low season $250–$750 double. Meal plan, including breakfast and dinner, for $60 per person per day is mandatory during the high season, and is optional, costing $45 during summer season. 3-night minimum stay generally required. AE, MC, V.*

Villa Vera Puerto Mio

$$$$–$$$$$ Zihuatanejo Centro

This idyllic inn is located on 25 acres of beautifully landscaped grounds apart from the rest of the hotels in Zihuatanejo. Technically not in *el centro,* Villa Vera Puerto Mio is on the farthest end of the bay, almost directly across from Playa Las Gatas. All rooms are decorated with hand-crafted details from around Mexico, and all enjoy beautiful views of either Zihuatanejo's bay or the Pacific Ocean. The rooms are divided into three main areas: Casa de Mar, the cliffside mansion closer to the main entrance where most of the rooms are located; the Peninsula, located on the tip of the bay; and a more secluded area with two deluxe suites. (These two suites have no TVs to disturb the tranquility.) Three other suites, located between Casa de Mar and the Peninsula, have recently been added and have private pools. The upper-level suite is the largest in size. One of the hallmarks of Villa Vera Puerto Mio is its seclusion — the location sets the hotel apart, and you can only reach the small private beach below by going through the hotel. The hotel has two restaurants, plus a small marina with a sailboat that's available for charters. Children under 16 are welcome only during the summer.

Paseo del Morro 5. ☎ *and fax:* **755-553-8165.** *23 units. Rack rates: High season $225–$315 double, $425–$475 villa suite; low season prices drop by $25 per room. AE, MC, V.*

Villas Miramar

$–$$$ Zihuatanejo Beaches/Playa Madera

A lovely hotel with beautiful gardens, Villas Miramar offers a welcoming atmosphere, attention to detail, and superb cleanliness. For the price, you may expect less, but the rooms are colorful and well equipped, and some have kitchenettes. Several of the suites are built around a shady patio that doubles as a restaurant, which serves a basic menu for breakfast, lunch, and dinner. Suites across the street face a swimming pool and have private balconies and sea views. A terrace with a view to Zihuatanejo Bay has a bar that features a daily happy hour from 5 to 7 p.m. Of all the more budget-priced accommodations around, Villas Miramar is the most welcoming to children. To find Villas Miramar, follow the road leading south out of town toward Playa La Ropa, take the first right after the traffic circle, and then hang a left on Adelita.

Calle Adelita, Lote 78. ☎ **755-554-2106** *or 755-554-3350. Fax: 755-554-2149. E-mail:* villasm@prodigy.net.mx. *18 units. Free enclosed parking. Rack rates: High season $95 suite for 1 or 2 or $100 with ocean view, $130 2-bedroom suite; low season $60 suite for 1 or 2 or $70 with ocean view, $90 2-bedroom suite. AE, MC, V.*

Villas San Sebastián

$$–$$$ Zihuatanejo Beaches/Playa La Ropa

A nine-villa complex nestled on the mountainside above Playa La Ropa, Villas San Sebastián offers great views of Zihuatanejo's bay and an indulgent sense of seclusion. The villas, all with beautiful ocean views, are surrounded by tropical vegetation and border a central swimming-pool area. Each comes complete with kitchenette and its own spacious, private terrace. The personalized service is one reason these villas come so highly recommended; owner Luis Valle, whose family dates back decades in the community, is always available to help guests with any questions or needs.

Bulevar Escénico, across from the Dolphins Fountain. ☎ **755-554-4154.** *Fax: 755-554-3220. 9 units. Rack rates: High season $155 1-bedroom, $250 2-bedroom; low season $105 1-bedroom, $155 2-bedroom. No credit cards.*

Chapter 19

Settling into Ixtapa and Zihuatanejo

By Lynne Bairstow

. . . .

In This Chapter

▶ Knowing what to expect when you arrive

▶ Finding your way around

▶ Discovering helpful information and resources

. . . .

*O*ne of the pleasures of a vacation in Ixtapa and Zihuatanejo is how easy finding your way around really is. The airport is a breeze to navigate, and the towns are just as simple to figure out; both are basically oriented around one main road each.

In this chapter, I cover the basics of getting around the towns, and I provide you with tips on everything from exchanging money to Internet access. Truly, the Ixtapa-Zihuatanejo area is a place for complete relaxation, and it almost seems like the towns have trivialized the everyday details of life to make everything just a little bit easier.

Arriving in Ixtapa and Zihuatanejo

Your arrival at the Ixtapa-Zihuatanejo airport is likely to set the tone for your trip here — arrivals are usually easy, uncomplicated, and hassle-free. But the airport lacks any real source of tourist information or currency exchange, so you're on your own until you reach town.

In recent years, the airport has been in a more-or-less constant state of renovation, but it's a generally simple building to navigate. When you exit the plane, head down the portable stairway to the tarmac and walk to the airport building.

The climate change is likely to be intense upon your arrival, especially if you're heading here during the winter months. Remember to wear layered clothes so that you're not unbearably hot when you get off the plane.

Navigating passport control and customs

Your task upon entering the airport is to clear immigration. At the immigration booth, an officer will ask you to show your passport (or other proof of citizenship) and your completed tourist card, the **FMT** (see Chapter 7 for all the FMT and entry details).

Your FMT is an important document, so take good care of it. You're supposed to keep the FMT with you at all times because you may be required to show it if you run into any sort of trouble. You also need to turn it back in upon leaving Mexico, or you may be unable to leave without replacing it.

After you pass through immigration, you go through glass doors to the baggage claim area — essentially one carousel, so finding your bags should be simple enough. Here, porters stand by to help with your bags, and they're well worth the price of the tip — about a dollar a bag. After you collect your luggage, you pass through another checkpoint. Something that looks like a traffic light awaits you here. You press a button, and if the light turns green, you're free to go. If it turns red, you need to open each of your bags for a quick search. It's Mexico's random search procedure for customs. If you have an unusually large bag, or an excessive amount of luggage, you may be searched regardless of the traffic-light outcome.

Finally, you pass through a second set of sliding-glass doors that open to the general airport-arrival area. This is where you find transportation to your hotel. Booths sell tickets for *colectivos* (shared van service) and private taxis. The fares for both are based on distance (see the following "Getting to your hotel" section). Taxis are always around, but *colectivos* gather only for the larger flights. Clear, well-marked signs indicate the way to the taxis.

Getting to your hotel

The **Ixtapa-Zihuatanejo airport** is 11km (7 miles) from Zihuatanejo and 13km (8 miles) from Ixtapa. Taxi fares into town range from $19 to $22.

The least expensive way to make the trip to either town is by using the *colectivos,* operated by **Transportes Terrestres.** For transportation to any of the hotels in Zihuatanejo and Ixtapa, purchase a ticket at the booth located just outside the baggage-claim area. Cost depends on distance, but fares generally run between $6.50 and $8.

Several **car-rental agencies** also have booths in the airport. These companies include **Dollar** (☎ **800-800-4000** in the U.S., or 755-554-2255; www.dollar.com) and **Hertz** (☎ **800-654-3131** in the U.S., or 755-554-2590 or 755-554-2952; www.hertz.com).

Getting Around Ixtapa and Zihuatanejo

Zihuatanejo is both a fishing village, in the traditional sense of the term, and a resort town. The town spreads out around the beautiful Bay of Zihuatanejo, which is framed by the downtown *(el centro)* to the north and a beautiful, long beach and the Sierra foothills to the east. The heart of Zihuatanejo is the waterfront walkway, **Paseo del Pescador** (also called the *malecón*), bordering the Playa Municipal.

One aspect of Zihua (as the locals call Zihuatanejo) that I enjoy most is that the town centerpiece isn't a plaza, as it is in most Mexican villages, but a **basketball court,** which fronts the beach. It's a useful point of reference for directions. The main thoroughfare for cars is **Juan Alvarez,** a block behind the *malecón.* The town has designated several sections of the main streets as the *zona peatonal* (pedestrian zone blocked off to cars). The *zona peatonal* follows a zigzag pattern, and to us, it seems to block parts of streets haphazardly.

A cement-and-sand walkway, lit at night, runs from the downtown-Zihuatanejo *malecón* along the water to **Playa Madera** making it easy to walk between these two points. Access to **Playa La Ropa** is via the main road, **Camino a Playa La Ropa.** Playa La Ropa and **Playa Las Gatas** are connected only by boat. Playa La Ropa and Playa Madera are connected by car (the rocks between the two beaches are dangerous). Skip to Chapter 21 for a description of these beaches.

Highway 200 connects Zihua to **Ixtapa,** which is located 6km (4 miles) to the northwest. The 18-hole **Ixtapa Golf Club** marks the beginning of the inland side of Ixtapa. Tall hotels line Ixtapa's wide beach, **Playa el Palmar,** against a backdrop of palm groves and mountains. The main street, **Bulevar Ixtapa,** provides access to the beach. A large expanse of small shopping plazas (many of the shops are air-conditioned) and restaurants lie opposite the beach. At the far end of Bulevar Ixtapa, **Marina Ixtapa** has excellent restaurants, private yacht slips, and an 18-hole **golf course.** Condominiums and private homes surround the marina and golf course, with exclusive residential communities in the hillsides past the marina en route to **Playa Quieta** and **Playa Linda.** Ixtapa also has a great paved bicycle track that begins at the marina and continues around the Marina Ixtapa Golf Course and on toward Playa Linda.

Getting around the two resorts is easy — **taxis** are the preferred form of transportation. Rates are reasonable, but from midnight to 5 a.m., they increase by 50%. The average fare between Ixtapa and central Zihuatanejo is $4.50; a trip from Playa La Ropa (just east of Zihuatanejo) to downtown Zihuatanejo is about $2.50; and it costs approximately $2.50 to get from one end of the Ixtapa Hotel Zone to the other.

A **mini bus** (35¢) goes back and forth between Zihuatanejo and Ixtapa every 15 or 20 minutes from 5 a.m. to 11 p.m. daily, but it's generally very hot and crowded with commuting workers. In Zihuatanejo, it stops near the corner of Morelos-Paseo Zihuatanejo and Juárez, about 3 blocks north of the market. In Ixtapa, it makes numerous stops along Bulevar Ixtapa.

The highway leading from Zihuatanejo to Ixtapa is now a broad, four-lane highway, which makes driving between the towns easier and faster than ever. Street signs are becoming more common in Zihuatanejo, and good signs now lead you in and out of both towns. However, both locations have an area called the **Zona Hotelera** (Hotel Zone), so if you're trying to reach Ixtapa's Hotel Zone (the area alongside Bulevar Ixtapa), signs in Zihuatanejo pointing to that village's own Hotel Zone (the area alongside Playa Madera and Playa La Ropa) may confuse you.

Fast Facts: Ixtapa and Zihuatanejo

American Express

The main office (☎ 755-544-6242; Fax: 755-544-6242) is located in the Plaza San Rafael, Local 7, on Av. Colegio Heroico Militar 38. It's open Monday to Friday from 9 a.m. to 6 p.m.

Area Code

The telephone area code is **755.**

Babysitters

Most of the larger hotels in Ixtapa can arrange babysitters, but many speak limited English. Rates range from $4 to $10 per hour. Babysitting services may be more difficult to come by in Zihuatanejo because the more upscale places tend to discourage children and the smaller ones simply may not have the resources.

Banks, ATMs, and Currency Exchange

Ixtapa's banks include Bancomer, located in the La Puerta shopping center. The most centrally located Zihuatanejo bank is Banamex, located on Cuauhtémoc 4. Banks change money during normal business hours, which are now generally 9 a.m. to 6 p.m. Monday to Friday and Saturday 9 a.m. to 1 p.m. ATMs and *casas de cambio* (currency exchange booths) are available during these and other hours, and they generally have the best rates. Most establishments accept U.S. dollars as readily as pesos but at reduced exchange rates, so you're better off using local currency whenever possible. The airport has a currency exchange booth, so upon arrival, exchange just enough to pay for your cab fare and have a bit of cash to move around until you make it to a bank.

Business Hours

Most offices maintain traditional Mexican hours of operation (10 a.m. to 2 p.m. and 4 p.m. to 8 p.m. daily), but shops remain open throughout the day. Offices tend to close on Saturday and Sunday, but shops are open on Saturday, at least, and increasingly offer limited hours of operation on Sunday.

Climate

Although the climate is always quite warm, summer is particularly hot and humid, but sea breezes and brief showers temper the heat. September is the peak of the tropical rainy season, and showers are concentrated in the late afternoons.

Consular Agency

A U.S. Consular Agency is located in Zihuatanejo (☎ 755-553-2100; fax 755-557-1106).

Emergencies

Police (☎ 755-554-2040, 755-554-5370); **fire department** (☎ 755-554-0012); **Red Cross** (☎ 755-554-2009).

Hospitals

The larger hotels in Ixtapa have a doctor on premises or on-call. The **Hospital de la Marina Ixtapa** is at Bulevar Ixtapa s/n, in front of the Hotel Aristos (☎ 755-553-0499). In Zihuatanejo, try the **Clinica Maciel** (Calle de la Palma 12; ☎ 755-554-2380); its staff also includes a reliable dentist.

Information

The **State Tourism Office** (☎ 888-248-7037 from the U.S., or ☎ and fax: 755-553-1967, 755-553-1968) is in the **La Puerta** shopping center in Ixtapa across from the Presidente Inter-Continental Hotel. It's open Monday to Friday 8 a.m. to 8:30 p.m. This location is mainly a self-service office where you can collect brochures; the staff is less helpful than in other offices in Mexico.

The **Zihuatanejo Tourism Office Module** is on the main square by the basketball court at Alvarez. It's open Monday to Friday 9 a.m. to 8 p.m. and serves basic, tourist-information purposes.

Note: According to recent regulations, the very few timeshare sales booths that exist in both towns must be clearly marked with the names of the businesses and can't display signs claiming to be tourist-information centers.

Internet Access

Several cybercafes are located in the Los Patios Shopping Center in Ixtapa. **Comunicación Mundial** is in Local 105 (☎ 755-553-1177). Go to the back of the shopping center and take the stairs to the second level; Comunicación Mundial is to your right. You can find many Internet cafes in Ixtapa, and the average fee is $3 per hour.

Maps

One of the best around is the free American Express map, usually found at the tourist information offices and hotel concierge desks.

Pharmacy

Farmacias Coyuca are open 24 hours a day and deliver. The Ixtapa branch doesn't have a phone number; in Zihuatanejo, call ☎ 755-554-5390.

Post Office

The post office for both towns (☎ 755-554-2192) is in the SCT building (called Edificio SCT) behind El Cacahuate. It's open Monday to Friday 8 a.m. to 3 p.m. and Saturday 9 a.m. to 1 p.m.

Safety

Generally speaking, both Ixtapa and Zihuatanejo are quite safe, and you should feel very comfortable walking around here — even at night.

The one main safety warning applies to travelers who elect to drive: Motorists planning to follow Highway 200 northwest up the coast from Ixtapa or Zihuatanejo toward Lázaro Cárdenas and Manzanillo should be aware of reports of car and bus hijackings on that route, especially around Playa Azul. Bus holdups are more common than car holdups. Before heading in that direction, ask locals, the police, or the tourism office about the status of the route. Don't drive at night. According to tourism officials, police and military patrols of the highway have increased recently, and the number of incidents has dropped dramatically.

As is the case anywhere, tourists are vulnerable to thieves, especially so when shopping in a market; lying on the beach; wearing jewelry; or visibly carrying a camera, purse, or bulging wallet.

Taxes

There's a 15% value-added tax (IVA) on goods and services, and it's generally included in the posted price.

Taxis

Always establish the price of a ride with the driver before starting out. Taxi rates are reasonable, but from midnight to 5 a.m., rates increase by 50%. The average fare between Ixtapa and Zihuatanejo is $4.50.

Telephones

Avoid the phone booths that have signs in English advising you to call home using a special 800 number — these are absolute rip-offs and can cost as much as $20 per minute. The least expensive way to call is by using a Telmex (LADATEL) prepaid phone card, available at most pharmacies and mini-supers, using the official Telmex (Lada) public phones.

In Mexico, you need to dial 001 prior to a number to reach the United States, and you need to preface long distance calls within Mexico by dialing 01.

Time Zone

Ixtapa and Zihuatanejo operate on central standard time, but Mexico's observance of daylight savings time varies somewhat from that in the United States.

Chapter 20

Dining in Ixtapa and Zihuatanejo

By Lynne Bairstow

. . . .

In This Chapter

▶ Uncovering some local institutions and bargains

▶ Discovering the best restaurants in Ixtapa and Zihuatanejo

. . . .

Dining destinations in this area are divided as neatly as the accommodations: You can find more modern, stylized places in Ixtapa, and eateries with more local color (and flavor) tend to be located in neighboring Zihuatanejo (Zihua for short). Although you find the majority of the best-known restaurants in Ixtapa inside the larger hotels, Zihua's top spots are small, mostly family-owned treasures. The restaurants on Zihuatanejo's Playa Madera and Playa La Ropa run the gamut from *palapa*-topped (thatched-roof) seafood shacks to elegant, upscale bistros.

From sunset to dinner, cocktails are the highlight of the nocturnal action here, and although these towns may lack the nightclub action of other resorts, they do offer a varied and excellent selection of restaurants. Seafood is the star, of course, but the preparations vary wildly, and in other cuisines, the influences of the European expatriate community are evident.

Mexico's 15% value-added tax (IVA) is added into most restaurant bills, but the tip isn't, and the wait-staff in Mexico depends on tips for the majority of their income — the usual tip here is 15%.

Finding Fast and Cheap Eats

Zihuatanejo's **central market,** located on Avenida Benito Juárez (about 5 blocks inland from the waterfront), is a perfect place for cheap and tasty food at breakfast and lunch before the market activity winds down in the afternoon. Look for what's hot and fresh. The market area is one of the best places on this coast for shopping and people-watching.

Two excellent **bakeries** in Zihua — smaller Mexican towns are known for their fresh pastries and *bolillos* (freshly baked, crusty mini-loaves) — are also noteworthy. Try **El Buen Gusto** (Guerrero 4, a half block inland from the Museo de Arqueología; ☎ 755-554-3231), which is open daily 7:30 a.m. to 10 p.m. and sells banana bread, French bread, doughnuts, and cakes. For more fresh-baked bread aroma, head for **Panadería Francesa** (González 15, between Cuauhtémoc and Guerrero; ☎ 755-554-2742) — open daily 7 a.m. to 9 p.m. You can buy sweet pastries or grab a long baguette or loaf of whole-wheat bread to munch on for a picnic.

Ixtapa and Zihuatanejo's Best Restaurants

I list the following restaurants alphabetically with references to price and location. Please refer to the Introduction of this book for an explanation of the price categories.

Because restaurants price shrimp and lobster so much higher than other entrees, I note the price ranges exclusive of these dishes unless they make up the major part of the menu. And, unless otherwise specified, reservations aren't accepted or aren't necessary.

Please see Appendix C for more information on Mexican cuisine.

Beccofino
$–$$ Ixtapa   NORTHERN ITALIAN

Beccofino is a standout not only in Ixtapa but also in all of Mexico. Owner Angelo Rolly Pavia serves up the flavorful northern Italian specialties he grew up enjoying. The breezy location is under a covered slip overlooking the marina's yachts. The menu is strong on pasta. Ravioli, a house specialty, comes stuffed with the freshest seafood, whether swordfish or shrimp. The garlic bread is terrific, and the wine list is extensive with an impressive selection of imported wines to choose from. It's a popular place, and the restaurant tends to be loud when crowded, which is often. Beccofino is increasingly becoming a popular breakfast spot.

Marina Ixtapa, near the lighthouse. ☎ *755-553-1770. Main courses: $14–$30; breakfast $5–$7. AE, MC, V. Open: Daily 9:30 a.m. to midnight.*

Zihuatanejo and Ixtapa Area Dining

Airport ✈
Bus ▣
Post Office ⊠

Beccofino **5**
Casa Puntarenas **4**
Coconuts **2**
Golden Cookie Shop **7**
Kau-Kan **9**
La Perla **10**
La Sirena Gorda **3**
Nueva Zelanda **1**
Ruben's **6**
Villa de la Selva **8**

Casa Puntarenas

$ Zihuatanejo Centro MEXICAN/SEAFOOD

A modest spot with a tin roof and nine wooden tables, Puntarenas is one of the best places in town for fried whole fish served with toasted *bolillos* (crusty, white-bread mini-loaves), sliced tomatoes, onions, and avocado. The place is renowned for *chile rellenos,* served mild and stuffed with plenty of cheese, and the pork chops are divinely inspired. Although it may appear a little too rustic for less experienced travelers to Mexico, Casa Puntarenas is very clean, and the food is known for its freshness. To get to Puntarenas from the pier, turn left on Alvarez and cross the footbridge on your left. Turn right after you cross the bridge; the restaurant is on your left.

Calle Noria s/n. No phone. Main courses: $4.50–$8.50. No credit cards. Open: Daily 6:30–9 p.m.

Coconuts

$–$$$ Zihuatanejo Centro INTERNATIONAL/SEAFOOD

What a find! Not only is the food innovative and delicious but also the restaurant is housed in a historic building — the oldest in Zihuatanejo. This popular restaurant set in a tropical garden was the former weigh-in station for Zihua's coconut industry in the late 1800s. Fresh is the operative word on this creative, seafood-heavy menu. Chef Patricia Cummings checks the market daily for the freshest foods and uses only top-quality ingredients to prepare dishes such as seafood pâté and grilled fillet of snapper Coconuts. The house specialty is chiles rellenos Luduvina, chile poblanos stuffed with shrimp and potatoes and topped with a tomato coulis. The bananas flambé has earned a loyal following of its own — with good reason. Expect friendly, efficient service here.

Augustín Ramírez 1, at Vicente Guerrero. ☎ 755-554-2518. Fax: 755-554-7980. Main courses: $11–$34. AE, MC, V. Open: Daily lunch 11:30 a.m–4:30 p.m.; dinner 6–11 p.m. during high season. Closed during rainy season.

Golden Cookie Shop

$ Ixtapa PASTRIES/INTERNATIONAL

Although the name is misleading — they sell more than cookies here — Golden Cookie's fresh baked goods beg for a detour, and the coffee menu is the most extensive in town — and includes iced-espresso drinks for those sultry Ixtapa days. Although the prices are high for the area, the breakfasts are particularly noteworthy, as are the deli sandwiches. Large sandwiches, made with fresh soft bread, come with a choice of sliced deli meats, such as smoked ham. Chicken curry is among the other specialty items, and the Golden Cookie folks serve up a hearty German buffet every Friday evening at 7 p.m. They have recently expanded their menu to include sugar-free options for diabetics and the dieting. To get to the shop, walk to the rear of the Los Patios shopping center as you face Mac's

Prime Rib; walk up the stairs, turn left, and the restaurant is on the right. An air-conditioned area is reserved for nonsmokers.

Los Patios shopping center. ☎ *755-553-0310. Main courses: $6–$8; breakfast $4–$6; sandwiches $4–$6. MC, V. Open: Daily 8 a.m.–3 p.m.*

Kau-Kan

$–$$ Zihuatanejo Beaches/Playa La Ropa   NUEVA COCINA/ SEAFOOD

Open architecture, stunning views of the bay, and refined cuisine are among the hallmarks of this popular restaurant. Head chef Ricardo Rodriguez supervises every detail of this elegantly understated operation from the ultra-smooth background music that invites after-dinner conversation to the spectacular presentation of all the dishes. The baked potato with baby lobster and the mahi-mahi carpaccio are two of my favorites, but consider the daily specials — Ricardo always gets the freshest seafood available and prepares it with great care. For dessert, the pecan and chocolate cake served with a dark chocolate sauce is simply delicious. During high season, reservations are essential. Located on the road to Playa La Ropa, the restaurant is on the right-hand side of the road past the first curve coming from downtown.

Camino a Playa La Ropa. ☎ *755-554-8446. Reservations recommended during high season. Main courses: $13–$25. AE, MC, V. Open: Daily 5–11:30 p.m.*

La Perla

$ Playa La Ropa   SEAFOOD

Along Playa La Ropa, you can find any number of casual, *palapa*-style restaurants, but La Perla, with its tables under the trees and a thatched roof, is the most popular. Although it's known more as a tradition than for the food or service, somehow, this long stretch of pale sand and groups of wooden chairs under *palapas* (thatched roof umbrellas) have made a charming combination. Some diners joke that getting a waiter's attention at La Perla can be so hard that, if you get take-out food from a competitor and bring it here to eat, they won't even notice. Still, La Perla is considered the best spot around for tanning and socializing and serves a whopper of a *gringo* (American) breakfast. Lunches are lighter — *cerviche* (fresh fish cocktail made with finely cubed raw fish that is marinated with lime, vinegar and spices) are the specialty. In the evening, casual dinners and cold *cervezas* (beers) are accompanied by satellite-dish-delivered sports. La Perla is located near the southern end of Playa La Ropa. Take the right fork in the road; a sign is in the parking lot. The kitchen doesn't open until 10 a.m. but the restaurant is open at 9 a.m. for customers who arrive early to get the best spots on the beach!

Playa La Ropa. ☎ *755-554-2700. Main courses $6.00–$11.00; breakfast $2.50–$5. AE, MC, V. Open: Daily 9 a.m.–10 p.m.; breakfast served 10 a.m. to noon.*

La Sirena Gorda

$ Zihuatanejo Centro   MEXICAN

Head to La Sirena Gorda (the chubby mermaid) for one of the most popular breakfasts in town. Choose from a variety of eggs and omelets, hotcakes with bacon, or fruit with granola and yogurt. The house specialty is seafood tacos — fish in a variety of sauces plus lobster — but I consider these selections overpriced at $3 for the fish and $20 for the lobster. To me, a taco is a taco is a taco, but they did earn rave reviews in *Bon Appétit* a few years back. Instead, I recommend something from the short list of daily specials such as blackened red snapper, steak, or fish kebabs. The food is excellent and patrons enjoy the casual sidewalk-cafe atmosphere. To get here from the basketball court, face the water and walk to the right along the *Paseo;* La Sirena Gorda is on your right just before the town pier.

Paseo del Pescador. ☎ *755-554-2687. Main courses: $3–$6; breakfast $2–$4. MC, V. Open: Thurs–Tues 7 a.m.–10 p.m.*

Nueva Zelanda

$ Zihuatanejo Centro   MEXICAN

Rich cappuccinos sprinkled with cinnamon, fresh fruit *liquados* (kind of a smoothie), and pancakes with real maple syrup draw patrons to this open-air snack shop. The mainstays of the menu are tortas and enchiladas, and everything is offered with friendly, efficient service. Dine indoors and watch your food get prepared in the spotless open kitchen, or choose a seat at one of the sidewalk tables for a pleasant people-watching session. You can easily find Nueva Zelanda by walking three blocks inland from the waterfront on Cuauhtémoc; the restaurant is on your right. A second location (☎ **755-553-0838**) is located in Ixtapa in the back section of the Los Patios shopping center.

Cuauhtémoc 23 at Ejido. ☎ *755-554-2340. Main courses: Tortas $2.50–$3.50; enchiladas $2.50–$5; fruit-and-milk liquados $2.50; cappuccino $2. No credit cards. Open: Daily 8 a.m.–10 p.m.*

Ruben's

$ Ixtapa   BURGERS/VEGETABLES

If time in Ixtapa also means a vacation from decision making, then check out Ruben's. The choices are easy — you can order a big, juicy burger made from top-sirloin beef grilled over mesquite or a foil-wrapped packet of baked potatoes, chayote, zucchini, or sweet corn. Ice cream, beer, and soda fill out the menu, which is posted on the wall by the kitchen. The place is kind of a do-it-yourself affair: Guests snare a waitress and order, grab their own drinks from the cooler, and tally their own tabs. But because of the ever-present crowds, it can still be a slow process. For years, Ruben's was a popular fixture in the Playa Madera neighborhood, but it moved to two locations in Ixtapa. The food remains as dependable as ever, even if the locale has expanded and spiffed up a bit.

Flamboyant shopping center, next to Bancomer. Also on Bulevar Ixtapa across from the Radisson. ☎ *755-553-0055. Main courses: Burgers $3–$5; vegetables $2; ice cream $1.50. No credit cards. Open: Daily 6–11 p.m. Delivery service also available.*

Villa de la Selva

$$–$$$ Ixtapa   MEXICAN/CONTINENTAL

Once the summer home of one-time Mexican president Luis Echevarria, this exquisite restaurant is set into the edge of a cliff overlooking the sea. Elegant and romantic, it offers diners the most spectacular sea-and-sunset view in Ixtapa. Candlelit tables are arranged on three terraces; try to come early in hopes of getting one of the best vistas — my favorite is the lower terrace. The cuisine is delicious, artfully appointed, and classically rich: *Filet Villa de la Selva* is red snapper topped with shrimp and hollandaise sauce. The cold avocado soup or hot lobster bisque make a good beginning; finish with chocolate mousse or bananas Singapore. The restaurant is just above Las Brisas Resort, overlooking Vista Hermosa beach.

Paseo de la Roca. ☎ *755-553-0362. Reservations recommended during high season. Main courses: $15–$44. AE, MC, V. Open: Daily 7–11 p.m.*

Chapter 21

Having Fun on and off the Beach in Ixtapa and Zihuatanejo

By Lynne Bairstow

In This Chapter

▶ Soaking up the sun

▶ Enjoying the best sports — on land and by sea

▶ Sightseeing and shopping like a licensed professional

▶ Getting *really* away from it all with a side trip to Troncones

▶ Living it up at night

*W*hile you're in Ixtapa and Zihuatanejo, life isn't just a beach; it's a choice of beaches! From rocky coves to smooth stretches of golden sand, this chapter gives you the rundown on all the key beaches in the area and highlights the beaches that are best for watersports and safest for swimming so that you can choose the patch of sand that's perfect for you. If you're looking for adventure beyond the sea, I also have some recommendations for you — along with tips on the best shopping and nightlife.

All beaches in Zihuatanejo are safe for swimming because undertow is rarely a problem, and the municipal beach is protected from the Pacific Ocean's main surge. Beaches in Ixtapa are more dangerous for swimming because of frequent undertow problems, so keep an eye on the safety flags posted in front of the hotel beaches.

Hitting the Beaches

This section contains the skinny on the area's beaches, traveling from the beaches northwest of Ixtapa to those south of Zihuatanejo. Even if you fall in love at first sight with the stretch of sand immediately in front of your hotel, explore a bit to see what other beauties are out there.

Playa Linda and **Playa Quieta** are about as far out as you're likely to travel to find a beach in this area. Playa Linda, about 13km (8 miles) north of Ixtapa (about 10 minutes by taxi), is the departure point for the inexpensive water taxis that ferry passengers to Isla Ixtapa. It's also the primary out-of-town beach, a long stretch of flat sand with water-sports equipment and horseback-riding rentals. Along with a collection of small stands selling trinkets, the La Palapa restaurant makes a good place to spend the afternoon. Playa Linda faces the open ocean but also lies near a freshwater estuary that's home to birds, iguanas, and the occasional alligator — visible through a safety fence. Club Med and Qualton Club have largely claimed neighboring Playa Quieta directly across from Isla Ixtapa. The beach at Playa Quieta is beautiful, but unless you're staying at either of those resorts, you won't find shade, drinks, or any sort of beach club facilities. If you're not staying on Playa Quieta, skip it. The other beaches are just as beautiful and a lot easier to get to.

Around the Punta Ixtapa peninsula lies **Playa Las Cuatas,** a pretty beach and cove a few miles outside of Ixtapa. It has heavy surf and a strong undertow, so I don't recommend it for swimming.

Ixtapa's main beach, **Playa el Palmar,** is a lovely white-sand arc on the edge of the Hotel Zone. Almost 3 miles long, this beach features dramatic rock formations by the sea. The surf here can be rough; use caution and don't swim when a red flag is posted. Several of the nicest beaches in the area are essentially closed to the public — resort developments rope them off exclusively for their guests. Although by law all Mexican beaches are open to the public, it's a common practice for hotels to create artificial barriers (such as rocks or dunes) to preclude entrance to their beaches.

Next up is lovely **Playa Vista Hermosa,** framed by striking rock formations and bordered by the Las Brisas Resort high on the hill. Although very attractive for sunbathing or a stroll, this patch of sand is also known for its heavy surf and strong undertow, so use extreme caution if swimming or snorkeling here.

Local fishermen still use the Zihuatanejo town beach, **Playa Municipal,** to pull their colorful boats up onto the sand — a fine photo-op. The small shops and restaurants lining the waterfront here are great for people-watching and absorbing the flavor of daily village life.

Ixtapa and Zihuatanejo Area

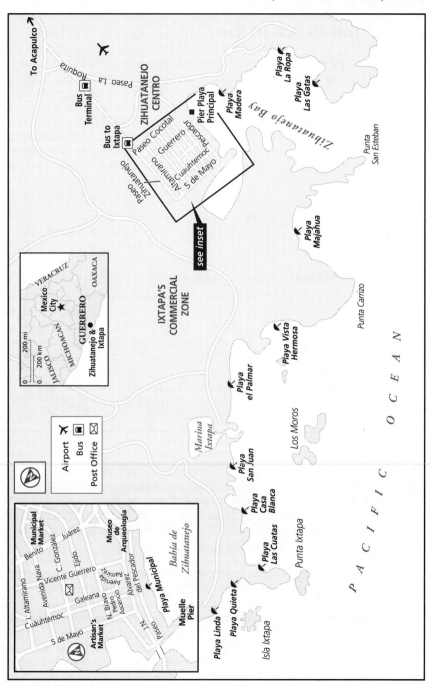

To Acapulco

Paseo La Roqueta

ZIHUATANEJO CENTRO

Bus Terminal

Bus to Ixtapa

Paseo Zihuatanejo

Paseo Cocotal

Guerrero

Av. Altamirano

Cuauhtemoc

5 de Mayo

Pescador

Pier Playa Principal

Playa Madera

Playa La Ropa

Playa Las Gatas

Punta San Esteban

Zihuatanejo Bay

see inset

IXTAPA'S COMMERCIAL ZONE

Playa Majahua

Punta Carrizo

VERACRUZ

OAXACA

Mexico City ★

GUERRERO

MICHOACAN

JALISCO

Zihuatanejo & Ixtapa ●

200 mi

200 km

0

Airport ✈

Bus ▣

Post Office ⊠

Playa Vista Hermosa

Playa el Palmar

Los Moros

Marina Ixtapa

Playa San Juan

Playa Casa Blanca

Playa Las Cuatas

Punta Ixtapa

Municipal Market

Benito Juárez

C. González

Museo de Arqueologia

Ejido

C.I. Altamirano

Avenida Nava

Vicente Guerrero

Galeana

Cuáuhtémoc

N. Bravo

N. Pedro Ascencio

Alvarez

Avenida Ramírez

Paseo del Pescador

5 de Mayo

N.T.I.

Artisan's Market

Playa Municipal

Muelle Pier

Bahía de Zihuatanejo

Playa Linda

Playa Quieta

Isla Ixtapa

P A C I F I C   O C E A N

Finding fun in the sun off the mainland

Some notable beaches, along with clear water, snorkeling, and a few nature trails, are out on **Isla Ixtapa**. You can find four small beaches on the island, the busiest of which is **Playa Cuachalatate,** named for a native tree. It's the arrival point for the ferryboats and has a selection of *palapa*-topped restaurants. **Playa Varadero,** with calm clear waters that make it a favorite for snorkeling, is along a paved walkway to the right of Playa Cuachalatate. Group tours here usually include lunch at El Marlin restaurant. El Marlin is one of several restaurants on the island, but it's not appreciably better than the others, so feel confident in making your way on your own.

Continue to the right along the same path past Playa Varadero and you come to **Playa Coral,** which true to name, offers the most varied groupings of underwater coral in the area — it's excellent for snorkeling. The most isolated of the beaches on Isla Ixtapa is **Playa Carey** — to the left of the Playa Cuachalatate dock. It doesn't have any facilities but makes a great spot for a picnic. (Be sure to take your trash with you as you leave — no containers are available here for disposal.)

Boats leave the dock at Playa Linda for Isla Ixtapa every 10 minutes between 11:30 a.m. and 5 p.m., so you can depart and return at your own pace. The round-trip boat ride is $2.50 and takes anywhere from 20 to 35 minutes (depending on the boat and the boat's captain). Along the way, you pass dramatic rock formations, and you can see **Los Moros de Los Pericos islands** in the distance where a great variety of birds nest on its rocky points jutting out into the blue Pacific. When you reach Isla Ixtapa, you can find snorkeling, diving, and other watersports gear available for rent. Be sure to catch the last water taxi back at 5 p.m., but double-check that time upon arrival on the island.

Just east of Playa Municipal lies **Playa Madera**, which is accessible by following a lighted concrete-and-sand walkway that cuts through the rocks for about 100 yards from the Paseo del Pescador. The beach itself is open to the Pacific surf but is generally peaceful. A number of attractive budget lodgings overlook this area from the hillside, and beachside restaurants line the shore.

South of Playa Madera is Zihuatanejo's largest and most beautiful beach, **Playa La Ropa,** a long sweep of sand with a great view of the sunset. Some lovely, small hotels and restaurants nestle into the hills; palm groves edge the shoreline. Although it's also open to the Pacific, waves are usually gentle. A taxi from town costs $3. The name "Playa La Ropa," *ropa* means clothing, comes from an old tale of a *galeón* that sunk during a big storm. The silk clothing that the boat was carrying back from the Philippines all washed ashore on this beach — hence the name.

The nicest beach for swimming and the best beach for children is the secluded **Playa Las Gatas**. You can see this delicate ribbon of sand, which is speckled with minute seashells, across the bay from Playa La Ropa and Zihuatanejo. The small coral reef just offshore is a nice spot for snorkeling and diving, and a few small dive shops on the beach rent gear. The waters at Las Gatas are exceptionally clear and there's no undertow or big waves, which is due in large part to a rock wall surrounding the beach that turns the waters into a virtual wading pool. The pre-Hispanic emperor Calzonzin, who chose this beach as his private playground more than 500 years ago, constructed the wall. Open-air seafood restaurants on the beach make it an appealing lunch spot. (Two of the restaurants are now open for dinner as well.) Small, shaded *pangas* (small boats) make the voyage to Las Gatas from the Zihuatanejo town pier, a 10-minute trip. The captains can take you across whenever you want between 8 a.m. and 4 p.m. Evening ferries are less predictable, so check for the current schedule. A round-trip fare generally runs about $3.50.

Finding Water Fun for Everyone

The beaches here are so appealing because the waters are crystal clear and obviously free of pollution and over-fishing. Snorkel, dive, cast a line, or take a dip — it's a slice of heaven. And there are other ways to enjoy splashing around . . . or cruising above the deep blue.

Skiing and surfing

Rental stands with **sailboats, windsurfers,** and other **watersports equipment** are located at numerous points along Playa La Ropa and Playa Las Gatas in Zihuatanejo, Playa el Palmar in Ixtapa, and even on Isla Ixtapa. You can **parasail** (about $20 for a 15-minute ride) at La Ropa and Palmar. **Kayaks** are available for rent at the **Zihuatanejo Scuba Center** (Cuauhtémoc 3; ☎ **755-554-3873;** www.divemexico.com), hotels in Ixtapa, and some watersports operations on Playa La Ropa. A few places also have **WaveRunners,** which rent for about $30 per half-hour.

Exploring the deep blue

These clear waters, with more than 30 deep-dive sites, just beg to be explored! Water visibility frequently is more than 100 feet, especially from December through May when the temperature is usually comfortably warm. You're likely to see an abundance of sea life — as well as the possibility of spotting an old anchor or other artifacts from the days of the Spanish conquistadors.

Arrange your **scuba-diving trip** through the **Zihuatanejo Scuba Center** (Cuauhtémoc 3; ☎ **755-554-3873**; www.divemexico.com). Fees start at around $80 for two dives including all equipment and lunch. Marine biologist and dive instructor Juan Barnard speaks excellent English and is known as a very fun guide. He's quite knowledgeable about the area, which has excellent dive sites, including walls and caves, for all experience levels. Certification courses are available, and the dive-guide-to-diver ratio is an outstanding one-to-three.

I suggest that you make advance reservations for dives during Christmas and Easter.

The diving here is great, but you can also enjoy many of the underwater sites without going to such depths. **Snorkeling** is best at Zihuatanejo's Playa Las Gatas, Isla Ixtapa's Playa Varadero, and Playa Vista Hermosa in front of the Las Brisas Resort. Equipment rentals are available at all locations and range from $5 to $15 a day.

Reeling in the big one

Looking for the big one? Billfish — notably blue and black marlin and Pacific sailfish — swim in the waters off Zihuatanejo. And, when you catch the big one, release it. It may sting a bit, but this conservation effort is increasingly popular in Mexico, and I encourage it. You can arrange **fishing trips** with the **boat cooperative** (☎ **755-554-2056**) at the Zihuatanejo town pier. Excursions cost $140 to $300 per trip depending on boat size, trip length, and other factors. Most trips last about 6 hours; no credit cards are accepted. The price includes ten soft drinks and ten beers, bait, and fishing gear. Lunch is on your own.

You pay more for a trip arranged through a local travel agency; the least expensive trips are on small launches called *pangas* — most have shade. Outfits offer both small-game and deep-sea fishing. The fishing here is adequate, but it's not on par with that of Mazatlán or Baja.

You can also arrange trips that combine fishing with a visit to the nearly deserted ocean beaches that extend for miles along the coast north and south of the towns of Zihua and Ixtapa. Sam Lushinsky at **Ixtapa Sportfishing Charters** (19 Depue Lane, Stroudsburg, PA 18360; ☎ **570-688-9466**; Fax: 570-688-9554; www.ixtapasportfishing.com; E-mail: ixtsptf@epix.net) is a noted fishing outfitter.

Boating and fishing expeditions from the **Marina Ixtapa,** a bit north of the Ixtapa Hotel Zone, can also be arranged. As a rule, everything available in or through the marina is more expensive, in addition to being more "Americanized."

Tipping the captain 10% to 15% of the total price of your charter is customary, depending on the quality of the service. Give the money to the captain, and he'll split it with the mates.

Cruising Ixtapa and Zihuatanejo

The area's most popular boat trip is probably the voyage to **Isla Ixtapa** for snorkeling and lunch at the El Marlin restaurant or one of several other restaurants on the island. You can book this outing as a tour through any local travel agency or your hotel tour desk, or you can head out on your own from Playa Linda, which allows you to follow your own schedule. (Check out the "Finding fun in the sun off the mainland" sidebar, earlier in this chapter, for more info on getting to Isla Ixtapa from Playa Linda.)

Local travel agencies can also arrange day-trips to **Los Moros de Los Pericos** islands for **bird-watching,** though it's less expensive to rent a boat with a guide at Playa Linda. These islands are located offshore from Playa el Palmar; however, you must leave from Playa Linda because no boats depart from Playa el Palmar.

Day cruises and **sunset cruises** on the *trimaran* (a catamaran with an extra hull) *TriStar* can be arranged through **Yates del Sol** (☎ 755-554-2694 or 755-554-8270) or through any travel agent (with no difference in price). Both day and sunset cruises depart from the Zihuatanejo town pier at Puerto Mío.

The day cruise sails to Playa Manzanillo, where you have time for swimming, snorkeling, and shell collecting. On the return trip, the boat anchors off Playa La Ropa. The price of $59 includes lunch, an open bar, and round-trip transportation from your hotel. Snorkeling gear is $5 extra. There's also a day-trip to Isla Ixtapa on this very comfortable and rarely crowded yacht that begins at 10 a.m., costs $49, and includes an open bar and lunch. The sunset cruise, generally running from 5 to 7:30 p.m., costs $39 and includes an open bar and snacks. Because schedules and special trips vary, call for current information.

Enjoying Land Sports

Ixtapa and Zihuatanejo offer plenty of popular land sports for vacationers. In this section, I cover golf, tennis, and horseback riding. If you're looking for an activity I don't list here, be sure to consult your hotel or resort concierge for more information.

Teeing off

Ixtapa has two locations where you can tee off. One spot is the **Club de Golf Ixtapa Palma Real** (☎ **755-553-1062** or 755-553-1163), located in front of the Barceló Hotel at the entrance to Ixtapa's Hotel Zone as you arrive from Zihuatanejo. Robert Trent Jones, Jr., designed the 18-hole course, and much of the land here is protected as a wildlife preserve, so you may see flamingos or cranes near the lagoon at the 15th hole. Greens fees are $70; caddies cost an additional $20 for 18 holes or $11 for 9 holes. Electric carts are $25, and club rentals are $20. Tee times begin at 7 a.m., but the club doesn't take reservations. Another option is the **Marina Ixtapa Golf Course** (☎ **755-553-1410**), which was designed by Robert von Hagge and features 18 challenging holes. It's located at the opposite end of Hotel Zone from the Palma Real — the courses kind of form two bookends. The greens fees are $120; carts, caddies, and club rentals are $20 each. The first foursome tees off at 7 a.m. Call for reservations 24 hours in advance. (Both courses accept American Express, MasterCard, and Visa.)

Taking time for tennis

If you want to work on your tennis game in Ixtapa, both the **Club de Golf Ixtapa Palma Real** (☎ **755-553-1062** or 755-553-1163) and the **Marina Ixtapa Golf Course** (☎ **755-553-1410**) have lighted public courts and equipment available for rent. Fees are $10 per hour during the day and $12 per hour at night. In addition, the **Dorado Pacífico** and most of the better hotels on the Playa el Palmar have courts. Although priority play is given to guests, most hotel courts are also open to the public.

Galloping along

For **horseback riding, Rancho Playa Linda** (☎ **044-755-557-0222** wireless) offers guided trail rides from the Playa Linda beach (about 13km/ 8 miles north of Ixtapa). Guided rides begin at 8:30, 9:45, and 11 a.m. and 3, 4, and 5 p.m. The early morning ride is the coolest, and it's a beautiful way to start a day; the 5 p.m. trip offers a view of the sunset. Groups of three or more riders can arrange their own tour, which is especially nice a little later in the evening around sunset (though you need mosquito repellent). Riders can choose to ride along the beach to the mouth of the river and then follow the river back through coconut plantations, or they can hug the beach for the whole ride (which usually lasts between an hour and an hour and a half). The fee is around $30, cash only. Travel agencies in either town can arrange your trip but do charge a bit more for transportation. During the high season, I suggest that you make reservations. Another good place to go horseback riding is at **Playa Larga.** There's a ranch on the first exit coming from

Zihuatanejo on Highway 200 going south (no phone, but you can't miss it — it's the first corral to the right as you drive toward the beach). The horses are in excellent shape, and the fee is $30 for 45 minutes.

Sightseeing in Ixtapa and Zihuatanejo

One of the most enjoyable things to do here doesn't even cost a peso — stroll along Zihuatanejo's **Paseo del Pescador** and take in the local life. Fishing boats bob in the waters, gulls circle overhead, and the basketball court is constantly in use.

The **Museo de Arqueología de la Costa Grande** (no phone), which traces the area's history from Acapulco to Ixtapa and Zihuatanejo from pre-Hispanic times through the colonial era, is at the east end of the Paseo del Pescador near Vicente Guerrero. Most of the museum's pottery and stone artifacts provide evidence of extensive trade between the peoples of this area and far-off cultures and regions, including the Toltec and Teotihuacán cultures near Mexico City, the Olmec culture on both the Pacific and Gulf coasts, and areas along the northern Pacific coast. This museum easily merits the half-hour or less it takes to stroll through; information signs are in Spanish, but an accompanying brochure is available in English. Admission is $1, and it's open Tuesday to Sunday from 10 a.m. to 6 p.m.

Shopping in Ixtapa and Zihuatanejo

Shopping isn't especially memorable in Ixtapa — T-shirts and Mexican crafts make up most of the offerings. Several of the town's numerous plazas have air-conditioned shops that carry resort wear — as well as the requisite T-shirts and silver jewelry. These shops are within the same area on Bulevar Ixtapa, across from the beachside hotels, and most are open 9 a.m. to 2 p.m. and 4 to 9 p.m. including Sunday.

However, the terrific shop **La Fuente** (in the Los Patios shopping center; ☎ 755-553-0812) is worth a stop in Ixtapa. The shop carries gorgeous Talavera pottery, jaguar-shaped wicker tables, hand-blown glassware, masks, tin mirrors and frames, hand-embroidered clothing from Chiapas, and wood and papier-mâché miniatures.

Zihuatanejo, like other resorts in Mexico, also has its quota of T-shirt and souvenir shops, but it's becoming a better place to buy Mexican crafts, folk art, and jewelry. The **artisan's market** on Calle Cinco de Mayo is a good place to start your shopping before moving on to specialty shops. A **municipal market** is located on Avenida Benito Juárez (about 5 blocks inland from the waterfront, sprawling over several blocks), but most of the vendors offer the same things — *huaraches* (Mexican-style sandals made of hard leather), hammocks, and baskets — with little variety. Numerous small shops spread inland from the waterfront some 3 or 4 blocks and are well worth exploring.

Shops are generally open Monday to Saturday 10 a.m. to 2 p.m. and 4 to 8 p.m.; many of the better shops close on Sunday, but some smaller souvenir stands stay open, although the hours vary.

I recommend the following shops:

- ✔ If you find your wardrobe isn't weathering the heat very well, **Boutique D'Xochitl** (Ejido at Cuauhtémoc; ☎ 755-554-2131) is the place to find crinkle-cotton clothing that's perfect for tropical climates.

- ✔ The small **Casa Marina** complex (Paseo del Pescador 9, along the waterfront heading in the direction of Alvarez near Cinco de Mayo; ☎ 755-554-2373) houses four shops, each specializing in handcrafted wares from all over Mexico including handsome rugs, textiles, masks, colorful woodcarvings, and silver jewelry. Café Marina, the small coffee shop in the complex, has shelves and shelves of used paperback books in several languages for sale.

- ✔ **Coco Cabaña Collectibles** (Guerrero and Alvarez, next to Coconuts Restaurant; ☎ 755-554-2518) is filled with carefully selected crafts and folk art, including fine Oaxacan woodcarvings, from all across the country. Owner Pat Cummings once ran a gallery in New York, and the inventory reveals her discriminating eye.

- ✔ **Viva Zapatos** (Guerrero 33, three doors down from Amueblados Valle; ☎ 755-554-4649) carries bathing suits to fit every shape and fashion trend, great casual and not-so-casual resort wear, sunglasses, and just about everything else for looking good in and out of the water.

Taking a Side Trip

About 32km (20 miles) northwest of Ixtapa, the tiny fishing hamlet of **Troncones,** with its long beaches, has become a favorite escape for visitors to Ixtapa and Zihuatanejo — when that pace of life becomes too hectic. Troncones is so remote that only a few people have phones. Strolling the empty beach, swimming in the sea, and hiking in the jungle and to nearby caves is about the extent of the action. When you've built up an appetite, satisfy it with fresh seafood at one of the fisherman-shack restaurants.

No public buses serve this area, so you must join a tour or hire a taxi to take you to Troncones. For about $30, the taxi driver can take you to the area and return at the hour you request to bring you back to town. Some travel agencies have day-trips here for about $25, which usually include lunch; it's cheaper, but less flexible than a taxi.

If you're only spending the day in Troncones, you can use the restaurant **El Burro Borracho** (☎ **755-553-2834** or 755-553-2800) as your head-quarters and have the taxi return for you there. This casual beachfront establishment isn't your ordinary beach-shack restaurant. Owned by a former chef from San Francisco, it offers fish, shrimp, and lobster as well as steak and grilled meat. Try the shrimp tacos for a uniquely Troncones treat. Wash the tasty grub down with a frosty margarita, an iced cappuccino, a glass of wine, or a cold beer. Remember that El Burro Borracho doesn't accept credit cards, and it's open daily from 8 a.m. to 9 p.m.

Discovering Ixtapa and Zihuatanejo after Dark

With an exception or two, Zihuatanejo nightlife dies down around 11 p.m. or midnight. For a decent selection of clubs, discos, hotel fiestas, and special events, head for Ixtapa. Just keep in mind that shuttle-bus service ends at 11 p.m., and a taxi ride back to Zihuatanejo after midnight costs 50% more than the regular price. During low season (after Easter and before Christmas), club hours vary: Some places are open only on weekends, and others are closed completely. In Zihuatanejo, the liveliest nightspot on weekends is **D'Latinos,** at the intersection of Nicolás Bravo and Vicente Guerrero in Zihuatanejo Centro (☎ 755-554-2230). A dance club with the lowest drink prices in town, it's popular with 20- to 30-year-olds. The most popular hang-out for local residents and ex-pats is **Paccolo,** around the corner from Amueblados Valle (no phone). It's the one place where you can find a lively crowd of locals almost every night.

Many Ixtapa hotels hold Mexican fiestas and other special events that include dinner, drinks, live music, and entertainment for a fixed price (generally $33). The **Barceló Ixtapa** (☎ **755-553-1858**) hosts the most popular fiesta, held each Wednesday night. Call for reservations or book your seats through your hotel's travel agency.

Many discos and dance clubs in Zihua and Ixtapa stay open until the last customers leave, so closing hours depend upon the revelers.

Most discos have a ladies night at least once a week — admission and drinks are free for women, making it easy for men to buy them a drink.

The Anderson chain of festive restaurants is a standard in Mexican nightlife, and Ixtapa has two of them. **Carlos 'n Charlie's** (Bulevar Ixtapa, just north of the Best Western Posada Real; ☎ 755-553-0085) runs knee-deep in nostalgia, bric-a-brac, silly sayings, and photos from the Mexican Revolution. This restaurant-nightclub boasts a party ambiance and good food. The eclectic menu includes iguana in season (with antacids and aspirin on the house). Out back by the beach is an open-air section (partly shaded) with a raised wooden platform for "pier-dancing" at night. The recorded rock-and-roll mixes with sounds of the ocean surf. The restaurant is open daily from 10 a.m. to midnight; pier dancing is held nightly from 9 p.m. to 3 a.m. The second tried-but-true Mexican nightspot from the Anderson lineup is **Señor Frog's** (Bulevar Ixtapa, in the La Puerta Center; ☎ 755-553-2282), which features several dining sections and a warehouse-like bar with raised dance floors. The rock-and-roll playing from large speakers sometimes prompts even dinner patrons to shimmy by their tables between courses. The restaurant is open daily 6 p.m. to midnight; the bar is open until 3 a.m.

Of all the clubs in Ixtapa, **Christine** (Bulevar Ixtapa, in the Hotel Krystal; ☎ 755-553-0456) is both the best known and the glitziest. A throwback to the days of disco, Christine is famous for its midnight light show, which features classical music played on a mega sound system. A semi-circle of tables arranged in tiers overlooks the dance floor. No tennis shoes, sandals, or shorts are allowed, and reservations are advised during high season. It's open nightly during high season from 10 p.m. to the wee hours of the mornin' (off-season hours vary). Cover varies depending on the day of the week from free to $20, and all major credit cards are accepted.

Ixtapa's newest and most progressive nocturnal option is **Liquid** (☎ 755-553-1725), located behind D'Rafaello restaurant in the Las Fuentes shopping center. A chill-out club in the true European tradition, Liquid opens at 1 a.m., plays the most progressive of electronic tunes, and stays open until 6 a.m. or so, although after you're inside, you'll never know a new day has dawned. With a cover charge ranging from free to $10, a very young, very hip crowd has claimed Liquid for its own.

Part VII
Acapulco

AFTER SAILING AROUND ACAPULCO BAY, RON AND DARLENE HEAD FOR THE INTERESTING GROTTOS OF NOSE CAY

In this part . . .

*1*t's a beach resort . . . and it's a big glittering city. The largest and most decadent of Mexico's beach resorts, Acapulco can be daunting at first glance.

With its 24-hour, nonstop action, Acapulco can overwhelm first-time visitors. But have no fear — this part helps you choose your accommodations and serves up insights on the best places to dine — from simply delectable fish-taco stands to cliff-side gourmet restaurants with views of Acapulco Bay's dazzling nightlights. Nightlife? You can't visit Acapulco without sampling this part of the action. The Acapulco club scene remains *the* super-hot attraction of this grande dame of Mexico's beach resorts.

Chapter 22

The Lowdown on Acapulco's Hotel Scene

By Lynne Bairstow

In This Chapter

▶ Laying out the hotel locations

▶ Evaluating the *numero uno* hotel choices

A capulco was the first Mexican beach town to attract tourism to its golden sands, warm waters, and sunny days. Since the late 1930s, this beach resort has welcomed visitors from around the world, and at one time, it rivaled Rio de Janeiro as the playground of the elite and famous. Today, Acapulco offers one of the widest ranges of hotel choices among Mexican beach resorts — something for every taste and budget.

Because Acapulco's heyday occurred somewhere between 1950 and 1970, many of the hotels are notably dated; however, others have been kept up admirably, offering a funky, kind of retro charm. To me, the single most striking feature of Acapulco is the view of the twinkling lights of the bay at night — an impressive sight that tends to draw you into its nocturnal energy, tempting you to come out and play. The best views are from the hilltop hotels and from the resorts on the bay's southern border, but any of the high-rise locations along Playa Condesa also offer prime views.

Choosing a Location

During my first encounter with Acapulco, I dismissed it as an outdated resort — a tired and ill-kempt relic most appropriate for those who enjoy a carnival-type atmosphere and sleeping all day to prepare for nights that last until sunrise. But my opinion was colored by where I was staying — in the heart of the rowdiest beach-bar action — which didn't suit my mood at the time. As I grew to know Acapulco and became acquainted with her other sides, it didn't take long for me to succumb to this diva's unique charms. Acapulco's energy is tireless (if occasionally tawdry), and her appeal lies somewhere between that of Las Vegas and Palm Beach. Your decision about where to stay plays a huge role in determining how happy you'll be with your Acapulco vacation.

Although Acapulco is an expansive city of several million residents, most visitors only come in contact with the area directly bordering Acapulco Bay and its beaches, which is easy to navigate and can be divided into three main areas. There's really no need to explore more — and you're not likely to have enough time to take in all the sights, activities, and options for dining and nightlife in these areas during a typical weeklong stay anyway.

Running from north to south, the first principal area is **Old Acapulco,** the historic section with a true downtown and plenty of budget accommodations.

Old Acapulco — the original heart of this grande dame of Mexico's beach resorts — has a great selection of basic, inexpensive hotels, and lots of local color. Travelers familiar with Acapulco — or comfortable with travel in Mexico — tend to prefer this area. Numerous budget hotels dot the streets fanning out from the *zócalo* (Acapulco's official and original central plaza). These accommodations are among the best values in Acapulco but, with the exception of the **Hotel Los Flamingos** — one of my favorite places to stay in Mexico — generally offer only the most basic of comforts.

Next comes the **Costera Hotel Zone.** The mid-range, high-rise hotels — lined up side by side, looking much like Miami Beach — are concentrated along this golden stretch of Playa Condesa. The area offers plenty of options for shopping, dining, and nightlife, and is easy to navigate, so it's the best choice for first-time visitors.

If you're looking to spoil yourself, the hotels in the southern neighborhoods and up in the hillsides overlooking the bay are your best bets. The hillside neighborhood bordering the curve of the southern edge of Acapulco Bay is **Las Brisas,** *the* elegant address in town and home of Acapulco's exclusive villas and lusher hotels. Encompassing the Las Brisas area, south of Acapulco Bay, as you travel toward the airport, are the neighborhoods of Punta Diamante and Revolcadero Beach, which fronts the Pacific Ocean. This is where you find the most expensive and luxurious resorts, complete with golf courses.

Las Brisas is several miles from the heart of Acapulco; anytime you want to travel into the Hotel Zone to enjoy its restaurants, shopping malls, or nightclubs, you're looking at a round-trip taxi fare of anywhere from $12 to $20.

Acapulco's Best Accommodations

Each hotel listing includes specific rack rates for two people spending one night in a double room during high season (Christmas to Easter), unless otherwise indicated. *Rack rates* simply mean published rates and tend to be the highest rate paid — you can do better, especially if you're purchasing a package that includes airfare (see Chapter 3 for tips on avoiding paying rack rates). Please refer to the Introduction of this book for an explanation of the price categories.

It's not unusual for many hotels to double their normal rates during Christmas and Easter weeks, but low-season rates can be anywhere from 20% to 60% below high-season rates. Note that some rates may seem much higher than others, until you realize that they're *all inclusive,* meaning that your meals and beverages are included in the price of your stay. These rates also include all tips, taxes, and most activities and entertainment.

All hotels have air conditioning unless otherwise indicated.

Camino Real Acapulco Diamante
$$$$$ Punta Diamante/Puerto Marqués

I love this hotel — it's an oasis of tranquility in the middle of Acapulco's nonstop energy. This relaxing, self-contained resort is an ideal choice for families or for travelers who already know Acapulco and don't care to explore much. If swimming in the ocean is a priority, this is your best bet in the area — it's located on the clean and safe-for-swimming Playa Puerto Marqués — but you do miss out on the compelling views of Acapulco Bay. In terms of contemporary decor, services, and amenities, I consider this to be one of Acapulco's finest hotels. The Camino Real is tucked in a secluded, 81-acre location — part of the enormous Punta Diamante development. From Carretera Escénica, you wind down a handsome brick road to the site of the hotel overlooking Puerto Marqués Bay. The spacious rooms have balconies or terraces, small sitting areas, marble floors, a safe-deposit box in the closet, and comfortable, classic furnishings. A bonus: The Camino Real offers 24-hour room service with a terrific menu at very reasonable prices — competitive with area restaurants after you figure in the cost of a round-trip taxi ride. The property also offers special amenities for children including the kid's "Mischief Club" and a children's pool. For adults, a small health club, spa, and tennis court are on-site.

Carretera Escénica Km 14 and Baja Catita 18. ☎ *744-435-1010. Fax: 744-435-1020.* www.caminoreal.com/acapulco. *146 rooms. Free parking. Rack rates: High season $300 double, $410 master suite (includes American breakfast); low-season and midweek discounts available. AE, MC, V.*

Acapulco Bay Area Accommodations

Camino Real Acapulco Diamante **11**
Costa Linda Hotel **3**
Elcano Hotel **8**
Fiesta Americana Condesa Acapulco **6**
Hotel Caleta **2**
Hotel Los Flamingos **1**

Hotel Misión **12**
Hotel Sands **5**
Hyatt Regency Acapulco **9**
Las Brisas **10**
Plaza Las Glorias/El Mirador **4**
Villa Vera Hotel, Spa, and Racquet Club **7**

Estrella de Oro Bus

To México City

Massieu
Navegante
Pizarro
Reyes
Católicos
Cosa
Pinzón
Universidad
Peg

Playa
Paraíso

5

6

Playa
Condesa

Morro

Herradura

Costera M. Alemán

Picuda

Sola

Del Mar

Deportes

El Morro

Golf Club

7

8

Las Palmas

Victoria
Trinidad

Cristóbal Colón

9

Santa María

Playa Icacos

Yucatán

Bravo

Cook

Av. Alm. Horacio Nelson

■ Icacos Naval Base

Playa
Guittarón

10

Carretera Escénica

To Oaxaca ↗

Playa
Puerto Marqués

11

To Airport ↘

Puerto Marqués

Old Acapulco (Downtown)

Vicente Guerrero

Nicolás

A. Serdán

Cuauhtémoc

Flecha
Roja Bus Stop

Nación

Escudero

Galeana

Progreso

V. de León

5 de Mayo

Lerdo Tejada

Galeana

La Quebrada

Iglesias

Valle

Hornitos

Hidalgo

Carranza

La Paz

B. Juárez

Morelos

Fuerte de
San Diego

La Pinzon

Arteaga

Bretón

Costera Miguel
Alemán

To Playa Hornos →

commercial
wharfs

Bahía de Acapulco

Playa Caleta ↓

UNITED STATES

Gulf of
Mexico

MEXICO

*PACIFIC
OCEAN*

Mexico
★ City

Acapulco

0   500 mi

0   500 km

Beach ↖
Bus Station ▣
Golf ⛳

Costa Linda Hotel

$$ Playa Caleta/Old Acapulco

Budget-minded American and Mexican couples are drawn to the clean, sunny, and well-kept rooms of the Costa Linda, one of the area's best values. Playa Caleta is just a 1-block walk from the property. All rooms have a minifridge, and some have a small kitchenette, making it a good choice for longer stays or for those who want to save vacation dollars by preparing a few of their own meals. Although the Costa Linda is cozy, it's situated adjacent to one of the busier streets in Old Acapulco, so traffic noise can be bothersome. Rooms surround a small pool with lounge chairs and tropical plants. Choose an upstairs room for more privacy. A tennis court is also available.

Costera Miguel Alemán 1008, just above the entrance to Caleta Beach pier. ☎ **744-482-5277** *or 744-482-2549. Fax: 744-483-4017. 44 units. Free parking. Rack rates: High season $80 double; low season $35 double. Two children under 8 stay free in parents' room. MC, V.*

Elcano Hotel

$$$–$$$$ Costera Hotel Zone

An Acapulco classic and a personal favorite of mine, the Elcano is known for its prime location near the convention center on a broad stretch of golden-sand beach. Its retro-style, turquoise-and-white lobby, and its beachfront pool area are the closest you can get to a South Beach Miami atmosphere in Acapulco, and its popular open-air restaurant adds to the lively waterfront scene. On the whole, the Elcano reminds me of a set from a classic Elvis-in-Acapulco movie — you almost expect to see the King among the tanned beach regulars here. The hotel's reputation is further enhanced by its exceptional service. The continually upgraded rooms, featuring classic navy-and-white accents, are bright and very comfortable, and most offer ample oceanfront balconies. This place is ideal if you attend a convention in Acapulco or want the optimal location between hillside nightlife and the Costera beach zone.

Costera Miguel Alemán 75, just west of the convention center. ☎ **800-972-2162** *in the U.S., or 744-435-1500. Fax: 744-484-2230.* http://hotel-elcano.com. *180 units. Rack rates: $132 studio and standard room, $170 junior suite, $213 master suite. AE, DC, MC, V.*

Fiesta Americana Condesa Acapulco

$$–$$$ Costera Hotel Zone

The location of this hotel — in the absolute heart of Playa Condesa — is perfect for travelers who don't want to miss a beat and who look to be right in the middle of the casual beach-bar action. The 18-story structure, located just east of and up the hill from the Glorieta Diana (a landmark traffic circle with a statue of Diana the Huntress — which is a duplicate of the one in Mexico City — at its center), towers above Playa Condesa.

The unremarkable but comfortable rooms tend to be loud (depending on the crowd) — as music from the pool wafts up into the rooms. All rooms have a private terrace or balcony with an ocean view. In addition to a beachfront pool, an adults-only hilltop swimming pool offers one of the finest views of Acapulco in the city, plus the hotel has a smaller children's pool and a sundeck.

Costera Miguel Alemán 97. ☎ *800-FIESTA1 in the U.S., or 744-484-2828. Fax: 744-484-1828.* www.fiestamericana.com. *500 units. Free parking. Rack rates: High season $112–$150 double; low season $93–$124 double. Ask about "Fiesta Break" packages, which include meals. AE, DC, MC, V.*

Hotel Caleta
$$ Playa Caleta/Old Acapulco

If you prefer the authentic feel of a Mexican holiday with all its boisterous, family-friendly, and spirited charms, then the Hotel Caleta (formerly known as the Grand Meigas Acapulco Resort) is a great choice. It's also a great value. The rooms at this all-inclusive property are simple — stark even — but the hotel itself is usually heavily populated and teeming with activity. This high-quality, nine-floor resort is built into a cliff on the Caleta peninsula and is located adjacent to one of the liveliest beaches in Old Acapulco. Successions of stepped terraces are home to tropical gardens, restaurants, and pools — both saltwater and freshwater. A private beach and boat dock are located down a brief flight of stairs. Rooms surround a central plant-filled courtyard topped by a glass ceiling, and all rooms have large terraces with ocean views, although some layouts lack separation from the neighboring terrace. As is traditional in all-inclusive resorts, meals and drinks are available at almost any hour, and the resort has a changing agenda of theme nights and evening entertainment.

Cerro San Martín 325, just east of Caleta Beach. ☎ *744-483-9940 or 744-483-9140. Fax: 744-485-9228. E-mail:* meigaca@prodigy.net.mx. *255 units. Rack rates: High season $82–$120 per person, all-inclusive; low season $50–$80 per person, all-inclusive. Room-only prices are sometimes available upon request. AE, DC, MC, V.*

Hotel Los Flamingos
$$ Old Acapulco

What a find! You can't help but fall in love with Los Flamingos as soon as you see it — I couldn't! — with its funky charm that transports you back to the days when there was a Hollywood jet set and Acapulco was their playground. Perched on a cliff 500 feet above Acapulco Bay, this hotel was frequented by such former Hollywood stars as John Wayne, Cary Grant, Johnny Weissmuller, Fred McMurray, Errol Flynn, Red Skelton, Roy Rogers, and a host of others. In fact, the stars liked the Flamingos so much that at one point they bought it and converted it into a private club. Though it enjoys a colorful history, it's in excellent shape and is exceptionally clean. Los Flamingos offers visitors a totally different perspective of Acapulco because it maintains all the charm of that grand era gone by. Photos of movie stars grace the lobby, especially those of Wayne, Grant, and Weissmuller — who constructed the large "Tarzan Suite" (also known as the "Round House") as his part-time residence. All rooms have dramatic ocean views with either a large balcony or terrace, but most of them aren't air-conditioned (those that are also have TVs). Still, the constant sea breeze is cool enough. Rooms are colorful with mosaic-tile tables and mirrors and brightly painted walls. A small pool is the popular gathering point during the day; the large bar is the place to be in the evening. I don't recommend this hotel for small children though — the same dramatic setting that produces such spectacular views can also inspire a constant state of panic for parents. A weekly *pozole* (a special stew made from hominy, served with shredded pork or chicken and an assortment of toppings) party makes Thursdays especially popular. Live music performed by a Mexican band that was probably around in the era of Wayne — note the seashell-pink bass — accompanies the festivities. Even if you don't stay here, plan to come for a margarita at sunset and a walk along the dramatic lookout point — not for the faint of heart!

Av. López Matéos s/n. ☎ *744-482-0690. Fax: 744-483-9806. 40 rooms. Rack rates: High season $80 double, $110 with A/C, $100 junior suite; low season $62 double, $88 with A/C, $80 junior suite. AE, MC, V.*

Hotel Misión
$ **Old Acapulco (Downtown)**

If this courtyard hotel reminds you of an old monastery, it may be because the original structure is more than a century old — truly and authentically "Old Acapulco"! Rooms are located in the L-shaped building that borders a plant-filled, brick courtyard shaded by two enormous mango trees. The hotel's location, on a narrow street surrounded by tiny shops, lends a distinctly different atmosphere to an Acapulco holiday here. You're in the center of town life just 2 blocks inland from the Costera, fishermen's wharf, *zócalo,* and La Quebrada — the site of the famous cliff divers. Playa Caleta is about a kilometer (half-mile) away. The rooms have colonial touches, such as colorful tile and wrought iron, and come simply furnished with a fan (no air conditioning here) and one or two beds with good mattresses. Unfortunately, the promised hot water isn't reliable — request a cold-water-only room and receive a discount. Breakfast is served on the patio.

Felipe Valle 12, between La Paz and Hidalgo. ☎ *744-482-3643. Fax: 744-482-2076. 27 units. Rack rates: $50 double. No credit cards.*

Hotel Sands
$ **Costera Hotel Zone**

Comfortable and unpretentious, the Hotel Sands is a great option for budget-minded travelers. The hotel's location on the inland side of the Costera translates to greatly reduced prices, and the fact that it's about a block off the main highway means it's far enough away from all the traffic noise to make your nights peaceful. Still, the Hotel Sands is close enough — walking distance — to the lively Costera Hotel Zone. From the street, you enter the hotel lobby through a stand of umbrella palms and an attractive garden restaurant — one that offers terrific, authentic Mexican food at rock-bottom prices. Rooms are light and airy in the style of a good, modern motel and have basic furnishings, wall-to-wall carpeting, and a terrace or balcony. The bungalow units are located across the street — all have kitchenettes. Two swimming pools (one for adults only), a kid's playground, a volleyball court, and complimentary coffee served in the lobby round out the features.

Costera Miguel Alemán 178, across from the Acapulco Plaza Hotel. ☎ *744-484-2260. Fax: 744-484-1053.* www.sands.com.mx. *93 units. Limited free parking. Rack rates: $58 standard room double, $47 bungalow double (all year except Christmas, Easter, and other major Mexican holidays). AE, MC, V.*

Hyatt Regency Acapulco
$$$ Costera Hotel Zone

The Hyatt is one of the largest and most modern hotels in Acapulco and about as sophisticated as they come here — which is still less sophisticated than most other resorts. It's a good choice for couples looking for a romantic break or for those attending conventions (it's close to the convention center). Two large, free-form pools meander through tropical gardens on the broad, golden-sand beachfront. The sleek lobby has an inviting sitting area and bar that hosts live music every evening and boasts the largest selection of tequilas in Acapulco. All rooms are large with sizable balconies overlooking the pool and ocean. Regency Club guests receive special amenities. (*Note:* Children aren't allowed in Regency Club rooms.) Kitchenettes are available in some rooms for an extra charge. Three outdoor tennis courts lit for night play and access to a nearby gym are included with your stay, making this hotel a good choice for travelers who prefer their vacations a little on the active side. The Hyatt Acapulco caters to a large Jewish clientele and offers a full-service kosher restaurant, an on-premises synagogue, and a special Sabbath elevator.

Costera Miguel Alemán 1. ☎ *800-633-7313 or 800-233-1234 in the U.S. and Canada or 744-469-1234. Fax: 744-484-3087.* www.hyattacapulco.com.mx. *640 units. Rack rates: High season $165 double, $175 Regency Club; low season $140 double, $150 Regency Club. AE, DC, MC, V.*

Las Brisas
$$$$$ Las Brisas

With its hilltop views, terrace pools, and 24-hour, pampering service, the pink-themed Las Brisas hotel is the quintessential Acapulco experience for many Acapulco veterans. A local landmark, Las Brisas is known for its tiered, pink-stucco facade and the 175 pink Jeeps rented exclusively to Las Brisas guests. If you stay here, you better like pink because the color scheme extends to practically everything. Las Brisas is also known for inspiring romance and is best enjoyed by couples indulging in time together — alone. Although the marble-floored rooms with mostly built-in furnishings are simple, they are each like separate villas and offer the most spectacular panoramic views of Acapulco Bay from the private balconies and terraces. Each room also has a private (or semi-private) swimming pool. (Altogether, Las Brisas boasts 250 swimming pools.) The more spacious Regency Club rooms are located at the apex of the property and offer the best views. You stay at Las Brisas more for the panache and setting than for the amenities. TVs are a recent addition, but they feature volume control so you don't disturb other guests. Early each morning, continental breakfast arrives in a discreet cubbyhole, so your coffee is ready when you are. Although the property isn't located on the beach, Las Brisas offers courtesy shuttle service to its own private beach club located five minutes away on the southwestern tip of Acapulco Bay. Here, freshwater and saltwater pools, plus a large restaurant and bar — though still not much of a real beach — compete for your attention. Five tennis courts, daily activities, and access to a nearby gym round out the action. A mandatory service charge takes care of the shuttle service from the hillside rooms to the lobby and all other service tips. The hotel is located on the southern edge of the bay overlooking the road to the airport and close to the hottest nightclubs in town.

Carretera Escénica 5255. ☎ *800-228-3000 in the U.S., or 744-469-6900. Fax: 744-446-5332. 263 units. Rack rates: High season $450 shared pool, $550 private pool, $650 Royal Beach Club; low season $230 shared pool, $345 private pool, $380 Royal Beach Club. $20 per day service charge extra (in lieu of all tips) plus 17% tax. Rates include continental breakfast. AE, DC, MC, V.*

Plaza Las Glorias/El Mirador

$$ Old Acapulco

The best part about staying here is watching those amazing Acapulco cliff divers every day and evening from the comfort of your room. It's an unforgettable sight and a real adrenaline rush. The hotel is built in a horseshoe shape at the apex of La Quebrada, the famous cove where the cliff divers perform. Rooms lack a little in the way of upkeep but offer a choice of double or queen-size beds, kitchenettes with a minifridge and coffeemaker, and large bathrooms with marble counters. Most have a separate living room, some have a whirlpool tub, and all feature colorful, Saltillo-tile accents and other Mexican decorative touches. Be sure to ask for a room with a balcony or ocean view. The restaurant and bar also offer great views of the cliff-diving shows and are popular with tourists from other hotels during the evening performances. The beach here is a steep jump down the cliff, but the resort does offer an alternative in the form of a saltwater pool as well as two freshwater pools. A protected cove with good snorkeling is located nearby.

Quebrada 74. ☎ *800-53-SUITE in the U.S., 744-483-1221, or 744-483-1155. Fax: 744-482-4564.* www.hotelelmiradoracapulco.com.mx. *132 units. Limited parking on street. Rack rates: High season $120 double; low season $98 double; suites with whirlpool year-round $140. An extra charge of $20 applies if you use the kitchenette. AE, MC, V.*

Villa Vera Hotel, Spa, and Racquet Club
$$$$–$$$$$ Costera Hotel Zone

Another "address of distinction" in Acapulco is the legendary Villa Vera, which is ideal for a romantic getaway. A smaller inn with a decidedly clubby feel to it, this property started off as a private home with adjacent villas serving as accommodations for houseguests. After a while, it became popular with stars such as Liz Taylor, who married Mike Todd here. Richard M. and Pat Nixon celebrated their 25th wedding anniversary here, and it also served as the set for much of Elvis's film, *Fun in Acapulco*. The hotel is located on a hill above the Costera Hotel Zone and offers the closest experience to Acapulco villa life that you can find on a public property. Several years ago, significant renovations and upgrades in facilities returned Villa Vera to a standard of excellence — in the style of today's more popular boutique-style hotels. Rooms are large, airy, and more sophisticated in decor than most others in Acapulco. Villa Vera offers exceptional spa facilities as well as two clay tennis courts, two lighted racquetball courts, and a small gym. The total of 14 pools includes eight private pools for the six villas and two houses. Most of the other rooms share pools, except for standard, least expensive rooms, which have the use of the large public pool located across from the restaurant.

Lomas del Mar 35 (from the Costera, take Av. de los Deportes inland and go left on Av. Prado, which curves right and turns into Av. Lomas del Mar). ☎ *888-554-2361 from U.S. or Canada, or 744-484-0334/35. Fax: 744-484-7479. E-mail:* hotel_villavera_aca@clubregina.com. *69 rooms including suites, villas, and 2 houses. Rack rates: High season $190 studio, $195–$260 double, $315–$350 suite, $380 villa, $1,095 Casa Teddy for 4 people, $1,210 Casa Julio for 6 people; low-season rates around 10% less than high season. AE, MC, V.*

Chapter 23

Settling into Acapulco

By Lynne Bairstow

. . . .

In This Chapter

▶ Knowing the scene before you arrive

▶ Finding transportation around town

▶ Reading up on all kinds of useful resources and tips

. . . .

Although most beach resorts have "relaxing" written all over them, Acapulco offers visitors nonstop, 24-hour-a-day energy. With so much to do, you won't want to lose a minute figuring out the details, so this chapter guides you through the fundamentals of settling into Acapulco. I help you get your bearings upon arrival at Acapulco's bustling airport, get settled into your hotel, and gain confidence in finding your way around the area. Finally, I give you tips on everything from currency exchanges to Internet access to finding the cheapest — and most entertaining — ways to get around town.

Arriving in Acapulco

No matter the time of year or where you're coming from, the first thing you're likely to notice about Acapulco when you get off the plane is the sizzling climate. You definitely feel the heat, but most travelers quickly adjust. Both immigration and customs are brief, generally easy procedures. Mexico's second-most important industry is tourism, so the country's aim is to be as welcoming as possible.

Navigating passport control and customs

The immigration clearance area is generally a lengthy walk from the plane's jetway and then down a flight of stairs. When you reach immigration, an officer asks you to show your passport (or other proof of citizenship) and your completed tourist card, the **FMT** (see Chapter 7 for all the FMT details).

Your FMT is an important document, so take good care of it. You're supposed to keep the FMT with you at all times because you may be required to show it if you run into any sort of trouble. You also need to turn it back in upon departure, or you may be unable to leave without replacing it.

Next up is the baggage claim area. Here, porters stand by to help with your bags, and they're well worth the price of the tip — about a dollar a bag. After you collect your luggage, you pass through another checkpoint. Something that looks like a traffic light awaits you here. You press a button, and if the light turns green, you're free to go. If it turns red, you need to open your bags for a quick search. It's Mexico's random search procedure for customs. If you have an unusually large bag, or an excessive amount of luggage, you may be searched regardless of the traffic-light outcome.

Getting to your hotel

The airport is 23km (14 miles) southeast of town — over the hills east of Acapulco Bay. Private taxis are the fastest option to get to downtown Acapulco. A taxi ride runs from $15 to $50 depending on your destination.

The major rental-car agencies all have booths at the airport, but I advise against getting a car unless you determine you really want one, say, for a side trip to Taxco (see Chapter 25) — they tend to be very expensive and generally more troublesome here than convenient.

Transportes Terrestres has desks at the front of the airport (just as you exit the baggage-claim area) where you can buy tickets for *colectivo* (shared minivan) transportation into town for $5 to $10 — rates are preset and based on the distance to your hotel. You must reserve return service to the airport through your hotel. Taxis to the airport tend to be much less expensive (about half the price) than taxis from the airport because the taxis that pick you up at the airport are federally chartered cars with exclusive rights to airport transportation — and the associated steep fares.

Getting Around Acapulco

Acapulco stretches for more than 6km (4 miles) around the huge bay. The most popular tourist areas are divided roughly into three sections: **Acapulco Viejo (Old Acapulco)**; the **Costera Hotel Zone,** which follows the main boulevard, Costera Miguel Alemán (or just "the Costera"); and **the southern shore,** whose exclusive neighborhoods border the scenic highway (Carretera Escénica) between the airport and the International Center.

Street names and numbers in Acapulco can be confusing and hard to find — many streets either aren't well marked or change names unexpectedly. Fortunately, you'll seldom have any reason to stray far from the Costera, so getting lost is difficult. But remember that street numbers on the Costera don't follow a logical order; you can't assume that similar numbers are necessarily close together.

Taking a taxi

Taxis, which are more plentiful than tacos in Acapulco (and practically as inexpensive if you're traveling in the downtown area only), are the best way to get around here.

Significant differences in prices for different types of taxis are common, so always establish the price with the driver before starting out. Hotel taxis may charge three times the rate of a taxi hailed on the street, and nighttime taxi rides cost extra, too. Taxis are also more expensive if you're staying in the Punta Diamante neighborhood, south of Las Brisas, which includes Puerto Marqués — these areas are along the southern highway (Carretera Escénica), between town and the airport. The minimum fare is $2 per ride for a roving VW bug–style taxi in town. The fare from Puerto Marqués costs $8 to the Hotel Zone and $10 into downtown. *Sitio* taxis are nicer cars, but they're also more expensive — $4 minimum fare.

Acapulco's taxi fashion demands that drivers decorate their cars with flashy, Las Vegas–style neon lights — the more colorful and pulsating, the better. It almost appears to be a local competition. And there's no extra charge for the added embellishments. These decked-out rides are especially popular in Old Acapulco.

Catching a bus

Buses are another great option for traveling along the Costera — they're easy to use and inexpensive. Two kinds of buses run along this main drag: pastel, color-coded buses and regular "school buses." The difference is in the price: The newer, air-conditioned, color-coded, tourist buses (Aca Tur Bus) cost 35¢; the older "school buses" cost 3¢. Covered bus stops, with handy maps on the walls showing bus routes to major sights and hotels, are located all along the Costera. If you want to go downtown from the Costera, take the bus marked "Centro" or "Zócalo"; to get to the southeast side (the Punta Diamante area), take a bus marked "Base" (pronounced *bah*-say). Buses traveling these popular routes come along at least every ten minutes. Buses also head out to more distant destinations such as **Puerto Marqués** to the east (marked "Puerto Marqués-Basa") and **Pie de la Cuesta** to the northwest (marked "Zócalo-Pie de la Cuesta"). Be sure to verify the time and place of the last bus back if you hop on along one of these routes.

Renting a car

Rental cars are available at the airport and at hotel desks along the Costera, but I don't recommend one — they're expensive, and parking is hard to find. Unless you plan on exploring outlying areas, you're better off taking taxis or using the easy and inexpensive public buses. Besides, leaving the driving to someone else is much easier.

Fast Facts: Acapulco

American Express

The main office (Av. Costera Miguel Alemán 121, Hotel Continental Emporio Local 31; ☎ 744-435-2200) is open Monday to Friday 9 a.m. to 6 p.m. and Saturday 9 a.m. to 1 p.m.

Area Code

The local telephone area code is **744.**

Babysitters

Though most of the larger hotels can easily arrange for them, many babysitters speak limited English. Rates range from $4 to $10 per hour with an additional charge of about $5 for a taxi for the sitter if you stay out past 10 p.m.

Banks, ATMs, and Currency Exchange

Numerous banks are located along the Costera and are open Monday to Friday 9 a.m. to 6 p.m. and Saturday 10 a.m. to 1:30 p.m. Banks, and their ATMs, generally have the best exchange rates. *Casas de cambio* (currency exchange booths) along the street may have better exchange rates than hotels, and they're open late. Most establishments accept U.S. dollars as readily as pesos but at reduced exchange rates, so you're better off using local currency whenever possible.

Climate

Acapulco boasts sunshine 360 days a year and an average daytime temperature of 80° F (27° C). Humidity levels vary. Acapulco receives approximately 59 inches of rain per year — June through October is the rainy season, although July and August are relatively dry. Tropical showers are brief and usually occur at night.

Consular Agents

The **U.S. Consular Agency** office is at the Hotel Club del Sol on Costera Alemán at Reyes Católicos (☎ 744-469-0556), across from the Hotel Acapulco Plaza. The office is open Monday to Friday 10 a.m. to 2 p.m. The **Canadian Consulate** (Centro Comercial Marbella, Local 23; ☎ 01-800-706-2900 to ll-free emergency number inside Mexico, or 744-484-1305) is open Monday to Friday 9 a.m. to 5 p.m.

Hospitals

Hospital Magallanes (Avenida Wilfrido Massieu 2, on the corner with Colon, one block from the Costera; ☎ 744-485-6194 or 744-485-6197) has an English-speaking staff and doctors. Another option is **Hospital Pacífico** (Calle Fraile y Nao 4; ☎ 744-487-7180 or 744-487-7161).

Information

The **State of Guerrero Tourism Office** (☎ and fax: 744-484-4583 or 744-484-4416) operates the **Procuraduría del Turista** on the street level in front of the International Center, a convention center set back from Costera Miguel Alemán. (It's down a lengthy walkway with fountains.) The office offers maps and information about the city and state as well as police assistance for tourists; it's open daily 9 a.m. to 10 p.m.

Internet Access

A number of small Internet-access services are located along the Costera, but they seem to go out of business quickly. Internet access kiosks are available inside **Wal-Mart,** Costera Miguel Alemán 500 (☎ 744-469-0203), with varying rates depending on usage. Or you can try **Acanet,** Av. Cuatemoc 1632 Centro Commercial Monte Blanco, Local 2, in front of Papagayo Park, across from City Hall (Presidencia) (☎ 744-486-1803 or 744-486-2343); it's open Monday to Saturday from 10 a.m. to 9 p.m. Internet access costs $1 per hour. This is a computer shop that also offers Internet access and has a very helpful staff.

Maps

One of the best around is the free American Express map, usually found at tourist information offices and hotel concierge desks. Sanborn's or Wal-Mart may also have more detailed maps for sale.

Newspapers/Magazines

The larger Costera hotels generally carry a good selection of English-language newspapers (such as *USA Today*) and magazines in their gift shops, as well as the English-language *Mexico City News.* You can also find English-language paperbacks and magazines at **Sanborn's** department stores (Costera Miguel Alemán 209, downtown across from the ship docks, ☎ 744-484-4413; Costera Miguel Alemán 1226, in the Estrella Condo Tower, ☎ 744-484-4465; and Costera Miguel Alemán 163, at the Hotel Calinda, ☎ 744-481-2426).

Pharmacy

One of the largest drugstores in town is **Farmacia Daisy** (☎ 744-484-7664, 744-484-5950). The **Sam's Club** and **Wal-Mart** (open 24 hours) are both located on the Costera and have pharmacy services and lower prices on medicines.

Police

Policemen in white and light-blue uniforms belong to a special corps of English-speaking police established to assist tourists. For the main police department, call ☎ 744-485-0650.

Post Office

The central post office *(correo)* is located next door to Sears (close to the Fideicomiso office). Other branches are located in the Estrella de Oro bus station on Cuauhtémoc, inland from the Acapulco Qualton Hotel, and on the Costera near Playa Caleta.

Safety

Riptides claim a few lives every year, so pay close attention to warning flags posted on Acapulco beaches. Red or black flags mean stay out of the water, yellow flags signify caution, and white or green flags mean it's safe to swim.

As is the case anywhere, tourists are vulnerable to thieves, which is especially true when shopping in a market; lying on the beach; wearing jewelry; or visibly carrying a camera, purse, or bulging wallet.

Taxes

There's a 15% value-added tax (IVA) on goods and services, and it's generally included in the posted price.

Taxis

Always establish the price of a trip with the driver before starting out. Hotel taxis charge more than a taxi hailed on the street, and nighttime taxi rides cost extra, too. The minimum fare is $2 per ride for a roving VW bug–style taxi in town. The fare from Puerto Marqués costs $8 to the Hotel Zone and $10 into downtown. *Sitio* taxis are nicer cars, but they're also more expensive — $4 minimum fare.

Telephone

Phone numbers seem to change frequently in Acapulco — the most reliable source for telephone numbers is the **Procuraduría del Turista** (☎ 744-484-4583) where an exceptionally friendly staff can help you locate what you need. Avoid the phone booths that have signs in English advising you to call home using a special 800 number — these are absolute rip-offs and can cost as much as $20 per minute. The least expensive way to call is by using a Telmex (LADATEL) pre-paid phone card, available at most pharmacies and mini-supers, using the official Telmex (Lada) public phones.

In Mexico, you need to dial 001 prior to a number to reach the United States, and you need to preface long distance calls within Mexico by dialing 01.

Time Zone

Acapulco operates on central standard time, but Mexico's observance of daylight savings time varies somewhat from that in the United States.

Chapter 24

Dining in Acapulco

By Lynne Bairstow

- -

In This Chapter
▶ Discovering Acapulco's best restaurants

▶ Finding the best Mexican cuisine in Acapulco

- -

*B*eing the cosmopolitan city that it is, Acapulco offers world-class international cuisine, much of it served in the romantic restaurants located along the southern coast. The quintessential Acapulco dining experience is sitting at a candlelit table with a view of the glittering bay spread out before you. If, however, you're looking for simple, good food or an authentic, local dining experience, you're best off checking out the scene in Old Acapulco. Being a beach town, Acapulco restaurants serve up a ton of fresh seafood. My personal Acapulco favorites include a small place that specializes in fish tacos.

Despite the growing profusion of American-influenced chain restaurants, resist the temptation to go with what you know — trust me, the locally owned restaurants offer the best food and best value.

And, although most of Mexico's beach resorts fall on the casual side when it comes to dress, Acapulco goes against the trend, especially for women. Feel free to go all out with your sexy resort wear when dining here. Also note that dinner tends to be a late affair. Most Acapulco regulars wouldn't think of dining before 10 p.m. so that they can finish up just in time to hit the clubs, which open at midnight.

You can find American standards such as McDonald's, Tony Roma's, Burger King, and Hard Rock Cafe — good choices if you're traveling with kids — but you may also want to try the Mexican alternatives of Carlos 'n Charlie's and 100% Natural, both located along the Costera.

If you're visiting Acapulco on a Thursday, indulge in the local custom of eating *pozole,* a bowl of white hominy and meat in a broth garnished with sliced radishes, shredded lettuce, onions, oregano, and lime. The truly traditional version is served with pork, but a newer chicken version has also become a standard. You can also find green pozole, which is made by adding a paste of roasted pumpkin seeds to the traditional pozole base, giving the broth its green color. For a uniquely Acapulco experience, enjoy your Thursday pozole at the cliff-side restaurant of the Hotel Los Flamingos.

Acapulco's Best Restaurants

All the restaurants included in this chapter are arranged alphabetically with their location and general price category noted. Remember that tips generally run about 15%, and most wait-staff really depend on tips for their income, so be generous if the service warrants. See the Introduction of this book for an explanation of the price categories.

Please see Appendix C for more information on Mexican cuisine.

100% Natural
$ Costera MEXICAN/HEALTH FOOD

Healthful versions of Mexican standards are the specialty at this clean, breezy, plant-filled restaurant, located on the second level of the shopping center across from the Acapulco Plaza Hotel. (This chain has five other branches in Acapulco, including another one farther east on the Costera.) Especially notable are the fruit *liquidos,* blended fresh fruit and your choice of purified water or milk. Yogurt shakes, steamed vegetables, and cheese enchiladas are alternatives to their yummy sandwiches served on whole grain breads. If you've over-indulged the night before, get yourself back on track here. It's also a great place for families.

Costera Miguel Alemán 200, across from the Acapulco Plaza Hotel. ☎ 744-485-3982. Reservations not needed. Sandwiches: $2.80–$4.80; other food items $2–$8. No credit cards. Open: Daily 24 hours.

Baikal
$$–$$$$ Las Brisas FUSION/FRENCH/ASIAN

This exquisite and ultra-hot Baikal is the best place in Acapulco for an over-the-top dining experience. You enter from the street, and then descend a spiral staircase into the stunning bar and restaurant, awash in muted tan and cream colors of luxurious fabrics and natural accents of stone, wood, and water. The restaurant itself is constructed into the cliff, providing sweeping views of Acapulco Bay's glittering lights. The large dining room, with a two-story ceiling, has comfortable seating, including sofas that border the room. The creative menu combines traditional French and Asian fare, and then adds a dash of Mexican flare. Start with the scallops in a chipotle vinaigrette, or the black bean soup with duck foie gras. Notable entrees include steamed red snapper with lobster butter sauce, chicken breast rolled and stuffed with asparagus in a white wine reduction, or medallions of New Zealand lamb in a sweet garlic sauce. The service is as impeccable as the presentation. You can also choose from an extensive selection of wines, as well as enjoy live piano music nightly. Periodically during the evening, large projector screens descend over the floor-to-ceiling glass windows, and show short films of old Acapulco or cavorting whales and dolphins, providing a brief reprise from conversation and dining. A fashionably late dining spot (expect a crowd at midnight), the attire is chic resort wear, because most patrons are headed to the clubs following dinner. Baikal also has wheel-chair access, a private VIP dining room, and wine cellar, as well as an ample bar, ideal for enjoying a sunset cocktail or after-dinner drink. It's located east of town on the scenic highway just before the entrance to the Las Brisas hotel.

Carretera Escénica 16 & 22. ☎ *744-446-6845 or 744-446-6867.* www.baikal. com.mx. *Reservations required. Main courses: $20–$60. AE, MC, V. Open: Daily 7 p.m.–2 a.m. Closed Mondays during the summer.*

Casa Nova

$–$$$ Las Brisas   GOURMET ITALIAN

This long-standing favorite of Mexico City's elite is easily one of Acapulco's top spots for a romantic evening, and one of the cliff-side restaurants noted for its food as much as for its view. Enjoy an elegant meal and a fabulous view of glittering Acapulco Bay at this restaurant located east of town on the scenic highway just before the entrance to the Las Brisas hotel. You can dine in one of several elegantly appointed dining rooms awash in marble and stunning murals or outdoors on the terrace that features a dramatic view. The crowd here is generally decked out in fash-ionable resort attire, and the peak dining hour is 10 p.m. Notable dishes include veal scaloppini and homemade pastas, such as linguini with fresh clams. The service is stellar, and a changing tourist menu offers a sam-pling of the best selections for a fixed price. You can also enjoy an ample selection of reasonably priced national and imported wines as well as live piano music nightly.

Carretera Escénica 5256. ☎ *744-446-6237, 744-446-6238, or 744-446-6239. Reserva-tions required. Main courses: $14–$50; $39 fixed-price 4-course meal. AE, MC, V. Open: Daily 7–11:30 p.m.*

El Amigo Miguel

$–$$ Old Acapulco   MEXICAN/SEAFOOD

The ever-present crowd of locals is a sure sign that El Amigo Miguel, 3 blocks west of the *zócalo,* is a standout among Acapulco seafood restaurants — you can easily pay more elsewhere and not eat better. Impeccably fresh seafood reigns here, and the large, open-air dining room is usually brimming with seafood lovers. When it overflows, head to a second branch with the exact same menu across the street. Dining at

Acapulco Bay Area Dining

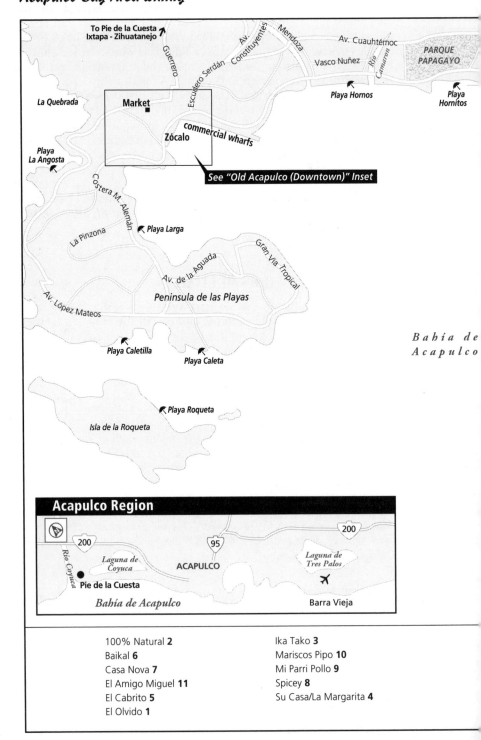

Acapulco Region

100% Natural **2**
Baikal **6**
Casa Nova **7**
El Amigo Miguel **11**
El Cabrito **5**
El Olvido **1**

Ika Tako **3**
Mariscos Pipo **10**
Mi Parri Pollo **9**
Spicey **8**
Su Casa/La Margarita **4**

Estrella de Oro Bus
To México City

Old Acapulco (Downtown)

Vicente Guerrero
Nicolás
A. Serdán
Cuauhtémoc
Flecha Roja Bus Stop
Nación
Progreso
Escudero
V. de León
5 de Mayo
Galeana
Lerdo Tejada
La Quebrada
Iglesias
Valle
Hornitos
Hidalgo
Carranza
La Paz
Morelos
Fuerte de San Diego
La Pinzon
Arteaga
Juárez
Costera Miguel Alemán
To Playa Hornos
A. Bretón
commercial wharfs
Playa Caleta
Bahía de Acapulco

Massieu
Navegante
Reyes Católicos
Pizarro
Cosa
Pinzón
Universidad
1
Playa Paraíso
2
Playa Condesa
Morro
Herradura
Picuda
Costera M. Alemán
Sola
Del Mar
Deportes
El Morro
3

Golf Club
Las Palmas
Victoria
Trinidad
Cristóbal Colón
Av. Alm. Horacio Nelson
4
5
Santa María
Yucatán
Playa Icacos
Bravo
Cook

Icacos Naval Base

Playa Guittarón
6
7
8
Carretera Escénica
To Oaxaca
Playa Puerto Marqués
To Airport
Puerto Marqués

UNITED STATES
MEXICO
Gulf of Mexico
Mexico City
PACIFIC OCEAN
Acapulco
0 500 mi
0 500 km

Beach
Bus Station
Golf

El Amigo Miguel is a casual way to enjoy the best of the bay's bounty. Try the delicious *camarones borrachos* (drunken shrimp) in a sauce made with beer, applesauce, ketchup, mustard, and bits of fresh bacon — the ingredients may not sound great when listed individually, but trust me, this stuff is heaven. The *filete Miguel* is red-snapper fillet stuffed with seafood and covered in a wonderful chipotle-pepper sauce. *Mojo de ajo* (grilled shrimp with garlic) and whole red snapper are also served at their classic best.

Juárez 31, at Azueta. ☎ *744-483-6981. Reservations not accepted. Main courses: $2.70–$20. AE, MC, V. Open: Daily 10 a.m.–11 p.m.*

El Cabrito

$ Costera   NORTHERN MEXICAN

A hacienda-inspired facade marks the entrance to this popular joint located in the heart of the Costera. El Cabrito is known for its authentic and well-prepared northern Mexican cuisine. Although the decor appears to shout out "tourist trap," this restaurant enjoys a strong reputation among Mexican nationals as well. Among the specialties are *cabrito al pastor* (roasted goat), *charro* beans (a dish made with pinto beans), Oaxaca-style *mole* (a complex sauce that uses a variety of ingredients ranging from chocolate to chiles — there are red, yellow, green, and black moles), and *burritos de machaca.*

Costera Miguel Alemán 1480, on the ocean side of the Costera opposite of Hard Rock Cafe. ☎ *744-484-7711. Reservations not accepted. Main courses: $5–$15. AE, MC, V. Open: Mon–Sat 2 p.m.–1 a.m.; Sun 1–11 p.m.*

El Olvido

$–$$$ Costera   MEXICANA

This stylish restaurant tucked in a shopping mall gives you all the glittering bay-view ambiance of the posh Las Brisas restaurants without the taxi ride from the Costera hotels. The menu is one of the city's most sophisticated. Each dish is a delight in both presentation and taste — truly some of the finest "new-style" Mexican cuisine in the country. Start with one of the 12 house specialty drinks such as Olvido — made with tequila, rum, Cointreau, tomato juice, and lime juice. Soups include a delicious cold melon and a thick, black bean and sausage. Among the innovative entrees are quail with honey and *pasilla chiles* and thick sea bass with a mild sauce of cilantro and avocado. For dessert, try the chocolate fondue or the *guanabana* (a tropical fruit) mousse in a rich *zapote negro* (black-colored tropical fruit) sauce. El Olvido is in the Plaza Marbella shopping center on Diana Circle. Aca Joe clothing store fronts the plaza. Walk into the passage to the right of Aca Joe and head left; it's in the back.

Plaza Marbella, at the Diana Glorieta (Circle). ☎ *744-481-0203, 744-481-0256, 744-481-0214, or 744-481-0240. Reservations recommended. Main courses: $14–$30. AE, DC, MC, V. Open: Daily 6 p.m.–2 a.m.*

Ika Tako

$ **Costera**   **SEAFOOD/TACOS**

This is my favorite place to eat in Acapulco, and I never miss it when I'm in town. Perhaps I have simple tastes, but these fresh fish, shrimp, and seafood tacos served in combinations that include grilled pineapple, fresh spinach, grated cheese, garlic, and bacon are addictive. Unlike most inexpensive eateries, the setting here is lovely — a handful of tables over-look tropical trees and the bay below. The lighting may be a bit bright, the atmosphere occasionally hectic, and the service dependably slow, but the tacos are delectable. You can also get beer, wine, soft drinks, and a dessert of the day. This restaurant is located along the Costera, next to Beto's lobster restaurant. A second branch of Ika Tako sits across from the Hyatt Regency hotel, but it lacks the atmosphere of this location.

Costera Miguel Alemán 99. No phone. Reservations not accepted. Main courses: $2.50–$8. No credit cards. Open: Daily 6 p.m.–5 a.m.

Mariscos Pipo

$–$$ **Old Acapulco**   **SEAFOOD**

Check out the photographs of Old Acapulco on the walls while relaxing in this airy dining room decorated with hanging nets, fish, glass buoys, and shell lanterns. The English-language menu lists a wide array of seafood, including *ceviche,* lobster, octopus, crayfish, and baby-shark quesadillas. This local favorite is 2 blocks west of the *zócalo* on Breton, just off the Costera. Another branch (☎ **744-484-0165**), open daily 1 to 9:30 p.m., is at Costera Miguel Alemán and Canadá, across from the con-vention center.

Almirante Breton 3. ☎ 744-482-2237. Reservations not accepted. Main courses: $5.50–$20 (though lobster will be a bit more). AE, MC, V. Open: Daily noon to 8 p.m.

Mi Parri Pollo

$ **Old Acapulco**   **MEXICAN/INTERNATIONAL**

Umbrella-covered tables on one of the coolest and shadiest sections of the *zócalo* comprise this tiny and typically Mexican restaurant. It's espe-cially popular for breakfast with specials that include coffee refills and a great fresh-fruit salad with mango, pineapple, and cantaloupe. Other spe-cials include fish burgers, *tortas,* a special rotisserie-grilled chicken, and steak *Milanesa.* Fruit drinks, including fresh mango juice, come in schooner-size glasses. To find the restaurant, enter the *zócalo* from the Costera and walk toward the kiosk. On the right, about midway into the *zócalo,* is a wide, shady passageway that leads onto Avenida Jesus Carranza and to the umbrella-covered tables under the shady tree.

Jesus Carranza 2B, Zócalo. No phone. Reservations not accepted. Breakfast: $1.50–$2.50; sandwiches $1–$2; fresh-fruit drinks $1.25; daily specials $2–$4. No credit cards. Open: Daily 7 a.m.–11 p.m.

Spicey
$$–$$$ **Las Brisas   CREATIVE CUISINE**

Of all the cliff-side restaurants, this one gets my vote for consistently delicious food, stellar views, and charming service. Diners can enjoy the air-conditioned indoor dining room or — better — the completely open rooftop terrace with a sweeping view of the bay. To begin, try the Shrimp Spicey in a fresh coconut batter with an orange marmalade and mustard sauce. Among the main courses, the grilled veal chop in pineapple and papaya chutney is a winner, as is the beef tenderloin prepared Thai- or Santa Fe–style or blackened. The *chiles rellenos* entree in mango sauce wins raves. An exceptional selection of premium tequilas for sipping is another highlight. Attire is resort dressy.

Carretera Escénica, next to Kookaburas. ☎ *744-481-1380. Reservations recommended on weekends. Valet parking available. Main courses: $19–$30. AE, DC, MC, V. Open: Daily 7–11:30 p.m.*

Su Casa/La Margarita
$–$$$ **Costera Zone (Inland)   INTERNATIONAL**

A comfortable setting, terrific food, and moderate prices are what you get at Su Casa. Owners Shelly and Angel Herrera created this pleasant and breezy open-air restaurant on the patio of their hillside home overlooking the city. Both are experts in the kitchen and stay on hand nightly to greet guests on the patio. The menu changes often, so each time you go there's something new to try. But some items are standard — shrimp *a la patrona* in garlic; grilled fish, steak, and chicken; and flaming *fillet al Madrazo*, a delightful brochette marinated in tropical juices. Most entrees come garnished with cooked banana or pineapple. The margaritas are big and delicious. Su Casa is the hot-pink building on the hillside above the convention center.

Av. Anahuac 110, up the hill from the convention center. ☎ *744-484-4350 or 744-484-1261. Reservations recommended. Main courses: $12–$40. MC, V. Open: Daily 6 p.m. to midnight.*

Chapter 25

Having Fun on and off the Beach in Acapulco

By Lynne Bairstow

· ·

In This Chapter

▶ Working on that tan at the best beaches

▶ Diving, fishing, golfing, and other fun stuff

▶ Checking out the sights and shops

▶ Visiting Taxco

▶ Partying like you're in Acapulco

· ·

*A*capulco's beaches aren't all created equal, and knowing that sun and sand are a key part of any vacation here, I use this chapter to guide you to the areas that are best for watersports and safest for swimming — and I throw in a few out-of-the-way recreational finds.

In and out of the water, Acapulco features a wealth of activities to do and see, so I point out the top attractions. Though the town is lacking in true cultural options, I've found a few hidden gems that I reveal in this chapter.

And then there's the nightlife! Oh, the nightlife! I wrap up this chapter with a guide of the top clubs in town, giving you a rundown of the typical crowd and type of action you're likely to encounter in each location. This info can help you pick a spot that best meets your tastes — without having to cough up a bunch of cover charges just to find the right scene.

Acapulco Bay Area

Cathedral Nuestra Señora de la Soledad **6**
Centro Acapulco (Convention Center) **4**
Centro Internacional de Convivencia Infantil **5**
Cliff Divers **3**
Fuerte de San Diego/Museo Histórico de Acapulco **8**

Mágico Mundo Marino **1**
Plaza de Toros **2**
Zócalo/Plaza Alvarez **7**

Estrella de Oro Bus

To México City

Massieu

Navegante

Pizarro

Reyes Católicos

Cosa

Pinzón

Universidad

Playa Paraíso

Playa Condesa

Morro

Herradura

Picuda

Costera M. Alemán

Sola

Del Mar

Deportes

El Morro

Old Acapulco (Downtown)

Vicente Guerrero

Nicolás

A. Serdán

Cuauhtémoc

Flecha Roja Bus Stop

Nación

Progreso

Escudero

V. de León

Galeana

5 de Mayo

Lerdo Tejada

La Quebrada

Iglesias

Valle

La Paz

Galeana

Hornitos

Hidalgo

Carranza

Arteaga

B. Juárez

Llave

6

7

Morelos

8

La Pinzon

A. Breton

Costera Miguel Alemán

To Playa Hornos

commercial wharfs

Bahía de Acapulco

Playa Caleta

Golf Club

Las Palmas

4

Victoria

Trinidad

5

Cristóbal Colón

Av. Alm. Horacio Nelson

Santa María

Yucatán

Playa Icacos

Bravo

Cook

Icacos Naval Base

Playa Guittarón

Carretera Escénica

To Oaxaca

Playa Puerto Marqués

To Airport

Puerto Marqués

UNITED STATES

Gulf of Mexico

MEXICO

Mexico ★City

PACIFIC OCEAN

Acapulco

0   500 mi

0   500 km

Beach

Bus Station

Golf

Hitting the Beaches

Acapulco Bay is a stunning sight — night or day — that practically cries out in temptation. But, before I dive into the best beaches, I have a few words of wisdom.

Acapulco's golden beaches, cobalt-blue bay, and sun-soaked climate lured so many people here that, by the late 1970s, Acapulco became a victim of its own success. Beaches began to lose their luster as waves of garbage and pollution started coming in with the tides. As the numbers of visitors sharply declined, authorities took notice, and over the past decade, the city has gone to great lengths (and great expense) to clean up the waters of its beautiful bay. Despite the notable success of these efforts, it still pays to be cautious in some areas. (Acapulco is an active, industrial port.) You may also notice the fleet of more than 20 power-sweeper boats that skim the top of the bay each morning to remove any debris or oil film or . . .

The tides in the area can be treacherous, especially in the open ocean north and south of Acapulco Bay. Each year, at least one or two unwary swimmers drown in the area because of deadly riptides and undertow, so heed any posted warnings — red or black flags mean stay out of the water altogether, and yellow warns you to exercise caution. The safest swimming is in either Acapulco Bay or Puerto Marqués Bay.

I'm glad I got that off of my chest; now I can tell you about the best places to play. In the old days, the downtown beaches were the focal point of Acapulco, but today, the resort developments stretch along the entire length of the shore. The beaches and coves tucked into Acapulco Bay go by as many as 50 different names, but I just focus on the best and most popular beaches from west to east.

Located 13km (8 miles) west of Acapulco Bay is **Pie de la Cuesta.** Traveling by taxi or car (this is the one day you may want to consider renting a car) is the best way to reach this beach because it's much faster than taking the bus. However, buses run regularly along the Costera, leaving every 5 or 10 minutes. A taxi costs about $22. The water here is too rough for swimming, but it's a great spot for checking out big waves and the spectacular sunset — especially over *coco locos* (drinks served in a fresh coconut with the top whacked off) at one of the rustic beachfront restaurants hung with hammocks. The area is known for excellent bird-watching and the surrounding coconut plantations.

Heading on the road northwest, beyond the bay, along the Pacific coastline, you come to **Coyuca Lagoon** on your right. *Colectivo* boat tours — or small boats that band together a group of people to comprise a tour — of the lagoon are offered for about $10.

Back toward Acapulco, around the area near La Quebrada (where the cliff divers perform), is **Playa La Angosta,** a small, sheltered, and often-deserted cove. If you're staying in Old Acapulco, this beach is great not only for its location, but also because it's much less crowded than public beaches in Old Acapulco, and much more dramatic in its setting — though generally too rough for swimming.

South of downtown on the Peninsula de las Playas lie **Caleta** and **Caletilla;** the image I hold in my mind of these sister beaches is one of bright colors, and plenty of laughter, kids, and an almost carnival-like atmosphere. A small outcropping of land that contains an aquarium and water park, **Mágico Mundo Marino** (open daily 9 a.m. to 7 p.m.; ☎ 744-483-1215), separates the two beaches. In this area, you find thatched-roofed restaurants, watersports equipment for rent, and brightly painted boats that ferry passengers to Isla de la Roqueta. You can also rent beach chairs and umbrellas for the day. Mexican families favor these beaches because they're close to several inexpensive hotels. In the late afternoon, fishermen pull their colorful boats up on the sand; you can buy the fresh catch of the day and, occasionally, oysters on the half shell.

Speaking of **Isla de la Roqueta,** this island has two small beaches amidst a hilly, forested terrain. **Playa Marin** is the more deserted of the two. **Playa Roqueta** has thatched-roof restaurants where you can enjoy a snack and a cold beer or rent snorkeling equipment. The island also has a small zoo of exotic animals kept in pitifully small cages — I kindly ask you to boycott it in the hope that these poor creatures will one day be released. You can get here via one of the *panga* boats (small, open-air fishing boats) departing from Playa Caletilla. The boat rides cost about $5 round trip and depart about every 20 minutes from 10 a.m. to 6 p.m. daily. You can purchase tickets directly from any boat that's loading.

You need to remember the name of **Playa Manzanillo** if you're planning to set out on a pleasure-boat excursion — including chartered fishing trips. This beach is where they dock. It's located just south of the *zócalo* (Acapulco's central plaza).

East of the *zócalo,* the major beaches are **Hornos** (near Papagayo Park and sometimes referred to as Playa Papagayo), **Hornitos, Condesa,** and **Icacos,** which merge one into the other. Icacos is the beach just beyond the Hyatt Hotel. Of the four beaches, it's closest to the naval base (La Base), which is directly opposite the bay from the *zócalo.* All these strips of sand are wide, and the surf is gentle, but I remain cautious about swimming along this interior curve of Acapulco Bay — based on my concerns about water cleanliness. Of these beaches, Condesa is the liveliest with watersports equipment for rent and a regular crowd of beach babes of both sexes.

As you travel around the bay, down the Costera to the Scenic Highway (Carretera Escénica), and past the legendary Las Brisas hotel, the road continues to **Playa Puerto Marqués,** located in the small, clean, and separate bay of **Puerto Marqués.** It's my top choice for beach swimming in Acapulco, and one key reason for staying at the Camino Real (see Chapter 22). The water is calm, and the bay is sheltered, meaning the water quality here is much better than in Acapulco Bay, and it's a great place for water-skiing — rentals are generally available. A row of *palapa*-topped, beachfront restaurants draws a sizable crowd every weekend, so arrive early; better yet, come during a weekday.

Past the bay lies **Playa Revolcadero,** a magnificent wide stretch of beach on the open ocean where you can find many of Acapulco's grandest resorts — including the Acapulco Princess, Mayan Palace, and Pierre Marqués. About 6km (4 miles) farther south lies **Barra Vieja,** a lovely, wide beach with firm sand (ideal for running on the beach) — but also strong waves. **Tres Palos Lagoon,** a fascinating freshwater jungle lagoon, is nearby. You can hire a boat for about $15 to take you around these wetlands, which are at the east end of the fishing village that adjoins Barra Vieja.

Finding Water Fun for Everyone

It seems like you can find more ways to have fun in Acapulco in the water than out of it — after all, this resort grew up around the bay. Whether it's plowing through the surf on a Jet Ski or diving below the surface, if you can do it in the water, you can find it in Acapulco!

Skiing and surfing

Acapulco watersports tend to lean toward the motorized variety — the louder the engine, the better the fun. In Acapulco's heyday, images of bronzed, muscled water-skiers were commonplace, and today, this sport remains as popular during the day as dancing is at night. An hour of water-skiing can cost as little as $35 or as much as $65. Boats and rental equipment are available at Playa Caletilla, Puerto Marqués Bay, and Coyuca Lagoon. You can also check out the **Club de Esquis** (Costera Miguel Alemán 100; ☎ **744-482-2034**); water-skiing rates run $50 per hour here.

You can find concessions for other watersports equipment on the beaches fronting the Costera hotels — most notably the Qualton Club, Acapulco Plaza, Fiesta Americana, and Hyatt hotels. Banana boats ($5 per person for about 15 minutes), parasail rides (about $30 for the longest 10 minutes of your life), and Jet Skis ($50 per hour) are usually available. Although these concessions are also available at Playa Caletilla and Coyuca Lagoon near Pie de la Cuesta, the equipment tends to be in better shape along the Costera hotel beaches.

The mother of all motorized watersports in Acapulco is, without a doubt, the **Shotover Jet.** These 12-person, soft-sided boats careen down the otherwise tranquil Laguna Puerto Marqués propelled by 8-liter, V-8 engines. You travel at speeds of 40 to 50 miles per hour and make 360-degree turns, so the ride is a thrill. Book these trips directly through the Shotover Jet office (Costera Miguel Alemán 121, in front of the Continental Plaza Hotel; ☎ **744-484-1154;** www. shotoverjet-acapulco.com). Tickets cost $44 for adults and $22 for children and include round-trip transportation from this departure point to the lagoon.

The Shotover Jet ride is a four-hour excursion, door-to-door. Be sure to bring a change of dry clothes — you'll get wet on this trip.

Exploring the deep blue

Scuba diving isn't as brilliant in Acapulco as it is in other parts of Mexico (the previous problems with pollution have resulted in fewer fish and less sea life), so it may disappoint. But, as an avid diver, I always say that there's no such thing as a bad dive. For novice divers, or those needing a refresher course, you can expect to pay $30 for 90 minutes of instruction if you book directly with an instructor on Playa Caleta. Two dive operators I recommend are **Divers de Mexico** (☎ **744-482-1398**) and **Aqua Mundo** (☎ **744-482-1041**), both located at Costera Miguel Alemán 100, near Club de Esquis. Typical prices are about $55 for equipment, a dive guide, and a boat for three hours. The best snorkeling sites are off **Isla de la Roqueta.** You can rent gear at a concession on the island, or you can take one of the regularly scheduled snorkeling trips from Playa Caleta to the island, which costs about $20 for two hours, including equipment.

Reeling in the big one

For deep-sea fishing excursions, go to the pale-pink building housing the fishing-boat cooperative **Pesca Deportiva** opposite the *zócalo* or book a day in advance (☎ **744-482-1099**). Charter fishing trips run from $150 to $200 for up to four people for six hours, tackle and bait included. Credit cards are accepted, and ice, drinks, lunch, and a fishing license (about $10) are extra. You can usually swing a better deal by paying cash. Generally, boats leave at 8 a.m. and return by 3 p.m. and travel anywhere from 3 to 10 miles offshore. Sailfish, marlin, and tuna are popular catches. If you book through a travel agent or hotel, fishing trips start at around $200 to $280 for four people, and again, fishing license, food, and drinks cost extra.

If you're into planning ahead, consider booking with either of these reliable sport-fishing outfitters: **Ixtapa Sportfishing Charters** (19 Depue Lane, Stroudsburg, PA 18360; ☎ **570-688-9466;** Fax: 570-688-9554;

www.ixtapasportfishing.com/acapulco) and **Fish-R-Us** (Costera Miguel Alemán 100; ☎ **877-3-FISH-R-US** in the U.S., or 744-482-8282; www.fish-r-us.com). Their boats range in size from 40- to 48-foot custom cruisers and are priced from $291 to $520 for up to eight people, including crew, tackle, and taxes.

Finding family fun

One of the best options for family fun is the **CICI water park** (Centro Internacional de Convivencia Infantil; Costera Miguel Alemán at Colón; ☎ **744-484-8033**). Located just east of the convention center, the park has swimming pools with waves, water slides, water toboggans, and sea-life shows. The park is open daily 10 a.m. to 6 p.m. with dolphin shows (in Spanish) taking place at noon, 2:30, and 5 p.m. A dolphin swim program includes 30 minutes of introduction and 30 minutes of swim time, for an additional $95. Swim times are at 10 a.m. and 12:30 and 4 p.m. Reservations are required, with a ten-person maximum per swim for the dolphin swim option. CICI, which recently underwent a $3 million renovation, also has a snack bar and restrooms. General admission is $6 during weekdays, and $8 on weekends; children under 2 are admitted free.

Cruising Acapulco's shores

Although a booze cruise may not technically qualify as a watersport (even though it requires extensive repetitions of the one-arm cocktail curl), I'll go out on a limb: Because the activity takes place on the water, it counts in my book. A booze cruise is one of the most popular ways to spend a day — or evening — in Acapulco, and the options are numerous. Choose from yachts, catamarans, and trimarans (single- and double-deckers) to take in the sun (and a few beverages) and enjoy expansive views of the bay. Cruises run morning, afternoon, and evening, and some offer buffets, open bars, and live music; others just have snacks, selected drinks, and taped music. You notice a difference in prices, too, which can range from $15 to $50. Your hotel's tour desk or any Acapulco travel agency can explain the current options, as well as provide brochures or recommendations.

Enjoying Land Sports

Acapulco has a number of ways to spend the day on land. From golf to tennis to horseback riding, you're sure to find an activity — or two — to suit your interests.

Teeing off

If you aim to hit the links during your stay, the best **golf** is at the courses at Playa Revolcadero. Both the **Acapulco Princess** (☎ 744-469-1000) and **Pierre Marqués** (☎ 744-466-1000) hotels have top-notch courses. The Princess's course is a rather narrow, level, Ted Robinson–design. The Marqués course, redesigned by Robert Trent Jones, Sr., in 1972 for the World Cup of Golf tournament, is longer and more challenging. A round of 18 holes at either course costs $105 for guests and $120 for non-guests; American Express, Visa, and MasterCard are accepted. Tee-times begin at 7:35 a.m. Make your reservations a day in advance. Club rental is available, and costs an extra $21. The **Mayan Palace Golf Club** (Geranios 22; ☎ 744-466-1924), designed by Latin American golf great Pedro Guericia, lies farther east. Greens fees are $75, and caddies are available for an additional $15.

The newest addition to Acapulco's golf scene is the spectacular Robert von Hagge–designed course at the exclusive **Tres Vidas Golf Club,** Carretera a Barra Vieja Km 7 (☎ 744-444-5138). The par-72, 18-hole course, right on the edge of the ocean, is landscaped with nine lakes, dotted with palms, and home to a flock of ducks and other birds. The club is open only to members, guests of members, and guests of certain hotels that have play privileges at the club. Greens fees are $144, including cart; a caddy costs $20. You can also enjoy a clubhouse with a restaurant, open from 7:30 a.m. to 7:30 p.m., as well as a pool and beach club. American Express, Visa, and MasterCard are accepted.

The main public course in town is the **Club de Golf Acapulco** (☎ 744-484-0781), located off the Costera next to the convention center. You can play 9 holes for $40 and 18 holes for $60, with equipment renting for $16. There are no carts, but caddies are available for about $14. To tell you the truth, the course isn't very well maintained.

Taking time for tennis

Tennis is vastly more popular in Acapulco than golf, and getting a game going is a fairly easy process. You can choose from several public tennis clubs — court time averages about $11 an hour. One option is the **Club de Tenis Hyatt** (Costera Miguel Alemán 1; ☎ 744-484-1225), which is open daily 6:30 a.m. to 7 p.m. Outdoor courts cost $15 an hour during the day and $22 per hour at night; the indoor courts costs $25. Rackets rent for $4, and a set of balls will set you back $2. Many of the hotels along the Costera have tennis facilities for their guests; the best are at the Acapulco Princess, Pierre Marqués, and Las Brisas hotels.

Galloping along

If you're not entirely comfortable swimming in Acapulco Bay, then try **horseback riding** along the beach. Independent operators stroll the Hotel Zone beachfront offering rides for about $20 to $40 for 1 to 2 hours. Horses for riding are also commonly found on the beach in front of the Acapulco Princess Hotel. There's no phone; you have to go directly to one of the beaches to make arrangements.

Experiencing Acapulco's Front Row Attractions

Traditionally called *Fiesta Brava,* **bullfights** are held during Acapulco's winter season at a ring (**Plaza de Toros**) up the hill from Playa Caletilla. Tickets purchased through travel agencies cost around $35 and usually include transportation to and from your hotel. The festivities begin at 5:30 p.m. each Sunday from December to March. Although bullfights in Acapulco tend to feature better matadors than those in other Mexican resort towns, you're still seeing amateur or up-and-coming matadors rather than the real pros who practice this sport in Mexico City.

The must-see spectacle in Acapulco is the renowned **cliff divers.** High divers perform at **La Quebrada** each day at 12:30, 7:15, 8:15, 9:15, and 10:15 p.m. for a $2.50 admission. From a spotlighted ledge on the cliffs, divers (holding torches for the final performance) plunge into the roaring surf 130 feet below — after wisely praying at a small shrine nearby. To the applause of the crowd, divers climb up the rocks and accept congratulations and cash tips from onlookers. This is the essential Acapulco experience, and no visit here is complete without watching these death-defying divers — this goes for jaded travelers as well.

The public areas have great views, but arrive early because all performances quickly fill up. Another option is to watch from the lobby bar and restaurant terraces of the **Hotel Plaza Las Glorias/El Mirador** (☎ 744-483-1155). At the bar, you have to pay an $18 cover charge, which includes two drinks. Reservations are recommended during the high season. The best way to reach La Quebrada is by taxi. It's located uphill from Avenida Lopez, 3 blocks west of the *zócalo.*

Sightseeing in Acapulco

Acapulco is best known for its beaches and bay, and sadly, few visitors bother to explore its traditional downtown area. But a trip to the shady *zócalo* (also called **Plaza Alvarez**) is an experience that offers a true glimpse of local life and color. Inexpensive cafes and shops border the plaza, and the cathedral **Nuestra Señora de la Soledad** — with its blue, onion-shaped domes and Byzantine towers — is at the north end. Though reminiscent of a Russian Orthodox church, the structure was originally built as a movie set and then later adapted for use as a house of worship. Take a taxi up to the top of the hill from the main plaza and follow the signs leading to **El Mirador** (lookout point) for an unparalleled view of Acapulco.

Of all the exclusive villas and homes in Acapulco, one stands far apart from the others. Though not as elegantly impressive as the villas of Las Brisas, the **home of Dolores Olmedo** in Acapulco's traditional down-town area is a veritable work of art. In 1956, the renowned Mexican artist Diego Rivera covered its outside wall with a mural of colorful mosaic tiles, shells, and stones. The work is unique, and one of the last he created. Rivera, considered one of Mexico's greatest artists, has been credited with being one of the founders of the 20th-century Mexican-muralist movement. The Olmeda mural, which took him 18 months to complete, features Aztec deities such as Quetzalcoatl and Tepezcuincle, the Aztec dog. Rivera and Olmeda were lifelong friends, and Rivera lived in this house for the last two years of his life during which time he also covered the interior with murals. However, because this home isn't a museum, you have to settle for enjoying the exterior masterpiece. The house is located a few blocks behind the Casablanca Hotel, a short cab ride from the central plaza, at Calle Cerro de la Pinzona 6. Have the driver wait while you look around because there's not much traffic and it's a steep climb back to the plaza.

Acapulco wasn't always a beach resort. Originally, it was an important port for the Spanish Empire, and because of the rich trade that took place here, the city was subject to frequent pirate attacks. In 1616, the **Fuerte de San Diego** was constructed to help protect Acapulco. Today, this fort is home to the **Museo Histórico de Acapulco** (☎ 744-482-3828). It contains exhibits that tell the story of Acapulco from its roles as a port in the conquest of the Americas, as a center for local Catholic conversion campaigns, and as a key site for trade with the Orient. The fort you see today was rebuilt after a large earthquake damaged the original structure in 1776, and it benefited from another renovation in 2000. To reach the fort, follow Costera Miguel Alemán from the Hotel Zone toward Old Acapulco and the *zócalo;* the fort is on a hill on the right. The museum is open Tuesday to Sunday from 10 a.m. to 5 p.m. The museum has exceptional bilingual exhibitions, and excellent air conditioning. The $3.50 admission is waived on Sunday.

Sightseeing on the water isn't limited to the ferryboats that take travel-ers to Isla de la Roqueta. Old, wooden glass-bottom boats circle the bay, and you can look down at a few fish and watch a diver or two swim down to the underwater sanctuary of the **Virgin of Guadalupe,** patron saint of Mexico. (The statue of the Virgin — created by sculptor

Armando Quesado — was placed at its submerged location in 1958 in memory of a group of divers who lost their lives at the spot.) You can purchase tickets (for approximately $5) at any loading boat or from the information booth on Playa Caletilla at a discount (☎ 744-482-2389).

Shopping in Acapulco

Shopping, like attractions in Acapulco, tends to favor the popular over the cultural — you're more likely to find a sexy swimsuit than a true artistic treasure here. Yet, Acapulco does have a few interesting shops. The best are found at the **Mercado Parazal** (often called the **Mercado de Artesanías**) on Calle Velázquez de León near Cinco de Mayo in the downtown *zócalo* area. (When you see Sanborn's, turn right and walk behind it for several blocks; ask for directions if you need to.) It's a collection of covered stalls selling unique curios from around the country including silver, embroidered cotton clothing, rugs, pottery, and papier-mâché. The market is open daily 9 a.m. to 6 p.m.

Markets such as the Mercado Parazal are made for bargaining, and the shopkeepers here test both your negotiating skills and your patience — they start with a steep price and then drag it down little by little. The more time you play their game, the better price you pay. As always, acting uninterested often brings down prices in a hurry.

What Acapulco does offer in abundance are stores selling resort wear, casual clothing, and the ever-present T-shirt. The Costera is crowded with shops and boutiques like these, including some brand-name locations such as Tommy Hilfiger that often have much lower prices than their stateside counterparts. If you find a sale, you can find incredible bargains.

For the serious shopper, Acapulco even has a few malls. One of the nicest, air-conditioned shopping centers on the Costera is **Plaza Bahía** (Costera Miguel Alemán 125; ☎ 744-485-6939 or 744-485-6992), which has four stories of shops, movie theaters, small fast-food restaurants, and a bowling alley. The center is located just west of the Costa Club Hotel. The bowling alley, **Bol Bahía** (☎ 744-485-0970 or 744-485-7464), is open Monday to Saturday noon to 1:30 a.m. and Sundays 10 a.m. to midnight. Another popular shopping strip is the **Plaza Condesa,** adjacent to the Fiesta Americana Condesa, with shops that include Guess, Izod, and Bronce Swimwear. **Olvida Plaza,** near the restaurant of the same name (see Chapter 24), has Tommy Hilfiger and Aca Joe.

Sanborn's is the hands-down standard in department stores in Mexico and offers an array of staples including cosmetics, drugstore items, electronics, music, clothing, books, and magazines. There are three branches in Acapulco:

✔ Downtown at Costera Miguel Alemán 209, across from the boat docks (☎ 744-484-4413)

✔ Costera Miguel Alemán 1226 at the Condo Estrella Tower, close to the convention center (☎ 744-484-2025, ext. 24/29)

✔ Costera Miguel Alemán 163 at the Hotel Calinda (☎ 744-481-2426 or 744-484-4465)

Acapulco also has a Sam's Club and a Wal-Mart located on the inland side of the main highway just prior to its ascent to Las Brisas.

Acapulco has a few notable fine-art galleries. My favorite, **Galería Espacio Pal Kepenyes,** Costera Guitarron 140, on the road to the Radisson (☎ 744-484-3738), carries the work of Pal Kepenyes, whose stunning bronzes are among Acapulco's most notable public sculptures. The gallery shows smaller versions, as well as signature pieces of jewelry in brass, copper, and silver, by appointment only.

Works by another notable Mexican artist, Sergio Bustamante, are available at his gallery and shop, **La Colección de Sergio Bustamante,** Costera Miguel Alemán 120-9, at Galerías Picuda (☎ 744-484-4992). You can see his capricious suns, moons, and fantasy figures in a variety of materials.

Taking a Side Trip to Taxco

The nearby colonial town of **Taxco** (*tahs*-ko) is known worldwide for its silver, but when you arrive, you may see that the town's geography and architecture are equally precious. Taxco sits at nearly 5,000 feet on a hill among hills, and almost any point in the city offers fantastic views.

The center of town is the tiny **Plaza Borda,** shaded by perfectly manicured Indian laurel trees. On one side is the imposing twin-towered, pink-stone **Santa Prisca y San Sebastián Church;** whitewashed, red-tile buildings housing the famous silver shops and a restaurant or two line the other sides. Beside the church, deep in a crevice of the mountain, is the **wholesale silver market** — absolutely the best place to begin your silver shopping, to get an idea of prices for more standard designs. You'll be amazed at the low prices. Buying just one piece is perfectly acceptable, though buying in bulk can lower the per-piece price. One of the beauties of Taxco is that its brick-paved and cobblestone streets are completely asymmetrical, zigzagging up and down the hillsides. The plaza buzzes with vendors of everything from hammocks and cotton candy to bark paintings and balloons.

The tiny, one-man factories that line the cobbled streets all the way up into the hills supply most of Taxco's silverwork. Your success at finding bargains depends somewhat on how much you know about the quality and price of silver, but Taxco's quantity and variety of silver can't be matched anywhere else in the country.

Getting to Taxco

It takes about four hours by bus to travel between Acapulco and Taxco, but the resulting bargains in exquisite silver and jewelry are well worth the trip — you won't be disappointed.

The best way to travel to Taxco from Acapulco is through one of the numerous day-trip charters that you can easily arrange at your hotel's tour desk or a local travel agent. Most excursions leave around 6:30 a.m. and return at 9 p.m. for a cost of about $60. You can also venture on your own — but I strongly recommend taking a bus over renting a car because the bus drivers know the route and much of the trip is along narrow, curvaceous roads through steep mountains.

Exploring Taxco

Shopping for jewelry and other items is the major pastime for tourists. Prices for silver jewelry at the more than 300 shops in Taxco are about the best in the world, and everything is available, from $1 trinkets to artistic pieces costing hundreds of dollars. You can get your fill of silver and an idea of what Taxco is like by spending an afternoon here, but this picturesque town has a lot more to offer than just the Plaza Borda and the shops surrounding it. For example, Taxco is the home of some of Mexico's finest stone sculptors and is also a good place to buy masks. However, beware of so-called "antiques" — there are virtually no real ones for sale.

Stay overnight and give yourself time to wander the steep cobblestone streets and discover the little plazas, fine churches, cultural attractions, and of course, the silversmith shops. If Acapulco is all you've seen during your vacation, a visit here will make you feel that, at last, you're in "Mexico." Take time to visit the following sites:

- ✔ **Santa Prisca y San Sebastián Church,** Plaza Borda (☎ 762-622-0183/4), is Taxco's centerpiece parish church; completed in 1758 after eight years of labor, it's one of Mexico's most impressive baroque churches. The church is open daily from 6:30 a.m. to 8 p.m., and admission is free.

- ✔ Stroll along Ruíz de Alarcón and look for the **Humboldt House/ Museo Virreynal de Taxco,** Calle Juan Ruíz de Alarcón 12 (the street behind the Casa Borda; ☎ 762-622-5501), where the renowned German scientist and explorer Baron Alexander von Humboldt (1769–1859) spent a night in 1803. The museum houses 18th-century memorabilia pertinent to Taxco. Admission is $3 for adults and $1.15 for students and teachers with ID; the museum is open Tuesday to Saturday 9 a.m. to 7 p.m., and Sunday 9 a.m. to 4 p.m.

✔ **The Silver Museum,** Plaza Borda (☎ **762-622-0658**), operated by a local silversmith, is a relatively recent addition to Taxco. After entering the building next to Santa Prisca (upstairs is Sr. Costilla's restaurant), look for a sign on the left; the museum is downstairs. It's not a traditional public museum; nevertheless, it does the much-needed job of describing the history of silver in Mexico and Taxco, as well as displaying some historic and contemporary award-winning pieces. Time spent here seeing quality silver work can make you a more discerning shopper in Taxco's silver shops. Admission is $1.50 for adults and $1 for children; the museum is open daily 10 a.m. to 5:30 p.m.

✔ A plaque in Spanish explains that most of the collection of pre-Columbian art displayed at the **Museo de Taxco Guillermo Spratling,** Calle Porfirio A. Delgado 1 (☎ **762-622-1660**), as well as the funds for the museum, came from William Spratling. You'd expect this to be a silver museum, but it's not. This museum's entrance floor and the second floor display a good collection of pre-Columbian statues and implements in clay, stone, and jade. The lower floor has changing exhibits. To find the museum, turn right out of the Santa Prisca Church and right again at the corner; continue down the street, veer right, then immediately left. The museum is facing you. The museum is open Tuesday to Saturday 10 a.m. to 5 p.m., and Sunday 9 a.m. to 3 p.m. Admission is $3.35 for adults and free for children under 13, with free admission for all on Sundays.

Staying a night

Taxco is an overnight visitor's dream: charming and picturesque, with a respectable selection of pleasant, well-kept hotels. Hotel prices tend to rise at holiday times (especially Easter week). The following are some suggestions in case you decide to spend a night or two.

✔ The **Hacienda del Solar,** Paraje del Solar s/n (Apdo. Postal 96), 40200 Taxco, Gro. (☎ and fax **762-622-0323**), comprises several Mexican-style cottages, all on a beautifully landscaped hilltop with magnificent views of the surrounding valleys and the town. The decor is slightly different in each cottage, but most contain plenty of beautiful handcrafts, red-tile floors, and bathrooms with hand-made tiles. Several rooms have vaulted tile ceilings and private terraces with panoramic views. Rates are $130 double and $130 to $150 for a junior or deluxe suite.

- **Hotel Los Arcos,** Juan Ruíz de Alarcón 4, 40200 Taxco, Gro. (☎ 762-622-1836; Fax: 762-622-7982), with rooms for $39 double, occupies a converted 1620 monastery. The handsome inner patio is bedecked with Puebla pottery and has a lively restaurant area, all around a central fountain.

- Each room at the delightful **Posada de los Castillo,** Juan Ruíz de Alarcón 7, 40200 Taxco, Gro. (☎ and fax **762-622-1396**), is simply but beautifully appointed with handsome carved doors and furniture; bathrooms have either tubs or showers. Rate is $40 double.

- The **Rancho Taxco Victoria,** Carlos J. Nibbi 5 and 7 (Apdo. Postal 83), 40200 Taxco, Gro. (☎ **762-622-0004;** Fax: 762-622-0010), clings to the hillside above town, with stunning views from its flower-covered verandas. It exudes the charm of old-fashioned Mexico. The comfortable furnishings, though slightly run-down, evoke the hotel's 1940s heyday. Even if you don't stay here, come for a drink in the comfortable bar and living room, or sit on the terrace to take in the fabulous view. Rooms cost $62 for a standard double, $89 for a deluxe double, and $100 for a junior suite.

- The **Santa Prisca,** Cenaobscuras 1, 40200 Taxco, Gro. (☎ **762-622-0080** or 762-622-0980; Fax: 762-622-2938), is one of the town's older and nicer hotels. Rooms are small but comfortable, with standard bathrooms (showers only), tile floors, wood beams, and a colonial atmosphere. A reading area in an upstairs salon overlooks Taxco, as well as a lush patio with fountains. Rooms range from $46 double to $52 superior to $74 suite.

Dining in Taxco

Taxco gets a lot of day-trippers from Mexico City and Acapulco, most of whom choose to dine close to the Plaza Borda. Prices in this area are high for what you get. Just a few streets back, though, you can find some excellent, simple restaurants.

- In a moderate price range is **Cielito Lindo,** Plaza Borda 14 (☎ 762-622-0603), probably the most popular place on the plaza for lunch. The menu is ample — there's something for every taste — but the best choices are the classic Mexican dishes. You can get anything from soup to roast chicken, enchiladas, tacos, steak, and dessert, as well as frosty margaritas.

- The spectacular view of the city from **La Ventana de Taxco,** in the Hacienda del Solar hotel, Paraje del Solar s/n (☎ 762-622-0587), makes it one of the best places to dine in Taxco. The food — standard Italian fare — is also quite good, if not predictable. The pasta dishes are the most recommendable. Lasagna is a big favorite, and Sicilian steak is also popular.

✔ An inexpensive alternative is **Restaurante Ethel,** Plazuela San Juan 14 (☎ 762-622-0788). This family-run place is opposite the Hotel Santa Prisca, a block from the Plaza Borda. It has colorful cloths on the tables and a tidy, homey atmosphere. The hearty *comida corrida* (essentially, a daily special) consists of soup or pasta, meat (perhaps a small steak), dessert, and good coffee.

✔ Another favorite is **Sotavento Restaurant Bar Galería,** Juárez 8, next to City Hall (no phone), which offers many Italian specialties — try deliciously fresh spinach salad and large pepper steak for a hearty meal; or Spaghetti Barbara, with poblano peppers and avocado, for a vegetarian meal. To find this place from the Plaza Borda, walk downhill beside the Hotel Agua Escondida, and then follow the street as it bears left (don't go right on Juan Ruíz de Alarcón) about a block. The restaurant is on the left just after the street bends left.

✔ **Toni's,** in the Hotel Monte Taxco (☎ 762-622-1300), is an intimate, classic restaurant (albeit a tad expensive) enclosed in a huge, cone-shaped *palapa* with a panoramic view of the city. The menu, mainly shrimp or beef, is limited, but the food is superior. Try tender, juicy prime roast beef, which comes with Yorkshire pudding, creamed spinach, and baked potato. Lobster is sometimes available. To reach Toni's, it's best to take a taxi. *Note:* Toni's is only open for dinner.

Discovering Taxco after dark

Paco's (no phone) is the most popular place overlooking the square for cocktails, conversation, and people-watching, all of which continue until midnight daily. Taxco's version of a disco, **Windows,** is high up the mountain in the **Hotel Monte Taxco** (☎ 762-622-1300). The whole city is on view, and music runs the gamut from the hit parade to hard rock. For a cover of $6.70, you can dance away Saturday night from 10 p.m. to 3 a.m.

Completely different in tone is **Berta's** (no phone), next to the Santa Prisca Church. Opened in 1930 by a lady named Berta, who made her fame on a drink of the same name (tequila, soda, lime, and honey), it's the traditional gathering place of the local gentry and more than a few tourists. Spurs and old swords decorate the walls, and a saddle is casually slung over the banister on the stairs leading to the second-floor room, where tin masks leer from the walls. A Berta (the drink, of course) costs about $2; rum, the same. It's open daily from 11 a.m. to around 10 p.m.

National drinks (not beer) are two-for-one nightly between 6 and 8 p.m. at the terrace bar of the **Hotel Rancho Taxco Victoria** (☎ 762-622-0004), where you can also drink in the fabulous view.

Discovering Acapulco after Dark

If there's anything Acapulco is more famous for than its beaches, it's the nightlife. Even if you feel that your "clubbing" days are behind you — trust me — give it a try. The views from the hillside clubs are among the best in town, and it's an equally fascinating scene inside. As is typical with clubs, the names and crowds change with the seasons, and places don't remain "hot" forever, but the ones I list tend to always be in the upper end of popularity. In addition, here are some general tips:

✔ Every club seems to have a cover charge of around $20 in high season and $10 in low season; drinks can cost anywhere from $3 to $10. Women can count on paying less or entering for free. Don't even think about going out to one of the hillside discos before 11 p.m., and don't expect much action until after midnight. The party goes on until 4 or 5 a.m. — and occasionally until 8 a.m. On weekends, the live dance shows — bordering on performance art — are well worth the lack of sleep.

✔ Many discos periodically waive their cover charge or offer some other promotion to attract customers. Another popular option is to have a higher cover charge but an open bar. Look for promotional materials displayed in hotel reception areas, at travel desks or concierge booths, and in local publications. You may also be hit up with promotions for nightclubs as you take in the sun at the local beaches.

✔ Besides nightclubs, you have other options. The **Gran Noche Mexicana** combines a performance by the Acapulco Ballet Folklórico with one by Los Voladores from Papantla. One of the few options to experience some authentic Mexican culture in town, it's held in the plaza of the convention center every Monday, Wednesday, and Friday at 7 p.m. With dinner and an open bar, the show costs $50; general admission (including three drinks) is $30. Call for reservations (☎ **744-484-7046** or 744-484-7098) or consult a local travel agency. Many major hotels also host Mexican fiestas and other theme nights that include dinner and entertainment.

✔ If you're brave enough — or inebriated enough — you can try out the **bungee jump** (Costera Miguel Alemán 101; ☎ **744-484-7529**) in the midst of the beach bar zone. For $62, you get one jump, plus a T-shirt, diploma, and membership. Additional jumps are $28, and your fourth jump is free. For $67, you can jump as many times as you like from 4 to 11 p.m.

Acapulco has essentially two different club scenes: the strip of beach bars along the Costera Hotel Zone and the glitzier club scene in the hillsides near Las Brisas.

The younger crowd seems to prefer a little fresh air with their nightlife and favor the growing number of open-air, oceanfront dance clubs along Costera Miguel Alemán. These establishments are concentrated between the Fiesta Americana and Continental Plaza hotels; tend to feature techno, house, or alternative rock; and are an earlier and more casual option for nightlife. Faves include the jammin' **DiscoBeach, El Sombrero** (you'll know it when you see it), **Tabu,** and the pirate-themed **Barbaroja.** These places generally offer an open bar with cover charge (around $10). Women frequently drink for free or with a lesser charge. (Men may pay more, but then, the young and tanned beach babes are here. So who's complaining?)

Of the more traditional clubs, here's my alphabetical rundown of the current scene including some uniquely entertaining options:

- ✔ Exterior reflection pools and flaming torches mark the entrance to **Alebrijes** (Costera Miguel Alemán 3308, across the street from the Hyatt Regency Acapulco; ☎ 744-484-5902). Inside, booths and round tables with a seating capacity of 1,200 surround the vast dance floor — the disco doubles as a venue for concerts and live performances by some of Mexico's most notable singers. Usually, you'll join a Mexican crowd in their mid-20s here, but the crowd may vary with featured performers. Alebrijes is open nightly 11 p.m. to 5 a.m. Cover (including open bar) for women is $5 to $25; for men it's $5 to $35. On Mondays, the open bar is for tequila drinks only.

- ✔ A long-time favorite in Acapulco is **Baby-O's** (Costera Miguel Alemán, across the street from the Hotel Romano Days Inn; ☎ 744-484-7474), which has kept current and maintained its place among the top clubs. This hangout is a great choice for those who shun mammoth clubs in favor of a more intimate setting. The mid- to late-20s crowd dances to everything from swing to hip-hop to rock 'n' roll on the small dance floor surrounded by several tiers of tables and sculpted, cave-like walls. Drinks are more moderately priced than in most Acapulco clubs and cost $3 to $5. Baby-O's is open 10:30 p.m. to 5 a.m. Cover for women is $5 to $10; for men, it's $10 to $15. Both covers include two national drinks.

- ✔ Venture into the stylish chrome-and-neon extravaganza that is **Enigma** (Carretera Escénica; ☎ 744-446-5712 or 744-446-5711) for a true Acapulco-nightlife experience. Perched on the side of the mountain between Los Rancheros Restaurant and La Vista Shopping Center, the club is easy to spot with its neon and laser lights pulsating in the night. The plush, dim interior dazzles patrons with a sunken dance floor and a panoramic view of the lights of Acapulco Bay. The club also has a more intimate Cuban bar upstairs overlooking the disco, which draws a more mature and moneyed crowd. Downstairs, the club alternates between pumping in mood smoke and fresh oxygen to keep you dancing. The door attendants wear tuxedos indicating that they encourage a more sophisticated dress — tight and slinky is the norm for ladies; no shorts for gentlemen. The club opens nightly at 10:30 p.m. Fireworks rock the usually full house at 3 a.m., which is when a stylized dance performance takes place on weekends in the style of Euro clubs. During peak season, call to find out if you need reservations. Cover varies but is around $15 to $40, and all major credit cards are accepted.

✔ **Palladium** (Carretera Escénica; ☎ 744-481-0330) is just down the road from Enigma, but it lacks both the style and the classy clientele of the neighboring club. A younger, rowdier crowd enjoys the equally fabulous views and the dancing platforms set in the large glass windows overlooking the bay. Cover is $5 to $15 for women, $8 to $25 for men.

✔ Billing itself as "the cathedral of salsa," **Salon Q** (Costera Miguel Alemán 3117; ☎ 744-481-0114) is known as the place to get down to the Latin rhythms when in Acapulco. Frequently, management raises the cover and features impersonators doing their thing as the top Latin American musical acts. Cover runs from $10 to $15.

✔ Across the street from Enigma is **Zucca** (Carretera Escénica 28, in the La Vista Shopping Center; ☎ 744-446-5691 or 744-446-5690), which offers up yet another fantastic bay view. It claims to cater to a slightly more mature crowd — stating that only those older than 25 are admitted — but seems to bend the rules, especially for younger women. Zucca is particularly popular with the moneyed Mexico City set. Periodically during the evening, the club projects a laser show across the bay. The dress code prohibits shorts, jeans, T-shirts, or sandals. The club is open nightly 10:30 p.m. to 2:30 a.m., but it stays open later (until 4 a.m.) on weekends or when the crowd demands it. The cover charge, which ranges from $10 to $15, is occasionally waived, at least until a sufficient crowd builds.

Part VIII

Huatulco and the Southern Pacific Coast

The 5th Wave   By Rich Tennant

SHELLING ON MEXICO'S SOUTHERN PACIFIC COAST

© RICHTENNANT

"Oooo! Back up Robert. There must be a half dozen Lightening Whelks here."

In this part . . .

The southern beach resorts of Huatulco and Puerto Escondido are Mexico's purest eco-tourism beach resorts. Unspoiled nature and a laid-back sentiment combine to offer up the uninterrupted experience of Mexico's pure, natural splendor. Puerto Escondido is a little-known paradise of exceptional values and unique, independent accommodations. Neighboring Huatulco puts on a bit of a different face as it combines indulgent hotels and modern facilities with pristine beaches and jungle landscapes.

The following chapters take you through these lesser-known treasures among Mexico's beach resorts and help you uncover their unique and worthwhile charms.

Chapter 26

Bahías de Huatulco

By Lynne Bairstow

. . . .

In This Chapter

▶ Surveying Huatulco's hotel scene

▶ Getting to know Huatulco

▶ Finding great places to dine

▶ Embarking on an adventure

. . . .

*L*ocated in the state of Oaxaca (wah-*hah*-cah), Huatulco's nine bays encompass 36 beaches and countless inlets and coves. The resort as a whole is a staged development project by the Mexican government's tourism development arm (FONATUR) that aims to cover 52,000 acres of land with more than 40,000 acres remaining as ecological preserves. Huatulco hasn't grown as rapidly as Cancún, the previous planned-development resort, so plenty of undeveloped stretches of pure white sands and isolated coves are still around to enjoy.

Huatulco has increasingly become known for its eco-tourism attractions — including river rafting, rappelling, and jungle hiking. It's not a destination for travelers who care a lot about shopping, nightlife, or even dining because its options for these pursuits are fewer than other beach resorts in Mexico. However, if you're especially drawn to snorkeling, diving, boat cruises to virgin bays, and simple relaxation, you may quickly find that Huatulco fits the bill perfectly.

The planned opening of a new cruise-ship dock in Santa Cruz Bay may change the level of activity in Huatulco, providing the sleepy resort with an important business boost. The new dock's plans call for it to handle up to two 3,000-passenger cruise ships at a time (tenders used to ferry passengers to shore).

In this chapter, I describe the layout of Huatulco and review some of the region's best hotels. I also take you from the plane, through the airport, and to your hotel, helping you quickly get your bearings in this easy-to-navigate resort situated along successive bays. I also offer tips on everything from transportation to dining out to enjoying the best of the numerous natural treasures of this pristine part of Mexico.

Choosing a Location

Unspoiled nature can be an idyllic retreat from the stress of daily life — and for some people, it's even more attractive when viewed from a luxury-hotel balcony. Huatulco is for vacationers who want to enjoy the beauty of nature during the day and then retreat to well-appointed comfort by night. Slow-paced and still relatively undiscovered, the hotels located among the nine bays of Huatulco enjoy the most modern infrastructure of any resort destination along Mexico's Pacific coast.

The area is divided into three sections: **Santa Cruz, Crucecita,** and **Tangolunda Bay.** These locations offer enough variety in accommodations that you're sure to find something to satisfy your vacation expectations regardless of your taste or budget.

The main differences between locations here can be simply summarized: Tangolunda Bay hotels are the newest, most deluxe properties in the area offering full-service pampering. Hotels in Santa Cruz are older, simpler in style, and lower in price. The village of Crucecita by far offers the best value, but you must take a shuttle to the beach. Although you certainly may find that the part of town you stay in impacts your overall experience, understand that everything is relatively close by, and getting around is both easy and inexpensive.

Moderate- and budget-priced hotels in Santa Cruz and Crucecita are generally higher in price compared to similar hotels in other Mexican beach resorts. But the luxury beach hotels in Tangolunda Bay have rates comparable to similar properties in other destinations, especially when these hotels are part of a package that includes airfare. The trend is toward all-inclusive resorts, which in Huatulco are a good option given the lack of memorable dining and nightlife options around town. Hotels that aren't oceanfront generally have an arrangement with one of the beach clubs at Santa Cruz or Chahué Bay and provide shuttle service to the beach. Low-season rates refer to the months of August through November only.

Evaluating the Top Accommodations

As far as prices go, I note *rack rates* (the maximum that a hotel or resort charges for a room) for two people spending one night in a double room during high season (Christmas to Easter). You can usually do better, especially if you're purchasing a package that includes airfare (read Chapter 5 for tips on avoiding paying rack rates). Prices quoted here include the 17% room tax. Note that some rates may seem much higher than others — until you realize that they're

Bahías de Huatulco

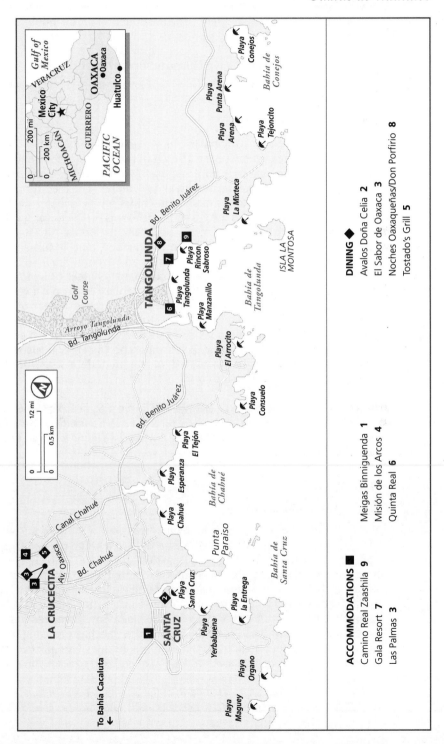

"all inclusive" — your meals and beverages are included in the price of your stay. These rates also include all tips, taxes, and most activities and entertainment. Please refer to the Introduction of this book for an explanation of the price categories.

All hotels have air conditioning unless otherwise indicated.

Camino Real Zaashila
$$$$$ Tangolunda Bay

One of Tangolunda Bay's original hotels — and my top choice here — the Camino Real is located on a wide stretch of sandy beach secluded from other beaches by small rock outcroppings. With calm water, it's perfect for swimming and snorkeling and ideal for families. The Mediterranean-style white-stucco building is washed in colors on the ocean side, looking a little like a scene from the Greek isles. Rooms on the lower levels — 41 of them — each have their own sizable dipping pools. All rooms are large and have an ocean-view balcony or terrace, marble tub/shower-combination bathrooms, wicker furnishings, and decors with bold colors. The main pool is a freeform design that spans 400 feet of beach with chaises built into the shallow edges. Well-manicured, tropical gardens surround the pool and the guest rooms. You have your choice of three restaurants here, including Chez Binni, noted for its excellent regional Oaxacan cuisine (featuring pork dishes and *moles*), plus room service and a lobby bar with live music. A full watersports center is also on its exceptional stretch of beach. Other pluses include a large outdoor whirlpool and a lighted tennis court.

Bulevar Benito Juárez No. 5. ☎ *800-722-6466 in the U.S., or 958-581-0460. Fax: 958-581-0461.* www.caminoreal.com/zaashila. *130 units. Rack rates: High season $300 double, $360 Camino Real Club; low season $165 double, $205 Camino Real Club. AE, DC, MC, V.*

Gala Resort
$$$$ Tangolunda Bay

With all meals, drinks, entertainment, tips, and a slew of activities included in the price of admission, the Gala is a value-packed experience. It caters to adults of all ages (married and single) who enjoy both activity and relaxation. An excellent kids' activities program probably makes it the best option in the area for families. Rooms have tile floors and Oaxacan wood trim, large tub/shower-combination bathrooms, and ample balconies — all with views of Tangolunda Bay. Three restaurants serve both buffet and a la carte meals, and the Gala has changing theme nights. A large, free-form pool, a complete beachfront watersports center, four lighted tennis courts, and a full gym are on-hand to keep you active.

Bulevar Benito Juárez s/n, located north of the Sheraton, south of Quinta Real. ☎ *958-581-0000. Fax: 958-581-0220. 290 units. Rack rates: $250 double, $100 per* *extra adult, $51 per child 7–11, $76 per child 12–15. Children under 7 stay free in parents' room. AE, MC, V.*

Las Palmas
$ Crucecita

The central location and accommodating staff are an added benefit to the clean, bright, but very basic rooms at Las Palmas. Located half a block from the main plaza in the town of Crucecita, the hotel is also connected to the popular El Sabor de Oaxaca restaurant (see the "Dining in Huatulco" section, later in this chapter), which offers room service to guests. Rooms have tile floors, cotton textured bedspreads, tile showers, and cable TV.

*Av. Guamúchil 206. ☎ **958-587-0060**. Fax: 958-587-0057. 10 units. Free parking. Rack rates: High season $37 double; low season $24 double. AE, MC, V.*

Meigas Binniguenda
$$ Santa Cruz

This property was Huatulco's first hotel, and it retains the Mexican charm and comfort that originally made it memorable. A recent addition has more than doubled the hotel's size. Rooms have Mexican-tile floors, artisan-crafted bedspreads, and colonial-style furniture; French doors open onto tiny wrought-iron balconies overlooking the main street of Juárez or the pool and gardens. The newer rooms have more modern teak furnishings and are generally much nicer — request this section. A nice shady area surrounds the hotel's small pool in back of the lobby. The hotel is away from the marina at the far end of Juárez, only a few blocks from the water. These folks offer free transportation every hour to the beach club at Santa Cruz Bay.

*Bulevar Santa Cruz 201. ☎ **958-587-0077** or 958-587-0078. Fax: 958-587-0284. E-mail: binniguenda@prodigy.net.mx. 165 units. Rack rates: High season $110 double; low season $70 double. Ask about special packages that include breakfast. AE, MC, V.*

Misión de los Arcos
$–$$ Crucecita

This exceptional hotel, just a block from the central plaza, has a similar style to the elegant Quinta Real — at a fraction of the cost. The hotel is mostly white and accented with an abundance of greenery (no flowering plants), which gives it a fresh, clean, and inviting feel. Rooms, washed in white with cream and beige bed coverings and upholstery, have the same ambiance. Built-in desks, French windows, and minimal but interesting decorative accents give this budget hotel a true sense of style. A new cafe with international magazines and high-speed Internet access (open 7:30 a.m. to 11:30 p.m.) is at the right side of the entrance level. Guests can enjoy the services of an adjacent restaurant. Although the hotel has no pool, guests have the use of a beach club, to which the hotel provides a complimentary shuttle. Its central location is ideal for sampling Crucecita's shops and restaurants.

Gardenia 902. ☎ ***958-587-0165.*** *Fax 958-587-1904.* www.misiondelosarcos.com. *13 rooms. Rack rates: High season $59 without A/C, $65 with A/C, suites $70–$130; low season $30 without A/C, $35 with A/C, suites $40–$85. AE, MC, V.*

Quinta Real
$$$$$ **Tangolunda Bay**

The most romantic of Huatulco's hotels, the Quinta Real is known for its understated elegance and efficient service. Double Moorish domes mark this relaxed hotel that has a richly appointed cream-and-white decor. The Quinta Real cascades down a hillside — from the welcoming reception area to the luxurious beach club below. The small groupings of suites are built into the sloping hill down to Tangolunda Bay and offer spectacular views of the ocean and golf course. (Rooms on the eastern edge of the resort sit above the highway and have some traffic noise.) Interiors are elegant and comfortable with stylish Mexican furniture, wood-beamed ceilings, marble tub/shower-combination bathrooms with whirlpool tubs, and original artwork. Telescopes grace many of the suites. Balconies have overstuffed seating areas and floors of stone inlay. Selected suites have private pools of their own. One restaurant serves breakfast and dinner, and the beach club poolside-casual restaurant is open for lunch. The beach club has two pools — one for children — as well as showers and *palapas* on the beach with chair and towel service. The elegant, library-style bar offers up a stunning view and makes a great place for a drink even if you're not staying here. The Quinta Real is perfect for weddings, honeymoons, or small corporate retreats.

Bulevar Benito Juárez No. 2. ☎ ***888-561-2817*** *in the U.S., or 958-581-0428. Fax: 958-581-0429.* www.quintareal.com. *28 units. Rack rates: High season $320 Master Suite, $370 Grand Class Suite, $420 with private pool; low season $220 Master Suite, $270 Grand Class Suite, $320 with private pool. AE, DC, MC, V.*

Settling into Huatulco

In Huatulco, getting into the swing of things is easy. From the small airport, the ride into town along well-paved roads is quick. You're likely to encounter exceptional graciousness and a truly warm welcome from everyone from taxi drivers to bellhops.

Arriving in Huatulco by air

Huatulco's international airport (☎ **958-581-9004** or 958-581-9017) is located about 19km (12 miles) northwest of the Bahías de Huatulco. As you deplane, you go down some stairs onto the tarmac and take a brief walk into the terminal — important to know if you're carrying on any heavy luggage. After you're inside the small terminal, you reach the immigration clearance area. At the immigration booth, an officer asks you to show your passport (or other proof of citizenship) and your completed tourist card, the **FMT** (see Chapter 7 for all the FMT details).

Your FMT is an important document, so take good care of it. You're supposed to keep the FMT with you at all times because you may be required to show it if you run into any sort of trouble. You also need to turn it back in upon departure, or you may be unable to leave without replacing it.

Next, grab your baggage from the baggage-claims carousel. If needed, porters are available to help with your bags for a tip of about a dollar a bag. After you collect your luggage, you pass through another check-point. Something that looks like a traffic light awaits you here. You press a button, and if the light turns green, you're free to go. If it turns red, you need to open each of your bags for a quick search. It's Mexico's random search procedure for customs. If you have an unusually large bag, or an excessive amount of luggage, you may be searched regardless of the traffic-light outcome.

With your bags, exit the terminal where taxis and other transportation services are waiting.

Getting from the airport to your hotel

From the airport, private **taxis** charge $4.50 to Crucecita, $5 to Santa Cruz Bay, and $9 to Tangolunda Bay. **Transportes Terrestres** *colectivo* (shared) minibus fares range from $3.50 to $5 per person.

When returning to the airport, make sure to specifically ask for a taxi unless you have a lot of luggage. Taxis to the airport run $4, but unless you request one, companies send a sport-utility vehicle, which costs $6 for the same trip.

Because this beach destination is so spread out and has excellent roads, you may want to consider a rental car (at least for a day or two for a bit of exploring). The bays are spread out, and having a car allows you to see more of them, and explore a bit on your own on the modern and well-paved roads. If you opt for a rental, consider timing it so that you either pick up your car upon arrival or return it as you depart, saving an extra trip to the airport. **Budget** (☎ **800-322-9976** in U.S., 958-587-0010 or 958-581-9000) and **Advantage** (☎ **958-581-1379**) share an office at the airport, which is open when flights arrive. Daily rates run around $56 for a Volkswagen sedan, $79 for a Nissan Sentra or Geo Tracker, and $100 for a Jeep Wrangler. **Dollar** has rental offices at the Royal and Barceló hotels and downtown, and offers one-way drop service if you're traveling on to Puerto Escondido.

Knowing your way around town

Bahías de Huatulco include all nine bays of this resort area. The town of Santa María de Huatulco, the original settlement in this area, is 27km (17 miles) inland. **Santa Cruz Bay,** usually just called Santa Cruz, was the first area on the coast to be developed. It has a central plaza with a bandstand kiosk that has been converted into a cafe serving regionally grown coffee. Santa Cruz also has an artisan's market on the edge of the plaza that borders the main road, a few hotels and restaurants, and a marina from which bay tours and fishing trips set sail. **Juárez** is Santa Cruz's main street. It's about 4 blocks long in all and anchored at one end by the Hotel Castillo Huatulco and at the other by the Meigas Binniguenda hotel. Opposite the Hotel Castillo is the marina, and beyond the marina are restaurants housed in new, colonial-style buildings facing the beach. The area's banks are on Juárez. Getting lost is impossible; you can take in almost everything at a glance.

About 2.5km (1.5 miles) inland from Santa Cruz is **Crucecita,** a planned city that sprang up in 1985 centered on a lovely grassy plaza edged with flowering hedges. Crucecita is the residential area for the resorts. Neighborhoods of new stucco homes are mixed with small apartment complexes. The town has evolved into a lovely, traditional town where you can find the area's best — and most reasonably priced — restaurants, plus some shopping and several clean, less-expensive hotels.

Tangolunda Bay, 5km (3 miles) east of Crucecita, is the focal point of bay development. Over time, half the bays should have resorts. But for now, Tangolunda has the lion's share, with an 18-hole golf course; the elegant Las Brisas Resort; and the Quinta Real, Barceló Huatulco, Gala Resort, Casa del Mar, and Camino Real Zaashila hotels, among others. Small strip centers with a few restaurants occupy each end of Tangolunda Bay. **Chahué Bay,** between Tangolunda and Santa Cruz, is a small bay with a beach club — and a marina under construction — along with houses and three new hotels.

Walking between any of the three destinations (Crucecita, Santa Cruz, and Tangolunda) is too far, but **taxis** are inexpensive and readily available. The fare between Santa Cruz and Tangolunda is roughly $2; between Santa Cruz and Crucecita, $1.50; and between Crucecita and Tangolunda, $2.50.

Minibus service between towns costs 50¢. In Santa Cruz, catch the bus across the street from Castillo Huatulco; in Tangolunda, it stops in front of the Grand Pacific; and in Crucecita, the bus stop is cater-corner from the Hotel Grifer.

Fast Facts: Huatulco

Area Code

The telephone area code is **958**.

Babysitters

Most of the larger hotels can easily arrange babysitters, but many sitters speak limited English. Rates range from $4 to $10 per hour.

Banks, ATMs, and Currency Exchange

All three areas have banks, including the main Mexican banks Banamex and Bancomer, with ATMs. Banks change money during business hours, which are 9 a.m. to 5 p.m. Monday to Friday and 9 a.m. to 1 p.m. on Saturdays. Banks are located along Calle Juárez in Santa Cruz and surround the central plaza in Crucecita.

Business Hours

Most offices maintain traditional Mexican hours of operation (10 a.m. to 2 p.m. and 4 p.m. to 8 p.m., daily), but shops remain open throughout the day. Offices tend to be closed on Saturday and Sunday, but shops are open on Saturday, at least, and increasingly offer limited hours of operation on Sunday.

Emergencies

Police emergency (☎ 060); **local police** (☎ 958-587-0815); **transit police** (☎ 958-587-0186); and **Red Cross** (Bulevar Chahué 110; ☎ 958-587-1188).

Information

The **State Tourism Office** (Oficina del Turismo; ☎ 958-581-0176 or 958-581-0177; E-mail: sedetur6@oaxaca.gob.mx) has an information module in Tangolunda Bay near the Grand Pacific hotel, and another inside the Gala Resort.

Internet Access

Two Internet cafes are located in Crucecita. One is on the ground-floor level of the **Hotel**

Plaza Conejo (Av. Guamúchil 208, across from the main plaza; ☎ 958-587-0054 or 958-587-0009; E-mail: conejo3@mexico.com). The other is **Portico's** (Gardenia 902; ☎ 958-587-0165).

Maps

One of the best around is the free American Express map, usually found at the tourist information offices.

Medical Care

Dr. Ricardo Carrillo (☎ 958-587-0687 or 958-587-0600) speaks English.

Pharmacy

Farmacia del Carmen (☎ 958-587-0878), one of the largest drugstores in Crucecita, is located just off the central plaza. **Farmacia La Clinica** (☎ 958-587-0591) is located at Sabalí 1602 in Crucecita and offers both 24-hour service and home/hotel delivery.

Post Office

The post office at Bulevar Chahué 100, Sector R (☎ 958-587-0551) is open Monday to Friday 9 a.m. to 3 p.m. and Saturdays 9 a.m. to 1 p.m.

Safety

Huatulco enjoys a very low crime rate. Most crime or encounters with the police are linked to pickpocket thefts, so use common sense and never leave your belongings unattended at the beach.

Taxes

A 15% IVA (value-added tax) on goods and services is charged, and it's generally included in the posted price.

Taxis

In Crucecita, a taxi stand is opposite the Hotel Grifer and another is on the Plaza Principal. Taxis are readily available in

Santa Cruz and Tangolunda through your hotel. The fare between Santa Cruz and Tangolunda is roughly $2; between Santa Cruz and Crucecita, $1.50; and between Crucecita and Tangolunda, $2.50. You can also rent taxis by the hour (about $15 per hour) or for the day if you want to explore the area.

Telephone

Avoid the phone booths that have signs in English advising you to call home using a special 800 number — these are absolute rip-offs and can cost as much as $20 per minute. The least expensive way to call is by using a Telmex (LADATEL) prepaid phone card, available at most pharmacies and mini-supers, using the official Telmex (Lada) public phones. Remember, in Mexico you need to dial 001 prior to a number to reach the United States, and you need to preface long distance calls within Mexico by dialing 01.

Time Zone

Huatulco operates on central standard time, but Mexico's observance of daylight savings time varies somewhat from that in the United States.

Dining in Huatulco

Contrary to conventional travel wisdom, many of the better restaurants in the Tangolunda Bay area — or from a practical standpoint, most of the restaurants, period — are located in the hotels. Outside the hotels, the best choices are in Crucecita and on the beach in Santa Cruz.

Like many of Mexico's beach resorts, even the finest restaurants in town can be comfortably casual when it comes to dress. Men seldom wear jackets, although ladies frequently wear dressy resort garb — basically, everything goes.

I list the following restaurants alphabetically and note their location and general price category. Remember that tips generally run about 15%, and most wait-staff really depend on these for their income, so be generous if the service warrants. Please refer to the Introduction of this book for an explanation of the price categories.

Please see Appendix C for more information on Mexican cuisine.

Avalos Doña Celia
$–$$ Santa Cruz Bay   SEAFOOD

For years, Doña Celia, an original Huatulco resident, chose to stay in business in the same area where she started her little thatch-roofed restaurant. Now, she's in a new building at the end of Santa Cruz's beach serving the same good eats. Among her specialties are *filete empapelado,* a foil-wrapped fish baked with tomato, onion, and cilantro, and *filete almendrado,* a fish fillet covered with hotcake batter, beer, and almonds. The *ceviche* is terrific (one order is plenty for two), as is the *platillo a la huatulqueño* (shrimp and young octopus fried in olive oil with chile and onion and served over white rice). The ambiance is basic, but the food is the reason for its popularity. If you dine here during the day, beach chairs and shade are available, so you can make your own "beach club" away from your hotel in this more traditional and accessible part of Huatulco.

Santa Cruz Bay, at the end of Playa Santa Cruz. ☎ 958-587-0128. Reservations not needed. Seafood prices: $4–$25; breakfast $2.50–$3.50. MC, V. Open: Daily 8:30 a.m.–11 p.m.

El Sabor de Oaxaca

$–$$ Crucecita   OAXACAN

El Sabor de Oaxaca is the best place in the area to enjoy authentic and richly flavorful Oaxacan food, which is among the best of traditional Mexican cuisine. This restaurant is a local favorite that also meets the quality standards of tourists. The mixed grill for two — with *chorizo* (a zesty Mexican sausage), Oaxacan beef filet, tender pork tenderloin, and pork ribs — is among the most popular items, and the Oaxacan special for two — a generous sampling of the best of the menu with tamales, Oaxacan cheese, pork *mole,* and more — is a can't-miss selection. Generous breakfasts are just $2.22 and include eggs, bacon, ham, beans, toast, and fresh orange juice. The colorful decor and lively music create a nice ambiance, and special group events are happily arranged.

Av. Guamúchil 206. ☎ 958-587-0060. Reservations not needed. Main courses: $5–$20. AE, MC, V. Open: Daily 7 a.m. to 11 p.m.

Noches Oaxaqueñas/Don Porfirio

$$$ Tangolunda Bay   SEAFOOD/OAXACAN

At this restaurant with a dinner show, local dancers perform the colorful, traditional folkloric dances of Oaxaca in an open-air courtyard reminiscent of an old hacienda despite being located in a modern strip mall. For dinner, I recommend the *plato Oaxaqueño,* a generous, flavorful sampling of traditional Oaxacan fare including a tamale, sope, Oaxacan cheese, a grilled fillet, a pork enchilada, and a chile relleno for $10. Other house specialties include shrimp with mezcal and spaghetti marinara with seafood. Meat lovers can enjoy American-style cuts of beef or a juicy *arrachera* (skirt steak).

Bulevar Benito Juárez s/n, across from Gala Resort. ☎ 958-581-0001. Reservations recommended. Show: $15; dinner and drinks available á la carte. Main courses: $15–$20. AE, MC, V. Open: Fri–Sun 12:30–10 p.m.; Tues and Thurs 8:30–10 p.m.

Tostado's Grill

$–$$ Crucecita   MEXICAN

This traditional family-oriented Mexican restaurant serves typical Mexican fare in a casual, friendly atmosphere. It's the place to dine if you're looking for a dose of local color with your meal and want something authentically Mexican. Especially delectable is the *Aztec soup* (tortilla soup), and the beef is known for its tenderness. It's one of the few restaurants in La Crucecita that is open late during low season.

Flamboyan No. 306, in front of La Crucecita's central plaza. ☎ *958-587-1697. Reservations not accepted. Main courses: $2–$20. AE, MC, V. Open: Daily 7 a.m. to midnight.*

Having Fun on and off the Beach

Attractions around Huatulco concentrate on the nine bays in the area and their related watersports. Huatulco is truly a nature-lover's paradise offering the more adventurous travelers activities from rafting to rappelling.

Hitting Huatulco's best beaches

Huatulco's major attraction is its coastline — that magnificent stretch of pristine bays bordered by an odd blend of cactus and jungle vegetation that runs right to the water's edge. The only way to really grasp its beauty is by taking a cruise of the bays, stopping at **Organo Bay** or **Maguey Bay** for a dip in the crystal-clear water and a fish lunch at one of the *palapa* restaurants on the beach.

As far as the more accessible, local beaches go, a section of the beach at **Santa Cruz** (away from the small boats), an inviting spot to soak in the sun, is the location of the beach clubs that guests of non-ocean-front hotels use. Several restaurants are also on this beach, and you can find *palapa* umbrellas down to the water's edge.

For about $15 one way, *pangas* (small boats) from the marina in Santa Cruz ferry passengers to **Playa La Entrega,** also in Santa Cruz Bay. A row of *palapa* restaurants, all with beach chairs out front, greet you at La Entrega. Find an empty *palapa,* call it home for the day, and in return, use that restaurant for your refreshment needs. A snorkel-equipment-rental booth is about midway down the beach, and there's some fairly good snorkeling on the end away from where the boats arrive.

Between Santa Cruz and Tangolunda bays is **Chahué Bay.** A beach club here has *palapas,* beach volleyball, and refreshments for an entrance fee of about $2. However, a strong undertow makes this a dangerous place for swimming.

Playa Tangolunda, fronting the best hotels, is wide and beautiful. Theoretically, all beaches in Mexico are public; however, if you're not a guest at a Tangolunda Bay hotel, you may have difficulty entering a hotel to get to the beach.

Cruising Huatulco

The most popular way to tour Huatulco's bays is to jump on a boat, such as the *Tequila,* and join one of the organized day-long bay cruises complete with guide, drinks, and on-board entertainment. You can call direct (☎ **958-587-0856**), or any travel agency can easily arrange these tours, which cost about $25 per person with an extra charge of $4 for snorkeling equipment rental and lunch. Another, more romantic option is the *Luna Azul,* a 44-foot sailboat that offers bay tours and sunset sails. Call ☎ **958-587-2276** or 587-0945 (at the Hotel Chahué) for reservations.

If you prefer to venture out on your own, arrange your own bay tour by going to the **boat-owners' cooperative** in the red-and-yellow tin shack at the entrance to the marina in Santa Cruz. Prices are posted there, and you can buy tickets for sightseeing, snorkeling, or fishing. Besides Playa la Entrega, other more distant beaches are noted for good offshore snorkeling, plus they also have *palapa* restaurants and other facilities. These strips of sand include **Playa Maguey** and **Playa San Agustín.** Just remember that several of these beaches are completely undeveloped and pristine, so you need to bring your own provisions. Boatmen at the cooperative can arrange return pick-up at an appointed time. Prices run about $15 for one to ten people to La Entrega and $35 for a trip to Maguey and Organo bays. The most distant bay is **San Agustinillo,** and that all-day trip runs $70 in a private *panga* (small boat).

Taking time for tennis or golf

For the more traditional sports aficionados, the 18-hole, par-72 **Tangolunda Golf Course** (☎ **958-581-0037**) is adjacent to Tangolunda Bay and has tennis courts as well. The greens fee is $37 and carts cost about the same. Tennis courts are also available at the **Barceló** hotel (☎ **958-581-0055**).

Sightseeing and shopping

A day in Crucecita can be enjoyable. Just off the central plaza is the **Iglesía de Guadalupe** with its large mural of Mexico's patron saint gracing the entire ceiling of this church's chapel. The image of the Virgin is set against a deep-blue, night sky, which includes 52 stars — a modern interpretation of the original cloak of Juan Diego.

Considering that **shopping** in Huatulco is generally limited, and unmemorable, the bays' best choices are in Crucecita — in the shops that surround the central plaza. The stores tend to stay open late and offer a good selection of regional goods and typical, tourist take-homes including *artesania* (local crafts), silver jewelry, Cuban cigars, and tequila. Plus, you can **dine** in Crucecita for a fraction of the price of dining in Tangolunda Bay and get the added benefit of some local color.

You can also check out the **Crucecita Market** (open from 10 a.m. to 8 p.m.) on Guamúchil, half a block from the plaza in Crucecita, and the Plaza Oaxaca, adjacent to the central plaza. This small shopping center has several clothing shops including **Poco Loco Club/Coconut's Boutique** (☎ 958-587-0279) for casual sportswear; **Mic Mac** (☎ 958-587-0565), featuring beachwear and souvenirs; and **Sideout** (☎ 958-587-0254) for active wear. **Coconuts** (☎ 958-587-0057) has English-language magazines, books, and music. A small, free trolley is available to take visitors on a short tour of the town. Hop on at the central plaza.

The other main option for shopping is the **Santa Cruz Market** (open 10 a.m. to 8 p.m.), located by the marina in Santa Cruz. Among all the typical souvenirs, you may want to search out regional specialties that include Oaxacan embroidered blouses and dresses and *barro negro,* a pottery made from a dark clay found exclusively in the Oaxaca region. Several shopping centers in Tangolunda Bay offer a selection of crafts and Oaxacan goods but are pricier than the markets.

The most worthwhile sightseeing excursion in the area is the daylong trip to **Oaxaca City** and **Monte Albán.** The tour includes round-trip airfare on Aerocaribe, lunch, admission to the archaeological sight of Monte Albán, and a tour of the architectural highlights of Oaxaca City — all for $100. Contact any travel agency or the **Aerocaribe** office (☎ 958-587-1220) for more information.

Brewing up some fun

Mexico's Huatulco region is known for its rich *pluma* coffee, grown in the region's mountainous areas. Centuries-old plantations, most of which continue to use traditional methods, grow and harvest coffee beans. The majority of the plantations are located around the mouth of the Río Copalita in small towns, including Pluma Hidalgo, Santa María de Huatulco, and Xanica, located roughly an hour to an hour and a half from Tangolunda Bay. Both day tours and overnight stays from Huatulco are available to select coffee plantations.

Café Huatulco (☎ 958-587-0339) is a unique project developed by the area's coffee producers' association to bring awareness to the region's coffee and to offer an unusual excursion for tourists. Café Huatulco, located in a kiosk in the central plaza of Santa Cruz, sells whole-bean, regional coffee and serves coffee and espresso beverages. The association can arrange coffee tastings for groups of six or more and overnight stays at the coffee plantations for travelers who are really serious about their coffee.

Enjoying the nightlife

Only a very limited selection of dance clubs is available around Huatulco — so everyone goes to these places. Note that these seem to change ownership and names almost annually, but the locations should be accurate. **Aqua Disco** (☎ **958-587-0017**), in Santa Cruz, is the area's longest-standing disco. It opens at 9 p.m. **El DexkiteLitros** (☎ **958-587-0971**) is the current hot spot, with open-air dancing on the Santa Cruz beachfront. Located next to the Marina Hotel on the beach, it spins techno and rock from 10 p.m. until 5 a.m. For live music, try **Magic Tropical,** Paseo Mitla 304, Santa Cruz (no phone).

Chapter 27

Puerto Escondido

By Lynne Bairstow

. . . .

In This Chapter

▶ Finding a place to stay

▶ Getting the lay of the land in Puerto Escondido

▶ Dining in Puerto Escondido

▶ Hitting the beach and checking out turtles

. . . .

*A*lthough it may be best known as Mexico's top surf break, Puerto Escondido has a much broader appeal — it simply offers the very best all-around value of any beach resort in Mexico. What's the attraction? Consider this: stellar beaches; friendly locals; and terrific and inexpensive dining, places to stay, and nightlife — plus an abundance of English-language speakers and a notable absence of beach vendors and timeshare salespeople. But if you're traveling with children, Puerto Escondido may not be the perfect fit — it's really a better choice for younger or more adventurous travelers.

In this chapter, I cover the best of Puerto Escondido — where to stay and dine and where to find the best adventures. I also offer tips on everything from transportation to where to find the best nightlife.

Evaluating the Top Accommodations

The town of Puerto Escondido is very small — all the hotels are in or bordering the town. The main pedestrians-only zone is known locally as the ***Adoquín*** after the hexagonal-shaped, interlocking bricks used in its paving. The hotels along Playa Zicatela really cater to surfers.

As far as prices go, I note *rack rates* (the maximum that a hotel or resort charges for a room) for two people spending one night in a double room during high season (Christmas to Easter). You can usually do better, especially if you're purchasing a package that includes airfare (read

Chapter 5 for tips on avoiding paying rack rates). Prices quoted here include the 17% room tax. Please refer to the Introduction of this book for an explanation of the price categories.

The hotels that I list here have both air conditioning and TVs, unless otherwise indicated; and if the review doesn't say anything to the contrary, you can safely assume that you can walk directly out of your hotel and onto the beach.

Arcoiris Hotel
$–$$ Playa Zicatela

This hotel offers a winning combination of Zicatela's laid-back charms, together with more amenities and services than the nearby bare-bones surfer hotels, making it a good choice for families. Rooms are located on three levels in this Mexican Colonial-style inn, and all have large balconies or terraces that face either Playa Zicatela or an interior garden. You can string a hammock up on the balcony — a common sight, with no air conditioning in the rooms — and relax away the afternoon. Ground-floor rooms are sans TV, while upper-level rooms have satellite TV. About half of the rooms have a small kitchenette. Hotel amenities include a smallish swimming pool, game room with satellite TV, bookstore, and pharmacy, as well as a restaurant and popular rooftop bar — one of Playa Zicatela's favorite spots for sunset-watching and happy hour. The attentive staff is a plus.

Calle del Morro s/n. ☎ *954-582-0432 or 954-582-1494. 33 units. Rack rates: First-floor rooms $52; upper-level rooms: $80. MC, V.*

Best Western Posada Real
$$$ Playa Bacocho

Set on top of a cliff overlooking Playa Bacocho just west of town, this property is the area's best choice for family travelers. The clean but smallish standard rooms are less enticing than the hotel grounds, which include an expansive, manicured lawn that is one of the most popular places in town for a sunset cocktail. A big plus here is the hotel's Coco's Beach Club — a half-mile stretch of soft-sand beach, a large swimming pool, a kid's playground, and a bar with swing-style chairs and occasional live music. A shuttle service (or a lengthy walk down a set of stairs) takes you to the beach club, which is also open to the public ($2.50 cover for non-guests). The hotel is located only 5 minutes from the airport and about the same distance from Puerto Escondido's Tourist Zone — you must take a taxi to get to town. In addition to Coco's, the hotel has two restaurants and a lobby bar plus two swimming pools — one is a wading pool for children — tennis courts, and a putting green. It's the most traditional (hotel-chain style) hotel I recommend in Puerto Escondido.

Av. Benito Juárez 11. ☎ *800-528-1234 in the U.S., 954-582-0133, or 954-582-0237. Fax: 954-582-0192.* www.bestwestern.com. *100 rooms. Rack rates: High season $130 double; low season $85 double. AE, DC, MC, V.*

Puerto Escondido

ACCOMMODATIONS ■
Arcoiris Hotel **10**
Best Western Posada Real **1**
Bungalows and Cabañas
Acuario **11**
Flor de María **7**
Hotel Casa Blanca **4**
Hotel Santa Fe **6**
Paraiso Escondido **2**
Rockaway Surfer Village **11**

DINING ◆
Cabo Blanco **8**
Carmen's La Patisserie **5**
El Cafecito **9**
Gota de Vida **12**
La Galería **3**
María's Restaurant **7**
Restaurant Santa Fe **6**

Airport ✈
Beach ⊀
Church ⊹
Information ⓘ
Post Office ⊠

Bungalows and Cabañas Acuario
$–$$ Playa Zicatela

Facing Playa Zicatela, this surfer's sanctuary offers clean, cheap accommodations plus an on-site gym, surf shop, vegetarian restaurant, and Internet cafe. The two-story hotel and the bungalows surround a pool shaded by great palms. Rooms are small and basic, but bungalows offer fundamental kitchen facilities. The *cabañas* are more open and have hammocks. Parking, public telephones, money-exchange facilities, a pharmacy, and the vegetarian restaurant (Mango's) are located in the adjoining commercial area. The well-equipped gym costs an extra $1 per day or $15 per month.

Calle del Morro s/n. ☎ *954-582-0357 or 954-582-1026. 40 units. Rack rates: High season $55 double without A/C, $70 double with A/C, $93 bungalow (no A/C); low season $25 double without A/C, $30 double with A/C, $40 bungalow (but you can often negotiate a better deal after you're there). No credit cards.*

Flor de María
$ Playa Marinero

Though not right on the beach, this hotel is a real find and very popular with older travelers. Canadians María and Lino Francato own this cheery, three-story hotel facing the ocean, which you can see from the rooftop. The structure is built around a garden courtyard, and each room is colorfully decorated with beautiful, realistic still lifes and landscapes painted by Lino. Two rooms have windows with a view; the rest face into the courtyard. All have double beds with orthopedic mattresses and small safes. The roof, in addition to the great view, has a small pool, a shaded hammock terrace, and an open-air bar (open 5 to 9 p.m. during high season) with a TV that receives U.S. channels. All in all, the roof is a great sunset spot. I highly recommend the first-floor María's Restaurant (see the "Dining in Puerto Escondido" section, later in this chapter). Ask about off-season discounts for long-term stays. The hotel is just steps from the center of town and up a sandy road from Playa Marinero on an unnamed street at the eastern end of the beach.

Playa Marinero. ☎ *and fax: 954-582-0536. 24 units. Rack rates: $35–$50 double. MC, V.*

Hotel Casa Blanca
$ Tourist Zone

If you want to be in the heart of the *Adoquín,* this hotel is your best bet for excellent value and clean, ample accommodations; plus it's just a block from the main beach. The courtyard pool and adjacent *palapa* (thatched roof) restaurant is a great place to hide away and enjoy a margarita or a book from the hotel's exchange rack. The bright, clean, and simply furnished rooms offer a choice of bed combinations, but all have at least two beds and a fan. Some rooms have air conditioning and a minifridge. The best rooms have a balcony overlooking the action in the street below. If you're a light sleeper, consider a room in the back. Some rooms can sleep up to five ($60), an excellent and economical choice for families.

Av. Pérez Gasga 905. ☎ *954-582-0168. 21 units. Rack rates: $30 double without A/C, $60 double with A/C. MC, V.*

Hotel Santa Fe
$$ Playa Zicatela

If Puerto Escondido is Mexico's best beach value, then the Santa Fe is without a doubt one of the best hotel values — and a personal, all-around favorite of mine. It has a winning combination of unique Spanish-colonial style, a welcoming staff, and clean, comfortable rooms. The hotel has grown up over the years alongside the surfers who came to Puerto in the 1960s and 1970s — and nostalgically return today. It's located about 1km (½ mile) southeast of the town center off Highway 200, at the curve in the road where playas Marinero and Zicatela join — a prime sunset-watching spot. The three-story, hacienda-style buildings have clay-tiled stairs, archways, and blooming vines surrounding the two courtyard swimming pools. The ample but simply stylish rooms feature large tile bathrooms, colonial furnishings, handwoven fabrics, Guerrero pottery lamps, and TVs with local channels only. Most rooms have a balcony or terrace — ocean views on upper floors. Bungalows are next to the hotel, and each has a living room, kitchen, and bedroom with two double beds. The Restaurant Santa Fe is one of the best on the southern Pacific coast (see the "Dining in Puerto Escondido" section, later in this chapter).

Calle del Morro s/n. ☎ *954-582-0170 or 954-582-0266. Fax: 954-582-0260. E-mail:* info@hotelsantafe.com.mx. *69 units. Free parking. Rack rates: High season $95.50 double, $120 bungalow; low season $56 double, $100 bungalow. AE, MC, V.*

Paraíso Escondido
$$–$$$ Tourist Zone

The curious collection of Mexican folk art, masks, religious art, and paintings on the walls make this eclectic inn an exercise in Mexican magic realism in addition to a tranquil place to stay. An inviting pool, surrounded by gardens, Adirondack chairs, a restaurant, and a fountain, has a commanding view of the bay — but it's several blocks to the main public beach in town. Each room has one double and one twin bed, a built-in desk, and a cozy balcony or terrace with French doors. Each has a slightly different decorative accent, and all are very clean. The suites, added in 2000, have a much more deluxe decor than the rooms and feature recessed lighting, desks set into bay windows with French-paned windows, living areas, and large private balconies. The penthouse suite has its own whirlpool tub and kitchenette plus a tile chessboard inlaid in the floor and murals adorning the walls — it's the owners' former apartment. Limited free parking is available in front of the hotel.

Calle Union 10. ☎ *954-582-0444. 25 units. Rack rates: $75 double, $150 suite. No credit cards.*

Rockaway Surfer Village
$ **Playa Zicatela**

Facing Playa Zicatela, this surfer's sanctuary offers very clean — and very cheap — accommodations geared for surfers. Every cabaña is equipped with a private bath, as well as floor fans and mosquito nets. In the central courtyard, there's a good-size swimming pool, palapa bar, and a 24-hour soft-drink fridge.

Calle del Morro s/n. ☎ *954-582-0668. Fax: 954-582-2420. 14 units. Rack rates: High season $25 double; low season $18 double. No credit cards.*

Settling into Puerto Escondido

Puerto Escondido's very small **airport** is about 4km (2.5 miles) north of the center of town near Playa Bacocho. A trip on the collective **minibus** to your hotel is $2.25 per person. **Transportes Terrestres** sells *colectivo* tickets to the airport through **Turismo Dimar Travel Agency** (☎ **954-582-1551;** Fax: 954-582-0737) on Avenida Pérez Gasga (the pedestrian-only zone) next to Hotel Casa Blanca. The minibus can pick you up at your hotel.

Flying directly into Puerto Escondido can sometimes be a challenge. I find it generally easier (and less expensive) to fly into the Huatulco airport via scheduled or charter flights. An airport taxi costs $85 between Huatulco and Puerto Escondido. If you can find a local taxi, rather than the government-chartered cabs, you can reduce this fare by about 50%, including the payment of a $5 mandatory airport exit tax. Frequent bus service also travels between the two destinations. **Budget Car Rental** has cars available for one-way travel to Puerto Escondido with an added drop charge of about $10. In Puerto Escondido, Budget is located at the entrance to Playa Bacocho (☎ **954-582-0312**). By car, the trip from Huatulco to Puerto Escondido takes just under two hours. Because the roads are unlit and frequently curvy through a mountainous zone, plan on traveling only during daylight hours.

Knowing your way around town

Looking out on the Bahía Principal and its beach, to your left is the eastern end of the bay consisting of a small beach, **Playa Marinero,** followed by rocks jutting into the sea. Beyond this is **Playa Zicatela,** unmistakably the main surfing beach. Playa Zicatela has really come into its own as the most popular area for visitors with restaurants, bungalows, surf shops, and hotels located well back from the shore-line. The western side of the bay, to your right, is about a mile long with a lighthouse and low green hills descending to meet a long stretch of fine sand. Beaches on this end aren't quite as accessible by land as those to the east, but hotels are overcoming this difficulty by con-structing beach clubs accessed by steep private roads and Jeep shuttles.

The town of Puerto Escondido has roughly an east-west orientation with the long Playa Zicatela turning sharply southeast. Residential areas behind (east of) Playa Zicatela tend to have unpaved streets; the older town (with paved streets) is north of the Carretera Costera (Highway 200). The streets are numbered — Avenida Oaxaca serves as the dividing line between east *(este)* and west *(oeste),* and Avenida Hidalgo acts as the divider between north *(norte)* and south *(sur).*

North of Zicatela is the old town, through which Avenida Pérez Gasga makes a loop. Part of this loop is a paved, pedestrians-only zone, known as the *Adoquín.* Hotels, shops, restaurants, bars, travel agencies, and other services are all conveniently located here. In the morning, taxis, delivery trucks, and private vehicles are allowed to drive here, but at noon it's closed off to all but foot traffic.

Avenida Pérez Gasga angles down from the highway at the east end of the *Adoquín;* on the west, where the *Adoquín* terminates, it climbs in a wide northward curve to cross the highway, after which it becomes Avenida Oaxaca.

The beaches — Playa Principal in the center of town and Marinero and Zicatela southeast of the town center — are interconnected. Walking from one to the other crossing behind the separating rocks is easy. Puerto Angelito, Carrizalillo, and Bacocho beaches are west of town, and you can reach them by road or water. Playa Bacocho hosts the few more-expensive hotels located in Puerto Escondido.

Getting around Puerto Escondido

Almost everything is within walking distance of the *Adoquín.* **Taxis** are inexpensive when traveling around town; call ☎ **954-582-0990** for service.

Hiring a boat is easy, but you can walk beside the sea from Playa Principal to the tiny beach of Puerto Angelito, though it's a bit of a hike.

Fast Facts: Puerto Escondido

Area Code

The telephone area code is **954**.

Banks, ATMs, and Currency Exchange

Banamex, Bancomer, Bancrear, and Banco Bital all have branches in town, and all exchange money during business hours; each bank's hours vary, but you can generally find one of them open Monday to Saturday 8 a.m. to 7 p.m. ATMs and currency-exchange offices are also located throughout town.

Business Hours

Most offices maintain traditional Mexican hours of operation (10 a.m. to 2 p.m. and from 4 p.m. to 8 p.m. daily), but shops remain open throughout the day. Offices tend to close on Saturday and Sunday. Shops are usually open on Saturday but still generally respect the tradition of closing on Sunday.

Hospitals

Try **Unidad Medico-Quirurgica del Sur** (Avenida Oaxaca 113; ☎ 954-582-1288), which offers 24-hour emergency services and has an English-speaking staff and doctors.

Information

The **State Tourist Office, SEDETUR** (☎ 954-582-0175), is about 1km (½ mile) from the airport at the corner of Carretera Costera and Bulevar Benito Juárez. It's open Monday to Friday 9 a.m. to 7 p.m. and Saturday 10 a.m. to 2 p.m. A kiosk at the airport is open for incoming flights during high season, and another, near the west end of the paved Tourist Zone, is open Monday to Saturday 9 a.m. to 2 p.m.

Internet Access

An excellent cybercafe is on the second floor of **Un Tigre Azul** (☎ 954-582-2855) on the *Adoquín.* It charges $2 per half hour or $4 per hour for Internet access; hours are

Monday to Friday 11 a.m. to 11 p.m. and Saturday to Sunday from 3 to 11 p.m. **Cyber-café** is a small, extremely busy Internet service at the entrance to the Bungalows and Cabañas Acuario (Calle de Morro s/n; ☎ 954-582-0357, ask for the cybercafe). It's open daily 8 a.m. until 9 p.m. The rate to get online is $1.50 for 15 minutes, $3 for a half hour, or $5 per hour.

Pharmacy

Farmacia de Mas Ahorro, on Primera Norte corner and Segunda Poniente (☎ 954-582-1911), is open 24 hours a day.

Post Office

The post office is on Avenida Oaxaca at the corner of Avenida 7 Norte (☎ 954-582-0959). It's open Monday to Friday 8 a.m. to 3 p.m.

Safety

Depending on whom you talk to, you need to be wary of potential beach muggings, primarily at night. However, the hope is that the new public lighting at Playa Principal and Playa Zicatela goes a long way in preventing these incidents. Local residents say most incidents happen after tourists overindulge and then go for a midnight stroll along the beach. Puerto Escondido is so casual that letting your guard down is easy, but don't carry valuables, and use common sense and normal precautions. Also, respect the power of the magnificent waves here. Drownings occur all too frequently.

Taxes

A 15% IVA value added tax (IVA) is charged on goods and services, and it's generally included in the posted price.

Taxis

Taxis are easy to find around town. They're also inexpensive, generally costing $1 to $3 for various parts of town; call ☎ 954-582-0990 for service.

Telephone

Numerous businesses offer long-distance telephone service. Many of these establishments are along the *Adoquín,* and several offer credit-card convenience.

Avoid the phone booths that have signs in English advising you to call home using a special 800 number — these are absolute rip-offs and can cost as much as $20 per minute. The least expensive way to call is by using a Telmex (LADATEL) prepaid phone card, available at most pharmacies and mini-supers, using the official Telmex (Lada) public phones. Remember, in Mexico, you need to dial 001 prior to a number to reach the United States, and you need to preface long-distance calls within Mexico by dialing 01.

Time Zone

Puerto Escondido operates on central standard time, although Mexico's observance of daylight savings time varies somewhat from that in the United States.

Dining in Puerto Escondido

I find dining in Puerto Escondido an absolute pleasure. The food is excellent — generous portions display innovative flavorings at some of the lowest prices I've ever seen anywhere. The atmosphere is exceedingly casual — but don't let that throw you. I've enjoyed some very memorable meals in these funky settings, starting with the mango éclairs at **El Cafecito.** In fact, Puerto Escondido is even more casual than Mexico's other beach resorts — no need to even think about bringing dressy attire or jackets. Personally, I think that Playa Zicatela has the highest concentration of great eats.

All the restaurants I include in the listings are arranged alphabetically with their location and general price category noted. Remember that tips generally run about 15%, and most wait-staff really depend on these for their income, so be generous if the service warrants.

In addition to the places I list in this section, the *palapa* restaurants on Playa Zicatela are a Puerto Escondido tradition for early-morning surfer breakfasts or casual dining and drinks by the sea at night. One of the most popular *palapa* restaurants is **Los Tíos,** offering very economical prices and surfer-sized portions.

Cabo Blanco
$ **Playa Zicatela   INTERNATIONAL**

"Where Legends Are Born" is the logo at this beachfront restaurant, and the local crowd craves chef Gary's special sauces that top his grilled fish, shrimp, steaks, and ribs. Favorites include his dill-Dijon mustard, wine-fennel, and Thai-curry sauces. But you can't count on these sauces always being on the menu because Gary buys what's fresh and then goes from there. An added bonus is that Cabo Blanco turns into a hot bar on Playa Zicatela with live music each Thursday and Saturday after 11 p.m.

Gary's wife Roxana and a top-notch team of bartenders keeps the crowd well served and well behaved.

Calle del Morro s/n. ☎ 954-582-0337. Reservations not accepted. Main courses: $4–$10. V. Open: Daily 6 p.m.–2 a.m.

Carmen's La Patisserie

$ **Playa Marinero   FRENCH PASTRY/SANDWICHES/COFFEE**

This tiny, excellent cafe/bakery has a steady and loyal clientele. Carmen's baked goods are unforgettable and go quickly, so arrive early for the best selection. La Patisserie is across the street from the Hotel Flor de María.

Playa Marinero. No phone. Pastries: $.50–$1.25; sandwiches $1.75–$2.25. No credit cards. Open: Mon–Sat 7 a.m.–3 p.m.; Sun 7 a.m. to noon.

El Cafecito

$ **Playa Zicatela   FRENCH PASTRY/SEAFOOD/VEGETARIAN/ COFFEE**

Carmen's second shop, with a motto of "Big waves, strong coffee!" opened several years ago on Playa Zicatela. Featuring all the attractions of Carmen's La Patisserie (see the previous entry), El Cafecito is also open for lunch and dinner. This restaurant actually spans two facing corners; the northern corner is set up more for coffee or a light snack with ocean-front bistro-style seating. The southern corner offers a more relaxed setting with wicker chairs and Oaxacan cloth-topped tables set under a *palapa* roof. Giant shrimp dinners are priced under $5, and the creative, daily specials are always a sure bet. An oversized mug of cappuccino is $1, a fresh and filling fruit smoothie goes for $1.50, and her mango éclairs — I'd pay any price — are a steal at $1.

Calle del Morro s/n. No phone. Reservations not accepted. Main courses: $1.75–$4.75; pastries $.50–$1.25. No credit cards. Open: Wed–Mon 6 a.m.–10 p.m.

Gota de Vida

$ **Playa Zicatela   VEGETARIAN/COFFEE**

This popular vegetarian restaurant, located just in front of the Bungalows Acuario, is generally packed — it's known for healthy food, ample portions, and low prices. Under a *palapa* roof and facing Playa Zicatela, Gota de Vida offers an extensive menu that includes fruit smoothies, espresso drinks, herbal teas, and a complete juice bar. These folks make their own tempeh, tofu, pasta, and whole grain bread. Creative vegetarian offerings are based on Mexican favorites like chiles rellenos, cheese enchiladas, and bean tostadas. Fresh seafood is also featured.

Calle del Morro s/n. No phone. Reservations not accepted. Main courses: $1.50–$4.50. No credit cards. Open: Daily 10 a.m.–11 p.m.

La Galería

$ Adoquín   ITALIAN

By far the best Italian restaurant in town, La Galería combines great food in an atmosphere of art, available for sale by local and regional artists. Open for breakfast, lunch, and dinner, the eatery is known for its brick-oven pizzas, homemade with fresh ingredients. La Galería also has a full selection of pastas, including exceptional lasagna. One of the *Adoquín*'s longstanding restaurants, La Galería recently opened a second location in Playa Zicatela (next to Casa Babylon and Arcoiris Hotel). Beautifully decorated with tiny mosaic tiles on the bar and in the bathrooms, the second Galería serves up the same great fare in a beautiful garden setting. Plans were progressing during my last visit to add an adjoining nightclub to the Zicatela locale.

Av. Pérez Gasga s/n. ☎ 954-582-2039. Reservations not accepted. Main courses: $4–$9. No credit cards. Open: Daily 8 a.m.–11 p.m.

María's Restaurant

$ Playa Marinero   INTERNATIONAL

This first-floor, open-air, hotel dining room near the beach is popular with the locals. The menu changes daily and features specials such as María Francato's fresh homemade pasta dishes. María's is in the Hotel Flor de María, just steps from the center of town and up a sandy road from Playa Marinero on an unnamed street at the eastern end of the beach.

Playa Marinero. ☎ 954-582-0536. Reservations not needed. Main courses: $3–$9; breakfast $2.50. MC, V. Open: Daily 8–11:30 a.m., noon to 2 p.m., and 6–10 p.m.

Restaurant Santa Fe

$–$$ Playa Zicatela   INTERNATIONAL

The atmosphere here (in the Hotel Santa Fe) is classic and casual with great views of the sunset and Playa Zicatela. Big pots of palms are scattered around, and fresh flowers grace the tables — all beneath a lofty *palapa* roof. The shrimp dishes are a bargain relative to the rest of the world, but at $15, they're a little higher-priced than in the rest of the town's eateries. Perfectly grilled tuna, served with homemade french-fried potatoes and whole-grain bread, is an incredible meal deal for under $7. A *nopal* (cactus leaf) salad on the side ($2) is a perfect complement. Vegetarian dishes are reasonably priced and creatively adapted from traditional Mexican and Italian dishes. A favorite is the house specialty, chiles rellenos. The bar offers an excellent selection of tequilas.

Calle del Morro s/n. ☎ 954-582-0170. Reservations recommended during high season. Main courses: $5–$15; breakfast $2.50–$6; AE, MC, V. Open: Daily 7 a.m.–11 p.m.

Having Fun on and off the Beach

Playa Principal is the main beach in town where small boats are available for fishing and tour services. Playa Principal and the adjacent **Playa Marinero** are the best swimming beaches. Beach chairs and sun shades rent for about $2, a charge that may be waived if you order food or drinks from the restaurants that offer them.

Playa Zicatela, a world-class surf spot, adjoins Playa Marinero about 2.5km (1.5 miles) from Puerto Escondido's town center and extends to the southeast for several miles. Due to the size and strength of the waves here, it's not a swimming beach, and only experienced surfers should attempt to ride Zicatela's powerful waves. A surfing competition is held each August, and Fiesta Puerto Escondido, held for at least three days each November, also celebrates Puerto Escondido's renowned waves. (The tourism office can supply exact dates and details; call ☎ 954-582-0175.) Beginning surfers often start out at Playa Marinero before graduating to Zicatela's awesome waves.

New, stadium-style lighting has recently been installed in both of these beach areas in an attempt to crack down on nocturnal beach muggings. The lights have diminished the appeal of the Playa Principal restaurants — you look into bright lights rather than at the nighttime sea now. Lifeguard service has recently been added to Playa Zicatela.

Barter with one of the fishermen on the main beach for a ride to **Playa Manzanillo** and **Puerto Angelito,** two beaches separated by a rocky outcropping (the best way to get here is by boat). Here, and at other small coves just west of town, swimming is safe and the overall atmosphere is calmer than it is in town. You can also find *palapas,* hammock rentals, and snorkeling equipment — the clear blue water is perfect for snorkeling. Enjoy fresh fish, tamales, and other Mexican dishes cooked right at the beach by local entrepreneurs. Puerto Angelito is also accessible by a dirt road that's a short distance from town, so it tends to be busier.

Playa Bacocho is on a shallow cove farther to the northwest and is best reached by taxi or boat rather than walking. It's also the location of Coco's Beach Club at the Best Western Posada Real. It's open to the public for a cover charge of $2.50, which gains you access to the pools, food and beverage service, and facilities.

An unusual spa experience

For terrific massage services — the ideal answer to a day spent in pounding surf — **Espacio Meditativo Temazcalli** (Calle Temazcalli Esq. Av. Infraganti; ☎ 954-582-1023; www.temazcalli.com) is the place to go. A variety of therapeutic massages range in price from $12 to $22.

Body Beauty treatments (priced from $27 to $33) and facials ($27) are designed to minimize the effects of too much sun. Bioenergetic Balance Techniques and the indigenous Mexican Temazcal steam bath (both individual and group) are treatments designed to purify body and soul. The center is a tranquil haven, lushly landscaped, with the sound of the nearby ocean prevalent in the treatment areas. On full moon nights, the spa has a special group Temazcal ceremony, a truly fascinating experience!

Embarking on an excursion

Ana's Eco Tours, located in Un Tigre Azul, an art gallery and Internet cafe on the *Adoquín* (☎ **954-582-2001;** E-mail: ana@anasecotours.com), is an exceptional provider of ecologically oriented tour services. "Ana" Marquez was born in the small, nearby, mountain village of Jamiltepec and has an intimate knowledge of the area's customs, people, flora, and fauna. She and her expert guides lead small groups on both eco-adventures and cultural explorations. Tours into the surrounding mountains include a five-hour horseback excursion up to the jungle region of the Chatino **healing hot springs** and a trip to **Nopala,** a Chatino mountain village, and a neighboring coffee plantation. An all-day trip to **Jamiltepec** (a small, traditional regional Indian community called a Mixtex village) offers the opportunity to experience day-to-day life in an authentic village. The visit includes stops at a market, the church, the cemetery, and the homes of local artisans.

Turismo Dimar Travel Agency (☎ **954-582-1551;** Fax: 954-582-0734), on the landward side of the *Adoquín,* is an excellent source of information and can arrange all types of tours and travel. It's open daily 8 a.m. to 10 p.m. Manager Gaudencio Díaz speaks English and can arrange individualized tours or more standard ones such as **Michael Malone's Hidden Voyages Ecotours.** Malone, a Canadian ornithologist, takes you on a dawn or sunset trip to **Manialtepec Lagoon,** a bird-filled mangrove lagoon about 19km (12 miles) northwest of Puerto Escondido. The cost is $32 and includes a stop on a secluded beach for a swim.

One of the most popular all-day tours offered by both companies is a trip to **Chacahua Lagoon National Park,** about 68km (42 miles) west of Puerto, at a cost of $38 with Dimar or $25 with Ana's. These excursions are true eco-tours — small groups treading lightly. You visit a beautiful sandy spit of beach and the lagoon, which has an incredible array of birds and flowers including black orchids. Locals provide fresh barbecued fish on the beach. If you know Spanish and get information from the tourism office, staying overnight under a small *palapa* is possible, but bring plenty of insect repellent.

An interesting and slightly out-of-the-ordinary excursion is **Aventura Submarina** (Avenida Pérez Gasga 601A, in front of the tourism office; ☎ **954-582-2353**). Jorge, who speaks fluent English and is a certified scuba instructor, guides individuals and small groups of qualified divers along the Coco trench just offshore. The price is $55 for a two-tank dive. This outfit offers a refresher scuba course at no extra charge. Jorge also arranges surface activities such as deep-sea fishing, surfing, and trips to lesser-known yet nearby swimming beaches.

Fishermen keep their colorful *pangas* (small boats) on the beach beside the *Adoquín*. A **fisherman's tour** around the coastline in a *panga* costs about $35, but a ride to Playa Zicatela or Puerto Angelito is only $10. Most hotels offer or gladly arrange tours to meet your needs.

Planning a side trip to Puerto Angel and Playa Zipolite

About 80km (50 miles) southeast of Puerto Escondido and 48km (30 miles) northwest of the Bahías de Huatulco is the tiny fishing port of **Puerto Angel** (not to be confused with Puerto Angelito, which is a beach in Puerto Escondido). Puerto Angel, with its beautiful beaches, unpaved streets, and budget hotels, is popular with the international backpacking set and travelers seeking an inexpensive and restful vacation. Its small bay and several inlets offer peaceful swimming and good snorkeling. The village follows a slow and simple way of life: Fishermen leave very early in the morning and return with their catch by late forenoon.

The golden sands and peaceful village life of Puerto Angel are the reasons to visit. **Playa Principal,** the main beach, lies between the Mexican navy base and the pier that's home to the local fishing fleet. Near the pier, fishermen pull their colorful boats on the beach and unload their catch in the late morning while trucks wait to haul it off to processing plants in Veracruz. The rest of the beach seems light years away from the world of work and purpose. Except on Mexican holidays, it's relatively deserted.

The beaches around Puerto Escondido and Puerto Angel (located between Huatulco and Puerto Escondido) are important **turtle nesting grounds** for the endangered Ridley sea turtle. During the summer months, tourists can sometimes see the turtles laying eggs or observe the hatchlings trekking to the sea. **Playa Escobilla,** near Puerto Escondido, and **Playa Barra de la Cruz,** near Puerto Angel, seem to be the favored nesting grounds of this species.

In 1991, the Mexican government established the Centro Mexicano la Tortuga, known locally as the **Turtle Museum,** for the study and life enhancement of the turtle. Examples of all species of marine turtles living in Mexico are on view, plus six species of freshwater turtles and two species of land turtles. The center is located on **Playa Mazunte** near the town of the same name. Hours are 10 a.m. to 4:30 p.m. Tuesday to Saturday and Sunday 10 a.m. to 2 p.m.; entry is $2.50.

Mazunte is also home to a unique shop that sells naturally produced shampoos, bath oils, and other personal-care products. The local community women make and package all the products as part of a project to replace the income lost from turtle poaching. The products are excellent in quality, and purchasing them goes a long way in ensuring the cessation of turtle poaching in the community. Buses go to Mazunte from Puerto Angel about every half-hour, and a taxi ride is around $5. You can fit this trip in with a visit to Playa Zipolite, the next one closer to Puerto Angel.

Playa Panteón is the main swimming and snorkeling beach. "Cemetery Beach," ominous as that sounds, is about a 15-minute walk from the center of town. Just walk straight through town on the main street that skirts the beach. The *panteón* (cemetery), which is also worth a visit with its brightly colored tombstones backed by equally brilliant blooming vines, is on the right.

In Playa Panteón, some of the *palapa* restaurants and a few of the hotels rent snorkeling and scuba gear and can arrange boat trips, but they all tend to be rather expensive. Check the quality and the condition of the gear — particularly scuba gear — that you rent.

Playa Zipolite and its village are 6km (4 miles) down a paved road from Puerto Angel. Taxis charge around $1 to $1.50 (taxis are relatively inexpensive here), or you can catch a *colectivo* on the main street in the town center and share the cost.

Zipolite is well known as a good surf break and nude beach. Although public nudity (including topless sunbathing) is technically against the law throughout Mexico, it's allowed here — one of only a handful of beaches in Mexico to allow it. This sort of open-mindedness has attracted an increasing number of young European travelers. Most sunbathers concentrate beyond a large rock outcropping at the far end of the beach. Police occasionally patrol the area, but they're much more intent on searching for drug users than harassing au natural sunbathers. Spots to tie up a hammock and a few *palapa* restaurants where you can grab a light lunch and a cold beer dot the beach.

In Zipolite, as in the rest of Mexico, the purchase, sale, or use of drugs is definitely against the law, no matter what the local custom may be (and their use is relatively customary here). Because the ocean currents are quite strong (that's why the surf is so good!), a number of drownings have occurred over the years — so, know your limits.

If you're traveling here by car, you arrive via Highway 200 from the north or south. Take coastal Highway 175 inland to Puerto Angel. The road is well marked with signs leading to Puerto Angel. From either Huatulco or Puerto Escondido, the trip takes about an hour.

Taxis are a readily available to take you to Puerto Angel, Playa Zipolite, the Huatulco airport, or Puerto Escondido for a reasonable price.

Shopping in Puerto Escondido

The *Adoquín* sports a row of tourist shops selling straw hats, post-cards, and Puerto Escondido T-shirts, and a few excellent shops feature Guatemalan, Oaxacan, and Balinese clothing and art. You can also get a tattoo or rent surfboards and bodyboards here. Pharmacies and mini-markets for basic necessities are interspersed among the shops, hotels, restaurants, and bars.

The largest of these mini-marts is **Oh! Mar** (Avenida Pérez Gasga 502; ☎ 954-582-3056), which not only sells anything you'd need for a day at the beach but also sells phone (LADATEL) cards, stamps, and Cuban cigars. Plus, the store has a mail drop box and arranges fishing tours.

During high season, businesses and shops are generally open all day, but during low season, they close between 2 and 5 p.m. Some highlights along the *Adoquín* include

- ✔ **Bazaar Santa Fe** (in the Hotel Santa Fe lobby, on Playa Zicatela, Calle del Morro s/n; ☎ 954-582-0170), which sells antiques including vintage Oaxacan embroidered clothing, jewelry, and religious artifacts.

- ✔ **Central Surf** shops are located on the *Adoquín* (☎ 954-582-0568) and on Playa Zicatela (Calle Morro s/n; ☎ 954-582-2285). The stores rent and sell surfboards and related gear and offer surf lessons.

- ✔ **Un Tigre Azul** (Avenida Pérez Gasga s/n; ☎ 954-582-2954) is the only true art gallery in town. It features quality works of art and a cafe-bar, plus Internet service upstairs.

- ✔ Just in front of the Rockaway Resort on Playa Zicatela, a 24-hour **mini-super** (no phone) sells the basic necessities: beer, suntan lotion, and basic food supplies.

Enjoying the nightlife

As hot as the daytime surf action is in Puerto Escondido, the nocturnal offerings offer some stiff competition that can make catching those first morning waves somewhat of a challenge.

Sunset-watching is a ritual to plan your day around, and good lookout points abound here. Watch the surfers at Zicatela and catch up on local gossip at **La Galería** (Calle del Morro s/n; ☎ 958-582-0432), upstairs on the third floor of the Arcoiris hotel. La Galería has a nightly happy hour (with live music during high season) from 5 to 7 p.m. For other great sunset spots, head to the **Hotel Santa Fe** at the junction of playas Zicatela and Marinero or the rooftop bar of **Hotel Flor de María.** For a more tranquil, romantic setting, take a cab or walk half an hour or so west to the **Best Western Posada Real.** The hotel's cliff-top lawn is a perfect sunset perch. You can also climb down the cliff (or take the Posada Real's shuttle bus) to Coco's on the beach below.

When it comes to bars and clubs, Puerto has a nightlife that satisfies anyone dedicated to late nights and good music. Along the *Adoquín,* here are some spots that may lure you in:

- ✔ **Bar Fly, The Blue Iguana,** and **Rayos X** cater to a younger surf crowd with DJs spinning alternative, house, and techno tunes.

- ✔ The **Bucanero Bar and Grill** has a good-sized bar and outdoor patio fronting Playa Principal.

- ✔ **Montezuma's Revenge** has live bands usually playing contemporary Latin American music.

- ✔ **Son y la Rumba** is home to live jazz featuring its house band with Andria Garcia playing each night 8 to 11 p.m. with a $1 cover. Wednesdays through Saturdays, it switches over to DJs playing house music after 11 p.m. This club is located beneath the Un Tigre Azul, on the western end of the *Adoquín.*

- ✔ **El Tubo** is an open-air, beachside disco just west of Restaurant Alicia on the *Adoquín.*

Out on Zicatela, don't miss **Cabo Blanco** (see the "Dining in Puerto Escondido" section, earlier in this chapter), where local musicians, alternating with DJs, get together and jam Thursdays and Saturdays during high season. An added benefit is the complimentary snacks with drink purchase, in the style of Mexico's cantina tradition. **Split Coco,** just a few doors down, has live music on Tuesdays and Fridays and TV sports on other nights. It has one of the most popular happy hours on the beach and serves barbecue as well.

Although it was under construction during my last visit, the new nightclub adjoining **La Galería** on Playa Zicatela should prove to be a great addition to this area. It plans to feature reggae and beach tunes to get you in the mood for the next day's surf action.

Most nightspots are open until 3 a.m. or until the customers leave.

Part IX

Los Cabos and Southern Baja

©RICHTENNANT

MEXICAN BEACH RESORT ACTIVITY TO AVOID

SWIM WITH THE GIANT SQUID

SWIM WITH THE MORAY EELS

SWIM WITH THE JELLYFISH

SWIM WITH OCTOP...

"SINCE WE LOST THE DOLPHINS, BUSINESS HASN'T BEEN QUITE THE SAME."

In this part . . .

Cabo San Lucas, San José del Cabo, and the stretch of coastline (the Corridor) that connects them are collectively known as Los Cabos (The Capes). They're located at the tip of Mexico's Baja Peninsula. "The end of the line," "the last resort," and "no man's land" are all terms used in the past to describe Mexico's remote but diverse Baja Sur, an exquisite setting that artfully blends desert landscapes with vibrant seascapes. With seven championship golf courses open for play, golf has overtaken sport-fishing as the main draw here. Other activities you can find in Cabos to keep you busy are sea kayaking, whale-watching, diving, surfing, and hiking.

In the next four chapters, you discover the differences between the three distinct parts of Los Cabos and their unique attractions. And you get clued in on the best places to stay and dine, great things to do, and the craziest spots for nighttime diversion.

Chapter 28

The Lowdown on the Hotel Scene in Los Cabos

By Lynne Bairstow

. . . .

In This Chapter

▶ Laying out the hotel locations

▶ Reviewing the top hotel choices in Los Cabos

. . . .

*P*art of the attraction of the towns of Los Cabos — on the tip of the Baja Peninsula — seems to be the feeling that they're an extension of Southern California's brand of American style — luxury accommodations, golf courses, shopping, franchise restaurants, and a spirited nightlife. **Cabo San Lucas** has retained its boisterous, party-town traditions, and **San José del Cabo** still has the appearance and ambiance of a quaint Mexican town, though it has become gentrified in recent years.

Nearly 30km (18 miles) of smooth highway, known as **the Corridor,** lie between the two Cabos. Along this stretch of pavement, major new resorts, including some of the world's finest golf courses and residential communities, have sprung up. And the area's signature natural beauty continues to beckon: Dozens of pristine coves and inlets with a wealth of marine life just offshore greet visitors.

The Los Cabos area has earned a deserved reputation for being much higher priced than other Mexican resorts. Although a boom in new hotel construction has occurred, these new properties have all been luxury resorts — solidifying Los Cabos' higher average room prices, not adjusting prices downward with the added supply of rooms. The other factor driving up prices here is that compared to mainland Mexico, little agricultural activity takes place in Baja; most foodstuffs (and other daily required items) must be shipped into the area. U.S. dollars are the preferred currency here, and seeing price listings in dollars rather than pesos isn't uncommon.

In this chapter, I review the two main towns, the Corridor between them, and the types of hotel rooms you're likely to find in each as well as the pros and cons of staying in each area. Then, I run down a selection of my favorite places to stay in Los Cabos. The accommodation options are so varied here that no matter your taste or budget, you're sure to find the perfect fit for a satisfying vacation.

Choosing a Location

Los Cabos is actually three destinations in one — the traditional town of San José, the rowdy party town of Cabo San Lucas, and the luxury-lined corridor between the two. Where you stay impacts your overall experience, although you can move around from one location to another — for a price. My hotel recommendations extend through this entire area.

San José del Cabo, located closest to the airport, has pastel cottages and flowering trees lining its narrow streets, retaining the air of a provincial Mexican town. Originally founded in 1730 by Jesuit missionaries, it's the seat of the Los Cabos government and the center of the region's business community. The main square, adorned with a wrought-iron bandstand and shaded benches, faces the cathedral, which was built on the site of an early mission.

San José is becoming increasingly sophisticated. A collection of noteworthy cafes, art galleries, and intriguing small inns adds a newly refined flavor to the central downtown area. Still, San José is the best choice for travelers who want to travel to this paradoxical Mexican landscape but still be aware that they're in Mexico. Most of the hotels I list here are found in the town — that is, away from the beaches of San José, but not so far away that it's an inconvenience.

The Corridor between the towns of San José del Cabo and Cabo San Lucas contains some of Mexico's most lavish resorts designed as self-contained dream getaways. Most growth in this area is occurring along the Corridor, which has already become a major international locale for championship golf. The three major resort areas are Palmilla, Cabo Real, and Cabo del Sol. Each location is a self-enclosed community with golf courses, elegant hotels, and million-dollar homes.

If you plan to explore the region while staying at a Corridor hotel, consider renting a car for at least a day or two for easier access; cars are available at the hotels. Even if you're not staying here, the beaches and dining options are worth the visit. All the hotels along the Corridor qualify as "very expensive" selections. Golf and fishing packages are available at most resorts.

The hundreds of luxury hotel rooms along the Corridor to the north of Cabo San Lucas have transformed the very essence of this formerly rustic and rowdy outpost. Although it still retains a boisterous nightlife that runs counter to the pampered services that surround it, Cabo San Lucas is no longer the simple town John Steinbeck wrote about and enjoyed. Once legendary for the big-game fish that lurk beneath the deep blue sea, Cabo San Lucas now draws more people for its nearby fairways and greens — and the world-class golf played on them. Today, it caters to a traveler getting away for a long weekend or indulgent stay of sport and relaxation. Cabo San Lucas has become Mexico's most elite resort destination.

Travelers here enjoy a growing roster of adventure-oriented activities, and playtime doesn't end when the sun goes down. The nightlife here is as hot as the desert in July and oddly casual, having grown up away from the higher-end hotels. It remains the raucous, playful party scene that helped put Cabo on the map. A collection of popular restaurants and bars, spread along Cabo's main street, stay open and active until the morning's first fishing charters head out to sea. Despite the growth in diversions, Cabo remains more or less a "one stoplight" town with most everything located along the main strip within easy walking distance.

Budget accommodations are scarce in Cabo San Lucas, but a growing number of small inns and B&Bs, with several notable ones, have opened in the past few years. Because most of the larger hotels are well maintained, and packages are available through travel agents, I focus on the smaller, more unique accommodations available in Cabo San Lucas.

Best Accommodations in Los Cabos

There's more demand than supply for hotel rooms in the Corridor, so prices tend to be higher than equivalent accommodations in other parts of Mexico. San José has only a handful of budget hotels, so call ahead for reservations if you want economical accommodations. A new trend throughout the region is toward smaller inns, or B&Bs, offering stylish accommodations in town. The beachfront Hotel Zone in San José often offers package deals that bring room rates down to the moderate range, especially during summer months. Shop around or check with your travel agent.

For each hotel, I include specific rack rates for two people spending one night in a double room during high season (Christmas to Easter), unless otherwise indicated. Keep in mind that summer rates are about 20% less. *Rack rates* simply mean published rates, and tend to be the highest rate paid — you can do better, especially if you're purchasing a package that includes airfare (read Chapter 5 for tips on avoiding paying rack rates). Please refer to the Introduction of this book for an explanation of the price categories.

Many hotels double their normal rates during Christmas and Easter weeks. Note that some rates may seem much higher than others — until you realize that they're "all-inclusive" — meaning that your meals and beverages are included in the price of your stay. This rate also includes all tips and taxes and most activities and entertainment.

All hotels I list here have both air conditioning and TVs, unless otherwise indicated; if the review doesn't say anything to the contrary, you can safely assume that you can walk directly out of your hotel and onto the beach.

The Bungalows

$$ Cabo San Lucas

The Bungalows is one of the most special places to stay in Los Cabos. Each "bungalow" is a charming retreat decorated with authentic Mexican furnishings. Terra-cotta tiles, hand-painted sinks, wooded chests, blown glass, and other creative touches make you feel as if you're a guest at a friend's home rather than in a hotel. Each room has a kitchenette, a private bath, purified water, a TV with VCR, and designer bedding. The varied bungalows, which include eight one-bedrooms, two deluxe one-bedrooms, and six two-bedrooms, surround a lovely heated pool with cushioned lounges and tropical gardens — but the nearest beach is a few miles away. You can enjoy fountains and flowers throughout the grounds, and a brick-paved breakfast nook serves a complete gourmet breakfast daily including fresh-ground coffee and fresh juices. The breakfast nook is also where guests become friends and share travel tips and experiences. Under the warm and welcoming management, this is Cabo's most spacious and comfortable full-service inn with exceptionally helpful service. A 100% smoke-free environment, the property is located 5 blocks from downtown Cabo.

Miguel A. Herrera s/n, in front of Lienzo Charro. ☎ *888-424-**CABO** from the U.S., 624-143-5035, or 624-143-0585.* www.cabobungalows.com. *16 units. Street parking available. Rack rates: High season $95 double, $115–$125 suites; low season $79 double, $99–$110 suites. Rates include complimentary full gourmet breakfast. AE.*

Cabo Inn

$ Cabo San Lucas

This three-story hotel on a quiet street is a real find, and it keeps getting better. The Cabo Inn is a rare combination of low rates, extra-friendly management, and great, funky style — not to mention extra clean — but you're about a mile to the nearest public beach. Rooms are basic and very small — this inn was a bordello in a prior life. All rooms have upgraded furnishings and those on the lower level also have a minifridge. Muted desert colors add a spark of personality, and rooms come with either two twin beds or one queen bed. The rooms surround a courtyard

San José del Cabo Accommodations

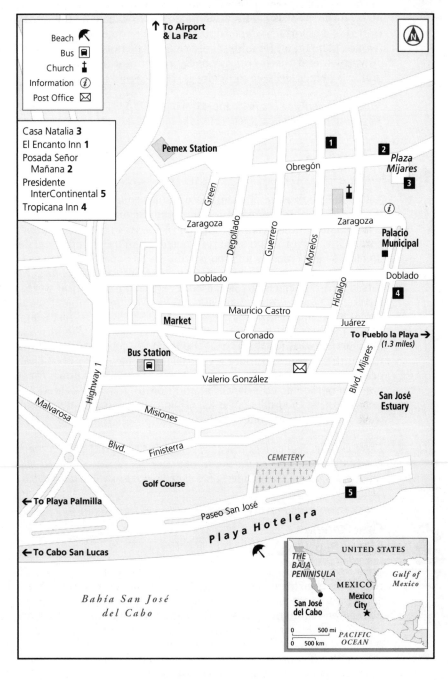

Beach
Bus
Church
Information
Post Office

Casa Natalia **3**
El Encanto Inn **1**
Posada Señor
    Mañana **2**
Presidente
    InterContinental **5**
Tropicana Inn **4**

To Airport
& La Paz

Pemex Station

Obregón

1

2 Plaza
Mijares

3

Green

Zaragoza

Zaragoza

Degollado

Guerrero

Morelos

Palacio
Municipal

Doblado

Hidalgo

Doblado

4

Mauricio Castro

Juárez

To Pueblo la Playa →
(1.3 miles)

Market

Coronado

Bus Station

Blvd. Mijares

San José
Estuary

Highway 1

Valerio González

Malvarosa

Misiones

Blvd. Finisterra

CEMETERY

← To Playa Palmilla

Golf Course

5

Paseo San José

Playa Hotelera

← To Cabo San Lucas

Bahía San José
del Cabo

THE
BAJA
PENINSULA

UNITED STATES

Gulf of
Mexico

MEXICO

San José
del Cabo

Mexico
City

0   500 mi
0   500 km

PACIFIC
OCEAN

where you can enjoy satellite TV, a barbecue grill, and free coffee. The third floor has a rooftop terrace with *palapa* and a small swimming pool. Also on this floor is Juan's Love Palace, also known as the honeymoon suite. It's a colorful, *palapa*-topped, open-air room with hanging *tapetes* (woven palm mats) for additional privacy. The hotel is just 2 blocks from downtown and the marina. A lively restaurant next door can deliver pitchers of margaritas and dinner to your room.

20 de Noviembre and Leona Vicario. ☎ *and fax: **624-143-0819**. 20 units. Street parking available. Rack rates: $58 double. Weekly rates are available. No credit cards.*

Casa del Mar
$$$$$ Corridor

A little-known treasure, this intimate resort is one of the best values along the Corridor, and it's one of my top recommendations for honeymooners. The hacienda-style building offers guests luxury accommodations complemented by an on-site spa. Located within the Cabo Real development, it's conveniently located by the 18-hole championship Cabo Real golf course. Gentle waterfalls lead to the adults-only pool area with hot tub, and a flowered path takes you farther along to the wide, sandy stretch of beach with a clear surf break. The Casa del Mar even has a "quiet area" on the lawn for those looking for a siesta. Guest rooms have a clean, bright feel to them with white marble floors, light wicker furnishings, separate sitting areas, and large hot tubs, plus separate showers on the raised bathroom level. Balconies have oversized chairs and ocean views beyond the pool. It's a romantic hotel known for its welcoming, personalized service. In addition to golf, two lighted Astroturf tennis courts, the full-service Avanti Spa, and a small but well-equipped workout room round out the offerings.

Carretera Transpeninsular (Hwy. 1), Km 19.5. ☎ ***800-221-8808*** *in the U.S., or 624-144-0030. Fax: 624-144-0034.* www.casadelmarmexico.com. *56 units. Rack rates: High season $470 double, $500 suite; low season $290 double, $340 suite. AE, MC, V.*

Casa Natalia
$$$$$ San José

This property may be Mexico's most exquisite boutique hotel, a former residence transformed into a beautiful combination of palms, waterfalls, and flowers that mirrors the beauty of the land. The inn itself is a completely renovated historic home, which now combines modern architecture with traditional Mexican touches. Each of the rooms has a name that reflects the decor such as Conchas (seashells), Azul (blue), or Talavera (ceramics); all have sliding glass doors that open onto small private terraces with hammocks and chairs, shaded by bougainvillea and bamboo. The two spa suites each have a private terrace with a hot tub and hammock. Thirty-nine tall California palms surround a small courtyard pool;

Cabo San Lucas Accommodations

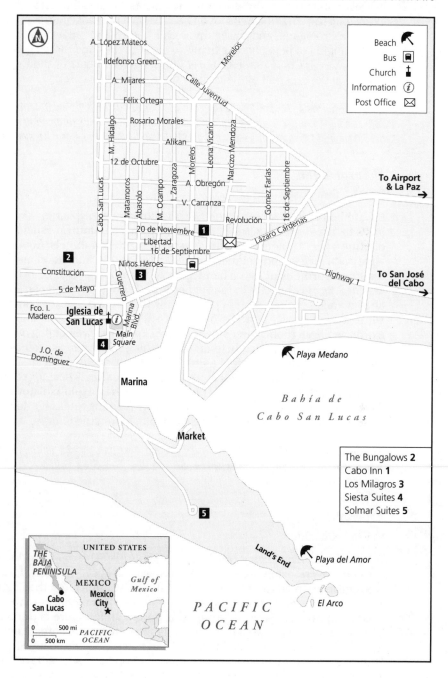

Beach ☂

Bus 🚌

Church ✝

Information ⓘ

Post Office ✉

A. López Mateos

Ildefonso Green

A. Mijares

Félix Ortega

Rosario Morales

Alikan

12 de Octubre

Morelos

Calle Juventud

M. Hidalgo

Leona Vicario

Narcizo Mendoza

Cabo San Lucas

Matamoros

Abasolo

M. Ocampo

I. Zaragoza

A. Obregón

V. Carranza

Gómez Farías

16 de Septiembre

Revolución

20 de Noviembre **1**

Libertad

16 de Septiembre

Niños Héroes

3

Constitución

5 de Mayo

Guerrero

Lázaro Cárdenas

To Airport & La Paz →

Highway 1

To San José del Cabo →

2

Fco. I. Madero

Iglesia de San Lucas ✝ ⓘ

Marina Blvd

Main Square

4

J.O. de Domínguez

Marina

Market

Playa Medano ☂

Bahía de Cabo San Lucas

The Bungalows **2**
Cabo Inn **1**
Los Milagros **3**
Siesta Suites **4**
Solmar Suites **5**

5

Land's End

☂ *Playa del Amor*

El Arco

UNITED STATES

THE BAJA PENINSULA

MEXICO

Gulf of Mexico

Cabo San Lucas

Mexico City ★

0 — 500 mi
0 — 500 km

PACIFIC OCEAN

PACIFIC OCEAN

the terraces face this view. The inn, however, is several miles from the nearest public beach, but does offer its guests a daily shuttle to a beach club along the corridor. In its favor, Casa Natalia offers its guests privacy, style, and romance, and it welcomes children 13 and older only. One of the highlights of being here is being so close to the exceptional gourmet restaurant, Mi Cocina (see Chapter 30). It's in the heart of the Bulevar Mijares action, just off of the central plaza.

Bulevar Mijares 4. ☎ *888-277-3814 in the U.S., or 624-142-5100. Fax: 624-142-5110.* www.casanatalia.com. *20 units including 2 spa suites. Rack rates: High season $295 double, $475 spa suite; low season $180 double, $305 spa suite. AE, MC, V.*

El Encanto Inn
$–$$$ San José

Located on a quiet street in the historic downtown district, this charming, small inn borders a grassy courtyard with a fountain and small pool, offering a very relaxing alternative to busy beachfront hotels. Rooms are all attractively — and uniquely — decorated with rustic wood and contemporary iron furniture. The nice-sized bathrooms have colorful tile accents. Rooms have two double beds, and suites have king-size beds and an added sitting room. A pool area with palapa bar and 14 poolside suites were recently added. These new suites have minibars and other extras, while all rooms offer satellite TV. El Encanto's welcoming owners, Cliff and Blanca, can also help arrange fishing packages, as well as golf and diving outings. Blanca is a lifelong resident of San José, so she's a great resource for information and dining tips. This inn is best for couples or singles looking for a peaceful place from which to explore historic San José. Continental breakfast is included with room rates. It's located between Obregón and Comonfort, half a block from the church.

Morelos 17. ☎ *624-142-0388.* www.elencantoinn.com. *26 units. Limited street parking available. Rack rates: $75 double, $85–$165 suites. Breakfast included. MC, V.*

Esperanza
$$$$ Corridor

Although this new luxury resort along Cabo's over-the-top Corridor sits on a bluff overlooking two small, rocky coves, the absence of a real beach doesn't seem to matter much to its guests — the hotel more than makes up for it in terms of pampering services and stylish details. Created by the famed Auberge Resorts group, this hotel's architecture is dramatic, elegant, and comfortable. The casitas and villas are spread across 17 acres, designed to resemble a Mexican village, and are connected to the resort facilities by stone footpaths. The top-floor suites have handmade palapa ceilings and a private outdoor whirlpool spa. All rooms are exceptionally spacious, with woven wicker and tropical wood furnishings, original art, rugs and fabrics in muted colors with jeweled-tone color accents, and Frette linens gracing the extra-comfortable feather

The Corridor Accommodations

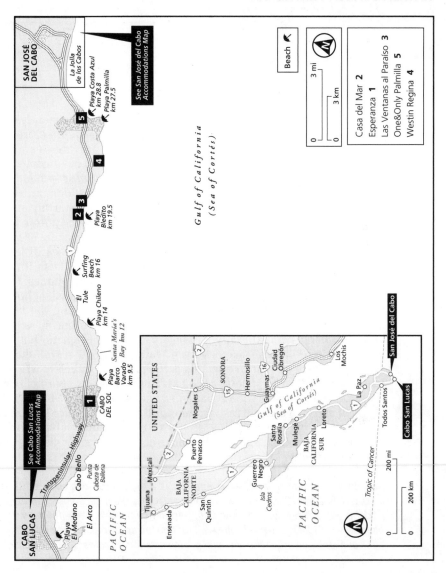

beds. Terraces are large, extending the living area to the outdoors, and all have hammocks and views of the Sea of Cortez. In-room amenities include fully stocked honor bars; plush bathrobes; high-speed Internet access; and entertainment centers with plasma televisions, stereos, and DVDs. The oversize bathrooms have a separate tub and shower with dual showerheads. You can also enjoy an acclaimed oceanfront restaurant, fitness center, full-service spa, gourmet market, infinity swimming pool, and the private beach.

Carretera Transpeninsular (Hwy. 1), Km 7, at Punta Ballena. ☎ *866-311-2226 in the U.S., or 624-145-6400. Fax: 624-145-6403.* www.esperanzaresort.com. *50 suites and 6 villas. Valet parking. Rack rates: High season $575–$950 double, $3,500–$5,000 villas; low season $350–$750 double, $2,000–$3,000 villas. AE, MC, V.*

Las Ventanas al Paraíso
$$$$$ Corridor

Mexico's most renowned luxury hotel, Las Ventanas consistently offers luxury accommodations and attention to detail. The architecture, with adobe structures and rough-hewn wood accents, provides a soothing complement to the desert landscape. The only burst of color comes from the dazzling *ventanas* (windows) of pebbled rainbow glass — handmade by regional artisans — that reflect the changing positions of the sun. Richly furnished, Mediterranean-style rooms are large (starting at 1,000 square feet) and appointed with every conceivable amenity, from wood-burning fireplaces to computerized telescopes for stargazing or whale-watching from your own room. Fresh flowers and glasses of tequila welcome each guest, and room standards include satellite TVs with VCRs and DVD players, stereos with CD players, and dual-line phones. Larger suites offer pampering extras such as rooftop terraces, sunken hot tubs on a private patio, or personal pools. The Spa is among the best in Mexico — particularly notable is its Sea and Stars nighttime massage for two, a relaxing aromatherapy massage with two therapists that takes place on the rooftop terrace of your private suite. With a staff that out-numbers guests by four to one, this is the place for travelers who want (and can afford) to be seriously spoiled. The ocean-view gourmet restaurant has an impressive wine cellar and an adjoining terrace bar with live classical music. A seaside casual-dining grill and a fresh-juice bar are also on the property. Guests enjoy access to the adjoining championship Cabo Real golf course. And Las Ventanas has its own sport-fishing boats and luxury yachts for charter.

Carretera Transpeninsular (Hwy. 1), Km 19.5. ☎ *888-767-3966 in the U.S., or 624-144-0300. Fax: 624-144-0301.* www.lasventanas.com. *61 suites. Complimentary valet parking. Rack rates: $575 double with partial ocean view, $800 double with full ocean view, $1,200 split-level suite with rooftop terrace. Special spa and golf packages available, as are inclusive meal plans and summer rates. AE, DC, MC, V.*

Los Milagros
$$ Cabo San Lucas

The elegant, white, two-level buildings that contain the 11 suites and rooms of Los Milagros (The Miracles) border either a grassy garden area or small pool. All rooms are different, but they're all decorated with contemporary iron beds with straw headboards, buff-colored tile floors, and artistic details — but no TVs. Some units have kitchenettes, and the master suite has a sunken tub. E-mail, fax, and telephone services are available only through the office, and morning coffee service takes place on the patio. In the evenings, candles light the garden, and classical music plays. Request a room in one of the back buildings because conversational noise is less intrusive. Los Milagros is located just a block and a half from the Giggling Marlin and Cabo Wabo nightclubs and a couple of miles from Cabo's main public beach.

Matamoros 116. ☎ *624-143-4566. Fax: 624-143-5004.* www.losmilagros.com.mx. *11 units. Limited street parking. Rack rates: $75 double; ask for summer discounts, group rates, and long-term discounts. No credit cards.*

One&Only Palmilla
$$$$$ Corridor

One of the most comfortably luxurious hotels in Mexico, the One&Only Palmilla is the grand dame of Los Cabos resorts, and it has recently completed (late 2003) a major renovation, making it among the most spectacular resort hotels anywhere. Perched on a cliff top above the sea (with beach access), the resort is a series of white buildings with red-tile roofs, towering palms, and flowering bougainvillea. The feeling here remains one of classic resort-style comfort, but the new sophisticated details bring it up-to-date with the most modern of resorts. The new decor features muted desert colors and luxury fabrics, with special extras such as flat-screen TVs, DVD/CD players, and Bose surround-sound systems. Bathrooms now feature inlaid stone rainshowers and sculpted tubs. Ample, private balconies or terraces have extra-comfortable, overstuffed chairs, and each room also has a separate sitting area. Guests receive twice-daily maid service, a personal butler, and an aromatherapy menu — to ensure you leave completely relaxed or rejuvenated. A new restaurant — simply named C — is under the direction of the renowned Chicago chef Charlie Trotter, and offers 24-hour in-room dining. A second, more casual dining choice is the palapa-topped Agua restaurant, with so-called Mexiterranean cuisine. The Palmilla has become renowned as a location for destination weddings and anniversary celebrations with a renewal of vows; ceremonies take place in its small, signature chapel that graces a sloped hillside. Across the highway, the resort's own championship golf course, designed by Jack Nicklaus, is available for guests, and the Palmilla also has two lighted tennis courts, a new 2,000 square-foot state-of-the-art fitness center, and a yoga garden. Also among the new additions is an exceptional spa, with 13 private treatment villas for one or two people.

Carretera Transpeninsular (Hwy. 1), Km 27.5. ☎ *866-829-2977 in the U.S., or 624-146-7000. Fax: 624-146-7001.* www.oneandonlypalmilla.com. *114 units. Rack rates: High season $475 double, $690 and up for suites and villas; low season $325 double, $435 and up for suites and villas. AE, MC, V.*

Posada Señor Mañana
$ San José

This comfortable two-story guest house, set in a grove of tropical fruit trees, offers basic rooms with tile floors and funky furniture and an abundance of hammocks strewn about the property. Younger travelers, surfers, and the backpack set are the mainstays here. Guests have cooking privileges in a large, fully equipped community kitchen set beside two palapas. Ask about discounts and weekly rates. It's next to the Casa de la Cultura, behind the main square in San José. A small swimming pool is on-site, but you're about 5km (3 miles) from the beach here.

Obregón 1. ☎ *and fax: 624-142-1372.* www.srmanana.com. *E-mail:* srmanana@ aol.com. *8 units. Rack rates: $35–$58 double. No credit cards.*

Presidente InterContinental
$$$$$ San José

The Presidente, set on a long stretch of beach next to the San José Estuary, is San José's most upscale all-inclusive property and an ideal choice for vacationers wanting to simply stay put on a lovely stretch of beach and have their every need attended to. Low-rise, Mediterranean-style buildings frame the beach and San José's largest swimming pool, which has a swim-up bar. If possible, select a ground-floor oceanfront room because the lower level offers spacious terraces as an alternative to a tiny balcony on upper-level units. The rooms have satellite TVs and large bathrooms; suites include a separate sitting area. The resort's all-inclusive nature makes it a good choice for families. In addition to the three restaurants and a garden cafe, theme-night buffet dinners take place a few nights per week. The roster of activities and facilities includes golf clinics, tennis, a small gym, bicycle rentals, and horseback riding. For a fee, the hotel also offers a twice-daily shuttle to Cabo San Lucas.

Bulevar Mijares s/n, at the very end of the road abutting the estuary. ☎ *800-327-0200 in the U.S., or 624-142-0211. Fax: 624-142-0232.* www.loscabos. interconti.com. *240 units. Rack rates: $285 double standard room, $315 double oceanfront room. Rates include all meals, beverages, and many sports. AE, DC, MC, V.*

Siesta Suites
$ Cabo San Lucas

Reservations are a must at this immaculate, small inn popular with return visitors to Cabo. (It's especially popular with fishermen.) The very basic rooms have white-tile floors and white walls, kitchenettes with seating areas, refrigerators, and sinks. The mattresses are firm, and the bathrooms are large and sparkling clean. Rooms on the fourth floor have two queen beds each. The accommodating proprietors offer free movies and VCRs, a barbecue pit and outdoor patio table on the second floor, and a comfortable lobby with TV. They can also arrange fishing trips. Weekly and monthly rates are available. The hotel is 1½ blocks from the marina, where parking is available.

Zapata at Hidalgo. ☎ *866-271-0952 from the U.S., or 624-143-2773.* www.cabo siestasuites.com. *20 suites (15 with kitchenette). Rack rates: $55 double. AE, MC, V.*

Solmar Suites
$$$$–$$$$$ Cabo San Lucas

Set against sandstone cliffs at the very tip of the Baja Peninsula, the Solmar is beloved by travelers seeking seclusion, comfort, and easy access to Cabo's diversions. The beach here is spectacular, though not for swimming. Suites are located in two-story, white-stucco buildings along the edge of the broad beachfront and have either a king bed or two double beds, satellite TVs, separate seating areas, and private balconies or patios on the sand. Guests gather by the pool and on the beach at sunset and all day long during the winter whale migration. With one of the best sport-fishing fleets in Los Cabos, including the deluxe *Solmar V* that is used for long-range diving, fishing, and whale-watching expeditions, the Solmar is especially popular with fishing enthusiasts. Every Saturday, Solmar hosts a popular Mexican fiesta; advance reservations are necessary almost year-round. A small timeshare complex adjoins the Solmar; some units are available for nightly stays. Rates include the hotel's mandatory 10% service charge.

Av. Solmar 1, past the marina. ☎ *800-344-3349 in the U.S., or 624-143-3535. Fax: 624-143-0410.* www.solmar.com. *194 units. Rack rates: $190–$330 double; $433 suite. AE, MC, V.*

Tropicana Inn
$$ San José

This small, colonial-style inn has been a long-standing favorite in San José and welcomes many repeat visitors. The Tropicana is considered "gringo central" in San José and caters to American tastes in a very traditional Mexican setting. Set just behind (and adjacent to) the Tropicana Bar and Grill (see review in Chapter 30), it frames a plant-filled courtyard with a graceful arcade bordering the rooms and inviting swimming pool. Each nicely furnished, medium-size room in the L-shaped building (which has both a two- and three-story wing) comes with tile floors, two double beds, a window looking out on the courtyard, a brightly tiled bathroom with shower, and a coffee pot. Each morning, the staff sets out freshly brewed coffee, delicious sweet rolls, and fresh fruit for hotel guests. You can order room service until 11 p.m. from the Tropicana Bar and Grill (owned by the hotel). The inn is a block south of the town square, and about 2.5km (1.5 miles) from the nearest beach.

Bulevar Mijares 30. ☎ *624-142-0907 or 624-142-1580. Fax: 624-142-1590.* www.tropicanacabo.com. *38 units. Free limited parking in back. Rack rates: High season $85 double; low season $79 double. AE, MC, V.*

Westin Regina
$$$$$ Corridor

Architecturally dramatic, the Westin Regina sits at the end of a long, paved road atop a seaside cliff. Vivid terra-cotta, yellow, and pink walls rise against a landscape of sandstone, cacti, and palms with fountains and gardens lining the long pathways from the lobby to the rooms. Electric carts carry guests and their luggage through the vast property. The rooms are gorgeous and feature air conditioning and ceiling fans, private balconies, satellite TVs, and walk-in showers separate from the bathtubs. This property is probably the best choice among my selections for families vacationing along the Corridor because of the wealth of activities available for children (plus babysitting). With six restaurants and two bars, you may never need to leave the resort. For golfers, both the Palmilla and Cabo Real golf courses are nearby, and the Westin also has two tennis courts, seven pools, two children's pools, a beach club, and complete fitness center with spa and massage services.

Carretera Transpeninsular (Hwy. 1), Km 22.5. ☎ **800-228-3000** *in the U.S., or 624-142-9000. Fax: 624-142-9050.* www.westin.com. *295 units. Rack rates: $308 double with partial ocean view, $347 double with full ocean view. Rates drop 20% in low season. AE, DC, MC, V.*

Chapter 29

Settling into Los Cabos

By Lynne Bairstow

. . . .

In This Chapter

▶ Knowing what to expect when you arrive

▶ Getting the lowdown on the layout

▶ Discovering helpful information and resources

. . . .

*E*ven though Los Cabos may feel like an extension of Southern California in spirit, it's still a foreign country, so a few things are important to know and keep in mind. Still, if you're a first-time traveler to Mexico, you'll immediately feel comfortable — English appears to be more accepted than Spanish in terms of languages, and U.S. dollars are the widely accepted currency.

In this chapter, I take you from the plane, through the airport and to your hotel, helping you quickly get your bearings in this easy-to-navigate area. I continue with tips on everything from where to find a babysitter to how to save a buck or two on transportation.

Arriving in Los Cabos by Air

Los Cabos International Airport is small and easy to navigate. It's located closest to San José del Cabo. From this town, continue down a long, well-paved stretch of highway known as the Corridor until you reach the proverbial "end of the line" — Cabo San Lucas and its rowdy charms. From the very beginning of your Cabo experience, everything should be smooth sailing — you can find both immigration and customs to be brief, generally easy procedures.

Navigating passport control and customs

When you arrive, you walk right from your plane straight into the immigration clearance area. Here, an officer asks you to show your passport (or other proof of citizenship) and your completed tourist card, the **FMT** (see Chapter 7 for all the FMT details).

Your FMT is an important document, so take good care of it. You're supposed to keep the FMT with you at all times because you may be required to show it if you run into any sort of trouble. You also need to turn it back in upon departure, or you may be unable to leave without replacing it.

Next up is the baggage claim area. Here, porters stand by to help with your bags, and they're well worth the price of the tip — about a dollar a bag. After you collect your luggage, you pass through another checkpoint. Something that looks like a traffic light awaits you here. You press a button, and if the light turns green, you're free to go. If it turns red, you need to open each of your bags for a quick search. It's Mexico's random search procedure for customs. If you have an unusually large bag, or an excessive amount of luggage, you may be searched regardless of the traffic-light outcome.

Inside the baggage claim are the rental-car booths, geared for people who haven't reserved a car in advance. If you do have a reservation, they can advise you where to go to pick up your car. After you're outside the baggage claim area and past the timeshare booths, you find an area with more rental-car information as well as taxi info and other transportation options. If you're part of a package tour that includes ground transportation to your hotel, this is where you look for your representative — generally carrying a sign with your name or the name of your tour company on it.

After you collect your bags, you may notice a corral-like area that you pass through, decorated with stunning photos of Los Cabos, and populated by lots of people waving you over. You may think this is a perfect place for tourism information, what with such exceptionally friendly locals; but you'd be wrong. These are timeshare salespeople — hot to offer you a deal on a rental car, transportation to your hotel, or some other ploy in exchange for a generally aggressive sales pitch. Trust me — settle in to the area first and then decide if a timeshare presentation is something you want to include in your vacation agenda.

Getting to your hotel

The one airport that serves both Cabos and the connecting Corridor is 12km (7½ miles) northwest of San José del Cabo and 35km (22 miles) northeast of Cabo San Lucas. Public transportation here is minimal — but improving — and taxis are expensive. This is one Mexican beach resort where I find having a rental car for even part of your stay not only can be practical but also may save you some green if you plan on exploring the area even a little bit. The main road connecting the two Cabos is a modern, well-paved stretch of road, and driving here is easy — getting lost is hard, and parking, though a challenge in the heart of the two towns, isn't impossible.

Renting a car

Advance reservations aren't always necessary, and don't be afraid of requesting a better price than the first one a representative quotes — bargaining sometimes works. You can, however, generally get a much better rate by booking your car in advance through a company's U.S. toll-free number. Before signing your name, be sure you understand the total price after insurance and taxes are added. Rates can run between $40 and $75 per day with insurance costing an extra $10 per day.

National Car Rental is my favorite here; its "all-inclusive" rate includes the insurance and taxes. I find this to be much clearer and preferable to trying to figure out the various options that other companies offer — that is, you don't have any surprises. The major car-rental agencies all have counters open at the airport during flight arrivals. Major car-rental services include

- ✔ **Avis** (☎ **800-331-1212** in the U.S., or 624-146-0201; www.avis.com; Open: 7 a.m. to 9 p.m.)

- ✔ **Budget** (☎ **800-527-0700** in the U.S., or 624-143-4190; www.budget.com; Open: 8 a.m. to 7 p.m.)

- ✔ **Hertz** (☎ **800-654-3131** in the U.S., or 624-146-1803 or 624-146-1821; www.hertz.com; Open: 7 a.m. to 9 p.m.)

- ✔ **National** (☎ **800-328-4567** in the U.S., or 624-142-2424; www.nationalcar.com; Open: 7 a.m. to 8 p.m.)

Of the local car-rental agencies, I find the most economical to be **Advantage Rent-A-Car** (Lázaro Cárdenas, between Leona Vicario and Morelos, downtown Cabo San Lucas; ☎ **624-143-0909**; Fax: 624-143-1060; E-mail: advantagecabo@grupoantyr.com.mx). Volkswagen sedan convertibles rent for $58 per day, and weekly rates include one free day. The collision damage waiver adds $14 per day to the rental price. If you pick up the car downtown, you can return it to the airport at no extra charge.

If you decide to rent a car, picking it up at the airport may be a good idea because doing so saves you the airport-to-hotel transportation expense. You don't have to drive to the airport to return it either — most of the car companies have pick-up service at your hotel or local offices within both towns. On the other hand, if you prefer to settle in first, plan your car rental for the last part of your vacation. The agency can deliver the car to your hotel, and then you can return it to the airport prior to departing (but allow as much as an extra 30 minutes for checking it in).

Hiring transportation

If you do opt to let someone else do the driving, buy a ticket inside the airport for a *colectivo* (shared minivan) or a taxi. *Colectivo* fares run about $9 to San José, about $10 to hotels along the Corridor, and $15 to Cabo for up to eight passengers, and they're only available from the airport. A private taxi can be shared by up to four people and costs about $25 to San José and about $85 to Cabo San Lucas.

If you prefer private transportation, but don't want to pay the high rates of a taxi, book through **Gray Line** (☎ **624-146-9410;** Fax: 624-146-9412; www.graylineloscabos.com), a company offering full tour services in Los Cabos. Rates from the airport to hotels range from $24 to $32 per person for shared rides, and include a bilingual driver who meets you with a sign bearing your name, luggage assistance, and bottled water. Private transportation ranges from $50 to $90, and includes all the previously mentioned items, plus extras such as a welcome kit of information. You can book in advance and prepay online (Visa and MasterCard are accepted).

Getting Around Los Cabos

You exit the airport onto Highway 1, also known as Carretera Transpeninsular. The first main town you come to is San José del Cabo. The highway continues west to the shore and then curves and heads south for about the next 32km (20 miles), where you reach Cabo San Lucas. In the center of Cabo, Highway 1 turns into Lázaro Cárdenas.

If you're staying in San José del Cabo, turn off Highway 1 on Zaragoza, the main street leading from the highway into town; Paseo San José runs parallel to the beach and is the principal boulevard of this hotel zone. The mile-long boulevard is the main street in San José with restaurants, shops, banks, and other services. San José has two principal zones: downtown, where sophisticated inns as well as traditional budget hotels are located, and the hotel zone along the beach. Note that no local bus service runs between downtown San José and the beach; a taxi is the only means of getting between the two places.

The road that connects San José del Cabo to Cabo San Lucas is the centerpiece of resort growth. Known as the Corridor, this stretch of four well-paved lanes offers cliff-top vistas but still has no nighttime lighting. You find the area's most deluxe resorts and renowned golf here, along with a collection of dramatic beaches and coves.

A toll-road expressway was recently added to bypass the traffic around San José, connecting the Corridor directly to the airport. The toll is $2.50 along this stunning — and mostly empty — stretch of road, and can be a faster way to reach the airport, or get to your destination, if you're in a hurry.

The small town of Cabo San Lucas, edged by foothills and desert mountains to the west and south, grew up around the harbor of Cabo San Lucas Bay and spreads out to the north and west. The main street leading into town from the airport and San José del Cabo is Lázaro Cárdenas. As Cárdenas nears the harbor, Marina Boulevard branches off from it and becomes the main artery that curves around the waterfront. Lázaro Cárdenas, the main street into town from Highway 1, splits off to the right and then loops back around a shady plaza, turning into Marina Boulevard, which runs along the waterfront. Most of the shops, restaurants, and nightlife in Cabo are all located within this loop.

Touring around town

Many of the Corridor hotels offer some sort of shuttle service into the two towns, usually for a $15 charge, but the hotels have to disguise it as a "tour" due to the strength of the taxi union.

Taking a taxi

Finding taxis may be easy, but comparing them to the high cost of everything else, they're expensive within Cabo. Expect to pay about $25 for a taxi between Cabo and the Corridor hotels, and about $35 if you're going all the way to San José.

Whenever you take a taxi, establish the price before setting out, because different taxis seem to have different charges. Your hotel should have the rates to various places posted in the lobby, enabling you to easily find out the average rates to and from different areas.

Considering a car rental

Because more than 32km (20 miles) separate the two Cabos — with numerous attractions in between — consider renting a car, even if it's only for a day. Transportation by taxi is expensive here, and if you're at all interested in exploring, a rental car is your most economical option. Each of the two towns has its own distinctive character and attractions, so make the most of this two-for-one resort.

See "Renting a car," earlier in this chapter, for car-rental information.

Fast Facts: Los Cabos

American Express

The representative in San José is at **Plaza La Misión,** Local 1-b, Bulevar Mijares/ Paseo Finisterra (☎ 624-142-1306). In Cabo, the office is located in the **Plaza Bonita Mall,** Local 48e/49e (☎ 624-143-5766).

Area Code

The local telephone prefix is **624.** Calls between Cabo San Lucas, San José del Cabo, and northern Corridor hotels are toll calls, so you must use the area code.

Beach Safety

Before swimming in the open water here, check whether the conditions are safe. Undertows and large waves are common. In Cabo, **Playa Medano** (close to the marina and town) is the principal beach that's safe for swimming. It has several lively beach-front restaurant-bars. It's also easy to find watersports equipment for rent here. The Hotel Melia Cabo San Lucas, on Playa Medano, has a roped-off swimming area to protect swimmers from Jet Skis and boats. *Note:* Colored flags signaling the safety of swimming conditions aren't generally used in Cabo, and neither are lifeguards.

Babysitters

Most of the larger hotels can easily arrange for babysitters, but many sitters speak limited English. Rates range from $4 to $10 per hour.

Banks, ATMs, and Currency Exchange

Banks exchange currency during normal business hours, generally Monday through

Friday from 9 a.m. to 6 p.m. and Saturday from 10 a.m. to 2 p.m. Currency-exchange booths, found all along Cabo's main tourist areas, aren't as competitive, but they're more convenient. ATMs are widely available and even more convenient, and they dispense pesos — and in some cases dollars — at bank-exchange rates.

Business Hours

Most offices maintain traditional Mexican hours of operation (10 a.m. to 2 p.m. and 4 p.m. to 8 p.m. daily), but shops remain open throughout the day. Offices tend to be closed on Saturday and Sunday, but shops are open on Saturday, at least, and increasingly offer limited hours of operation on Sunday.

Climate

It's warm all year; however, evenings and early mornings in the winter months can turn quite cool. Summers can be very hot, but tropical rainstorms may cool the afternoons.

Emergencies

You can try **060,** but generally, no one answers. The local city-hall number is ☎ 624-142-0361.

Hospitals

In Cabo, **Baja Medico** (Camino de la Plaza s/n, on the corner with Pedegral; ☎ 624-143-0127 or 624-143-0175) has a 24-hour walk-in clinic. Most of the larger hotels have a doctor on-call.

Information

In San José, the **city tourist information office** (☎ 624-142-0465) is in the old post-office building on Zaragoza at Mijares. It offers maps, free local publications, and other basic information about the area. It's open Monday through Friday from 8 a.m. to 3 p.m.

The **Los Cabos Tourism Office** is in San José, located in the Plaza San José, locals 3 & 4 (☎ 624-146-9628). *Note:* The many visitor-information booths along the street are actually timeshare sales booths, and their staffs aim to pitch a visit to their resort in exchange for discounted tours, rental cars, or other giveaways.

Internet Access

In San José, **Trazzo Internet,** on the corner of Zaragoza and Morelos, 1 block from the central plaza (no phone), is open Monday to Saturday from 10 a.m. to 8 p.m. and charges $2.50 for 30 minutes or less for high-speed access.

Access in Cabo San Lucas is available at **Onda Net Café & Bar** (Lázaro Cárdenas 7, Edificio Posada, across from the Pemex gas station; ☎ 624-143-5390). Access costs $5 for 15 minutes, $7 for 30 minutes, or $8 for an hour. It's open 8 a.m. to 6 p.m. Monday to Saturday.

Maps

One of the best around is the free American Express map, usually found at the tourist information offices and the hotel concierge desks.

Newspapers/Magazines

Most hotels and shops distribute the English-language *Los Cabos Guide, Los Cabos News, Cabo Life, Baja Sun,* and the irreverent and extremely entertaining *Gringo Gazette.* These publications have up-to-date information on new restaurants and clubs.

Books, Books, in Cabo San Lucas (☎ 624-143-3172 or 624-143-3173), sells a good selection of English- and Spanish-language reading material, with a specialty of regional guides and publications. It's located on Bulevar Marina #20, next to Carlos 'n Charlie's, and is open daily from 9 a.m. to 10 p.m. A second location is in San José at Bulevar Mijares #41 near the Tropicana Inn (☎ 624-142-4433), open daily 9 a.m. to 9 p.m.

English-language books and magazines are also generally available for sale in hotel gift shops.

Pharmacy

In San José, **Farmacia ISSTE** (Carretera Transpeninsular, Km 34, Plaza California; ☎ 624-142-2645) is the major pharmacy in the area. It's open from 8 a.m. to 8 p.m.

A long-standing drugstore in Cabo San Lucas, with a wide selection of toiletries as well as medicines, is **Farmacia Aramburo** (Lázaro Cárdenas at Zaragoza, Plaza Aramburo; ☎ 624-143-1489). It's open daily from 7 a.m. to 9 p.m.

Police

In San José, call ☎ 624-142-0361; in Cabo San Lucas, the number is ☎ 624-143-3977.

Post Office

In San José, the *correo* on Bulevar Mijares 1924 at Valerio González (☎ 624-142-0911) is open Monday through Friday 8 a.m. to 6 p.m. and Saturday 9 a.m. to noon.

The *correo* (☎ 624-143-0048) in Cabo San Lucas is at Lázaro Cárdenas and Francisco Villa on the highway to San José del Cabo, east of the El Squid Roe bar. It's open Monday through Friday 8 a.m. to 6 p.m. and Saturday from 9 a.m. to noon.

Special Events

The feast of the patron saint of San José del Cabo is celebrated on March 19 with a fair, music, dancing, feasts, horse races, and cockfights. October 12 is the festival of the patron saint of Todos Santos, a town about 65 miles north. October 18 is the feast of the patron saint of Cabo San Lucas, celebrated with a fair, feasts, music, dancing, and other special events.

Taxes

There's a 15% value-added tax (IVA) on goods and services, and it's generally included in the posted price.

Taxis

Taxis are plentiful but relatively expensive. Trips between the two towns average $35; trips between hotels along the Corridor average $20. Rides within San José cost around $5, but rides within Cabo cost between $8 and $12.

Telephone

Avoid the phone booths that have signs in English advising you to call home using a special 800 number — these are absolute rip-offs and can cost as much as $20 per minute. The least expensive way to call is by using a Telmex (LADATEL) prepaid phone card, available at most pharmacies and mini-supers, using the official Telmex (Lada) public phones. In Mexico you need to dial 001 prior to a number to reach the United States, and you need to preface long-distance calls within Mexico by dialing 01.

Time Zone

Los Cabos operates on mountain standard time, but Mexico's observance of daylight savings time varies somewhat from that in the United States.

Chapter 30

Dining in Los Cabos

By Lynne Bairstow

*P*aying a lot for mediocre food isn't uncommon in Los Cabos, so try to get a couple of unbiased recommendations before settling in for a meal. If people are only drinking and not dining, take that as a clue because many seemingly popular places are long on party atmosphere but short on food quality. Prices decrease the farther you walk inland from the waterfront.

With several exceptional choices and culinary offerings more representative of Mexico, San José is becoming known as the preferred dining town. Prices also tend to be more reasonable. If you're staying along the Corridor, remember to figure in transportation costs when calculating the price of your meal — you may just decide to dine at your hotel, which is likely to have a top-notch chef anyway. Cabo has the most restaurant offerings, but sad to say, few are truly spectacular.

Cabo is a very casual town, and shorts and jeans are accepted everywhere except the most upscale resort restaurants, but dressier resort wear is still acceptable, too. Despite the relaxed atmosphere, prices here are generally higher than you find in comparable restaurants in the United States or other parts of Mexico. This situation is due to the necessity of importing many ingredients from the mainland. Cabo has also imported some customs of "upper" California — it's becoming more common to have segregated nonsmoking areas in restaurants here due to the demand by visitors.

Besides the restaurants mentioned in this chapter, dozens of good, clean taco stands and taco restaurants dot the downtown area. To find additional good restaurants, explore Hidalgo and Cárdenas and the Marina at the Plaza Bonita. North-of-the-border tastes have heavily influenced Cabo's dining scene. The usual suspects (U.S. franchise chains such as KFC, Subway, Pizza Hut, and a host of others) are everywhere downtown. Note that many restaurants here automatically add the tip to the bill.

When it comes to welcoming young ones at restaurants, Los Cabos is more like the United States than Mexico — less than enthusiastic, except at the more traditional establishments and casual hotel restaurants. If your children are particular to American tastes, you can go with the standards such as McDonald's, Burger King, and Hard Rock Cafe — all good choices. But you may also want to try the Mexican alternatives of Carlos O'Brian's or Squid Roe, which seem to be fun at any age — and if you dine early, the atmosphere is less raucous.

The Best Restaurants in Los Cabos

I arrange the following restaurants alphabetically, noting their location and general price category. Remember that tips generally run about 15%, and most wait-staff really depend on these for their income, so be generous if the service warrants. Please refer to the Introduction of this book for an explanation of the price categories.

Please see the menu glossary in Appendix C for more information on Mexican cuisine.

Cafe Canela

$ **Cabo San Lucas** **COFFEE/PASTRY/LIGHT MEALS**

This cozy, tasty cafe and bistro is a welcome addition to the Cabo Marina boardwalk. Espresso drinks or fruit smoothies and muffins are good eye-openers for early risers. Enjoy a light meal or a tropical drink either inside or on the bustling waterfront terrace. The appealing menu also offers breakfast egg wraps, salads (for example, curried chicken salad with fresh fruit), sandwiches (such as blue-cheese quesadillas with smoked tuna and mango), and pastas — all reasonably priced. Full bar service is also available.

Marina boardwalk, below Plaza Las Glorias hotel. ☎ 624-143-3435. Reservations not accepted. Main courses: $4–$9; coffee $1.75–$3.50. AE, MC, V. Open: Daily 6 a.m.–5 p.m.

Casa Rafael's

$$–$$$$ **Cabo San Lucas** **INTERNATIONAL**

Although I consider it overpriced, Casa Rafael's is regarded as among the most romantic places in Cabo. Dine in one of the candlelit rooms and alcoves (air-conditioned) of this large house, or outside beside the small swimming pool. Piano music plays in the background while you enjoy a

San José del Cabo Dining

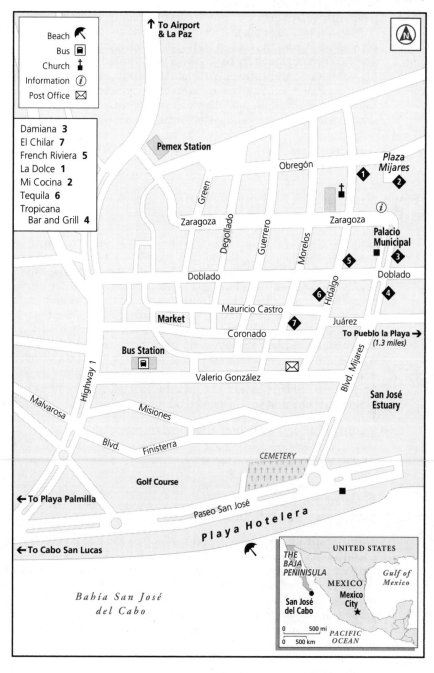

Beach
Bus
Church
Information
Post Office

Damiana **3**
El Chilar **7**
French Riviera **5**
La Dolce **1**
Mi Cocina **2**
Tequila **6**
Tropicana
  Bar and Grill **4**

↑ To Airport
& La Paz

Pemex Station

Obregón

Green

Plaza
Mijares

Zaragoza

Degollado

Guerrero

Morelos

Zaragoza

Palacio
Municipal

Doblado

Doblado

Hidalgo

Mauricio Castro

Market

Coronado

Juárez

To Pueblo la Playa →
(1.3 miles)

Highway 1

Bus Station

Valerio González

Blvd. Mijares

San José
Estuary

Malvarosa

Misiones

Blvd. Finisterra

CEMETERY

Golf Course

← To Playa Palmilla

Paseo San José

← To Cabo San Lucas

Playa Hotelera

*Bahía San José
del Cabo*

THE
BAJA
PENINISULA

UNITED STATES

Gulf of
Mexico

MEXICO

San José
del Cabo

Mexico
City ★

0   500 mi
0   500 km

PACIFIC
OCEAN

leisurely meal; the staff times the courses so that you don't feel rushed. To start, try the sublime smoked dorado paté or perhaps the hearts of palm with a raspberry vinaigrette dressing. House specialties include the chicken parmesan Sonia and scampi with pasta. The Black Angus steaks are imported from the United States; the lamb comes from New England. The rich desserts may make you wish you'd seen them first before stuffing yourself on the entrees. Wine and aperitif menus are extensive. To find Casa Rafael's, follow Hacienda Road toward the ocean; when you top the hill, look left. Turn left when you see the rosy-pink château with an arched front and patio with caged birds and a fountain.

Calle Medano and Camino el Pescador. ☎ 624-143-0739. Reservations suggested. Main courses: $19–$52. AE, MC, V. Open: Daily 7–10 p.m.

Damiana

$$$ **San José** **SEAFOOD/MEXICAN**

For one of the area's finest Mexican meals, this casually elegant restaurant in an 18th-century hacienda is a great bet. The 150-year-old colonial home is decorated in the colors of a Mexican sunset: walls painted a deep orange, and tables and chairs clad in bright rose, lavender, and orange cloth. Mariachis play nightly from 8 to 9 p.m. (mid-December through March) in the tropical courtyard where candles flicker under the trees and flowering vines. For an appetizer, try the mushrooms diablo — a moderately zesty dish of mushrooms with garlic and guajillo chiles. For a main course, the ranchero shrimp in cactus sauce or grilled lobster tail are flavorful choices. You can also enjoy brunch almost until the dinner hour. The interior dining room is nice, but the courtyard is the most romantic dining spot in San José. It's located on the east side of the town plaza.

San José town plaza. ☎ 624-142-0499 or 624-142-2899. Reservations recommended during Christmas and Easter holidays. Main courses: $30–$42; lunch $7.50–$20. AE, MC, V. Open: Daily 11 a.m.–10:30 p.m.

El Chilar

$–$$ **San José** **MEXICAN**

In this rustically casual restaurant, you may feel like you're dining at a friend's home, as welcoming as chef Armando Montano is. His passion for Mexican cuisine is evident, as he blends the traditional flavors of this country — including an array of chiles — into imaginative and heavenly offerings. Among the most popular dinner options are shrimp in a roasted garlic and guajillo chile sauce, or the creative grilled tortilla and salmon Napoleon accompanied by a mango pico de gallo. These choices may not be offered when you arrive, however, as chef Armando is known to frequently change his menu. At night, candlelight adds a sparkle of romance to the setting. El Chilar also offers a full bar and an ample selection of wines, with suggestions for pairings with your meal. Air-conditioned indoor dining is available.

Cabo San Lucas Dining

Beach ☂
Bus 🚌
Church ✝
Information ⓘ
Post Office ✉

A. López Mateos
Ildefonso Green
A. Mijares
Félix Ortega
Rosario Morales
Alikan
12 de Octubre
Calle Juventud
Morelos
M. Hidalgo
Leona Vicario
Narcizo Mendoza
I. Zaragoza
Morelos
Matamoros
Abasolo
M. Ocampo
A. Obregón
V. Carranza
Gómez Farías
16 de Septiembre
Revolución
20 de Noviembre
Libertad
16 de Septiembre
Niños Héroes
Lázaro Cárdenas
Cabo San Lucas
Constitución
5 de Mayo
Guerrero
Highway 1
Fco. I. Madero
Iglesia de San Lucas ✝
Marina Blvd
Main Square
J.O. de Domínguez
Marina
Playa Medano
Bahía de Cabo San Lucas
Market

To Airport & La Paz →
To San José del Cabo →

Cafe Canela **4**
Casa Rafael's **7**
La Dolce **2**
Mi Casa **1**
Mocambo **5**
Nick-San **3**
Peacocks **6**

Land's End
Playa del Amor

UNITED STATES
THE BAJA PENINSULA
MEXICO
Gulf of Mexico
Cabo San Lucas
Mexico City ★
El Arco
PACIFIC OCEAN
0   500 mi
0   500 km
PACIFIC OCEAN

Benito Juárez 1490, corner with Morelos, near the Telmex tower. ☎ **624-142-2544** *or 624-146-9798. Reservations suggested. Main courses: $5–$29. No credit cards. Open: Mon–Sat 3–10 p.m.*

French Riviera

$ San José FRENCH/PASTRIES/COFFEE

What a great place to start the day — or end it! This casual restaurant, located in a classic historic building in San José, not only serves tempting French fare but also absolutely irresistible sweets! Its on-site bakery, with an exhibition window for watching the pastry chefs at work, results in smells so delectable I dare you to leave without a sweet something. Start the day with a croissant and cappuccino, or any number of coffee and pastry choices, or end it with a full meal of delectable French fare. A second location in Cabo San Lucas (☎ **624-104-3125**) offers a more traditional restaurant setting, with a great selection of wines. You can find it in Plaza del Rey, next to the Misiones del Cabo entrance on the highway, Km 6; it's open from noon until 11 p.m.

Corner of Hidalgo and Manuel Doblado s/n. ☎ **624-142-3350.** www.french rivieraloscabos.com. *Breakfast $1.50–$4; dinner $2.50–$6.50. No credit cards. Open: Daily 7:30 a.m.–11 p.m.*

La Dolce

$–$$ Cabo San Lucas ITALIAN

This Cabo restaurant, with authentic Italian thin-crust, brick-oven pizzas and other specialties, is the offspring of Puerto Vallarta's La Dolce Vita. The food is some of the best in the Baja Peninsula, and the fact that 80% of La Dolce's business is from local customers underscores the point. It's known for its reasonable prices and attentive and welcoming service. The simple menu also features sumptuous pastas and calzones, beef or fish carpaccio, plus great salads. Due to its popularity, a second location (☎ **624-142-6621**) has opened in one of San Jose's historical buildings, right on the main Plaza Jardin Mijares. With a true bistro atmosphere, this La Dolce is open Tuesday through Sunday, from 6 p.m. to 11 p.m.

Corner of M. Hidalgo and Zapata. ☎ **624-143-4122.** *Reservations not accepted. Main courses: $8–$19. No credit cards. Open: Mon–Sat 6 p.m. to midnight. Closed Sept.*

Mi Casa

$$ Cabo San Lucas MEXICAN/NOUVELLE MEXICAN

The building's vivid, cobalt-blue facade is your first clue that this place celebrates Mexico; the menu confirms that impression. Mi Casa is one of Cabo's most renowned gourmet Mexican restaurants, although it's

The Corridor Dining

equally noted for its inconsistency. Traditional specialties, such as *man-chamanteles* (literally interpreted as "tablecloth stainers," it's a stew of meat and vegetables), *cochinita pibil* (a local pork dish), and *chiles en nogada* (chile peppers stuffed with a mixture of meat, nuts, and fruit) are everyday menu staples. Fresh fish is prepared with delicious seasonings from recipes found throughout Mexico. Especially pleasant at night, the restaurant's tables, scattered around a large patio, are set with colorful cloths, traditional pottery, and glassware. It's across from the main plaza.

Calle Cabo San Lucas at Madero. ☎ 624-143-1933. Reservations recommended. Main courses: $15–$25. AE, MC, V. Open: Mon–Sat 5:30 to 10:30 p.m.

Mi Cocina

$$ San José   NOUVELLE MEXICAN/EURO CUISINE

Without a doubt, Mi Cocina is currently the best dining choice in the entire Los Cabos area. From the setting to the service, a dinner here is sure to be unforgettable. The plant-filled courtyard, with its towering palms, dramatic lighting, and art-filled exposed brick walls, accommodates alfresco dining on several different levels. But it's not just the romantic setting that makes this restaurant special — the food is creative and consistently superb. Notable starters include steamed baby clams topped with a light creamy cilantro sauce and served with garlic croutons, or a healthy slice of Camembert cheese, fried and served with homemade toast and fresh grapes. Among the favorite main courses are the Provencal-style baked baby rack of lamb served with grilled vegetables, and the shrimp served with risotto, roasted tomato, basil, and cilantro-fish consommé. Save room for dessert; choices include the famous chocolate-chocolate cake and a perfect crème brûlée. The full-service palapa bar offers an excellent selection of wines, premium tequilas, and single-malt scotches. Be adventurous, and try one of the special martinis, such as the Flor de Mexico, an adaptation of the Cosmo, using hibiscus flower infusion rather than cranberry juice.

Bulevar Mijares 4, inside Casa Natalia. ☎ 624-142-5100. Reservations recommended. Main courses: $15–$28. AE, MC, V. Open: Daily 7 a.m.–4 p.m. to hotel guests only and 6:30–10:30 p.m. to the public.

Mocambo

$–$$ Cabo San Lucas   SEAFOOD

The location of this long-standing Cabo favorite isn't very inspirational — it's basically a large cement building — but somebody obviously likes the food. The place is always packed, generally with local diners tired of high prices and small portions. Ocean-fresh seafood is the order of the day here, and the specialty platter can easily satisfy the healthy appetites of four people. The restaurant is a block and a half inland from Lázaro Cárdenas.

Leona Vicario and 20 de Noviembre. ☎ 624-143-6070. Reservations not accepted. Main courses: $5–$23. MC, V. Open: Daily noon to 10 p.m.

Nick-San

$–$$$ Cabo San Lucas   JAPANESE/SUSHI

Exceptional Japanese cuisine and sushi are the specialties in this air-conditioned restaurant with a clean, minimalist decor. A rosewood sushi bar with royal blue-tiled accents invites diners to watch the master sushi chef at work. An exhibition kitchen behind the sushi chef demonstrates why this place has been honored with a special award for cleanliness.

Blvd. Marina, Plaza de la Danza. ☎ *624-143-4484. Reservations recommended. Main courses: $12–$30; sushi $3.50 and up. MC, V. Open: Tues–Sun 11:30 a.m.–10:30 p.m.*

Peacocks
$$–$$$ Cabo San Lucas   INTERNATIONAL

One of Cabo's most exclusive patio-dining establishments, Peacocks emphasizes creatively prepared fresh seafood. Start off with the house paté or a salad of feta cheese with cucumber, tomato, and onion. For the main course, try one of the pastas — linguini with grilled chicken and sun-dried tomatoes is one of my favorites. Heartier entrees include steaks, shrimp, and lamb, all prepared several ways.

Paseo del Pescador s/n, corner of Melia Hotel. ☎ *624-143-1858. Reservations recommended. Main courses: $15–$30. AE, MC, V. Open: Daily 6–10:30 p.m.*

Pitahayas
$$–$$$ Corridor   PACIFIC RIM

Pitahayas' beachfront setting in the Hacienda del Mar resort offers gourmet dining under a grand palapa or on open-air terraces under a starlit sky. Master chef Volker Romeike has assembled a creative — if not slightly pretentious — menu that blends Pacific Rim cuisine with Mexican native herbs and seasonings. Notable sauces include mango, black bean, and curry. The rotisserie-barbecued duck is a house specialty, along with anything done over a mesquite grill or in a wok — all prepared in an impressive exhibition kitchen. A dessert pizza with fresh fruit, chocolate, and marzipan makes a fitting finish to a stunning meal. Pitahayas also boasts a large wine cellar with vintages from around the world housed in an underground *cava*. Formal resort attire is requested, and reservations are an absolute must during high season.

Hacienda del Mar, Hwy. 1, Km 10. ☎ *624-145-8010. Reservations required during high season. Main courses: $20–$40. AE, MC, V. Open: Daily 5–10:30 p.m.*

The Restaurant (Las Ventanas al Paraíso)
$$$–$$$$ Corridor   INTERNATIONAL

It may just be called "The Restaurant," but that's where simplicity ends and the extraordinary begins. Where Los Cabos is known for its pricey dining, this is one Restaurant that is worth the price. Start off with a cocktail before dinner in The Lounge, the casually elegant bar area bordering Las Ventanas' stunning pool, lit from above with a constellation of tin stars illuminated by candles. When you move into the dining area, you get a sense of the Las Ventanas signature service — such as, if you're wearing black, your server gives you a black napkin. As remarkable as the service is, the dining itself is even better. First courses may include Ensenada steamed mussels served in coconut milk with a hint of chile arbol and a dash of tequila, or a stone crab salad with baby watercress, mango, phillo, and sweet mustard sauce. The constantly changing menu of main courses generally includes an ample selection of seafood, including lobster, done in creative presentations, but the grilled rack of lamb with garlic potatoes, or prime filet mignon in a Cabernet sauce, is as good as anywhere. A stellar selection of premium wines is served, and dress is resort attire. You have your choice of alfresco dining on the patio, or in indoor, air-conditioned comfort. Reserve early, because dinner at The Restaurant is quite popular in Cabo at any time during the year.

Las Ventanas al Paraíso, Hwy. 1, Km 19.5. ☎ *624-144-0300. Reservations required. Main courses: $35–$50. AE, MC, V. Open: Daily 5–11 p.m.*

Tequila
$–$$$$ San José   MEXICAN/ASIAN

The contemporary Mexican cuisine with a light and flavorful touch is the star attraction here, although the garden setting, with rustic leather and twine furniture and lanterns scattered among palms and giant mango trees, is also lovely. Start with a heavenly version of the traditional *chiles en nogada* stuffed with couscous, raisins, and papaya and seasoned with cinnamon. Grilled tuna with cilantro ginger sauce arrives perfectly seared; the whole-grain bread is fresh and hot; and seriously consider trying one of the specialties: shrimp in tequila sauce or the ribs in tamarind sauce. Attentive service complements the fine meal. An added touch: Cuban cigars and an excellent selection of tequilas are available.

M. Doblado s/n, near Hidalgo. ☎ *624-142-1155. Reservations recommended. Main courses: $10–$45. AE. Open: Daily 5:30–10:30 p.m.*

Tropicana Bar and Grill
$–$$ San José   SEAFOOD/MEAT

The Tropicana remains a popular mainstay, especially for tourists. The newly remodeled restaurant and bar promises to retain its steady clientele day and night, as well as its offerings of live music and special sporting events on satellite TV. The main dining area is in a garden (candlelit in the evening) with a tiled mural at one end, and a new interior area, in a rustic-chic decor, adds about 100 new seats to the restaurant. Cafe-style sidewalk dining is also available. The menu is too extensive to lay claim to any specialty; it aims to please everyone. All meats and cheeses are imported, and dinners include thick steaks and shrimp fajitas. The restaurant is a block south of the Plaza Mijares.

Bulevar Mijares 30. ☎ *624-142-1580. Reservations recommended. Main courses: $10–$25; breakfast $4–$6. AE, MC, V. Open: Daily 6 a.m.–11 p.m.*

Zipper's

$–$$ Corridor   BURGERS/MEXICAN/SEAFOOD

Enjoy a hearty, American-style lunch served seaside at this popular, casual hangout. Sitting at the far south end of the beach heading toward Cabo San Lucas and fronting the best surfing waters, Zipper's has become popular with gringos in search of American food and TV sports. Burgers have that back-home flavor — order one with a side of spicy curly fries. Steaks, lobster, beer-batter shrimp, deli sandwiches, and Mexican combination plates round out the menu, which is printed with U.S. dollar prices.

Playa Costa Azul, just south of San José. No phone. Main courses: $7–$18; burgers and sandwiches $7–$10. No credit cards. Open: Daily 8 a.m.–10 p.m.

Chapter 31

Having Fun on and off the Beach in Los Cabos

By Lynne Bairstow

- -

In This Chapter

▶ Checking out the beach scene

▶ Landing the big one and shooting a low score

▶ Venturing into the wild — and shopping, too

▶ Visiting La Paz and Todos Santos

▶ Saddling up to the bar

- -

Geographically, Baja California is set apart from mainland Mexico, which greatly contributes to its unique culture and personality, as well as to its many attractions and diversions. Volcanic activity created the craggy desertscape populated mainly by forests of cardón cactus, spiky Joshua trees, and spindly ocotillo bushes that you see today. Hard to believe such a formidable landscape could become home to a vacation haven, but it has. Today, Los Cabos offers visitors a ton of options for fun in the sun — eco-tours, golfing, sport-fishing, diving, and whale-watching, to name a few — amidst beautiful settings and posh resorts.

In this chapter, I give you an overview of the best beaches tucked into the miles of coastline between the two Cabos (and in the neighboring areas). I point out the most interesting sights in these twin towns, and I also offer a rundown of the best ways to spend an active day — or night — here.

Hitting the Beaches

The beaches of Los Cabos are stunning — cobalt-blue waters set against a backdrop of rugged desert terrain. The countless inlets and small coves in the Sea of Cortez have made Cabos a popular destination for ocean kayaking, and the abundant sea life attracts both divers and sport fishermen. And as for the beaches here (see the "Los Cabos" map, in this section), you can choose from dozens of tranquil coves or opt to take on the long stretches of challenging surf breaks. One after another, these beautiful patches of sand hug the shoreline between the two Cabos (San José del Cabo and Cabo San Lucas).

If you're a beach aficionado who wants to explore the beautiful coves and beaches along the 35-km (22-mile) coast between the two Cabos, consider renting a car for a day or so. Rental cars cost $40 to $75 per day and up. (Check out Chapter 29 for all the details on renting a car in Cabo.) Frequent bus service between San José del Cabo and Cabo San Lucas also makes it possible to take in the pleasures of both towns.

Cabo's northern beaches

The relaxed pace of San José del Cabo makes it an ideal place to unwind and absorb authentic Mexican flavor while enjoying a stretch of sand.

The nearest beach to San José that's safe for swimming is **Pueblo la Playa** (also called La Playita), located about 3km (2 miles) east of town. From Bulevar Mijares, turn east at the small "Pueblo la Playa" sign and follow the dusty, dirt road through cane fields and palms to a small village and beautiful beach where local fishermen pull their *pangas* (skiffs) ashore. The La Playita Resort and its adjacent restaurant (☎ **624-142-4166**) offer the only formal sustenance on the beach. Also note that the beach has no shade *palapas*.

The beach that forms the southern border of San José is a broad stretch of sand, but because hotels front most of it, hotel guests are the primary beachgoers here — it can be a hassle for non-guests to access the beach.

Corridor beaches

Traveling from San José to Cabo San Lucas along Highway 1, the first beach along the Corridor is **Playa Costa Azul** (Km 29) where Zipper's restaurant is located (see Chapter 30). It's a long stretch of sand next to the Mykonos and La Jolla condo developments. Most of the year, Costa Azul has a gentle, but regular, surf break; however, from late summer to early fall, a southwest swell brings consistent wave action with some truly exceptional surf conditions.

Playa Palmilla (Km 27.5), with its beautiful rock formations, is the nearest swimming beach after you've set off down the Corridor. It's located just west of Playa Costa Azul near the Spanish-colonial-style Hotel Palmilla — an elegant place to stay or dine. To reach Playa Palmilla, take a taxi to the road that leads to the Hotel Palmilla grounds. Then take the left fork in the road (without entering the hotel grounds) and follow the road to the beach.

Los Cabos

Playa Chileno (Km 14) is the largest and most popular of the public beaches along the corridor, and it has both public restrooms and showers — a rarity in Mexico. A watersports-equipment rental facility located at the southern end of the beach can come in handy — the rocky headlands at both ends of this small bay offer some good snorkeling. Nearby **Playa Santa María** (Km 12) has less in the way of facilities and shade, but it's better for snorkeling and diving. Both of these beaches are noted for their abundance of marine life.

Watching your feathered friends

Between Pueblo la Playa and San José's Presidente InterContinental Hotel lies the **Estero San José**, an estuary and protected ecological reserve with at least 270 species of birds. Across from the entrance to the InterContinental, a footpath leads you into the estuary for one heck of a bird-watching experience.

The remains of the Japanese tuna boat *Inari Maru* make **Playa Barco Varado** (Km 9–10) noteworthy and provide the beach with its name — Shipwreck Beach. The boat became stranded on the rocky shoals in 1966. It's now one of the main dive sites in the area. The hull and other wreckage lie 6½ to 85 feet underwater.

Although a few travel agencies run snorkeling tours to some of these beaches, no public transportation is available. If you want to explore these beaches on your own, your only option is to rent a car. To find these beaches, follow the blue-and-white signs along Highway 1. The signs are sometimes labeled "Acesso a Playa," but more often, they simply bear the international symbol for a swimmer or a snorkeler.

In addition to Playa Palmilla, the beaches of Chileno and Santa María are generally safe for swimming — but always be careful. The other beaches along the Corridor aren't safe. Experienced snorkelers may want to check them out, but other visitors should go for the view only. Always check at a hotel or travel agency for directions and swimming conditions.

Cabo's southern beaches

The main beach in Cabo San Lucas is a curving sweep of sand known as **Playa El Medano** and located on the east side of the bay. The swimming conditions here are generally safe. You can also rent snorkeling gear, boats, WaveRunners, kayaks, pedal boats, and windsurf boards and score some windsurfing lessons. The people-watching at El Medano is as hot as the action — take your pick from the many outdoor restaurants along the shore and settle in for a cold one.

Finding Water Fun for Everyone

It began with John Steinbeck's stories and continued with the tall tales of the early sport fishermen who came here in the 1940s and 1950s. With more than 3,000 estimated species of fish in the waters offshore Baja California and the title of undisputed bill-fishing capital in the world, Los Cabos enjoyed early fame among visitors who wanted to tackle these larger species, such as tuna, marlin, and swordfish (see "Reeling in the big one," later in this chapter). In the years that followed, travelers to Los Cabos have discovered an even greater number of ways to revel in the treasures of this deep, blue sea.

Cruising Los Cabos

Whether by day or in the fading light of the sunset, numerous cruises are available to take you around Land's End — the famed tip of Baja California — to enjoy this truly stunning sight. Boats depart from Cabo San Lucas. The cruise prices and offerings vary but usually include music, an open bar, and snacks for between $30 and $45 per person. Variables include the type of boat, duration of the cruise, and amenities.

The sunset cruise on the 42-foot catamaran *Pez Gato* (☎ 624-143-3797 or 624-143-5297; E-mail: pezgato@cabotel.com.mx) is always a favorite. The excursion departs from the Muelle Principal dock at 5 p.m. This two-hour cruise costs $30 and includes margaritas, beer, and sodas. Similar boats also leave from the Plaza las Glorias Hotel dock and from the marina. Almost any travel agency or hotel tour desk can make the arrangements for you, or you can call **Gray Line Los Cabos** (☎ 624-146-9410; www.graylineloscabos.com). Gray Line works with all the tour providers in the area and can give you the unbiased lowdown on which one will meet your individual needs.

Another great way to see the aquatic sights is aboard a **glass-bottom boat.** These boats leave from the Cabo San Lucas marina every 45 minutes between 9 a.m. and 4 p.m. daily. The cost is about $10 for an hour-long tour past sea lions and pelicans to the famous El Arco (Rock Arch, or simply "The Arch") at Land's End where the Pacific Ocean and the Sea of Cortez meet. Most boats make a brief stop at Playa del Amor or drop you off if you ask; you can use your ticket to catch a later boat back. (Be sure to find out what time the last boat departs.)

You don't want to miss the **whale-watching cruises** when the gray whales migrate to the Los Cabos area between January and March. In San José, fishermen at Pueblo la Playa take small groups out to see the whales; a four-hour trip runs about $45 per person. Another option is **Cabo Travel Advisors** in San José (☎ 624-142-4444; www.cabocta.com), which arranges whale-watching adventures for groups of four or more people; the two-and-a-half-hour trip costs $95 per person and includes snacks and beverages.

Sport-fishing boats, glass-bottom boats, and cruise catamarans also offer whale-watching trips at prices ranging from $35 to $60 for a half-day trip. You can also spot the whales from shore; good whale-watching spots include the beach by the Solmar Suites hotel on the Pacific (see review in Chapter 28) and the beaches and cliffs along the Corridor.

The ultimate whale excursion is an all-day trip to Magdalena Bay, a one-hour plane ride away. In a small skiff, you get close enough to touch the whales. The cost for the trip, including air transportation, is $380, available through most local travel agents. If you want to spend more time with the whales, **Sea Kayak Adventures** (☎ 800-616-1942; www.sea kayakadventures.com) offers an eight-day trip to Magdalena Bay, with kayaking among whales for four to five hours per day, hiking, and camping in remote coves. Prices start at $1,195 per person.

Preferring a paddleboat

Fully guided, ecologically oriented **sea-kayaking tours** are available through **Cabo Travel Advisors** (☎ 624-142-4444; www.cabocta.com). The tour runs from 8:30 to 11:30 a.m. and includes breakfast and beverages for a price of $70. No previous experience is necessary — guides provide complete instructions at the start of the tour. Kayaks are the most popular and practical way to explore the pristine coves that dot this shoreline.

Another excellent source for kayak tours is **BajaWild Expeditions** (☎ 624-142-5300; www.bajawild.com), specialists in adventure tours in the Cabos area. They offer a variety of kayaking and snorkeling tours to venues that include Cabo Pulmo, the Arch and Lover's Rock, and within the estuary. Prices range from $50 to $95.

Catching a wave

When summer hurricanes spin off the southern end of the peninsula, they send huge surf northward to beaches such as **Zippers, Punta Gorda,** and **Old Man's.** People have compared Zippers (near the Brisa del Mar Trailer Park and the Costa Azul surf shop outside San José del Cabo) with places such as Pipeline on the North Shore of Oahu. That may be a bit of an exaggeration, but this area does feature great waves nonetheless.

Playa Costa Azul (Highway 1, Km 29, just south of San José) is the most popular surfing beach in the area. A few bungalows are available for rent here, and surfers can camp on the beach. You can rent surfboards and surf racks for your rental car by the day here. Spectators can watch the action from the highway lookout point at the top of the hill south of Costa Azul.

You can find good surfing from March through November all along the beaches west of Cabo, and **Playa Chileno,** near the Cabo San Lucas Hotel east of town, has a famous right break. Other good surfing beaches along the corridor are **Acapulquito, El Tule,** and **La Bocana.**

The Pacific coast has yet to face the onslaught of development that has rapidly changed the landscape to the east. An hour-long drive up the coast to the little towns of Pescadero and Todos Santos can be a great surf journey, with a couple of good point breaks near here. You can reach **Playa San Pedrito** via the dirt road that begins about 7km (4.5 miles) south of the Todos Santos town limits. Follow the "San Pedrito Campground" signs. The point is very rocky and sharp, but it's a wonderful wave at the right swell direction and tide (north-west swell, rising tide). Farther down the road is **Playa los Cerritos,** located 13km (8 miles) south of Todos Santos. Cerritos is a lovely beach with a surfable point break off a big headland.

New to surfing? **Baja Wild** (☎ 624-142-5300; www.bajawild.com) offers surf lessons as well as surf tours, so you can get right to the best waves in the briefest amount of time. Trips take you to any of 15 breaks within the Sea of Cortez or to the big breaks on the Pacific Ocean, or you can even combine surfing and kayaking.

Exploring the deep blue

Diving in Los Cabos is so special because of the abundance of marine life, which includes giant mantas, sea turtles, dolphins, and tropical fish. You can choose between diving the coral reefs at the southern tip of the cape region or one of the shipwrecks in the area. April through November is the best time to dive, but diving is most crowded from October to mid-January. Making reservations in advance is important if you're planning to dive then. During the winter months, you're also likely to hear the moving, tonal songs of the humpback whales as you dive. Note that during the winter months, the water here can be quite cold, so a wet suit is necessary — even for most snorkelers.

Several companies offer snorkeling; a two-hour cruise to sites around El Arco costs $30, and a four-hour trip to Santa María costs $55. Both prices include gear rental. Certain beaches, such as Playa del Amor, Santa María, Chileno, and Barco Varado, have snorkeling gear for rent at the beach; it's generally priced between $10 and $15.

For scuba diving, contact **Amigos del Mar** (☎ 800-344-3349 in the U.S., or 624-143-0505; Fax: 310-454-1686 in the U.S., or 624-143-0887; www.amigosdelmar.com), located at the marina in Cabo San Lucas. Diving specialist Ricardo Sevilla has all the answers to your Cabo diving questions. Dives are made along the wall of a canyon in San Lucas Bay where you can see the "sandfalls" that even Jacques Cousteau couldn't figure out — no one knows its source or cause. Amigos del Mar also has scuba trips to Playa Santa María and places farther away including the Gordo Banks and Cabo Pulmo. Dive prices start at $40 for a one-tank dive and $66 for two tanks. Trips to the coral outcropping at Cabo Pulmo start at $125. Located two hours from Cabo San Lucas, Cabo Pulmo is rated for beginners and up. Gordo Banks, for advanced divers, is an underwater mountain about 5 miles offshore with a black-coral bottom and schools of game fish and manta rays at a rate of $125 for a two-tank dive. Resort courses cost $100 per person and open-water certification costs around $450.

In addition to Amigos del Mar in Cabo San Lucas, snorkeling and scuba trips can also be arranged through **Gray Line** (☎ **624-146-9410;** www.graylineloscabos.com) and Cabo Travel Advisors (☎ **624-142-4444;** www.cabocta.com) — both in San José.

Reeling in the big one

Superb sport-fishing put Cabo San Lucas on the map, and many travelers still come here with the dream of dropping a line and waiting for the big one. The fishing really lives up to its reputation — bringing in a 100-pound marlin is considered routine. Angling is good all year, though the catch varies with the season. Here's the fishing lineup by time of year and the most prevalent fish:

- ✔ **January to April:** Yellowtail

- ✔ **May to December:** Yellowfin tuna

- ✔ **June to November:** Sailfish and wahoo

- ✔ **July to December:** Black and blue marlin

- ✔ **All year:** Striped marlin

For most cruises and excursions, try to make fishing reservations at least a day in advance, keeping in mind that some trips require a minimum number of people. You can arrange your fishing trip through a travel agency or directly at one of the fishing-fleet offices at the marina's far south end in Cabo San Lucas.

The marina is located on the south side of the harbor. You can easily find fleet operators with offices near the docks. To choose a boat, take a stroll around the marina and talk with the captains — you may arrive at an economical deal. Try **ABY Charters** (☎ **624-143-0874;** Fax: 624-143-0831; www.abycharters.com) or **Picante/Bluewater Sportfishing** (☎ **624-143-2474;** www.picantesportfishing.com). Both companies have booths located at the sport-fishing dock at the marina's far south end.

The going rate for a day on a fully equipped cruiser with captain and guide (many of the larger hotels, such as the Solmar, have their own fleets) starts at around $700 for up to four people. For deluxe trips with everything included aboard a 40-foot boat, budget $1,250.

The *panga* **fleets** offer the best deals. Pair up with another angler and charter a *panga*, a 22-foot skiff used by local fishermen, at Playa la Puebla near San José. Several *panga* fleets offer up to six-hour sport-fishing trips, usually from 6 a.m. to noon, for $25 per hour (with a three-hour minimum). You can split the cost with one or two other people. For information, contact the fisherman's cooperative in Pueblo la Playa, or you can call **Victor's Sportfishing** (☎ **949-496-0960** in the U.S., or 624-142-1092; Fax: 624-142-1093) at the Hotel Posada Real. Victor's also has its own fishing fleet with both pangas ($175 for six hours) and cruisers ($380 to $495). Outfitters supply the boat and tackle, and the client buys the bait, drinks, and snacks.

You need daily fishing permits in Cabos, but your captain can take care of the details. Daily permits range from $4 to $10, and annual permits are also available. Check with your outfitter when you make your reservation to determine how he handles permits.

Catch and release is strongly encouraged in Los Cabos. Anglers reel in their fish, which are tagged and released unharmed into the sea. Anglers get a certificate that documents the catch, and they leave Los Cabos with the knowledge that plenty of billfish will still be in the sea when they return.

Enjoying Land Sports

The rugged terrain of Baja and the cape region once kept people out of the area. Now it seems to be a main lure, attracting travelers in search of an active vacation and true interaction with nature. If you prefer your nature somewhat on the tame side, you may find your game on one of Cabo's many famed golf courses. In fact, golf has overtaken sport-fishing in popularity in Cabo.

Lowdown on golfing in Cabo

Golf isn't always how you play the course, but how the course plays you. Los Cabos is now considered one of the world's finest golf destinations, which means some of the courses can be pretty challenging. Picking a course that matches your abilities is important so that a challenge doesn't become a frustration. Los Cabos has an ample and intriguing variety of courses for golfers of all levels.

Beyond the selection, quality, and beauty of the courses in Los Cabos, a key reason so many golfers choose to play here is the very reliable weather. The courses highlighted in this chapter compare to the great ones in Palm Springs and Scottsdale with the added beauty of the ocean views, as well as the wider variety of desert cacti and flowering plants.

✔ **Cabo del Sol:** A Jack Nicklaus Signature course, its dramatic, finishing, ocean-side holes have earned it the nickname "the Pebble Beach of Baja." Compared to the Palmilla course (also by Nicklaus), this layout is much more difficult with less room for error. Seven of the holes are set along the water. This course is

(continued)

(continued)

very challenging target golf with numerous forced carries — even from the red tees. The signature hole here is 17, which runs by the water. Don't be fooled by the wide and welcoming 1st hole.

✔ **Cabo Real:** This Robert Trent Jones, Jr., course is known for its holes along the Sea of Cortez that sit high on mesas overlooking the sea; exceptional among these holes is the frequently photographed 12th hole. Jones designed the course to test low handicappers, but multiple tees make it enjoyable for average players as well. The par-72 layout is 6,945 yards long and was designed with professional tournament play in mind. The most famous hole is the 14th, which sits right on the beach near the Melia Cabo Real resort.

✔ **El Dorado Golf Course:** Another Jack Nicklaus Signature course located at Melia Cabo Real, El Dorado is a links-style course in the Scottish tradition. The layout is challenging — 7 holes border the Sea of Cortez and 12 are carved out of two pristine canyons. The ocean isn't the only water you see on this course — manmade lakes are also a part of the scenery. El Dorado bills itself as the "Pebble Beach of Baja" — but then again, so does Cabo del Sol — you decide.

✔ **The Raven Club** (formerly known as the Cabo San Lucas Country Club): Different Dye family members designed the front and back nine here, so the course plays like two different courses. It has deep waste bunkers, subtle terracing up hillsides, and holes built into the natural desert terrain. The most challenging hole is the extremely long, 607-yard, par-five 7th around a lake; it's the longest hole in Mexico. The Dye family redid the whole course in 2002. Although the layout is essentially the same, some greens have moved slightly and some holes are a little shorter than before, but all the bunkers and hazards have remained, and the course is now considered better than before.

✔ **Palmilla Golf Club:** The original Cabo course is now a 27-hole layout. You must play the Arroyo (the original front nine) for your first nine holes, and then you choose between Mountain (the name given to the original back nine) and Ocean Nine (the new holes — although these newer holes lie closer to the water, only one of them has a true ocean view) for your back nine. If you play this course only once, choose the Mountain back nine — it offers better ocean views. The views at the mountaintop clubhouse are also pretty spectacular. The eventual plan is for this course to be exclusive to Palmilla Hotel guests and residents of the adjacent real estate development. It's beautiful, playable, and well maintained, and views of desert mountains and the cobalt ocean without any interfering construction are featured throughout. It's one of a handful of places in the world where a golfer can play by water, mountain, and desert views surrounded by flowering vegetation. Bermuda short-cut grass makes putting fast, and the signature hole is the Mountain 5 hole; you hit over a canyon and then down to the greens below over a forced carry. This is target golf, and as a Jack Nicklaus course, the layout was constructed with strategy in mind.

Teeing off

Los Cabos has become Mexico's golf mecca. The master plan for golf in Los Cabos calls for 207 total holes in the future. The fees I list in this section are for 18 holes of play during high season, including golf cart, water, club service, and tax. Summer rates are about 25% lower, and many hotels offer special golf packages. I list the courses in geographical order, starting in San José, heading down along the Corridor, and ending in Cabo San Lucas (for specifics on the playability of the various courses, see the "Lowdown on golfing in Cabo" sidebar in this chapter):

✔ As with many things in Los Cabos, visitors find that the most economical way to enjoy this sport is to play in San José. Greens fees at the nine-hole **Club Campo de Golf San José** (Paseo Finisterra, across from the Howard Johnson Hotel; ☎ **624-142-0900** or 624-142-0905) are just $54 for nine holes or $75 for 18 holes with carts costing an extra $30. The course is open daily from 6:30 a.m. to 4 p.m., and club guests can also use the swimming pool.

✔ The newest course to open in Los Cabos is **Querencia** (1 Querencia Blvd.; ☎ **624-145-6670**), a Tom Fazio–designed course, which includes an 18-hole championship course along with a 9-hole Fazio short course and practice facility. Although it's billed as a strictly private club with play limited to property owners and golf club members, increasingly, there are provisions for guests of the resort hotels along the Corridor.

✔ The 27-hole course at the **Palmilla Golf Club** (One&Only Palmilla resort, the Corridor; ☎**800-367-2226** in the U.S., or 624-144-5250) was the first Jack Nicklaus Signature layout in Mexico. The course was built in 1992 on 900 acres of dramatic oceanfront and desert. The 27-hole course offers you a choice between two back-nine options. High-season greens fees are $215 (lower after 1 p.m.), and low-season greens fees are between $120 and $210. Although Palmilla is currently a semiprivate club, most Corridor hotels have membership benefits.

✔ Just a few miles down the road from the Palmilla is another Jack Nicklaus Signature course, the 18-hole **Ocean Course at Cabo del Sol** (Cabo del Sol resort, the Corridor; ☎ **800-386-2465** in the U.S., or 624-145-8200). The 7,100-yard course is known for its challenging final three holes. Tom Weiskopf designed the new 18-hole Desert Course, also at Cabo del Sol. Greens fees are $208 to $228.

✔ Robert Trent Jones, Jr., designed this 18-hole, 6,945-yard course at **Cabo Real** (Melia Cabo Real resort, the Corridor; ☎ **624-144-0232**), which features holes that sit high on mesas overlooking the Sea of Cortez. Fees run $215 for 18 holes, $150 after 3 p.m.

✔ The **El Dorado Golf Course** (Melia Cabo Real resort, next to the Westin Regina hotel, the Corridor; ☎ **624-144-5451**) is a Jack Nicklaus Signature course. The course is open daily from 7 a.m. until dusk. Eighteen holes are $246. After 2 p.m., a twilight special offers a round for $168. Carts are included; caddies are available for $80.

✔ Located in Cabo San Lucas, the **Raven Club** (501 Palo Blanco; ☎ **888-328-8501** in the U.S., or 624-143-4653; Fax: 624-143-5809) features an 18-hole course designed by two members of the Dye family, so the front and back nines play like two different courses. The entire course overlooks the juncture of the Pacific Ocean and Sea of Cortez, including the famous Land's End rocks. The layout includes the 607-yard, par-five 7th hole — the longest hole in Mexico. Greens fees are $176 for morning tee times, $130 for the noon rate (noon to 2:30 p.m.), and $95 after 2:30 p.m.

The golf offerings in Los Cabos continue to expand — another five courses are currently under various phases of construction. All courses generally offer 50% off their rates if you play after 2 or 2:30 p.m. Actually, late afternoon is great to play because the temperatures are cooler and play is generally faster. Course fees are high in Cabo — generally more than $200 per round, but these courses are truly world class and worth the world-class price to play them.

Several specialty tour operators offer golf packages to Los Cabos, which include accommodations, greens fees, and other amenities. Among the best is **Sportours** (☎ **888-GOLF-MEX** from the U.S.; www. golfinmexico.com).

Making time for tennis

You can play tennis at the two courts of the **Club Campo de Golf Los Cabos** (Paseo Finisterra No. 1; ☎ **624-142-0905**) for $13 an hour during the day or $20 an hour at night. (Club guests can also use the swimming pool.) Tennis is also available at the **Hotel Palmilla** (two lighted courts) and the **Presidente InterContinental** (two lighted courts).

Taking Adventure and Nature Tours

Expeditions on all-terrain vehicles (ATVs) to the Cabo Falso lighthouse and La Candelaria (an Indian pueblo in the mountains) are among the most popular of the adventure tours available in Los Cabos. These excursions are a great way to explore the land, and they're available through most travel agencies.

✔ The three-hour tour to **Cabo Falso** includes a stop at the beach, a look at some sea-turtle nests (without disturbing them) and the remains of a 1912 shipwreck, a ride over 500-foot sand dunes, and a visit to the lighthouse. Guided tours cost around $45 per person on a single vehicle or $60 for two people riding on one ATV. You can also rent ATVs for $35 for three hours. Ask your hotel concierge for more information.

✔ **La Candelaria** is an isolated Indian village in the mountains 40km (25 miles) north of Cabo San Lucas. As described in *National*

Geographic, the old pueblo is known for the white and black witch-craft still practiced here. An underground river that emerges at the pueblo provides water for the lush landscape of palms, mango trees, and bamboo. The tour's return trip travels down a steep canyon, along a beach (giving you time to swim), and past giant sea-turtle nesting grounds. Departing at 9 a.m., the La Candelaria tour costs around $80 per person or $100 for two on the same ATV.

A variety of land- and water-based adventure and nature tours are available through **Tio Sports** (☎ 624-143-3399; www.tiosports.com), including the popular ATV tours to Cabo Falso and Candelaria and para-sailing at $50 single or $70 tandem. **Gray Line Tours** (☎ 624-146-9410) is a great contact for a complete rundown of what's available. They offer all the tours from all the local companies rather than working with only a select few.

For horseback riding, here are a couple of good options for the Los Cabos area:

✔ I highly recommend **Cuadra San Francisco Equestrian Center,** Km 19.5 along the Corridor, in front of the Casa del Mar resort (☎ 624-144-0160). Master horseman Francisco Barrena, with more than 30 years of experience in training horses and operating eques-trian schools, can assist any level rider in selecting and fitting a horse to his or her skill level. Your choice of English or Western sad-dles are available on well-trained, exceptional horses. A two-hour canyon ride in and around Arroyo San Carlos or Venado Blanco costs $70; a one-hour ride to the beach or desert is $35.

✔ **Rancho Collins** (☎ 624-143-3652) also has horses available for rent for $25 per hour, with guide. Rides include trotting along the beach and sunset tours to El Faro Viejo (the Old Lighthouse). They also take you to the Pacific for sunset-riding on the beach for a cost of $35 per person per hour. It's open daily from 8 a.m. to noon and 2 to 5 p.m. They're located in front of the parking lot of the Hotel Melia Las Cabos.

Sightseeing in Los Cabos

Sports and partying are Cabo's main attractions, but you can find a few — very few is a better description — cultural and historical points of interest. In San José, the Spanish missionary Nicolás Tamaral estab-lished the stone **Iglesia de San Lucas** (Church of San Lucas; Calle Cabo San Lucas, close to the main plaza; no phone) in 1730. According to local lore, the Pericúe Indians reportedly resisted Tamaral's demands that they practice monogamy and eventually killed the missionary. Buildings on the streets facing the main plaza in San José are being renovated to house restaurants and shops, and the picturesque neighborhood prom-ises to have the strongest Mexican ambiance of any place in town.

Shopping in Los Cabos

San José has the better shopping of the two towns when it comes to higher quality items, but if you're after a beer-themed T-shirt, Cabo San Lucas can't be topped. In San José, a growing selection of unique shops, hip boutiques, and collections of fine Mexican *artesanía* (handcrafts) is clustered around Bulevar Mijares and Zaragoza, the main street. The municipal market on Mauricio Castro and Green has edibles and utilitarian wares.

In Cabo San Lucas, the most notable shops are now concentrated in the **Puerto Paraíso Entertainment Plaza.** Opened in 2002, this truly world-class mall is now the focal point for shopping for tourists, complete with parking, a food court, movie theatres, and a video arcade. With more than 50,000 square meters (54,500 sq. yd.) of air-conditioned space on three levels, it's too bad that the shops don't live up to the promise of this attractive mall. Although it bills itself as having an array of designer shops, this claim is a bit misleading; you may find only one or two name-brand items within any store, and many of the locales are vacant. It *is* a good place to shop for swimwear or resort wear, and there are plenty of gift items to choose from, but don't expect the equivalent of a U.S. shopping mall experience. However, Puerto Paraíso does have some choice dining options, the best being the local branch of **Ruth's Chris Steak House** (adjacent to the marina; ☎ 624-144-3232) and the **Cinamomo Cocina and Lounge** (local 375; ☎ 624-144-4848). The plaza is located marina-side between the Plaza Bonita Mall and Marina Fiesta Resort — you couldn't miss it if you tried. Most other shops in Cabo are on or within a block or two of Bulevar Marina and the plaza.

Clothing

Escape (Plaza Florentine, Zaragoza #20, across from the cathedral in San José; ☎ 624-142-2799) features designer and casual sportswear and accessories including designer jeans, leather bags, belts, and a trendy selection of sunglasses. An interior-decor shop by the same name next door has a small cafe and espresso bar in the connecting courtyard.

Contemporary art

San José has a growing number of art galleries — mainly artist studios open to the public — and the town's creative ambiance is blossoming. The most notable gallery is **Galería Wentworth Porter** (Avenida Obregón 20; ☎ and fax: 624-142-3141), which features a selection of original fine art along with prints and art cards by local artists. As the name implies, the work of locally popular artist Dennis Wentworth

Porter figures prominently. The gallery is open Monday through Saturday 10 a.m. to 5 p.m.

The area's longest-standing art gallery, in Cabo San Lucas, is the **Golden Cactus Studio-Gallery** (Vicente Guerrero and Madero; ☎ 614-143-6399; www.goldencactusgallery.com), which shows original art by regional artists, including Chris MacClure, as well as reproductions and posters of popular Mexican works. It's open Monday to Saturday from 10 a.m. to 2 p.m. and 4 to 7 p.m.

Also in Cabo San Lucas, in the Medano Beach area, the handsome **Galería Gattamelata** (Hacienda Road; ☎ 624-143-1166) specializes in antiques and colonial-style furniture. It's open daily from 10 a.m. to 8 p.m.

Crafts, gifts, and jewelry

Copal (in San José at Plaza Mijares; ☎ 624-142-3070) features traditional and contemporary Mexican artesanía and silver jewelry in a former residence tastefully converted into a contemporary shop. You can shop here daily from 8:30 a.m. to 9:30 p.m.

Cuca's Blanket Factory (in Cabo San Lucas at Cárdenas and Matamoros; no phone) is an open-air stand that sells the standard, Mexican, cotton and woolen blankets with an added attraction — you can design your own blanket and have it ready the next day. The stand is open daily from 9 a.m. to 9 p.m.

For unusual and well-priced jewelry, visit **SAX** (Mijares #2 in San José; ☎ 624-142-6053; www.saxstyle.com), where two local designers create one-of-a-kind pieces using silver, coral, and semi-precious stones. They can even create a special request design for you, ready in 24 hours. Located next to Casa Natalia, SAX is open from 10 a.m. to 9 p.m., closed Sundays.

Decorative and folk art

Arte, Diseño y Decoración (ADD) (Zaragoza at Hidalgo, San José; ☎ 624-142-2777) sells creative home accessories and furnishings, mostly made of rustic wood, pewter, and Talavera ceramics, and offers shipping services back home for travelers who shop too much and can't carry it all.

El Callejon (Vicente Guerrero s/n, Cabo San Lucas, between Cárdenas and Madero; ☎ 624-143-1139; Fax: 624-143-9959) may just be the most eclectic shop in the area. It features antiques, unique gifts, paintings, and home furnishings. Local artists make most of the one-of-a-kind items. It's open Monday through Friday from 10 a.m. to 8 p.m., Saturdays 10 a.m. to 6:30 p.m.

Other stores

The Plaza Bonita Shopping Center (Bulevar Marina at Cárdenas) is an older shopping center that is still worth a visit. This large terra-cotta-colored plaza on the edge of the Cabo San Lucas marina has been around since 1990, and it finally has a group of successful businesses. A branch of **Dos Lunas** (☎ 624-143-1969) sells colorful casual sports-wear. **Cartes** (☎ 624-143-1770) offers hand-painted ceramic vases and dishes, pewter frames, carved furniture, and hand-woven textiles. Most shops in the plaza are open daily from 9 a.m. to 9 p.m.

One of the spiffiest (but commercial) shops in Los Cabos is **Mamma Eli's** (Calle Cabo San Lucas, west of the plaza at Madero; ☎ 624-143-1616), a three-level store packed with folk art, crafts, clothing, and furniture. It's open Monday through Sunday from 9 a.m. to 2 p.m. and 4 to 7 p.m.

Books, Books, in Cabo San Lucas (Bulevar Marina #20, next to Carlos 'n Charlie's; ☎ 624-143-3172 or 624-143-3173), sells a good selection of English- and Spanish-language books, magazines, and newspapers, as well as a fine collection of regional guides and publications. This location is open daily from 9 a.m. to 10 p.m. A second location in San José, at Bulevar Mijares #41 near the Tropicana Inn (☎ 624-142-4433), is open daily 9 a.m. to 9 p.m.

For fine Cuban cigars and cigarettes, as well as Veracruz cigars, a visit to **Los Amigos Smokeshop and Cigar Bar** (☎ 624-142-1138) in San José is a must. Here you can buy not only high-quality cigars but also a whole range of smoking accessories, including humidors and cutters, with friendly assistance from a knowledgeable staff. In a new, expanded location (M. Doblado and Morelos, across from the French Riviera bakery), they offer private lockers, a bar with an excellent selection of single malts, Wednesday evening cigar tastings, and a VIP club for frequent visitors. Los Amigos is open Monday to Wednesday 9 a.m. to 8 p.m. and Thursday to Saturday from 9 a.m. to 10 p.m.

Embarking on a Side Trip

You can book a day-trip to the city of **La Paz** through a travel agency or through **Cabo Travel Advisors** (☎ 624-142-4444; www.cabocta.com) for around $55, which includes beverages and a tour of the countryside along the way. The tours usually stop at the weaving shop of Fortunato Silva, who spins his own cotton and weaves it into wonderfully tex-tured rugs and textiles. Cabo Travel Advisors also offers a day-trip to **Todos Santos** for $95, including a guided walking tour of the Cathedral Mission, a museum, the Hotel California, and various artists' homes.

A few years back, Todos Santos became known as "Bohemian Baja." It found its way on the travel agendas of folks looking for the latest, the trendiest, and the hippest of artist outposts — and in the plans of travelers who were simply weary of the L.A.-ization of Cabo San Lucas. In no time, Todos Santos blossomed as a true gem of a place that seems to foster the creative spirit while retaining its pervasive beauty and lovely heritage that held the original attraction.

The art and artistry created here now — from the culinary plate to the canvas — cares less about commercial appeal than quality, and in doing so, it becomes more of a draw. Don't overlook the attendant arts of agriculture, masonry, and weavings that some of the town's original residents created. From the superb meals at **Café Santa Fe** to an afternoon spent browsing the numerous shops and galleries, Todos Santos is intriguing to its core. Following is a sampling of what the town has to offer:

✔ For me — and I suspect for many others — a meal at the **Café Santa Fe** (Calle Centenario 4; ☎ 612-145-0340) is reason enough to visit Todos Santos. Much of the attention the town has received in recent years can be directly attributed to this outstanding cafe, which opened 13 years ago; it continues to live up to its lofty reputation. Owners Ezio and Paula Colombo refurbished a large stucco house across from the plaza, creating an exhibition kitchen, several dining rooms, and a lovely courtyard adjacent to a garden of hibiscus, bougainvillea, papaya trees, and herbs.

The excellent Northern Italian cuisine emphasizes local produce and seafood. Try the homemade ravioli stuffed with spinach and ricotta in a Gorgonzola sauce or the ravioli with lobster and shrimp accompanied by one of their organic salads. In high season, the wait for a table at lunch can last quite a while. Everything is prepared fresh when ordered, and reservations are recommended. Main courses run between $10 and $15. The restaurant is open Wednesday through Monday from noon to 9 p.m., but it's closed September 29 to October 18.

✔ A more casual option, and a magical place to kick off a day in Todos Santos, is the garden setting of the **Caffé Todos Santos** (Calle Centenario 33, across from the Todos Santos Inn; ☎ 612-145-0300). Try the bowl-sized cafe latte with a freshly baked croissant or one of the cafe's signature cinnamon buns. Lunch or a light meal may include a frittata or a fish filet wrapped in banana leaves with coconut milk. Main courses average $3 to $6, and the cafe is open Tuesday through Sunday from 7 a.m. to 9 p.m. and Monday from 7 a.m. to 2 p.m.

✔ A new and notable addition is the **La Coronela** restaurant/bar (Calle Benito Juárez and Morelos; ☎ 612-145-0525), at the recently remodeled **Hotel California** (allegedly the inspiration for The Eagles' popular song of the same name). With its high-style design (think Philipe Stark meets Baja), the Belgian chef creates a changing menu to accompany the ever-present and very popular margaritas.

✔ At least a half dozen galleries are in town including the noted **Galería de Todos Santos** (Topete and Legaspi; ☎ 612-145-0040), which features a changing collection of works by regional artists.

✔ **El Tecolote Libros** (Hidalgo and Juárez; ☎ 612-145-0295), though tiny, gets my vote for the best bookstore in Mexico due to its exceptional selection of Latin American literature, poetry, children's books, and reference books centering on Mexico. You can purchase English- and Spanish-language books, both new and used, along with maps, magazines, cards, and art supplies. Adjacent to El Tecolote (you enter through the bookshop) is the whimsical **Traditions** shop that sells fun folk art and Mexican kitsch at its best. It's a great place for finding that perfect, creative, and inexpensive something to bring home.

Casual visitors can easily explore Todos Santos in a day, but a few tranquil inns welcome charmed guests who want to stay a little longer. You can arrange a day's visit through tour companies in Los Cabos or venture on your own with a rental car.

Discovering Los Cabos after Dark

San José's nightlife is nonexistent outside of the restaurant and hotel bars. The bars at Casa Natalia and Tropicana — the former catering to sophisticated romantics and the latter to those in search of rowdier good times — are particularly notable. On some weekends, Tropicana even brings in a live Cuban band for dancing. Several of the larger hotels along the beach have Mexican fiestas and other weekly theme nights that include a buffet (usually all-you-can-eat), drinks, live music, and entertainment for $25 to $35 per person. A large disco on Bulevar Mijares seems to be under different ownership each year — it was closed at press time but had a "re-opening soon" sign on the door. If you're looking for real nightlife, look to Cabo San Lucas, because even the restaurants in San José close between 9 and 10 p.m.

In fact, Cabo San Lucas is the undisputed nightlife capital of Baja and a contender for the title within all resort Mexico. After-dark fun is centered around the party ambiance and camaraderie found in the casual bars and restaurants on Bulevar Marina and those facing the marina, rather than around a flashy disco scene. You can easily find a happy hour with live music and a place to dance or a Mexican fiesta with mariachis.

To enjoy live music in a more sedate setting, check out the **Sancho Panza Wine Bar and Bistro** (see "Hanging out and happy hours," later in this chapter) and the new **Jazz on the Rocks** (Zaragoza and Niños Heroes; ☎ 624-143-8999), a restaurant and live jazz bar, open 6 p.m. to 1 a.m.; jazz starts at 8 p.m. Both locations offer classic jazz in a club-style atmosphere that accommodates conversations.

Enjoying a theme night

Some of the larger hotels have weekly fiesta nights, Italian nights, and other buffet-plus-entertainment theme nights that can be fun and a good buy. Check with travel agencies and the following hotels: the **Solmar** (☎ 624-143-3535), the **Finisterra** (☎ 624-143-3333), the **Hacienda** (☎ 624-143-0123), and the **Melia San Lucas** (☎ 624-143-0420). Prices generally range from $16 (drinks, tax, and tips are extra) to $35 (everything is covered including an open bar with national drinks).

Watching a sunset

At twilight, check out Land's End — where the Sea of Cortez meets the Pacific Ocean — and watch the sun sink into the Pacific. The **Whale Watcher's Bar** (Hotel Finisterra; ☎ 624-143-3333) is considered Los Cabos' premier place for sunset-watching. Its location at Land's End offers a truly world-class view of the setting sun. The high terrace offers vistas of both sea and beach as well as magical glimpses of whales from January to March. "Whale margaritas" cost $4, and beers set you back $3. The bar is open daily from 10 a.m. to 11 p.m.

Hanging out and happy hours

If you shop around, you can usually find an *hora alegre* (happy hour) somewhere in town between noon and 7 p.m. On my last visit, the most popular places to drink and carouse until all hours were the Giggling Marlin and El Squid Roe.

✔ Lounge-style bars are the new thing in Cabo, with The Blue Room, Aqua-Lounge, and Cinamomo leading the way. **Cinamomo Cocina and Lounge,** on the third level of the trendy new Puerto Paraíso mall (local 375; ☎ 624-144-4848), has an eclectic menu of food to complement the chic bar and satiate the hip crowd. It's open from 8 a.m. to 2 a.m.

✔ **El Squid Roe** (Bulevar Marina, opposite Plaza Bonita; ☎ 624-143-0655; www.elsquidroe.com) is one of the late Carlos Anderson's inspirations, and it still attracts wild, fun-loving crowds of all ages. This two-story bar features nostalgic decor and eclectic food that's far better than you'd expect from such a party place. As fashionable as blue jeans, El Squid Roe is a place to see and see what can be seen — women's tops are known to be discarded with regularity here as the tabletop dancing moves into high gear. A patio out back serves as a place to dance when the tables, chairs, and bar spots have all been taken. It's open daily from noon to 4 a.m.

✔ Live music alternates with recorded tunes at the **Giggling Marlin** (Cárdenas at Zaragoza, across from the marina; ☎ 624-143-0606; www.gigglingmarlin.com) to get the happy patrons dancing — and occasionally jumping up to dance on the tables and bar. A contraption of winches, ropes, and pulleys above a mattress provides entertainment as couples literally string each other up by the heels — just like a captured marlin. The food is only fair here; stick with nachos and drinks. It's open daily 9 a.m. to 2 a.m. Drinks are half-price during happy "hour," which in the tradition of excess that Cabo adores, lasts for four hours — 2 to 6 p.m.

✔ **Latitude 22+** (Cárdenas s/n; ☎ 624-143-1516) is a semi-seedy restaurant/bar that never closes. License plates, signs, sports caps, and a 959-pound blue marlin are the backdrop for U.S. sports events that play on six TVs scattered among pool tables, dart boards, and assorted games. The kitchen offers dishes from hamburgers to chicken-fried steak, or you can have breakfast any time. Latitude 22+ is a block north of the town's only traffic light.

✔ Finally, an alternative to beer bars! **Sancho Panza Wine Bar and Bistro** (Plaza Las Glorias boardwalk, next to the lighthouse; ☎ 624-143-3212; www.sanchopanza.com) combines a gourmet-food market with a wine bar that features live jazz music plus an intriguing menu of nuevo-Latino cuisine. The place has a cozy neighborhood feeling. Tourists and locals take advantage of the selection of more than 150 wines, plus espresso drinks. During high season, you need reservations. It's open daily, 4 p.m. until the last guest leaves (the kitchen remains open until 11 p.m.).

✔ The **Tropicana Bar and Grill** (Mijares 30, San José; ☎ 624-142-0907) is definitely the most popular place in San José. This long-standing bar was undergoing extensive renovations during my last visit, but promises to have a more elegant ambiance — rather than its previous "rustic chic." Don't worry though, the Tropicana will still feature all types of American sports events — on plasma TV screens — and a new area to segregate drinkers from diners. Live mariachi music plays nightly from 6 to 9 p.m., with live Mexican and Cuban dance music playing from 9:30 p.m. until about 1 a.m. Truly, this is your sole nightlife option in tranquil San José. The Tropicana is open daily from 7 a.m. to 1 a.m.

Going dancing

Owned by Sammy Hagar (formerly of Van Halen) and his Mexican and American partners, the **Cabo Wabo Cantina** (Vicente Guerrero at Cárdenas; ☎ 624-143-1188) packs in youthful crowds — especially when rumors fly that a surprise appearance by a vacationing musician is imminent. Rock bands from the United States, Mexico, Europe, and Australia frequently perform live on the well-equipped stage. When live music is absent, a disco-type sound system plays mostly rock but some alternative and techno music as well. Overstuffed furniture frames the dance floor. For snacks, the Taco-Wabo, just outside the club's entrance, stays up late too. The cantina is open from 11 a.m. to 4 a.m.

The best Web sites for Los Cabos and Baja

All About Cabo (www.allaboutcabo.com) features a weekly fishing report, live golf cam, and information on hotels, restaurants, golf courses, and more.

Baja Travel Guide (www.bajatravel.com) provides a good overview of activities and how to get around, but its extensive Yellow Pages are the most useful part of the site. The site can help you with tours, ground transportation, and outdoor excursions before you go.

Visit Cabo (www.visitcabo.com) is the official site of the Los Cabos Tourism Board. The site has plenty of details about activities to do, current news, and a lodging and dining guide. You can also book your reservations online for select hotels.

Part X
The Part of Tens

The 5th Wave   By Rich Tennant

"All I know is what the swim-up bartender told me. Wearing these should improve our game by 25 percent."

In this part . . .

We give you the ten most common myths and misconceptions about Mexico. For instance, if you think all Mexican food is fiery hot, keep reading. And, speaking of Mexican food, you also find ten picks for the most delicious Mexican dishes. We also pass along ten quintessential Mexican moments — those places and experiences that you can only find in this magical, charismatic culture. Just a few *Dummies*-friendly lists that can help ensure your trip is a breeze.

Chapter 32

Ten Top Mexican Moments

*W*ant to watch the sun sink into the horizon from the deck of a sailboat while balmy breezes swirl around you? Do you know the truly proper way to drink tequila? Care to be amazed by watching men leap into a narrow, rocky passage of surging ocean from a ledge 130 feet above the water's surface?

Along with all the classic, beach-going fun you can have at a Mexico beach resort, several singular experiences exist that you can only have here in grand old Mexico. These events become the unforgettable moments that make traveling to another country and another land a unique experience.

Enjoying a Mexican Fiesta

Mexican fiestas, colorful celebrations of Mexican food, dance, and fun, are mainstays among the entertainment options at Mexican beach resorts. Though the varieties of a *fiesta mexicana* can range from the cheesy to the sublime, a fiesta is generally a party that begins with a shot of tequila and an ample buffet, goes on to take you through presentations of different regional dances, and ends in a display of fireworks. ¡Viva Mexico!

Setting Sail at Sunset

Virtually every Mexican beach resort offers some variation of the sunset sail, which is just about the very best way to experience a Mexican beach resort. In Acapulco, Ixtapa, Huatulco, and Puerto Vallarta, these trips tend to be romantic bay cruises — with plenty of libations. In

Cancún, try a replica pirate cruise with a lobster dinner; in Los Cabos, make that sail at sunset around the famous *El Arco* (the Arch) at the end of the Baja Peninsula past Lovers Beach. No matter where you set sail from, an excursion at sunset provides memories that can make a vacation.

Mixing It Up with Mariachi Music

From the first impressive note of the trombone, to the last strum of the guitar, mariachi music is synonymous with Mexico. Strolling musicians, often dressed to the nines in charro outfits and sombreros, play mariachi music on the streets and in restaurants.

Sipping on Margaritas at Sunset

Actually, feel free to pick your poison, but a cocktail at sunset is the quintessential Mexican beach vacation experience. This plan works best when you're on the Pacific coast so that you can watch the sun sink into the horizon; however, sipping at sunset on the East coast doesn't seem to dampen the spirits either!

Strolling the Malecón

Call it a cheap thrill, but in most of Mexico's beach resorts, one of the best experiences is absolutely free — just stroll along the seaside walkway *(malecón)* in Puerto Vallarta or Zihuatanejo or sit in the plaza in San Jose de Los Cabos or Acapulco. You're certain to be both charmed and entertained by the parade of local life. And while you're at it, splurge on classic fare sold by vendors — we're talking corn on the cob and a colorful swirl of cotton candy.

Feasting on Fresh Fish under a Palapa

Eating fresh fish — or, more specifically, grilled fresh fish on a plate served under a *palapa* (a thatched umbrella) by the ocean's edge and accompanied by a cold *cerveza* and a balmy sea breeze — is an experience. We promise — you've never tasted anything more delicious.

Looking for Whales in Baja or Puerto Vallarta

Watching the majestic — and enormous — whales leap out of the water, splash their tail, or corral in their young is a thrill. Each winter, whales migrate to Mexico's Pacific shores. You can find the greatest concentration of whales in Baja California and in Banderas Bay, just offshore Puerto Vallarta. Ecologically sensitive whale-watching tours are becoming a favored Mexico-vacation experience.

Watching Cliff Divers in Acapulco

The only place in the world to see this sight is in Acapulco — bikini-brief-clad men dive from a rocky cliff into the roaring surf of a narrow crevice 130 feet below. Why? Because they can . . . and because you keep watching them do it! Don't miss this sight when in Acapulco.

Visiting Tulum

Although Tulum isn't the largest or most important Mayan ruin, it's the only one by the sea, which makes it the most visually impressive. Ancient Tulum is a stunning site — and our personal favorite of all the ruins — poised on a rocky hill overlooking the transparent, turquoise Caribbean Sea. You can't visually sum up Mexico's combination of exquisite beaches and a centuries-old culture more aptly.

Shopping — While Sunbathing

Call it Mexican multi-tasking, but you can make the most of your precious vacation time by doing a little shopping while soaking up the sun. Along Mexico's public beaches, being approached by strolling vendors, peddling everything from silver jewelry to Spiderman parachute dolls, is quite common. Woven baskets, colorful ceramics, and even woven rugs are also common finds. And the shopping isn't limited to tangibles — services are available as well! Have your hair braided, your portrait sketched, or even get a temporary tattoo, all from the comfort of your beach chair. Where else but Mexico?

Chapter 33

Ten (Or So) Myths and Misconceptions about Mexico

*I*f you've never visited Mexico, you may have some preconceptions about what you're likely to find here. Perhaps you think that the geography — apart from the beaches — is an arid landscape with a uniformly hot climate. Or you may think that you should only drink tequila as a shot — doused with lime and salt.

This chapter explains some of the most common misconceptions about this vast country and its rich culture. Read on — and the next time someone starts talking about how you shouldn't drink the water in Mexico, you can set them straight!

Mexico Is a Desert, and It's Hot Everywhere

Not true: Mexico's geography includes pine forests, and occasional snowfalls hit some of the country's higher elevations. Most of the beach resorts in this book, however, do enjoy sultry climates, but bringing along a sweater or light jacket for cool evenings, especially during winter months, is always wise.

Mexico Is the Land of Sombreros and Siestas

The common image of a Mexican napping under his sombrero exists in some minds, but this stereotype is mostly made of myth. Today, Mexico is a mix of contemporary business professionals and traditional agrarian populations. The afternoon break — between 2 and 4 p.m. — is still a wonderful tradition, but rather than being a time for *siesta,* it's the time when families come together for the day's main meal. The more familiar you become with Mexico, the more you find that the people are over-whelmingly hard-working, hospitable, and honest.

Mexico's Beaches Are All the Same

With more than 8,000 miles of coastline bordering this geographically diverse country, Mexico's beaches are as varied as they can possibly be. From the flat, white sand and translucent turquoise waters of the Caribbean coast to the jungle-draped mountains that descend to rocky coves along the Pacific coast, Mexico offers the ideal beach for every-one. The striking combo of desert and sea makes Baja California one of the most memorable sights in the world.

Mexico Has No Drinking or Drug Laws

When on vacation, many travelers tend to let loose — and some tend to overindulge. Because of the welcoming and casual nature of Mexico, many visitors believe that the sale of alcoholic beverages — or illegal drugs — is unregulated. This belief simply isn't true. The legal drinking age in Mexico is 18, and technically, you're not allowed to drink openly in public. However, if you're not acting intoxicated, you can generally enjoy a beer or even a cocktail while you stroll around town. As with most things in Mexico, it's not so much what you do but how you do it. Although you can drink on public beaches, you can't be inebriated in public, so once again, be aware of how much you drink and how well you can handle your alcohol intake. White-clad police patrolling Mexico's beaches are a common sight.

With regard to drugs, we want to get straight to the point: They're ille-gal, and carrying even a small amount of marijuana can earn you a very unpleasant trip to jail. So keep your trip free of undesired encounters with the law and don't carry, buy, or use any kind of drugs. Remember that Mexican law states that you're guilty until proven innocent.

If in Trouble, Pay a Mordida

The concept of paying off someone for a favor or to overlook a transgression is as clichéd as the image of the sleeping Mexican under his sombrero. Although the idea of paying a *mordida,* or "bite," may have been rooted in truth for a long time, in Mexico's new political era, an active campaign is underway to keep dishonesty to a minimum and to clean house of corrupt public servants. Many old-school traffic cops still take a bribe when offered; however, officers belonging to the new generation of federal policemen are tested for honesty, and the penalties for corrupt behavior are severe — as are the penalties for those civilians inducing corruption by offering bribes to police officers. Our suggestion is don't offer a "tip" or *mordida* to ease your way out of trouble; the best course of action is to just act politely and find out what the problem is.

All Mexican Food Is Spicy

Not all Mexican food is spicy — although Mexican food does include some of the most intriguingly flavored foods we've ever enjoyed. Although spicy sauces may likely be in the vicinity of the food you're served, the truth is that many delicious Mexican dishes don't include chile peppers among their ingredients.

Don't Drink the Water

In the past, visitors often returned home from Mexico with stomach illnesses, but this type of vacation souvenir is a rarity today. Massive investments in an improved infrastructure and a general increase in standards of cleanliness and hygiene have practically wiped out the problem. However, play it safe and drink bottled water. Ice served in tourist establishments is purified.

Tequila Is Best with a Pinch of Salt and Lime

Tequila is a drink to be appreciated and sipped — not slammed down in a shot, its flavor masked by salt and lime. If you need to do that, you're drinking the wrong tequila. Insist on only 100% blue agave tequila — the mark of a pure, quality tequila — and then discover how to appreciate the subtleties and nuances of this tasteful beverage.

A Jeep Rental Is Really $10 a Day

One of the most common lures a timeshare salesperson uses is the "Rent a Jeep for $10 per day" enticement. Sure, it's true that the Jeep is only $10, but only after you spend up to half a day listening to an often high-pressured sales pitch. You decide — what's your vacation time really worth? And always remember: *If it looks too good to be true. . . .*

Going Anywhere in Just Your Swimsuit Is Okay

Although you may be at a seaside resort, keep in mind that it's also a home and place of business for many Mexicans. Wearing swim trunks or a pareo skirt wrapped around your bikini is okay while you're on your way to the beach, but we recommend that you put on a shirt or a sundress when you plan to explore the town or when you take a tour that involves riding around in a bus. You can still go casual, but Mexicans frown upon tourists who can't tell the difference between beach and town attire — especially true when it comes to going into any church wearing inappropriate clothing. If you want to blend in, just take a few minutes to find out what the locals wear around town. Usually, walking shorts and T-shirts are fine everywhere.

One more thing: Nude or semi-nude sunbathing is neither customary nor legal in Mexico — avoid problems with the law and keep your top on.

Mexicans Who Don't Speak English Are Hard of Hearing

Or at least it appears that many tourists buy into this statement. Some travelers seem to believe that a native Spanish-speaker will somehow get over his or her inability to understand English if the English-speaking individual talks really loudly into the Spanish-speaker's face. The truth is that many Mexicans understand at least some English, especially in popular tourist areas. Try this (we guarantee it works): Instead of panicking and starting to yell in order to get your point across, ask nicely for help, and an English-speaking local will come to assist you.

Another thing to keep in mind is that should you voice any negative comments about Mexico or Mexicans, don't assume that no one around you can understand your comments — you may find yourself in a rather embarrassing situation.

Chapter 34

Ten Most Deliciously Mexican Dishes

. . . .

In This Chapter

▶ Knowing your Mexican meals and sauces

▶ Indulging in uniquely Mexican beverages

. . . .

Some like it hot . . . and then there's Mexican food! But true Mexican cuisine is noted more for its unique way of combining flavors — chocolate and chiles, sweet and hot — than for its fire appeal.

This chapter explains some of the most flavorful and traditional Mexican dishes that you're likely to find on a menu here — go ahead and be adventurous! Let your taste buds have a vacation from the foods you know — explore the favored flavors of Mexico.

Café de Olla

The popularity and tradition of drinking coffee is nothing new to Mexico, so to experience a taste of the past, try the traditional Mexican version called *café de olla*. The espresso-strength coffee is prepared in an earthenware pot. It's spiced with cinnamon, cloves, and raw brown sugar. It's certain to wake you up!

Ceviche

Ceviche is one of Mexico's more traditional ways to enjoy fish and seafood. *Ceviche* is usually made of fish, but it may also be made from seafood including shrimp, octopus, crab, and even conch. The fresh fish — or seafood — is marinated in lime and vinegar and mixed with chopped tomatoes, onions, and, depending on the region, cucumbers and carrots.

Chilaquiles

One of the most traditional and satisfying breakfast dishes in Mexico is *chilaquiles,* fried tortilla strips cooked in a mild or spicy red or green sauce. They're usually served with a fried egg or shredded chicken and topped with fresh cream, chopped onions, and shredded white cheese.

Liquados

Not quite a meal, yet much more than a beverage, *liquados* are essentially smoothies, blended drinks of fresh fruit, ice, and either water or milk. Popular flavors include mango, banana, pineapple, or watermelon. You can also make up your own combination of tropical fruit flavors!

Mole

Mole is a rich sauce that's often considered Mexico's most important culinary contribution. A thick, deeply colored sauce, mole comes in hues of green, red, yellow, and even black. Mole blends the flavors of fresh and dried peppers, nuts, and — depending on the area — fruits or chocolate. Mole is traditionally served with chicken but is sometimes found accompanying fish and pork. It truly reflects the spirit of Mexico — the ingredients are a combination of both European and pre-Hispanic elements. The final taste varies according to the individual chef. If we had to compare it with something, curry would be the closest association.

Pescadillas

Pescadillas, flour tortillas filled with melted cheese and fresh grilled fish, are truly succulent. Most places serve them with a mild tomato sauce.

Pescado Sarandeado or Pescado en Talla

You're at a Mexican beach resort, so you're almost certain to indulge in the fresh fish *(pescado).* One of the most traditional and tasty ways to prepare fish is *sarandeado* (the term used along the beaches of Puerto Vallarta) or *en talla* (as they refer to this dish in Acapulco and Huatulco). The fish is prepared by marinating it in a sauce of Worcestershire, lime, mild red-pepper paste, and other seasonings that vary slightly depending on the region. The fish is then cooked slowly over a wood fire. The Mexican-Caribbean variation of this fish is called *tikik-chik* or *tikin-chik,* and it includes a regional *achiote* (annatto seed) paste in the marinade.

Pozole

A traditional dish from the coastal states of Jalisco, Colima, and Guerrero, *pozole* represents the blending of the pre-Hispanic Mexican culture and European influences. It's a soup-like dish made with hominy and pork, but nowadays many places make it with chicken. You can find red, green, and white versions of *pozole,* depending on the area, and garnishes include shredded lettuce, radish slices, or cabbage.

Tacos al Pastor

When ordered from a street vendor, *tacos al pastor* are only for the more adventurous travelers, but they're truly a Mexican specialty. *Tacos al pastor* are made from shanks of marinated pork, which are skewered and slowly cooked on a vertical charcoal grill. The traditional ones are served with a chunk of fresh pineapple, diced onion, and cilantro. You may have heard about the dangers of eating tacos on the street; however, the common sense that you apply to purchasing food from any street vendor also applies here. If you want to be really safe, though, we recommend you enjoy them at a small taco restaurant rather than from a street stall.

Tamales

Tamales in Mexico are quite different from the ones you typically find in the United States, which tend to be compact and greasy. In Mexico, these tasty bundles of corn dough are fluffy and come with a variety of fillings ranging from spicy to sweet. One popular variety is *rajas con queso,* a filling of poblano pepper strips and cheese. Other possibilities are *rojos* (red) or *verdes* (green) tamales filled with shredded chicken or pork — the names refer to the type of sauce included. Sweet tamales may come filled with cinnamon and raisins, stewed mangos, or pineapple. On the southern-Pacific coast, tamales come wrapped in banana leaves and have a heavier consistency. Traditional *Oaxaqueño* (from Oaxaca) tamales are filled with mole and chicken and wrapped in palm leaves.

Part XI
Appendixes

The 5th Wave   By Rich Tennant

"Of all the stuff we came back from Mexico with,
I think these adobe bathrobes were the least
well thought out."

In this part . . .

*L*ooking for a quick phone number or Web site to help you finalize the details of your Mexican beach resort vacation? Want to bone up on a few common Spanish words and phrases? Or simply hoping to get your hunger pangs going for some authentic Mexican cuisine? You can search this part for that kind of information and more, including contact information for some reputable resort tourist associations and a helpful glossary of common Mexican dishes and ingredients.

Appendix A

Quick Concierge

• •

Fast Facts

Abbreviations

Common address abbreviations include *Apdo.* (post office box), *Av.* or *Ave.* (*avenida;* avenue), *Blvd.* (*bulevar;* boulevard), *c/* (*calle;* street), *Calz.* (*calzada;* boulevard), *Dept.* (apartments), and *s/n* (*sin numero;* without a number).

The "C" on faucets stands for *caliente* (hot), and "F" stands for *fría* (cold). "PB" *(planta baja)* means ground floor, and most buildings count the next floor up as the first floor (1).

American Express

All major resort destinations have local American Express representatives. For a detailed list of all representatives, visit the AmEx Web site at http://travel. americanexpress.com/travel/ personal/resources/tso/. For credit card and traveler's check information, call ☎ 800-504-0400 toll free inside Mexico. The local offices in the beach resorts covered in this guide are Acapulco (Av. Costera Miguel Alemán 121, Hotel Continental Emporio Local 31; ☎ 744-435-2200), Cabo San Lucas (Plaza Bonita Mall, Local 48e/49e; ☎ 624-143-5766), Cancún (Av. Tulum 208; ☎ 998-881-4025), Huatulco (Av. Carrizal 704, La Crucecita; ☎ 958-587-0811), Ixtapa and Zihuatanejo (Av. Heroico Colegio Militar 38, Plaza San Rafael Local 7, Col. Centro; ☎ 755-544-6242), Puerto Vallarta (Morelos 660; ☎ 322-223-2955), and San José del Cabo (Plaza La Misión, Local 1-b, Blvd. Mijares/Paseo Finisterra; ☎ 624-142-1306).

ATMs

Automated teller machines are widely available in all major resort towns, with fewer to be found in the smaller destinations. They're a great option to get cash at an excellent exchange rate. To find the closest ATM, visit the Web sites for the most popular networks: Plus (www.visa.com/pd/atm) and Cirrus (www.mastercard.com/atmlocator). (See Chapter 6 for further details.)

Business Hours

In general, businesses in resort destinations are open daily between 9 a.m. and 8 p.m.; although many close between 2 and 4 p.m. Smaller businesses also tend to close on Sundays. The larger resort destinations have extended business hours — many shops stay open until 10 p.m. Bank hours are Monday to Friday 8:30 or 9 a.m. to anywhere between 3 and 7 p.m. Increasingly, banks are offering Saturday hours in at least one branch for at least a half-day, usually from 10 a.m. until 2 p.m.

Credit Cards

Most stores, restaurants, and hotels accept credit cards. However, smaller destinations such as Puerto Escondido, where telephone lines aren't always available to process the authorization for the charge, may not be so credit-card friendly. The same goes for smaller, family-run shops and restaurants. You can withdraw cash from your credit card at most ATMs, but make sure that you know your PIN and you've cleared the card for foreign withdrawals with your bank. For credit-card emergencies, call the following numbers: **American Express** ☎ 001-800-221-7282, **MasterCard** ☎ 001-800-307-7309, and **Visa** ☎ 001-800-336-8472. These numbers connect you to the U.S. toll-free numbers to report lost or stolen credit cards; however, the call isn't toll free from Mexico.

Currency

The currency in Mexico is the Mexican peso. Paper currency comes in denominations of 20, 50, 100, 200, and 500 pesos. Coins come in denominations of 1, 2, 5, 10, 20, and 50 centavos (100 centavos equal 1 peso). The currency-exchange rate is about 11 pesos to US$1.

Customs

All travelers to Mexico are required to present proof of citizenship, such as an original birth certificate with a raised seal, a valid passport, or naturalization papers, and need to have a Mexican tourist card (FMT), which is free of charge and can be attained through travel agencies and airlines and at all border-crossing points going into Mexico. For more information, see Chapter 7.

Doctors/Dentists

Every embassy and consulate can recommend local doctors and dentists with good training and modern equipment; some of the doctors and dentists also speak English. See the list of embassies and consulates under the "Embassies/Consulates," section later in this appendix. Hotels with a large foreign clientele can often recommend English-speaking doctors as well. Most first-class hotels in Mexico's resort areas have a doctor on call.

Drug Laws

To be blunt, don't use or possess illegal drugs in Mexico. Mexican officials have no tolerance for drug users, and jail is their solution. If you go to jail, you have little hope of getting out until you complete the sentence (usually a long one) or pay heavy fines. Remember, in Mexico, the legal system assumes that you're guilty until proven innocent. (***Note:*** It isn't uncommon to be befriended by a fellow user, only to be turned in by that "friend," who's collected a bounty.) Bring prescription drugs in their original containers. If possible, pack a copy of the original prescription with the generic name of the drug.

U.S. Customs officials are also on the lookout for diet drugs that are sold in Mexico but illegal in the United States. Possession of these could land you in a U.S. jail. If you buy antibiotics over the counter (which you can do in Mexico) — say, for a sinus infection — and still have some left, you probably won't be hassled by U.S. Customs.

Electricity

The electrical system in Mexico is 110 volts AC (60 cycles), as it is in the United States and Canada. But in reality, it may cycle more slowly and overheat your appliances. To compensate, select a medium or low speed for hair dryers. Many older hotels still have electrical outlets for flat, two-prong plugs; you'll need an adapter for any modern electrical apparatus that has three prongs or an enlarged end on one of the two prongs. Many first-class and deluxe hotels have the three-holed outlets (*trifásicos* in Spanish). Hotels that don't have modern outlets may have adapters to loan, but to be sure, carry your own.

Embassies/Consulates

Embassies and consulates can provide valuable lists of doctors and lawyers, as well as regulations concerning marriages in Mexico. Contrary to popular belief, your embassy can't get you out of a Mexican jail, provide postal or banking services, or fly you home when you run out of money. However, consular officers can provide you with advice on most matters and problems. Most countries have a representative embassy in Mexico City, and many have consular offices or representatives in the provinces.

The embassy of the **United States** is in Mexico City (Paseo de la Reforma 305; ☎ 555-080-2000; fax: 555-525-5040). Its hours are Monday to Friday 8:30 a.m. to 5:30 p.m. You can visit the embassy's Web site at www.usembassy-mexico.gov fo a list of street addresses for the U.S. consulates inside Mexico. U.S. consular agencies are located in Acapulco (☎ 744-469-0556 or 744-484-0300), Cabo San Lucas (☎ 624-143-3566), Cancún (☎ 998-883-0272), Cozumel (☎ 987-872-4574 or 987-872-4485), Ixtapa (☎ 755-553-2100), and Puerto Vallarta (☎ 322-222-0069).

The embassy of **Australia** is in Mexico City at Rubén Darío 55, Polanco (☎ 555-531-5225; fax: 555-531-9552). It's open Monday to Friday 9 a.m. to 1 p.m. (www.mexico.embassy.gov.au).

The embassy of **Canada** is also in Mexico City (Schiller 529, in Polanco; ☎ 555-724-7900). It's open Monday through Friday 9 a.m. to 1 p.m. and 2 to 5 p.m. (At other times, the name of a duty officer is posted on the embassy door.) Visit the Web site at www.canada.org.mx for a complete list of the addresses of the consular agencies in Mexico. Canadian consulates are located in Acapulco (Centro Comercial Marbella, Local 23, Prolongación Farallón s/n; ☎ 744-484-1305; E-mail: acapulco@canada.org.mx), Cancún (Plaza Caracol 11, Blvd. Kukulkán; ☎ 998-883-3360; E-mail: cancun@canada.org.mx), Puerto Vallarta (Edificio Obelisco Local 108, Av. Francisco Medina Ascencio No. 1951; ☎ 322-293-0098 or 322-293-0099; E-mail: vallarta@canada.org.mx), and San José del Cabo (Plaza José Green, local 9, Blvd. Mijares s/n; ☎ 624-142-4333; E-mail: loscabos@canada.org.mx).

The embassy of **New Zealand** in Mexico City is at José Luis Lagrange 103, 10th floor, Col. Los Morales Polanco (☎ 555-283-9460; fax: 555-283-9480; E-mail: kiwimexico@compuserve.com.mx).

The embassy of the **United Kingdom** is in Mexico City at Río Lerma 71, Col. Cuauhtémoc (☎ 555-242-8500). The embassy's Web site, which you can visit at www.embajadabritanica.com.mx, has an updated list of honorary consuls in Mexico. There are honorary British consuls in Acapulco (☎ 744-484-1735), Cancún (☎ 998-881-0100), and Huatulco (☎ 958-587-2373 or 958-587-2372 — leave a message).

The embassy of **Ireland** is located in Mexico City on Blvd. Cerrada Avila Camacho 76, 3rd floor Forum Building, Col. Lomas de Chapultepec (☎ 555-520-5803; fax: 555-520-5892; E-mail: embajada@irlanda.org.mx).

The embassy of **South Africa** is also in Mexico City on Andres Bello 10 / 9th floor, Col. Polanco (☎ 555-282-9260; www.sudafrica.org.mx).

Emergencies

In case of emergency, always contact your embassy or consulate. For police emergencies, you must dial ☎ 060 — this number connects you to the local police department. Remember that in most cases the person answering the phone doesn't speak English. The 24-hour tourist help line from Mexico City (INFOTUR) is ☎ 800-903-9200 or 555-250-0151. A tourist legal assistance office *(Procuraduría del Turista)* is located in Mexico City (☎ 555-571-3600). Although the phones are frequently busy, they do offer 24-hour service, and an English-speaking person is always available.

Health

No special immunizations are required. As is often true when traveling anywhere in the world, intestinal problems are the most common afflictions experienced by travelers. Drink only bottled water and stay away from uncooked foods, especially fruits and vegetables. Antibiotics and anti-diarrheal medications are readily available in all drugstores.

Contact your embassy or consulate for a list of accredited doctors in the area.

Hotlines

While in Mexico, contact the 24-hour tourist help line, INFOTUR (☎ 800-903-9200), for information regarding hotels, restaurants, tourist attractions, hospitals with English-speaking staff, and so on.

Information

The best source of information is the tourist help line INFOTUR (☎ 800-903-9200); however, having a general idea of the information you're requesting — the approximate name of the hotel or restaurant, the name or subject matter of the museum, and so on — is important. You can also find telephone-number information inside Mexico by dialing ☎ 040; however, it's very common to find that the telephone numbers aren't listed under the known name of the establishment. A reminder: Very few information operators speak English.

Internet Access

In large cities and resort areas, a growing number of five-star hotels offer business centers with Internet access. You also find cybercafes in destinations that are popular with expatriates and business travelers. Even in remote spots, Internet access is very common now — it's often their best way of communicating with the outside world. Note that many Internet service providers automatically cut off your Internet connection after a specified period of time (say, 10 minutes) because telephone lines are at a premium. Some Telmex offices also have free-access Internet kiosks in their reception areas. If you plan to check your e-mail while in Mexico, register for a Web-based e-mail address, such as those from Hotmail or Yahoo!.

Language

The official language in Mexico is Spanish, but you find that a fair number of Mexicans who live and work in resort areas speak some English. Mexicans are very patient when it comes to foreigners trying to speak Spanish. See Appendix B for commonly used terms in Spanish.

Legal Aid

International Legal Defense Counsel (111 S. 15th St., 24th floor, Packard Building, Philadelphia, PA 19102; ☎ 215-977-9982) is a law firm specializing in legal difficulties of Americans abroad. Also, see the "Embassies/Consulates" and "Emergencies" sections, earlier in this appendix.

Liquor Laws

The legal drinking age in Mexico is 18; however, it's extremely rare that anyone is asked for identification or denied purchase. Grocery stores sell everything from beer and wine to national and imported liquors. You can buy liquor 24 hours a day, but during major elections and a few official holidays, dry laws often are enacted as long as 24 hours beforehand. The laws apply to foreign tourists as well as local residents, even though it's not uncommon to find a few hotels and nightclubs that manage to obtain special permits to sell alcohol. Mexico doesn't have any "open container" laws for transporting alcohol in cars, but authorities are beginning to target drunk drivers more aggressively. Driving defensively is a good idea.

Drinking in the street isn't legal, but many tourists do it. Use your better judgment and try to avoid carrying on while sporting beer bottles and cans — you're not only exposing yourself to the eyes of the authorities, but most Mexicans consider public intoxication to be tacky behavior. If you're getting too drunk, don't drink in the street because the police will most likely stop you. As is the custom in Mexico, it's not so much what you do, but how you do it.

Mail

Postage for a postcard or letter is 59¢, and the item may arrive at its destination anywhere between one to six weeks after you send it. A registered letter costs $1.90. Sending a package can be quite expensive — the Mexican postal service charges $8 per kilo (2.20 pounds) — and is unreliable — it takes between two and six weeks, if it arrives at all. Packages are frequently lost within the Mexican postal system, although the situation has improved in recent years. Federal Express, DHL, UPS, or any other reputable, international-mail service is the recommended option for a package or important letter.

Newspapers/Magazines

Newspaper kiosks in larger Mexican cities carry a selection of English-language magazines. Most resort towns have their own local publications in English, which provide helpful hints and fun reading tailored to tourists and foreigners who have made their homes in the different resort destinations around Mexico. In Puerto Vallarta, the *Vallarta Today* and *PV Tribune* are two of these newspapers — the former is a daily publication, and the latter is published weekly. In Los Cabos, you can find a wealth of information in the *Los Cabos Guide, Los Cabos News, Cabo Life, Baja Sun,* and the irreverent and extremely entertaining *Gringo Gazette.*

Pets

Taking a pet into Mexico is easy but requires a little pre-planning. For travelers coming from the United States and Canada, your pet's health needs to be checked within 30 days before arrival in Mexico. Most veterinarians in major cities have the appropriate paperwork — an official health certificate, to be presented to Mexican Customs officials, which ensures the pet is up-to-date on its vaccinations. When you and your pet return from Mexico, U.S. Customs officials will require the same type of paperwork. If your stay extends beyond the 30-day time frame of your U.S.-issued certificate, you need to get an updated certificate of health issued by a veterinarian in Mexico that also states the condition of your pet and the status of its vaccinations. To find out about any last-minute changes in requirements, consult a Mexican-government tourist office.

Pharmacies

Farmacias sell you just about anything you want, with or without a prescription. Most pharmacies are open Monday to Saturday 8 a.m. to 8 p.m. Generally, one or two 24-hour pharmacies are located in the major resort areas. Pharmacies take turns staying open during off-hours, so if you're in a smaller town and you need to buy medicine after normal hours, ask for the *farmacia de turno* (pharmacist on duty).

Police

It's quite common to find that the majority of police forces in tourist areas are very protective of international visitors. Several cities, including Cancún, Puerto Vallarta, and Acapulco, have gone so far as to set up a special corps of English-speaking tourist police to assist with directions, guidance, and more. In case of a police emergency, dial ☎ 060 to contact the local police department, keeping in mind that, unless you're dealing with tourist police, the force is very unlikely to speak English.

Restrooms

Public restrooms are usually more of an adventure than a service — you can never tell whether they'll be clean or toilet paper will be available. You can usually resort to using the restroom in a restaurant.

Safety

Most resort areas in Mexico are very safe; however, it's better to be prepared than sorry. A few points to keep in mind: Before you leave home, prepare for the theft or loss of your travel documents by making two photocopies of them. Keep each copy and the original documents in separate places. Lock your passport and valuables in the hotel safety-deposit box. Keep credit-card company phone numbers and the numbers of traveler's checks somewhere other than your purse or wallet. Don't dress or behave in a conspicuous manner. When visiting crowded places, be aware of your wallet or purse at all times. Leave your best jewelry at home — who wants jewelry tan lines anyway?

Taxes

Most of Mexico has a 15% value-added tax (IVA) on goods and services, and it's supposed to be included in the posted price. This tax is 10% in Cancún, Cozumel, and Los Cabos. Mexico charges all visitors an entry tax of $15, which is usually included in the price of your plane ticket. Mexico also imposes an exit tax of around $18 on every foreigner leaving the country, which again, is usually included in the price of airline tickets.

Telephone/Fax

In November 2001, telephone area codes were changed. Now, all telephone numbers in Mexico are seven digits plus a three-digit area code, except for Mexico City, Guadalajara, and Monterrey where local calls require that you dial the last eight digits of the published phone number. Many fax numbers are also regular telephone numbers — you have to ask whoever answers your call for the fax tone ("*Me da tono de fax, por favor.*"). Wireless phones are very popular for small businesses in resort areas and smaller communities. To dial a wireless number inside the same area code, dial 044 and then the number — depending on the area, you may need to dial the last seven digits or the seven digits plus the three-digit area code. To dial the cellular phone from anywhere else in Mexico, first dial 01, and then the ten-digit number, including the area code. To dial any number inside Mexico from the United States, just dial 011-52 plus the ten-digit number.

The country code for Mexico is 52. To call home from Mexico, dial 00 plus the country code you're calling and then the area code and phone number. To call the United States and Canada, you need to dial 001 plus the area code and the number. The country code for the United Kingdom is 44; the country code for New Zealand is 64, and the country code for Australia is 61.

To call operator assistance for calls inside Mexico, dial 020; for operator assistance for international calls, dial 090. Both numbers provide assistance for person-to-person and collect calls.

Time Zone

Central standard time prevails throughout most of Mexico. The west-coast states of Sonora, Sinaloa, and parts of Nayarit are on mountain standard time. The state of Baja California Norte is on pacific time, but Baja California Sur is on mountain time. Most of Mexico observes daylight savings time, but the time change lasts for a shorter period of time than it does in the rest of the world. Mexico doesn't spring forward until June, and the country falls back in early October. This time-change pattern has created a lot of political arguments, and the guidelines may change again.

Tipping

Most service employees in Mexico count on tips for the majority of their income — especially true for bellboys and waiters. Bellboys should receive the equivalent of 50¢ to $1 per bag; waiters generally receive 10% to 20%, depending on the level of service. In Mexico, tipping taxi drivers isn't customary, unless you hire them by the hour, or they provide guide or other special services. Don't use U.S. coins to tip.

Water

Most hotels have decanters or bottles of purified water in the rooms, and the better hotels have purified water from regular taps or special taps marked *agua purificada.* Some hotels charge for in-room bottled water. Virtually any hotel, restaurant, or bar brings you purified water if you specifically request it, but they usually charge you for it. Bottled, purified water is sold widely at drugstores and grocery stores. Some popular brands are Santa María, Ciel, and Bonafont. Evian and other imported brands are also widely available.

Toll-Free Numbers and Web Sites

Airlines serving select Mexican destinations

Aeroméxico
☎ 800-237-6639
www.aeromexico.com
Acapulco, Cancún, Huatulco, Los Cabos,
Ixtapa-Zihuatanejo, Puerto Vallarta

Air Canada
☎ 888-247-2262
www.aircanada.ca
Cancún, Cozumel, Puerto Vallarta

Alaska Airlines
☎ 800-426-0333
www.alaskaair.com
Cancún, Ixtapa-Zihuatanejo, Los Cabos,
Puerto Vallarta

American Airlines
☎ 800-433-7300
www.aa.com
Acapulco, Cancún, Cozumel, Ixtapa-
Zihuatanejo, Los Cabos, Puerto Vallarta

America West Airlines
☎ 800-235-9292
www.americawest.com
Acapulco, Cancún, Ixtapa-Zihuatanejo, Los
Cabos, Puerto Vallarta

ATA Airlines
☎ 800-225-2995 or 800-435-9282
www.ata.com
Cancún, Ixtapa-Zihuatanejo, Puerto Vallarta

British Airways
☎ 800-247-9297
www.britishairways.com
Flights from London to Cancún

Continental Airlines
☎ 800-525-0280
www.continental.com
Acapulco, Cancún, Cozumel, Ixtapa-
Zihuatanejo, Los Cabos, Puerto Vallarta

Delta Air Lines
☎ 800-221-1212
www.delta.com
Cancún, Los Cabos, Puerto Vallarta

Frontier Airlines
☎ 800-432-1359
www.frontierairlines.com
Cancún, Ixtapa-Zihuatanejo, Los Cabos,
Puerto Vallarta

United Airlines
☎ 800-864-8331
www.united.com
Cancún, Los Cabos

Serviced through Aeroméxico

Mexicana
☎ 800-531-7921
www.mexicana.com
Acapulco, Cancún, Cozumel, Huatulco,
Ixtapa-Zihuatanejo, Los Cabos, Puerto
Vallarta

Northwest Airlines
☎ 800-225-2525
www.nwa.com
Seasonal flights to Acapulco, Cancún,
Cozumel, Los Cabos, Puerto Vallarta

US Airways
☎ 800-428-4322
www.usairways.com
Cancún, Cozumel

Major car-rental agencies

Advantage
☎ 800-777-5500
www.advantagerentacar.com
Cancún, Huatulco, Los Cabos,
Puerto Vallarta

Alamo
☎ 800-227-7368 or 800-327-9633
www.goalamo.com
Acapulco, Cancún, Cozumel, Huatulco,
Ixtapa-Zihuatanejo, Los Cabos,
Puerto Escondido, Puerto Vallarta

Avis
☎ 800-331-1212 in the continental U.S.
☎ 800-TRY-AVIS in Canada
www.avis.com
Acapulco, Cancún, Cozumel, Los Cabos,
Puerto Vallarta

Budget
☎ 800-527-0700
www.budgetrentacar.com
Acapulco, Cancún, Cozumel, Huatulco,
Ixtapa-Zihuatanejo, Los Cabos, Puerto
Escondido, Puerto Vallarta

Dollar
☎ 800-800-4000
www.dollar.com
Cancún, Huatulco, Ixtapa-Zihuatanejo,
Los Cabos, Puerto Vallarta

Hertz
☎ 800-654-3131
www.hertz.com
Acapulco, Cancún, Cozumel, Ixtapa-
Zihuatanejo, Los Cabos, Puerto Vallarta

National
☎ 800-CAR-RENT
www.nationalcar.com
Cancún, Cozumel, Ixtapa-Zihuatanejo,
Los Cabos, Puerto Vallarta

Payless
☎ 800-PAYLESS
www.paylesscarrental.com
Los Cabos

Thrifty
☎ 800-367-2277
www.thrifty.com
Cancún, Ixtapa-Zihuatanejo, Los Cabos,
Puerto Vallarta

Major and select local hotel and motel chains

Best Western
☎ 800-528-1234
www.bestwestern.com
Acapulco, Cancún, Cozumel, Huatulco,
Ixtapa-Zihuatanejo, Los Cabos,
Puerto Escondido, Puerto Vallarta

Blue Bay Getaway
☎ 800-BLUE-BAY
www.bluebayresorts.com
Cancún, Puerto Vallarta

Camino Real
☎ 800-722-6466
www.caminoreal.com
Acapulco, Cancún, Huatulco, Puerto Vallarta

Days Inn
☎ 800-329-7466
www.daysinn.com
Cozumel

Fiesta Americana
☎ 800-FIESTA-1
www.fiestaamericana.com
Acapulco, Cancún, Cozumel, Los Cabos,
Puerto Vallarta

Hilton Hotels
☎ 800-HILTONS
www.hilton.com
Cancún, Los Cabos

Holiday Inn
☎ 800-HOLIDAY
www.ichotelsgroup.com
Cancún, Puerto Vallarta

Hyatt Hotels and Resorts
☎ 800-233-1234
www.hyatt.com
Acapulco, Cancún

Inter-Continental Hotels and Resorts
☎ 888-567-8725
www.ichotelsgroup.com
Cancún, Cozumel, Los Cabos,
Puerto Vallarta

Le Méridien Hotel
☎ 800-543-4300
www.lemeridien.com
Cancún

Marriott Hotels
☎ 800-228-9290
www.marriott.com
Cancún, Puerto Vallarta

Plaza Las Glorias
☎ 800-800-2424

www.mexicoissoeasy.com
Cancún, Cozumel, Ixtapa-Zihuatanejo,
Los Cabos, Puerto Vallarta

Quinta Real
☎ 800-323-7500
www.quintareal.com
Acapulco, Huatulco, Puerto Vallarta

Radisson Hotels International
☎ 800-333-3333
www.radisson.com
Acapulco, Cancún, Ixtapa-Zihuatanejo

Ritz-Carlton Hotel
☎ 800-241-3333
www.ritzcarlton.com
Cancún

Sheraton Hotels and Resorts
☎ 800-325-3535
www.sheraton.com
Cancún, Los Cabos, Puerto Vallarta

Westin Hotels and Resorts
☎ 800-228-3000
www.westin.com
Cancún, Los Cabos, Puerto Vallarta

Where to Get More Information

The following **tourist boards** and **embassies** provide valuable information regarding traveling in Mexico, including information on entry requirements and customs allowances:

✔ **Mexico Tourism Board:** There are several offices in major North American cities, in addition to the main office in Mexico City (☎ 55-5203-1103; www.visitmexico.com). The toll-free information number is ☎ **800-44-MEXICO.**

Locations in the United States: Chicago (300 N. Michigan, 4th floor, Chicago, IL 60601; ☎ 312-606-9252); Houston (4507 San Jacinto, Ste. 308, Houston, TX 77074; ☎ 713-772-2581 ext. 105); Los Angeles (2401 W. 6th St., Los Angeles, CA 90057; ☎ 213-351-2069; Fax: 213-351-2074); Miami (5975 Sunset Dr., Ste. 305, Miami, FL 33143; ☎ 786-621-2909); New York (375 Park Ave., Ste. 1905, New York, NY 10152; ☎ 212-308-2110; Fax: 212-308-9060); and the Mexican Embassy Tourism Delegate in Washington D.C. (1911 Pennsylvania Ave., Washington, DC 20006; ☎ 202-728-1750).

Locations in Canada: Montreal (1 Place Ville-Marie, Suite 1931, Montreal, PQ H3B 2C3; ☎ 514-871-1052; Fax: 514-871-3825); Toronto (2 Bloor St. W., Ste. 1502, Toronto, ON M4W 3E2; ☎ 416-925-0704; Fax: 416-925-6061); Vancouver (999 W. Hastings, Ste. 1110, Vancouver, BC V6C 2W2; ☎ 604-669-2845; Fax: 604-669-3498); and the embassy office in Ottawa (Ste. 1500 ,45 O'Connor St., Ottawa, ON K1P 1A4; ☎ 613-233-8988; Fax: 613-235-9123).

✔ **U.S. State Department:** Travel information from the U.S. State Department and the Overseas Citizens Services division (☎ 202-647-5225) offers a consular information sheet on Mexico that contains a compilation of safety, medical, driving, and general travel information gleaned from reports by official U.S. State Department offices in Mexico. In addition to calling, you can request the consular information sheet by fax at ☎ 202-647-3000. The State Department is also on the Internet: Check out `http://travel.state.gov/mexico.html` for the consular information sheet on Mexico; `http://travel.state.gov/travel_warnings.html` for other consular information sheets and travel warnings; and `http://travel.state.gov/tips_mexico.html` for the State Department's *Tips for Travelers to Mexico.*

✔ **INFOTUR (24-hour tourist help line):** Dial ☎ 01-800-903-9200 toll free inside Mexico, and you can get information from English-speaking operators as to where to go for medical assistance and other types of assistance. It's also a great source for general tourism information. You can always find helpful operators who will try to get the information that you need. To call this office from the United States, dial ☎ 800-482-9832.

✔ **Centers for Disease Control (CDC):** A source for medical information for travelers to Mexico and elsewhere, the Centers for Disease Control (☎ 800-311-3435 or 404-639-3534; `www.cdc.gov/travel`) provides detailed information on health issues for specific countries. For travelers to Mexico and Central America, the number with recorded messages about specific health issues related to this region is ☎ 877-FYI-TRIP. The toll-free fax number for requesting information is ☎ 888-232-3299.

Local **tourist information offices** offer all kinds of information to travelers, including brochures, maps, and destination-specific magazines and posters. If you want them to mail information to you, allow four to six weeks for the mail to reach you.

✔ **Acapulco's State of Guerrero Tourism Office** (Costera Miguel Aleman 4455, Centro Internacional Acapulco, Acapulco, Guerrero, located on the Costera side of the convention center; ☎ 744-484-4416; Fax: 744-484-4583; `www.acapulco.gob.mx`; E-mail: `procurador2000@yahoo.com`). Note that the Web site is currently available in Spanish only.

✔ **Cancún Convention and Visitors Bureau** (Ave. COBA Esq. Ave. Nader S.M.5, Cancún, Quintana Roo, Mexico 77500; ☎ 998-884-6531 or 998-881-0400; www.cancun.info).

✔ **Huatulco Hotels Association** (Blvd. Santa Cruz 303 Local 5, interior Hotel Castillo Huatulco, Bahías de Huatulco, Oaxaca, 70989; ☎ 866-416-0555 from the U.S. or 958-587-0848; Fax: 958-587-0686; www.hoteleshuatulco.com.mx; **E-mail:** info@hoteleshuatulco.com.mx).

✔ **Huatulco State Tourism Office** (Blvd. Benito Juarez s/n Bahía de Tangolunda, Bahías de Huatulco, Oaxaca, 70989; ☎ 958-581-0176 or 958-581-0177; www.oaxaca.gob.mx/sedetur; **E-mail:** sedetur6@oaxaca.gob.mx). The Web site offers information about the whole state of Oaxaca, including some information on Huatulco; however, the information is in Spanish and not very consumer-oriented.

✔ **Isla Mujeres Tourism Office** (Av. Rueda Medina 130, Isla Mujeres, Quintano Roo, Mexico, C.P. 77400) across from the main pier between Immigration and Customs; ☎ 998-877-0767; www.isla-mujeres.com.mx; **E-mail:** infoisla@prodigy.net.mx).

✔ **Ixtapa Tourism Office** or Subsecretaría de Fomento Turístico (Centro Comercial La Puerta, Locales 2, 3, 8, and 9, Ixtapa, Guerrero, 408880; ☎ 755-553-1967; Fax: 755-553-1968).

✔ **Los Cabos Tourism Office** (Bolivar Mauricio Castro, Plaza San Jose Local 3 and 4 Col. 1 de mayo, Cabo San Lucas, BCS; ☎ 624-142-3310; www.visitcabo.com). You can try to call the office for information, and who knows, someone may even be there to answer the phone; however, you're better off visiting the Web site.

✔ **Puerto Escondido State Tourism Office** (SEDETUR, Blvd. Benito Juarez s/n Fraccionamiento Bacocho, Puerto Escondido, Oaxaca, 71980; ☎ 954-582-0175; www.oaxaca.gob.mx/sedetur; **E-mail:** sedetur7@oaxaca.gob.mx).

✔ **Puerto Vallarta Tourism Board and Convention and Visitors Bureau** (Local 18 Planta Baja, Zona Comercial Continental Plaza, Puerto Vallarta, Jalisco, 48310; ☎ 888-384-6822 from the U.S., or 322-224-1175; Fax: 322-224-0915; www.visitpuertovallarta.com; **E-mail:** info@visitpuertovallarta.com).

✔ **State of Jalisco Tourism Office in Puerto Vallarta** (Centro Comercial Plaza Marina Locales 144 and 146, Marina Vallarta, Puerto Vallarta, Jalisco, 48321; ☎ 322-221-2676 or 322-221-2677; Fax: 322-221-2678).

✔ **Zihuatanejo Tourism Office or Dirección de Turismo Municipal** (located in the city-hall building in Zihuatanejo; ☎ 755-554-4455, ask for the tourism office; **E-mail:** presidencia@ixtapa-zihuatanejo.com).

Following is a list of several Web sites where you can find updated information about Mexico and traveling to the most popular beach resorts; however, keep in mind that most of the companies that these Web sites recommend received this lofty status by paying some sort of advertising fee.

- ✔ The **Mexico Ministry of Tourism's** official Web site (www.mexico-travel.com) offers ample information (15,000 pages worth) about Mexico. However, the pages are slow to load and the information is a little outdated.

- ✔ The **Mexico Tourism Board** developed another official site (www.visitmexico.com) with more current information on the different destinations in Mexico. Again, the pages are slow to load, but the navigation is a lot easier. The site features sections for travelers divided by region; a good search engine usually takes you to the information you're looking for.

- ✔ For low-impact travel planning, visit the **Eco Travels in Mexico** section of the award-winning Web site **Planeta.com** (www.planeta.com/mexico.html). You can find up-to-date information on reliable eco-tour operators in Mexico. This site also offers an excellent source to find banks and telephone services. Planeta.com is one of the best sources for current information because it's updated monthly.

- ✔ The electronic version of *Mexico Connect* magazine (www.mexconnect.com) offers a wealth of information and is the ideal site to begin a more in-depth, online exploration about when and where to visit Mexico. The site offers a great index where you can find everything from out-of-the-way adventures to Mexico's history to recommended accommodations.

- ✔ **Cancun South** (www.cancunsouth.com) is a great site for independent travelers looking to explore the Riviera Maya. The site is easy to navigate and offers a wealth of information specific to the area.

- ✔ **Cozumel.net** (www.cozumel.net) provides detailed information about the island's life. In our opinion, this site has the most reliable information about Cozumel and it even lists ferry schedules in the "About Cozumel" section.

- ✔ Two good sites feature information on Los Cabos: **Baja Travel Guide** (www.bajatravel.com) and **All about Cabo** (www.allaboutcabo.com). We prefer the factual and less flashy presentation of the Baja Travel Guide site; however, if you want to find out a bit more about activities such as golf and fishing and get an up-to-date beach forecast, All About Cabo is the site to visit.

Following is a selection of Web sites that can help you with all the important stuff related to your Mexican beach resort vacation, such as figuring out where to get cash, how to ask for a cold beer, where to go to send an e-mail to your friends back home, how to find really great deals, and so on.

- ✔ **Cybercafes** (www.cybercafes.com): Search this interactive database to find Internet and cybercafes worldwide, though given the fluxuating state of these businesses, locations change frequently. For Mexican cybercafes, you have to search by state, rather than city or resort.

- ✔ **Foreign Languages for Travelers** (www.travlang.com): Find out what basic terms mean in more than 70 languages and click on any underlined phrase to hear what it sounds like. *Note:* Free audio software and speakers are required.

- ✔ **Intellicast** (www.intellicast.com): **Get** weather forecasts for all 50 United States and cities around the world. *Note:* Temperatures are in Celsius for many international destinations.

- ✔ **Mapquest** (www.mapquest.com): Choose a specific address or destination, and in seconds, get a map and detailed directions.

- ✔ **Travel Secrets** (www.travelsecrets.com): This site is one of the best compilations around. The site offers advice and tips on how to find the lowest prices for airlines, hotels, and cruises, and it also provides a listing of links for airfare deals, airlines, booking engines, discount travel, resources, hotels, and travel magazines.

- ✔ **Universal Currency Converter** (www.xe.net/ucc): See what your dollar or pound is worth in more than 100 other countries.

- ✔ **Visa ATM Locator** (www.visa.com/pd/atm) or **MasterCard ATM Locator** (www.mastercard.com/atmlocator): Find ATMs in hundreds of cities in the United States and around the world.

Appendix B

Glossary of Spanish Words and Phrases

● ●

*M*ost Mexicans are very patient with foreigners who try to speak their language. And your trip can be much easier and more enjoyable if you know a few basic Spanish phrases.

In this glossary, we include a few lists of simple words and phrases for expressing basic needs.

English-Spanish Phrases

English	*Spanish*	*Pronunciation*
Good day (Good morning)	**Buenos días**	*bway*-nohss *dee*-ahss
Good evening/afternoon	**Buenas tardes**	*bway*-nahss *tar*-days
Good night	**Buenas noches**	*bway*-nahss *noh*-chase
How are you?	**¿Cómo está?**	*koh*-moh ess-*tah?*
Very well	**Muy bien**	mwee byen
Thank you	**Gracias**	*grah*-see-ahss
You're welcome	**De nada**	day *nah*-dah
Good-bye	**Adiós**	ah-dee-*ohss*
Please	**Por favor**	pohr fah-*vohr*
Yes	**Sí**	see
No	**No**	noh
Excuse me	**Disculpe**	dees-*kool*-peh
Give me	**Déme or Dame**	*day*-may *or dah*-may

(continued)

English-Spanish Phrases *(continued)*

English	Spanish	Pronunciation
Where is...?	¿Dónde está...?	*dohn*-day ess-*tah?*
the station	la estación	lah ess-tah-*seown*
a hotel	un hotel	oon oh-*tel*
a gas station	una gasolinera	*oon*-uh gah-so-lee-*nay*-rah
a restaurant	un restaurante	oon res-tow-*rahn*-tay
the toilet	el baño	el *bahn*-yoh
a good doctor	un buen médico	oon bwayn *may*-dee-co
the road to...	el camino a...	el cah-*mee*-noh ah
To the right	A la derecha	ah lah day-*reh*-chah
To the left	A la izquierda	ah lah ees-ky-*ehr*-thah
Straight ahead	Derecho	day-*reh*-cho
I would like	Quisiera	key-see-*ehr*-ah
I want	Quiero	*kyehr*-oh
to eat	comer	ko-*mayr*
a room	una habitación	*oon*-nuh ha-bee-tah-*seeown*
Do you have...?	¿Tiene usted...?	*tyah*-nay oos-*ted?*
a book	un libro	oon *lee*-bro
a dictionary	un diccionario	oon deek-see-on-*ar*-ee-oh
How much is it?	¿Cuánto cuesta?	*kwahn*-to *kwess*-tah?
When?	¿Cuándo?	*kwahn*-doh?
What?	¿Cómo?	*koh*-moh?
There is (Is there ...?)	(¿)Hay(?)	eye?
What is there?	¿Qué hay?	kay eye?
Yesterday	Ayer	ah-*yer*
Today	Hoy	oy
Tomorrow	Mañana	mahn-*yahn*-ah
Good	Bueno	*bway*-no
Bad	Malo	*mah*-lo

English	Spanish	Pronunciation
Better (best)	**Mejor**	meh-*hor*
More	**Más**	mahs
Less	**Menos**	*may*-noss
No smoking	**Se prohibe fumar**	say pro-*ee*-bay foo-*mahr*
Postcard	**Tarjeta postal**	tar-*heh*-ta pohs-*tahl*
Insect repellent	**Repelente contra insectos**	reh-peh-*lehn*-te *cohn*-trah een-*sehk*-tos

More Useful Phrases

English	Spanish	Pronunciation
Do you speak English?	**¿Habla usted inglés?**	*ah*-blah oo-*sted* een-*glays?*
Is there anyone here who speaks English?	**¿Hay alguien aquí que hable inglés?**	eye *ahl*-gyen ah-*key* kay ah-blay een-*glays?*
I speak a little Spanish.	**Hablo un poco de español.**	*ah*-blow oon *poh*-koh day ess-pah-*nyol*
I don't understand Spanish very well.	**No entiendo español muy bien.**	noh ehn-tee-*ehn*-do ess-pah-*nyol* mwee byen
The meal is good.	**Me gusta la comida.**	may *goo*-sta lah koh-*mee*-dah
What time is it?	**¿Qué hora es?**	kay *oar*-ah ess?
May I see your menu?	**¿Puedo ver el menú?**	*puay*-tho veyr el may-*noo?*
The check, please.	**La cuenta, por favor.**	lah *quayn*-tah pohr fa-*vorh*
What do I owe you?	**¿Cuánto le debo?**	*kwahn*-toh leh *day*-boh?
What did you say?	**¿Mande?** (formal)	*mahn*-day?
	¿Cómo dijo? (informal)	*koh*-moh dee-ho?
I want (to see)	**Quiero (ver)**	key-*yehr*-oh vehr
a room	**un cuarto** or **una habitación**	oon *kwar*-toh *or* oon-nah ah-bee-tah-*see-on*
for two persons	**para dos personas**	*pahr*-ah doss pehr-*sohn*-as
with (without) bathroom	**con (sin) baño**	kohn (seen) *bah*-nyoh

(continued)

More Useful Phrases *(continued)*

English	Spanish	Pronunciation
We are staying here only	**Nos quedamos aquí solamente**	nohs kay-*dahm*-ohss ah-*key* sohl-ah-*mayn*-tay
one night	**una noche**	*oon*-ah *noh*-chay
one week	**una semana**	*oon*-ah say-*mahn*-ah
We are leaving	**Partimos or Salimos**	pahr-*tee*-mohss; sah-*lee*-mohss
Do you accept ...?	**¿Acepta usted...?**	ah-*sayp*-tah oo-*sted*
traveler's checks?	**... los cheques de viajero?**	los-*chay*-kays day bee-ah-*hehr*-oh
credit cards	**...las tarjetas de crédito**	lahs-tar-*hay*-tahs day *kray*-dee-toh
Is there a Laundromat (or laundry)?	**¿Hay una lavandería?**	eye *oon*-ah lah-*vahn*-day-*ree*-ah
Is...near here?	**Es...cerca de aquí?**	*sehr*-ka day ah-*key*
Please send these clothes to the laundry.	**Hágame el favor de mandar esta ropa a la lavandería.**	*ah*-ga-may el fah-*vhor* day mahn-*dahr ays*-tah *rho*-pah a lah lah-*vahn*-day-*ree*-ah

Numbers

1	**uno** (*ooh*-noh)
2	**dos** (dohs)
3	**tres** (trayss)
4	**cuatro** (*kwah*-troh)
5	**cinco** (*seen*-koh)
6	**seis** (sayss)
7	**siete** (*syeh*-tay)
8	**ocho** (*oh*-choh)
9	**nueve** (*nway*-bay)
10	**diez** (dee-*ess*)
11	**once** (*ohn*-say)
12	**doce** (*doh*-say)

13	**trece** (*tray*-say)
14	**catorce** (kah-*tor*-say)
15	**quince** (*keen*-say)
16	**dieciseis** (de-*ess*-ee-sayss)
17	**diecisiete** (de-*ess*-ee-*syeh*-tay)
18	**dieciocho** (dee-*ess*-ee-*oh*-choh)
19	**diecinueve** (dee-*ess*-ee-*nway*-bay)
20	**veinte** (*bayn*-tay)
21	**veinteuno** (*bayn*-tay-*ooh*-noh)
30	**treinta** (*trayn*-tah)
40	**cuarenta** (kwah-*ren*-tah)
50	**cincuenta** (seen-*kwen*-tah)
60	**sesenta** (say-*sen*-tah)
70	**setenta** (say-*ten*-tah)
80	**ochenta** (oh-*chen*-tah)
90	**noventa** (noh-*ben*-tah)
100	**cien** (see-*en*)
200	**doscientos** (*dos*-se-en-tos)
500	**quinientos** (keen-ee-*ehn*-tos)
1,000	**mil** (meal)

Transportation Terms

English	*Spanish*	*Pronunciation*
Airport	**Aeropuerto**	ah-ay-row-*por*-tow
Arrival gates	**Llegadas**	yay-*gah*-dahs
Departure gate	**Puerta de embarque**	*por*-tow day em-*bark*- kay
Baggage	**Equipajes**	eh-key-*pah*-hays
Baggage-claim area	**Recibo de equipajes or reclamo de equipajes**	ray-*see*-boh day eh-key-*pah*-hay *or* ray-*klah*-moh day eh-key-*pah*-hay

(continued)

Transportation Terms *(continued)*

English	*Spanish*	*Pronunciation*
First class	**Primera clase**	pree-*mehr*-oh *klah*-say
Second class	**Segunda clase**	say-*goon*-dah *klah*-say
Flight	**Vuelo**	*bway*-low
Nonstop	**Directo or sin escala**	dee-*reck*-toh or seen ess-*kah*-lah
Rental car	**Coche de alquiler**	co-*chay* day ahl-*key*-layr
Bus	**Autobús**	ow-toh-*boos*
Bus or truck	**Camión**	ka-mee-*ohn*
Intercity	**Foraneo**	fohr-ah-*nay*-oh
Lane	**Carril**	kah-*rreal*
Luggage storage area	**Guarda equipaje**	gwar-dah eh-key-*pah*-hay
Originates at this station	**Local**	loh-*kahl*
Originates elsewhere	**De paso**	day *pah*-soh
Stops if seats available	**Para, si hay lugares**	*pahr*-ah see eye loo-*gahr*-ays
Waiting room	**Sala de espera**	*saw*-lah day ess-*pehr*-ah
Ticket window	**Taquilla**	tah-*key*-yah
Toilets	**Baños**	*bahn*-yohs

Appendix C

Authentic Mexican Cuisine

*A*uthentic Mexican food differs quite dramatically from what is frequently served up in the United States under that name. For many travelers, Mexico is new and exciting culinary territory. Even grizzled veterans are pleasantly surprised by the wide variation in specialties and traditions offered from region to region.

Despite regional differences, you can make some generalizations. In fact, Mexican food usually isn't pepper-hot when it arrives at the table (though many dishes must have a certain amount of spiciness, and some home cooking can be very spicy, depending on a family's or chef's tastes). The piquant flavor is added with chiles and sauces after the food is served; you never see a table in Mexico without one or both of these condiments. Mexicans don't drown their cooking in cheese and sour cream (which is the case in many Tex-Mex restaurants), and they use a great variety of ingredients. But the basis of Mexican food is simple — tortillas, beans, chiles, squash, and tomatoes — the same as it was centuries ago, before the Europeans arrived.

Knowing the Basic Dishes

Traditional **tortillas** are made from corn that has been cooked in water and lime, and then ground into *masa* (a grainy dough), patted and pressed into thin cakes, and cooked on a hot griddle known as a *comal*. In many households, tortillas take the place of fork and spoon; Mexicans merely tear the tortillas into wedge-shaped pieces, which they use to scoop up their food. Restaurants often serve bread rather than tortillas because it's easier to prepare, but you can always ask for tortillas. A more recent invention from northern Mexico is the flour tortilla, which you don't see as frequently in the rest of Mexico.

Dishes made with tortillas

The tortilla is the basis of several Mexican dishes, and the most famous dish is the **enchilada.** The original name for this dish was *tortilla enchilada,* which simply means a tortilla dipped in a chile sauce. In a similar manner, there's the *entomatada* (tortilla dipped in a tomato sauce) and the *enfrijolada* (tortilla dipped in a bean sauce). The enchilada began as a very simple dish: A tortilla is dipped in chile sauce (usually with ancho chile) and then into very hot oil, and then is quickly folded or rolled on a plate and sprinkled with chopped onions and a little *queso cotija* (crumbly white cheese) and served with a few fried potatoes and carrots. You can get this basic enchilada in food stands across the country. If you come across them in your travels, give them a try. In restaurants, you get the more elaborate enchilada, with different fillings of cheese, chicken, pork, or even seafood, and sometimes in a casserole.

A **taco** is anything folded or rolled into a tortilla, and sometimes a double tortilla. The tortilla can be served either soft or fried. *Flautas* and *quesadillas* are offshoots of tacos. For Mexicans, the taco is the quintessential fast food, and the taco stand *(taquería)* — a ubiquitous sight — is a great place to get a filling meal. See the section, "Eating Out: Restaurants, Taquerías, and Tipping," later in this appendix for information on taquerías.

All about beans

An invisible "bean line" divides Mexico: It starts at the Gulf Coast in the southern part of the state of Tamaulipas and moves inland through the eastern quarter of San Luis Potosí and most of the state of Hidalgo, and then goes straight through Mexico City and Morelos and into Guerrero, where it curves slightly westward to the Pacific. (Check out the map of Mexico on the inside back cover of this book to gain a little perspective about this bean line.) To the north and west of this line, the pink bean known as the *flor de mayo* is the staple food; to the south and east, the standard is the black bean.

In private households, beans are served at least once a day and, among the working class and peasantry, with every meal, if the family can afford it. Mexicans almost always prepare beans with a minimum of condiments — usually just a little onion and garlic and perhaps a pinch of herbs. Beans are a contrast to the heavily spiced dishes. Sometimes they're served at the end of a meal with a little Mexican-style sour cream, which is basically just cream.

Mexicans often fry leftover beans and serve them on the side as *frijoles refritos*. *Refritos* is usually translated as refried, but this translation is a misnomer — the beans are fried only once. The prefix *re* actually means *well* (as in thoroughly), and what Mexicans actually mean is the beans are well fried.

Getting to know tamales

You make a *tamal* by mixing corn *masa* with a little lard, adding one of several fillings — such as meats flavored with chiles (or no filling at all) — and then wrapping it in a corn husk or in the leaf of a banana or other plant, and finally steaming it. Every region in Mexico has its own traditional way of making *tamales*. In some places, a single *tamal* can be big enough to feed a family, although in other places, they're barely 3 inches long and an inch thick.

Understanding the chile pepper

Many kinds of chile peppers exist, and Mexicans call each of them by one name when they're fresh and another when they're dried. Some are blazing hot with only a mild flavor; some are mild but have a rich, complex flavor. They can be pickled, smoked, stuffed, stewed, chopped, and used in an endless variety of dishes.

Eating Out: Restaurants, Taquerías, and Tipping

First of all, we feel compelled to debunk the prevailing myth that the cheapest place to eat in Mexico is in the market. Actually, this is almost never the case. You can usually find better food at a better price without going more than two blocks out of your way. Why? Food stalls in the marketplace pay high rents, they have a near-captive clientele of market vendors and truckers, and they get plenty of business from many Mexicans for whom eating in the market is a traditional way of confirming their culture.

On the other side of the spectrum, avoid eating at those inviting sidewalk restaurants that you see beneath the stone archways that border the main plazas. These places usually cater to tourists — so authenticity may be suspect — and they don't need to count on getting any return business. But they're great for getting a coffee or beer.

In most nonresort towns, you can usually find one or two restaurants (sometimes it's a coffee shop) that are social centers for a large group of established patrons. These establishments over time become virtual institutions, and change comes very slowly to them. The food is usually good standard fare, cooked as it was 20 years ago; the decor is simple. The patrons have known each other and the staff for years, and the *charla* (banter), gestures, and greetings are friendly, open, and unaffected. If you're curious about Mexican culture, these places are fun to eat in and observe the goings-on.

During your trip, you're going to see many *taquerías* (**taco stands**). These are generally small places with a counter or a few tables set around the cooking area; you get to see exactly how they make their tacos before deciding whether to order. Most tacos come with a little chopped onion and cilantro, but not tomato and lettuce. Find one that seems popular with the locals and where the cook performs with *brio* (a good sign of pride in the product). Sometimes you see a woman making the tortillas right there (or working the *masa* into *gorditas, sopes,* or *panuchos* if the taquería serves them). You'll never see men making tortillas — this is perhaps the strictest gender division in Mexican society. Men do all other cooking and kitchen tasks, and work with already-made tortillas, but they never work with *masa*.

For the main meal of the day, many restaurants offer a multicourse blue-plate special called **comida corrida** or **menú del día.** This dish is the most inexpensive way to get a full dinner. In Mexico, you need to ask for your check; Mexican culture generally considers presenting a check to someone who hasn't requested it as inhospitable. If you're in a hurry to get somewhere, ask for the check when your food arrives.

Tips are about the same as in the United States. You sometimes find a 15% **value-added tax** on restaurant meals, which shows up on the bill as "IVA." If you're an arithmetically challenged tipper, you may be (slightly) thankful for this tax, saving you from the undue exertion of trying to calculate a 15% tip in your head.

To summon the waiter, wave or raise your hand, but don't motion with your index finger, which is a demeaning gesture that may even cause the waiter to ignore you. Or if you want your check, you can motion to the waiter from across the room using the universal pretend-like-you're-writing gesture.

Most restaurants don't have **nonsmoking sections;** when they do, we mention it in the restaurant reviews throughout this book. But Mexico's wonderful climate allows for many open-air restaurants, usually set inside a colonial house's courtyard, or in rooms with tall ceilings and plenty of open windows.

Drinking in Mexico

All over Mexico you find shops selling *jugos* **(juices)** and *liquados* **(smoothies)** made from several kinds of tropical fruit. They're excellent and refreshing; while in Mexico, take full advantage of them. You also come across *aguas frescas* — water flavored with hibiscus, melon, tamarind, or lime. Soft drinks come in more flavors than in any other country we know. Pepsi and Coca-Cola taste the way they did in the United States years ago, before the makers started adding corn syrup. The coffee is generally good, and **hot chocolate** is a traditional drink, as is *atole,* a hot, corn-based beverage that can be sweet or bitter.

Of course, Mexico has a proud and lucrative **beer**-brewing tradition. A lesser-known brewed beverage is *pulque,* a pre-Hispanic drink: the fermented juice of a few species of maguey or agave. Mostly you find it for sale in *pulquerías* in central Mexico. It's an acquired taste, and not every gringo acquires it. **Mezcal** and **tequila** also come from the agave. Tequila is a variety of mezcal produced from the *A. tequilana* species of agave in and around the area of Tequila, in the state of Jalisco. Mezcal comes from various parts of Mexico and from different varieties of agave. The distilling process is usually much less sophisticated than that of tequila, and, with its stronger smell and taste, mezcal is much more easily detected on the drinker's breath. In some places such as Oaxaca, it comes with a worm in the bottle; you're supposed to eat the worm after polishing off the mezcal. But for those teetotalers who are interested in just the worm, we have good news — you can find these worms for sale in Mexican markets when in season.

Glossary of Spanish Menu Terms

The following is a list of common menu items and a description for each to take some of the guesswork out of ordering meals on your vacation.

Achiote: Small, red seed of the annatto tree.

Agua fresca: Fruit-flavored water, usually watermelon or cantaloupe where ingredients such as lemon and hibiscus flower are added.

Antojitos: Typical Mexican supper foods, usually made with masa or tortillas and containing a filling or topping such as sausage, cheese, beans, and onions; includes such items as *tacos, tostadas, sopes,* and *garnachas* (thick tortillas).

Atole: A thick, lightly sweet, hot drink made with finely ground corn and usually flavored with vanilla, pecan, or chocolate.

Botana: An appetizer.

Buñuelos: Round, thin, deep-fried, crispy fritters dipped in sugar.

Carnitas: Pork that's been deep-cooked (not fried) in lard, then simmered, and then served with corn tortillas for tacos.

Ceviche: Fresh, raw seafood marinated in fresh lime juice, garnished with chopped tomatoes, onions, chiles, and sometimes cilantro, and served with crispy, fried, whole-corn tortillas or crackers.

Chayote: A type of spiny pear-shaped squash boiled and served as an accompaniment to meat dishes.

Chiles en nogada: Poblano peppers stuffed with a mixture of ground pork and chicken, spices, fruits, raisins, and almonds, fried in a light batter, and covered in a walnut-and-cream sauce.

Chiles rellenos: Usually poblano peppers stuffed with cheese or spicy ground meat with raisins, rolled in a batter, and fried.

Churro: Tube-shaped, bread-like fritter, dipped in sugar and sometimes filled with *cajeta* (caramel) or chocolate.

Enchilada: A tortilla dipped in a sauce and usually filled with chicken or white cheese; sometimes topped with mole sauce *(enchiladas rojas or de mole),* tomato sauce and sour cream *(enchiladas suizas,* or Swiss enchiladas*),* a green sauce *(enchiladas verdes),* or onions, sour cream, and guacamole *(enchiladas potosinas).*

Escabeche: A lightly pickled sauce used in Yucatecán chicken stew.

Frijoles charros: Beans flavored with beer; a northern Mexican specialty.

Frijoles refritos: Pinto beans mashed and cooked with lard.

Gorditas: Thickish fried-corn tortillas, slit and stuffed with choice of cheese, beans, beef, or chicken; served with or without lettuce, tomato, and onion garnish.

Gusanos de maguey: Maguey worms, considered a delicacy; delicious when deep-fried to a crisp and served with corn tortillas for tacos.

Horchata: Lightly sweetened, refreshing drink made of ground rice or melon seeds, and ground almonds. Also known as *agua de arroz* in certain destinations on the Pacific coast, such as Puerto Vallarta and Ixtapa.

Huevos Mexicanos: Scrambled eggs with chopped onions, hot peppers, and tomatoes.

Huevos rancheros: Fried eggs on top of a fried corn tortilla covered in a spicy or mild tomato sauce.

Huitlacoche: Sometimes spelled "cuitlacoche." A mushroom-flavored black fungus that appears on corn in the rainy season; considered a delicacy.

Machaca: Shredded, dried beef scrambled with eggs, onion, and a mild red sauce; a specialty of northern Mexico.

Masa: Ground corn soaked in lime used as the basis for tamales, corn tortillas, and soups.

Menudo: Stew made with the lining of the cow's stomach. It can be served in a red or white broth. A traditional hangover cure.

Pan dulce: Lightly sweetened bread in many configurations, usually served at breakfast or bought in any bakery.

Pibil: Pit-baked pork or chicken in a sauce of tomato, onion, mild red pepper, cilantro, and vinegar.

Pipián: A sauce made with ground pumpkin seeds, nuts, and mild peppers.

Poc chuc: Slices of pork with onion marinated in a tangy, sour, orange sauce and charcoal-broiled; a Yucatecan specialty.

Pozole: Pork or chicken broth with hominy and shredded pork or chicken. The traditional recipe calls for the pork's head, but now it's commonly prepared with chicken or pork loin. Pozole is served red in Jalisco and white in Guerrero. Thursdays are the traditional day to eat pozole in Acapulco and Ixtapa.

Quesadilla: Corn or flour tortillas stuffed with melted white cheese and lightly fried.

Queso relleno: "Stuffed cheese"; a mild yellow cheese stuffed with minced meat and spices; a Yucatecan specialty.

Rompope: Delicious Mexican eggnog, invented in Puebla, made with eggs, vanilla, sugar, and rum.

Salsa verde: A cooked sauce using the green tomatillo puréed with spicy or mild hot peppers, onions, garlic, and cilantro; on tables countrywide.

Sopa de lima: A tangy soup made with chicken broth and accented with fresh lime; popular in Yucatán.

Sopa de Tortilla: A traditional chicken broth-based soup, seasoned with chilies, tomatoes, beans, onion, and garlic, with crispy fried strips of corn tortillas.

Sope: Pronounced "*soh*-pay;" an *antojito* similar to a *garnacha* (a thick tortilla), except spread with refried beans and topped with crumbled cheese and onions.

Tacos al pastor: Thin slices of flavored pork roasted on a revolving cylinder dripping with onion slices and the juice of fresh pineapple slices. Served in small corn tortillas, topped with chopped onion and cilantro.

Tamal: Incorrectly called a "tamale" (*tamal* singular; *tamales* plural). A meat or sweet filling rolled with fresh *masa,* wrapped in a corn husk or banana leaf, and then steamed; many varieties and sizes throughout the country.

Torta: A sandwich, usually on *bolillo* bread, typically comprising sliced avocado, onions, and tomatoes with a choice of meat and often cheese.

Tostadas: Crispy, fried corn tortillas topped with meat, onions, lettuce, tomatoes, cheese, avocados, and sometimes sour cream.

Making Dollars and Sense of It

Expense	Daily cost	x	Number of days	=	Total
Airfare					
Local transportation					
Car rental					
Lodging (with tax)					
Parking					
Breakfast					
Lunch					
Dinner					
Snacks					
Entertainment					
Babysitting					
Attractions					
Gifts & souvenirs					
Tips					
Other					
Grand Total					

Fare Game: Choosing an Airline

When looking for the best airfare, you should cover all your bases — 1) consult a trusted travel agent; 2) contact the airline directly, via the airline's toll-free number and/or Web site; 3) check out one of the travel-planning Web sites, such as www.frommers.com.

Travel Agency _____ Phone _____

    Agent's Name _____ Quoted fare _____

Airline 1 _____ Quoted fare _____

    Toll-free number/Internet _____

Airline 2 _____ Quoted fare _____

    Toll-free number/Internet _____

Web site 1 _____ Quoted fare _____

Web site 2 _____ Quoted fare _____

Departure Schedule & Flight Information

Airline _____ Flight # _____ Confirmation # _____

Departs _____ Date _____ Time _____ a.m./p.m.

Arrives _____ Date _____ Time _____ a.m./p.m.

Connecting Flight (if any)

Amount of time between flights _____ hours/mins

Airline _____ Flight # _____ Confirmation # _____

Departs _____ Date _____ Time _____ a.m./p.m.

Arrives _____ Date _____ Time _____ a.m./p.m.

Return Trip Schedule & Flight Information

Airline _____ Flight # _____ Confirmation # _____

Departs _____ Date _____ Time _____ a.m./p.m.

Arrives _____ Date _____ Time _____ a.m./p.m.

Connecting Flight (if any)

Amount of time between flights _____ hours/mins

Airline _____ Flight # _____ Confirmation # _____

Departs _____ Date _____ Time _____ a.m./p.m.

Arrives _____ Date _____ Time _____ a.m./p.m.

Sweet Dreams: Choosing Your Hotel

Make a list of all the hotels where you'd like to stay and then check online and call the local and toll-free numbers to get the best price. You should also check with a travel agent, who may be able to get you a better rate.

Hotel & page	Location	Internet	Tel. (local)	Tel. (Toll-free)	Quoted rate

Hotel Checklist

Here's a checklist of things to inquire about when booking your room, depending on your needs and preferences.

- ❑ Smoking/smoke-free room
- ❑ Noise (if you prefer a quiet room, ask about proximity to elevator, bar/restaurant, pool, meeting facilities, renovations, and street)
- ❑ View
- ❑ Facilities for children (crib, roll-away cot, babysitting services)
- ❑ Facilities for travelers with disabilities
- ❑ Number and size of bed(s) (king, queen, double/full-size)
- ❑ Is breakfast included? (buffet, continental, or sit-down?)
- ❑ In-room amenities (hair dryer, iron/board, minibar, etc.)
- ❑ Other_____

Menus & Venues

Enter the restaurants where you'd most like to dine. Then use the worksheet below to plan your itinerary.

Name	Address/Phone	Cuisine/Price

Places to Go, People to See, Things to Do

Enter the attractions you would most like to see and decide how they'll fit into your schedule. Next, use the "Going My Way" worksheets that follow to sketch out your itinerary.

Attraction/activity	Page	Amount of time you expect to spend there	Best day and time to go

Going "My" Way

Day 1

Hotel _____ Tel. _____

Morning _____

_____

Lunch _____ Tel. _____

Afternoon _____

_____

Dinner _____ Tel. _____

Evening _____

_____

Day 2

Hotel _____ Tel. _____

Morning _____

_____

Lunch _____ Tel. _____

Afternoon _____

_____

Dinner _____ Tel. _____

Evening _____

_____

Day 3

Hotel _____ Tel. _____

Morning _____

_____

Lunch _____ Tel. _____

Afternoon _____

_____

Dinner _____ Tel. _____

Evening _____

_____

Going "My" Way

Day 4

Hotel_____ Tel._____

Morning_____

_____

Lunch_____ Tel._____

Afternoon_____

_____

Dinner_____ Tel._____

Evening_____

_____

Day 5

Hotel_____ Tel._____

Morning_____

_____

Lunch_____ Tel._____

Afternoon_____

_____

Dinner_____ Tel._____

Evening_____

_____

Day 6

Hotel_____ Tel._____

Morning_____

_____

Lunch_____ Tel._____

Afternoon_____

_____

Dinner_____ Tel._____

Evening_____

_____

Going "My" Way

Day 7
Hotel_____ Tel._____
Morning_____
_____
Lunch_____ Tel._____
Afternoon_____
_____
Dinner_____ Tel._____
Evening_____
_____

Day 8
Hotel_____ Tel._____
Morning_____
_____
Lunch_____ Tel._____
Afternoon_____
_____
Dinner_____ Tel._____
Evening_____
_____

Day 9
Hotel_____ Tel._____
Morning_____
_____
Lunch_____ Tel._____
Afternoon_____
_____
Dinner_____ Tel._____
Evening_____
_____

Index

• E •

• *M* •

FOR DUMMIES®

A world of resources to help you grow

TRAVEL

0-7645-5453-0

0-7645-5438-7

0-7645-5444-1

Also available:

America's National Parks For Dummies
(0-7645-6204-5)

Caribbean For Dummies
(0-7645-5445-X)

Cruise Vacations For Dummies 2003
(0-7645-5459-X)

Europe For Dummies
(0-7645-5456-5)

Ireland For Dummies
(0-7645-6199-5)

France For Dummies
(0-7645-6292-4)

Las Vegas For Dummies
(0-7645-5448-4)

London For Dummies
(0-7645-5416-6)

Mexico's Beach Resorts For Dummies
(0-7645-6262-2)

Paris For Dummies
(0-7645-5494-8)

RV Vacations For Dummies
(0-7645-5443-3)

EDUCATION & TEST PREPARATION

0-7645-5194-9

0-7645-5325-9

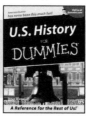

0-7645-5249-X

Also available:

The ACT For Dummies
(0-7645-5210-4)

Chemistry For Dummies
(0-7645-5430-1)

English Grammar For Dummies
(0-7645-5322-4)

French For Dummies
(0-7645-5193-0)

GMAT For Dummies
(0-7645-5251-1)

Inglés Para Dummies
(0-7645-5427-1)

Italian For Dummies
(0-7645-5196-5)

Research Papers For Dummies
(0-7645-5426-3)

SAT I For Dummies
(0-7645-5472-7)

U.S. History For Dummies
(0-7645-5249-X)

World History For Dummies
(0-7645-5242-2)

HEALTH, SELF-HELP & SPIRITUALITY

0-7645-5154-X

0-7645-5302-X

0-7645-5418-2

Also available:

The Bible For Dummies
(0-7645-5296-1)

Controlling Cholesterol For Dummies
(0-7645-5440-9)

Dating For Dummies
(0-7645-5072-1)

Dieting For Dummies
(0-7645-5126-4)

High Blood Pressure For Dummies
(0-7645-5424-7)

Judaism For Dummies
(0-7645-5299-6)

Menopause For Dummies
(0-7645-5458-1)

Nutrition For Dummies
(0-7645-5180-9)

Potty Training For Dummies
(0-7645-5417-4)

Pregnancy For Dummies
(0-7645-5074-8)

Rekindling Romance For Dummies
(0-7645-5303-8)

Religion For Dummies
(0-7645-5264-3)
